To Joyce, as always, and to Stan Gershman, professor emeritus, colleague, friend, and tireless advocate for quality education of legal paraprofessionals.

— *L.M.O.*

To the memory of my father, Henry Kelly.

— *M.A.K.*

Contents

List of figures

Preface to the first edition

In the past, when we taught civil litigation subjects to students in law clerk programs, we both noticed that students were able to master individual rules of procedure but were often unable to see how these rules fit into the process of getting a case to trial. In short, students were unable to see the forest for the trees. To solve this problem, members of faculty contributed to a collection of materials that supplemented the commercially published annual edition of the *Rules of Civil Procedure*. When the supplemental materials grew to the size and weight of the Toronto telephone book, but with much less coherence, we realized that we had better do something.

This book is our solution. Using a case study, which involves the misadventures of the fictional Abigail Boar, you will follow the process of a typical civil action, looking at both the forest and the trees, and using exercises at the back of each chapter to practise analytic and drafting skills. We hope that you will gain an understanding of the process as a whole, as well as a grasp of specific procedures.

This book would probably not have appeared without our students' helpful comments on what was lacking in our teaching materials and the encouragement of our colleagues in the School of Legal and Public Administration and the School of Office Administration at Seneca College. The suggestions of students and colleagues, both solicited and otherwise, were welcome even if the proffered advice was not always followed. Any errors or omissions are, of course, the responsibility of the authors, and we welcome your assistance in correcting them. An e-mail to laurence.olivo@senecac.on.ca or maryann.kelly@senecac.on.ca will bring any problems to our attention.

The text reflects the law generally and the *Rules of Civil Procedure* in particular as of February 2003. The Rules Committee of the Superior Court is not inactive. Changes to the rules are to be expected from time to time, and care must be taken to see that your knowledge remains current. This text is designed to be used in conjunction with one of the commercially published annual versions of the *Rules of Civil Procedure*, and you should always refer to the text of the rules when examining a particular procedure or step in the process.

Laurence Olivo
Mary Ann Kelly
Toronto, February 2003

Preface to the second edition

Law texts are not like fine wines. Fine wines improve with age. Law books become obsolete and are soon fit only to be used as doorstops. Thus it is with the first edition of *Civil Litigation*. While the format and approach to the subject developed in the first edition continues to meet the test of time, the content is now in need of revision and a new edition is necessary.

The Rules Committee of the Superior Court has continued to be active in refining and revising the rules of procedure and the associated forms, and this edition keeps pace with those changes. In this connection, as we were going to press in early 2009, the government announced that it would proceed with a number of reforms to the civil court system, to take effect in January 2010. Because many of these changes will not come into effect until a year after publication, we have created new sections in relevant chapters, noting what the changes are generally, and what their intended effect is, when that can be discerned. The devil is, as usual, in the details, and the details are in O. reg. 438/08 (amendments to the *Rules of Civil Procedure*) and in O. reg. 439/09 (increase of the Small Claims Court monetary jurisdiction from $10,000 to $25,000 as of January 1, 2010).

These new amendments to the superior court rules introduce a new concept, the principle of proportionality, in which the complexity and cost of proceedings must be in proportion to the value to the client. This has led to a more complex simplified procedure, the introduction of a form of case management to the discovery process, new controls and requirements for pretrials, details on when and how case management is to be used, new restrictions on the use of expert reports, and, generally, the introduction of more conferencing, timetabling, and compulsory cooperating. Good lawyers have been doing most of this already; whether those who did not will be made to "behave" by the rule changes remains to be seen. One suspects that the process has simply been made more complicated, and the extra complexities will make things no quicker or cheaper for litigants. Time will tell us whether we have turned a corner in the struggle with cost and delay, or whether we have been tinkering and making matters worse.

One of the more noticeable changes we made in this edition, as a result of changes to the law in Ontario, was the decision to omit chapter 25, "Motor Vehicle Insurance Claims in Ontario." There were several reasons for this. First, in a text designed for basic litigation courses in a law clerk diploma program, this topic seemed too broad, complex, and specialized for basic litigation courses. It really deserves a book of its own. Second, the establishment of licensing regulations for paralegals has, in our view, taken this practice area away from law clerks (the majority of our readers) and given it over to paralegals — law clerks will no longer have the right of audience before adjudicative bodies of the Financial Services Commission of Ontario. In the circumstances, it seemed sensible to delete a chapter that was of marginal use.

And, of course, we listened to the feedback we received from instructors and our students, and made corrections and provided clarification where necessary.

Laurence Olivo
Mary Ann Kelly
Toronto, January 2009

PART I

An overview of the civil litigation process

CHAPTER 1

Overview of a civil law suit

This chapter presents the "big picture" of how a civil proceeding unfolds. The balance of the book fills in the details. In order to help you see both the big picture and later the details, we start by setting out a fact situation involving Abigail Boar and her various difficulties. Using Abigail's story, we demonstrate how a civil case progresses from the initial stage of hiring a lawyer to the final stage of appealing a trial judgment.

FACT SITUATION: THE SAD TALE OF ABIGAIL BOAR
Introduction

It is now time to introduce you to the unfortunate Abigail Boar, who set out to buy a sports car and ended up with serious injuries resulting from the apparent negligence of others involved in what lawyers usually refer to as a "slip and fall case." We will follow Abigail's case from the time Abigail consults a lawyer, through the various pretrial stages, to trial in the Ontario Superior Court.[1] As we proceed, we will discuss the steps that are taken, including the preparation of many of the documents that are required in a civil action. The facts set out here present a broad outline of what occurred. As we proceed we will add more detail where it is required.

Facts

Abigail Boar is a 28-year-old securities analyst employed by Megadoon Investments Ltd. She is earning more money than she ever thought she would and decides the time has come to do some conspicuous consuming, so she buys her first car. After talking to friends, she decides the right kind of car for her is a two-seater sports coupe. On September 14, year 0, she decides to go after dinner to look at the hot new line of sports coupes manufactured by the Skank Motorcar Company Ltd., which are being sold at Rattle Motors Ltd. After work, she stops at Barbeerians, a trendy bar frequented by financial types, where she has a quick dinner and two glasses of wine. She then walks over to Rattle Motors Ltd. at 1240 Bay Street, Toronto.

At about 6 p.m., Fred Flogem, a salesperson employed by Rattle Motors Ltd., notices that there is some oil on the floor next to the Super Coupe model. He peers underneath the car and discovers oil leaking from underneath the engine. Because this is hardly good advertising for a new car, Fred does not want to draw customers' attention to the problem by cleaning up the mess immediately. Instead, he shuts off two of the four spotlights that illuminate the Super Coupe, hoping that no one looking at the car will notice the mess on the floor. Fred intends to clean up the mess when there are no customers in the showroom, or when the showroom closes for the day.

Abigail walks in the front door of the showroom at about 7:30 p.m. There are several sports cars on display. On seeing her come in, two salespersons get up from their desks and make a beeline for Abigail. Linda Lucre gets there first, so the second salesperson, Fred Flogem, sits down again and busies himself with some paperwork. Abigail tells Linda what she is looking for, and Linda shows her the floor models. Abigail looks at one car and then walks over, with Linda behind her, to look at another. The second car is in an area of the showroom where two of the four spotlights on the car are off so that the side of the car near to the wall is in relative darkness. As Abigail walks around to the darker side of the car, she steps into some oil, slips, loses her balance, and falls, striking the left side of her head against the side of the car. Abigail is knocked unconscious. Her body twists as she falls heavily to the floor with the result that she fractures her right wrist and several bones in her right arm.

Linda goes to her office and phones for an ambulance. Abigail is taken to Toronto Hospital, where she is treated. She remains there for four days. The broken bones in her wrist and right arm are set in a cast. Because of the head injury, Abigail remains for neurological observation and is then sent home, where she remains for a further six weeks until the cast is taken off her arm. After that, she goes to physiotherapy once a week for ten weeks.

After she is released from hospital, Abigail has no memory of slipping and falling. She continues to have chronic lower back pain and headaches. She is unable to walk long distances or sit at her desk at work for prolonged periods. Abigail, who is right-handed, has limited mobility in her right arm and is unable to work at her computer for more than ten minutes at a time without experiencing pain.

She returns to work on March 1, year 1 for a month. However, because of chronic pain and her difficulty using a computer, which is essential for her job, Abigail then goes on long-term disability.

Before her accident, Abigail was an avid tennis player and a good amateur violinist. After her accident, she is unable to enjoy these activities and is far less active, both physically and socially, than she had been. She used to be a lively individual: cheerful, with a good sense of humour. She has, since the fall, become quieter and more withdrawn and has difficulty sleeping. Her family physician has begun treating her for depression, prescribing an antidepressant and painkillers.

At the time of the accident, Abigail was earning $80,000 gross per year. Her employer does not have a short-term sick leave plan but does have a long-term disability plan that pays Abigail 60 percent of basic monthly earnings after four months' absence from work resulting from illness or injury.

Abigail has consulted I.M. Just, a lawyer, and intends to sue Rattle Motors Ltd. and Fred Flogem because she believes they are responsible for the injuries she sustained.

AN OVERVIEW OF THE CIVIL LITIGATION PROCESS

Now that you have met Abigail, we can consider some preliminary matters and turn to a general description of what happens after she decides to sue.

What is civil litigation?

When we send Abigail off to a lawyer, we should note that she is about to involve herself in what lawyers call civil litigation. Civil litigation describes the court process used to resolve disputes and conflicts where one person claims that the acts of another have caused harm. If the harm is of a type that the law recognizes, then the party who caused the harm will be ordered by the court to compensate the party who was harmed, usually by paying money to the injured party. The general goal of civil litigation is to compensate a person for his or her injuries or losses — to restore a person to the position that he or she was in prior to harm being done — to the extent that the payment of money damages can accomplish this.

Civil litigation cases can take various forms. Debt collection cases, personal injury claims, wrongful dismissal, disputes over property use or ownership, and shareholder disputes are all examples of civil litigation cases. These disputes usually involve private rights and obligations, as opposed to public ones, although there may be public interest and public policy aspects to civil cases. In this context, the government can be a party to a civil litigation case. Consider, for example, a recent case in which several parents of autistic children sued the Ontario Government for failure to pay for a specific and expensive educational program. On the surface this was a private dispute where one party said the other was legally obliged to compensate it, but the outcome would also determine health and education funding obligations of the Crown, generally.

People are often more familiar with criminal litigation than they are with civil litigation. They often assume that what goes on in one process goes on in another, but in fact they are very different. Criminal litigation involves the prosecution by the Crown of actions that have been legally defined as criminal and harmful to the public in general, so that the object of criminal law is to protect the public generally, rather than to protect the rights of those individuals who may have been harmed by criminal acts. While in some cases the criminal accused may be ordered to pay restitution, which is like paying civil damages, that is not the primary purpose of the criminal law. The goal of criminal law is to punish wrongdoing and maintain public order, usually by the imposition of fines payable to the Crown (and not the person harmed) or by the imposition of terms of imprisonment.

There are also vast differences between civil and criminal procedure. In a civil case, the plaintiff is obliged to make out a case and prove each factual and legal element on the balance of probabilities. This means that if the plaintiff is successful, his or her version is more than likely the correct version. If the plaintiff fails to show this, the defendant wins, and the case is dismissed. In criminal cases, the accused is presumed to be innocent, unless the Crown can prove its case beyond reasonable doubt, a much higher standard of proof and a much greater burden for the Crown than for the plaintiff in a civil case. These differences also explain some of the differences in civil and criminal procedure. For example, because a criminally accused person is presumed to be innocent, he or she can sit back and say nothing and provide no information to the court. The Crown is obliged to prove its case on

FIGURE 1.1   STEPS IN AN ACTION

its own, and is not permitted to extract information from the accused. In civil cases, both parties are obliged to make full disclosure of everything that is relevant to the issues in dispute, both helpful and harmful. So if you have some familiarity with criminal law and procedure, you may find civil litigation to be quite different, driven by quite different purposes and goals.

What happens when Abigail decides to sue?

Generally, a civil proceeding can be divided into the following stages:

1. hiring of a lawyer,

2. preliminary investigations and research,

3. commencement of proceedings,

4. exchange of pleadings (statement of claim and statement of defence),

5. examinations for discovery of the parties and discovery of documents,

6. motions,

7. pretrial conference and trial preparation,

8. trial, and

9. appeals.

Figure 1.1 lists the principal rules of procedure that relate to these steps.

Hiring of a lawyer

Unless she is suing in Small Claims Court, where people often represent them-selves, as a practical matter Abigail needs to hire a lawyer either to negotiate a settlement or to take her case to trial. Rattle Motors Ltd. and Fred Flogem, the likely defendants in a personal injury case, are probably covered by insurance taken out by Rattle Motors Ltd. to cover its own torts and those of its employees. If so, Rattle Motors Ltd.'s obligation is to notify the insurer immediately of a potential claim. The insurance company will then hire and direct lawyers to act for Rattle Motors Ltd. and Fred because it is the insurance company that will have to pay Abigail if the case settles or if she wins at trial. For that reason, the insurance company controls the conduct of the case and instructs the lawyers even though Rattle Motors Ltd. and Fred are the defendants. If Rattle Motors Ltd. is not insured, it must hire and in-struct its own lawyer to represent it and Fred. If there is a conflict between Fred and Rattle Motors Ltd. concerning any issue in dispute, Fred must be separately repre-sented. If not, one lawyer can act for both.

How does Abigail go about choosing a lawyer? She could seek a recommenda-tion from friends or relatives, call the lawyer referral service at the Law Society of Upper Canada, or look in the Yellow Pages. Any lawyer can take her case, but she would be wise to choose one who practises personal injury law. Because many people are injured in circumstances that give rise to legal remedies, personal injury law is a high-volume area with many lawyers to choose from.

Once Abigail has made a choice, she should formally engage the lawyer's services by signing a retainer. A retainer is a contract between a lawyer and a client that sets out a description of the work to be done by the lawyer and the terms and conditions for the payment of **fees** and **disbursements** by the client. The lawyer may also ask Abigail to pay a deposit to be applied to future fees and disbursements. This deposit is also called a retainer.[2] Abigail and her lawyer may make other arrangements for the paying of legal fees. It is not uncommon for personal injury lawyers to take no fees or disbursements at the beginning of a case; instead, they are often paid what they are owed out of the trial judgment or settlement. A lawyer who loses a case is still entitled to be paid for services rendered. However, collecting fees from clients in these circumstances is not easy, particularly if clients do not have the resources to pay and feel that the lawyer's services have produced nothing of value. Note that a **contingency fee**, where a lawyer is paid a percentage of the judgment *only* if he or she wins the case, is permitted in Ontario as of 2003.[3] Contingency fees have long been permitted in most other Canadian provinces and in the United States.

In deciding what to charge Abigail, the lawyer may consider several factors:

- the amount of money at stake in the action,

- Abigail's ability to pay,

- the amount of time the lawyer will spend on the pretrial stage and the trial,

- the degree of complexity of the legal and/or factual issues, and

- the degree of success the lawyer is able to achieve.

Once Abigail has retained a lawyer, she will be interviewed at some length by the lawyer or the law clerk to determine the facts of the case, who the witnesses are, and who the other parties are. From this information, the lawyer has to decide whether Abigail has a good **cause of action** or not.

Preliminary investigations and research
DETERMINING THE CAUSE OF ACTION

In order for the lawyer to decide if there is a good cause of action, the lawyer has to ask whether or not the facts, as related by the client, identify a legal right or issue that gives rise to a legal remedy for the client. If there is a cause of action, the lawyer must then consider whether there is sufficient evidence to prove the facts. In the end, the evidence must lead the **trier of fact** to conclude that it is more probable than not that the facts set out by the client are correct. To put it another way, facts are conclusions that can be drawn by assessing the evidence.

If there is not enough evidence to prove the facts, the lawyer may have to advise the client not to continue with the case. The facts as Abigail relates them disclose that there is probably negligence on the part of Fred Flogem, for which Fred's employer, Rattle Motors Ltd., is vicariously liable and perhaps directly liable. Negligence is Abigail's cause of action.

fees
payment to lawyers for services rendered

disbursements
amounts lawyers pay on behalf of clients to third parties that lawyers can recover from clients

contingency fee
fee payable to a lawyer only if he or she wins the case for a client

cause of action
legal right to sue to obtain a legal remedy

trier of fact
judge or jury whose job is to determine the facts of the case from the evidence

RELATIONSHIP BETWEEN PROOF AND EVIDENCE

In a civil case, the burden of proof is on the plaintiff, who is obliged to prove her case on the balance of probabilities — that is, the plaintiff must show the court that it is more likely than not that her version of the case is true. The plaintiff establishes her version of the facts through the evidence of witnesses and other types of evidence. The facts, and the evidence that proves those facts, focus on two issues: who is liable or at fault and how much is to be paid to compensate the plaintiff for the damage done.

There are four main types of evidence:

1. *Testimonial evidence.* The lawyer will determine from Abigail who the likely witnesses are and will interview any witness who is willing to talk to him or her. It is unlikely that the defendants, Fred and Rattle Motors Ltd., would be willing to talk to Abigail's lawyer, and they certainly would be advised by their lawyer not to. If the lawyer can discover the identity of any bystanders who saw the accident, the lawyer will want to interview them. Abigail's doctors will be interviewed about the injuries she sustained. Any witness interviewed should be asked to sign a statement setting out what they said in the interview. This can be used as a reference for the lawyer and as notes to refresh the memory of the witness at trial. If a witness says he or she saw nothing, a signed statement to that effect will prevent the witness from surfacing later with damaging information.

2. *Documentary and demonstrative evidence.* Any document, diagram, photograph, video tape, or audio tape may contain relevant evidence. In Abigail's case, there may be accident reports written by Fred or Linda, medical emergency admission reports, reports from Abigail's physician, from the rehabilitation staff, and from Abigail's employer concerning her return to work. Demonstrative evidence is also included, such as a diagram of the car showroom, photographs of the showroom taken with the floodlights around the car turned on and off, and photographs of Abigail in her cast and showing her injuries. These documents are all admissible in evidence once the person who made the record proves their authenticity. In some cases, such as a doctor's report, a document is admissible without having its maker give evidence.

3. *Physical evidence.* This evidence consists of physical objects, such as the car's leaking engine or oil pan.

4. *Expert evidence.* This evidence usually consists of the reports and testimony of experts asked to comment on some aspect of the case where specialized knowledge and interpretation of evidence is required. Normally, a witness is restricted to evidence about what they actually observed. An expert can go beyond that and give opinions and offer speculation. The report of a lighting engineer on the lights in the showroom might constitute expert evidence.

CLOSE OF PRELIMINARY INVESTIGATION: CONSIDERATION OF WHETHER AND HOW TO PROCEED

damages
compensation awarded by a court for harm done

At this point, Abigail has retained a lawyer, I.M. Just, who has found out the basic facts and made some preliminary investigations from which he can give Abigail advice on how to proceed. Abigail finds out that if she is successful in her action, she will obtain a judgment in her favour in which she will receive monetary compensation called **damages**. As a successful litigant, Abigail will also recover some of her legal fees and disbursements from the defendants because an award of costs is usually given to the party who is successful at trial. However, if Abigail loses, she will not recover any money for her injuries, and she will have to pay some of the legal costs incurred by the successful defendant. She will also have to pay her own legal fees and disbursements in full. (In some cases, a lawyer might accept a case on a contingency fee basis. *If the plaintiff wins*, the lawyer is paid a percentage of the judgment; if the plaintiff loses, the lawyer is paid nothing.)

It is important that Abigail consider her options carefully. The outcome of her case may be uncertain for a variety of reasons. The legal issues involved may not be clearly resolved. There may be conflicting decisions on the point in issue. More usually, the problem lies with the facts: Is there convincing evidence that will prove the facts of Abigail's case? If, on the lawyer's advice, Abigail thinks she has a good case, she may elect to start a legal proceeding to recover the remedy she seeks.

THE CONCERN WITH COST AND DELAY

An additional concern for Abigail is how much this might cost her, and how long it will take to bring the case to a conclusion. Over the past 15 years, there has been increasing concern that civil litigation in the Superior Court has become slow and expensive. Civil case management (discussed in chapter 21) and simplified procedure (discussed in chapter 23) are two attempts to control cost and delay that have not been entirely successful. The Civil Justice Reform Project made further recommendations that are to take effect on January 1, 2010.[4] It will be interesting to see whether these changes are any more effective than earlier reforms.

principle of proportionality
requires that the time spent on and the expense of a lawsuit be in proportion to the value of the case that is at stake for the parties

The civil court rules will now contain a general **principle of proportionality** to guide lawyers and the courts in applying the rules, generally. The time and expense devoted to any step in a proceeding, and to the proceeding generally, will now have to reflect what is at stake for the parties. Cases that are legally and factually straightforward and of lower value should not take as long or cost as much as large, complex cases. While this has always been a rule of thumb, the principle of proportionality is now incorporated in the *Rules of Civil Procedure* (rule 1.04(1.1)). For Abigail, this would mean that if her case were worth $250,000 rather than $50,000, her lawyer might hold extensive and lengthy discoveries and bring motions that he otherwise might not bring if the case were worth less.

Commencement of proceedings

COURT JURISDICTION

As a plaintiff in a civil proceeding, Abigail must choose between two possible courts: the Small Claims Court and the Ontario Superior Court of Justice. In order to decide which court Abigail should sue in, it is necessary to understand the basis for a court's jurisdiction — its power to hear a case and grant remedies.

There are three types of jurisdiction:

1. *Jurisdiction over the subject matter of the lawsuit.* Does the court have the power to hear this type of case and provide the remedies Abigail seeks? For example, if the court has jurisdiction only over criminal law matters, it does not have jurisdiction to hear Abigail's lawsuit. Similarly, if Abigail were seeking an injunction as a remedy, she could not do so in Small Claims Court because this court has no authority to grant this remedy. In Ontario, the Superior Court of Justice can hear civil cases dealing with any subject other than a subject over which the Federal Court of Canada has exclusive jurisdiction or a subject that has been allocated by statute to a particular court. It can also grant any civil remedy known to law: injunctions, declarations of rights, orders for the return of property, and monetary damages. The Small Claims Court, by contrast, is restricted to making orders for the return of personal property and the payment of money.

2. *Jurisdiction over the monetary amount claimed in the lawsuit.* The issue here is whether a court has the power to order payment of the amount of money being claimed. The Small Claims Court's monetary jurisdiction as of 2008 is $10,000 (expected to rise to $25,000 in 2009 or 2010). This means that the court may grant a judgment for the payment of money for any amount up to and including $10,000 exclusive of interest and costs. However, it has no authority to give judgment for more than that amount. The Superior Court, on the other hand, has an unlimited monetary jurisdiction. It can grant judgment for any amount of money, including an amount within the jurisdiction of the Small Claims Court.[5] Because Abigail's injuries are serious, she will choose the Superior Court because her damages exceed $10,000. The lawsuit will be more expensive to conduct than it would be in Small Claims Court, where proceedings are simpler and less formal.

3. *Territorial jurisdiction.* Does the court have the power to hear a case where the events the case is based on or the parties' residence is outside its geographical jurisdiction? In general, courts in Ontario have territorial jurisdiction over cases where the event giving rise to the lawsuit or the parties are in Ontario. But questions will arise if some of the events took place in another jurisdiction or if one or more of the parties resides outside Ontario. For example, if Abigail had gone to Buffalo, New York to buy her car and had been injured there, if events leading up to the injury occurred in Buffalo, or if the defendants resided there, could Abigail or should Abigail sue in Ontario or New York? The answer to this kind of question is often complicated. As an issue of private international law, it is often determined on a case-by-case basis on a test of the balance of convenience to the parties.[6]

Even within Ontario, there can be issues of territorial jurisdiction that may arise as a result of the plaintiff's choice of place to sue, or the forum. Abigail, as plaintiff, has the right to commence her proceeding in the Superior Court office in any county or region in Ontario, unless a statute requires that it be commenced in a particular county or region. However, if her choice is much more inconvenient to other parties than to her, or it is impossible to get a fair trial, any party may apply to the court to have the case transferred to another county or region. For example, if she and the defendants were all in Toronto and she chose to start her proceeding in Thunder Bay, it is likely that the defendants would bring a motion to move the trial to Toronto on the balance of convenience. Note that her case will be tried in the county or region where it was commenced, unless the court orders otherwise.

RULES OF CIVIL PROCEDURE

In commencing proceedings, Abigail must use the appropriate court forms and follow the procedural rules for conducting a civil case. These rules are set out in the Ontario *Rules of Civil Procedure*. (We will refer to these henceforth as "the rules," as lawyers do.) The rules are actually regulations made pursuant to the *Courts of Justice Act*. The power to make the rules is vested in the Civil Rules Committee, consisting of staff from the Ministry of the Attorney General, members of the judiciary, and lawyers. Rule 1.07 provides a procedure for creating practice directions. The purpose of a practice direction is to allow the senior judge in a judicial region to customize the rules and create additional procedures to deal with problems that are specific to that region and are not covered by existing rules. For example, because of difficulties in scheduling trials in the Toronto region, there is a practice direction under rule 52 that requires counsel to complete certain forms to facilitate the trial-scheduling process there. The additional procedures in this practice direction are presumably not necessary for the administration of justice in other judicial regions, where they do not apply. It is now clear that a practice direction carries the force of law and must be followed. Previously the status and validity of practice directions were questioned because there was no clear authority for creating them. Rule 1.07 now sets out a procedure for creating practice directions. To bring some consistency and uniformity to practice directions, the power to authorize and approve a practice direction is vested in the chief justice of the Superior Court.

You should become familiar with the practice directions that operate in the judicial region where cases you work on are heard. When these are created, they appear in the *Ontario Gazette* and are posted in the regional courthouses. They are also announced in the *Ontario Reports*, the law society's publication of Ontario cases, which all lawyers receive. The *Ontario Annual Practice* reproduces practice directions next to the rules to which they apply. It also contains an index of published practice directions, so you can easily locate the one you are looking for. Other commercially published versions of Superior Court practice materials also contain this information.

MOTIONS

At first glance, it seems that all you need to do is read a rule and follow it. The rules appear to be clear, but like all legal rules they require interpretation. Because the parties are in an adversarial position, both Abigail's lawyer and the defendants' lawyers are likely to use the rules to attempt to gain the upper hand or assert a position that will be helpful to them. Where one party seeks to use a rule against another party that is allegedly violating the rule, there is a procedural dispute that the court must sort out at the pretrial stage. This is done when one party brings a motion. A motion is a proceeding brought within the main action to settle a procedural issue that has arisen at the pretrial stage. A judge, or in some cases a junior judicial official called a master, will hear submissions from counsel on a motion, read submitted material, and decide the issue by making an order. An order on a motion usually does not dispose of a case on its merits, although this can happen. For example, if Abigail had made a claim not recognized by the law, the defendants could bring a motion to strike out her statement of claim and dismiss her action. If the court was persuaded by the defendants that Abigail did not have a legal reason for suing, the court could strike out her statement of claim, and that would be the end of her case. But this is most unusual. Motions are discussed in more detail later in this chapter.

ACTIONS AND APPLICATIONS

Abigail's lawyer is now ready to start the case or, in the language of the rules, to "commence proceedings." In Ontario, there are two ways for a plaintiff to commence proceedings. Abigail can start an **action** by issuing a statement of claim, or she can start an **application** by issuing a notice of application. Usually a party commences an action. Applications are used when a statute or the rules require them, or when it is unlikely that there will be any material facts in dispute and the matter turns on an interpretation of law. Otherwise, a plaintiff must proceed by way of an action. An action has a much longer and more complex pretrial procedure than an application. It is largely devoted to giving the parties the opportunity to review evidence and determine facts before trial. In an application, where there is usually little in the way of factual disputes, we have a much simpler and less time-consuming pretrial procedure. There is no need to conduct discovery or otherwise investigate the facts exhaustively. The trial is more like a hearing with no oral evidence. Each party's lawyer spends most of the hearing time on legal arguments, with the evidence introduced by the use of sworn written statements called affidavits.

The facts and issues in Abigail's case are complex and crucial to her proving negligence against the defendants. It is appropriate that her case proceed as an action rather than as an application.

action
one of the two procedures by which a civil matter is commenced in the Superior Court; the other such procedure is an application

application
one of the two procedures by which a civil matter is commenced in the Superior Court; the other such procedure is an action

Exchange of pleadings: Statement of claim and statement of defence

STATEMENT OF CLAIM

I.M. Just is now ready to commence proceedings by starting an action with a statement of claim. He prepares this document, which sets out

- the remedies Abigail is asking for, referred to as the "claim for relief";

- the identification of the parties in terms of their legal status — for example, Abigail and Fred are individuals, and Rattle Motors Ltd. is a corporation; and

- the facts on which Abigail relies, as well as statements of the laws that entitle her to a remedy.

With the statement of claim, he also files a form called "Information for Court Use," which provides the court with information about the causes of action and whether the case is using any special procedure. Once it is prepared, the document is taken by a law clerk or office courier to the local office of the Superior Court to be issued. After the law office courier pays the prescribed fee for issuing a claim, the

FIGURE 1.2   GENERAL HEADING OF STATEMENT OF CLAIM (FORM 4A)

Court file no. 01-CV-1234

ONTARIO
SUPERIOR COURT OF JUSTICE

BETWEEN:

ABIGAIL BOAR

Plaintiff

and

RATTLE MOTORS LTD. and FRED FLOGEM

Defendants

---

true copy
copy of an original document that is like the original in every particular, including copies of alterations, signatures, and court file numbers

notice of action
document informing defendants that they have been sued

general heading
heading on all court documents identifying the court, the parties, and the status of the parties

title of proceedings
part of the general heading that identifies the parties and their status in a lawsuit

backsheet
part of every court document, it contains the name, LSUC number, address, and telephone and fax numbers of the lawyer who prepared the document, the short title of proceedings, the court and court file number, the fax number of the person to be served (if known), and a large space reserved for court officials to make entries on

registrar opens a court file, assigns the case a court file number which is placed on the document, and issues the statement of claim by sealing and signing the document on behalf of the registrar of the court. As the registrar is doing this to the original, the lawyer's clerk makes a **true copy** of the statement of claim. The lawyer's clerk does this by copying on a copy of the statement of claim the information the court clerk has put on the original. The true copy goes into the court file, and the lawyer's clerk brings the original back to the law office. The lawyer pays the prescribed fee of $181.00[7] to the court on Abigail's behalf. If Abigail's case were urgent and I.M. Just did not have time to draft a statement of claim, I.M. Just could issue a **notice of action**, and file the statement of claim later. This might happen if Abigail had not sued until the limitation period for her cause of action had almost run out. To preserve a client's rights before the limitation period expires, a lawyer can use a notice of action to start the lawsuit and "stop the clock" on the soon-to-expire limitation period.

Once the statement of claim is issued, all further filed documents must bear the appropriate **general heading** identifying the court, the court file number, and the names of the parties. The names of the parties and the status in which they are suing or being sued that appears within the general heading is referred to as the **title of proceedings**. If there are many defendants or plaintiffs, the case is generally referred to by the short title of proceedings, used on the **backsheet** of the court forms. In Abigail's case, the short form is *Boar v. Rattle Motors Ltd. et al.* Figure 1.2 shows the general heading of the statement of claim, including the title of proceedings, where Abigail sues Rattle Motors Ltd. and Fred Flogem in the Superior Court.

Figure 1.3 shows the backsheet for this statement.

Now that I.M. Just has issued the statement of claim, he must serve a copy of it on the defendants within six months from the date on which the claim was issued. Because defendants do not know they have been sued until they are served with the first document in the lawsuit against them, the rules are strict about ensuring that they are properly served with the first or originating document.

SERVING THE STATEMENT OF CLAIM

The statement of claim, the originating document in this case, must be served personally on the defendants or must be served by a permitted alternative to personal

FIGURE 1.3 BACKSHEET (FORM 4C)

ABIGAIL BOAR

Plaintiff(s)

(Short title of proceeding)

and

RATTLE MOTORS LTD. ET AL.

Defendant(s)

Court file no. 01-CV-1234

ONTARIO SUPERIOR COURT OF JUSTICE

Proceeding commenced at Toronto

STATEMENT OF CLAIM

Name, address and telephone number of plaintiff's lawyer or plaintiff:

I.M. Just
LSUC #12345R

Just & Coping
Barristers and Solicitors
365 Bay Street - 8701
Toronto, Ontario, M3J 4A9

tel. 416-762-1342
fax 416-762-2300

Lawyers for the Plaintiff

service. Personal service means that the statement of claim must be handed direct-ly to the defendant if the defendant is an individual. Service is effective even if the defendant refuses to take the document, tears it up, or throws it away. Therefore a process server can simply hand a copy of the document to Fred. But what about serving Rattle Motors Ltd.? There are special rules for serving individuals on behalf of a corporation. Here, a process server can serve the corporate defendant by handing a copy of Abigail's statement of claim to the manager of Rattle Motors Ltd., or a director or officer.

It is also possible to use one of the three alternatives to personal service to serve an originating document.

1. If I.M. Just knows that Rattle Motors Ltd. and Fred have lawyers acting for them in this lawsuit, he can serve the lawyers' office. This is valid service, provided that the lawyers sign a document stating that they accept service on behalf of the defendants. To do that, the lawyers should have instructions from the clients to accept service on their behalf.

2. I.M. Just can send a copy of the claim to the defendants' last-known addresses by ordinary mail with an acknowledgment of receipt form, which is provided by the post office. Service is valid and effective if the recipient signs the acknowledgment card and mails it back to the sender.

3. If he has first attempted personal service, I.M. Just can deliver the statement of claim in an envelope to the defendant's residence and leave it with an apparently adult person who appears to be a member of the household. He can then mail a copy of the claim to the defendant the next day. This mode of service applies only when serving an individual, such as Fred Flogem.

SUBSTITUTED SERVICE

All of the methods of service that we have discussed so far assume that I.M. Just knows or can find out the defendants' last-known addresses and that the defend-ants are actually there. But what if Fred has moved and no longer works at Rattle Motors Ltd.? Or what if he is evading service? I.M. Just may have tried personal ser-vice and the alternatives to personal service and failed to serve him. If I.M. Just does not know exactly where Fred is, the other modes of service will be ineffective. In these situations, plaintiffs can ask the court to permit them to use substituted ser-vice. I.M. Just must suggest a method of service that satisfies the court that there is a reasonable probability that Abigail's statement of claim will come to Fred's atten-tion. Depending on what seems likely to be most effective, the court may order ser-vice by registered mail, or service on a close relative or friend with whom the defendant appears to be in touch, or service by an announcement in the news-paper. Whatever method is ordered by the court, once I.M. Just does what the order says, Fred is presumed to be served, even if he did not actually receive a copy of the statement of claim. Abigail can continue with her lawsuit. If substituted service will not be effective, a court may order that service be dispensed with altogether, although this is rare.

OTHER FORMS OF SERVICE

There are special rules for personally serving corporations and other legal entities, such as estate executors, trustees, mentally incompetent persons, and children. There is another set of rules for serving a party who does not reside or carry on business in Ontario. There are often special procedural rules that must be followed when serving someone who lives in a foreign country. Those who reside outside Ontario are given more time to respond to the lawsuit.

Once the originating document is served, the rules for service are relaxed, as those parties with an interest in the lawsuit are now presumed to know about it and about their obligations to respond. Subsequent documents may be served in a variety of ways:

- by mailing a copy to the opposite party's lawyer's office (this document is deemed to be served on the fifth day after it is mailed);

- by physically delivering a copy to the lawyer's office and leaving it with an employee, usually a receptionist;

- by depositing a copy at a document exchange of which the lawyer is a member if the copy is date-stamped as received by the document exchange (this document is deemed to be served on the day after the document exchange receives it);

- by faxing a copy to the lawyer's office, including a cover sheet setting out information that the document is being served by fax and showing who served it (some documents may not be served this way);

- by sending a copy to the lawyer's office by courier (this document is deemed to be served two days later); and

- by e-mailing a document to the lawyer's office, provided that the sender indicates in the e-mail message who he or she is and provided that the lawyer served in this way e-mails back an acceptance of the document served (this document is deemed to be served on the day following the day the message is sent).

PROOF OF SERVICE

Someone who is served with a document, whether originating or not and whatever the mode of service, may deny that he or she was served. If so, that person claims to have no notice of the lawsuit. This can be problematic. A defendant who does not respond to a claim will find that the plaintiff may still proceed in that defendant's absence.

A defendant who claims he or she was not served, and finds that he or she has been sued or that a judgment has been obtained, may move to set aside the proceedings or set aside the judgment. If the defendant is successful, the plaintiff may have to start all over from the beginning with added expense and delay. It is therefore important that I.M. Just is careful to ensure that he serves the defendants and can prove it. This is particularly important for originating documents, such as a statement of claim, which give notice to the defendant that he or she has been sued. It is less crucial with subsequent documents because a misadventure of service does not mean the action has to be restarted.

Proof usually consists of an affidavit of service, in which the person who served the document swears that he or she did so and describes the method of service, the date, and other details. The rules permit the affidavit of service to be written right on the backsheet of the originating or subsequent document. Where a lawyer accepts service, his or her endorsement is proof of service. Where service is through a document exchange, the document exchange's date stamp is sufficient evidence to prove service. No additional affidavit is required.

STATEMENT OF DEFENCE

Now that I.M. Just has served Fred and Rattle Motors Ltd. with Abigail's statement of claim by personally serving the defendants or by using an alternative to personal service, the defendants must respond to the statement of claim by serving and filing a statement of defence. If they are served in Ontario, they have 20 days to serve and file a statement of defence. If they are served elsewhere in Canada or in the continental United States, they have 40 days. If they are served anywhere else on the planet, they have 60 days to serve and file a defence. If time is running out before they have finished preparing a defence, they may file a notice of intent to defend. This extends the time for filing the statement of defence for a further 10 days.

Generally, plaintiffs in the same proceeding do not have conflicts of interest and are represented by the same lawyers. A plaintiff cannot be forced to have others join him or her as plaintiff. One lawyer may also represent multiple defendants, provided that their defences do not conflict. For example, if one defendant says the plaintiff's injuries were caused by the acts of the other defendant, there is a clear conflict if the other defendant denies liability. Fred and the manager of Rattle Motors Ltd. will have to decide if one lawyer can represent both. In this case, Rattle Motors Ltd. will be vicariously liable for the acts of its employee even if it did not itself commit separate acts of negligence. In cases like this, where both the employer and employee are sued, they are usually represented by one lawyer because it is likely that the employer or its insurer will end up paying any damages. If a conflict develops between the defendants, however, a lawyer is obliged to tell both defendants that he or she can no longer act for either of them and to help arrange for separate representation.

Let us assume that one lawyer represents both defendants. This lawyer reviews Abigail's claim, which sets out a concise statement of the facts but not the evidence by which these facts are to be proven. The claim should also identify the cause of action and set out the legal principles that Abigail relies on. Finally, the claim should set out the remedies sought. After reviewing this document the lawyer may advise one of three possible responses to the claim:

1. *Do nothing.* In this case, Abigail will obtain a default judgment, after noting that the defendants have defaulted on their defence.

2. *Bring a motion to dismiss on the ground that the claim discloses no known cause of action.* This type of motion is rare and unlikely in our case because Abigail's claim is not unusual.

3. *Serve and file a statement of defence.* In this statement, a lawyer sets out defences which, if proved, will result in Abigail's claim being dismissed. The defendants must admit those paragraphs in Abigail's claim with which

they agree. They must then deny those paragraphs that contain statements with which they disagree. Then, if applicable, they must identify those paragraphs in the claim about which they have no knowledge. They must also set out their own version of the facts and the law they rely on. This last requirement is sometimes referred to as an affirmative defence because it consists of more than denials of the plaintiff's claim. Those paragraphs of Abigail's claim that the defendants admit are deemed to be proved and need not be proved at trial. This is one of the ways in which the pleadings serve to narrow the issues before trial.

After the statement of defence has been served on Abigail's lawyer and filed in court, I.M. Just reviews it. If he finds that the statement of defence has raised an issue or facts related to that issue that were not dealt with in the statement of claim, Abigail may serve and file a reply to the statement of defence. For example, if the defence states that Abigail showed up at the showroom in an intoxicated state, the defendants may argue that there was contributory negligence on Abigail's part. Abigail may need to serve and file a reply denying that she was intoxicated if those facts and issues were not covered in the statement of claim. If the plaintiff simply wishes to deny the defendant's defence generally, there is no need to serve and file a formal reply.

OTHER PLEADINGS

In some cases, there are other types of legal issues that may result in other pleadings. Suppose Abigail sues Fred and Rattle Motors Ltd. but not Skank Motorcar Company Ltd., the manufacturer of the Super Coupe. If the two defendants think that it was not their negligence but the negligent manufacturing of the Super Coupe that caused Abigail's damages, they may issue a third party notice to add Skank Motorcar Company Ltd. to the proceedings. This is a notice to the manufacturer which says that the defendants hold Skank Motorcar Company Ltd. wholly or partly responsible for Abigail's damages, so that if they are found liable, they will argue to have that liability transferred to the manufacturer, whom they are adding as a third party. They must send Skank Motorcar Company Ltd. all the pleadings to date, and Skank Motorcar Company Ltd. may serve and file a defence against the claim made by the defendants against it. Skank Motorcar Company Ltd. is also entitled to raise any defence against the plaintiff's claim in the main action that the other defendants did not raise but could have raised. Thereafter, Skank Motorcar Company Ltd. is treated as a defendant in the main proceeding, and the third party issues are part of the trial of the main action, although in some cases they may be tried separately. It is also possible for a third party to deny liability and claim that the fault, if any, is that of a fourth party. This would result in the issuing of a fourth party notice with the fourth party having the same rights as the third party.

If one defendant has a claim against the other defendant that is related to events or transactions in the main action, the defendant with the claim should file a crossclaim against the other defendant. In a case like Abigail's, this is most likely to occur with respect to a claim for contribution by one defendant against the other under the *Negligence Act*. That Act permits one defendant to have the degree of liability between the defendants assessed to determine how much each should pay, and it allows a defendant that settles the action to claim financial contributions from other defendants. In our case, Fred may wish to argue that if the defendants are liable to Abigail, Rattle Motors Ltd. is 90 percent responsible for Abigail's injuries. If Fred seeks to pin most of the responsibility on Rattle Motors Ltd., he needs to do it by crossclaim against Rattle Motors Ltd. The recipient of a crossclaim may counterclaim against the crossclaimant or serve and file a defence to the crossclaim. A crossclaim is not dependent on the main action but is usually tried with it.

If either defendant can argue that Abigail acted in some way to cause them a legally recognized injury (unlikely in this case), the defendant can file a counterclaim with the statement of defence. Abigail would then have to respond with her own defence to counterclaim.

Once a reply has been made to every defence filed, or the time for replying has expired, the pleading stage is complete. Facts that are admitted do not have to be proved at trial. Facts that are not admitted must be proved. For example, if Rattle Motors Ltd. and Fred admit that Abigail sustained the injuries and suffered the damages she claims but deny that the damages resulted from their negligence, damages are admitted and need not be proven at trial. However, Abigail will still have to prove negligence because liability is not admitted. Both parties will have to advance evidence to prove facts on the issue of negligence.

Because a party can only introduce evidence relevant to the facts as pleaded, evidence relating to facts that were not pleaded but should have been pleaded cannot be admitted. This happens rarely, but when it does happen it can be fatal to the party who forgot to plead a necessary fact to support his or her case. Sometimes the party can ask the judge to let the party amend the pleadings, but the other party will object, and the judge may decide that it is too late to permit amendments and reopen the pretrial stage for discovery on these "new" facts if the case is already at trial. This is one of the reasons it is necessary to read statements of claim and defence carefully to ensure that the pleadings fit the theory of your case.

Examinations for discovery of parties and discovery of documents

The pleadings should set out the case from each party's point of view. You should now know the basic facts in dispute, the legal issues, the case your law firm has to prove, and the case it has to meet. The pleadings are a concise statement of material facts — a lot of the details are missing. For this reason each party is entitled to have discovery of the other party's case to obtain more information about the supporting evidence and details. There are a number of different types of discovery available, including medical examinations and inspections of places or property. For example, Fred and Rattle Motors Ltd. may request Abigail to submit to a medical or psychological examination about her neurological problems by a medical professional of its choice. The evidence from that examination can be received in

***viva voce* evidence**
oral evidence

the form of the doctor's ***viva voce* evidence** or the doctor's report. Abigail, on the other hand, may wish to have a lighting expert and an expert on flooring examine Rattle Motors Ltd.'s showroom. Discovery in the form of inspection of property is available to her because she does not have possession of the property or a right to enter it for the purposes of inspecting it. These types of discovery are used only in those actions where they are helpful. The main types of discovery used in almost every civil case are discovery of documents and oral examination for discovery.

DISCOVERY OF DOCUMENTS

The rules require all parties to prepare an affidavit of documents in which they disclose under oath the identity and nature of every document that might be relevant to the action they now have or had previously. Documents also include information stored electronically. In recent years, issues have arisen over how extensive a search of electronic files must be to discover relevant documents. Because the number and length of electronic files on disks and hard drives are often great, a search can be daunting, particularly given the time, money, and effort required to conduct the search. Fortunately, in Abigail's case there are unlikely to be voluminous electronic records to review. Abigail, for example, must disclose all of the subsequent medical records that underlie her claim that she suffered specific serious injuries. Rattle Motors Ltd. must disclose any reports it has concerning leaking oil pans on the Super Coupe. Documents are given a broad interpretation and may include computer disks, audio and video tapes, photographs, and other media of communication. All documents that a party has or had must be listed. If the document is still in existence and obtainable, it must be produced for inspection by the other side. Usually, each side provides the other with copies of its own documents.

An exception to the disclosure rule exists with respect to documents for which a party claims legal privilege. For example, lawyer–client correspondence is routinely claimed as privileged based on the lawyer–client privilege. Similarly, documents or reports prepared specifically because of the litigation are also privileged and need not be produced. If privilege is claimed for a document, it must be listed but does not have to be produced at trial. If a party decides to waive the privilege and rely on the document for the party's own case at trial, then the privilege is lost, and the document must be disclosed. However, where a document is not privileged it must be listed in the affidavit of documents and produced.

EXAMINATION FOR DISCOVERY

Once documentary discovery has taken place, the parties usually arrange for an examination for discovery. Here, each party's lawyer is entitled to question the other party under oath about the case, the statement of claim or defence, and the documents disclosed in the discovery of documents process. Questions can be wide ranging. If a party does not know the answer to a question, he or she may be asked to undertake to provide an answer or produce a document later. On a lawyer's advice, the party either accepts or rejects the undertaking. If the undertaking is rejected, the party asking the question may bring a motion to compel the other party to re-attend at his or her own expense to answer the question, provided that the judge on the motion agrees that the question is a proper question.

These examinations are held outside court, usually in an office rented for the purpose. Abigail would be present with her lawyer to answer questions put to her by the lawyer for Rattle Motors Ltd. and Fred. Fred and a representative of Rattle Motors Ltd. may attend to observe and to advise their lawyer. Abigail may also be present when her lawyer questions the defendants in their lawyer's presence. Also present is a court reporter or stenographer to take down a record of the proceedings. This record can be used in preparing both for cross-examination of a party and for preparing a client for examination-in-chief at trial. Where a party gives different answers or tells a different story from the one given at discovery, the discovery transcript can be used to challenge the credibility of the evidence given by the party at trial. The transcript can also be used to "read in" admissions by the opposite party on issues and facts in the case, although this is more likely to be done on a "request to admit" before trial. We discuss "requests to admit" later in this chapter.

Motions

Thus far, we have been describing how a civil action proceeds. It appears to be orderly and without any procedural disputes. On occasion, we have made reference to one or the other of the parties applying to the court for an order concerning the conduct of the action. For example, if a lawyer omits an essential fact or legal issue from a statement of claim, he or she can ask the court for permission to amend the claim to add the missing information. But how do you ask the court? The answer is that you bring a motion to obtain the relief or remedy you request. Motions are generally proceedings within an action and may be brought at any time during the proceedings, including at trial. Their purpose is to settle a dispute about some procedural point that the parties are unable to resolve themselves. On a motion, the court hears argument by the parties and then issues an order that resolves the problem. Such orders rarely decide the case on the merits and bring it to an end. Instead, the parties usually do as the order directs and get on with the case. Appeals from orders made on motions are rare. The right to appeal this kind of order is restricted, and it is usually too expensive and time-consuming since the issues are often procedural and not crucial to ultimate success. Examples of procedural motions include motions to extend the time for filing pleadings, motions for particulars (details) of allegations in a statement of claim or defence, and motions to compel a party to produce documents or attend discovery. Occasionally, a motion may decide the case without a trial: A motion for default judgment will do this where a defendant has failed to file a defence. A motion to strike out a statement of claim as disclosing no cause of action may do this as well.

Motions are usually made on notice to the other party. The party who brings the motion, called "the moving party" whether plaintiff or defendant, serves the "the responding party" with a notice of motion. The notice of motion tells the responding party what the moving party wants the court to do and provides a brief statement of the reasons why the moving party is entitled to the order. The notice of motion also sets out the documents or sources of information relied on. Evidence on the motion is usually given by affidavit rather than orally. The affidavit sets out the facts that entitle the moving party to the relief claimed in the notice of motion. The responding party may also file an affidavit or other documents to support its case and may bring a crossmotion if it also has related issues that it wishes resolved. Counsel then appears before a judge or master of the Superior Court and presents the motion orally. The judge or master decides the issues raised in the motion and issues an **order**. If a motion is made at trial, it is not necessary to use formal notices of motions because the parties are already before the court. While motions are generally made on notice, some motions may be made without notice to the other side. An example is a motion for substituted service of a claim when the other party cannot be located for service.

One motion that might occur when pleadings have been exchanged is a motion for summary judgment. While a default judgment may be obtained if the defendant

order
generic term used in the
Rules of Civil Procedure to
describe commands
issued by courts on
motions and at trials

files no statement of defence, a summary judgment is obtained when a party argues that the other party's pleadings disclose no triable issue. If the motion is successful, a judgment should be issued — to dismiss the action if a defendant brings the motion, or to grant judgment if a plaintiff brings the motion. If the issue is one of law alone, the judge may decide it. If it involves questions of credibility or facts which are disputed, the judge is more likely to use the motion to narrow the issues, establish facts, and order a speedy trial. If, for example, the defendants bring a motion for summary judgment to dismiss Abigail's action on the basis that the limitation period for tort actions has expired, they must file affidavits as to when the accident occurred and when the action was commenced, with reference to the pleadings and perhaps discovery transcripts. On a motion for summary judgment, the facts of a case must be simple and unambiguous. There are heavy cost penalties for a party that brings a futile and unnecessary motion.

Pretrial conference and trial preparation

The parties have now exchanged pleadings, discoveries have been completed, and usually any motions necessary to ensure compliance with the rules have been brought, heard, and determined. The parties need no more information before trial. At this point, lawyers and their clients often assess their chances for success at trial, weighing the pros and cons of their case. Most cases get this far because there is a dispute about the facts. No lawyer will tell a client with certainty that he or she will win or lose; when facts are disputed, much will depend on the credibility of witnesses, which is hard to assess.

In this atmosphere and at this stage, either side or both sides may attempt to settle the case. If the parties reach a settlement, they file a consent to dismiss the action on the basis of the terms of the settlement. If the settlement involves payments by one side to the other, the action is not dismissed until the payment is made to prevent the payer from reneging on the promise. The parties may pursue informal discussions, or they may make formal written offers — the latter have some important consequences if they are rejected. Briefly, if a formal offer to settle is made, it is made in writing to the other side, and a sealed copy is filed with the court. If the other side accepts the offer on its terms and within the time during which the offer is open for acceptance, the case is over. But if the offer is rejected and the party who rejected the offer does not do as well at trial as he or she would have done had he or she accepted the offer, there are negative cost consequences.

For example, if Abigail is offered $300,000 to settle but thinks she can get $500,000 at trial, she may reject the offer. However, if she recovers only $200,000, she will receive costs only to the date the offer was made, and she will be deprived of costs thereafter. Further, the defendant is entitled to the usual costs from the date the offer was made to the date of judgment. If Abigail made an offer to Fred and Rattle Motors Ltd. and they rejected it, and if Abigail received a judgment that was equal to or better than the offer she made, Abigail will receive costs to the date the offer was made and a higher cost award from the day the offer was made to the date of judgment. In a long and complex lawsuit, legal costs can reach a significant amount. This may make litigants think twice about forging ahead when they find that a large part of the judgment is eaten up by their obligations to pay their own and part of their opponent's legal costs.

SETTING THE CASE DOWN FOR TRIAL

If the case does not settle on the close of discoveries, either party may signal that he or she has completed all necessary information-gathering steps, all motions, and is ready to go to trial. This is done by filing a trial record after serving it on the other party. Sixty days after that is done, the court registrar will put the action on the trial list by setting the case down for trial. If no party sets the matter down for trial, there are provisions for the registrar to force the action on for trial, or to dismiss the action for want of prosecution after giving notice to the parties. Cases are tried in the order in which they are placed on the trial list. There are three separate lists: one for jury trials, one for non-jury trials, and one for speedy trials.

TRIAL RECORD

The trial record is a booklet with grey cardboard covers. It is prepared for the use of the trial judge by the party who sets the action down for trial. It contains a table of contents, a copy of each of the pleadings filed, and a copy of any orders made at the pretrial stage as a result of motions. The back cover of the record is set up as a backsheet, with a large blank space for the judge to write his or her **endorsement**. The endorsements are handwritten notes recording the judge's decision, though not usually the judge's reasons for his or her decision.

endorsement
judge's handwritten order or judgment from which a successful party is expected to prepare a formal draft of the order or judgment

PRETRIAL CONFERENCE

After the matter has been set down, either party may request a pretrial conference. Though not mandatory under the rules, the parties are encouraged to avail themselves of the opportunity to use a pretrial conference. Each party serves on the other and files with the court a pretrial conference memorandum that sets out the issues between the parties. The lawyers, with the parties, appear before a pretrial conference judge. The role of the judge is to listen to the lawyers, review the issues with them, and give a frank assessment of the case. The idea here is that an impartial judge may inject a dose of reality that may facilitate settlement, particularly where the parties are being obstinate. The judge's goal is to promote settlement and, failing that, to narrow the issues in order to speed up and simplify the trial. Unless the parties consent, the judge who conducts a pretrial conference does not preside at the trial of the matter.

REQUESTS TO ADMIT

As a means to speeding up the proof of facts at the trial, either party at any time may serve on the other a **request to admit**. The party served with a request to admit is being asked to admit the truth of a fact or the authenticity of a document. The party receiving the request must admit, deny, or refuse to admit, and explain any refusal to admit. Failure to respond leads to a finding that the fact is deemed to be admitted, or the document is deemed to be authentic. An admission, as noted earlier, eliminates the need to prove that fact at trial and can reduce the time it takes to try the case.

request to admit
document in which one party requires the other to admit the truth of a fact or the authenticity of a document

ASSIGNMENT COURT

After the pretrial conference or after both parties have consented to dispense with the pretrial conference, the action is placed on a controlled list for trial. As the case gets closer to the top of the list, it goes to a weekly assignment court, where the lawyers appear and, with the judge, set a specific date for trial. However, if cases ahead of it on the list settle on the eve of trial, the list may collapse, and the parties may suddenly find that their trial date has moved up. Similarly, another trial may take longer than estimated, and the parties' case may be delayed. Note that the procedures for trial lists vary from one judicial region to another.

PRETRIAL PREPARATION

Once you know your client is going to trial, there is much to do. I.M. Just needs to decide what witnesses he will call to provide the evidence that will prove the facts alleged. Abigail will obviously give evidence of what happened to her. In addition, I.M. Just will have to use a **summons to a witness** to ensure that other witnesses attend trial and give evidence. If a witness has relevant documents that he or she can speak about, the summons should direct the witness to bring those documents to court. Because Abigail's medical reports are important evidence on the issue of damages, I.M. Just must give notice of his intent to produce these records at trial. The records will be admitted in evidence unless the opposite party wishes to cross-examine the doctor or maker of the report. There are other notices that might have to be served, though perhaps not in this case — for example, one party may serve a notice to introduce business records, such as invoices or an account record. As with medical reports, business records may be admissible without the maker of the record having to prove their validity and authenticity. I.M. Just and the defendants' lawyer may wish to prepare a trial brief. This brief includes a list of witnesses, what they will say, what opposing witnesses are likely to say, and contains points about cross-examining witnesses. It may also include matters for opening and closing argument and a guide for proving each fact necessary to the case.

Time must then be spent preparing witnesses for their examinations-in-chief and cross-examinations and preparing demonstrative and other physical and documentary evidence for trial.

summons to a witness
order of a court telling the person named on the summons to attend a trial and give evidence

A VARIATION: CASE MANAGEMENT SYSTEM

You should be aware that in Windsor and Ottawa, under rule 77, there is a mandatory case management system for most civil actions. In Toronto, under rule 78, case management is currently (2008) an option: either full case management or modified case management can be used. Case management does not change the basic steps in an action, but it does two things that the rules do not require. First, it imposes mandatory time limits on completion of steps in a proceeding by establishing a timetable immediately after the action commences. The timing and scheduling of the case is now in the hands of the courts rather than in the hands of the parties or their lawyers. The result is that cases are thought to move through the system much more quickly than they did when lawyers controlled the timing. Second, it simplifies and in some cases eliminates some of the procedural aspects that most contribute to wasting time and increasing cost. For example, the process for motions is greatly simplified. It also introduces some steps not otherwise required by the rules: Both case mediation and pretrial conferences are mandatory under case management. The ultimate goal of case management is to move a case rapidly through the system, structuring opportunities for settlement and getting the matter tried quickly if settlement is unsuccessful.

Trial

Because Abigail is the plaintiff, her lawyer opens her case, perhaps with an opening statement to explain what the case is about. The statement may be brief because it is presumed that the trial judge has read the trial record and knows that this is a "slip and fall" negligence case with issues concerning both liability and damages. But it will be necessary to have an opening statement if this is a jury trial, because jurors know nothing of the case until the lawyers tell them in the opening statements. I.M. Just then calls his witnesses, probably starting with Abigail. He examines Abigail in chief, and the defendant's counsel cross-examines her. The same sequence is followed with the plaintiff's other witnesses. When I.M. Just has finished presenting Abigail's case through the testimony of witnesses, he closes the case. At this time, the defendants open their case. If their lawyers think that the evidence adduced from the plaintiff's witnesses does not prove the facts alleged by the plaintiff, they may move that the action be dismissed and elect not to call evidence. But it is more likely that they will not run this risk, and that they will call the first witness. The case then proceeds with examination and cross-examination of the defence witnesses. When the defendants close their case, each side sums up, the plaintiff going first.

Having heard the evidence, read the documents, and heard counsel, the trial judge may then decide the case on the spot. But if the judge needs to think about the issues, he or she reserves judgment and gives judgment on a later date. If the judge reserves judgment, he or she may also issue written or oral reasons for judgment. These reasons may be reported in the law reports or be available through an online service such as Quicklaw.

JURY TRIALS

If Abigail had wanted a jury trial, she would have been required to issue a jury notice before the close of pleadings and discovery. The defendants could then have moved to have the jury notice struck out on the ground that the case was not appropriate for a jury. This usually happens when the evidence is technical or complex, although it is harder to strike out a jury notice on these grounds than it once was.

If the matter proceeds before a jury, the trial takes longer than it does before a judge sitting alone. This is because juries are not experienced in trying cases or knowledgeable about the law. Lawyers may have to move more slowly in questioning witnesses and be more thorough in their summing up and in their opening remarks. At the end of the trial, the judge charges the jury, giving a neutral summing up of the evidence and explaining how the law is to be applied to whatever facts the jury finds. The judge carefully drafts the charge, bearing in mind suggestions by the lawyers. It is up to the jury to assess the evidence to determine what facts have been proven from the evidence it has heard. The judge tells the jury what the law is in his or her charge. Unlike the situation in the United States, civil juries are relatively rare in Canada.

JUDGMENT

At the end of the trial, the judge gives judgment. If there is a jury, it gives a verdict on which the judgment is based.[8] If Abigail is successful, she will be given a judgment requiring Fred and Rattle Motors Ltd. to pay her damages for her injuries. Each defendant may be ordered to pay a specific share if the judge assesses liability for each of them, or they may be jointly and severally liable to pay. Abigail is likely to receive general damages for her pain and suffering, and special damages for her out-of-pocket expenses, which cover her actual out-of-pocket expenses and other **pecuniary** losses caused by the defendants' negligence. She will receive prejudgment interest from the date that she was injured to the date of judgment, and she will also be awarded postjudgment interest on the amount of the judgment from the day of judgment to the day of payment of that judgment. If Abigail wins her case, she is likely to be awarded partial indemnity costs, which amount to one-third to two-thirds of her actual legal costs, based on a cost grid or table. If Abigail is not successful, her claim will be dismissed. She will not receive anything. The successful defendants will receive their partial indemnity costs, which Abigail will have to pay.

A judgment in Abigail's favour does not mean that she will simply receive a cheque. A judgment is a command to pay, but if the defendants choose not to pay up voluntarily, Abigail will have to take steps to enforce her judgment. Abigail can file **writs of seizure and sale** against Fred and Rattle Motors Ltd. She can then direct the sheriff of Toronto or the sheriff of any county in which she has filed a writ and the defendants have property to seize and sell the property under the authority of the writ. Abigail then satisfies her judgment from the proceeds of the sale. For example, the sheriff could seize Fred's bank account or sell his car or house. The sheriff could also seize the property on which Rattle Motors Ltd. has its building, as well as its inventory of cars. Alternatively, Abigail could **garnishee** Fred's wages or any amounts due to either defendant from third parties. A garnishee order is sent to third parties who owe money to either defendant, telling them to pay the funds due to the defendant to the sheriff to be held to satisfy the judgment.

EFFECT OF THE JUDGMENT

Once a judgment is given, it is final and may not be challenged unless it is appealed. The matter is then said to be *res judicata*, which means that any issue tried and decided in a court proceeding cannot be relitigated in a subsequent proceeding.

Appeals

The rules and the *Courts of Justice Act* provide for an appeal from almost any trial court's decision. In some circumstances, appeals are heard by the Divisional Court, a branch of the Superior Court. In Abigail's case, which originated in the Superior Court, the appeal (if the damages are substantiated) is heard in the Ontario Court of Appeal, the highest court in the province. If, for example, the defendants felt that the damage award for Abigail's pain and suffering was excessive and not supported by legal principle or the evidence, they could appeal by filing a notice of appeal in which they set out the grounds on which the appeal is based. Here the defendants are called the "appellants" in the title of proceedings because they are appealing the trial decision. Abigail will be called the "respondent" on the appeal.

pecuniary
of monetary value

writ of seizure and sale
order from a court to a sheriff to enforce the court's order by seizing and selling the defendant's property and holding the proceeds to satisfy the judgment debt to the plaintiff; also known as a writ of execution

garnishee
order directed to a third party who owes money to a defendant as a means of enforcing a judgment

res judicata
Latin phrase meaning that a matter decided by a court is final and incapable of being relitigated in a subsequent proceeding

The appellants are required to file with the court a statement of fact and law, which sets out the facts of the case, the legal issues raised on appeal, and a brief resume of the law on which they rely. I.M. Just will file a statement of fact and law in reply. The appellants will also order those parts of the trial transcript that are required to support their factual and legal arguments. The transcripts and documents that were exhibits at trial are the only evidence. No witnesses are heard on an appeal.

The Court of Appeal has very broad powers, but it exercises them sparingly and with discretion. The court may affirm the trial decision, reverse it, or vary it. It may substitute its own decision for that of the trial judge, though this is unusual. More often, a new trial is ordered. In most cases, the appeal is dismissed and the trial decision affirmed. The major reason why most appeals fail is because the appeal court will not interfere with the findings of fact made by the trial court, even if the appellate judges would have come to a different conclusion if they had been adjudicating at trial. The appellate judges will not substitute their findings of fact for those of the trial judge if there was any reasonable basis for the trial judge's drawing the conclusions that he or she did from the evidence at trial. The reasoning is that the trial judge saw and heard the witnesses and, from personal observation, was able to draw conclusions about credibility which the Court of Appeal, having only the transcripts of evidence, is not in the position to do. Therefore, errors of fact rarely give rise to a successful appeal, leaving major errors of law as the main basis of a successful appeal. If the trial judge misapplied the law, the appellate court can identify the error and vary the judgment without a new trial. If a jury was improperly charged on the law and reaches an erroneous verdict, a new trial is ordered because a jury's reasoning process is unknown.

If appealing to the Ontario Court of Appeal is difficult, appealing from that court to the Supreme Court of Canada is even more so. Anyone who can pay for it can appeal from a Superior Court trial judgment. You do not need the appellate court's permission. While your chances may be poor, they worsen at the Supreme Court of Canada. In order to appeal from the provincial appellate court to this court, you need the Supreme Court's permission, which is called "leave to appeal." To get leave to appeal, you need to show that there are conflicting lines of case authority in different provinces or that the matter you are raising is a public policy issue of great importance.

You have had a broad overview of how a civil action proceeds through to trial and appeal. We can now begin to examine the process in more detail in subsequent chapters.

CHAPTER SUMMARY

In this chapter, using Abigail Boar's claim for negligence against the defendants Rattle Motors Ltd. and Fred Flogem, we have followed the conduct of a civil action through the Ontario Superior Court of Justice to the Court of Appeal. The procedure began when Abigail hired I.M. Just to sue on her behalf. I.M. Just conducted preliminary investigations to determine if there was a good cause of action against the defendants. Once the decision to sue was made, proceedings were commenced with the issuing of a statement of claim. The defendants answered with a statement of defence. When both sides exchanged pleadings, the pleading stage closed, and the parties proceeded to oral examinations for discovery and discovery of each other's documents. Until the end of discovery, the parties could bring motions to resolve disputes concerning the application of procedural rules in this case. Once discovery ended, the matter was set down for trial by filing a trial record, and a pretrial conference was held. The parties then proceeded to prepare for trial. At the end of the case, the judge gave judgment, and the parties considered their options on appeal.

KEY TERMS

fees	title of proceedings
disbursements	backsheet
contingency fee	*viva voce* evidence
cause of action	order
trier of fact	endorsement
damages	request to admit
principle of proportionality	summons to a witness
action	pecuniary
application	writ of seizure and sale
true copy	garnishee
notice of action	*res judicata*
general heading	

NOTES

1 Civil cases where the remedy sought is less than $10,000 (expected to rise to $25,000 in 2009 or 2010) may be tried in Small Claims Court. This court has its own rules of procedure, which are less formal and complex than those used in the Superior Court. This text is about the civil process in the Superior Court. For a discussion of the rules of procedure in Small Claims Court, see Laurence Olivo and DeeAnn Gonsalves, *Debtor–Creditor Law and Procedure*, 3rd ed. (Toronto: Emond Montgomery, 2008).

2 The use of the word "retainer" to describe both the contract for services and the deposit paid by a client for services to be rendered is confusing. The reason for this usage is that the payment of a deposit served to retain the services of a lawyer, even if there was no written contract of retainer. Hence, the deposit was often described as "the retainer" even where a separate "contract of retainer" was signed. To further the confusion, however, some retainers are not deposits to be set off against future accounts rendered by the lawyer but are payments made directly to a lawyer for agreeing to be available to provide unspecified

services for a given period of time. This practice is common in commercial law, where a company may have a law firm on an annual retainer.

3 A contingency fee is permitted in a class action under the *Class Proceedings Act, 1992*, SO 1992, c. 6, for example, as well as in other civil actions.

4 Some of the amendments came into force immediately, in December 2008. These generally extend the revocation dates of pilot projects involving general case management (rule 77), case management in Toronto (rule 78), and mandatory mediation (rule 24.1) from various dates in 2009 to January 1, 2010. There is a good chance that some or all of these pilot projects may be extended beyond January 1, 2010, and this would be done through further amendments to the *Rules of Civil Procedure.*

5 A claim within the monetary jurisdiction of the Small Claims Court usually goes there, and there can be cost penalties for suing in the Superior Court for a small amount of money. However, there are reasons for suing for small sums in Superior Court that the court will recognize as appropriate: a test case on which many other similar cases depend, or a novel cause of action should be brought in the higher court.

6 "Balance of convenience" is a practical, fact-based test in which the court examines how difficult, expensive, or time consuming it is for the parties to try the case in one location rather than another. If the plaintiff has chosen a location, a defendant who wishes to change location needs to show that he or she is at a great disadvantage because of the residence of witnesses, travel costs, and similar matters.

7 As of the time of writing; the fees increase from time to time.

8 Unless the verdict is completely against the weight of the evidence, in which case the judge will set the jury's verdict aside and substitute the verdict that should have been given. This is unusual, however.

REFERENCES

Carthy, James J., W.A. Derry Millar, and Jeffrey G. Cowan, *Ontario Annual Practice* (Aurora, ON: Canada Law Book, published annually).

Class Proceedings Act, 1992, SO 1992, c. 6.

Courts of Justice Act, RSO 1990, c. C.43.

Negligence Act, RSO 1990, c. N.1.

Olivo, Laurence and DeeAnn Gonsalves, *Debtor–Creditor Law and Procedure*, 3rd ed. (Toronto: Emond Montgomery, 2008).

Ontario Gazette

Ontario Reports

Rules of Civil Procedure, RRO 1990, reg. 194.

REVIEW QUESTIONS

1. What are the principal steps in a civil lawsuit?

2. How does Abigail Boar go about retaining a lawyer?

3. What is a retainer?

4. What are the usual terms of a retainer?

5. What is a contingency fee and can a lawyer accept one?

6. How are legal fees determined?

7. What does it mean to have a good cause of action?

8. What is the standard of proof in a civil matter, and what kinds of evidence meet this standard?

9. Give examples of the kinds of evidence in question 8 that may arise in Abigail's case.

10. What matters are considered in determining a court's jurisdiction? Which court should Abigail sue in?

11. What is the relationship between a practice direction and the *Rules of Civil Procedure*?

12. What are the two types of civil procedure, and how do they differ?

13. How does an action commence, and what is the function of the first document?

14. How is a statement of claim issued?

15. What are originating documents and how are they served?

16. What happens if you cannot find a defendant for service because he or she has moved or gone on vacation?

17. What might happen if the defendant never saw the statement of claim and the plaintiff signed default judgment when no defence was filed?

18. What choices do Fred and Rattle Motors Ltd. have when served with a statement of claim?

19. What other pleadings might one find in a civil case, and what is their function?

20. What is discovery?

21. What is a motion, and what is its purpose?

22. When the parties have completed pleadings and discovery, how do they get on the list for trial?

23. What is case management?

24. If Abigail obtains a judgment in her favour, does she sit back and wait for the defendants to send her a cheque?

25. What does it mean when we say the issue of liability in Abigail's case is *res judicata*?

26. Why is an appeal from a decision in Abigail's case based on an error of fact unlikely to succeed?

DISCUSSION QUESTIONS

1. The primary purpose of the *Rules of Civil Procedure* is to reduce cost and delay. Discuss.

2. Suppose Abigail arrived drunk at the showroom and was staggering when she slipped on the oil. Suppose that she took a fancy to Fred and made unwelcome physical advances. Suppose Fred felt he had not been negligent in any way. And suppose that Rattle Motors Ltd. discovered that there had been numerous incidents of leaking oil pans on the Super Coupe. How might these situations change the type of pleadings used?

PART II

From commencement of proceedings to close of pleadings

CHAPTER 2

Procedure before commencement of proceedings

INTRODUCTION

When a client brings a civil litigation matter to the law office, there are a number of steps that both the lawyer and the legal staff must complete before going to the court office to issue the statement of claim. Before the claim issues, the apparent facts must be assessed to figure out what the cause of action is. Is the lawyer commencing the action in time or has the limitation period passed? You will have to perform a number of checks: Is the defendant solvent and worth suing? Have you named the defendant correctly for the purposes of the suit? Is any of the claim covered by insurance? You must prepare a retainer for the client to sign if he or she is to retain your firm's services. Then you will have to set up a client account or have the firm's accounts office or bookkeeper do it. Finally, you will open and set up an office file.

DETERMINING THE CAUSE OF ACTION AND OTHER PRELIMINARY STEPS

Is there a good cause of action?

After Abigail tells I.M. Just the story of her misfortune, I.M. Just must decide if the facts as related by Abigail amount to the breach of a legal right that gives rise to a remedy. In Abigail's case that is not difficult. The facts as disclosed indicate that some acts of Fred Flogem, Rattle Motors Ltd., and Skank Motorcar Company Ltd. caused her injuries and may amount to negligence. Therefore, in Abigail's case, the breach of the duty of care that caused her injuries amounts to a breach of a legal right and gives rise to the remedy of monetary damages. This breach is her legal reason for suing, or her cause of action.

Although this is a straightforward situation where the cause of action is easy to identify, it is not always so simple to determine the cause of action from the facts. For example, in what is now a landmark case,[1] a woman (known by the name Jane Doe to preserve her privacy) sued the Toronto Police and various individual officers in tort for failing to warn her of the danger of sexual assault she faced from a serial rapist. This man sexually assaulted Doe. Her argument was that the police had a duty to warn her, given their knowledge of the case, particularly because she alleged that the police used her as bait to catch the perpetrator. When she commenced her proceeding, the defendants brought a motion to dismiss her statement of claim on the grounds that it disclosed no reasonable cause of action. Their argument was that the police had by statute and at common law a general duty to the public, but that they had no specific duty to an individual in Doe's situation. To hold otherwise, they argued, would put them in the position of being an insurer of everyone's safety and liable to everyone who was a victim of crime. On the face of things they had a good argument, and the decision on the motion went through several stages of appeal.

Many lawyers would have told Doe that while she may have been treated badly, she had no reasonable cause of action because the duty owed by the police had never been extended as far as Doe was claiming it should be extended. However, she persevered and eventually won her case. While Doe faced an uphill fight on this issue, the common law does evolve; old principles and established causes of action are refined and extended. The courts are aware of this and scrutinize a novel cause of action carefully. Just because courts have not previously granted remedies, there is no reason why they cannot extend the law. In *Doe*, the court held that if the claim discloses a cause of action — a tort — the fact that it is novel is of no concern. For the purpose of assessing a case of this type, the facts in the pleadings are presumed to be true. If they disclose a cause of action with some chance of success, though novel, the action should proceed to trial.

Not every claimed cause of action will succeed, even if the facts are proved. For example, if I invite you to dinner, and you promise to come but do not show up, I may be mortified, humiliated, and have my feelings hurt, but the law of contract does not enforce this type of promise. Neither will the tort of deceit be applicable in this situation. The courts are not ready to extend legal rights and remedies to take into account what the law currently regards as a trifling matter or bad manners — although that could change.

You need to be aware that even if there is a good cause of action, the client might be advised not to sue. Suppose Abigail were fired by her employer without just cause. She could then sue for salary in lieu of having been given reasonable notice.[2] If, however, the day after she was fired, she landed another job that paid more than the job she had been dismissed from, Abigail did not suffer any damages. Instead, she improved her position. Although she has a good cause of action in that her contract of employment was breached, she suffered no damages and would receive no remedy. There is therefore no rational basis for her to continue with the suit.

Correctly naming individual defendants

Suing in the wrong name can result in an unenforceable judgment. For example, if you are suing Fred Flogem and obtain a judgment in that name, the judgment is useless if it turns out that Fred's real first name is Frederico, but that he informally changed it to Fred. Legally, Frederico Flogem exists, but Fred Flogem does not, at least for the purposes of enforcing a judgment. Therefore, getting the proposed defendant's name right is important.

Verifying a name
NAME SEARCH: CONSUMER DEBTORS

If you are suing an individual consumer rather than a business, you should verify the legal name of the defendant. Suing in the wrong name can result in an unenforceable judgment. For example, if you are suing Murray Benek and obtain a judgment in that name, the judgment will be useless if it turns out that Murray's legal first name is really Miroslav, but that he informally changed it to Murray years ago. Legally, Miroslav Benek exists; Murray Benek does not, at least for the purposes of obtaining and enforcing a judgment. Getting the defendant's name right at the outset is important both to obtaining a judgment against the defendant in the right name, and to conducting searches to determine whether the defendant is worth suing.

There are several ways in which you can verify a defendant's correct name.

Statement of Driving Record

If you have the individual's driver's licence number, you can request a Statement of Driving Record, which provides a three-year history of the driver, including the name of the driver, licence status information (including a physical description and date of birth), and a record of driving offence convictions. The person's driving record can help you verify the name of the individual and verify that you have the right person. In this connection, the information about height, gender, and date of birth might be useful in performing other searches. For example, having the date of birth makes it easier to verify who an individual is on a *Personal Property Security Act* (PPSA) search. A driving record search may be especially useful with someone who has a common last name, like Smith or Wong. Note, however, that this search will not provide an address for the licence holder — privacy restrictions keep addresses out of the public record. An authorized requester may obtain the driver's address. You may become an "authorized" requester if

1. you apply for authorization and enter into an agreement with the Ministry of Transportation, and

2. your search is conducted for one of the purposes for which authorization will be granted, such as debt collection, litigation, claims, and accidents. Authorized investigators may include private investigators, security guards, lawyers, and others acting for these purposes.

For further information about authorization to obtain personal information, including addresses, contact:

Supervisor
Driver and Vehicle Licensing Call Centre
Licensing Administration Office
Ministry of Transportation
2680 Keele Street
Downsview, ON M3M 3E6
Tel. 416-235-2999

You may conduct your search online, paying by credit card, and receiving an online report. You can access the search site from the Ontario government website at http://www.gov.on.ca. Click on Choose a Ministry on the left-hand side, and select Transportation. On the left-hand side of the Ministry of Transportation page under Ministry Offices, click on Online Services, which will direct you to online searches. From there, you can order licence and vehicle abstracts.

To see what a Statement of Driving Record abstract looks like, see figure 2.1.

Plate History and Vehicle History Abstracts

If you have the Vehicle Identification Number (VIN) or the licence plate number for a vehicle you think is owned by the defendant, you can use either number to do a plate or VIN search, either of which will provide the name of the owner, his or her driver's licence, the date the vehicle was registered, and whether it has changed owners recently.

Again, the address of the owner will not be provided unless you have obtained the authorization described in the previous section, Statement of Driving Record. You may also do these searches online using the web addresses provided in the previous section.

You can see what a Certified Plate Search — Recent Owner looks like in figure 2.2. The VIN search record is similar.

Online Searches

In the last several years various search engines and other online sources have been expanded and refined to allow you to submit the name of an individual to obtain addresses, telephone numbers, and other information about an individual that can help you verify a name, obtain other identifying information, and locate the person. These searches can be used to find both individuals and other legal entities, such as businesses operating under a business name. You may also do a **reverse search** on many of these sites by submitting a telephone number, address, e-mail address, or other information that will help you to obtain the correct name of a defendant, as well as other information. Reverse searches of phone numbers will often identify the subscriber of unlisted landlines and cellphones. Many sites are free, but some charge for information, in which case you can pay by credit card. The following websites were useful at the time of publication.

reverse search
a reverse search allows you to submit an address, telephone number, or e-mail address to obtain the name of a resident or subscriber

- *Search Detective:* http://www.searchdetective.net This site allows you to search by phone number and will turn up account holder names and addresses, including those for unlisted landlines and cellphones. Searches may also be done by name, but it is useful only when your subject has a US address.

- *Yahoo People Canada:* http://ca.people.yahoo.com You may search by name, with or without the city or province. This may turn up addresses and other miscellaneous information, some of which could be useful. Also includes an e-mail address search.

- *Canada411:* http://www.canada411.ca Submitting a name to this site can turn up a telephone number. Reverse searching is also available.

FIGURE 2.1   STATEMENT OF DRIVING RECORD

Transportation Information Productions System (TIPS)   09/20/2007 04:34 PM

 Ontario

Ministry of
Transportation
| central site | feedback | search | site map | français |

Location: <u>Ministry Home</u> > <u>Drivers & Vehicles</u> > <u>Ministry Online Service</u> > Order

<u>Back</u>

Ministry	Ministère	Safety and	Division de la
of	des	Regulation	sécurité et des
Transportation	Transports	Division	règlements

Ontario

Ministry No./No. Du Ministère Search Date/Date de recherche (Y/A M D/J)
0000-0000-0 1994/08/19

STATEMENT OF DRIVING RECORD/RELEVÉ DU DOSSIER DE CONDUITE PAGE 01

DRIVER INFORMATION/DONNÉE DE CONDUCTEUR

Name/Nom **PUBLIC, JOHN, Q.**
Address/Adresse *

Reference No. or Driver's Licence No./
No de référence ou du permis de conduire **P0000-00000-00000**
Date of Birth/Date de naissance (Y/A M D/J) **1962/12/10**
Sex/Sexe **MALE/HOMME**
Height/Taille **175**
Class/Catégorie **G*****
Condition/Restriction *******
Expiry Date/Date d'expirition (Y/A M D/J) **1985/08/31**
STATUS/STATUT **UNLICENCED/PERMIS DE CONDUIRE EXPIRÉ**
UNRENEWABLE/NON RENOUVELABLE SUSPENDED/SUSPENDU

DATE CONVICTIONS, DISCHARGES AND OTHER ACTIONS
Y/A M D/J CONDAMNATIONS, LIBÉRATIONS ET AUTRES ACTIONS

93/10/12 NO DRIVERS LICENCE OR IMPROPER CLASS OF LICENCE
ABSENCE OU MAUVAISE CATÉGORIE DE PERMIS DE CONDUIRE
93/10/26 NO DRIVERS LICENCE OR IMPROPER CLASS OF LICENCE
ABSENCE OU MAUVAISE CATÉGORIE DE PERMIS DE CONDUIRE

FIGURE 2.1   CONCLUDED

93/11/10 SPEEDING 82 KMH IN 50 KMH ZONE
EXCÈS DE VITESSE 82KMH DANS ZONE DE 50 KMH
93/11/10 NO DRIVERS LICENCE OR IMPROPER CLASS OF LICENCE
ABSENCE OU MAUVAISE CATÉGORIE DE PERMIS DE CONDUIRE
93/11/15 SPEEDING 100 KMH IN 70 KMH ZONE
EXCÈS DE VITESSE 100 KMH DANS ZONE DE 70 KMH
93/11/15 NO DRIVERS LICENCE OR IMPROPER CLASS OF LICENCE
ABSENCE OU MAUVAISE CATÉGORIE DE PERMIS DE CONDUIRE
93/12/04 SUSPENDED UNTIL JAN. 3, 1994, DEMERIT POINT
TOTAL - PROBATIONARY DRIVER
SUSPENDU JUSQU'AU 3 JANV. 1994, TOTAL DES
POINTS D'INAPTITUDE, STAGIAIRE

FIGURE 2.2   CERTIFIED PLATE SEARCH — RECENT OWNER

 Ontario

Ministry of
Transportation
| central site | feedback | search | site map | français |

Location: <u>Ministry Home</u> > <u>Drivers & Vehicles</u> > <u>Ministry Online Service</u> > Order

<u>Back</u>

| Ministry of Transportation **Ontario** | Ministère des Transports | Safety and Regulation Division | Division de la sécurité et des règlements |

MINISTRY CONTROL NO./NO. DE CONTRÔLE DU MINISTÈRE SEARCH DATE/DATE DE RECHERCHE
000000 94/10/24

SEARCH TYPE/TYPE DE RECHERCHE INQUIRY KEY/ CRITÈRE DE RECHERCHE

PLATE/PLAQUE PLATE/PLAQUE - **AAAAAA**
==
REGISTRANT/CONDUCTEUR
NAME/NOM - **PUBLIC, JOHN, Q.**
ADDRESS/ADRESSE - * STAGGER/ÉCHELONNER - **0509**

-VEHICLE/VÉHICULE
VEHICLE IDENTIFICATION NO./NO D'IDENTIFICATION DU VÉHICULE - **OAOAAOOAOAAOOOOOO**
CLASS/CATÉGORIE - **PASSENGER/VOITURE PARTICULIÈRE** MAKE/MARQUE - **PONT**
MODEL/MODÈLE - **FRS**
BODY TYPE/TYPE DE CARROSSERIE - **2 DOOR SEDAN/COUPÉ**
NO. OF CYLINDERS/NO DE CYLINDRÉE-**04**
MOTIVE POWER/FORCE MOTRICE - **GASOLINE/ESSENCE**
COLOUR/COULEUR - **WHITE/BLANC** YEAR/ANNÉE - **84**
STATUS/STATUT - **FIT/EN ÉTAT DE MARCHE** WEIGHT EMPTY/POIDS À VIDE -
NO. OF AXLES/NO D'ESSIEUX -

-PLATE/PLAQUE
PLATE/PLAQUE - **000YYY** YEAR/ANNÉE -
SERIES/SÉRIE - **OWN CHOICE PASSENGER/PERSONNALISÉE VOITURE PARTICULIÈRE**
STATUS/STATUT - **ATTACHED/FIXÉE**
FORMAT -
PLATE REGISTRATION DATE/DATE D'ENREGISTREMENT DES PLAQUES - **910122**

-VALTAG NO./NO DE VIGNETTE - **0000000** REGISTERED WEIGHT/POIDS ENREGISTRÉ -
DECLARATION/DÉCLARATION -
STAGGER/ÉCHELONNER - **93/05/10** EXPIRY/EXPIRATION - **94/05/09**
PERMIT NO./NO DE CERTIFICAT - **49815715** DATE ISSUED/DATE DE DÉLIVRANCE - **91/05/09**

- *Lycos Search:* http://www.whowhere.com This site can find individuals with a name search for locations in the United States. You can also do reverse searches. The results will yield information about who has the phone or e-mail account, or who owns premises or lives at an address. It may also provide other personal information.

- *NetTrace:* http://www.nettrace.com.au/resource/search/people.html This Australian site is a gateway to a variety of search sites that allow you to search in various countries, including Canada, by inputting phone numbers, addresses, e-mail addresses, names, and other data. Many of the sites will search various public and private databases, including many in Canada. Some charge fees.

- *Telus:* http://www.mytelus.com/phonebook This site allows you to submit names to obtain addresses and phone numbers, including unlisted cellphone numbers. You may also do reverse searches on phone numbers and addresses to identify and locate individuals.

- *WhitePages.ca:* http://www.whitepages.ca This site allows you to look up names to obtain addresses and phone numbers and also allows you to do reverse directory searches of addresses and phone numbers to identify and locate individuals.

Correctly naming businesses

To get the name of a business right you must know the form of business entity used by the proposed defendant. If the business is a sole proprietorship — that is, a business carried on by an individual using the individual's name — then searching the individual's name may be sufficient.

However, suppose that the proposed defendant carries on business using a business name:

- If the business is incorporated, you must sue the corporation in its legal corporate name.

- If the business is a sole proprietorship, you may sue the individual sole proprietor in his own name, or sue in the business name.

- If the business is a partnership, you may sue in the partnership name or sue the partners individually in their own names.

Naming the proper parties to a lawsuit will be discussed in chapter 5. For now, we will concentrate on verifying the names of proposed defendants that are businesses.

Unless a business is carried on in the owner's name, it must register its business name with the Companies and Personal Property Security Branch, Ministry of Government and Consumer Services (the Companies Branch). If you submit a business name on a search, it will result in the identification of the individual person if the business is a sole proprietorship. If the business is a partnership, submission of the business name will result in identification of the partners registered at the time of the search. Similarly, if the business is a corporation, submission of the business name will get you the correct legal corporate name. Remember that when you sue a corporation, you have no choice concerning how to name the company: Its proper legal name must be used. Do not be surprised if the corporate name that turns up has no relation to the business name used. If Rattle Motors Ltd. was simply a name used to carry on business as a trade name, it could turn out to be a "numbered company," for example, 1234 Ontario Ltd. There is nothing sinister about this. If the company intends to use the business name that it used before its incorporation, it does not matter what the limited company is called, and the number initially assigned to a new corporation by the Companies and Personal Property Security Branch of the Ministry of Government and Consumer Services will do as well as anything else, because the company will use the name under which it was carrying on business.

A business name search can be done in two ways. You can attend in person at the public search office of the Companies and Personal Property Security Branch, Ministry of Government Services (MGS), 375 University Avenue, 2nd floor, Toronto, Ontario M5G 2M2 or you can conduct an online search. You can access the Ministry of Government and Consumer Services and Service Ontario at http://www.mgs .gov.on.ca. Click on English and then, on the right, click Business Services. From there, you can get to Service Ontario or Business Gateway, which seem to have everything needed for name searches, registration, and so on.

An online search can be inexpensively done, provided that the name you are searching has been registered with the Companies and Personal Property Securities Branch. At the Service Ontario website, follow the links to the search application, and select Enhanced Business Name Search. You can see a sample Enhanced Business Name Search — Search Criteria online form in figure 2.3. You can search the exact business name, words within the name, or use the business identification number (if you have it) that all businesses are given when their names are registered. You can pay for the search online by credit card. Searching can also be done, for a fee, through Oncorp, a recognized provider of service to the Ontario government. You can access their search services and also view samples of documents such as a Corporation Profile Report (which contains a corporation's address and the names of its directors) at http://www.oncorp.com/home/services_onbis_corp.asp. You can see a sample Corporation Profile Report in figure 2.4.

Because detailed web addresses (called URLs) often change, another way to conduct a search when a precise URL does not work is to do a broad search. Start with http://www.gov.on.ca, and on the homepage do a search using the name of the form or the name of the procedure you want to use. If you are successful, that will take you to the URL you need. If you know the government department that administers the information or procedures you are interested in, start at the Ontario government website, choose the appropriate ministry, and search its homepage. In the case of business name searches, you could start with http://www.gov.on.ca, click on Ministry, click on Government and Consumer Services, click on Search, Register and Renew a Business (which takes you to the Service Ontario Business Gateway site), and follow the links to the search application site. For business searches, you can also start at the Ministry of Government and Consumer Services website at http://www.mgs.gov.on.ca and follow the links to the various searches you wish to make.

There are companies that will conduct searches for you for a fee. You may also do your own online searches by using one of two private search and registration services: http://www.oncorp.com or http://www.cyberbahn.ca. Start at the home-page and follow the directions and links. These search sites will also allow you to conduct a variety of other searches of other public business records maintained by the federal and provincial governments. Note that if a corporation is carrying on business in Ontario but is incorporated in another province or is a federally incorporated company, an Ontario corporate search will not be useful. However, either of these search sites can be used to obtain information about companies incorporated federally or in other provinces.

A business names report will identify individual persons using a business name with their address. If the business name is not registered, you can obtain a certificate of non-registration showing that a business name that may be in use has not been registered. (There are penalties for failure to register a business under the *Business Names Act*, although this will not directly affect a lawsuit against the defendant who failed to register; however, if the plaintiff is suing in a name that is not registered, her lawsuit will be **stayed** until the name is registered.)

If a business name search shows that the business is actually a corporation, or you know that you are dealing with a corporation, you can verify that you have the correct corporate name, obtain the corporation's address for service, and the names and addresses of officers and directors of the corporation, all of which is set out in the Initial Return/Notice of Change by an Ontario Corporation, which must be filed by every corporation incorporated in Ontario. A sample of a completed Initial Return/Notice of Change is set out in figure 2.5.

Impecunious clients and opponents

Cost is a factor in determining whether to sue or not. The probable costs should be discussed candidly with the client in relation to the probable relief to be obtained. If Abigail's chances of establishing liability are good, she is likely to be awarded substantial damages. Because the corporate defendant is likely to carry insurance, the chances of being paid those damages are very good. Consequently, even if Abigail does not have a lot of spare cash, I.M. Just may be prepared to take his payment at the end of the case, as is common in many personal injury actions. Her lawyer may also take the case on a contingency-fee basis, which is now permissible in Ontario. In this case, Abigail would pay nothing, but if she won, I.M. Just would be paid by taking 20–30 percent of the damage award as his fee.

If the case is more speculative or uncertain, the client can be billed on a periodic basis. Payment by instalments the client can handle is common in litigation cases. A client who cannot pay may have to go without a remedy unless the lawyer is prepared to act on a **pro bono** basis. Legal aid is virtually unobtainable in civil cases. "Justice," as an English appeals judge once observed, "is like the Ritz Hotel. Anyone who has the price of a room may stay there."

If your opponent is **impecunious**, there is another set of problems to consider. If you get a judgment against the defendant, will he or she be able to pay it? If Rattle Motors Ltd. has no assets and is teetering on bankruptcy, it may be better not to sue and to make a claim in the ensuing bankruptcy instead. Otherwise, you may spend both money and effort to win a case and then be left with a paper judgment — that is, a judgment that is of no more value than the paper it is written on because the client has no money or assets to pay it.

---

stayed
a legal proceeding may be stopped from proceeding further, or stayed by a judge, until one of the parties does something they are obliged to do; for example, a plaintiff who is suing using an unregistered business name will have the proceeding stayed until he proves that he has registered the name as he is legally required to do

pro bono
abbreviation of a Latin term *pro bono publico*, meaning "for the public good," used where a lawyer takes on a case without charging a fee as part of a duty to see that justice is done

impecunious
insolvent

FIGURE 2.3   ENHANCED BUSINESS NAME SEARCH — SEARCH CRITERIA

ServiceOntario

| ministry | central site | feedback | search | site map |

| français |

| SEARCH / REGISTER / RENEW | CHANGE / CLOSE YOUR BUSINESS | MyBIS |

Caution: The Integrated Business Services Application does not support the Browser's Back button.

Help With This Page

Enhanced Business Name Search - Search Criteria

You must enter either a Business Name or the Ontario Business Identification Number.

Note: It will take approximately 45 seconds to process your search.

Business Name	Fly-By-Night Enterprises
City	BARRIE
Ontario Business Identification Number	
Type of Search *(Required)*	⦿ Enhanced Search ◯ Exact Search
Type of Report	Detailed Business Names Report ⬍

FIGURE 2.4   CORPORATION PROFILE REPORT

Request ID: 000177620	Province of Ontario	Date Report Produced: 2005/10/21
Transaction ID: 12871109	Ministry of Consumer and Business Services	Time Report Produced: 14:38:07
Category ID: UN/E	Companies and Personal Property Security Branch	Page: 1

CORPORATION PROFILE REPORT

Ontario Corp Number	Corporation Name		Incorporation Date
1990004	TEST		1993/02/25

Jurisdiction

ONTARIO

Corporation Type	Corporation Status	Former Jurisdiction
ONTARIO BUSINESS CORP.	ACTIVE	NOT APPLICABLE

Registered Office Address	Date Amalgamated	Amalgamation Ind.
	NOT APPLICABLE	NOT APPLICABLE
2 QUEEN STREET	New Amal. Number	Notice Date
Suite # 222		
TORONTO	NOT APPLICABLE	NOT APPLICABLE
ONTARIO		
CANADA M6M 6M6		Letter Date
Mailing Address		NOT APPLICABLE
	Revival Date	Continuation Date
2 QUEEN STREET	NOT APPLICABLE	NOT APPLICABLE
Suite # 222		
TORONTO	Transferred Out Date	Cancel/Inactive Date
ONTARIO		
CANADA M6M 6M6	NOT APPLICABLE	NOT APPLICABLE
	EP Licence Eff.Date	EP Licence Term.Date
	NOT APPLICABLE	NOT APPLICABLE

	Number of Directors	Date Commenced	Date Ceased
	Minimum Maximum	in Ontario	in Ontario
	UNKNOWN UNKNOWN	NOT APPLICABLE	NOT APPLICABLE

Activity Classification

NOT AVAILABLE

FIGURE 2.4 CONTINUED

Request ID: 000177620 Transaction ID: 12871109 Category ID: UN/E	Province of Ontario Ministry of Consumer and Business Services Companies and Personal Property Security Branch	Date Report Produced: 2005/10/21 Time Report Produced: 14:38:07 Page: 2

CORPORATION PROFILE REPORT

Ontario Corp Number

1990004

Corporation Name

TEST

Corporate Name History

TEST

Effective Date

1993/02/25

Current Business Name(s) Exist:

Expired Business Name(s) Exist:

YES

YES - SEARCH REQUIRED FOR DETAILS

Administrator:
Name (Individual / Corporation)

ADAM

EVE

Address

77 5TH STREET

KINGSTON
ONTARIO
CANADA   N5N 5N5

Date Began

2004/07/01

First Director

NOT APPLICABLE

Designation

DIRECTOR

Officer Type

Resident Canadian

Y

FIGURE 2.4 CONTINUED

Request ID: 000177620	Province of Ontario	Date Report Produced: 2005/10/21
Transaction ID: 12871109	Ministry of Consumer and Business Services	Time Report Produced: 14:38:07
Category ID: UN/E	Companies and Personal Property Security Branch	Page: 3

CORPORATION PROFILE REPORT

Ontario Corp Number

1990004

Corporation Name

TEST

Administrator:
Name (Individual / Corporation)

ADAM

EVE

Address

77 5TH STREET

KINGSTON
ONTARIO
CANADA   N5N 5N5

Date Began

2004/07/01

First Director

NOT APPLICABLE

Designation

OFFICER

Officer Type

GENERAL MANAGER

Resident Canadian

Y

Administrator:
Name (Individual / Corporation)

JANE

JANENE

Address

99 15TH AVENUE

OTTAWA
ONTARIO
CANADA   L7L 6K5

Date Began

2003/02/28

First Director

NOT APPLICABLE

Designation

DIRECTOR

Officer Type

Resident Canadian

Y

FIGURE 2.4   CONTINUED

Request ID: 000177620 Transaction ID: 12871109 Category ID: UN/E	Province of Ontario Ministry of Consumer and Business Services Companies and Personal Property Security Branch	Date Report Produced: 2005/10/21 Time Report Produced: 14:38:07 Page: 4

CORPORATION PROFILE REPORT

Ontario Corp Number

1990004

Corporation Name

TEST

Administrator:
Name (Individual / Corporation)

JANE

JANENE

Address

99 15TH AVENUE

OTTAWA
ONTARIO
CANADA   L7L 6K5

Date Began

2003/02/28

First Director

NOT APPLICABLE

Designation

OFFICER

Officer Type

PRESIDENT

Resident Canadian

Y

Administrator:
Name (Individual / Corporation)

JAMES

JONES

Address

2 KING STREET WEST

TORONTO
ONTARIO
CANADA   M7M 7M7

Date Began

1999/05/05

First Director

NOT APPLICABLE

Designation

DIRECTOR

Officer Type

Resident Canadian

Y

FIGURE 2.4 CONTINUED

Request ID:	000177620	Province of Ontario	Date Report Produced:	2005/10/21
Transaction ID:	12871109	Ministry of Consumer and Business Services	Time Report Produced:	14:38:07
Category ID:	UN/E	Companies and Personal Property Security Branch	Page:	5

CORPORATION PROFILE REPORT

Ontario Corp Number

1990004

Corporation Name

TEST

Administrator:
Name (Individual / Corporation)

JOHN
P.
SMITHEX

Address

88 QUEEN STREET NORTH

TORONTO
ONTARIO
CANADA   L7L 5M5

Date Began	First Director
2004/07/01	NOT APPLICABLE

Designation	Officer Type	Resident Canadian
DIRECTOR		Y

Administrator:
Name (Individual / Corporation)

JOHN
P.
SMITHEX

Address

88 QUEEN STREET NORTH

TORONTO
ONTARIO
CANADA   L7L 5M5

Date Began	First Director
2004/07/01	NOT APPLICABLE

Designation	Officer Type	Resident Canadian
OFFICER	SECRETARY	Y

FIGURE 2.4 CONCLUDED

Request ID: 000177620	Province of Ontario	Date Report Produced: 2005/10/21
Transaction ID: 12871109	Ministry of Consumer and Business Services	Time Report Produced: 14:38:07
Category ID: UN/E	Companies and Personal Property Security Branch	Page: 6

CORPORATION PROFILE REPORT

Ontario Corp Number   Corporation Name

1990004   TEST

Last Document Recorded

Act/Code Description   Form   Date

CIA   CHANGE NOTICE   1   2005/08/30 (ELECTRONIC FILING)

THIS CORPORATION HAS RECEIVED A NOTICE OF INTENTION TO DISSOLVE ON THE DATE INDICATED IN THE "NOTICE DATE" FIELD AND IS SUBJECT TO CANCELLATION.

THIS REPORT SETS OUT THE MOST RECENT INFORMATION FILED BY THE CORPORATION ON OR AFTER JUNE 27, 1992, AND RECORDED IN THE ONTARIO BUSINESS INFORMATION SYSTEM AS AT THE DATE AND TIME OF PRINTING. ALL PERSONS WHO ARE RECORDED AS CURRENT DIRECTORS OR OFFICERS ARE INCLUDED IN THE LIST OF ADMINISTRATORS.

ADDITIONAL HISTORICAL INFORMATION MAY EXIST ON THE COMPANIES AND PERSONAL PROPERTY SECURITY BRANCH MICROFICHE.

The issuance of this report in electronic form is authorized by the Director of Companies and Personal Property Security Branch

FIGURE 2.5   INITIAL RETURN/NOTICE OF CHANGE

Ontario

Ministry of Government Services	Ministère des Services gouvernementaux	Companies and Personal Property Security Branch 393 University Ave Suite 200 Toronto ON M5G 2M2	Direction des compagnies et des sûretés mobilières 393 av., University, bureau 200 Toronto ON M5G 2M2

For Ministry Use Only
À l'usage du ministère seulement
Page/Page 1   **of/de** _____

Form 1 - Ontario Corporation
Formule 1 - Personnes morales de l'Ontario

Initial Return/Notice of Change/
Rapport initial/Avis de modification
Corporations Information Act/*Loi sur les*
renseignements exigés des personnes morales

1.

	Initial Return Rapport initial	Notice of Change Avis de modification
Business Corporation/ Société par actions	☐	☐
Not-For-Profit Corporation/ Personne morale sans but lucratif	☐	☐

Please type or print all information in block capital letters using black ink.
Prière de dactylographier les renseignements ou de les écrire en caractères d'imprimerie à l'encre noire.

2. Ontario Corporation Number
Numéro matricule de la personne morale en Ontario

114836

3. Date of Incorporation or Amalgamation/
Date de constitution ou fusion

Year/Année	Month/Mois	Day/Jour
2006	12	11

For Ministry Use Only
À l'usage du ministère seulement

4. Corporation Name Including Punctuation/Raison sociale de la personne morale, y compris la ponctuation

CHEN GOLF LTD.

5. Address of Registered or Head Office/Adresse du siège social

c/o / a/s

MARY CHEN

Street No./N° civique   Street Name/Nom de la rue   Suite/Bureau
60   **CENTRE ST.**   **#3**

Street Name (cont'd)/Nom de la rue (suite)

City/Town/Ville
TORONTO   **ONTARIO, CANADA**

Postal Code/Code postal
M6Z 3A5

For Ministry Use Only/
À l'usage du ministère seulement

6. Mailing Address/Adresse postale

☑ Same as Registered or Head Office/ Même que siège social

☐ Not Applicable/ Ne s'applique pas

Street No./N° civique

Street Name/Nom de la rue   Suite/Bureau

Street Name (cont'd)/Nom de la rue (suite)

City/Town/Ville

Province, State/Province, État   Country/Pays   Postal Code/Code postal

7. Language of Preference/Langue préférée

English - Anglais   ☑   French - Français   ☐

8. Information on Directors/Officers must be completed on Schedule A as requested. If additional space is required, photocopy Schedule A./**Les renseignements sur les** administrateurs ou les dirigeants doivent être fournis dans l'Annexe A, tel que demandé. Si vous avez besoin de plus d'espace, vous pouvez photocopier l'Annexe A.

Number of Schedule A(s) submitted/Nombre d'Annexes A présentées   **1**   (At least one Schedule A must be submitted/Au moins une Annexe A doit être présentée)

9. (Print or type name in full of the person authorizing filing / Dactylographier ou inscrire le prénom et le nom en caractères d'imprimerie de la personne qui autorise l'enregistrement)

I/Je   **MARY CHEN**

certify that the information set out herein, is true and correct.
atteste que les renseignements précités sont véridiques et exacts.

Check appropriate box
Cocher la case pertinente

D) ☑ Director/Administrateur

O) ☐ Officer /Dirigeant

P) ☐ Other individual having knowledge of the affairs of the Corporation/Autre personne ayant connaissance des activités de la personne morale

NOTE/REMARQUE : Sections 13 and 14 of the **Corporations Information Act** provide penalties for making false or misleading statements or omissions. Les articles 13 et 14 de la *Loi sur les renseignements exigés des personnes morales* prévoient des peines en cas de déclaration fausse ou trompeuse, ou d'omission.

07200E (04/2007)

FIGURE 2.5   CONCLUDED

Form 1 - Ontario Corporation/Formule 1 - Personnes morales de l'Ontario Schedule A/Annexe A

For Ministry Use Only
À l'usage du ministère seulement
Page/Page _____ of/de _____

Please type or print all information in block capital letters using black ink. Prière de dactylographier les renseignements ou de les écrire en caractères d'imprimerie à l'encre noire.	Ontario Corporation Number Numéro matricule de la personne morale en Ontario 114836	Date of Incorporation or Amalgamation Date de constitution ou fusion Year/Année Month/Mois Day/Jour 2006 | 12 | 11

DIRECTOR / OFFICER INFORMATION - RENSEIGNEMENTS RELATIFS AUX ADMINISTRATEURS/DIRIGEANTS
Full Name and Address for Service/Nom et domicile élu

Last Name/Nom de famille	First Name/Prénom	Middle Names/Autres prénoms
CHEN	MARY	A

Street Number/Numéro civique: 60   Suite/Bureau: #3

Street Name/Nom de la rue: CENTRE ST.

Street Name (cont'd)/Nom de la rue (suite):

City/Town/Ville: TORONTO

Province, State/Province, État: ON   Country/Pays: CANADA   Postal Code/Code postal: M6Z 3A5

*OTHER TITLES (Please Specify)
*AUTRES TITRES (Veuillez préciser)
Chair / Président du conseil
Chair Person / Président du conseil
Chairman / Président du conseil
Chairwoman / Présidente du conseil
Vice-Chair / Vice-président du conseil
Vice-President / Vice-président
Assistant Secretary / Secrétaire adjoint
Assistant Treasurer / Trésorier adjoint
Chief Manager / Directeur exécutif
Executive Director / Directeur administratif
Managing Director / Administrateur délégué
Chief Executive Officer / Directeur général
Chief Financial Officer / Agent en chef des finances
Chief Information Officer / Directeur général de l'information
Chief Operating Officer / Administrateur en chef des opérations
Chief Administrative Officer / Directeur général de l'administration
Comptroller / Contrôleur
Authorized Signing Officer / Signataire autorisé
Other (Untitled) / Autre (sans titre)

Director Information/Renseignements relatifs aux administrateurs

Resident Canadian/ [ ] YES/OUI   [ ] NO/NON   (Resident Canadian applies to directors of business corporations only.)/
Résident canadien   (Résident canadien ne s'applique qu'aux administrateurs de sociétés par actions)

Date Elected/Date d'élection: Year/Année __ Month/Mois __ Day/Jour __   Date Ceased/Date de cessation: Year/Année __ Month/Mois __ Day/Jour __

Officer Information/Renseignements relatifs aux dirigeants

	PRESIDENT/PRÉSIDENT			SECRETARY/SECRÉTAIRE			TREASURER/TRÉSORIER			GENERAL MANAGER/DIRECTEUR GÉNÉRAL			OTHER/AUTRE		
	Year/Année	Month/Mois	Day/Jour	Year/Année	Month/Mois	Day/Jour	Year/Année	Month/Mois	Day/Jour	Year/Année	Month/Mois	Day/Jour	Year/Année	Month/Mois	Day/Jour
Date Appointed/Date de nomination	2006	12	11												
Date Ceased/Date de cessation															

DIRECTOR / OFFICER INFORMATION - RENSEIGNEMENTS RELATIFS AUX ADMINISTRATEURS/DIRIGEANTS
Full Name and Address for Service/Nom et domicile élu

Last Name/Nom de famille	First Name/Prénom	Middle Names/Autres prénoms
PARTEN	JOHN	E

Street Number/Numéro civique: 25   Suite/Bureau:

Street Name/Nom de la rue: STIPPARD RD.

Street Name (cont'd)/Nom de la rue (suite):

City/Town/Ville: TORONTO

Province, State/Province, État: ON   Country/Pays: CANADA   Postal Code/Code postal: M4R 1M6

*OTHER TITLES (Please Specify)
*AUTRES TITRES (Veuillez préciser)
Chair / Président du conseil
Chair Person / Président du conseil
Chairman / Président du conseil
Chairwoman / Présidente du conseil
Vice-Chair / Vice-président du conseil
Vice-President / Vice-président
Assistant Secretary / Secrétaire adjoint
Assistant Treasurer / Trésorier adjoint
Chief Manager / Directeur exécutif
Executive Director / Directeur administratif
Managing Director / Administrateur délégué
Chief Executive Officer / Directeur général
Chief Financial Officer / Agent en chef des finances
Chief Information Officer / Directeur général de l'information
Chief Operating Officer / Administrateur en chef des opérations
Chief Administrative Officer / Directeur général de l'administration
Comptroller / Contrôleur
Authorized Signing Officer / Signataire autorisé
Other (Untitled) / Autre (sans titre)

Director Information/Renseignements relatifs aux administrateurs

Resident Canadian/ [✔] YES/OUI   [ ] NO/NON   (Resident Canadian applies to directors of business corporations only.)/
Résident canadien   (Résident canadien ne s'applique qu'aux administrateurs de sociétés par actions)

Date Elected/Date d'élection: Year/Année 2006 Month/Mois 12 Day/Jour 11   Date Ceased/Date de cessation: Year/Année __ Month/Mois __ Day/Jour __

Officer Information/Renseignements relatifs aux dirigeants

	PRESIDENT/PRÉSIDENT			SECRETARY/SECRÉTAIRE			TREASURER/TRÉSORIER			GENERAL MANAGER/DIRECTEUR GÉNÉRAL			OTHER/AUTRE		
	Year/Année	Month/Mois	Day/Jour	Year/Année	Month/Mois	Day/Jour	Year/Année	Month/Mois	Day/Jour	Year/Année	Month/Mois	Day/Jour	Year/Année	Month/Mois	Day/Jour
Date Appointed/Date de nomination															
Date Ceased/Date de cessation															

07200E (04/2007)

Determining solvency

If the solvency of the potential defendant is an issue, there are some searches that can be done to determine whether or not the defendant is worth suing.

If the defendant has been successfully sued before, but the judgment has never been paid, there is likely to be a writ of seizure and sale (also called a writ of execution) on file in the sheriff's office in the county or judicial region where the defendant resides or carries on business. If the writ has been unsatisfied for some time, you know that a previous judgment creditor has sued and been unsuccessful in recovering anything on the judgment debt. In addition to providing information about the likelihood of the judgment being paid, the writ of execution can confirm the proper name or spelling of the name of the defendant so that he, she, or it will be correctly named in the statement of claim if you do proceed.

A number of outstanding writs of execution indicate that the proposed defendant has generally been defaulting on claims. They may also indicate that the proposed defendant is adept at hiding assets.

If the writs are all recently filed, it may mean that judgment creditors are closing in and that bankruptcy may be imminent. Suing is a waste of time if the proposed defendant is **judgment-proof**. If the proposed defendant goes bankrupt, the plaintiff may obtain more by making a claim as an unsecured creditor in the bankruptcy proceedings.

judgment-proof
unlikely to be able to pay any amount of a judgment

Finding no writs of execution on file may indicate that the proposed defendant is solvent, but it may also indicate that you may not have searched the regions where the writs are lodged. The problem with searching writs of execution is that there is no province-wide system that can be searched. You need to search the files in each county or judicial region where the proposed defendant has or is likely to have had assets.

Even if there are writs on file, if the proposed defendant has not gone bankrupt, it may be useful to sue anyway and obtain judgment. The reason for taking this approach is that the *Creditors' Relief Act* requires that execution creditors (all those who have filed writs of execution) share on a pro rata basis if any execution creditor succeeds in seizing and selling assets. When assets are seized and sold, the sheriff is obliged to distribute a share of the money to each of the execution creditors in proportion to what they are owed. This means that execution creditors with large judgments receive a larger share of the money than those who have judgments for smaller amounts. There are some exceptions: family support creditors and tax authorities take precedence over other creditors.

HOW TO CONDUCT A SEARCH OF EXECUTIONS

When a plaintiff obtains a judgment in a lawsuit, the judgment orders the defendant to pay money, but the judgment is not self-enforcing. If the defendant does not pay, it is necessary for the plaintiff to file a writ of seizure and sale (also referred to as a "writ of execution") with the sheriff of the county or district where the defendant has assets. Unfortunately, the province has no centralized file of all writs of seizure and sale. This means that you might have to file duplicate writs of execution in sheriff's offices in more than one county or district if you have reason to believe the defendant has assets in more than one county or district. Once filed, a writ of execution can be used in one of two ways: (1) if the judgment creditor knows of an asset that can be seized and sold, so that the proceeds of sale can be used to satisfy the judgment, she can direct the sheriff to seize and sell the goods; or (2) the judgment creditor can simply leave the execution sitting on file. Others who do business with the judgment debtor, or who may be lending the judgment debtor money, often search executions to assure themselves that the person they are dealing with is a good credit risk. They may be reluctant to lend or extend credit to a business once they learn of an outstanding writ of execution. In these circumstances, the judgment debtor may be pressured to pay off the execution creditor. The writ, once filed, is enforceable for six years and can be renewed. Sheriff's offices used to send renewal notices, but now they do not. You will need to diarize the renewal date.

It is a good idea to do an execution search against the name of the defendant, because a lot of useful information will be revealed. For example:

- It can be used to verify the defendant's name or the spelling of the name.

- A number of outstanding writs of execution may indicate that the defendant has been sued before and that the judgment creditors have not been able to collect on the judgment.

- Recent writs of execution may indicate that all of the creditors are closing in and that the defendant is likely to be "judgment-proof" with little likelihood that assets will be available to satisfy the judgment. This pattern may also indicate that the defendant has just gone, or is about to go, bankrupt. Suing may be a waste of time and the creditor may obtain more through bankruptcy.

- Many outstanding writs that are several years old may indicate that the defendant has successfully avoided paying creditors for some time and either has no assets or is adept at hiding them.

- No executions may indicate that there are no prior unsatisfied judgments and that there will be assets available to seize; it may also indicate that the defendant's assets are not located in the county or district where you searched executions.

Even where you find a number of writs on file, it may still be useful to try to obtain a judgment and add your own writ of execution to those on file. The reason for this is that the *Creditors' Relief Act* requires that execution creditors (all those who have filed writs of execution) share on a pro rata basis if any execution creditor succeeds in seizing and selling assets. When assets are seized and sold, the sheriff is obliged to distribute a share of the money to each of the execution creditors in proportion to what they are owed. This means that execution creditors with large judgments receive a larger share of the money than those who have judgments for smaller amounts (as the box below shows). There are some exceptions to the rule about pro rata distributions. Support creditors and the Crown in respect of unpaid taxes take priority over other judgment creditors.

To conduct a search of executions against the name of a defendant, at the sheriff's office, request a certificate indicating whether there are writs of seizure and sale on file in that office. The Sheriff's Office is usually located in the local Superior Court of Justice courthouse. The local court office and the Sheriff's Office are listed in the blue government pages of the local telephone directory.

Illustration of a Pro Rata Distribution of the Proceeds of Execution

Amount owing to execution creditor A	$500
Amount owing to execution creditor B	$200
Amount owing to execution creditor C	$100
Total	$800

Execution creditor C levies execution and recovers $300 as a net amount after the costs of execution have been deducted from the gross amount.

Formula:

$$\text{amount recovered on levy} \times \frac{\text{amount owing to creditor}}{\text{amount owing to all creditors}} = \text{share paid to creditor}$$

A will receive	$300	×	$500/800$	=	$187.50
B will receive	$300	×	$200/800$	=	$75.00
C will receive	$300	×	$100/800$	=	$37.50

In Toronto, execution searches at the Sheriff's Office are done online after payment of the prescribed fee. You key in the same kind of information you would provide for the certificate and the system produces an on-screen response, and, if desired, a printout of that response. In time, this system will extend to other parts of Ontario, and may one day be available online from your office computer.

Give the full name of the defendant; if the defendant is an individual, give middle names as well as the first name, if possible. If the defendant is a business, be sure to give the business's proper legal name. With sole proprietorships and partnerships, it may be wise in most cases to list the name of the individual who is the sole proprietor or the names of the partners. File the certificate in the Sheriff's Office for the county or district where the defendant is likely to have assets, lived, or carried on business. In Toronto, it is possible to use a computer to do your own search, which will give you immediate information on writs on file. Once you have results you can ask for copies of the writs to find out the particulars, such as the name of the judgment creditor, the amount owing, and the length of time the debt has been unsatisfied. You can also call the judgment creditor's lawyer whose name appears on the writ to find out about any attempts to collect that have been made.

You can pay to have an online writ of execution search carried out by using the writs search service provided by Bar-Ex. To access this service you need to register as a member at http://www.bar-ex.com. Membership is free.

BANKRUPTCY AND INSOLVENCY ACT SEARCH

A bankruptcy search is useful to determine if the defendant has gone bankrupt or is about to go bankrupt. If a defendant is bankrupt, there is no point in suing the defendant because any action would be automatically stayed. Instead, the creditor will file a proof of debt claim with the defendant's trustee in bankruptcy. The trustee will review the claim and, if it is in order, the creditor may recover some of the money owing but is unlikely to ever see all of it. Secured creditors are entitled to seize their secured property to satisfy the debt owing to them and to do so ahead of the claims and rights of unsecured creditors claiming through the trustee. Unsecured creditors, which include ordinary judgment creditors, get what is left over. After all of the bankrupt's creditors, both secured and unsecured, have had their interests attended to, the defendant is usually discharged from bankruptcy, free and clear of the debts incurred before bankruptcy, with some exceptions.[3]

As a result of the bankruptcy rules, there is often little of value left for unsecured creditors of the bankrupt. For this reason, unsecured creditors may recover no more than 10 or 20 cents on each dollar owed, because the secured creditors have already taken all the major assets.

There are two ways to go bankrupt: (1) in certain circumstances, an unpaid creditor can put a debtor into bankruptcy using a petition for bankruptcy, or (2) the debtor can make an assignment in bankruptcy. As an alternative to bankruptcy, a debtor who owes up to $75,000 (excluding a mortgage) may make a consumer proposal to his creditors through a trustee in bankruptcy. All bankruptcy searches are done through the Office of the Superintendent of Bankruptcy. All bankruptcies and proposals filed in Canada since 1978 are on file. The Office of the Superintendent of Bankruptcy is represented in each province by its Offices of the Official Receiver. Official Receivers are individuals authorized to handle various functions under the *Bankruptcy and Insolvency Act*.[4] There are four offices of the Official Receiver in Ontario. Their locations and telephone numbers are as follows:

- 55 Bay Street North, 9th Floor, Hamilton, Ontario L9R 3P7, 905-572-2847

- 451 Talbot Street, Room 303, London, Ontario N6A 5C9, 519-645-4034

- 160 Elgin Street, 11th Floor, Rm B-119, Ottawa, Ontario K2P 2P7, 613-995-2994

- 25 St. Clair Avenue East, 6th Floor, Toronto, Ontario M4T 1M2, 416-973-6486.

The national insolvency database, which includes information on bankruptcies, proposals, and receiverships, may be searched online through the Office of the Superintendent of Bankruptcy using the Insolvency Name Search Service available at http://osb-bsf.gc.ca, by calling 613-941-2863, or by faxing 613-941-9490. In order to conduct searches you must establish a Name Search Account with the Office of the Superintendent of Bankruptcy. An account can be established by faxing a letter, on letterhead, to 613-941-9490. The letter should set out your name, mailing address, fax and telephone numbers, and e-mail address, along with the name of the person responsible for the payment of the account, and a password. If you wish to search online you must also register on the Strategis secure website at https://strategis.ic.gc.ca. For online access, after you register and have received your OSB client number you must call 613-941-2863 to have your client number linked with your Secure Registration Preferred username. There is a search fee of $8 for each group of ten matches against the name that you are searching.

A bankruptcy search will also reveal if the defendant is in receivership. This may happen when a business debtor has defaulted on a loan, which gives the creditor the right, on default, to appoint a receiver to run the debtor's business or take it over to liquidate assets. Unless your client has some priority right over the secured lender in this situation, she is unlikely to recover any money, because the secured lender will dispose of virtually all of the assets free of any claim by your client. The Office of the Superintendent of Bankruptcy maintains online records of receiverships nationwide since 1993.

Insurance

Always review a client's insurance policies. Rattle Motors Ltd. is likely to have occupier's insurance covering precisely the kind of situation that arises in Abigail's case. Subject to a deductible, damage awards must be paid by the insurance company. If so, you should advise the insurer immediately that there is a claim. Insurance companies usually have their own lawyers and prefer to have them defend the case. Your firm should not be taking steps to defend unless the insurer instructs you to do so or unless it is necessary in order to preserve a defendant's rights.

The insurer may resist providing coverage on the ground that the client has failed to comply with the terms of the policy or on the ground that the claim falls outside the terms of the policy. The lawyer for Rattle Motors Ltd. should try to persuade the insurer to defend on a non-waiver basis. This means that the insurer defends, but it reserves the right to make a claim against the insured for any amount the insurer has to pay out on the insured's behalf. If this happens, Rattle's lawyer may still act for its client, not against Abigail, but against Rattle's insurers on the issue of whether the insurance company is obliged to cover the claim. If the insurance company refuses to honour a claim, Rattle's lawyer should proceed to defend and serve a third party notice on the insurer.

I.M. Just should check to see if Abigail's homeowner's insurance, workplace health insurance, or any other policy of insurance provides any coverage. Sometimes homeowner's policies are very broad and may provide full or partial coverage for her losses. If so, this may eliminate some issues and remedies in the case, or it may make it unnecessary to sue if the loss is completely covered by the insurer. Abigail must be assisted in making a claim as quickly as possible, and I.M. Just's office should take steps to see that she fully complies with the terms of the policy. If Abigail's insurance company seeks to recover from the defendants what it paid to Abigail, you may need to take initial steps to safeguard Abigail's right to sue until the insurance company takes control of the litigation.

Conflicts of interest

Your law firm will need to ensure that in representing a client it does not have a conflict of interest. The rules about conflicts of interest have become more complicated as large law firms merge, join international networks, and acquire partners from professions other than law. The new rule 2 of the law society's rules of professional conduct make several things clear:

- A lawyer cannot act against a former client on the same or a similar matter on which he or she acted for that client previously.

- When one lawyer in a firm acted for a former client, his or her partners cannot later act against that client unless the former client consents or the interests of justice demand it.

- A lawyer can act for two clients on the same matter on a joint retainer; however, if a conflict develops, the lawyer must cease acting for both clients. Further, there is no confidentiality between the two clients so that information given to one client cannot be withheld from the other. If a lawyer is acting for both Fred and Rattle Motors Ltd. and the lawyer has a continuous and ongoing professional relationship with Rattle Motors Ltd., Fred must be advised of that fact.

- When a lawyer transfers from firm A to firm B and discovers that firm B is acting against firm A's client *and* the lawyer has actual knowledge of confidential matters about firm A's client, firm B must transfer the case to another firm, unless firm A's client consents to firm B's staying on the case. The former client may consent if the transferring lawyer agrees not to communicate with the lawyers handling the case against firm A's client.

Fortunately, our case is simpler. I.M. Just is practising with one salaried lawyer employed as an associate and can easily tell if he has any conflict of interest. If he did have such a conflict, he would be obliged to tell Abigail at once and help her find another lawyer.

When a case comes into the office, the names of the defendants and the client should be cross-checked against names on closed files, using either client cards or computerized client lists. There is software available that is designed to run conflict checks of this sort. However, this may not catch all conflicts.

For example, in one case lawyer A, an associate in a firm, sued a charitable organization on behalf of an employee. The organization was headed by B, and the lawsuit turned on B's conduct toward the employee. There was no apparent conflict between the parties because lawyer A and the firm had never acted for either party before. However, a chance remark by a partner led to the discovery by lawyer A that the partner had acted for B in another matter and knew a great deal about B. At that point, there was a conflict of interest, although the case was well underway. The parties agreed that the partner with knowledge of B's affairs would not discuss any aspect of the case with A.

LIMITATION PERIODS

Care should be taken to determine when the cause of action is complete. In Abigail's case, this occurs at the moment she comes to rest in a pool of oil on the showroom floor. All the acts that caused her damages have occurred, so an action may now be commenced against the defendants, although the extent of those damages may not be known for some time. Lawyers sometimes say at this point that "the cause of action has accrued." From this moment, the clock begins to tick and the limitation period begins to run.

Negligence is a tort. At common law, the limitation period was six years, but under the new Ontario *Limitations Act, 2002* the basic limitation period for almost all causes of action, including Abigail's, will be two years from the time the events occurred (s. 4) or could reasonably be discovered (s. 5).

Sometimes it is difficult to tell when the cause of action is complete. For example, if you are negligently exposed to excessive radiation that might cause cancer, you may not be able to sue because the cause of action does not accrue until you are actually diagnosed with cancer. If you never get cancer, you cannot sue because the cause of action did not accrue.

There are other issues concerning the discovery of the cause of action. Usually, time begins to run when the act or omission occurs. But, as noted above, the

Limitations Act, 2002, in s. 5, sets out situations where time does not begin to run when the act or omission occurs. Rather, it begins to run when the plaintiff can show that a reasonable person knew or ought reasonably to have known that the act occurred and they could move to obtain a legal remedy.

When a client has given you the basic facts, you then have to determine the specific cause of action and the applicable limitation period. Under the *Limitations Act, 2002*, the period is almost always two years from the time the cause of action arose, or from when it could reasonably be discovered.

However, there are exceptions. Some of the more notable exceptions are:

- Minors and persons under disability: limitation periods are generally suspended until a litigation guardian is appointed; at that point the limitation period begins to run (ss. 6 to 9).

- Where the cause of action involves assault or sexual assault, limitation periods are suspended while the plaintiff is physically, mentally, or psychologically unable to act. The plaintiff in such a case is presumed to be unable to act. If the defendant thinks the limitation period should be running, he or she must present evidence to rebut the presumption (s. 10).

- In some circumstances, where a limitation period is suspended, the limitation period runs for a maximum of 15 years, with some exceptions. Where a person is mentally, physically, or psychologically incapable of starting proceedings, or where a person is a minor and not represented by a litigation guardian, the limitation-period suspension might exceed 15 years (s. 15).

- For some causes of action there is no limitation period: proceedings for a declaration of a right where there is no damage claim, proceedings to enforce or obtain a family law domestic agreement for support, and proceedings by the Crown to collect taxes, reclaim welfare benefits, or recover on defaulted student loans (s. 1).

- If a limitation period is set out in another act, it does not apply unless it is set out as an exception in the schedule at the back of the act (s. 19).

retainer
contract between a lawyer and client describing the services to be provided by the lawyer and the terms of payment by the client; also refers to a cash deposit to be used by a lawyer to pay future fees and disbursements as they are incurred

fiduciary relationship
one-sided relationship where one party relies on the other party's honesty and advice given in the reliant party's best interests

There is also a transition rule to cover transitions between the old limitation rules and those under the new Act.

Note that the new *Limitations Act* only affects causes of action arising under Ontario law. If a lawsuit involves a federal statute, you need to look at the limitation periods set by federal statutes.

RETAINERS

Once Abigail has decided to retain I.M. Just to represent her, and I.M. Just has agreed to act, their agreement should be incorporated into a contract of **retainer**. The retainer should be more than just a brief notation of a contractual relationship. It should set out all of the major terms governing the relationship. Because the lawyer is an expert in these matters, and the client is dependent on the lawyer for sound and honest advice, there is said to be a **fiduciary relationship**: the lawyer is

FIGURE 2.6 RETAINER

DATE: Sept. 16, year 0

CONTRACT OF RETAINER

BETWEEN:

JUST & COPING, BARRISTERS AND SOLICITORS

and

ABIGAIL BOAR

1. I, Abigail Boar, retain you as my lawyers to commence proceedings against Fred Flogem and Rattle Motors Ltd. in respect of injuries sustained by me in an accident on September 14, year 0.

2. I understand that I have retained the firm, and not just an individual lawyer, and that other lawyers and staff may work on my case.

3. I understand that the hourly rates of those who may work on my file are as follows:

   I.M. Just, lawyer: $250/hour

   N.O.T. Coping, lawyer: $200/hour

   Edward Egregious, law clerk: $75/hour

4. I understand that the hourly rates of office staff may increase by no more than 5 percent on the first day of March, Year 1, and on the first day of March in subsequent years. I agree to pay the increased amount for work done after the date on which the rates change.

5. I understand that if I am dissatisfied with the amount of the account, I have the right to have that account assessed by the court.*

6. I understand that before work begins under this retainer, I am required to pay a deposit of $3,000 to be credited against accounts when rendered. I understand that I may be required to furnish future deposits from time to time to cover future fees and disbursements.

7. I understand that I must pay accounts promptly when they are rendered and that interest is chargeable on overdue accounts at the rate of 18 percent per year.

8. In the event settlement funds are received, I direct that they be paid to I.M. Just in trust, and that you may deduct any fees or disbursements owing at the time settlement funds are received, on rendering an account to me, and that the balance of the settlement funds will then be paid to me.

9. I understand that it is my obligation, on receiving advice and being asked for instructions, to provide you with instructions as requested.

Signed: *Abigail Boar*   *September 16, year 0*

---

* We have yet to see this in a retainer or hear of a lawyer who conveys this information as a matter of course to clients; but in our view, given the fiduciary nature of the relationship, this information should be in the retainer.

obliged to ensure that the client is treated fairly and scrupulously. One of the ways to ensure this is to explain the terms of the retainer and spell out the corresponding duties and obligations of both lawyer and client.

The retainer must:

- identify the names of the parties (law firm and client);

- identify the work to be done ("to commence proceedings against Rattle Motors for personal injuries arising out of an incident"); and

- be signed by the client to indicate that she has agreed to retain the firm.

The retainer should:

- make clear that other members of the law firm, such as other lawyers, clerks, and staff, may work on the file;

- set out the hourly rate for these individuals;

- indicate that the rate changes periodically, and the client is obliged to pay at the new rate for work done after the date on which the rate changes;

- indicate that if the client is dissatisfied with an account, he or she has the right to have the account assessed by the court;

- indicate the amount of the deposit required before work under the retainer begins;

- indicate that the client will be billed at stated intervals, that the client will be required to pay further deposits, and that interest will be charged on overdue accounts;

- make clear that deposits will be used to pay accounts when rendered;

- make clear that any settlement funds are paid to the law firm, from which accounts will be paid before the balance is paid to the client; and

- indicate that the lawyer will advise the client and that it is the client's obligation, on being given advice, to give the lawyer instructions when asked to do so.

Recently, there have been a number of incidents where lawyers found themselves acting for clients who were using false identities to engage in mortgage fraud or other criminal activity. Law Society bylaw 7.1 now requires lawyers and paralegals to verify the identification of clients, both individuals and organizations. In particular, this is required whenever a lawyer or paralegal transfers funds on behalf of a client, with some exceptions if the money is transferred to a public body, public company, or financial institution, or when it is transferred to or from another licencee's trust account.

When your office agrees to be retained, you will need to obtain identity information from the client, which you must then verify. For individuals, you inspect the original and make a copy of a birth certificate, driver's licence, health card, or passport. You must retain a copy of these documents in your records. If the client is a business, obtain copies of the articles of incorporation or partnership agreement, as the case may be.

CLIENT ACCOUNTS

Once the client has retained the firm, a client account must be opened. A bookkeeper or the bookkeeping department may do this, or you or other office staff may do it. The law society has strict rules about keeping the lawyer's own money separate from money the lawyer holds on behalf of clients. Clients' money is to be kept in a separate trust account or accounts. A lawyer's own money is kept in a general account. If a large sum is being held for a client for more than a few days, the lawyer may open a separate trust account; otherwise trust funds are deposited into one trust account for all clients.

Funds held in trust include settlement payments and retainer deposits made by clients. Abigail's $3,000 deposit, for example, does not go into I.M. Just's general account but into the firm's trust account. Part of it can be transferred from the trust to the general account when I.M. Just renders his account. If there is any of the deposit left, it remains in trust as a credit on any amount the client may owe in future.

In order to accurately record client money transactions, the firm sets up a client ledger card or a computer version of one. On this card, all monies received on behalf of the client and all debits for expenses chargeable to the client are recorded. Each firm has a method of tracking client expenses so they eventually can be billed to the client ledger card, using petty cash vouchers for cash transactions on behalf of the client, and cheque requisitions for cheques for the client's case (for example, to pay the court fee to issue the claim). These forms authorize a withdrawal from the firm's general account and allow the expense to be tracked so it can be debited to the client on the ledger statement. In addition, there is a disbursement journal in which all in-office expenses are recorded so they can be charged to the client's account. Included, for example, are photocopying charges, long distance telephone calls, and delivery of documents by office staff.

Chapter 18 examines how this information is used to assess or fix costs if a party has been awarded costs. Chapter 19 shows how the information is used to prepare a client's account.

Docketing

While actual disbursements incurred on the client's behalf can be tracked and recorded from cheque requisitions, petty cash vouchers, and disbursement journal entries, all of which are recorded on the ledger card, we still need to record the fees to be charged. As you may recall, the lawyers and law clerks charge an hourly rate. In order to determine how many hours they put in on Abigail's file, they need to keep track of their time. They do this by using either a computerized or manual docketing system. Units of time are broken down into tenths of an hour, each tenth being a six-minute block of time. On a docket, the time and the nature of the work are recorded. When a client account is billed, the dockets are referred to and the time is totalled.

If the law clerk, Edward Egregious, spent about 45 minutes doing a first draft of the statement of claim on September 28, his docket slip would look something like the one in figure 2.7. Whoever has charge of the file collects the docket slips. It is also important not to discard the docket slips when the account is rendered. Should the client move to assess the account, the burden is on the lawyer to justify the amount of time spent on the case. That is a lot easier to do, and the lawyer will be much more believable, if he or she has docket slips that were made at the time

FIGURE 2.7   DOCKET SLIP

Boar, A.		Rattle Motors Ltd. et al.		28/09/yr0		.7	
Client		Matter		Date		Time	
X						Edw E.	
Drafting	Meeting	Court	Research	Telephone	Misc.	Initial	
First draft of statement of claim							

the work was done and show what work was done. It is also easy to forget to docket. Interestingly, when dockets are not kept carefully, many lawyers tend to underestimate and undercharge clients for the time spent on the matter.

It is important for law clerks to document their time. For one thing, it can be charged to clients on an account. For another, a clerk who has docketed his or her time is making a case for a raise by showing the chargeable value of the work done by that clerk.

FILE ORGANIZATION

A file must be opened for Abigail's case. In a small firm, this may be an informal process, done by the lawyer, law clerk, or office assistant. In a larger firm, a central file office may do it. However it is done, there are certain practices that, with variations, are usually followed.

The case must be assigned a file number and case name. This may be as simple as the name of the client, "A. Boar," or the name followed by further information. In this case, it might be "Boar v. Rattle et al.," using a short form of the title of the proceedings. This will be useful if Abigail has several files dealing with different legal matters with this law firm. If Abigail were the defendant, the name on her file might read "Boar ats Rattle." The letters "ats" mean "at the suit of" and indicate that the client is being sued by Rattle. After the name, a file number is assigned. It may be as simple as a sequential number, followed by the year the file was opened. For example, "231/08" indicates the 231st file opened in 2008. In larger firms, the system may also record the category or subject matter, identity of the lawyer opening the file, and provide other such information. For example, "231/08-FL-IMJ" indicates the 231st file opened in 2008, that this file is a family law file, and that it was opened by I.M. Just.

Because it is difficult to work on the case if the file or part of it goes missing, a law firm may have rules about how files are stored. In a small firm, the lawyer who has carriage of the file may simply store it in his or her filing cabinet, where anyone who is working on it can find it. In larger firms, where there are more people working on a case and centralized filing is used, the centralized filing office may control the file. This means files must be checked in and out like library books. It may also mean that files cannot remain out overnight or leave the office unless special procedures are followed. This prevents inadvertent loss or the misplacing of files and is also a security measure. Files contain original documents, some of which may be valuable, and are full of confidential and privileged information. Access to them needs to be controlled.

Once opened, the file must be set up and organized. The main file is a large file folder with the case name and file number on the outside. Inside the main folder are subfiles with differently coloured subfolders to identify them at a glance. The office should have a system for maintaining a consistent colour code for subfiles. Otherwise confusion reigns.

The main file should include a file management checklist, such as the one shown in figure 2.8, for noting when necessary steps have been taken or are to be taken. Anyone in the office who picks up the file will know at a glance what the status is and what has to be done next. You will also find the file management checklist useful as a study guide for your course because it provides a practical step-by-step overview of the litigation process.

Subfiles

The following list describes the subfiles usually used in a litigation case and their contents. The contents of subfiles vary from law firm to law firm:

- correspondence: includes all correspondence sent and received in sequential order, with the oldest correspondence on the bottom of the pile;

- pleadings: includes copies of all pleadings, including motions;

- evidence: includes witness statements, factual memos, expert reports, photographs, and other demonstrative evidence;

- discovery: includes all discovery transcripts, documents produced with the affidavit of documents, and discovery exhibits in sequential order;

- law: includes research memoranda, copies of relevant cases, and research notes;

- client documents: includes all original client documents;

- opponents documents: includes all originals and copies not in other subfiles; and

- accounts: includes all statements of account, dockets, and disbursement records.

FIGURE 2.8   FILE MANAGEMENT CHECKLIST

Court file no.: _____   Lawyer: _____

Reference: _____   File no.: _____

Document	Date served	Date filed	Document	Date served	Date filed
Notice of action			Request for other side's answers to undertakings		
Statement of claim			Answers to undertakings received		
Notice of intent to defend			Security for costs		
Statement of defence			Motions		
Reply					
Defence and counterclaim					
Defence and crossclaim			Trial record and setting down for trial		
Third party claim			Waiver of privilege (10 days) (rules 30.09, 31.07)		
Third party defence			Notice of expert witness (10 days) (rule 53.03)		
Offer to settle			Notice for business records (7 days) (rule 35)		
Affidavit of documents (plaintiff)			Notice for medical reports (7 days) (rule 52)		
Affidavit of documents (defendant)			Trial brief		
Notice to admit			Authorities brief		
Notice of examination			Summons		
Examination for discovery					
List of undertakings					
Client's answers to undertakings					

Tickler systems

A file management checklist is not a substitute for an automatic reminder of crucial deadlines. The law society and the Lawyer's Professional Indemnity Corporation (the law society's malpractice insurance body) require all lawyers to maintain a reminder system as a form of protection against professional negligence claims by clients arising from missed deadlines, especially missed limitation periods.

The reminder system may take the form of a desk calendar or day book, or it may be a computerized reminder system. It should give several reminders before the crucial date comes for doing something: 30 days, 1 week, 3 days before the date, and then the date itself. Lawyers, clerks, and office assistants must take responsibility for checking the tickler system daily. At the time a file opens, the law clerk should note the expiry date of the limitation period, as well as the dates for serving and receiving pleadings and taking other steps in the proceeding. If the file falls under the case management system, it will also be necessary to enter the dates of the mandatory timetable for steps in the proceeding. Failure to set up, maintain, and check a tickler system may amount to professional misconduct and can lead to malpractice claims and higher insurance premiums for the lawyer.

CHAPTER SUMMARY

In this chapter, we discussed some of the steps taken by a law firm when it accepts a client's case. We began by assessing the facts as related by the client to determine if there was a good cause of action based on whether rights of the client had been breached and whether damages arose from the breach. We then conducted various searches to identify and name the right individuals or businesses as parties so that the correct person is sued on behalf of the client. We then determined whether the potential party was solvent and able to pay a judgment or was "judgment-proof" and not worth suing. Various searches were identified to determine whether the proposed defendant was insolvent. We also determined if the client could afford to pay for a lawsuit, noting that civil litigation is rarely funded by legal aid. The issue of insurance coverage was explored with the client because insurance may cover the claim and make a lawsuit unnecessary for a plaintiff. If acting for an insured defendant, proper notice of a claim must be given to the insurer. We explored whether a conflict of interest arose for the lawyer with the new or a former client. If so, the lawyer might need to turn the case over to someone else. Next, limitation periods were checked to see if the lawsuit was timely. We observed that once a firm decides to act for a client, the client needs to sign a formal retainer setting out the contractual relationship between the lawyer and the client. Office systems were activated for the client. An account ledger card was opened to record receipts and disbursements on this client's behalf, and methods of tracking the client's costs and expenses were identified. We noted that of particular importance is the need to docket all work done so that fees can be charged accurately. Suggestions were made about how a litigation file should be organized and maintained, and how time limits in the file can be kept track of.

KEY TERMS

reverse search	judgment-proof
stayed	retainer
pro bono	fiduciary relationship
impecunious	bill of costs

NOTES

1 *Doe v. Metropolitan Toronto (Municipality) Commissioners of Police* (1990), 74 OR (2d) 225 (Gen Div.).

2 An employer can terminate an employee if the employee's services are no longer necessary or desired but must pay an amount equal to the salary for the period that would have been required had notice been properly given. If an employer has just cause to dismiss an employee, however, no notice need be given.

3 Although most debts are extinguished on the discharge of the bankrupt, some, like child support debts, are not.

4 This Act and other federal legislation is available online at http://laws.justice.gc.ca.

REFERENCES

Bankruptcy and Insolvency Act, RSC 1985, c. B-3, as amended.

Business Names Act, RSO 1990, c. B.17.

Creditors' Relief Act, RSO 1990, c. C.45.

Doe v. Metropolitan Toronto (Municipality) Commissioners of Police (1990), 74 OR (2d) 225 (Gen. Div.).

Execution Act, RSO 1990, c. E.24.

Law Society of Upper Canada, *Rules of Professional Conduct* (Toronto: LSUC, 2000, as amended) (also available at http://www.lsuc.on.ca).

Limitations Act, 2002, SO 2002, c. 24, sched. B.

Mew, G., *The Law of Limitation of Actions*, 2nd ed. (Toronto: LexisNexis Canada, 2004).

Personal Property Security Act, RSO 1990, c. P.10.

REVIEW QUESTIONS

1. Roger Redoubt was hit by a car while walking along the left side of a road. Roger has always been tone deaf. As a result of the accident, he suffered some painful injuries to his legs, which have now healed, and a concussion. However, since the accident, he is no longer tone deaf and is able to play the violin like a maestro. Does Roger have a good cause of action?

2. If a client is advancing a cause of action that has not been previously recognized, should a lawyer tell him or her to sue anyway?

3. Why is it important to be accurate about the names of the parties you are suing or on whose behalf you are suing?

   MONEY, TIME, MUST SUE RIGHT PERSON,

4. Why does a plaintiff need to know if a defendant has judgment creditors or is bankrupt?

   WHETHER IT IS WORTH PROCEEDING OR NOT. IF BANKRUPT THE PLAINIFF CAN BE ADDED TO THE BANKRUPTCY AS A UNSECURED CREDITOR, PROOF OF DEBT CLAIM FILED WITH TRUSTEE ANY ACTION WOULD BE AUTOMATICALLY STAYED.

5. What searches should a law clerk make in the ordinary course of preparing to commence proceedings?

6. Does it matter whether the defendant went into bankruptcy voluntarily or was petitioned?

7. What insurance issues should be covered with the client?

8. Describe two situations that might give rise to conflicts of interest in a law office.

9. What steps do you need to take to safeguard a client from the expiry of limitation periods?

10. What should be included in a retainer?

11. What needs to be done to set up and maintain a client's account?

12. Describe how a client file is organized.

DISCUSSION QUESTIONS

1. Read the following memorandum:

    To: Edward Egregious, law clerk
    From: I.M. Just, lawyer
    Re: Boar v. Rattle Motors et al.

    We have been retained by Abigail Boar. I wish you to conduct the usual searches to verify the name of the individual defendant, known to us as Fred Flogem, and to make sure we have the correct business name for Rattle Motors. I suspect Rattle is a limited company. Please prepare the necessary search forms in draft.

    I have heard rumours that Rattle is in financial difficulty and want to ensure it is solvent before suing it. Please prepare the documentation to search executions, and tell me what I need to do for a bankruptcy search.

2. Using your own name or that of a friend, business, or parent, find out as much information as you can from one or more of the "people searches" search sites.

CHAPTER 3

Client management and interviewing

INTRODUCTION

In many law offices, it is the law clerk who has the most ongoing contact with the client as the case proceeds. It is often the law clerk who is involved in preliminary interviewing of the client and who speaks to him or her on the telephone. Therefore, it is important that the law clerk have some basic interviewing and some effective client management skills. It is important to remember that client contact is not just about getting information. It is also about conveying information to the client.

OBTAINING INFORMATION FROM THE CLIENT

Much of the initial and ongoing contact with the client involves information gathering. A lawyer needs to know as much about the facts of the case as possible in order to plan the case.

When clients come to the office for a meeting, make certain they are seen in private. They should also have an appointment time that is uninterrupted by telephone calls. A law office may be very busy but clients need to know that the office will not be so busy that staff cannot spend time on their case. The best way to convey this is to give clients undivided attention during their arranged appointments. Be alert, make eye contact, and listen to what they are telling you.

Interviewing is a skill, and there are many books written on the subject. Here is a short overview of some techniques that may be helpful.

Ask the client **open-ended questions**. Questions such as "What would you like to tell me about the case?" or "Is there something more I should know about the facts?" are open-ended questions. They do not box clients in. Open-ended questions encourage clients to tell the story in their own way and to convey information that is important to them. Sometimes clients may talk too much about matters that are of no consequence to the case. It is a good idea to try to redirect clients back to the issues by asking short clarifying questions to help them focus. A question that starts with, "So, what you're saying is" may be enough to turn their minds back to their narrative.

open-ended questions
questions that allow the persons interviewed to choose what they want to talk about to the interviewer

Once clients have finished relaying their story, you can then ask questions that tend to narrow the issues and focus on matters that require more elaboration. While the client has been talking, you have been deciding what parts of the story are more important or what further information you may need about certain points. **Narrow questions** tend to direct the conversation. By asking narrow questions, the questioner can get at specific points. For instance, Abigail Boar may have related her story to you about the slip and fall in the Rattle Motors Ltd. showroom. You may want to ask some details about the lighting or how many drinks she had before ambling over to look at cars.

narrow questions
questions in which the interviewer tries to elicit specific information

Listen carefully to what the client is saying. Taking notes is a good idea, but try to do so unobtrusively. You can encourage a client to continue by nodding or making small verbal responses such as "uh-huh." If clients are upset or expressing their feelings, you can show empathy by saying things like, "So, you are frustrated and angry." Litigation is often a very emotional experience for clients, and it is perfectly acceptable to acknowledge your clients' feelings if they are raising them.

There are some common mistakes made by many people who are "listening." Some of these are:

- jumping in to add comments when clients are telling their stories;

- fidgeting with paper or tapping a pencil or pen;

- answering a question with a question;

- pretending to understand a situation when they do not understand it; and

- using clichés, such as "I hear you."

COMMUNICATING WITH THE CLIENT

Taking a case through the litigation process can take a long time. You know what has happened on the file, but the client does not. One of the major complaints that clients have about litigation is that their lawyer's office does not keep them informed of the progress of the case or that no one returns their telephone calls. Therefore, it is important to establish, right at the beginning, when and how their lawyer or you will be communicating with them.

There are several issues in establishing proper communications with clients. It is wise at the outset to advise clients how often during the litigation process you will be providing them with updates. Tell clients how the office will keep them informed. The method of communication must fit a client's understanding and ability to understand. It is useless to tell a client that you will fax or e-mail information if the client has no equipment for receiving fax or e-mail messages. It is not safe to assume that all clients have access to a computer.

Ask clients how they wish to receive communications. Do they prefer telephone contact or written communications? If they prefer to speak to someone on the telephone, it is a good idea to send a confirming letter to ensure that there is no misunderstanding about what was said.

Ensure that all the client contact information is correct. Do you have the correct mailing address and postal code, the correct e-mail address, the correct telephone or fax number? If your clients have both a home and a business telephone number, find out which number is the most convenient for them. Do not call clients at their place of business unless they indicate that that is the best manner of communicating with them. If you telephone, ensure that you do not leave too much information with whoever answers the telephone. Clients may not have advised people that they are involved in litigation and may not be happy to have it revealed to a co-worker in a message from the lawyer's office. It should be sufficient to say no more than, "This is Joe Clerk calling from Susie Seneca's office. Would you please ask Ms. Client to call me?" There is no need to say that Susie Seneca is a lawyer or that you are her law clerk.

Once the method of communication has been settled, it is a good idea to determine how often clients can expect to hear from the law office. Will you update them once a month? Will you contact them only at certain milestones in the process? If so, determine what the milestones are and approximately when they will occur. Let clients know whether to expect a formal written report or an informal telephone chat.

One effective method for communicating with clients is sending them copies of relevant documents as they come into or leave the office. In this way, clients are kept abreast of developments as they occur. Some documents that may be sent to clients are:

- copies of all correspondence the office sends or receives on the matter,

- pleadings and court documents, and

- memorandums to file confirming communications or meetings.

Find out if your law office has a standard maximum length of time that it takes to return a client's telephone call. If such a standard exists, make sure you adhere to it. Often the standard is one business day. Whether there is an office standard or not, it may be a good personal policy to try to return client calls within 24 hours. If a lawyer is tied up in court and unable to return the call, make certain that this information is conveyed to the client.

It is also important to establish how clients will keep the office informed of developments in the case or new information pertaining to the litigation. They should be advised if there are certain things they should be watching for in terms of facts or situations.

When a practical and effective method and time frame of communication with the client is set up, the client has more confidence in the process and is less likely to inundate the office with telephone calls that interrupt work and create stress for all involved.

CHAPTER SUMMARY

This chapter introduced some general techniques and practices used in dealing with clients in a law office. It set out practical suggestions to guide you in interviewing clients and witnesses, including the appropriate use of open-ended and narrow questions to elicit information relevant to a case. The chapter also discussed appropriate techniques for maintaining communication with clients to ensure that the client receives necessary information in a timely fashion.

KEY TERMS

open-ended questions

narrow questions

REVIEW QUESTIONS

1. Give three examples of open-ended questions:

2. Considering the Boar case, give three examples of narrow questions you might ask Abigail.

3. What should you not do while interviewing a client or a witness?

4. Why is it important to maintain communication with the client as the case progresses?

5. What sort of information should clients receive from a law firm?

DISCUSSION QUESTION

1. Work in pairs for the following listening exercise. Look at the list of comment starters below. One student chooses any of the statements listed and uses it to begin speaking for a few minutes.

   When the first student is finished, the second student paraphrases the first student's comments. Take turns speaking and listening.

   - I would like to take a trip to ... because ...

   - One thing that I feel strongly about is ...

   - I am taking this course in college because ...

   - My favourite television show is ... because ...

   - When I go to a party ...

   - This college is ...

   - When I graduate, I would like to ...

   - My ideal job is ...

CHAPTER 4

Introduction to the Rules of Civil Procedure and the Courts of Justice Act

INTRODUCTION

The Courts of Justice Act and the law of equity

The *Courts of Justice Act* sets out the jurisdiction of the Ontario courts, the way those courts function, and other matters related to the makeup and operation of the courts. For instance, the Act tells you the route from court to court that must be followed on an appeal, it provides for the use of French and English as the official languages of the court, it spells out the names of the courts and their jurisdiction, and it requires that court hearings be open to the public except in special circumstances. It even tells you how to address judges in the courtroom.

Until the late 19th century, there were two types of courts: the common law courts and the courts of equity. The common law courts applied **common law** principles, and the courts of equity dealt with the **law of equity**. These two separate sets of legal rules created a complicated and sometimes rigid system that made it difficult for litigants and lawyers. A major court reform about a hundred years ago merged the two courts. This was a statute that joined the courts and was a predecessor to the *Courts of Justice Act*. Now any Superior Court in Ontario can apply both the common law and the law of equity. Superior Court judges have the power to give an equitable remedy to a party in a proceeding. They can grant injunctions and specific performance of contracts.

common law
law that is made by judges following precedents set by higher courts; often called "case law"

law of equity
type of law developed several hundred years ago in England wherein judges, rather than following precedents, look at the issues in a case and apply certain principles to ensure a fair outcome

The Rules of Civil Procedure

The *Courts of Justice Act* requires that a Civil Rules Committee be set up. This committee has the responsibility for making the rules of practice for the Superior Court of Justice and the Court of Appeal. The *Rules of Civil Procedure* are actually regulations to the *Courts of Justice Act*.

Under s. 66(2) of this Act, the rules committee may make rules for the Superior Court of Justice and the Court of Appeal in relation to the practice and procedure of those courts in all civil proceedings. Other committees set the rules for family law matters and criminal matters. The Small Claims Court also has its own rules; therefore the rules made by the Civil Rules Committee do not apply in that court.

It is the Civil Rules Committee that makes and amends the *Rules of Civil Procedure*. Because the committee is made up of judges, lawyers, representatives of the provincial attorney general and court administrators, its members are familiar with the manner in which courts operate from a number of different perspectives.

WORKING WITH THE RULES

The rules tell you everything you need to know about preparing a civil case for court. Your first task is therefore to learn how to use them.

Structure of the rules

Rule 1 tells us how to cite the rules, that is as the *Rules of Civil Procedure*. In addition, this rule provides an explanation as to how the rules are numbered and subdivided.

All of the rules with the same starting number comprise a rule. For instance, rules 1.01, 1.02, 1.03, etc., are all part of rule 1. However, most major rules are broken down into subdivisions and each of these subdivisions are rules themselves. The major subdivision of the rule follows the main number and a decimal point, for example, rules 1.01, 1.02, and 1.03.

Each major subdivision may be subdivided as well into

- subrules, indicated by a number in parentheses (for example, subrule 1.01(2));

- clauses, indicated by a lower case letter in parentheses (for example, clause 1.01(2)(c) or 2.02(a));

- subclauses, indicated by a lower case Roman numeral in parentheses (for example, subclause 1.01(2)(c)(iii) or 7.01(c)(i));

- paragraphs (for example, paragraph 1 of subrule 52.07(1)), and

- definitions (for example, the definition of "originating process" in rule 1.03).

The layout of the rules generally follows the steps that are taken in a court case from start to finish. In addition, lawyers, law clerks, judges, and court officers and staff become familiar with the rules and come to know very quickly that rule 37 deals with motions and rule 77 with case management. However, from time to time, the rules are amended to add new rules or subrules, or revoke existing ones.

To avoid confusion, the rules use a numbering system that allows the insertion of new rules in the appropriate order without having to renumber those that follow. For example, in 2004, a new rule was created to deal with a proceeding that is to be commenced. The appropriate place for this rule to fall was right before existing rule 14, which deals with the commencement of proceedings. The new rule is designated by the major rule number followed by a decimal point. A further decimal point then indicates any major subdivision of the rule. Therefore, the new rule's number looks like this: rule 13.1, and its subdivisions look like this: subrule 13.1.01(1). The number following the first decimal point is crucial to designating the rule and distinguishing it from existing rule 13.

Using Ontario Annual Practice

As discussed above, the *Rules of Civil Procedure* are a regulation to the *Courts of Justice Act*. Like most Ontario legislation, this regulation can be found on the Ontario government's e-laws website. *Ontario Annual Practice* publishes the *Rules of Civil Procedure* along with additional material that is helpful to litigators, law clerks, and court officials and staff.

In another example, a new rule governing the use of information obtained from discovery, "the implied undertaking" rule, was added to the rules by amendment. It was placed next to the rule it was most closely associated with, rule 30, and was made rule 30.1.

THE PROCEDURAL CHARTS

There is a Procedural Guide in *Ontario Annual Practice* that offers a number of procedural guides that take you through the various steps for a number of types of proceedings under the rules. Included in the guide, among other proceedings, are charts for steps in actions, motions, the simplified procedure and various types of appeals. Until you become familiar with the steps to be taken in a specific type of proceeding, these charts can be invaluable because they tell you the nature of the step required, when it must be taken, and who must take it.

SYNOPSIS, COMMENT, AND ADVOCACY NOTES

There is an introduction to each rule, provided by the editors. A synopsis summarizes the content of the rule in easy-to-read language. In addition to the synopsis of the rule, there may also be a comment by the editor or advocacy notes — sometimes they both appear. A comment draws attention to any recent changes in that rule and it is here that the editors provide helpful comments. Advocacy notes offer useful tips. You should not overlook these valuable tools while working with the rules.

ANNOTATIONS

Annotations are the short summaries of cases that follow most rules. These cases provide court interpretations and applications of the rule.

Finding rules

The index at the back of the rules can lead to a long roundabout search if you do not know what you want to find. A preferable way to find a rule is to use the following three-step technique:

1. Look at the "summary of contents" at the beginning of the rules, and choose a rule that looks relevant.

2. Go to the "table of contents," which follows the summary of contents; look at the outline of what is covered in that rule, and choose a section.

3. Turn to the rule, and look through the section to find the information that is required.

The summary of contents provides a general overview of the rules. The table of contents breaks the summary into smaller components according to the various subsections of the rule. Because the summary allows an overview of the rules, it also assists you in seeing where the particular component you are searching for fits into the entire scheme.

Some rules are much easier to find and read than others and do not require all three steps, but until you are familiar with the rules, it is best to follow this technique.

Definitions and application of the rules: Rules 1 and 2

A court case runs in a fairly predictable manner from start to finish. The rules, for the most part, are set out in the same chronological order that a court case follows. The first steps you must take are set out in the first rules. In fact, the very first rules tell you the basic things that you need to know.

Rules 1.01 and 1.02 tell you how to cite the rule and where and how they are to be applied.

Rule 1.03 is one of the most important rules because it is the definition rule. There are many words and terms used continually throughout the rules, and this rule defines those terms. You must be careful when reading the rules that you do not automatically apply everyday interpretations to the words in them. An ordinary word may have a different meaning in the context of the *Rules of Civil Procedure*. For instance, the word "holiday" means not only statutory holidays, as you might expect, but rule 1.03 also defines a "holiday" to mean a Saturday and a Sunday.

Over time, you will become familiar with the list of words that are defined in rule 1.03, but until you do, every time that you read a new rule, you should go back to rule 1.03 to check that there are no words in the rule you are reading that have a special definition.

Rule 2 spells out the consequences of not following the rules properly. The rules do not set up a system of proceeding that is so rigid that parties lose the right to continue with their case if they do not comply with the them. On the contrary, the court usually allows parties to correct their mistakes or to bring their documents or steps into compliance. However, such mistakes or failures in compliance cost your client money and time, and it is therefore essential that you always try to comply with the requirements of the rules.

Practice directions

The rules are applied in the same manner throughout the Ontario Superior Court of Justice. However, there are courts all over Ontario, and the administrative needs of one court may be quite different from those of another. For instance, jurisdictions with a high volume of cases, such as Toronto and Ottawa, may require special procedures to facilitate the management and organization of courts in those regions. These special procedures would make no sense in a court that has many fewer cases. Therefore, rule 1.07 provides that the chief justice of the court may give a **practice direction** to the other judges and lawyers who are active in that region. A practice direction is like a memorandum that outlines how a particular court operates in specified areas. The practice directions are signed by the Chief Justice of

practice direction
instructions set out by a chief justice to inform lawyers about special procedures that must be followed in particular courts as a result of administrative needs

the appropriate court, filed with the secretary of the Civil Rules Committee, published in the *Ontario Reports*, and posted on the website for the court: http://www.ontariocourts.on.ca. The practice direction is operable only in the courts named in the practice direction and not in all Ontario courts. Nevertheless, the practice direction must be followed in the courts where it applies.

In the *Ontario Annual Practice*, the practice directions precede the rule to which they relate. As an example, there are a number of different practice directions that apply to the procedure for bringing motions in various judicial regions in the province. These precede rule 37, which is the rule dealing with motions.

You must always check to find out if there is a practice direction relating to the litigation step you wish to take in the court where you are proceeding with your client's case. The court may refuse to file your documents if they do not comply with what is required under a practice direction.

The difference between "shall" and "may"

The words "shall" and "may" are used throughout the rules. In legal interpretation, the world "shall" is an imperative. This means that when the word "shall" is used, the procedure must be followed — it is mandatory. There is no discretion to do something else. For example, rule 20.04 deals with a motion for summary judgment. (The procedure for summary judgment is dealt with in depth in chapter 11.) Rule 20.04(2) uses the word "shall," and the court is therefore required to grant summary judgment if it is satisfied that there is no genuine issue for trial or the parties consent to the procedure.

In legal interpretation, the word "may" is permissive. This means that the procedure can be used or not — it is discretionary. Rule 20.04(3) uses the word "may," and the court therefore has discretion as to whether or not it orders summary judgment if the only genuine matter at issue is the amount of money to be paid.

This interpretation of the words "shall" and "may" is set out in s. 29(2) of the Ontario *Interpretation Act*.

COMPUTATION OF TIME: RULE 3

The rules require that many steps in a court proceeding be taken within certain time limits. For instance, there are time limits for the service and the filing of documents. Rule 3 tells you how to compute the time. You might ask why there needs to be a special rule to tell you how to count time when it is something everyone knows how to do. Counting time, according to the rules, is different from counting time in ordinary life. For instance, if someone told you on Thursday that you had three days to do something, you would probably think that meant you had until Sunday. However, if you were counting in the time prescribed by the rules, your answer would be different.

Under rule 3.01(1)(a), when you count days, do not count the first day, but count the last day. For example, rule 34.05 requires you to give a party who lives in Ontario not less than two days' notice of the time and place for examinations for discovery. If you give notice on Monday, you do not count Monday as the first day. Tuesday is the first day, and Wednesday is the second. Since you count the last day as a full day, the earliest you can require the party to attend for examination is Wednesday.

Where the rules have a time limit of *less* than seven days, holidays are not counted as days (rule 3.01(1)(b)). If the time limit required by the rule is more than seven days, you do count the holidays. Under rule 1.03, "holiday" includes Saturdays and Sundays. This means that if a rule requires three days to do something, you do not count Saturdays, Sundays, or other holidays listed under the definition of "holiday" in rule 1.03.

When the last day for taking a step in the court proceeding falls on a holiday, the step may be taken on the first day afterward that is not a holiday (rule 3.01(1)(c)). Therefore, if the third day falls on a Saturday, the deadline is extended until Monday, assuming that Monday is not a holiday. If Monday is a holiday, then the next day that is not a holiday after Saturday is the following Tuesday.

If you serve a document other than an originating process after 4 p.m. or on a holiday, the document is regarded as served on the next day that is not a holiday (rule 3.1(1)(d)). This means that if you served a document on Friday afternoon at 4:15 p.m. and the following Monday is Labour Day, the rules regard the document as being served on the Tuesday after Labour Day.

Although rule 3.02(1) permits the court to extend or shorten the time, you must bring a motion to ask for the court to do this, and it will cost the client more money. Therefore, it is important to try to keep the time limits as required by the rules.

FORMAT FOR COURT DOCUMENTS

The rules tell you what a court document should look like. Rule 4 prescribes in specific detail the format and content of court documents, provides for the use of electronic documents, tells you how to issue and bind documents, and gives all the other information you need to make your documents easy to read. Although instructions on how to prepare documents might seem far removed from conducting a court hearing, the documents are an integral part of the proceeding. The first impression that a judge has of your client's case arises when he or she reads your documents in preparation for a hearing or a trial.

In addition, during the court proceeding, it is necessary for the lawyers to refer the judge to parts of the documents that have been filed. It can be very irritating to a judge to try to find his or her way around a set of court documents that are not properly formatted or are badly written. Court documents may reflect on the lawyer and the law firm. Therefore, you want to make them as professional and as reflective of the seriousness of the client's case as you can.

Format of documents: Rule 4.01

Rule 4.01 gives specific requirements for the set up of documents to be filed in any court proceeding. Documents are to be typewritten and double spaced with a margin of 40 mm on the left side of the text. The font must be at least 12 point or 10 pitch size. Remember that fonts that are too small are extremely difficult to read. White paper must be used and the pages must be 216 mm by 279 mm. This is standard 8.5 × 11 inch stationery. Do not be tempted to use legal-sized paper. It is not acceptable in part because it is difficult to fit into the court files. You may use single-sided or double-sided pages.

Contents of documents: Rule 4.02

Every document in a court proceeding must have both a general heading and a backsheet. In addition, there are requirements for the contents of the body of the particular document.

GENERAL HEADING: RULE 4.02(1)

This is a standard beginning for every document. There is a precedent for the general heading in the forms that are attached to the rules. The general heading for an action is in Form 4A and for an application is in Form 4B. Note that the form number is the same as the rule number related to it. Each general heading must contain:

- the name of the court;

- the court file number, if one has been issued by the court (if you are preparing the first document in the case and it has not yet been served or filed, there will be no court file number, but if you are preparing documents in an ongoing case, you must make sure that the file number is properly put on the document so that it will make its way to the proper court file); and

- the title of the proceeding (this is a fancy way of saying "the name of the case"). The title of the proceeding is sometimes called the "style of cause." This is an old-fashioned term that some lawyers still use. What is the title of the proceeding? If Abigail Boar is suing Rattle Motors Ltd., the title of the proceeding is *Abigail Boar v. Rattle Motors Ltd.*

If there are more than two parties on documents that are not originating process (a statement of claim or notice of application), or a court order, report, or record, you can use the name of one plaintiff and one defendant. For example, *Boar v. Rattle Motors Ltd. and others* is the short title of proceedings where Abigail Boar sues Fred Flogem and Rattle Motors. However, on originating process, and court orders, reports, and records, all the parties must be named in full.

BODY OF THE DOCUMENT: RULE 4.02(2)

The body of each document must contain:

- the title of the document (is it a notice of motion, an affidavit?);

- the date the document was prepared;

- the name, address, and telephone number of the person filing the document; and

- the address of the court.

If the person filing the document is a lawyer, the lawyer's name, address, and telephone number appears on the document. If a party has no lawyer and is representing himself or herself, the party's name, address, and telephone number goes on the document. It is a good idea to put a fax number on the document as well since some documents can be served by fax.

BACKSHEET: RULES 4.02(3) AND 4.07

Every court document must have a backsheet. The prescribed form for a backsheet is form 4C. Judges usually write their endorsements on the backsheet, so it is an important part of the document. Figure 1.3 in chapter 1 shows an example of a backsheet. An endorsement is a short summary of the order that the court has made.

The backsheet must contain:

- the short title of the proceeding;

- the name of the court and the court file number;

- the location of the court office where the proceeding is commenced;

- the title of the document (is it a notice of motion, an affidavit?);

- the name, address, telephone, and fax number of the lawyer serving or filing the document;

- if the person filing is a lawyer, the Lawyer's Law Society ID number; and

- the fax number, if possible, of the person being served.

In addition, if the document is an affidavit, the backsheet must also contain the name of the deponent and the date when he or she swore that the document was true.

There are usually many types of documents filed in a court proceeding. In a long case with many parties, the documents are often brought into the court on trolleys. The rules prescribe a method for telling the documents apart. They are given different coloured backsheets. Being able to tell the documents apart is very useful in a proceeding because it makes for easier access. The judge and lawyers do not need to search through a stack of documents that all look the same.

Records for motions, applications, trials, and appeals must have a light blue backsheet. Transcripts of evidence must have a light grey backsheet, except for transcripts that are to be used on an appeal. Those must have a red backsheet. Although not all court documents require a special colour for the backsheet, you should check rule 4.07 to make certain that the document that you are preparing does not require a special colour. If it does not, you can use ordinary white bond for the backsheet.

CHAPTER SUMMARY

In this chapter, we looked at the *Courts of Justice Act*, and you were introduced to the *Rules of Civil Procedure*. These rules provide a detailed set of directions as to how a court proceeding is conducted in the Ontario Superior Court of Justice and the Ontario Court of Appeal. For the most part, the rules are laid out in the same order as the chronological progress of a court case. It is essential to learn how to use the rules. Until you are familiar with them, we suggest that you use the "three-step" approach described in this chapter.

Rule 1 tells you how to cite the rules and where and how they are to be applied. It also contains a list of definitions that are crucial to your understanding of the rest of the rules. Rule 1 also provides that the chief justice may give practice directions about certain court procedures to the judges and lawyers in a particular court region. These directions must be followed.

Rule 2 spells out the consequences of not complying with the *Rules of Civil Procedure*. Although every effort must be made to follow the rules properly, the court has the ability to dispense with compliance if the interests of justice make it appropriate to do so. However, seeking the court's permission to dispense with compliance after a mistake has been made is costly to a client and should be avoided.

Many steps in the litigation process involve time limits. Rule 3 tells you how to count time when the rules prescribe a time limit. You must be able to use this rule in reference to the definition section in rule 1.03 to ensure that you are applying the correct usage of the terms and mechanisms contained in rule 3.

Rule 4 prescribes the format and general content of all court documents. It also tells you the size, colour, and type of paper that is required for each type of court document. Your documents provide the material for a judge's first impression of your client's case, and it is therefore essential that the documents be presented in a professional manner.

KEY TERMS

common law

law of equity

practice direction

REFERENCES

Carthy, James J., W.A. Derry Millar, and Jeffrey G. Cowan, *Ontario Annual Practice* (Aurora, ON: Canada Law Book, published annually).

Courts of Justice Act, RSO 1990, c. C.43.

Interpretation Act, RSO 1990, c. I.11.

Rules of Civil Procedure, RRO 1990, reg. 194.

REVIEW QUESTIONS

1. Using the three-step process outlined in this chapter, find the rule (or rules) that:

   a. provides for service of a document on a corporation,

b. permits the amendment of pleadings,

c. prescribes how to commence a proceeding in the Ontario Superior Court of Justice,

d. requires a title of proceeding on all court documents,

e. requires that service of originating process must be personal,

f. permits service of court documents on a party's lawyer,

g. tells when an appointment for an examination for discovery can first be served,

h. determines the contents of a motion record, and

i. determines the contents of a trial record.

2. To what courts do the *Rules of Civil Procedure* apply? Name the rule that tells you that.

SUPERIOR COURT OF JUSTICE } PRACTICE & PROCEDURES FOR ALL
COURT OF APPEAL   CIVIL LITIGATIONS.

3. What rules apply in Small Claims Court? How do you know?

RULES MADE BY THE CIVIL RULES COMMITTEE DO NOT APPLY
IN SMALL CLAIMS COURT BECAUS SCC HAS ITS OWN
RULES, SEPARATE

4. What is the definition of "judgment"?

COURT DECISION (USUALLY) AGAINST A PARTY IN A PROCEEDING

5. Are there special forms that you must use under the rules? If so, where do you find them?

YES   THEY ARE FOUND IN THE RULES OF CIVIL PROCEDURE.
RULE # 4.

6. What form gives you a precedent for a backsheet?

RULES 4.02(3) AND 4.07

7. Must you include a fax number in your documents?

NO BUT IT IS A GOOD IDEA BECAUSE SOME DOCUMENTS
CAN BE SERVED BY FAX.

8. What rule applies to the contents of an affidavit?

RULE 4.02

9. What colour backsheet belongs on an application? What rule applies?

LIGHT BLUE   RULE 4.07

10. What rule tells you who should make an affidavit for a corporate party?

11. How and where do you issue and file a document?

12. Who must sign a practice direction for the Superior Court of Justice?

CHIEF JUSTICE

DISCUSSION QUESTIONS

1. A motion record is served on Brad Pout on Friday May 10 at 4:25 p.m. It is returnable — that is, it is to come to court — on May 20. However, Brad is entitled to six days' notice of the return date. Was he served in time?

2. Your firm wants to have a motion in court on Tuesday July 3 and must give three days' notice. What is the last possible day you can serve the opposite party with the motion record?

FRIDAY

CHAPTER 5

Identification of parties, joinder of claims and parties

INTRODUCTION

We know that the parties to an action are called "plaintiff" and "defendant." But it is not always clear who the plaintiff or defendant is, or who should be included as a party. Can Abigail's boyfriend be a plaintiff because he has lost the pleasure of the company of the pre-accident Abigail? Can Skank Motorcar Company Ltd. be a party defendant? Can you join Barbeerian's, where Abigail had two glasses of wine before going to the car showroom? How about Abigail's employer: Haven't Abigail's injuries cost Megadoon Investments something? Would it make a difference procedurally if Abigail were under 18 or mentally disabled? If any of the defendants were partnerships, are there things you would need to do?

In this chapter, we examine the relevant rules of procedure to determine the answers to some of these questions. Set out below are the rules we examine and the issues they address:

- rule 5: who should be included as a party to a lawsuit;

- rule 5: which claims can be included together in one lawsuit;

- rule 6: how separate proceedings may be joined together into one proceeding;

- rule 7: how parties who are under a disability are represented in proceedings;

- rule 8: how partnerships and sole proprietorships are named as parties;

- rule 9: how estates and trusts sue and defend civil suits;

- rule 10: how unidentified persons with an interest in the issues are joined to civil suits;

- rule 11: how an interest in a lawsuit may be transferred by a party to a non-party, who then joins the proceeding;

- rule 12: how many persons who have the same interest in a lawsuit may be joined together to be represented by one plaintiff or defendant; and

- rule 15: whether a party to a lawsuit must be represented by a lawyer.

Our primary focus is on joinder of claims and parties (rule 5), consolidation of claims (rule 6), parties under disability (rule 7), and proceedings on behalf of and against sole proprietorships and partnerships (rule 8). You will encounter these basic rules for procedural matters often. The other rules and procedures are encountered less often unless you work in specialized areas of practice, such as estate litigation. We nevertheless include a general discussion so that if you find yourself working in these areas, you will have some familiarity with the procedural requirements.

JOINDER OF CLAIMS AND PARTIES: RULE 5

Abigail is suing Rattle Motors Ltd. and Fred Flogem for negligence concerning the failure to clean up the oil spill. But she may also have a claim against Skank Motorcar Company Ltd. arising from the defective design or manufacture of the oil pan on the Super Coupe. Should Skank Motorcar Company Ltd. and Abigail's claim against it be joined to a lawsuit against Flogem and Rattle Motors Ltd. that is, in some respects, about something else? Must all defendants be involved with all issues in the main lawsuit, whether their personal interest in them is minor or major? Rule 5 provides guidance in answering these questions.

Remember the basic principle in rule 1.04(1): the aim of the rules is to reduce cost and delay in the process of resolving disputes. Rule 5 is a more specific version of that general principle tied to the issues of what claims can be joined together in a lawsuit and what parties can be included as either plaintiffs or defendants. The thrust of rule 5 is that all parties with an interest in an issue in the litigation should be before the court in one hearing, so that all persons with an interest have a chance to be heard and are bound by one judgment. Generally, the rules frown on multiple proceedings involving common events, transactions, or factual issues. However, where inclusion of several parties in one proceeding would be prejudicial to the rights of a party, issues may be tried separately.

Joining claims

There are three procedural guidelines for joining claims set out in rule 5.01:

1. If a plaintiff has several claims against one party, he or she may join those claims together in one proceeding.

2. If a plaintiff has different claims against different defendants, he or she may include all of the claims against the defendants in one proceeding, even if some defendants have no interest in some claims made against other defendants.

3. A plaintiff may sue in more than one capacity. For example, a party may have been injured and sue for his or her own injuries, but that party may also be the litigation guardian for a child injured in the same accident. In that case, in the capacity of litigation guardian, the party makes claims for the child's injuries, and in a personal capacity, the party makes claims on his or her own behalf.

For example, if Abigail sued Fred and Rattle Motors Ltd. for negligence, she might also sue Barbeerian's for continuing to serve her alcohol when she was intoxicated. These are separate incidents of negligence involving different parties. The only link the defendants have to each other is Abigail. But indirectly the issues involving the separate defendants are linked because they are part of the same transaction, event, or series of events. If Abigail were partly intoxicated, some of the liability for her injuries may lie with Barbeerian's, so she would include all claims she may have against any defendant. This is particularly important since the court might have to apportion liability among all defendants who were causally linked to Abigail's injuries.

However, the rule is flexible, and the court may refuse to join all of the plaintiff's claims together if some of the claims are disconnected from the others. For example, after the accident, Abigail's change in personality may have had a negative impact on her relationship with her boyfriend, to whom she had just become engaged. Suppose he breaks off the engagement? If she has a claim against him for engagement gifts she gave him, demanding their return, should she join that claim to her negligence action against the other defendants? There is some link between the claims. But for the accident, the relationship would likely have continued. The fact that the claim against the boyfriend might be in contract rather than in tort is not important. But a causal link such as this may be so remote that a court would hold it to be prejudicial to the other defendants to require them to spend time and money on a contractual issue in which they have no interest, direct or indirect, and that does not affect their cases. In this situation, the court might order that the contractual issue be severed from the negligence issues, and that the action against the boyfriend be tried separately. This means that if Abigail pursues both claims, she must do so in two separate lawsuits, which may raise costs and result in more stress for her. In considering whether to join claims or sever them, a court must balance the prejudice and relative inconvenience to all parties.

Joinder of parties

At least initially, the plaintiff can decide what claims to include in a lawsuit, with the understanding that where it is both fair and possible, all claims that are logically related should be disposed of in one proceeding. We now turn to rule 5.02 and the issue of when parties can join or be joined in a lawsuit.

PLAINTIFFS

To be joined as plaintiffs in the same proceeding, the plaintiffs or applicants must have the same lawyer of record and must assert claims arising out of the same event, series of transactions, or occurrence where a common question of law or fact may arise or where joining the parties may "promote the convenient administration of justice." There are two essential requirements. First, the same lawyer must represent all plaintiffs in the proceeding. This means that while the plaintiffs may advance different claims, there are no conflicts of interest among them with respect to those claims. Second, the claims must be related because they arise out of the same events where either it is convenient in terms of cost and delay to join the plaintiffs or there is a common question of fact and law that links the plaintiffs, even if some of the claims are different.

For example, suppose Abigail were a key employee so that her injuries caused loss of profits to her employer because she was unable to work. Abigail might sue for her injuries, and the employer might sue for its profit loss. The claims are different, but there is no conflict of interest between the plaintiffs. There is a common question of fact or law (whether the defendants were negligent), and the claims arise out of the same occurrence (the accident). This case might well proceed with the two plaintiffs, represented by one lawyer, making claims in one proceeding. Otherwise, each plaintiff would need to sue separately. They would also have to sue separately if any conflict between them made them adverse in interest to each other. Lawyers must be alert to this and warn multiple plaintiffs that if a conflict develops, other lawyers must represent them both separately, and their cases must be divided and tried separately.

DEFENDANTS

While plaintiffs must be united and not in conflict to proceed together, this is not the case for defendants. Defendants may have little interest in each other, be at each other's throats, and be separately represented. If defendants are in agreement on their defence, are united against the plaintiff's claim, and have no conflict of interest with each other, they may be represented by the same lawyer, subject to the development of a conflict of interest. But it is the plaintiff who decides who the defendants are, simply because it is the plaintiff who decides whom to sue. Most lawyers follow the "sue everybody in sight" approach, particularly in the early stages of a case. Everyone who might be liable or who should be bound by the judgment is included initially. Later, often after discovery when the plaintiff has assessed his or her case, the plaintiff may discontinue proceedings against some of the defendants, though he or she may have to pay some costs to do so.

Guidelines as to who may be added as defendants are set out in rule 5.02(2)(a) to (e).

1. *Persons against whom the plaintiff makes claims arising out of "the same transaction or occurrence, or series of transactions or occurrences" may be joined as defendants.* These claims may be made against defendants who acted together or who acted separately from each other. If a claim against one defendant fails, it can be made alternatively against another defendant. The uniting factor is not the relationship between the defendants or between the defendants and the plaintiff; it is the relationship of all to an occurrence or transaction. For example, Abigail may sue Barbeerian's, Fred, Rattle Motors Ltd., and Skank Motorcar Company Ltd. Her reason for suing each is different, but they are each connected to an occurrence: the accident that gave rise to damages for which they are allegedly liable in various ways.

2. *Persons who are linked together by a common fact or issue of law may be joined as defendants.* For example, if a plaintiff seeks to determine who among several people share an interest in property, all of those people may be made defendants because of their link to and interest in an issue of law (the ownership of property). In this case, the plaintiff may seek a declaration as to who is entitled to the property rather than damages.

3. *All potential defendants may be joined in the proceeding when the plaintiff is not sure who is liable and from whom a remedy can be obtained.* This

is the basis for the "sue everybody in sight" rule. In medical malpractice, there may be several medical practitioners who are responsible for the plaintiff's injury, but because of the nature of treatment or the patient's state or both, the patient may not know who among all the doctors, nurses, and other medical professionals caused the damage. The plaintiff therefore sues them all.

4. *All potential defendants may be joined when the plaintiff has sustained a loss caused by more than one defendant, even where there is no factual connection between the potential defendants* and *there is doubt as to which defendant caused what damage.* This rule applies to a situation where, for example, a plaintiff was physically injured in an accident and then taken to a hospital where negligent medical staff caused further physical damage. The nature of the physical damage may prevent the plaintiff from knowing which potential defendant caused what part of the damage. In this case, this rule permits the plaintiff to sue everyone involved. This situation differs from that contemplated by the previous subrule. Here we think various defendants each did some damage. In the previous situation, we think that one or more defendants did all the damage, but we do not know which one was responsible. While the rules seems to contemplate distinct situations giving rise to joinder of defendants, you will find that often several of the subrules can apply to a case.

5. *Notwithstanding the failure of a case to come within the first four rules, defendants may be joined if joinder promotes the convenient administration of justice.* The term "convenient" incorporates the concept of "balance of convenience." The court, in examining balance of convenience, looks to see if joinder will cause the proceeding to be less expensive and less time-consuming for the parties, on the whole, without prejudicing a party's right to a fair trial.

Joinder of necessary parties: Rule 5.03

As a general rule, the court has the power to join in a proceeding any person whose presence is necessary to decide the issues in the case. This means, for example, that if a person who is not a party to the proceeding will be affected by a decision, that person should have standing as a party in the proceeding.

If a plaintiff claims a remedy to which another person is also entitled, the plaintiff is obliged to join the other person to the proceeding. If there is no conflict of interest and if the "add-on" agrees by filing a consent under rule 5.04(3), the add-on is joined as a plaintiff. If the add-on does not consent or objects, he or she is added as a defendant so as to be bound by the decision, even though no claim is made against the add-on. While the add-on cannot be compelled to be a plaintiff, he or she cannot easily prevent being made a defendant. In general, if a person who is not a party to the proceeding could be affected by the decision, he or she should be added as a defendant. As a general rule, if a plaintiff is in doubt, the plaintiff should add the person as a defendant, even if there is no claim made against that defendant, so that the defendant is bound by the judgment. This is important because a **judgment *in personam*** is more common than a **judgment *in rem***. A judgment *in*

judgment *in personam*
judgment that is binding only on the parties to the proceeding

judgment *in rem*
judgment that is binding on everyone, whether a party to the proceeding in which the judgment is pronounced or not

personam arising, for example, from a negligence action is binding only on the parties; a judgment *in rem* arising, for example, from a declaration of land ownership, binds the parties, but it also binds non-parties. If you are declared the owner of Pink Acre, then you have an interest superior to the whole world, even though the whole world was not a party to the proceeding.

In the event that a plaintiff fails to include a necessary party, any person can apply to the court to be made a party, or the court can add a party on its own motion. The ground for such addition brings us back to the main principle: a party is added where his or her presence is necessary for the court to completely determine the issues in the proceeding. Similarly, under rule 5.03(6) the court may also permit someone who ought to be joined to be relieved of that obligation. Remember that being joined to a lawsuit is expensive and time-consuming. Rule 5.04(1) confronts this issue as well.

Rule 5.04 generally recognizes that the naming of parties to a lawsuit is primarily left to the plaintiff, not to the court. Plaintiffs can make errors in including people who should have been left out and in omitting people who should have been included. Rule 5.04 gives the court broad powers to correct the errors of litigants. It does not require the dismissal of a case where persons have been wrongfully included or omitted. It allows the court to determine the dispute without the presence of a person who should have been added, but without prejudice to that person's rights, which may be litigated in a subsequent proceeding. The court may also add, substitute, or drop parties, or correct the name of a party who was incorrectly named in the lawsuit, without the lawsuit having to be dismissed and restarted against the correct parties. This power is consistent with rule 2.01, which treats procedural errors as irregularities rather than nullities. However, if the failure to include a party is so prejudicial that it cannot be compensated for by costs and an adjournment, then the failure may result in a nullity notwithstanding rule 2.01. For example, if a party was omitted and the limitation period has expired, it may be prejudicial to add the party at that time.

Claim by an assignee of a chose in action

Rule 5.03(3) contains specific provisions about assignments of the right to sue. An **assignee** is a person to whom a right, usually a contractual right, has been transferred. A **chose in action** is a type of property that is intangible — that is, its value does not lie in its physical properties but in what it represents. For example, a cheque is a chose in action; its value lies not in the printed piece of paper that it physically is, but in what it represents: the promise to pay the sum written on it.

Where an **assignor** has assigned his or her right to a debt or other chose in action, the assignee acquires all the rights the assignor had, including the right to sue to collect the debt or the value of a chose in action. However, rule 5.03 requires that the assignor be added as a party. But the assignor need not be added if the assignment was absolute, so that the assignor retains no further rights in the asset *and* notice in writing of the assignment has been given to the person obliged to pay the debt or deliver up the chose in action. If, for example, the assignor assigned a chose in action as security for a loan, the assignor may redeem the security on payment of the loan. In that case, the assignor must be included as a party. Also, if the debtor or defendant was not given notice of the assignment, the assignor is still a necessary party.

assignee
person to whom rights, usually contract benefits, are granted by an assignor

chose in action
intangible personal property whose value lies in what it represents

assignor
person who grants contract rights to an assignee

Relief against joinder

We have already noted, under rule 5.04, how a court has the power to correct joinder errors without making the lawsuit a nullity. But sometimes, the correct joinder of parties results in a cumbersome proceeding that causes judges and lawyers to flee in horror. Relief from this situation is available under rule 5.05. Where a case is unduly complicated or will be delayed or prejudice a party because of joinder of multiple claims or parties, the court may take a number of procedural steps. It can order separate hearings. For example, if Abigail sued Fred, Rattle Motors Ltd., and Skank Motorcar Company Ltd. for negligence, and her employer for wrongful dismissal all in one proceeding, the court could break the matter into two separate proceedings: negligence and wrongful dismissal. It could also order claims in one proceeding to be transferred to another proceeding or allow costs to a party compelled to attend part of a proceeding in which it has no interest. It can also **stay proceedings** against one defendant while a proceeding against another defendant is completed and bind the party against whom proceedings are stayed by the findings of fact and law made in the previous proceeding. This rule may be invoked when the same issues affect both defendants, so that trying both is repetitious, and the decision in the first case is justly binding on the defendant in the stayed proceeding.

stay proceedings
stop proceedings for a given or indefinite period, pending the fulfillment of a condition, without dismissing the proceedings

CONSOLIDATION OR HEARING TOGETHER: RULE 6

Just as the court may order parties or issues to be severed from a proceeding and tried separately when convenient, so may the court order the consolidation of separate proceedings. As a means of reducing cost and delay, the court will combine separate proceedings, where possible, rather than have several related proceedings continue separately. An additional reason for consolidation is that the courts wish to avoid two or more decisions on an issue or fact that is common to both proceedings. Inconsistent decisions are to be avoided because they lead to further proceedings by way of appeal, instability, and uncertainty — all things that the common law tries to eliminate.

Under rule 6.01(1)(a) to (c), proceedings may be consolidated when:

- there is a common question of law or fact (not just common issues or questions raised by litigants);

- the relief claimed arises out of the same fact situation; or

- there is some other good reason for consolidation, leaving the court broad discretion to deal with each case on its facts within the confines of the principles stated above.

Rule 6.01 also goes on to give the court broad powers to direct how a consolidated proceeding is to be conducted justly in relation to the parties with minimal cost and delay. The two proceedings can be consolidated to be heard together as one proceeding, with the plaintiff presenting all its issues and evidence and the defendants following. However, if it is logical to have one issue or set of issues heard first because this is necessary to render a decision on a second set of issues, the court may order the cases to be consolidated but tried one after the other.

For example, if Abigail sues Fred in one proceeding and Rattle Motors Ltd. in another, it may make sense to consolidate the two into one proceeding but to try the case against Fred first. If Fred turns out not to be liable for failing to mop up the oil, there may be no case against Rattle Motors Ltd. to answer. If Rattle is allegedly liable for failing to direct Fred and Fred is not liable, neither logically is Rattle Motors Ltd. If the plaintiff's first case fails, her second case can be dismissed without further evidence being heard, saving time and money for all of the parties.

The court also has the power to stay one proceeding until the other is heard or asserted as a counterclaim by the defendant in the plaintiff's action. In practical terms, the court is free under rule 6.01(1)(d) and (e) to control its own process and customize consolidation orders to save time and money and to yield a just result. In rule 6.01(2), the court is given the power to make an order for directions that may dispense with service of a notice of listing for trial and abridge the waiting time for placing a case on the trial list. In fact, the court can order the matter to proceed immediately and fix a date for trial. Note the use of the motion for directions to break procedural log-jams and clean up procedural messes. Lawyers generally have carriage of how an action proceeds, who gets sued, and what issues are included. Each lawyer is focused on his or her client's needs, and if there are multiple issues and parties, there needs to be some objective supervision. If a case is going from a straightforward matter to chaos with multiple parties, proceedings, and issues, a party may use a motion for directions to sort out the mess. In Ottawa and Windsor, where proceedings are subject to case management under rule 77, this should be less of a problem. Case management judges and masters, assigned to a case from the beginning, have more control over how the case progresses than in non-case-managed proceedings. They have charge of the timetable, and they can see problems developing and head them off at an early stage, probably on their own initiative. In Toronto, where case management is an option under rule 78, the complex case scenario may trigger transfer to a modified or full case management.

PARTIES UNDER A DISABILITY: RULE 7

The common law has long barred parties who are not of "full age and capacity" from initiating and defending lawsuits on their own. The reasoning here is that children and mentally ill adults do not have the judgment, experience, or resources to engage in litigation on their own, just as they may not contract on their own in some cases. They are not barred from suing and being sued, however, since access to the courts is a fundamental right. Instead, they may exercise rights as litigants but must have a mentally competent adult or a public body assist them in the enterprise. The rules governing the duties and procedures to be followed by a **litigation guardian** are set out in rule 7.

litigation guardian
competent adult who directs and takes responsibility for the litigation of a legally disabled party, such as a minor, an absentee, or a mentally disabled person

Minors and mentally incapacitated persons are generally referred to in rule 7 as "persons under disability"; this term replaces the now-derogatory terms "infant," "imbecile," or "lunatic" previously used at common law and under older statutes. Persons under disability must have a litigation guardian. Such people include:

- a minor;

- a person who is mentally incapable of understanding proceedings and instructing counsel on an issue in those proceedings, whether the person has a guardian or not;[1] and

- an **absentee** under the *Absentees Act*.

The court can dispense with litigation guardians in an appropriate case. A sophisticated minor, almost 18 years of age, may be allowed to proceed without a litigation guardian if the court thinks this is appropriate. The other instance where a litigation guardian is not needed involves an application for a declaration that a person is incompetent. Where a litigant seeks to declare someone mentally incompetent so as to appoint a guardian to make decisions about the alleged incompetent's property and person under the *Substitute Decisions Act, 1992*, the alleged incompetent need not have a litigation guardian appointed under rule 7 unless the court requires it.

To make some sense of the law in this area, you need to understand that, under legislation, if a person is unable to manage his or her own assets because of mental illness or another infirmity, the law provides for a procedure to have the person declared mentally incompetent. Such a declaration means that the person could not manage day-to-day life decisions, especially concerning his or her money and assets. Note that not all mental illness is equivalent to legal mental incapacity. A person may be a schizophrenic and suffer specific delusions but be able to manage his or her own business affairs. If so, the court does not often intervene to appoint a guardian. But if the person cannot manage his or her business affairs, to prevent waste to the person's estate or harm to him or her physically, the court can order one or more people to act as the committee of the incompetent person, after making a finding of mental incompetence. This is the route that is often followed if someone suffers from Alzheimer's disease or some other form of dementia.

In addition, a person who recognizes that he or she can no longer handle his or her own affairs or who wishes to provide for that situation when it occurs, may voluntarily, without a finding of mental incompetence, make his or her own arrangements for someone to manage his or her estate. This is done by appointing a person to take on this task under a power of attorney. No court order is or was required for this. The person granted power of attorney has the power to enter into contracts and generally deal with the assets of the person who made the appointment. In addition, the law also provides for a power of attorney for personal care, in which an individual may appoint a person to make decisions about personal care, including medical decisions, when and if the person making the appointment is no longer able to do so. Again, no court order is required. It is not uncommon for an elderly person to grant a younger, trustworthy relative both a power of attorney regarding property and a power of attorney for personal care to make decisions about health care.

Rule 7.01(3) is a transition section that takes into account new legislation in the mental health area introduced between 1990 and 1995. A person who was named as the committee of a mental incompetent in the older legislation, to represent the incompetent in proceedings, continues as a litigation guardian. Where there was no individual to do this and the public trustee was appointed to act for the mental incompetent under the *Mental Health Act*, the public guardian and trustee continues to act as litigation guardian. You should note that the rules generally are littered with such transition provisions when older legislation is amended or repealed and replaced. Often only the terminology is changed, but read the relevant rule and the legislation referred to carefully because there may be substantive changes as well.

absentee
person whose rights or interests are being determined in a proceeding and whose whereabouts are unknown

Litigation guardians for plaintiffs

Rules 7.02(1) and (2) lay out a complete code governing litigation guardians for a plaintiff or applicant. Any person who is not under a disability may act as the litigation guardian of a person under a disability. No court order is required. The assumption is that a person under a disability who has a cause of action also has friends or relatives who will step in. This is almost always the case for minors. Where a person is mentally incapable, it may be more complicated, especially if the mental incapacity is connected to homelessness or substance abuse and the individual has become disconnected from friends and family. If Abigail were a minor, she would be identified in the title of proceedings as "Abigail Boar, a minor, by her litigation guardian, Henrietta Boar, Plaintiff." If she were mentally incapacitated, she would be identified in the proceedings as "Abigail Boar, a mentally incapable person, by her litigation guardian, Henrietta Boar, Plaintiff." See figure 5.1.

If Henrietta were suing for her own damages as well as acting as litigation guardian for Abigail, the title of proceedings would read "Abigail Boar, by her litigation guardian, Henrietta Boar, and Henrietta Boar personally." The same formats would be used if Abigail and Henrietta were defendants instead of plaintiffs.

Mentally incapable persons may have existing representatives act as litigation guardians without a court order unless the court orders otherwise. If a mentally incapable person has a guardian, or had a committee under older legislation, or voluntarily appointed an attorney[2] to manage his or her affairs under a power of attorney, that person may act as litigation guardian. However, in the case of a power of attorney, the power to act as a litigation guardian must have been included as one of the powers under the power of attorney appointing him or her. If the public guardian and trustee acted for an incompetent, as would be the case where there was no relative to appoint as committee or attorney under a power of attorney, and the person was sued, the public guardian and trustee would act as litigation guardian.

While no court order is required to appoint a plaintiff's litigation guardian, an individual who seeks such an appointment must file a certificate or a sworn affidavit setting out the nature of the disability. The affiant must also generally show that he or she is a proper person to act as litigation guardian and that there is no conflict of interest. The affiant must also agree to pay any costs awarded against him or her or against the plaintiff. If neither the affiant nor the plaintiff resides in Ontario, they may be asked to provide security for costs as well (rule 7.02(2)).[3]

The body of a sample affidavit to be filed with the court pursuant to rule 7.02(2) is set out in figure 5.1.

This affidavit uses the provisions of rule 7.02(2) as an outline to set out the information required. The affidavit also uses the language and vocabulary of the rule with simple modifications. Why make the job of drafting harder than it is?

Litigation guardians for defendants

Rule 7.03(1) provides a detailed code governing the appointment of litigation guardians for defendants or respondents. A defendant's litigation guardian must be an appropriate person: someone willing and able to act on behalf of the defendant. There must be no conflict of interest with the defendant, and the person cannot be under disability. As with plaintiffs, if the defendant is a minor, a parent, guardian, or other close relative, he or she will likely be approved as litigation guardian. If the

FIGURE 5.1   AFFIDAVIT FILED PURSUANT TO RULE 7.02(2) (FORM 4D)

Court file no. 01-CV-5678

ONTARIO
SUPERIOR COURT OF JUSTICE

BETWEEN:

ABIGAIL BOAR, A MENTALLY INCAPABLE PERSON,
BY HER LITIGATION GUARDIAN,
HENRIETTA BOAR

Plaintiff

and

RATTLE MOTORS LTD. and FRED FLOGEM

Defendants

AFFIDAVIT OF HENRIETTA BOAR

I, Henrietta Boar, of the City of Toronto, in the Province of Ontario, MAKE OATH AND SAY:

1. I consent to act as litigation guardian for Abigail Boar, the plaintiff in this action.
2. I have given written authority by way of a retainer signed on September 16, year 0 to I.M. Just to act as lawyer in this proceeding.
3. The plaintiff, as a result of her injuries, is unable to concentrate, understand complex concepts, or take any interest in her surroundings. She is depressed and passive. Dr. Alice Wunderkind, a psychologist who has examined the plaintiff, advises me that the plaintiff is unable to instruct her lawyer in this proceeding. Now marked exhibit A to my affidavit is a copy of the medical report of Dr. Wunderkind dated September 29, year 0, when this assessment was made.
4. Both the plaintiff and I are ordinarily resident in Ontario.
5. I am the mother of the plaintiff.
6. I have no interest in the proceeding adverse to that of the plaintiff.
7. I acknowledge that I have been informed by my lawyer that I may be liable to personally pay any costs awarded against me or against the plaintiff.

Sworn before me at the	)
City of Toronto,	)
Province of Ontario,	)
on October 16, year 0.	)

Henrietta Boar
Henrietta Boar

I.M. Just

I.M. Just
Commissioner for Taking Affidavits   )

defendant is mentally incapable, a close friend or relative is likely to be approved to act as litigation guardian. Unlike the case with plaintiffs under disability, a defendant's litigation guardian must apply to the court by motion to be approved as litigation guardian. However, a court appointment is not necessary if:

- the defendant is a minor with an interest in an estate or trust (in which case he or she is represented by the **children's lawyer**);

- the defendant is mentally incapable or an absentee and either has a guardian, attorney under a power of attorney, or a committee, all with authority to act as litigation guardian; or

- the defendant is mentally disabled, in which case he or she is represented by the public guardian and trustee.

children's lawyer
official of the Ontario Ministry of the Attorney General whose office oversees the rights of some minors involved in civil litigation and custody disputes

A person who is to act as a litigation guardian for a mentally incapable defendant, must file a certificate or affidavit under rule 7.03(10) signifying ability and willingness to act. If the litigation guardian is the public guardian and trustee or the children's lawyer, the affidavit is abbreviated and omits material dealing with potential conflict of interest between the guardian and the disabled party.

A person who seeks to act as a litigation guardian must file a notice of motion asking to be appointed before acting for the disabled defendant, and must support the motion with the affidavit or certificate referred to in rule 7.03(10). If a litigation guardian is already acting for a plaintiff, he or she may defend a counterclaim without bringing a motion (rule 7.03(3)).

A sample affidavit to be filed pursuant to rule 7.03(10) is set out in figure 5.2.

If no one moves to become litigation guardian for a defendant, the plaintiff may move for the appointment of a litigation guardian for the defendant. The moving party must also serve a request to appoint a litigation guardian on the defendant, personally or by an alternative to personal service. This notice may be served with the originating documents, but must be served at least ten days before the **return date** of the motion. The motion may be made without notice to a defendant, but it is necessary to move to dispense with notice in the notice of motion to appoint a litigation guardian. This may be done as part of the motion to appoint by asking for leave to proceed without serving the disabled defendant and, if leave is granted, for an order appointing a litigation guardian. This eliminates the need for bringing a motion to dispense with service separately. If the goal is to appoint the children's lawyer or the public guardian and trustee as the defendant's litigation guardian, those bodies must be served with the motion (rule 7.03(4) to (9)).

return date
the date on which the motion will be heard by the court

Figure 5.3 sets out form 7A, the notice to appoint a litigation guardian for a defendant. With modifications, it can be used to appoint a litigation guardian for the plaintiff.

Representation of a party under disability when no one volunteers to be litigation guardian

Being a litigation guardian is not considered one of life's joys. There are disabled plaintiffs and defendants with no relatives, no friends, and no one to step in and help. Where no one comes forward for the plaintiff or defendant, and where a

FIGURE 5.2   AFFIDAVIT FILED PURSUANT TO RULE 7.03(10) (FORM 4D)

Court file no. 01-CV-7890

ONTARIO
SUPERIOR COURT OF JUSTICE

BETWEEN:

HENRY SMOKE

Plaintiff

and

ABIGAIL BOAR

Defendant

AFFIDAVIT OF HENRIETTA BOAR

I, Henrietta Boar, of the City of Toronto, in the Province of Ontario, MAKE OATH AND SAY:

1. This is an action for breach of contract brought against the defendant.

2. The cause of action arose on or about April 10, year 0, and the action was commenced on July 19, year 0.

3. The defendant was served with a statement of claim and a notice requesting appointment of a litigation guardian on July 24, year 0.

4. The defendant suffers from Alzheimer's disease. As a result, she often behaves impulsively, suffers from delusions, and is unable to understand the issues in this lawsuit or give instructions to counsel.

5. The defendant ordinarily resides in Ontario.

6. I, the proposed litigation guardian, am the daughter of the defendant.

7. I am ordinarily resident in Ontario.

8. I consent to act as litigation guardian in this proceeding. I am a proper person to be appointed as litigation guardian. I have no interest in the proceeding that is adverse to that of the defendant. I understand that I may incur costs that may not be recovered from the other party.

Sworn before me at the	)
City of Toronto,	)
Province of Ontario,	)
on November 24, year 0.	)

Henrietta Boar
Henrietta Boar

I.M. Just

I.M. Just
Commissioner for Taking Affidavits)

FIGURE 5.3   REQUEST FOR APPOINTMENT OF LITIGATION GUARDIAN (FORM 7A)

Court file no. 01-CV-1011

ONTARIO
SUPERIOR COURT OF JUSTICE

BETWEEN:

ABIGAIL BOAR

Plaintiff

and

MAXIM FURTWANGLER

Defendant

THE PLAINTIFF BELIEVES THAT YOU ARE UNDER A LEGAL DISABILITY. As a party under disability, you must have a litigation guardian appointed by the court to act on your behalf in defending this proceeding.

YOU ARE REQUIRED to have some proper person make a motion to this court forthwith to be appointed as your litigation guardian.

IF YOU FAIL TO DO SO WITHIN TEN DAYS after service of this request, the plaintiff may move without further notice to have the court appoint a litigation guardian to act on your behalf.

Date: July 14, year 0

Just & Coping
Barristers and Solicitors
365 Bay Street - 8701
Toronto, Ontario, M3J 4A9

I.M. Just
LSUC #12345R
tel. 416-762-1342
fax 416-762-2300

Lawyers for the Plaintiff

TO: Maxim Furtwangler
123 DeCory Street
Toronto, Ontario, M4R 1Z6

plaintiff moves to have someone appointed as a litigation guardian for a defendant where there is no likely person available, the court may appoint:

- the children's lawyer to represent a minor, or

- the public guardian and trustee to represent a person who is mentally incapable and has no guardian or attorney under a power of attorney.

If the disabled party is both a minor and mentally incapable, the court may appoint either the public guardian and trustee or the children's lawyer (rule 7.04(1)). Where a disabled person is not a party and the court deems that he or she should be, then the party must be added. The children's lawyer or the public guardian and trustee, as the case may be, is appointed as litigation guardian.

The children's lawyer and the public guardian and trustee are government officials. Their departments operate with high case loads and with limited resources. This is particularly true for the public guardian and trustee, where staff have large workloads. In dealing with people's property, they also often have contentious and adverse relationships with the relatives of mentally disabled persons.

Powers of the litigation guardian

Once appointed, a litigation guardian may make any decision and take any step a litigant of full capacity can make. This includes retaining and dismissing counsel and being advised by and instructing counsel. A litigation guardian may take further proceedings, such as counterclaims, crossclaims, and third party claims. A litigation guardian, other than the children's lawyer and the public guardian and trustee cannot act on his or her own. He or she must retain a lawyer to represent the disabled party in court (rule 7.05).

Removing a litigation guardian

Being a family member or friend of a person under disability does not necessarily make a person capable as a litigation guardian. There are provisions to remove a litigation guardian where the court thinks it is appropriate or it is otherwise required. If a minor reaches the age of majority, the litigation guardian may file an affidavit setting out that fact, and the registrar will grant an order authorizing the action to continue without the litigation guardian. The order will be served on all other parties.

An order in form 7B to continue a proceeding where a party has reached the age of majority is set out in figure 5.4. It can be modified for a party whose incapacity has ended.

Note that this is one of the few instances where the title of proceedings changes after litigation commences. Similarly, if a person is under disability for other reasons — mental incapacity, for example — and the incapacity ends, the litigation guardian or the party may move to continue the proceeding without the litigation guardian. This order is served on all other parties

If the court is of the opinion that the litigation guardian is not acting in the best interest of the party under disability, the court may remove the litigation guardian and substitute the children's lawyer, the public guardian and trustee, or any other person (rule 7.06).

FIGURE 5.4   ORDER TO CONTINUE (FORM 7B)

Court file no. 01-CV-1415

ONTARIO
SUPERIOR COURT OF JUSTICE

BETWEEN:

EMILY BOAR, A MINOR, BY HER
LITIGATION GUARDIAN, ABIGAIL BOAR

Plaintiff

and

J.S. BACH LTD.

Defendant

ORDER TO CONTINUE

On the requisition of the plaintiff, Abigail Boar, and on reading the affidavit of Abigail Boar, filed, which states that the minor, Emily Boar, has reached the age of majority on August 14, year 0,

IT IS ORDERED that this proceeding continue by Emily Boar, without a litigation guardian and that the title of the proceeding be amended accordingly in all documents issued, served, or filed after the date of this order.

Date: August 17, year 0

Signed by: _____

Address of
court office: Court House
393 University Avenue
Toronto, Ontario, M5G 1E6

Protection against default judgment

When a defendant fails to defend an action, the plaintiff can note the defendant in default and move without notice for default judgment. If the claim is for a liquidated amount that is easily calculated by objective standards — such as a debt and interest on it — the clerk may sign immediate judgment. Because a litigation guardian may inadequately represent a disabled party or there may be difficulty in finding a litigation guardian or getting him or her to respond, it is easy for a plaintiff to move quickly for a default judgment. However, if a plaintiff moves for default judgment and the responding party is under disability, the defendant may not be noted in default without leave of a judge of the court. If the plaintiff knows of the disability, he or she is obliged to serve a motion to note (the defendant) in default, on the litigation guardian of a person under disability, and on the children's lawyer if the defendant is a minor, unless the public guardian and trustee is the litigation guardian (rule 7.07).

Often, however, a defendant, who is a minor or mentally incapable may not appreciate or understand the need to file a defence and by doing nothing, defaults. The plaintiff may be unaware that the defendant is under disability until he or she attempts to enforce the judgment. At that point, a family member or friend of the defendant may become involved, leading to the appointment of a litigation guardian who has a right to move to set the default judgment aside on the ground of the incapacity of the defendant, with leave to defend.

Approval of settlements for parties under disability

Neither a party under a disability nor a litigation guardian has the power to settle a proceeding on behalf of a disabled party or make a settlement before proceedings are commenced without the approval of the court. This reflects a long-standing common law rule that the courts need to oversee and supervise settlements made by parties under disability to ensure that they are not taken advantage of. An unapproved settlement is not binding on the disabled party, who may have up to six years after the disability ends to sue again. For example, a minor who is injured at age 4 by the defendant's negligence can, after turning 18, sue the defendant and may have as long as six years from the time he or she turns 18 to do so before the limitation period expires.

Rule 7.08 sets out a procedural code for obtaining approval of a settlement for a disabled party. If a claim is settled before proceedings are commenced, the parties must, by application to a judge, ask for approval of the settlement by the court. If proceedings have been commenced, approval of the court must be obtained on a motion within the proceedings. The application or motion for approval must be accompanied by an affidavit of the litigation guardian, setting out the facts, the reasons for settling, and the opinion of the litigation guardian as to the proposed settlement. The lawyer acting for the litigation guardian must, by affidavit, set out his or her position on the proposed settlement. This requirement is intended as a safeguard against an improvident agreement by a litigation guardian who ignores a lawyer's advice. It puts the court on notice to examine the matter further. If the litigation guardian is acting on a lawyer's advice, the lawyer's affidavit will usually mirror the litigation guardian's.

If the person under disability is a minor over the age of 16, the consent of the minor should be filed unless the court orders otherwise.

If a judge has any qualms or questions about the propriety of the settlement, he or she may direct the material to be served by the moving party on the public guardian and trustee or on the children's lawyer, depending on the circumstances. The official served must report back to the court orally on the return date of the motion or in writing with recommendations. Reasons for recommendations in connection with the proposed settlement must also be provided.[4]

PARTNERSHIPS AND SOLE PROPRIETORSHIPS: RULE 8

There are special rules for suing sole proprietorships and partnerships. These two forms of business organizations share an important legal characteristic. The individuals who own the businesses are personally liable for the business debts, and the liabilities generally of the business. The business, regardless of its name, is not a separate entity from the individuals who own it. By contrast, the liability of shareholders as the owners of a corporation for the corporation's acts is limited; the corporation is a legal person separate from its owners, so that only the corporation is liable for its actions.[5]

Suing partnerships

If your law firm is going to sue a partnership, the suit is usually brought in the partnership's name, which you verify by a business name search. If so, the judgment may be enforced only against the partnership's assets. If Rattle Motors Ltd. were a partnership, you could seize its property — for example, its land and showroom, office furniture and equipment, bank account, income from sales, automobiles, and other inventory. But you could not seize the personal assets of partner A, B, or C. If partner A had a house, bank account, and car, none of which was used in the partnership business, this property could not be seized to enforce the judgment against the partnership (rule 8.06(1)).

However, a plaintiff may be interested in seizing partnership assets *and* personal assets of the partners to enforce and satisfy a judgment. After all, partners are liable at common law for the debts and liabilities of the partnership, and the rules of procedure do not change the substantive law. Rule 8 makes provision for a plaintiff to claim against partnership assets and a partner's personal assets. If your law firm wishes to enforce a judgment against an individual partner, when it serves originating process against a partnership on the partner, it must also serve on the partner a notice to an alleged partner, in form 8A, stating that the individual partner was a partner at the time stated in the notice (usually when the cause of action arose). The person is then deemed to be a partner unless he or she files a statement of defence in his or her own name, denying that he or she was a partner at the relevant time. An example of a notice to an alleged partner is set out in figure 5.5.

When suing partnerships, how the parties are named in the title of proceedings depends on whether you wish to enforce a judgment against partnership assets alone, or against partnership assets and the assets of individual partners. It also depends on whether you use the procedure in rule 8 or not, when claiming against individual partners.

- Assuming for the moment that Rattle Motors is a partnership, if you are claiming against the partnership and intend to enforce a judgment only against the partnership, name the parties as follows: ABIGAIL BOAR, Plaintiff v. RATTLE MOTORS.

- Under rule 8, if you are claiming against the partnership and the partners and intend to enforce a judgment against the assets of the partnership and the personal assets of the individual partners, name the parties in the same way as in the preceding example, but remember to serve a notice in Form

FIGURE 5.5   NOTICE TO ALLEGED PARTNER (FORM 8A)

Court file no. 01-CV-1516

ONTARIO
SUPERIOR COURT OF JUSTICE

BETWEEN:

ABIGAIL BOAR

Plaintiff

and

RATTLE MOTORS

Defendant

NOTICE TO ALLEGED PARTNER

YOU ARE ALLEGED TO HAVE BEEN A PARTNER on Sept. 14, year 0 in the partnership of Rattle Motors, named as a party to this proceeding.

IF YOU WISH TO DENY THAT YOU WERE A PARTNER at any material time, you must defend this proceeding separately from the partnership, denying that you were a partner at the material time. If you fail to do so, you will be deemed to have been a partner on the date set out above.

AN ORDER AGAINST THE PARTNERSHIP MAY BE ENFORCED AGAINST YOU PERSONALLY if you are deemed to have been a partner, if you admit that you were a partner or if the court finds that you were a partner, at the material time.

Date: October 4, year 0

```
                              I.M. Just
                              LSUC #12345R
                              Just & Coping
                              Barristers and Solicitors
                              365 Bay Street - 8701
                              Toronto, Ontario, M3J 4A9
                              tel. 416-762-1342
                              fax 416-762-2300


                              Lawyers for the Plaintiff
```

TO: Adolphus Ambrose
     123 Elm Street
     Scarborough, Ontario, M8Y 2Z8

8A on the individual partners you seek to enforce against at the same time you serve originating process on them.

- If you wish to claim against the individual partners only, simply sue the individuals: ABIGAIL BOAR v. SAM SLIPP and BOB CHATERJEE.

- If you are not using rule 8, but wish to claim against both the partnership and the individual partners, then name each party you seek to enforce the judgment against: ABIGAIL BOAR v. SAM SLIPP and BOB CHATTERJEE carrying on business as RATTLE MOTORS. Usually, however, you will sue in the business name and use rule 8 to expand enforcement rights against the individual partner's assets.

If you seek to fix personal liability on partners by giving them notice under form 8A, you need to know who they are. Think about a large law firm. Of the 200 lawyers, perhaps 150 may be partners. Further, as lawyers pursue career opportunities, several lawyers may become partners and several may leave the partnership in a given year. The firm name may not be any help. Most large firms use the names of just one or two partners, and other types of businesses may use commercial names that do not include the names of any partners. If you wish to know who the partners were five or six years ago, the business records of the Companies Branch will not be helpful because they contain mostly current records. Rule 8.05 provides the answer to a plaintiff's problem. Where there is a proceeding brought by or against a partnership, rule 8.05 entitles any party to serve a notice on the partnership requiring the partnership to set out the names and addresses of partners for the time period or date specified in the notice. In this way, a party can find out who the partners are, and then serve partners individually with the notice in form A, provided that this is done within 15 days of receiving the information. If the partnership wants to stall and prevent liability from resting on the individual partners by not providing the information, the rule provides a solution: The action will be stayed if the partnership is a plaintiff, and the defence will be struck out if it is a defendant.

Suppose a claim against a partnership gives rise to crossclaims between partners, where one partner, for example, claims that the other promised to indemnify him or her from suits by the plaintiff, or claims that he or she was not a partner when the plaintiff's cause of action arose. If one partner's defence is different from or adverse to the positions of other partners or the partnership, that partner may apply to the court on motion for leave under rule 8.02 to file a separate defence. If the partner denies being a partner at the relevant time, he or she may file a separate defence pursuant to rule 8.03(2) and rule 8.04(a).

Once the plaintiff has a judgment in a proceeding against a partnership, he or she may enforce it against partnership assets. If a partner was named individually, the plaintiff may also enforce against that person's personal property, provided that the procedure for giving the individual partner notice under rule 8.03 was followed. Rule 8.06(3) provides further relief for a plaintiff who failed to name an individual under rule 8.03. Here, if the plaintiff obtains judgment against the partnership and then seeks to enforce it against a defendant not previously named, the plaintiff must apply to a judge on a motion for leave to enforce against a named individual. The order is granted if the individual admits or is found to be a partner at the relevant time.

Sole proprietorships

Sole proprietorships are treated in the same way as partnerships, as if the sole proprietor were a partner. Rule 8.07(1) indicates that you can sue a person carrying on a sole proprietorship in the business name, and that is the approach usually taken. Rule 8.07(2) then tells you that the rules for giving notice to individual partners and demanding the identity of partners at the relevant time apply to sole proprietorships. This will allow you to pursue the individual's personal assets as well as their business assets, as was the case for partnerships. However, the details for dealing with sole proprietors are not spelled out, so you have to use rules 8.01(1) to (6) as models and guidelines for procedures; similarly, you have to adapt and modify the forms used for partnerships for use in dealing with a sole proprietorship. So, if you wish to expand enforcement rights by giving notice to the individual sole proprietor that he or she was the sole proprietor at the relevant time, you have to edit the partnership version of the form. And the sole proprietor could answer by claiming not to have been the sole proprietor at the relevant time. Similarly, you can demand that a sole proprietorship reveal who the sole proprietor was at the relevant time, and the sole proprietor must respond in the same way that a partner would. While this might sound strange, if the plaintiff is dealing with a business entity that uses a business or trade name, the plaintiff might be uncertain as to who the actual sole proprietor is, especially if the cause of action arose in the past, and the business was sold to someone else as an ongoing business operation, including its business name. At the time the lawsuit begins, the new owner may have no personal liability, and finding the "old" owner may be required in order to expand liability to include enforcement of a judgment against the "old" owner's assets.

Suing corporations

A corporation is required by law to include in its name some indication that it is a corporation with limited liability. It does this by having the words "Limited," "Incorporated," "Ltd." or "Inc."[6] following its name or as part of its name. However, your client may have dealt with what he or she thought was a business called "Prissy's Plants." You will need to search that name, which will tell you whether you are dealing with a sole proprietorship, partnership, or corporation, and who its principals are. If the defendant turns out to be a corporation, the plaintiff *cannot* sue in the business name. He or she must sue in the proper corporate name as revealed in your search.

ESTATES AND TRUSTS AS PARTIES: RULE 9

We now turn to some rules governing the naming, joining, and severing of parties and issues in litigation involving trusts and estates. A trust is a means of holding property where the legal owner is acting for the benefit, not of himself or herself, but for the benefit of beneficiaries of the trust, who are also the beneficial owners of the trust assets. If a grandmother wants to give a minor grandchild the benefit of a large capital fund, she may, as the grantor, set up a trust, where the person she names as trustee is the legal owner and controls the assets for the benefit of the minor, who cannot directly get at the capital and waste the assets. An estate is

executor

person appointed by a will maker to administer an estate under the provisions of the will; a female executor is sometimes called an executrix

estate administrator

person appointed by a court to administer an estate where there is no will or where the appointment of an executor is ineffective

personal representative

under the *Estates Administration Act*, this term refers to the person charged with administering an estate, whether the person is an executor appointed by the deceased, or an administrator appointed by the court

similarly structured, though the grantor who creates the trust through a will is deceased. The **executor** or **estate administrator** acts in the interest of the estate beneficiaries. The same is true for trusts, where the trustee acts for the benefit of beneficiaries. Note that while rule 9 still uses the general terms "executor" and "administrator" with reference to estates, recent amendments to the *Estates Administration Act* have resulted in some changes in terminology. An executor or estate administrator is now referred to as a **personal representative** of the estate. However, as of the date of writing, this terminology has not made it into rule 9.

Rule 9 sets out procedural rules for naming parties. The general rule is that an estate or trust may sue or be sued by naming the administrator, executor, or trustee as the estate representative, without naming the beneficiaries specifically because they are deemed to be included. There are some exceptions where beneficiaries must be named:

- a suit to contest the validity of a will;

- a suit brought to interpret a will;

- a suit to remove the personal administrator of an estate;

- a suit alleging fraud against a personal representative of an estate, or a trustee; and

- a suit to force the administration of an estate or the carrying out of the terms of a trust where the trustee, executor, or administrator has failed to or refused to act (rule 9.01(1), (2)).

Where there is more than one executor, administrator, or trustee, what happens if one does not agree to join the others as plaintiff? Because they may have some liabilities and an interest in the outcome, they are joined as respondents or defendants even though no claim is made against them. This is done so that they will be in the lawsuit and bound by the judgment. In addition, the court may order any creditor or beneficiary to be added as a separate party (rule 9.01(3), (4)).

If an estate has no personal representative, your law firm will sue the estate in its own name and apply to the court for the appointment of a litigation administrator (rule 9.02). The proceeding can then continue, and any order will be binding on the estate and its beneficiaries. A litigation administrator can be an estate creditor with an interest in defending the plaintiff's lawsuit, a relative or business partner of the deceased, or a trust company that will accept the appointment. Estate departments of trust companies routinely administer estates under wills and charge a fee for doing so. The appointment of a litigation administrator will depend on the facts and circumstances of the case and whether there are estate assets that make the effort worthwhile.

Rule 9.03 is a child of rule 2.01 in that it prevents accidental slips, omissions, and errors from derailing a lawsuit by making it a nullity. An error is treated as an irregularity that can be cured by the court, subject to costs or an adjournment to compensate the other side from being unduly disadvantaged.

If a personal representative commences proceedings on behalf of an estate before the grant of probate has confirmed the appointment, the proceeding is deemed to be properly constituted, provided that the administrative grant is approved. The title of proceedings for an action commenced by or against an estate by naming the estate as a party — for example, the Estate of Abigail Boar — results in an irregularity, and the court may simply order that the action continue against the personal representative of the estate, with the title of proceedings being amended accordingly. If your law firm sues a deceased person in his or her own name, or if a party it has sued dies before it starts the suit, the court can order that the title of proceedings be amended so that the personal representative of the estate is the named party. If the court appoints a litigation administrator and then finds there was a personal representative already appointed under a will or otherwise, the action continues against the previously appointed personal representative.

In the event that an action is not properly constituted, as noted in the situations above, the court may order that the case be properly constituted and continue, but the proceeding is stayed until the errors are corrected. If the corrections are not made — for example, by applying for a litigation administrator — the proceeding can be dismissed. The court may also order that a personal representative of an estate be relieved of personal liability if he or she paid money out of an estate to beneficiaries before becoming aware of a proceeding against the estate, provided that he or she acted in good faith (rule 9.03).

UNIDENTIFIED AND UNASCERTAINED PARTIES AND REPRESENTATION ORDERS: RULE 10

In cases like Abigail's, there is no difficulty in determining who the parties are or might be. Abigail's claim against Barbeerian's or Skank Motorcar Company Ltd. may be more speculative and uncertain than the one against Fred Flogem and Rattle Motors Ltd. However, you can identify these entities as parties, and define and describe the claim against them, including the damages for which they may be responsible.

But consider, for example, an estate where the beneficiaries include grandchildren and great grandchildren of specific persons named in a will. If someone challenges the validity of the will, rule 9(2)(a) requires that the beneficiaries be made parties to the proceeding. The persons named in the will can easily be added, but what about the class of grandchildren? It is possible that we may not know at the time who all of the individuals in the class are. Some of these persons are not yet born or may never be born but may have an interest. Rule 10 provides a procedure for representing those who have an interest in the outcome of a proceeding where either the interest or the person cannot be ascertained at the time of the suit, or the person cannot otherwise be represented.

The provisions of the rule apply to certain types of proceedings:

- the interpretation of documents, such as contracts and wills, that create rights and interests, and proceedings that interpret the provisions of a statute, regulation, or other Act of a government body that affect rights and interests;

- the interpretation of a question or issue that has arisen in the administration of an estate or trust;

- the approval of a sale, purchase, settlement, or other transaction involving interests that cannot be ascertained or where the members of a class of persons are not known;

- the variation of the terms of a trust because the provisions did not take into account some state of affairs that prevents the trust's objects from being carried out (for example, if the trust authorizes payments to a class of beneficiaries to "advance their station in life," does this authorize flying lessons for one of the beneficiaries?);

- the administration of an estate where a question about its administration arises; and

- any other matter where it appears necessary to make a representation order.

Rule 10.01(1) gives the court considerable leeway in deciding when to make such an order. Generally, when there appears to be a present, future, or even a contingent interest (an interest contingent on the fulfillment of a condition precedent) of persons who are unborn or not yet ascertained, a representation order can be made. An order may also be made if a person is a member of a class whose interests may be affected even if the identity of the individual is not yet known. Where a large number of people are affected by the interpretation of a government regulation or a provision of a pension fund, for example, you may not know whether the class member is still alive or whether he or she still qualifies as having an interest. You may know who the persons in the class are but may not be able to find them or serve them all. In these cases, the procedural shortcut is to have one person represent the interests of all. Rule 10 governs situations similar to class proceedings, which are covered by rule 12, but rule 10 is a broader provision.

Once a representation order is made, the person named in it becomes a party, representing the class of persons identified in the order — the unborn grandchildren of Fred Flogem, for example. The person or class of persons named in the order as being represented is bound by any judgment or order made in the proceeding. This means that one of Fred's grandchildren cannot come forward and say that he or she was not consulted, had no notice, and is therefore not bound. If a settlement offer is made to, and accepted by, the representative of the class, the members of the class are bound by the settlement. An individual class member may escape from the settlement in some circumstances, although the test for doing so is a difficult one to meet (see rule 10.01(3)).

If an estate of a deceased person has an interest in an issue in a case and there is no executor or administrator, the judge may order the proceeding to continue in the absence of an estate representative. The judge may also name a representative for the purpose of the proceeding, in which case the estate of the deceased person is bound by the outcome (rule 10.02).

Although a judge may make a representation order in an appropriate case, the judge in the case or in a subsequent case can order the person or estate not to be bound provided that

- the order was obtained by fraud,

- the interests of the person appointed and the estate or person represented were in conflict, or

- there is a good reason to set the representation order aside (rule 10.03).

Because a court's discretion under rule 10 is broad, we need to look at case law. The purpose of rule 10 is to encourage a quick means of resolving contentious proceedings without having to resort to the more cumbersome class proceeding procedure covered by rule 12. The test that should be applied by the court in considering whether or not to make a representation order is not whether the members of the group can be found or ascertained, but whether it is more convenient to issue a representation order than to insist that each member of the class be served and allowed to participate. The court must also check to see that there is no conflict between the members of the class and the representative (rule 10.03).[7] In fact, the representative of the class should have all of the crucial characteristics of the class members. In a pension case, for example, the representative of the class of retirees must have the same characteristics as the retirees in the class who are affected by the issue in question: The representative must be a retiree, from the same occupation, with a right to the same types of benefits.

TRANSFER OR TRANSMISSION OF INTEREST: RULE 11

Rule 11 gives you directions about what to do if the legal status of a party changes in the course of an ongoing proceeding. For example, if Abigail Boar starts an action as a plaintiff in her own name and then dies, her legal status changes. The lawsuit must be continued in the name of her estate's personal representative. Another example occurs where the rights being litigated are transferred by assignment from one person to another. For example, a person becoming bankrupt transfers his or her property to a trustee in bankruptcy for the general benefit of creditors. Whatever the reason, rule 11.01 requires a proceeding to be stayed until the court makes an order to continue the proceeding by or against the "new" litigant — for example, the estate's personal representative or the trustee in bankruptcy. The new litigant is not usually personally liable: The estate is the focus of the judgment, not the estate's personal representative who is the "new" party.

The order is obtained on requisition from the registrar, on the filing of an affidavit by any party setting out the fact that the interest or liability of a party has been transferred. A formal motion is not necessary because the matter is usually a procedural formality. If, however, the transmission is contested, the requisition may be challenged by bringing a motion to set aside the order to continue. An example of the registrar's order to continue, form 11A, is set out in figure 5.6.

CLASS PROCEEDINGS: RULE 12

While rule 11 gives the court general powers to make one person the representative of a class in ordinary litigation, it is also available for the less complex representative or class proceeding. Rule 12 contains specific procedures that apply to actions certified as class proceedings under the *Class Proceedings Act, 1992*. The Act and rule 12 are designed to deal with proceedings more complex than those to which rule 11 applies. It is necessary to know something about the Act before we examine rule 12. What follows is an overview of the highlights that make a class proceeding or class

FIGURE 5.6 ORDER TO CONTINUE (FORM 11A)

Court file no. 01-CV-1234

ONTARIO
SUPERIOR COURT OF JUSTICE

BETWEEN:

ABIGAIL BOAR

Plaintiff

and

RATTLE MOTORS LTD. and FRED FLOGEM

Defendants

ORDER TO CONTINUE

On the requisition of Henrietta Boar and on reading the affidavit of Henrietta Boar, filed, which indicates that on July 24, year 1 Abigail Boar, the plaintiff in this action, died, and her right of action was transferred to her estate, of which Henrietta Boar is the representative, as the executrix of the estate of Abigail Boar,

IT IS ORDERED that this proceeding continue and that the title of the proceeding in all documents issued, served, or filed after the date of this order be as follows:

Henrietta Boar, Estate Trustee, With a Will of the Estate of Abigail Boar

Date: February 6, year 3

Signed by: _____

Address of
court office: Court House
393 University Avenue
Toronto, Ontario, M5G 1E6

A party who wishes to set aside or vary this order must make a motion to do so forthwith after the order comes to the party's attention.
Where a transmission of interest occurs by reason of bankruptcy, leave of the bankruptcy court may be required under section 69 of the *Bankruptcy Act* (Canada) before the proceeding may continue.

action different from other types of civil proceedings. If you are involved in a class pro-ceeding, there are other resources you should use that provide detailed procedural guides.[8]

Overview of the Class Proceedings Act

Suppose Abigail Boar bought a Super Coupe in its first model year, along with several thousand others. Within the first year the car was on the market, there were fre-quent reports of sudden engine failure. In about 30 percent of the cases, the engine failure also led to car fires, which caused serious injuries. Approximately 10 percent of the engine failures involved serious accidents, with injuries, but no car fires. In Abigail's case, let us suppose that the engine failed, but Abigail was able to steer her car off the road, so that she was uninjured. When she consulted I.M. Just, she dis-covered that there have been a number of incidents involving the Super Coupe.

The purpose of the *Class Proceedings Act, 1992* is to allow numerous potential plaintiffs or defendants to have their claims considered as members of a class rep-resented by one plaintiff or defendant. This allows justice to be done by allowing many small claims to be considered. Otherwise, no claim might ever have been made because of the expense. The Act also eliminates the possibility of the courts having to deal with a torrent of separate lawsuits.

I.M. Just, or the lawyer of any claimant, can apply to certify a proceeding as a class proceeding, in which case Abigail and all others with claims against the defend-ant, Skank Motorcar Company Ltd., may be separated into classes and subclasses. Here all would be included in the class claiming for product failure, but there would also be subclasses for those who were injured in car fires and for those who were otherwise injured. Because Abigail suffered only from product failure, she is a member of the main class but not the subclasses. The purpose of this arrangement is to require class members to incur expense only on issues that affect them. Each class or subclass would have a representative plaintiff. The representative must have all the relevant attributes or qualities of the class on the issues that concern the class. Often the court will have to sort out competing class action claims by a vari-ety of plaintiffs.

The lawyers for the plaintiff whose action is certified by the court face prob-lems and opportunities. The firm will require staff and resources to administer the proceeding, identify the members of the class, and process their claims. At the same time, if the suit is successful, the fees, which are payable on a contingency basis, will be lucrative for the firm.[9]

Under the *Class Proceedings Act, 1992*, a potential plaintiff cannot be involun-tarily joined to another plaintiff's proceeding and can opt out of a class proceeding (s. 9). If Abigail wants to go it alone, she may apply to the court to do so.

Once a proceeding is certified, potential plaintiffs need to know about it so that they can contact the lawyer for the class representative and have their claims in-cluded. To facilitate the process, the court requires that a public notice be prepared, approved by the courts, and published as a legal notice, or sent by mail or by any other means (ss. 17 to 22). In Abigail's case, the court may require the defendant to furnish a list of all purchasers, in which case Abigail may receive a registered letter or a couriered letter giving her notice of the proceeding.

Individual legal or factual issues involving a class or subclass may be tried separately. Thus, one class proceeding may give rise to several subproceedings (see s. 27). Abigail, for example, may be included in the class that suffered property damage but not in the classes that sustained personal injuries.

If the representative party agrees to settlement, the court must approve the settlement because it affects other class members (s. 29). Abigail will receive notice of the settlement and be entitled to voice objections as a class member.

Because running a representative proceeding is speculative and expensive, s. 33 of the Act permits lawyers for a class to be paid their costs on a contingency-fee basis. And of course, this is now generally permitted in civil proceedings.

class proceeding fund
public fund of the Law Foundation of Ontario, administered by the Law Society of Upper Canada, to provide funding for the costs of class actions which otherwise might be beyond the financial reach of the parties

Because the costs incurred before trial by a law firm are high, the Act permits the law firm for a class representative to apply for funding for disbursements at various points in the class proceeding from the **class proceeding fund**. This fund, which is administered by the Law Society of Upper Canada, was set up to provide funding for class proceedings, especially where there are many individual class members with small claims.

If the plaintiff receives assistance from the class proceedings fund, a successful defendant in the proceeding is entitled to claim payment of costs awarded by the court from the fund.

Application of rule 12 to class proceedings

Rule 12 deals with certain procedural requirements of class proceedings. After the names of the parties and as part of the title of proceedings, there must appear the words "Proceeding under the *Class Proceedings Act, 1992*." These words must be included in all court documents, commencing with the notice of motion to certify the proceeding as a class proceeding (rule 12.02). An example is set out in figure 5.7.

A class member as well as the class representative may be examined for discovery. Only parties are usually subject to examination for discovery. Admissions in the class member's discovery transcript can be read into the record at trial (rule 12.03(1)). Parts of rule 31, setting out the basis for examining non-parties, do not apply because that matter is covered in rule 12. Similarly, the sanctions under rule 34 for a class member who does not cooperate in the discovery process do not apply because they include dismissal of the proceeding. If Abigail were summoned as a class member and refused to cooperate in the discovery process, the proceeding should not be dismissed against the class representative, who is the actual party, because of Abigail's misconduct.

If the plaintiff has received financial support from the class proceedings fund, the Law Foundation of Ontario is entitled to notice of any motion or request for an order for costs or an assessment of costs after costs have been awarded. The fund's representative is entitled to make submissions, cross-examine witnesses, and present evidence on the issue of costs, including appeals on the issue of costs (rule 12.04). This makes sense because the fund may well be paying the costs that are being disputed.

Judgments and orders made in a class proceeding, including an order approving a settlement, must contain provisions

- detailing how the award will be distributed to class members and how the costs of making the distribution will be paid,

FIGURE 5.7   GENERAL HEADING UNDER THE CLASS PROCEEDINGS ACT, 1992

Court file no. 00-00-0000

ONTARIO
SUPERIOR COURT OF JUSTICE

BETWEEN:

ABIGAIL BOAR

Plaintiff

and

SKANK MOTORCAR COMPANY LTD.

Defendants

Proceeding under the Class Proceedings Act, 1992

- outlining the payments owing on a contingency agreement between the lawyer and a representative party,

- detailing the payment of costs of the proceeding, and

- detailing payments of any levy to the fund (rule 12.05).

Defendants with the same interest may defend a proceeding on behalf of or for the benefit of all defendants and may be authorized as a class in a class proceeding for that purpose (rule 12.07).

Where there are many members of an **unincorporated association** or a trade union and it would be unduly expensive and complicated to apply to certify a class proceeding, one or more of the members may be authorized to commence a proceeding on behalf of and for the benefit of all (rule 12.08). Note that this rule is restricted to unincorporated associations and trade unions, so that a mass of individuals with a common interest is not able to use this rule. Rule 12.08 is also only available to plaintiffs. A plaintiff suing a voluntary association or trade union would have to name all the members of the association as defendants or commence a class proceeding.

unincorporated association
association of persons formed to carry out a specific purpose and not formally incorporated

REPRESENTATION BY A LAWYER: RULE 15

As a general rule, an individual is entitled to represent himself or herself in every court in Canada, including the Supreme Court of Canada. This does not mean it is a good idea. There is a saying among lawyers that "a lawyer who represents himself has a fool for a client." As you already can see, knowledge of and experience with both substantive law and procedure is necessary to conduct a case, as is detachment and objectivity. Advocacy skills are also necessary. Most non-lawyers lack these skills and experiences. If you are dealing with a party who is acting in person, be prepared for the proceeding to go more slowly and for there to be numerous irregularities as parties stumble through the pretrial stages. Abigail could represent herself, and might do so if she cannot afford to hire a lawyer. Legal aid is very difficult to obtain in civil proceedings.

There are some parties that *must* be represented by a lawyer in proceedings in the Superior Court:[10] they include parties who are acting in a representative capacity, parties under a disability, and parties that are corporations unless the court grants leave for someone else to represent the corporation. Where, for example, an individual is sued along with a corporation that he or she controls, the individual has a right to represent himself or herself and may be granted the right to represent the corporation as well.

Once Abigail has retained I.M. Just and instructed him to commence proceedings, I.M. Just and his firm have the authority to proceed. I.M. Just's name, address, telephone, fax number, and Law Society registration number appear on the backsheet of every court document, starting with the originating process. Since I.M. Just is a member of a firm, both his name and the firm's name must be disclosed, along with his individual phone number or extension. Once the proceeding is commenced, the court will note and record I.M. Just's name and the firm name from the backsheet, making I.M. Just the **lawyer of record**. I.M. Just or a member of his firm is then obliged to appear for Abigail unless she fires him or he obtains the court's permission to be removed from the record.

lawyer of record
lawyer recognized by the court as the legal representative of a party in a proceeding

Requiring a lawyer to prove authority to act

Anyone may require a lawyer of record to state in writing whether he, she, or the client authorized the commencement of proceedings. If there is no authority to proceed, the court may stay or dismiss the proceeding (rule 15.02). This rule is not often used, but it may be resorted to, for example, where there are warring factions in a privately held company or association and one such faction questions the company's proceedings.

Changing lawyers

What happens if Abigail is unhappy with I.M. Just and wishes to fire him and hire Brenda Smart to carry on the case? What usually happens is that once Brenda Smart agrees to take the case, she prepares a notice of change of lawyer (form 15A), indicating that Abigail has changed lawyers, and serves it on I.M. Just and every other party or the lawyer for every other party, if the other party is represented by counsel (rule 15.03(1)). Then, with an affidavit of service or other proof of service, the notice is filed in the court office. The court amends its records to show who the new lawyer of record is. A notice of change of lawyer in Abigail's case is set out in figure 5.8.

Similarly, a party who has been representing himself or herself must also give notice, and serve on all other parties and file with the court, a notice of appointment of a lawyer in form 15B, with proof of service (rule 15.03(2)). An example of the notice is set out in figure 5.9.

A party who has a lawyer but who wishes to dispense with the lawyer's services and represent himself or herself may do so by serving his or her lawyer and all other parties with a notice of intention to act in person in form 15C (rule 15.03(3)). The notice should be filed in court with proof of service. An example of the notice is set out in figure 5.10.

Lawyer's lien

When a client changes lawyers, the former lawyer is entitled to a lien on the client's documents in the former lawyer's possession until the client has paid his or her account with the law firm. A party may bring a motion for an order to determine what, if any, right the former lawyer has to maintain and enforce the lien (rule 15.04).

Lawyer's request to be removed as lawyer of record

A client is free to change or remove a lawyer at will, but how does a lawyer get rid of a client? Once the lawyer is "on the record" as lawyer of record, he or she is expected to represent and protect the client's interest until the matter is concluded, the client serves a notice under rule 15.03, or the court makes an order relieving the lawyer of the responsibilities as lawyer of record. The lawyer cannot "fire" a client just because the client is difficult or obnoxious.

There are two primary reasons for a court's granting an order relieving a lawyer of the obligation to act for a party: the client has refused to pay the lawyer's account or the client refuses to give the lawyer instructions when asked for them. Refusal to give instructions also includes giving instructions that are unlawful and that would require the lawyer to breach the rules of professional conduct or his or her duties as an officer of the court. In this case, because of rules requiring the lawyer to keep the client's confidence, the lawyer cannot usually reveal what the client has requested. Instead, the lawyer states that he or she is unable to obtain instructions.

To do this, a lawyer must serve the client with a notice of motion for an order to be removed as lawyer of record. The client must be served personally, by an alternative to personal service, or by mailing the motion to the client's last-known address. There are special rules for serving parties under a disability: The litigation guardian must be served along with the children's lawyer if the party is a minor, and the public guardian and trustee must be served in every other case. Corporations are also given notice in the motion to remove the lawyer from the record that they must retain new counsel or other suitable representation within 30 days after being served with the order removing the lawyer. The notice must inform the corporation that failure to obtain new representation may result in the case being dismissed, or the corporation's defence being struck out. For other parties, an order removing a lawyer must include the client's last known address and any other address where service might be effective. Also, the client must be warned that a new lawyer must be retained within 30 days of the order being served or the claim may be struck out, or the defence dismissed, as required under rule 15.04(8) and (9).

The affidavit to support the motion must give the court some reason to take the lawyer off the record because leaving the client unrepresented can have serious consequences for the client. The affidavit need not give details and should not violate lawyer–client privilege by revealing the contents of any disagreement on strategy or tactics between the lawyer and the client. A sample affidavit is set out in figure 5.11.

While rule 15.05 does not explicitly provide for other parties to apply to remove one party's lawyer of record, other parties may do this if there is a conflict of interest, using the rule 15 procedure with necessary modifications. For example, if I.M. Just had previously acted for Fred Flogem or Rattle Motors Ltd., the defendants could bring a motion to have I.M. Just removed as lawyer for Abigail on the grounds of there being a conflict of interest.[11]

CHAPTER SUMMARY

This chapter was primarily concerned with joinder and severance of parties and issues from one proceeding into other proceedings. We began by examining the rules for determining who can be a party to a lawsuit and which claims can be included in a lawsuit. We noted that, where possible, unless it is prejudicial or inconvenient, all proper parties and claims should be included in one proceeding rather than several because this usually reduces cost and delay. We then turned to special rules governing lawsuits for and against parties under disability. We noted that minors and those with a mental incapacity must be represented by litigation guardians. If none can be found, the parties must be represented by the children's lawyer and public guardian and trustee, respectively.

Partnerships and sole proprietorships can sue or be sued in their business name or in the name of the owners. There are special provisions to assist you in finding out who the owners are or were at the relevant time. There are also provisions to include them as parties, particularly if you want their individual as well as their business assets available to satisfy a judgment.

Estates and trusts, unascertained persons, and the transmission by assignment of an interest in a lawsuit from a party to a non-party were also examined with respect to who is, or who represents, a party in proceedings. For more complex representative actions, we set out the highlights of the *Class Proceedings Act, 1992* and examined the specific procedural rules governing some aspects of class proceedings. Finally, we examined the circumstances in which a party can represent himself or herself as well as the circumstances in which a party must have a lawyer. We also examined the procedure for both lawyers and clients where someone wished to change lawyers once proceedings had started.

KEY TERMS

judgment *in personam*

judgment *in rem*

assignee

chose in action

assignor

stay proceedings

litigation guardian

absentee

children's lawyer

return date

executor

estate administrator

personal representative

class proceeding fund

unincorporated association

lawyer of record

FIGURE 5.8   NOTICE OF CHANGE OF LAWYER (FORM 15A)

Court file no. 01-CV-1234

ONTARIO
SUPERIOR COURT OF JUSTICE

BETWEEN:

ABIGAIL BOAR

Plaintiff

and

RATTLE MOTORS LTD. and FRED FLOGEM

Defendants

NOTICE OF CHANGE OF LAWYER

The plaintiff, formerly represented by I.M. Just of Just & Coping, Barristers and Solicitors, has appointed Brenda Smart as lawyer of record.

Date: July 25, year 1

Brenda Smart
LSUC #45678L
Barrister and Solicitor
1201 Bay Street - 458
Toronto, Ontario, M1P 2B9

tel. 416-203-7798
fax 416-203-7797

Lawyer for the Plaintiff

TO:
I.M. Just
LSUC #12345R
Just & Coping
Barristers and Solicitors
365 Bay Street - 8701
Toronto, Ontario, M3J 4A9

tel. 416-762-1342
fax 416-762-2300

Former Lawyers for the Plaintiff

AND TO:
Huey Sue
LSUC #23456T
Barrister and Solicitor
65 False Trail
Toronto, Ontario, M6Y 1Z6

tel. 416-485-6891
fax 416-485-6892

Lawyer for the Defendants

FIGURE 5.9   NOTICE OF APPOINTMENT OF LAWYER (FORM 15B)

Court file no. 01-CV-1234

ONTARIO
SUPERIOR COURT OF JUSTICE

BETWEEN:

ABIGAIL BOAR

Plaintiff

and

RATTLE MOTORS LTD. and FRED FLOGEM

Defendants

NOTICE OF APPOINTMENT OF LAWYER

The plaintiff, Abigail Boar, formerly acting in person, has appointed I.M. Just of Just & Coping, Barristers and Solicitors, as lawyer of record.

July 25, year 1.

Just & Coping
Barristers and Solicitors
365 Bay Street – 8701
Toronto, Ontario, M3J 4A9

I.M. Just
LSUC #12345R
tel. 416-762-1342
fax 416-762-2300

Lawyers for the Plaintiff

TO:
Huey Sue
LSUC #23456T
Barrister and Solicitor
65 False Trail
Toronto, Ontario, M6Y 1Z6

tel. 416-485-6891
fax 416-485-6892

Lawyer for the Defendants

FIGURE 5.10   NOTICE OF INTENTION TO ACT IN PERSON (FORM 15C)

Court file no. 01-CV-1234

ONTARIO
SUPERIOR COURT OF JUSTICE

BETWEEN:

ABIGAIL BOAR

Plaintiff

and

RATTLE MOTORS LTD. and FRED FLOGEM

Defendants

NOTICE OF INTENTION TO ACT IN PERSON

The plaintiff, Abigail Boar, formerly represented by I.M.
Just as lawyer of record, intends to act in person.

Date: July 26, year 1

Abigail Boar
72 Sumach Street
Toronto, Ontario, M4R 1Z5
tel. 416-928-0001
fax. 416-928-0002

TO:
Just & Coping
Barristers and Solicitors
365 Bay Street - 8701
Toronto, Ontario, M3J 4A9

I.M. Just
LSUC #12345R
tel. 416-762-1342
fax 416-762-2300

Former Lawyers for the Plaintiff

AND TO:
Huey Sue
LSUC #23456T
Barrister and Solicitor
65 False Trail
Toronto, Ontario, M6Y 1Z6

tel. 416-485-6891
fax 416-485-6892

Lawyer for the Defendants

FIGURE 5.11   AFFIDAVIT IN SUPPORT OF MOTION FOR REMOVAL AS LAWYER OF RECORD (FORM 4D)

Court file no. 01-CV-1234

ONTARIO
SUPERIOR COURT OF JUSTICE

BETWEEN:

ABIGAIL BOAR

Plaintiff

and

RATTLE MOTORS LTD. and FRED FLOGEM

Defendants

AFFIDAVIT

I, I.M. Just, **lawyer in the law firm of** Just & Coping, **of the** City of Toronto, **in the Province of Ontario, MAKE OATH AND SAY:**

1. I am the lawyer of record for Abigail Boar, the plaintiff in this proceeding and, as such, have knowledge of the matters deposed to in this affidavit.
2. I commenced proceedings on behalf of the plaintiff with a statement of claim and have received the statement of defence filed by the defendants. The defendants have served a notice for examination for discovery to be held on February 10, year 1. I have repeatedly called and left messages for the plaintiff, and have written to advise her of the date for discovery and the need to prepare for it. She has not answered my letters, nor has she returned my calls or otherwise contacted me or given me instructions.
3. I am unable to act on behalf of the plaintiff without instructions from her.
4. The plaintiff's last-known address is 72 Sumach Street, Toronto, Ontario, M4R 1Z5.
5. I make this affidavit for an order to be removed as lawyer of record for the plaintiff.

Sworn before me at the	)	
City of Toronto,	)	*I.M. Just*
Province of Ontario,	)	I.M. Just
on February 1, year 1.	)	
U.R. Merely		
U.R. Merely		
Commissioner for Taking Affidavits	)	

NOTES

1   See ss. 6 and 45 of the *Substitute Decisions Act, 1992*, SO 1992, c. 30, as amended.

2   "Attorney" as used here does not mean lawyer; it means a person who is authorized to act as an agent for another person.

3   If a person does not reside in Ontario, he or she probably has no assets in Ontario against which to enforce an order to pay costs. For that reason, a non-resident may be asked to post security for costs by depositing an asset or title to an asset with the court.

4   The children's lawyer has issued a memorandum setting out the information it requires and how it should be contacted. This document is reproduced in most commercially published versions of the rules.

5   There are some narrow exceptions. A shareholder may be liable for a corporate act in some circumstances for an amount equal to the value of his or her shares. Where the owner of all shares is also the directing mind of the corporation and uses it to shield himself or herself from liability, the court may "lift the corporate veil" and allow a plaintiff to sue the owner directly. But this is very unusual.

6   Or the French equivalent of these words.

7   See *Police Retirees of Ontario Inc. v. Ontario Municipal Employees' Retirement Board* (1997), 35 OR (3d) 177 (Gen. Div.); *Bruce (Township) v. Thornburn* (1986), 57 OR (2d) 77 (HC).

8   W. Branch, *Class Actions in Canada* (Aurora, ON: Canada Law Book, 2001) (looseleaf updates).

9   See s. 5 of the *Class Proceedings Act, 1992*.

10 A party is free to represent himself or herself or use a lawyer or paralegal in Small Claims Court.

11 See, for example, *Harding v. Fraser* (2006), 81 OR (3d) 708, 23 MPIR (4th) 288 (SCJ).

REFERENCES

Absentees Act, RSO 1990, c. A.3.

Bankruptcy and Insolvency Act, RSC 1985, c. B-3, as amended.

Branch, W., *Class Actions in Canada* (Aurora, ON: Canada Law Book, 2001) (looseleaf updates).

Bruce (Township) v. Thornburn (1986), 57 OR (2d) 77 (HC).

Class Proceedings Act, 1992, SO 1992, c. 6.

Estates Administration Act, RSO 1990, c. E.22; 2006, c. 19, sched. C, s. 1.

Mental Health Act, RSO 1990, c. M.7.

Police Retirees of Ontario Inc. v. Ontario Municipal Employees' Retirement Board (1997), 35 OR (3d) 177 (Gen. Div.).

Rules of Civil Procedure, RRO 1990, reg. 194.

Substitute Decisions Act, 1992, SO 1992, c. 30.

REVIEW QUESTIONS

1. Abigail Boar would like to sue Fred Flogem for negligence in one proceeding, Rattle Motors Ltd. for negligence in another, and Skank Motorcar Company Ltd. in a third. Can she do this?

2. Can Abigail force defendants into the same lawsuit when the defendants have claims against each other?

3. In deciding to join or sever parties or issues, the court uses the balance of convenience test. Explain what this test is.

4. What are judgments *in personam* and *in rem*?

5. Can a party avoid joinder?

6. Can the court order two or more proceedings to be consolidated?

7. Suppose Abigail is 6 instead of 26 and wants to sue. Can she?

8. Why might a litigation guardian have to post security for costs?

9. How is a litigation guardian for a defendant appointed?

10. Who acts as litigation guardian if no one comes forward on behalf of the party under disability?

11. What obligations does a litigation guardian have toward a party under disability and toward the opposite party?

12. What happens if no one comes forward to act as litigation guardian for a defendant?

13. What happens if the court is not satisfied that there is an appropriate person to appoint as litigation guardian?

14. Can a litigation guardian be removed?

15. Suppose Fred Flogem is a party under disability and fails to file a statement of defence. Can Abigail sign default judgment?

16. Can a litigation guardian settle a case on behalf of the party under disability?

17. If Rattle Motors is a sole proprietorship owned by Fred Flogem, who should Abigail sue?

18. Would it make a difference if Regina Rattle and Fred Flogem owned Rattle Motors as partners?

19. When does a partner file a separate statement of defence from that of the partnership?

20. Suppose you do a name search of Rattle Motors and discover that Rattle is a trade name. The business is owned by 1234 Ontario Ltd. What party do you sue?

21. Whom does I.M. Just sue if he discovers that Abigail's estate has no personal representative?

22. If your law firm sues Abigail and she dies after the action is commenced, can you continue to sue her?

23. How does a class proceeding differ from other types of representative proceedings?

24. What must be done to turn a lawsuit into a class proceeding?

25. May any litigant represent himself or herself in a proceeding?

26. What does the phrase "on the record" mean?

27. What does Abigail need to do if she wishes to change lawyers or remove her lawyer and represent herself?

DISCUSSION QUESTIONS

1. Herkimer Spittoon, aged 26, is an electrical engineer and brother of Sam Spittoon. On August 4, year 2, Herkimer suffered brain injuries when he was involved in an automobile collision. As a result of the injuries, he suffers from mood swings and impulsive behaviour, when he goes on wild spending sprees. He has little sense of financial reality, and does not understand that he is living on a small disability allowance and does not have the income he once had. He also does not understand or accept advice on the management of his financial affairs. A creditor has sued him for purchases he made on April 4, year 0. The claim was issued on June 4, Year 0 and served on June 6, year 0. Both Sam and Herkimer live in Toronto. Sam has just become aware that Herkimer has been sued. Sam has come to the law office you work in for some advice because Herkimer is ignoring the whole business.

    a. Explain to Sam why Herkimer cannot defend this action by himself, and explain what must be done.

    b. Explain to Sam what his duties are as litigation guardian.

    c. Draft the body of Sam's affidavit, assuming he is moving to be appointed litigation guardian.

2. Johnson Eversharp retained Huey Sue to act for him in a complicated piece of commercial litigation. The pleading stage has closed, and the opposition has served Huey with a notice of examination for discovery of Johnson to be held on August 14, year 0. On August 3, year 0, Huey's law clerk phoned Johnson but got the answering machine. This happened on four subsequent days. Phone calls and e-mails to Johnson's home got no better results. The date of discovery is rapidly approaching. Huey decides that this client is not cooperating and wants to get off the record before there are further difficulties. The client still has $1,000 to his credit in the law office trust account, which will cover services to date. Draft the body of Huey's affidavit.

CHAPTER 6

Commencing proceedings

INTRODUCTION

In Ontario, court cases proceed in one of two ways, by action or by application. The steps to be taken and the pleadings are generally different if you are proceeding by action rather than by application, and in this chapter we will look at each of these ways of proceeding.

Rule 14.02 requires that a matter proceed by action unless a specific rule or statute requires otherwise. Rules 65, 67, and 68, for example, provide that proceedings commenced under those rules are to be by application. Rule 66 allows that the proceeding under that rule may be either by action or application. However, the vast majority of proceedings are by action.

Rule 14.01 requires that all proceedings, whether actions or applications, are commenced by the **issuing** of originating process.

ISSUING AND FILING

The pleadings that are originating process are listed in the definition of originating process in rule 1.03. Generally, an originating process can be described as the first document or pleading in a court case. Although the parties in a proceeding may have had extensive contact and been involved in lengthy negotiations before the first steps were taken to bring the matter to court, the court has no knowledge of a case until it receives the first court document or pleading. The step that notifies the court that a proceeding is being commenced is called "issuing."

The process of issuing is dealt with in rule 4.05. The originating process is drafted in the law office and is then taken to the court office to have the registrar sign, date, and put a seal on it. It is the court seal that lets the other side know that the court proceeding is genuine. During issuing, the registrar also assigns a court file number to the proceeding and it is at this point that the court opens a file, which will later hold other court documents relating to the case. Until the registrar assigns a court file number, the space on the origination process for the number remains blank. Once a number is assigned, this number must appear on every other pleading when it is prepared in the law office.

issuing
official commencement of court proceedings whereby documents that are originating processes are signed by the registrar, dated, sealed with a court seal, and given a file number

It is only in very small court offices that the registrar personally signs each originating process. In big court offices, such as Toronto, numerous court staff who work in the issuing office are designated by the registrar to sign the documents on his or her behalf.

Issuing the document also requires the payment of a fee. The person from the law office who takes the document to the court to be issued must also bring a cheque from the law firm made out to the Minister of Finance in the required amount. The fees charged by the Superior Court of Justice for the processing of documents are set out in a regulation to the *Administration of Justice Act*. The current fee for various court functions can be obtained by referring to the regulation on the e-laws website at http://www.e-laws.gov.on.ca, by calling the court office, or by checking on the Ontario government's website under the Ministry of the Attorney General, Court Services, which can be found at http://www.attorneygeneral.jus.gov.on.ca/english/courts. You should take two copies of your document with you. Only one copy will be signed and sealed. The original signed and sealed document will be returned to you and the court will keep a copy in its file.

While the court clerk is signing and preparing the original, you need to create a true copy for the court to keep in its file. This is done by copying by hand everything that the clerk is writing on the original. You put the signature of the registrar in quotation marks to indicate that it is a copy of the signature and not the original. On your copy, put a circle on the document in the same place that the clerk affixes the court seal. Inside the circle, write the word "seal." This process of making a true copy at the court counter, while your document is being issued, is called "**truing up**" the document. Once the original has been issued, the clerk will give it back to you and take your trued-up copy for the court file. The original, sealed document is kept in the client's file in the law office. You can then make copies of it on a photocopier for serving on the other side.

Once the originating process has been issued, only then can it be served on the other parties in the case. "Serving" a document, in very general terms, involves giving a copy to the other party or parties. Service must be done according the rules, and this process is dealt with in detail in chapter 8.

Only originating process need go through the process of issuing. All the other documents in the proceeding may be served on the other parties and then filed with the court office. Filing involves merely taking a document to the court, with the appropriate fee, and having the court staff place a copy on the court file.

truing up
making a handmade copy of a document at the court counter, usually by adding a seal and the registrar's signature inside quotation marks, by hand, to a photocopy of the original document

PROCEEDINGS BY WAY OF ACTION

Generally, the originating process that starts an action is a statement of claim, the precedent of which can be found in form 14A (general actions) or form 14B (mortgage actions). Some exceptions to this can be found in rule 14.03(1)(a) to (e).

Abigail Boar's case does not fit into the exceptions under rules 14.02 or 14.03, so it will proceed by way of action and the originating process will likely be a statement of claim. But perhaps Abigail has been uncertain whether she wants to sue the defendants. She spends so much time thinking about what she is going to do that the limitation period for starting an action against Rattle Motors and Fred Flogem may be running out.

It takes time to properly draft a statement of claim and perhaps Abigail only goes to see a lawyer three days before the limitation period on her case is about to expire. This is a relatively common situation because most people without any legal training do not realize that limitation periods exist.

A **limitation period** is the time in which a plaintiff may sue another person whom he or she believes may be legally responsible for causing him or her damage. The limitation period in most cases is two years, but once the limitation period has passed, a plaintiff loses forever his or her right to sue. It is therefore very important that the court proceeding be started before the limitation period expires.

limitation period
specified time within which court proceedings must be commenced

If I.M. Just, Abigail's lawyer, does not have enough time to draft a lengthy and detailed statement of claim before the limitation period expires, he can instead issue a notice of action under rule 14.03(2). Figure 6.1 sets out a notice of action for Abigail's case.

The issuing of a notice of action stops the limitation period and gives Abigail 30 more days from the date the notice of action is issued to serve and file the statement of claim. If a notice of action is used, the form for the statement of claim changes a bit. Instead of using the general form 14A, the plaintiff who files a notice of action first must file a statement of claim using the prescribed form 14D. The claim made by the plaintiff in the notice of action is usually the same as the claim that is later made in the statement of claim. But sometimes more information about the plaintiff's claim comes to light after the notice of action has been filed. In that case, rule 14.03(5) allows the plaintiff to alter or extend the claim stated in the notice of action.

If you start your action with a notice of action instead of a statement of claim, it is only the notice of action that is issued. The statement of claim is filed with the court when it is ready. This means that the court seal is on the notice of action and not on the statement of claim.

Whether the action is started by a statement of claim or a notice of application, you must also file form 14F, Information for Court Use (see figure 6.2).

Time limits for serving the statement of claim

Once the statement of claim is issued, you can serve it on the other side. Chapter 8 deals with the specific steps required to serve a court document. Very simply, service of a document means giving a copy of the document to the other side. Abigail's lawyer will have to ensure that both Rattle Motors Ltd. and Fred Flogem are given copies of the claim according to the methods prescribed in the rules.

Rule 14.08(1) requires that the statement of claim be served within six months after it is issued. This means that you want to be certain of the defendant's location before you issue the statement of claim. Otherwise, you may spend more than six months looking for him or her. If your statement of claim cannot be served within six months, you will have to bring a motion before the court to extend the six-month time period. Usually, if there is a good reason why the statement of claim could not be served within the time period, an extension of time will be granted. In Abigail's case, we know the location of Rattle Motors and Fred Flogem.

If Abigail's lawyer must start the proceeding with a notice of action because a limitation period is about to expire, the notice of action is not served separately on the defendant. Both the notice of action and the statement of claim in form 14D are

FIGURE 6.1   NOTICE OF ACTION (FORM 14C)

Court file no. 01-CV-1234

ONTARIO
SUPERIOR COURT OF JUSTICE

BETWEEN:

ABIGAIL BOAR

Plaintiff

and

RATTLE MOTORS LTD. and FRED FLOGEM

Defendants

NOTICE OF ACTION

TO THE DEFENDANT

A LEGAL PROCEEDING HAS BEEN COMMENCED AGAINST YOU by the plaintiff. The claim made against you is set out in the statement of claim served with this notice of action.

IF YOU WISH TO DEFEND THIS PROCEEDING, you or an Ontario lawyer acting for you must prepare a statement of defence in Form 18A prescribed by the Rules of Civil Procedure, serve it on the plaintiff's lawyer or, where the plaintiff does not have a lawyer, serve it on the plaintiff, and file it, with proof of service, in this court office, WITHIN TWENTY DAYS after this notice of action is served on you, if you are served in Ontario.

If you are served in another province or territory of Canada or in the United States of America, the period for serving and filing your statement of defence is forty days. If you are served outside Canada and the United States of America, the period is sixty days.

Instead of serving and filing a statement of defence, you may serve and file a notice of intent to defend in Form 18B prescribed by the Rules of Civil Procedure. This will entitle you to ten more days within which to serve and file your statement of defence.

IF YOU FAIL TO DEFEND THIS PROCEEDING, JUDGMENT MAY BE GIVEN AGAINST YOU IN YOUR ABSENCE AND WITHOUT FURTHER NOTICE TO YOU. IF YOU WISH TO DEFEND THIS PROCEEDING BUT ARE UNABLE TO PAY LEGAL FEES, LEGAL AID MAY BE AVAILABLE TO YOU BY CONTACTING A LOCAL LEGAL AID OFFICE.

IF YOU PAY THE PLAINTIFF'S CLAIM, and $500.00 for costs, within the time for serving and filing your statement of defence, you may move to have this proceeding dismissed by the court. If you believe the amount claimed for costs is excessive, you may pay the plaintiff's claim and $400.00 for costs and have the costs assessed by the court.

FIGURE 6.1 CONCLUDED

Date: January 4, year 1

Issued by: _____

Address of
court office: Court House
393 University Avenue
Toronto, Ontario, M5G 1E6

TO:
Rattle Motors Ltd.
1240 Bay Street
Toronto, Ontario, M8H 0K8

AND TO:
Fred Flogem
21 Cypress Boulevard
Scarborough, Ontario, M8Q 1P3

CLAIM

1. The plaintiff claims against both defendants:

    a. General damages in the amount of $200,000;

    b. Special damages in the amount of $3,649 to the date
       of this pleading;

    c. Prejudgment and post judgment interest pursuant to
       the *Courts of Justice Act*, RSO 1990, c. C.43

    d. Costs of this action

    e. Such further relief as seems just to this court.

2. The plaintiff's claim is a result of a slip and fall
    that occurred on September 14, year 0.

Date of Issue: _____

Just & Coping
Barristers and Solicitors
365 Bay Street, Suite 8701
Toronto, Ontario M3J 4A9

I.M. Just
LSUC #12345R
tel.: 416-762-1342
fax: 416-762-2300

Lawyers for the Plaintiff

FIGURE 6.2   INFORMATION FOR COURT USE (FORM 14F)

SUPERIOR COURT OF JUSTICE

BETWEEN:

ABIGAIL BOAR

Plaintiff

and

RATTLE MOTORS LTD. AND FRED FLOGEM

Defendants

INFORMATION FOR COURT USE

This proceeding is an: [x] action   [ ] application

Has it been commenced under the *Class Proceedings Act, 1992*?   [ ] yes   [x] no

---

(If the proceeding is an action, answer all of the following:)

Rule 76 (Simplified Procedure) applies: [ ] yes   [x] no
Note: *Subject to the exceptions found in subrule 76.01(1), it is MANDATORY to proceed under Rule 76 for all cases in which the money amount claimed or the value of real or personal property claimed is $50,000 or less.*

Rule 77 (Civil Case Management) applies: [ ] yes   [x] no

If Rule 77 applies, choice of track is: [ ] Fast   [ ] Standard

Rule 78 (Toronto Civil Case Management Pilot Project) applies: [ ] yes   [x] no

---

The claim in this proceeding (action or application) is in respect of:

*(Select the **one** item that **best** describes the nature of the main claim in the proceeding.)*

Bankruptcy or insolvency law	[ ]	Motor vehicle accident	[ ]
Collection of liquidated debt	[ ]	Municipal law	[ ]
Constitutional law	[ ]	Partnership law	[ ]
Construction law (other than construction lien)	[ ]	Personal property security	[ ]
Construction lien	[ ]	Product liability	[ ]
Contract law	[ ]	Professional malpractice (other than medical)	[ ]
Corporate law	[ ]	Real property (including leases; excluding mortgage or charge)	[ ]
Defamation	[ ]	Tort: economic injury (other than from medical or professional malpractice)	[ ]
Employment or labour law	[ ]		
Intellectual property law	[ ]	Tort: personal injury (other than from motor vehicle accident)	[x]
Judicial review	[ ]	Trusts, fiduciary duty	[ ]
Medical malpractice	[ ]	Wills, estates	[ ]
Mortgage or charge	[ ]		

CERTIFICATION

I certify that the above information is correct, to the best of my knowledge.

Date: _____ January 4, year 1 _____   _____ *I.M. Just* _____
                                                                                Signature of lawyer

served on the defendant together. You have six months to serve the documents together, but the six months starts running as soon as the notice of action is issued, not when the statement of claim is filed later with the court.

PROCEEDINGS COMMENCED BY APPLICATION

A court proceeding in the Ontario Superior Court of Justice may also be by application instead of action. Although proceeding by application is much faster and more expeditious than proceeding by action, the use of applications is limited. A proceeding must be by action unless a statute or the rules say it is to be commenced in some other manner (rule 14.02).

There are a number of rules that require a proceeding by application instead of by action.[1] In addition, rule 14.05(3) provides a list of types of situations where plaintiffs can proceed by application. Therefore, the first step is deciding whether or not the case you are commencing is one that can proceed by application. If it does not fit in one of the categories provided by the rules and no statute authorizes you to proceed by application, then you must proceed by action and follow the steps outlined above in relation to actions.

There has been a recent change to the rules. Rule 14.05(3)(h) now permits an application to be brought on any matter where it is unlikely that there will be any material facts in dispute. Material facts are those central to the case.

If you can commence the action by application, you use a different originating process than you do with an action. In an application, you start the proceedings with a notice of application. The general form for a notice of application is form 14E, but there is a special notice of application if your application is for judicial review under rule 68 or is a proceeding to register an order from the United Kingdom for enforcement by the Ontario court under rule 73. For judicial review, you commence the application with a notice of application for judicial review using form 68A. For the registration of an order from the United Kingdom, you must use form 73A. An example of the general notice of application, form 14E, is set out in figure 6.3. In addition to the notice of application, form 14F, information for court use, must also be filed (see figure 6.2).

In addition to rule 14, rules 38 and 39 spell out the procedure and the evidence to be used on applications.

In an application, the parties are not called the plaintiff and the defendant. Instead, they are the applicant and the respondent. The application must state the rule or statute under which it is commenced and set out the precise relief sought and the grounds for the relief. It should list the documentary evidence that will be used in the hearing of the application. All applications are brought before a judge. A master has no jurisdiction to hear an application (rule 38.02).

Because a notice of application is an originating process, the court must issue it before it is served on the other side. It must then be served on all parties at least 10 days before the date of the hearing unless it is served outside Ontario. Then it must be served at least 20 days in advance.

One of the reasons that an application is a much faster procedure than an action is that it relies mostly on **affidavit** evidence. The affidavit is usually served on the respondent along with the notice of application. An affidavit is a sworn document

affidavit
written statement setting out the evidence of the person who swears or affirms its contents are true

that lays out the facts that a party is relying on. It is evidence in the proceeding. It must be clear, precise, and based on the knowledge or belief of the person who is swearing that the facts in the affidavit are true. See chapter 9 for more information on drafting affidavits.

A respondent who has been served with a notice of application serves and files a notice of appearance in form 38A. An example of a notice of appearance is set out in figure 6.4. A respondent who does not serve and file the notice of appearance cannot file material, examine a witness, or take other steps in the proceeding, and is not entitled to any further notice of other steps in the application.

Place and date of hearing of the application

The applicant names the place of hearing, which is usually the court nearest the place where the applicant resides, unless a statute or rule requires that the application be brought in a specific location.

You may pick any date for the hearing of the application when a judge is scheduled to hear applications as long as the hearing is estimated, by the lawyer, to take less than two hours. You need not obtain the date from the court before you complete and serve the notice of application (rule 38.03(2)). However, if the hearing is to take longer than two hours, a date must be obtained from the court office first unless it is an urgent case (rule 38.03(3)). An urgent matter may be scheduled for any day that applications are being heard in the court, even if it is going to take more than two hours to argue. In some courts, practice directions apply to the scheduling of applications, and you must therefore check whether a practice direction exists for the court in which you wish to bring an application.

Figure 6.3 sets out a notice of application in form 14E.

Material for use on the application

factum
document that sets out the facts, statutes, and cases that a party relies on to obtain a favourable decision

The applicant is required to serve and file an application record and a **factum**, along with proof of service, at least four days before the hearing of the application. A factum is a document that sets out the facts and the law on which the party relies. Rule 38.09 provides that an application record must contain the following information:

- a table of contents describing each document by its nature, date, and, if it is an exhibit, its exhibit number;

- a copy of the notice of application;

- a copy of all affidavits and other material served by any party for use on the application;

- a list of all relevant transcripts of evidence in chronological order, but not necessarily the transcripts themselves; and

- a copy of any other material in the court file that is necessary for the hearing of the application.

All of the above must be bound together in consecutively numbered pages and be in the order specified above. The application record will have a light blue backsheet and the applicant's factum will be bound, front and back, with white covers.

The respondent must serve and file his or her factum, stating the facts and the law on which the respondent relies, at least two days before the hearing. The respondent's factum must be bound both front and back with green cover stock paper. For more information about factums, refer to chapter 20 on appeals.

If the respondent believes that the applicant's record is incomplete, he or she may serve and file his or her own application record. The respondent's application record must contain a table of contents, the exhibits relied on, and copies of any other material that the respondent intends to rely on at the hearing.

If for any reason either or both parties believe that an application record or a factum is not necessary for the hearing of the case, they may bring a motion before a judge, asking for an order dispensing with the application record and factum.

A party who wishes to rely on a transcript of evidence must file a copy of the transcript in accordance with rule 34.18. It must be filed at least two days before the hearing of the application.

Confirmation of an application

An applicant who brings an application on notice must confer or attempt to confer or discuss the application with the respondent no later than 2 p.m. two days before the date for the hearing. The purpose of this discussion is for the parties to determine whether the application will proceed as scheduled, whether an adjournment is being sought, or whether the parties can settle the matter completely or in part. Then the applicant must send a confirmation of application, form 38B, to the registrar of the court, confirming that the application will be proceeding as scheduled, or advising whether an adjournment, or another type of order listed on the form, is being sought. Form 38B may be sent to the court in person, by fax, or by e-mail (if the court has an available e-mail address). A copy must also be sent to the respondent by fax or e-mail.

If the confirmation is not sent as required, the application will not be heard on the date originally scheduled, unless the court orders otherwise. The applicant must also ensure that if the situation changes after the confirmation is sent, that the court is provided with updated information.

Disposition of an application

After the judge has heard the application, he or she may grant the relief the applicant is seeking, dismiss the application, adjourn the application, or direct that the matter go to trial. If the application is ordered to trial, it is turned into an action.

Evidence on an application

Evidence on an application is presented in an affidavit, which is a sworn document laying out the facts in the case. It must be based on the personal knowledge or belief of the person who makes it and swears it to be true. The person who makes the affidavit is called the **deponent**. Although the evidence is written down and not given in court through witnesses, the opposite party has a right to cross-examine the deponent on the facts he or she claims to be true. On cross-examination, a lawyer for the opposite party asks questions to test the credibility of the deponent. The cross-examination takes place in the office of an official examiner or a reporting

deponent
person who makes an affidavit

service (rule 34.02(1)). The evidence is recorded word-for-word, and a transcript is prepared. If a party wishes to present the cross-examination at the hearing, it does so by filing a copy of the transcript.

A lawyer who wants to cross-examine a witness on an affidavit must serve and file all the affidavits he or she intends to rely on in the hearing of the application. It is only then that he or she may cross-examine a deponent for the other side. Once a lawyer has conducted a cross-examination, he or she cannot file any more affidavits for his or her client without permission from the court.

For more information on affidavits and cross-examinations, you may refer to chapter 9 on motions and chapter 14 on discovery.

CHAPTER SUMMARY

In Ontario, we have seen that all civil proceedings are commenced by application or by action. The rules require a proceeding to be commenced by action unless a statute or the rules require that it should be commenced by way of application.

The document that starts a court proceeding is called an originating process. There are different types of originating processes, depending on the type of court proceeding that is being started. All of the originating processes are listed under the definition in rule 1.03. Generally, the originating process that starts an action is a statement of claim. All originating processes, including a statement of claim, must be issued by the registrar of the court. A statement of claim must be served on the defendant within six months after it is issued. If the action is commenced by a notice of action, it is served along with the statement of claim.

If the case is one that is proceeding by application, the originating process is a notice of application. We noted that it must also be issued before it is served, and it must be served at least 10 days before the hearing of the application. Once the application has been commenced, rule 38 dictates how the application proceeds through the court process. Rule 39 specifies what evidence can be brought. An application record and a factum must be filed in all applications.

After the parties have presented their cases at the hearing of the application, the judge may dismiss the application, grant the relief the applicant is seeking, or adjourn the matter. These resolutions are similar in any other type of hearing. However, the judge has an additional option on an application: he or she may order that the application be turned into an action. If this occurs, any further steps in the case must follow the procedural requirements for an action.

FIGURE 6.3   NOTICE OF APPLICATION (FORM 14E)

Court file no. 03-CL-8926

ONTARIO
SUPERIOR COURT OF JUSTICE

BETWEEN:

DINGLEHOOFER OFFICE SUPPLIES LTD.

Applicant

and

DONALDSON PRINTING CORPORATION

Respondent

APPLICATION UNDER the *Business Corporations Act*, RSO 1990,
c. B.16, ss. 207-18 and s. 248, as amended.

NOTICE OF APPLICATION

TO THE RESPONDENT

A LEGAL PROCEEDING HAS BEEN COMMENCED by the applicant.
The claim made by the applicant appears on the following page.

THIS APPLICATION will come on for a hearing on March 10, year 2,
at 10:00 a.m., at Osgoode Hall, 130 Queen Street West, Toronto,
Ontario, M5H 2N5.

IF YOU WISH TO OPPOSE THIS APPLICATION, to receive notice of
any step in the application or to be served with any documents in the
application you or an Ontario lawyer acting for you must forthwith
prepare a notice of appearance in Form 38A prescribed by the Rules of
Civil Procedure, serve it on the applicant's lawyer or, where the applicant
does not have a lawyer, serve it on the applicant, and file it, with proof of
service, in this court office, and you or your lawyer must appear at the
hearing.

IF YOU WISH TO PRESENT AFFIDAVIT OR OTHER
DOCUMENTARY EVIDENCE TO THE COURT OR TO EXAMINE OR
CROSS-EXAMINE WITNESSES ON THE APPLICATION, you or your
lawyer must, in addition to serving your notice of appearance, serve a
copy of the evidence on the applicant's lawyer or, where the applicant
does not have a lawyer, serve it on the applicant, and file it, with proof of
service, in the court office where the application is to be heard as soon
as possible, but at least two days before the hearing.

IF YOU FAIL TO APPEAR AT THE HEARING, JUDGMENT MAY BE
GIVEN IN YOUR ABSENCE AND WITHOUT FURTHER NOTICE TO
YOU. IF YOU WISH TO OPPOSE THIS APPLICATION BUT ARE
UNABLE TO PAY LEGAL FEES, LEGAL AID MAY BE AVAILABLE TO
YOU BY CONTACTING A LOCAL LEGAL AID OFFICE.

FIGURE 6.3   CONCLUDED

Date: February 26, year 2

Issued by: _____

**Address of
court office:** Court House
393 University Ave.
Toronto, Ontario, M5G 1E6

TO:

Donaldson Printing Corporation
3276 College Street North,
Toronto, Ontario, M7Y 4F7

APPLICATION

1. **The applicant makes application** pursuant to the Ontario
    Business Corporations Act, RSO 1990, c. B.16, s. 207, for
    a. an order that the voluntary winding up of the
       respondent corporation be continued under supervision
       of the court;
    b. the costs of the application; and
    c. such other order as seems just to this court.

2. **The grounds for the application are:**
    a. the applicant is a creditor of the respondent
       corporation, which is currently in the process of
       being voluntarily wound up;
    b. the respondent corporation owes the applicant a debt
       for supplies in the amount of $5,000.
    c. it is not in the interests of the contributories and
       creditors that the proceedings should be continued
       under the supervision of the court for the following
       reasons:
       i. (*here set out reasons*)
    d. the applicant relies on the provisions of the
       Business Corporations Act, RSO 1990, c. B.16,
       ss. 207-218 and s. 248.

3. **The following documentary evidence will be used at the hearing of
    the application:**
    affidavit of Bradley Pittbottom, president of the
    applicant corporation, dated February 20, year 2 and the
    exhibit referred to therein.

Date of issue: February 26, year 2

Fair and Duguid
Barristers and Solicitors
50 Justice Way
Suite 1000
Toronto, Ontario, M9V 6J2

Bonnie Fair
LSUC #98765D
tel. 416-555-1225
fax 416-555-1226

Lawyers for the Applicant

FIGURE 6.4   NOTICE OF APPEARANCE (FORM 38A)

Court file no. 03-CL-8926

ONTARIO
SUPERIOR COURT OF JUSTICE

BETWEEN:

DINGLEHOOFER OFFICE SUPPLIES LTD.

Applicant

and

DONALDSON PRINTING CORPORATION

Respondent

APPLICATION UNDER the *Business Corporations Act*, RSO 1990,
c. B.16, ss. 207-18 and s. 248, as amended.

NOTICE OF APPEARANCE

The respondent intends to respond to this application

Date: March 10, year 2

Tilley Townsend
LSUC #76543U
Barrister and Solicitor
10 Winding Road
Newmarket, Ontario N0M 1D0

tel. 905-666-1010
fax 905-666-1011

Lawyer for the Respondent

TO:
Fair and Duguid
Barristers and Solicitors
50 Justice Way
Suite 1000
Toronto, Ontario M9V 6J2

Bonnie Fair
LSUC #98765D
tel. 416-555-1225
fax 416-555-1226

Lawyers for the Applicant

KEY TERMS

issuing	affidavit
truing up	factum
limitation period	deponent

NOTE

1 See rules 65.01, 66.01, 67.01, and 68.01.

REFERENCES

Administration of Justice Act, RSO 1990, c. A.6.

Limitations Act, 2002, SO 2002, c. 24, sched. B.

Rules of Civil Procedure, RRO 1990, reg. 194.

REVIEW QUESTIONS

1. What are the two ways that a court case may be commenced in Ontario?

2. What is the originating process that usually commences an action? Can another originating process be used to start an action?

3. What is an issued document?

4. What do you have to do to "true up" an issued document, and when do you do it?

5. Why is it important to get as much information about the location of the defendant as possible before you issue the statement of claim?

6. Your client was one week away from the expiry of the limitation period under the *Limitations Act, 2002* when she contacted your office. You did not have time to prepare a statement of claim so you filed a notice of action to stop the limitation period from running out. Twenty-nine days after you issued the notice of action, you filed your statement of claim. How much time do you have left to serve the statement of claim?

7. Must you serve the notice of action on the other side?

8. Will Abigail Boar commence her court case by way of application or by way of action?

9. What is the procedure for obtaining a hearing date for an application?

10. What are the contents of an application record?

11. Under what circumstances would a respondent file an application record?

DISCUSSION QUESTION

1. Brad Pout, an avid horse enthusiast, met an experienced horse trader, Tom Craze. They discussed their mutual interests over lunch on several occasions and decided to go into partnership to carry on the business of buying horses. Brad contributed $100,000 to the partnership and Tom was to buy the horses, but he contributed no money. They did buy and sell many horses and made a big profit but they eventually had a falling out. Tom now wants to dissolve the partnership. There is $300,000 in the partnership bank account. Tom wants his half of the $300,000 because he says that he contributed all the work. Brad says Tom is only entitled to $100,000, which amounts to 50 percent of the profit after Brad deducts the money he put into the partnership in the beginning. Tom is relying on s. 5 of the *Partnership Act*, which allows a partner to make an application to the court for a dissolution of the partnership when circumstances have arisen that make it fair for the partnership to be dissolved. He wants the court to order that he receive $150,000 from the partnership's remaining assets. Draft a notice of application for Tom.

CHAPTER 7

Drafting pleadings

INTRODUCTION

In this chapter, we turn to some of the matters you must consider in drafting statements of claim and defence as well as replies to statements of defence. Drafting issues involving notices of application are dealt with in chapter 9 because procedurally and in terms of format notices of application have more in common with motions than they have with statements of claim. The procedural aspects of commencing an action are discussed in chapter 6.

GENERAL DRAFTING CONSIDERATIONS

Getting organized

Before you start to draft a statement of claim or other pleading, you need to think about what you wish to say and organize your material. As a law clerk, you will usually be working under the supervision of a lawyer. Speak to him or her to be sure you understand your instructions and the theory of the case. The theory of the case is the focus or basis of liability on which you organize the facts and decide which facts are relevant. For example, if I.M. Just's theory is that Abigail Boar was injured solely because of the negligence of Fred Flogem, you include only allegations about what Fred did or did not do properly. You do not include statements to show that Rattle Motors Ltd. or Skank Motorcar Company Ltd. is liable. If, on the other hand, I.M. Just's theory is that Fred was negligent, Rattle Motors Ltd. is responsible for Fred's acts, and Skank Motorcar Company Ltd. negligently manufactured the car that caused the oil leak, you include allegations about Skank Motorcar Company Ltd. and statements of law that Rattle Motors Ltd. is responsible for the negligent acts of its employees. What you plead depends on the theory of the case.

Assemble and review the interview notes from meetings with the client and with any witnesses. Also review client documents, expert reports, or any other evidentiary material you have. Summarize the evidence on the facts that you will plead. If there is no hope of proving a fact because there is no evidence to support it, the fact should not be pleaded, and the supervising lawyer may need to revise his or her theory of the case.

Peruse precedents for other statements of claim in the firm's files. Most firms keep precedent binders, and you should too, starting with the forms and documents you create in this course and other courses as assignments and projects. A precedent can show you the proper format, act as a guide for drafting an outline, and sometimes give you the language to express a certain claim or principle of law. But precedents should be used with caution. You are unlikely to find a statement of claim into which you can simply plug in Abigail's name. You need to look at precedents critically, being prepared to use your own language to express your meaning and purpose. Be aware that many precedents, particularly older ones, use what is called the common law drafting style — an archaic legal style that is repetitious and full of jargon. Mercifully, it is fast disappearing as young lawyers in Ontario are trained to use plain language drafting techniques. Plain language has been part of the bar admission curriculum since 1990 and has had some impact on drafting. This style, also referred to as the Citibank style, originated with loan agreements used by the First National City Bank of New York, a major American commercial bank. The simpler and clearer documents used by the bank have been credited with reducing the volume of the bank's litigation by reducing the ambiguity of the documents. Plain language drafting has since spread throughout the common law world. This plain language style is also used in modern Ontario statute drafting, and the contrast with older statutes is startling. Do not be afraid to use simple language to express your meaning. Cut to the chase. Avoid legal jargon such as "the plaintiff states and the fact is" or "the defendant alleges." Instead, say "the plaintiff states" or "the defendant states."

Prepare an outline. The format of the statement of claim and defence as outlined in forms 14A and 18A sets this out in part, but you still need to outline the facts and law you rely on.

Type out or dictate a first draft. With minimal polishing, this can be forwarded to a client for comment and feedback. A client will often have important corrections to make to basic facts as pleaded. As you revise and go to later drafts, be sure to label the draft with the date so you do not mistakenly rely on an earlier imperfect draft.

Revise and polish the draft after getting client and lawyer feedback. A law clerk should forward what he or she thinks is the final draft to the lawyer for approval before serving and filing the pleading in question.

Check for internal consistency. If you make a cross-reference to another paragraph in the claim or to a fact alleged elsewhere in the claim, be sure your reference is in the right place.

Give the document a fast read to see that it flows logically and that the facts and law as pleaded support the theory of the case.

Language and tone

You already know that you should avoid jargon and legalese. Most commentators think that it is best to use simple language in pleadings. Facts should be simply stated as facts. You need not search the thesaurus for a string of colourful adjectives to describe Abigail's pain. It is sufficient to describe it as "chronic and severe pain in the neck and back," for example. Use relatively short, blunt sentences that are devoid of flowery language. If a fact is material, it should be stated positively, and if possible, in a separate sentence. Tell the story in a logical way so that the reader can follow it. Usually, telling a story chronologically works well. Use an outline to be sure that you have included everything that is material and that the story flows logically.

DRAFTING STATEMENTS OF CLAIM
Format

The format of a claim is in part prescribed by rule 14 and form 14A.[1] It consists of the following, discussed in sequential order:

GENERAL HEADING AND TITLE OF PROCEEDINGS

The format for this is prescribed by form 4A. It must head every court document, including a statement of claim.

PRESCRIBED TEXT

Generally referred to as **boilerplate**, this is the part of the statement of claim that follows the general heading and title of proceedings. It begins with the words "TO THE DEFENDANT." The language here is prescribed by the rules, and the wording must appear in every claim. Fortunately, there is litigation software available that reproduces this and eliminates the need for copy typing and pre-printed forms. The boilerplate for the generic statement of claim, form 14A, is reproduced in figure 7.1 at the end of the chapter.

> **boilerplate**
> standard wording that is part of every copy of a particular type of document

The only information you need to plug into the boilerplate is the address of the court office, the date that the claim is issued, an amount for costs, the name and address of the defendant, and the name, address, and telephone number of the plaintiff's lawyer. The amount for costs should not be an astronomical sum and should reflect the cost of an uncontested action where the claim is paid right after it issues. An amount approximating $500 or $600 should be sufficient.

You will also need to prepare form 14F: information for court use. This form indicates what the main claim in the action is for and whether rule 76 (simplified procedure), rule 77 (case management), and rule 78 (case management — Toronto) apply. If rule 77 applies, you also need to indicate whether the proceeding will be on the fast or standard track. Form 14F must be filed with every statement of claim. Figure 6.2 in chapter 6 sets out a completed form 14F.

Format of pleadings: Rule 25.02

The body of the pleadings following the boilerplate is set out in consecutively numbered paragraphs. As far as possible, each allegation should be set out in a separate paragraph. This may make for some two- or three-sentence paragraphs, which may seem short to you, but they are appropriate for pleadings.

Claim for relief: Rule 25.09

The claim for relief, which is paragraph 1, begins with the words "The plaintiff claims." In it, you set out each head of damage together with an amount, where that amount is known, in separate subparagraphs. Other relief claimed, such as an injunction or a declaratory judgment, must be specified as well. If there is more than one plaintiff, the claims for each must be set out separately. If there is more than one defendant, you are obliged to set out how much you claim from each defendant for each claim you make unless the claim is made against all defendants jointly. Remember that each defendant is entitled to know the details of the claim made against him or her by each plaintiff.

general damages

monetary damages for pain and suffering that cannot be determined on the basis of a formula

special damages

monetary damages that are specific, ascertainable, and measured on an objective basis; sometimes referred to as out-of-pocket expenses

Abigail is likely to claim **general damages** and **special damages**. It is not always possible at the beginning of a lawsuit to determine what special damages will be at trial. For example, Abigail has become depressed and may be prescribed anti-depressants. At the time the claim issues, she may have spent $300 for these, but she does not know how much she will have spent by the time of trial. Rule 25.06(9) provides a solution. The plaintiff is permitted to claim special damages calculated to the date of pleading and undertake to deliver particulars of further claims when known and, in any event, within 10 days of the start of the trial.

You should always claim prejudgment and postjudgment interest, which are available under ss. 127–130 of the *Courts of Justice Act* but will not be awarded unless they are specifically claimed. Prejudgment interest runs from the date the cause of action arises until judgment or payment, so you need to set out the date the cause of action arose in the pleadings. In this case, the cause of action arose on September 14, year 0, when Abigail was injured. Postjudgment interest runs from the date of judgment until payment. Because you do not know these dates, the bare claim for postjudgment interest is sufficient.

You must also claim costs: Failure to claim them means they may not be awarded. The practice has developed among some lawyers of claiming costs on a substantial indemnity basis. This is a punitive costs award, and judges award it when one party has behaved badly or improperly in the course of the litigation. In our view, you should simply claim costs without elaborating unless you believe this is a case for a punitive costs award — for example, where one side has tried to hide evidence or has behaved maliciously. In that case, a claim for substantial indemnity costs is appropriate. Otherwise, you should refrain from overstating your claim. When you do that, you raise your client's expectations, which cannot be fulfilled, and you fool neither your opponent nor the judge.

Most lawyers include a final claim for "such further relief as seems just to this court." This is probably unnecessary, but nearly all lawyers do it. It amounts to a security blanket to cover claims you should have made but did not. In fact, if you seek specific relief, you must state it in your claim, or the court cannot grant the relief at trial. This is because your opponent will say, with justification, that he or she is prejudiced in his or her defence because if the defendants had been aware of the claim at the beginning of the case, they would have prepared to defend it and presented their case differently. In a situation like this, the security blanket in the claim for relief will not help you. If there is a variation on a claim that is made within the scope of the pleadings, the security blanket is probably unnecessary. But most lawyers continue to put it in as if it were some kind of legal rabbit's foot or lucky charm. So, with misgivings, we include it too.

Abigail Boar's claim for relief against Fred Flogem and Rattle Motors Ltd. is set out in paragraph 1 of her statement of claim, which appears in figure 7.2 at the end of the chapter.

Cast of characters

After the claim for relief, which is set out in paragraph one, you identify in subsequent numbered paragraphs each plaintiff and each defendant. If a party is an individual, you say so. If it is relevant, you may wish to add a party's occupation, and you should add a general address, consisting of a town or city and province or state.

Street addresses are not used as a matter of custom. The purpose of setting out the residence of an individual or, in the case of a party that is not an individual, the place where it carries on business, is to identify whether a party is a non-resident for purposes of service, determine whether the party should post security for costs, and identify other territorial jurisdiction issues. If the party is not an individual, its status should be set out: corporation, non-profit corporation, Crown corporation, or government agency, for example. This paragraph may also briefly describe the party's involvement in the case. An example of a cast of characters appears in paragraphs 2 to 4 of Abigail Boar's statement of claim, which is set out in figure 7.2.

Facts and law underlying the claim

In the subsequent paragraphs, you tell Abigail's story. Before doing this, however, we need to discuss a number of basic rules of pleading that apply to the drafting of claims and defences. There are also some rules that apply only to the drafting of defences, which we will discuss later in this chapter.

Plead material facts but not evidence: Rule 25.06(1)

You must plead a concise statement of material facts on which the party relies, but not the evidence that will be used to prove the facts of your case. There are three elements to this rule:

- Be concise.
- Plead material facts.
- Do not plead evidence.

"Concise" tells you not to use 15 words when 5 will do. Avoid flowery language and excessive use of adjectives. Keep sentences and paragraphs reasonably short, confining a material fact to a single sentence where possible. Don't be surprised to find yourself writing paragraphs of two to three sentences. This is probably not what you learned in English class, but then you weren't being asked to do this kind of specialized writing.

"Material facts" are the facts that are necessary to prove or defend the claim based on your theory of the case. Before you can know what the material facts are, you must be familiar with both the events involved in the case and the law that applies to the situation. For example, in Abigail's case, the material facts concern her slipping and falling on the oil on the floor. Because the law involved is the law of negligence, material facts will be those that show negligence by the defendants. Here your facts include the lawful entry of Abigail into the area where the oil spill was, the lack of lighting, the fact that Fred knew about the spill, the fact that he did nothing to clean it up, the fact that Abigail was not warned or protected, the fact that she fell, and the fact that she was injured. What may not be relevant in this instance, though it may be interesting, are the facts that Fred is married with five children, that Abigail is very fond of the colour red, and that she had a happy childhood. Similarly, it is of no relevance to Abigail's claim that Rattle Motors Ltd. has sold far fewer cars this year than last and is teetering on bankruptcy. This last fact may be relevant in enforcing a judgment against Rattle Motors Ltd., but it is irrelevant to making a claim for negligence against it. Some of these facts may be relevant in some situations but not others. For example, if Abigail were going to participate in a psychological study relating colour preference to personality, then her preference for the colour red would be relevant indeed.

"Not pleading evidence" is the last element of this rule. Evidence of a material fact is information from which a material fact may be proven or deduced. For example, to state "the plaintiff fell because there was oil on the floor" is to state a material fact. But to go on to say "Abigail knew Fred was negligent because Fred admitted to Abigail that he knew about the spill and had not cleaned it up" is to set out the evidence (the admission) used to prove the material fact.

Pleading points of law: Rule 25.06(2)

Rule 25.06(2) permits you to plead any point of law in a claim or defence that is relevant to your case. If you are drawing a legal conclusion, the rule requires you to set out the facts on which that conclusion is based. For example, suppose Abigail wishes to claim against Rattle Motors Ltd. by raising the issue that it is vicariously liable for the acts of its employees. To plead this principle of law, she needs to set out the material facts that underlie it: that Fred is an employee of Rattle Motors Ltd. and that the acts of negligence complained of were done by Fred in the course of his employment. If you are pleading a statute or regulation as part of a point of law, be sure to give the full citation.

Pleading conditions precedent: Rule 25.06(3)

A condition precedent is something that must be done before one is legally entitled to do something else. For example, if one party refuses to close a real estate transaction, the other party may tender on the party refusing to close. In order to successfully tender, the tendering party must have met the conditions precedent for tendering by showing that he or she was ready, willing, and able to close the transaction before tendering. In an action, if one party alleges that he or she tendered on the other, this rule says that the allegation alone is sufficient, and that it is not necessary to also plead that the party was ready, willing, and able to close the transaction. In other words, you need not plead the performance of the conditions precedent to tendering. by setting out all of its elements. The performance of the conditions precedent are presumed without your having to state them. If the opposing party believes that the tendering process was defective because you had not fulfilled the conditions precedent, that party must say so in his or her response to your pleading, specifying the nature of the defect.

Inconsistent pleadings: Rule 25.06(4)

It is considered appropriate to plead inconsistent or apparently contradictory allegations in a claim or defence, provided that it is clear that the statements are made in the alternative. For example, in a negligence action involving a car accident, it is not always clear to the plaintiff, especially in the early stages of an action, exactly what acts of the defendant constitute negligence. The other driver may have failed to apply the brakes in time, or he may have been talking on his cell phone and not paying proper attention, or his car may have been poorly maintained. In this situation, it is permissible to plead as follows: "the defendant failed to keep a proper lookout; or in the alternative, he failed to apply his brakes; or in the further alternative, his brakes malfunctioned because he had not properly maintained and serviced his vehicle." In this case, evidence on discovery or at trial may show that one or the other of these facts is correct.

The important thing is that the evidence at trial has to correspond to the case as pleaded. If the evidence shows that the negligence of the defendant was different from what the plaintiff said it was in his or her claim, the plaintiff may have his or her case dismissed for failing to prove the claim as pleaded. You are therefore encouraged to plead broadly and in the alternative where there is factual uncertainty of the type described here so that the range of possibilities pleaded will cover what is revealed at trial to have occurred.

The rule about pleading alternative versions presumes that of five versions pleaded in the alternative, one will be factually correct. But go back to our example of a motor vehicle collision: What if it turns out that the car had malfunctioning brakes *and* the driver was talking on his cell phone and was not paying attention to the road. In this case, your pleading will catch the problem because you have covered both causes of the collision. However, if you suspect there is more than one cause but you are not sure which it is at the time of pleading, it is permissible to plead "the defendant failed to keep a proper lookout. *Further or in the alternative*, he failed to properly maintain his brakes so that they functioned properly."

No contradicting an allegation in a previous pleading: Rule 25.06(5)

Rule 25.06(5) identifies a situation where inconsistent or alternative pleading is not permitted. You may not in your reply to the statement of defence plead facts that contradict the facts in your statement of claim or raise a new cause of action. If you wish to do so, you must move to amend your earlier pleading to include the new cause of action or to amend the facts in your previous pleading so that the facts in the claim are consistent with those in the reply. If you were allowed to plead different versions of the facts in the claim and the reply, you can see what the problem would be for the defence. The defendants have no procedural vehicle to counter the contradictory allegation (there is no defendant's reply to a plaintiff's reply) nor do they know the case they have to meet, which is the prime purpose of pleadings. The purpose of a reply is not to permit the plaintiff to split her case, but to allow her to reply to issues raised in the statement of defence that were not covered in the claim.

At the same time, you do sometimes have to deal with a fact that is relevant but occurred after the statement of claim was issued. For example, if Abigail Boar recited her injuries as the basis for her damages in her claim, and then later more symptoms developed that indicated more serious injuries, she can get the new facts before the court. Rule 14.01(4) allows a party to rely on a fact that occurs after a proceeding commences, even though it is not specifically pleaded. However, the party relying on a new fact not connected to a fact previously pleaded should move to amend pleadings to include it. The purpose of this rule is to allow a party who has sustained damage to include damage discovered after pleadings where there is some relationship between the facts as pleaded and the facts as discovered later.

Pleading notice: Rule 25.06(6)

You can usually plead that notice was given by simply saying so: "The plaintiff gave the defendant notice to quit the premises." However, if the form of notice is material, you need to go into more detail. For example, if notice to a tenant to quit commercial premises must be given by registered mail, it is appropriate to plead it: "The plaintiff gave the defendant notice to quit the leased premises by giving notice in writing sent by registered mail to the defendant."

Pleading documents or conversations: Rule 25.06(7)

This rule echoes the requirement in rule 25.06(1) that pleadings be concise. If you are pleading the contents of a conversation, you need merely state the effect or purpose of a conversation or a document without repeating the precise conversation or document in its entirety. The exception to this rule occurs where the exact language is material; for example, in a libel action, in which case the precise wording should be set out and surrounded by quotation marks.

Pleading the nature of an act or a state of mind: Rule 25.06(8)

This rule states that where the intentional torts of fraud, misrepresentation, or breach of trust are pleaded, the full facts underlying these allegations must be pleaded with more particularity or detail than pleading usually requires. The second branch of the rule says that if you are pleading a mental element such as malice, intent, or acting knowingly, it is permissible to state that the party acted with malice, or acted knowingly, or with intent without explicitly connecting the relevant allegations to specific factual events. The reason for this is that there is rarely a smoking gun when an allegation of malice is made — that is, the allegedly malicious party is unlikely to say, "I am motivated by my malice to act in this way." Instead, malice must be inferred from surrounding circumstances, which may be pleaded in some detail, as noted above, as facts. It is then up to counsel, in his or her submissions at trial, to use the facts as pleaded to make the appropriate inferences and draw the appropriate conclusions.

Body of a statement of claim

The narrative part of Abigail Boar's claim begins at paragraph 5 and continues to the end of figure 7.2. Paragraphs 5 to 9 take you chronologically and sequentially through the events immediately leading up to the accident. They omit a lot from the original summary of Abigail's story as immaterial and irrelevant to the cause of action. It does not matter, for example, what Abigail's motivations were in deciding to buy the Super Coupe, nor whom she worked for, nor what her age was. These matters are not material to the issue of negligence.

At paragraph 10, we switch to describing Abigail's injuries and their effects. We provide the particulars of the damages, both general and special, that are described briefly in the claim for relief in paragraph 1. Paragraphs 10 to 11 describe the injuries themselves in a crisp matter-of-fact way, and paragraphs 12 to 15 describe the consequences for Abigail. The consequences are described chronologically in the sense that the earliest known consequences are described first, but information is also grouped by its effect on Abigail's lifestyle — an important factor in determining the extent of general damages. We do not connect specific injuries to special or general damages. That will be done in submissions later in the proceedings, although some lawyers do plead by identifying special and general damages. There is nothing wrong with that approach; it is simply a style preference. There is lots of room for good pleading in a variety of styles.

DRAFTING STATEMENTS OF DEFENCE

A statement of defence must follow the format prescribed by form 18A. It begins with the same general heading (the court file number, court name, and title of proceedings) as used in the statement of claim. It then sets out the title, "STATEMENT OF DEFENCE." Paragraph 1 sets out admissions of allegations in the statement of claim, paragraph 2 sets out denials of allegations in the statement of claim, and paragraph 3 sets out allegations in the claim of which the defendants have no knowledge. After that, defendants set out in consecutively numbered paragraphs each allegation on which they rely for their defence, containing their version of the facts. All of the general rules of pleading in rule 25.06 apply to drafting statements of defence. Also applicable are some specific rules in rule 25.07.

Pleading admissions: Rule 25.07(1)

The defendant must admit every allegation of fact in the statement of claim that he or she deems to be correct by admitting that the paragraph containing it is accurate. For example, Fred and Rattle Motors Ltd. will probably admit the allegations in paragraphs 2, 3, and 4 of Abigail Boar's statement of claim, set out in figure 7.2, because these paragraphs accurately describe the legal status of the parties. But they probably will not admit much else. Many of the allegations that they may admit are in paragraphs that have allegations that they will not admit because their admission would hamper the defence. For example, look at paragraph 8: "The Super Coupe model was in an open area of the showroom, where two of the four spotlights trained on the car were off, so that one side of the car was well illuminated, and the other was not well illuminated."

The defendants may wish to admit that the car was in an open area and that some of the lights were off. But they may hotly deny that the area was not well illuminated. They may allege, for example, that there was other perfectly adequate lighting. If so, their best bet is to deny the allegation in the paragraph altogether and plead their own version later in the statement of defence. This gives them more control as to how they present their defence in terms of both substance and content, and it prevents them from inadvertently admitting something while trying to admit part of a paragraph. Rule 25.02 asks that you confine each allegation to one paragraph so that a paragraph can be admitted if the allegation is true. But often, as in our case, a paragraph will contain an allegation that cannot be admitted in its entirety. In that case, deny it and proceed.

Figure 7.3 (at the end of the chapter) presents the joint statement of defence of Rattle Motors Ltd. and Fred Flogem. In it, Fred and Rattle Motors Ltd. admit Abigail's allegations in paragraph 1. We are assuming there is no conflict between the defendants on any issue.

Pleading denials and pleading "no knowledge": Rule 25.07(2)

If there are allegations that the defendant denies are true, he or she must deny the allegations by identifying the paragraph in the claim that contains them. Again, if some of the contents of the paragraph are to be admitted and some denied, then it is best to deny the whole paragraph and plead your version later in the defence. If you are silent on the allegations in a paragraph, they are deemed to be admitted. Each paragraph of the claim must be scrutinized carefully and critically. When in doubt, deny. Most lawyers follow this practice with the result that after (usually) admitting the paragraphs identifying the parties, they deny most, and often all, of the other paragraphs in the claim. You will note below that the defendants have neither admitted nor denied paragraph 1, the claim for relief, and paragraphs 5 and 6, which are non-controversial facts that may be omitted from the list of denials and can be admitted. It follows logically, and also according to the rule, that an allegation which is not denied or admitted is deemed to be admitted. But what happens when a defendant comes across an allegation that he or she cannot deny or admit because he knows nothing of it? In that case, it is permissible for the defendant to state that he or she has no knowledge of the allegation, in which case the plaintiff must prove it. It is not necessary for the defendant to deny the claim for relief if damages are claimed because damages are deemed to be in issue unless the defendant admits them (rule 27.07(6)).

Paragraph 2 of Fred and Rattle Motors Ltd.'s statement of defence, set out in figure 7.3, contains their denial of Abigail's allegations.

Different version of the facts must be pleaded: Rule 25.07(3)

It is not sufficient for the defendant merely to deny the plaintiff's version of the facts. If the defendant has a different view of the facts, he or she is obliged to set it out in consecutively numbered paragraphs after having dealt with admissions and denials in paragraphs 1 and 2 of the statement of defence.

This is an appropriate place to deal with paragraphs in the statement of claim where the defendant wishes to deny some and admit other allegations: "The defendants admit that some of the spotlights on the Super Coupe were not lit but deny that the area around the car was not well illuminated." The rule explicitly prohibits a bare denial without an explanation. Before the creation of this rule, you might have seen statements of defence which simply denied the plaintiff's allegations: "The defendants deny every allegation in the statement of claim and put the plaintiff to the strict proof of them." This rule eliminates that approach.

Plead affirmative defences: Rule 25.07(4)

If a defence is more than a denial of the legal basis for the plaintiff's claim — for instance, a denial by the defendants that they were negligent — it is necessary to set out further defences and the facts on which they rest. For example, Abigail did not mention that she had two glasses of wine before coming to the defendants' premises. But if the defendants know of it, they may want to plead contributory negligence specifically. In the alternative, they may want to claim that Abigail became the sole author of her own misfortunes when she voluntarily put herself into an intoxicated state and, for that reason, fell and injured herself. If the defendants take this route, they are introducing a new issue, with new facts to support their position on that issue. As we will see, the plaintiff is entitled to deal with it in her reply to the statement of defence.

Effect of denying the existence of an agreement: Rule 25.07(5)

Where an agreement is alleged in a statement of claim, a denial of it in the statement of defence is deemed to be no more than a denial of the making of the agreement or a denial of facts from which an agreement can be implied by law. It is not to be construed as a denial that the alleged agreement was legal or sufficient in law to have an effect. If the defendant wishes to deny the legality or legal sufficiency of an agreement, he or she must set out the particulars on which he or she relies. For example, if a defendant denies entering into a lease with a plaintiff, it is sufficient to deny that there is a lease between the parties. If, however, the defendant wishes to allege that the lease is invalid, he or she must state that the lease is invalid and give particulars — for example, it was not signed by the parties or a copy was not delivered to the defendant as required under its terms.

DRAFTING REPLIES

A reply to a statement of defence is necessary only when the defendant has pleaded a version of the facts or raised issues in the statement of defence that are different from the facts pleaded in the claim. A reply should be used in the following two situations:

1. Where a plaintiff contests the version of the facts as pleaded in the statement of defence, he or she should deliver a reply to the statement of defence, setting out his or her version of the facts unless this has been covered in the claim (rule 25.08(1)).

2. Where the defendant has raised a defence with which the statement of claim does not deal, the plaintiff should respond to this defence in the reply.

Other than in these two situations, no reply should be issued. If no reply is issued, the plaintiff is deemed to have denied the allegations in the statement of defence. In dealing with the version of facts set out in the defence, the plaintiff should admit any allegation of fact in the defence that is correct. If the defence alleges an agreement, the reply may deny it, in which case the denial is a denial of the making of an agreement or of the facts from which an agreement may be implied by law. It is not to be construed as a denial of the legality or legal sufficiency of the agreement (rule 25.09(2)). This must be pleaded specifically, as is the case under rule 25.07(5).

Figure 7.4 (at the end of the chapter) sets out Abigail Boar's reply to the statement of defence. You will notice in this example that the plaintiff does not bother to deny allegations she has already dealt with in the claim, but she denies those new allegations that allege intoxication, contributory negligence, exaggeration of damages, malingering, and failure to mitigate. None of these issues were raised in the claim, but having been raised in the defence, they must be answered if there is a version that the plaintiff wishes to advance — as is the case here, where Abigail states that her drinking did not contribute to her injuries. She also deals with the defendant's allegations about malingering, exaggerating her injuries, and failing to take steps to mitigate her damages. Remember that allegations in the reply cannot be inconsistent with or contradict statements in the claim. The defendant has to know which version of the facts the plaintiff is relying on. Where a reply is inconsistent with the claim, it is likely that the claim needs to be amended.

DEMAND FOR PARTICULARS

While a pleading must be a concise statement of material facts, it must not be so skimpy that it is impossible to respond to. While the modern version of the rules emphasizes the need to give full disclosure before trial to promote settlements, lawyers, for strategic reasons, often try to hold back as much information as possible. One of the ways of doing this is to plead enough to cover an issue without revealing important details. Those adopting this strategy hope that the lack of specificity will not be noticed and that the opponent can then be taken by surprise. This is a risky approach because a court may conclude that this kind of strategy amounts to trial by ambush. Penalties may await those who pursue this strategy. One should not assume that the other side is stupid. Other lawyers also know these strategies, and your opponent has a remedy when facing a pleading that is too general. Rule 25.10 permits a party to request particulars. If you receive such a request, you must supply the details requested. The initial request and the response to it may be by letter between law offices. But if the request is not answered within 10 days or if a party refuses to comply because he or she believes the request is unwarranted, the party making the request may ask the court on a notice of motion to order particulars. In considering the motion, the court asks itself whether the pleading is clear enough so that the opposite party can frame an answer to the issues raised and will not be surprised at trial. The additional information provided should constitute further detail of material facts, but not be so detailed as to amount to evidence.

Suppose Abigail had pleaded that as a result of her fall, she suffered "severe and catastrophic injuries that prevented her from working." This does not indicate what the injuries were or how they prevented Abigail from working, so the defendants cannot determine whether the damages claimed have any basis in fact. The defendants might then write to I.M. Just and ask him to provide details. They will likely be interested in knowing what specific injuries she sustained, the treatment for those injuries, the specific activities that the injuries prevent her from engaging in, the prognosis, her attempt to mitigate her damages, and whether she attempted to return to work.

STRIKING OUT PLEADINGS

Occasionally a pleading is so defective in failing to follow rule 25 that, on a motion by the other side, the court may strike out all or part of the pleading (rule 25.11). Usually the court gives leave to amend the pleading, but on occasion it strikes out a wholly unmeritorious pleading without leave to amend, in which case plaintiffs may have their claim dismissed or defendants may have judgment signed against them.

There are three general grounds for the court to strike all or part of a pleading or other document under rule 25.11:

- the contents of the pleading "may prejudice or delay the fair trial of an action";

- the contents are "scandalous, frivolous or vexatious"; and

- the contents constitute an "abuse of the process of the court."

A pleading may be defective because it violates all or one of these grounds. Generally, allegations that cannot be proven are deemed to be prejudicial because the opponent is being asked to respond to allegations or issues on which no proof can or will be offered. For example, if Abigail pleads the contents of documents that are not admissible in court, she cannot prove the allegations because she cannot present admissible evidence on them.[2] Therefore, the defendants should not have to respond to those allegations: it would not be fair, and that is what "prejudicial" really means. Similarly, allegations that stray well beyond the issue involved in the lawsuit may simply lengthen the pretrial and trial without being relevant to the matter being decided. A barrage of allegations only tenuously connected may be deemed to be improperly delaying proceedings if the issue being litigated involves only one allegation in the barrage of allegations.

A pleading is scandalous, frivolous, or vexatious when a fact is set out that could be proved but that would not be allowed to be proved. For example, if Fred and Rattle Motors Ltd. wanted to undermine Abigail's credibility by showing her to be a person of low character, they might make various allegations about her general dishonesty. If these allegations are not relevant to the issues raised in the proceeding, then while they may be true and could be proved, they would likely not be allowed to be proved. This is not because they are scandalous[3] or shocking in the ordinary sense, but because they are irrelevant and immaterial to the issues being tried and are introduced solely to add "atmosphere." Some courts have asked whether the allegation can have any effect on the outcome. If not, it is probably scandalous, frivolous, or vexatious. If the issue in the lawsuit concerned Abigail's allegedly fraudulent behaviour, allegations about her general honesty, no matter how embarrassing or scandalous in the ordinary sense, are relevant and ought not to be struck out.

Any of the "bad" pleading behaviour described in the preceding paragraphs may also constitute an abuse of process, particularly when it is done knowingly or intentionally.

Where a pleading is attacked on an issue that goes to the court's jurisdiction or otherwise might lead to a final order disposing of the case in its entirety — either through dismissal of the action, or granting of judgment on the motion to strike a pleading — the motion should be brought before a judge, not a master. Masters have the jurisdiction to deal with procedural matters, but they do not usually have the power to make orders that finally dispose of the rights of the parties.

CHAPTER SUMMARY

In this chapter, you were introduced to the rules and conventions governing the drafting of claims, defences, and replies. We examined some of the steps that must be taken to organize material and information, develop a theory of the case, prepare outlines, and use sample precedents before drafting the document. When drafting you should try to use simple language that is clear and direct.

We then examined specific rules in rule 25, which governs all pleadings, as well as specific rules governing defences and replies. We illustrated how these rules work by setting out a claim, defence, and reply in Abigail Boar's case. Finally, we looked at what may be done if pleadings are inadequate, examining demands for particulars as well as motions to strike out pleadings that are manifestly defective.

KEY TERMS

boilerplate

general damages

special damages

NOTES

1   Form 14A is the generic version of a statement of claim. The subsequent versions of form 14 deal with various specialized types of claims.

2   *F. (M.) v. Sutherland* (July 5, 2000), doc. CA C32601 (Ont. CA).

3   Some cases use the word "embarrassing" in the same way that the word "scandalous" is used. The words have roughly the same meaning: immaterial, irrelevant, and introduced to create an atmosphere so as to make the other side look bad. Similarly, the terms "scandalous," "frivolous," and "vexatious" tend to be used synonymously in cases.

REFERENCES

Courts of Justice Act, RSO 1990, c. C.43.

F. (M.) v. Sutherland (July 5, 2000), doc. CA C32601 (Ont. CA).

Occupiers' Liability Act, RSO 1990, c. O.2.

Rules of Civil Procedure, RRO 1990, reg. 194.

REVIEW QUESTIONS

1. Edward Egregious, I.M. Just's law clerk, has just interviewed a client and intends to transcribe his notes into a statement of claim and issue it. Have you any advice for him?

2. Can Edward claim $15,000 for costs in the space provided on the boilerplate for costs?

3. Edward thinks that paragraphs in a pleading should be lengthy and detailed. Is he correct?

4. Edward wants to know the order in which you present information in the claim. Tell him what that order is.

5. In the following paragraphs, indicate which parts are material facts and which parts are evidence.

   a. The plaintiff states that the area was not properly lit. A lighting expert who examined the site confirmed this.

   b. The plaintiff states that the area was not properly illuminated. The defendant admitted this to the plaintiff at the time of the accident.

c. The standard of care exercised by the defendant was well below the standard followed by other engineers. One engineer referred to the standard as "antique," claiming no one she knew used it.

d. The defendant drove her car down Mill Lane at an excessive rate of speed for the road conditions. The speed was in excess of the stated speed limit.

e. In borrowing from the plaintiff, the defendant failed to disclose that he was about to be petitioned into bankruptcy. The defendant knew this because he had had a letter from another creditor advising him that he would be petitioned into bankruptcy if he did not pay what was owing.

6. In drafting Abigail's claim, suppose Edward set out the facts leading to Abigail's fall, the damages sustained, and then followed with a statement that the defendant Fred was negligent and caused harm to the plaintiff, for which the corporate defendant is legally responsible. How would you advise him in improving his efforts?

7. Suppose Elizabeth Egret placed an order to buy some Framitses. The contract requires a 10 percent deposit before Egmont Pigeon will ship the goods. In her claim for delivery of the goods, Elizabeth states that she demanded delivery in accordance with the terms of the contract but that the defendant neglected or refused to deliver the goods. Is that a sufficient statement of her right to delivery?

8. Edward wants to plead that Fred was negligent in turning off the spotlights or in the alternative that he did it knowingly or with reckless intent. Can he do this?

9. Is it permissible for Edward to plead negligence in the claim and to state in the reply to the statement of defence that the defendants conspired to injure Abigail intentionally?

10. If Abigail has a claim that rests on the contents of a 10-page contract, does she need to quote the whole contract in the statement of claim?

11. If Abigail wants to claim that Fred attempted to defraud her, is it sufficient for her to state that Fred acted fraudulently?

12. If Abigail commences the proceeding in Brampton but wishes to have it tried in Toronto, what does she do?

13. Fiona Flapdoodle must prepare the defendant's statement of defence. She wants to know what she needs to include and in what order.

14. If a defendant wishes to deny that he or she entered into an agreement, how does the defendant do it?

15. When should a reply be delivered?

16. In what situations should you demand particulars?

17. When might a lawyer move to strike all or part of a pleading?

DISCUSSION QUESTIONS

1. Sarah Jacobs, her husband Jack Jacobs, and her 15-year-old daughter Mary kept their boat at Tom's Marina near their cottage. Since summer was approaching, they wanted to arrange to get their boat ready for the season. The Jacobs went to Tom Shanks's marina on May 24, 1999. When the Jacobs arrived at the marina, Tom Shanks, the owner and sole proprietor, was not there, but his long-time employee Kevin Coaster was in the main office. Kevin said that he would take them down the dock to their boat. He knew a shortcut along a dock at the side of the marina office. The Jacobs followed Kevin. As they were walking along the dock, several planks gave way because they were rotten. Sarah fell against a support beam, hitting the lower part of her face and then her arm as she fell backwards into the water. Mary injured her ribs when she also fell against the support beam. The Jacobs have come to your law firm. They want to sue for their injuries. Draft a statement of claim.

2. Your law firm is acting for Tom Shanks. He is very annoyed with Kevin Coaster since he had told Kevin repeatedly that Kevin was not to take the shortcut because the dock is a mess and there are a lot of rotten boards. He also says Kevin was not supposed to be at work that day and that the marina was to be shut and locked until he arrived later. Tom wants you to draft his defence.

FIGURE 7.1   STATEMENT OF CLAIM (GENERAL) (FORM 14A)

[General Heading]

STATEMENT OF CLAIM

TO THE DEFENDANT

A LEGAL PROCEEDING HAS BEEN COMMENCED AGAINST YOU by the plaintiff. The claim made against you is set out in the following pages.

IF YOU WISH TO DEFEND THIS PROCEEDING, you or an Ontario lawyer acting for you must prepare a statement of defence in Form 18A prescribed by the Rules of Civil Procedure, serve it on the plaintiff's lawyer or, where the plaintiff does not have a lawyer, serve it on the plaintiff, and file it, with proof of service in this court office, WITHIN TWENTY DAYS after this statement of claim is served on you, if you are served in Ontario.

If you are served in another province or territory of Canada or in the United States of America, the period for serving and filing your statement of defence is forty days. If you are served outside Canada and the United States of America, the period is sixty days.

Instead of serving and filing a statement of defence, you may serve and file a notice of intent to defend in Form 18B prescribed by the Rules of Civil Procedure. This will entitle you to ten more days within which to serve and file your statement of defence.

IF YOU FAIL TO DEFEND THIS PROCEEDING, JUDGMENT MAY BE GIVEN AGAINST YOU IN YOUR ABSENCE AND WITHOUT FURTHER NOTICE TO YOU. IF YOU WISH TO DEFEND THIS PROCEEDING BUT ARE UNABLE TO PAY LEGAL FEES, LEGAL AID MAY BE AVAILABLE TO YOU BY CONTACTING A LOCAL LEGAL AID OFFICE.

(Where the claim made is for money only, include the following:)

IF YOU PAY THE PLAINTIFF'S CLAIM, and $_____ for costs, within the time for serving and filing your statement of defence, you may move to have this proceeding dismissed by the court. If you believe the amount claimed for costs is excessive, you may pay the plaintiff's claim and $500.00 for costs and have the costs assessed by the court.

Date: _____ Issued by: _____

Address of
court office: _____
_____

TO: *(Name and address of each defendant)*

FIGURE 7.2 STATEMENT OF CLAIM OF ABIGAIL BOAR (FORM 14A)

Court file no.

ONTARIO
SUPERIOR COURT OF JUSTICE

BETWEEN:

ABIGAIL BOAR

Plaintiff

and

RATTLE MOTORS LTD. and FRED FLOGEM

Defendants

STATEMENT OF CLAIM

TO THE DEFENDANTS

A LEGAL PROCEEDING HAS BEEN COMMENCED AGAINST YOU by the plaintiff. The claim made against you is set out in the following pages.

IF YOU WISH TO DEFEND THIS PROCEEDING, you or an Ontario lawyer acting for you must prepare a statement of defence in Form 18A prescribed by the Rules of Civil Procedure, serve it on the plaintiff's lawyer or, where the plaintiff does not have a lawyer, serve it on the plaintiff, and file it, with proof of service, in this court office, WITHIN TWENTY DAYS after this statement of claim is served on you, if you are served in Ontario.

If you are served in another province or territory of Canada or in the United States of America, the period for serving and filing your statement of defence is forty days. If you are served outside Canada and the United States of America, the period is sixty days.

Instead of serving and filing a statement of defence, you may serve and file a notice of intent to defend in Form 18B prescribed by the Rules of Civil Procedure. This will entitle you to ten more days within which to serve and file your statement of defence.

IF YOU FAIL TO DEFEND THIS PROCEEDING, JUDGMENT MAY BE GIVEN AGAINST YOU IN YOUR ABSENCE AND WITHOUT FURTHER NOTICE TO YOU. IF YOU WISH TO DEFEND THIS PROCEEDING BUT ARE UNABLE TO PAY LEGAL FEES, LEGAL AID MAY BE AVAILABLE TO YOU BY CONTACTING A LOCAL LEGAL AID OFFICE.

IF YOU PAY THE PLAINTIFF'S CLAIM, and $500.00 for costs, within the time for serving and filing your statement of defence, you may move to have this proceeding dismissed by the court. If you believe the amount claimed for costs is excessive, you may pay the plaintiff's claim and $400.00 for costs and have the costs assessed by the court.

FIGURE 7.2   CONTINUED

Date: January 4, year 1

Issued by: _____

Address of
court office: Court House
393 University Avenue
Toronto, Ontario, M5G 1E6

TO:

Rattle Motors Ltd.
1240 Bay Street
Toronto, Ontario, M8H 0K8

AND TO:

Fred Flogem
21 Cypress Boulevard
Scarborough, Ontario, M8Q 1P3

CLAIM

1. The plaintiff claims, against both defendants:
   a. general damages in the amount of $200,000;
   b. special damages in the amount of $3,649 to the date
   of this pleading. The full extent of special damages is
   not yet known, but full particulars will be furnished
   before the date of trial.
   c. prejudgment interest from September 14, year 0 to the
   date of payment or judgment pursuant to the *Courts of
   Justice Act*, RSO 1990, c. C.43;
   d. postjudgment interest from the date of judgment to
   the date of payment pursuant to the *Courts of Justice
   Act*, RSO 1990, c. C.43;
   e. costs of this action; and
   f. such further relief as seems just to this court.
2. The plaintiff is an individual who resides in the City
   of Toronto, in the Province of Ontario, and at the
   relevant time was a customer lawfully on the premises of
   the corporate defendant.
3. The defendant Fred Flogem is an individual who resides
   in the City of Toronto, in the Province of Ontario, and
   at the relevant time was an employee of the corporate
   defendant.
4. The defendant Rattle Motors Ltd. is a business
   corporation, incorporated under the laws of Ontario with
   business premises in the City of Toronto, in the
   Province of Ontario.
5. On September 14, year 0, at about 7:30 p.m., the
   plaintiff entered the retail automobile premises owned
   and operated by the defendant Rattle Motors Ltd. at 1240
   Bay Street, in the City of Toronto, in the Province of
   Ontario, in order to view a Super Coupe, which she was
   thinking of purchasing, in the showroom.

FIGURE 7.2   CONTINUED

6. She was met at the door by Linda Lucre, a salesperson employed by the corporate defendant, who showed her some of the automobiles displayed on the showroom floor.

7. The plaintiff saw a Super Coupe model on the showroom floor and walked over to have a better look at it.

8. The Super Coupe model was in an open area of the showroom, where two of the four spotlights trained on the car were off, so that one side of the car was well illuminated while the other was not well illuminated.

9. The plaintiff walked around to the side of the car near the wall, which was in relative darkness. She walked onto a part of the floor that was covered with oil. Because of the restricted lighting, she did not see the oil, slipped on it, lost her footing, and fell.

10. As a result of the fall, she struck her head, suffered a concussion, and lost consciousness. She also fractured her right wrist and several bones in her right arm.

11. Following the fall, the plaintiff was hospitalized for 4 days and the plaintiff's arm was in a cast for 6 weeks; she suffered much pain and discomfort. In addition, she was required to attend for physiotherapy for 10 weeks after her cast was removed.

12. As a result of these injuries, the plaintiff suffers from pain in her arm and head as well as chronic lower back pain, and is unable to walk long distances or sit at a desk for long periods. She has limited mobility in her right arm and is unable to work at a computer keyboard for more than 10 minutes without experiencing pain. The plaintiff is right-handed and severely disadvantaged by these injuries.

13. Since she sustained these injuries, and as a result of them, the plaintiff has become far less active physically than she had been before the accident, and she is far less cheerful and gregarious than she had been. She is now quieter, more withdrawn, and has difficulty sleeping. She also suffers from depression. Before being injured, the plaintiff was an avid tennis player and a competent amateur violinist. Since sustaining the injuries, and as a result of them, she is unable to engage in either activity. She also has suffered some memory loss. In particular, she has no memory of sustaining the injuries complained of.

14. Since the plaintiff sustained these injuries, she has been unable to return to her work as a securities analyst. She returned to work for the month of March, year 1, but because of chronic pain, and difficulty using a computer which is essential to her work, she was unable to continue. She has been off work since April 1, year 1, and on long-term disability, where she remains at the time of pleading.

15. The plaintiff has suffered catastrophic and permanent injuries, and it is unlikely that she will ever be able to return to work as a securities analyst. At the time

FIGURE 7.2   CONTINUED

of injury, she earned $80,000 per year in this occupation. She would likely have had a lengthy career with a high level of income, had she not been injured.

16. The defendant Fred Flogem, a salesperson employed by the corporate defendant, caused the plaintiff's injuries through his negligence, for which the corporate defendant is at law responsible. The particulars of negligence are as follows:

    a. He was aware that there was oil on the floor and knew or ought to have known that the oil constituted a danger to the safety of persons such as the plaintiff.

    b. He knew or ought to have known that he had a duty to see that persons such as the plaintiff did not come to harm while on the premises.

    c. He failed to clean up or remove the spill expeditiously, although he had the opportunity and the means to do so.

    d. He turned off lighting that illuminated the area where the plaintiff fell, with the intention of making the oil spill less visible or noticeable to persons such as the plaintiff. By so doing, he negligently, or in the alternative knowingly, created a situation of danger for the plaintiff.

    e. He knowingly created a situation of danger for the plaintiff by deliberately not taking steps to clean up the spill so as to hide a defect in the automobile from the plaintiff and other customers.

17. The defendant Flogem was an employee of the corporate defendant, for whose acts of negligence the corporate defendant is vicariously liable.

18. The corporate defendant is also directly responsible for the injuries sustained by the plaintiff as a result of its negligence, the particulars of which are as follows:

    a. It failed to take such care as was reasonable to see that the plaintiff entering the corporate defendant's showroom would be reasonably safe while on the property. The plaintiff pleads and relies on the *Occupier's Liability Act,* RSO 1990, c. O.2.

    b. It failed to instruct its employees, including the individual defendant, in maintaining safe premises.

    c. It knew or ought to have known that the floor area where the plaintiff fell was unsafe for the plaintiff.

    d. It failed to maintain a system of inspection to ensure that the showroom was safe for persons on the premises, including the plaintiff.

    e. In the alternative, it knowingly permitted the area where the plaintiff fell to remain in an unsafe condition so as not to attract customer attention to a defect in the car it was selling.

FIGURE 7.2   CONCLUDED

Date of issue: January 4, year 1

Just & Coping
Barristers and Solicitors
365 Bay Street - 8701
Toronto, Ontario M3J 4A9

I.M. Just
LSUC #12345R
tel. 416-762-1342
fax 416-762-2300

Lawyers for the Plaintiff

FIGURE 7.3 STATEMENT OF DEFENCE (FORM 18A)

Court file no. 01-CV-1234

ONTARIO
SUPERIOR COURT OF JUSTICE

BETWEEN:

ABIGAIL BOAR

Plaintiff

and

RATTLE MOTORS LTD. and FRED FLOGEM

Defendants

STATEMENT OF DEFENCE

1. The defendants admit the allegations contained in paragraphs 2, 3, 4, 5, and 6 of the statement of claim. ✓

2. The defendants deny the allegations contained in paragraphs 7, 8, 9, 10, 11, 12, 13, 14, 15, 16, and 17 of the statement of claim.

3. The plaintiff entered the corporate defendant's premises at about 7:30 p.m. on September 14, year 0. She indicated to Linda Lucre, a salesperson on the showroom floor at that time, that she was interested in purchasing a Super Coupe.

4. Lucre showed the plaintiff several automobile models. Then the plaintiff walked over, on her own, to look at another model. She walked around the car and fell.

5. The defendants admit that there was a small pool of oil on one side of the car but claim that it was easily visible to any reasonably prudent person who could have avoided it without difficulty.

   [handwritten: ADMIT SNOW ON ROOF BUT CLAIM EASILY VISIBLE]

6. The defendants admit that two of the four spotlights were off but deny that the area was not well illuminated. The defendants state that the area was well and clearly illuminated. Any hazard, if there was one, which is specifically denied, could easily be seen and avoided.

7. The defendants admit that the plaintiff fell and appeared to lose consciousness momentarily. She also appeared to injure her lower right arm in the fall.

8. The defendants state that the plaintiff, before coming to the corporate defendant's place of business, had consumed two glasses of wine and that she was intoxicated when she entered the defendant's premises.

   [handwritten: PLAINTIFF DRANK EARLIER THAT MORNING]

9. The plaintiff fell solely as a result of her intoxication. Any injuries she sustained were solely the result of her own intoxicated state and not the result of any acts of the defendants.

   [handwritten: USE THIS PHRASE?]

10. With respect to paragraphs 10, 11, 12, 13, 14, and 15 of the statement of claim, the defendants deny that the plaintiff suffered such injuries as described. Further

FIGURE 7.3 CONCLUDED

or in the alternative, the defendants state that the plaintiff has exaggerated both the extent of her injuries and the consequences of them.

11. With respect to the plaintiff's allegation that she cannot return to work, the defendants state that the plaintiff is exaggerating her injuries and that she is a malingerer. In the alternative, the defendants state that the plaintiff has failed to mitigate her damages.

12. With respect to the allegations of negligence in paragraph 16, the defendant Flogem states that he knew there was oil on the floor but that it was contained and did not constitute a danger to any reasonably prudent person. The defendant Flogem admits that he turned off two of the four spotlights, but he specifically denies that he created a situation of danger for the plaintiff because the area in question remained well illuminated and safe for a reasonably prudent person.

13. The defendants therefore request that this action be dismissed with costs.

Date: January 12, year 1

Huey Sue
LSUC #23456T
Barrister and Solicitor
65 False Trail
Toronto, Ontario M6Y 1Z6

tel. 416-485-6891
fax 416-485-6892

Lawyer for the Defendants

TO:
Just & Coping
Barristers and Solicitors
365 Bay Street – 8701
Toronto, Ontario M3J 4A9

I.M. Just
LSUC #12345R
tel. 416-762-1342
fax 416-762-2300

Lawyers for the Plaintiff

FIGURE 7.4   REPLY TO STATEMENT OF DEFENCE

Court file no. 01-CV-1234

ONTARIO
SUPERIOR COURT OF JUSTICE

BETWEEN:

ABIGAIL BOAR

Plaintiff

and

RATTLE MOTORS LTD. and FRED FLOGEM

Defendants

REPLY

1. The plaintiff admits to the allegations in paragraphs 1, 3, and 4 of the statement of defence.
2. The plaintiff denies the allegations in paragraphs 2, 5, 6, 7, 8, 9, 10, 11, 12, and 13 of the statement of defence.
3. The plaintiff admits that she had two glasses of wine at dinner, well before she entered the corporate defendant's premises, and she denies that she was intoxicated. She neither contributed to nor solely caused her fall and subsequent injuries.
4. The plaintiff states that she has made every effort to fully regain the good health she enjoyed before being injured, following medical advice and undertaking therapy and treatment as advised. Further, she was eager to return to work and did so for a period of one month but was unable to carry out her duties, which required extensive use of a computer, solely because of her injuries. The plaintiff specifically denies that she has exaggerated the extent and consequences of her injuries and denies that she has been malingering or has failed to mitigate her damages.

Date: February 2, year 1

Just & Coping
Barristers and Solicitors
365 Bay Street - 8701
Toronto, Ontario M3J 4A9

I.M. Just
LSUC #12345R
tel. 416-762-1342
fax 416-762-2300

Lawyers for the Plaintiff

TO:

Huey Sue
LSUC #23456T
Barrister and Solicitor
65 False Trail
Toronto, Ontario M6Y 1Z6

tel. 416-485-6891
fax 416-485-6892

Lawyer for the Defendants

CHAPTER 8

Service of court documents

INTRODUCTION

Once the initiating documents have been prepared, Abigail, as plaintiff, must let the court know that she wants to begin a court case, and she must let the defendants know about the details of the case that she is bringing against them. The process in which the plaintiff lets the court know about the case is called "issuing." We looked at issuing documents in chapter 6. The process in which she gives a copy of her pleadings or documents to the defendants is called "**service**."

As soon as the defendants know about Abigail's case against them, they will have a chance to prepare their defence to the allegations that Abigail is making. The defendants must give Abigail a copy of any documents they prepare in the case. (All the documents that are prepared in a court proceeding must be given to the other side.) It is through service of the documents that the parties exchange formal information about the court case. When service of the documents has been completed according to the rules, we say that service has been "effected."

Not only must the defendants know the details of the case that is brought against them, the court must also be satisfied that each side has provided the other side with their pleadings. Therefore, when pleadings are served, an additional document, proving service according to the rules, must be filed in the court along with the documents. This process is called providing "proof of service." Service is proven by way of affidavit. The person who served the document must, in writing, provide the details of how the document was served and swear that the details are true. The affidavit is called an affidavit of service, which appears as form 16B. If service is performed by the Sheriff's Office, the sheriff's officer provides a certificate of service by sheriff, form 16C.

Rule 16 tells you how documents are to be served within Ontario. Rule 17 tells you how they are to be served if the other party is not in the Province of Ontario. Rule 4.05 tells you how documents are to be issued and filed in the court.

Although all documents in the court proceeding must be served on the other side, the rules require different methods of serving the document depending on the type of document. If a document is an originating process, it must be served in a different manner than other pleadings.

service
process by which documents are brought to the attention of a party in accordance with the rules or a court order

SERVICE OF AN ORIGINATING PROCESS

originating process
first document in a
lawsuit that tells parties
that they are being sued

A document that is an **originating process** must be served either personally or by an alternative to personal service (rule 16.01(1)). If you are not certain whether the document with which you are working is an originating process, you must look at the definition of originating process in rule 1.03. If a pleading is an originating process, it will be listed there. Any document not listed there is not an originating process and therefore does not need to be served using personal service or an alternative to personal service.

Personal service

According to rule 16.02(1)(a), personal service on an individual can be made by leaving a copy of the document with the person that you wish to serve. But if the individual is a person under a disability, there are special provisions as to how they are to be served personally (rule 16.02(1)(j) and (k)). For instance, if a party is a minor, the document is served on the minor's litigation guardian or, if there is no litigation guardian, on the minor *and* a parent who has custody of the child. Leaving the document with either the parent or the litigation guardian of the minor qualifies as personal service on the minor.

There are also specific provisions in rule 16.02 governing personal service on a corporation, a municipality, a partnership, a sole proprietorship, and other entities. When you are serving a document that requires personal service under the rules and the party is not a competent adult individual, refer to rule 16.02 to determine the manner in which you are required to serve your document.

Service by way of alternative service

If an originating process is not specifically required by the rules to be served personally, it can be served by means of an alternative to personal service. When a rule says a particular document can be served either personally or by an alternative to personal service and you decide to serve it by an alternative to personal service, you must look at rule 16.03, which lists the only alternatives to personal service permitted by the rules. There are three general alternatives to personal service and a fourth special provision for alternative service that relates only to corporations in Rule 16.03.

1. *Acceptance of service by a lawyer: Rule 16.03(2).* If the party to the proceeding has a lawyer, you may serve the lawyer with the document. However, this type of alternative to personal service is valid only if the lawyer agrees to accept the service on behalf of his or her client and signs a copy of the document acknowledging that he or she has accepted service. Most lawyers are not willing to do this unless they have specific permission from their client because by accepting service for their client, they are representing to the court that they have the authority to do so.

2. *Service by mail to the last-known address: Rule 16.03(4).* Service by mail is an effective alternative to personal service only if the person who is being served signs and returns the acknowledgment of receipt card, form 16A, which is sent along with the document that is being served. Form 16A appears in the exhibit attached to figure 8.5. If the party fails to return the card,

service is not valid.[1] Do not use this method unless you know beforehand that the party you are serving is cooperative and will return the card.

3. *Service at place of residence: Rule 16.03(5).* You may use this alternative method of service only if you have attempted, at least once, to serve the document personally. Then you may leave the document, in a sealed envelope, at the residence with a person who appears to be an adult. However, the same day or the day after you leave the document with someone at the residence, you must also send another copy of the document by mail to the person to be served.

4. *Service on a corporation: Rule 16.03(6).* This rule applies only when you wish to serve a corporation by an alternative to personal service. You may use this alternative method only after you have tried to effect personal service on the corporation and you find that the corporation is not at its last address registered with the Ministry of Government and Consumer Services, Companies and Personal Property Security Branch. In that case, you may mail the document to the last registered address. It is quite possible that the corporation will not receive the document. However, because a corporation is required by statute to keep its records with the ministry up to date, the corporation's own failure to comply with legal requirements is the cause of this situation.

For example, if Abigail Boar tried to serve Rattle Motors Ltd. and found that it was no longer at its last-known address, her lawyer's clerk would do a search for the corporation's records with the Ministry of Government and Consumer Services. If the corporation had registered a new address with the ministry, Abigail would need to effect service at the new address. However, if Rattle Motors Ltd. had failed to notify the ministry of its new address, Abigail's lawyer could simply have mailed the documents to that address and service would have been effected in accordance with the rules.

DOCUMENTS THAT CAN BE SERVED ON A PARTY'S LAWYER OF RECORD

Although a document that is an originating process can only be served personally or by an alternative to personal service, there is an additional service option available for a document that is not an originating process. A document that is not an originating process can usually be served on a lawyer of record for the party. This means that there are three options for the service of a document that is not an originating process:

1. it can be served personally,

2. it can be served by an alternative to personal service listed in the rules, or

3. it can be served on a party's lawyer of record.

Service can only be on a lawyer of record, not on a lawyer that the party may have consulted or retained in the past for a case. A lawyer becomes a lawyer of record only if he or she has either filed documents in a particular proceeding on behalf of the party or if he or she has appeared in court in this proceeding for the party.

Rule 16.05(1)(a) to (f) sets out how a lawyer of record may be served with documents that would otherwise require personal service or an alternative to personal service. These methods are:

- mailing a copy of the document to the lawyer's office,

- leaving a copy of the document with the lawyer or an employee in the lawyer's office,

- faxing a copy to the lawyer's office,

- e-mailing a copy of the document to the lawyer's office,

- sending a copy to the lawyer's office by courier, or

- depositing a copy of the document at a document exchange of which the lawyer is a member.

Service by fax on a lawyer of record

If you serve a lawyer of record by fax, there are special conditions under rule 16.05 to make this method of service effective.

- You must attach a cover page that includes all of the information required in rule 16.05(3).

- If a document is longer than 16 pages, you may serve it by fax only between 4 p.m. and 8 a.m. unless the party gives prior consent for you to serve it during another time period (rule 16.05(3.1)).

- If you serve by fax between 4 p.m. and midnight, service is not effective until the next day (rule 16.05(1)(d)).

- You may not serve a motion record, application record, trial record, appeal book, compendium, or book of authorities by fax unless the party being served gives prior permission for you to do so (rule 16.05(3.2)).

Service by e-mail on a lawyer of record

To effect valid service on a lawyer of record by e-mail under rule 16.05(1)(f), the following conditions must be met:

- The message to which the court document is attached must contain all the information required by rule 16.05(4), including the name of the person transmitting the message and his or her address, telephone number, fax number, and e-mail address; the date and time of the message; and the name and telephone number of a contact should there be transmission problems.

- The lawyer of record who is being served provides an e-mail response saying that he or she is accepting service and giving the date of the acceptance.

- If the e-mail acceptance of service by the lawyer of record is received between 4 p.m. and midnight, service is deemed to have occurred the next day.

Service on a lawyer of record by courier

Since someone must sign for a courier delivery, there is an independent record of receipt of the document in the lawyer of record's office, but it is important to note that service is effective on the second day following the day the courier was given the document to serve unless the second day is a holiday. In this case, service is deemed to have occurred in the next day that is not a holiday (rule 16.05(2.1)).

Service on a lawyer of record through a document exchange

A document exchange is a centralized service that has been formally set up by lawyers to send and receive court documents. At one time it was a common method of serving documents, but with service by fax and e-mail now permitted, these exchanges are not as widely used as they once were. Many law firms still use them, however. For service on a lawyer of record through a document exchange to be valid, the lawyer of record must be a member of that document exchange, and a copy of the document being served must be date stamped by the document exchange in front of the person who is depositing the copy for service (rule 16.05(1)(c)). Service then becomes effective on the first day that is not a holiday after the document has been deposited and date stamped.

SUBSTITUTED SERVICE AND DISPENSING WITH SERVICE

Sometimes it is extremely difficult to effect service according to the rules. It may be that parties cannot be located despite the best of efforts, or it may be that parties are doing everything they can to avoid service. The fact that you have not been able to serve the opposite side does not mean that you cannot proceed with a lawsuit. If every effort has been made to serve a party and service has not been possible, the lawyer for the party trying to serve the documents may bring a motion for an order for substituted service or for an order dispensing with service.

A party that obtains an order dispensing with service has the court's permission to proceed with its case without serving the other side. It is only in the most exceptional circumstances that a party is granted an order dispensing with service. The reason is that the other side would have no notice of the party's court proceeding and therefore no opportunity to answer the allegations made against it.

However, an order for substituted service is relatively common in litigation. Such an order permits a party to use a method of service not prescribed by the rules. When the court makes an order for substituted service, it will also make an order specifying exactly what method of service may be substituted for the method required by the rules. Often this means that the party requesting substituted service may place a notice in a newspaper or serve by ordinary mail. An order for substituted service specifies when the service becomes effective (rule 16.04(2)). For example, the order might say service is effective on the 10th day following the publishing of the notice in the newspaper.

PROOF OF SERVICE

Once you have served the document according to the rules, you must prepare another document that proves to the court that you have served your document on the other parties. The court requires this proof because if parties fail to file documents or to appear in court, if it can be proven that they had proper service of all relevant documents, the court will be prepared to make a decision about the case in their absence. The court does not accept any document for filing unless you file proof of service at the same time.

There are three methods of proving service:

1. affidavit of service,

2. certificate of service by the Sheriff, or

3. proof of acceptance or admitting of service by the other side.

Affidavit of service

Documents are usually served by a person hired specifically to effect service or by a member of the law firm, usually the law clerk dealing with the file. The server must provide evidence to the court that the party whom they served was served according to the rules. The server does this by way of an affidavit of service. An affidavit is a document sworn under oath or affirmed that can constitute evidence in a court proceeding. The person who serves the document must give details of the steps he or she took to effect service.

An affidavit of service is set out in form 16B. Figures 8.1 to 8.5 provide precedents for affidavits of service in various circumstances. The affidavit of service need not be a separate document. Many law offices use a stamp that is put on the backsheet of the copy of the document that is to be filed with the court. When documents must be served in a hurry, these stamps are often used. The stamp is completed when the document is served, and it can be signed and commissioned at the court office.

Certificate of service by sheriff

sheriff
official appointed by the provincial government to assist in various court-related functions, such as the enforcement of orders and judgments

Each judicial area in the province has a **sheriff**. He or she is a judicial official who is appointed under the *Public Service Act* and who has certain duties involving the courts and the judicial system. Each sheriff has numerous people who work under his or her supervision.

At one time, one of the duties of the sheriff was to serve court documents. The party serving the document would be charged a fee to have a sheriff's officer go out and serve the documents. Now the sheriff's duties have been changed, and sheriffs only serve documents involving the enforcement of judgments and orders. This means that if you have documents that involve enforcement — for example, a writ of seizure and sale or a garnishment — you may either have them served by a private process server or have them served by the sheriff.

When the document is served through the sheriff's office, the sheriff's officer prepares a certificate of service by sheriff. This precedent is form 16C, which appears as figure 8.6. It contains much of the same information that an affidavit of service contains. All the details concerning the steps taken to effect service are included in

FIGURE 8.1 AFFIDAVIT OF SERVICE BY LEAVING COPY WITH ADULT AT RESIDENCE (FORM 16B)

Court file no. 01-CV-1234

ONTARIO
SUPERIOR COURT OF JUSTICE

BETWEEN:

ABIGAIL BOAR

Plaintiff

and

RATTLE MOTORS LTD. and FRED FLOGEM

Defendants

AFFIDAVIT OF SERVICE

I, Joe Splitz, **of the** City of Toronto, **in the** Province of Ontario,
MAKE OATH AND SAY:

1. I am the process server for the law firm of Just &
   Coping, Barristers and Solicitors, and as such have
   knowledge of the matters to which I herein depose.

2. I served Fred Flogem with the statement of claim by
   leaving a copy on January 6, year 1, at 2:30 p.m., with
   Belinda Flogem, who appeared to be an adult member of
   the same household in which Fred Flogem is residing, at
   21 Cypress Blvd., Scarborough, Ontario, M8W 1P3 and by
   sending a copy by regular lettermail on January 6,
   year 1 to Fred Flogem at the same address.

3. I ascertained that the person was an adult member of the
   household by means of the fact that she identified
   herself as Fred Flogem's wife and confirmed that she was
   over 18 years of age.

4. Before serving the documents in this way, I made an
   unsuccessful attempt to serve Fred Flogem personally at
   the same address on January 5, year 1.

Sworn before me at the	)	
City of Toronto,	)	*Joe Splitz*
in the Province of Ontario,	)	Joe Splitz
on January 6, year 1.	)	

I.M. Just

I.M. Just
Commissioner for Taking Affidavits)

FIGURE 8.2 AFFIDAVIT OF SERVICE ON LAWYER OF RECORD (FORM 16B)

Court file no. 01-CV-1234

ONTARIO
SUPERIOR COURT OF JUSTICE

BETWEEN:

ABIGAIL BOAR

Plaintiff

and

RATTLE MOTORS LTD. and FRED FLOGEM

Defendants

AFFIDAVIT OF SERVICE

I, Cynthia Patel, of the City of Toronto, in the Province of Ontario, law clerk for Huey Sue, lawyer for the Defendant, **MAKE OATH AND SAY:***

1. I served Abigail Boar, the plaintiff, with the statement of defence, dated January 14, year 1, by sending a copy by fax to 416-762-2300 on January 14, year 1 to I.M. Just, Just & Coping, Barristers and Solicitors, the lawyers for the plaintiff.

Sworn before me at the)	
City of Toronto,)	*Cynthia Patel*
in the Province of Ontario,)	Cynthia Patel
on January 15, year 1.)	

Huey Sue

Huey Sue
Commissioner for Taking Affidavits)

* *When serving a lawyer by mail, substitute the following:*

1. I served Abigail Boar, the plaintiff, with the statement of defence, dated January 12, year 1, by sending a copy by regular lettermail on January 14, year 1 to I.M. Just, Just & Coping, Barristers and Solicitors, the lawyers for the plaintiff, at 365 Bay Street - 8701, Toronto, Ontario, M3J 4A9.

When serving a lawyer by courier, substitute the following:

1. I served Abigail Boar, the plaintiff, with the statement of defence, dated January 12, year 1, by sending a copy by UPS to I.M. Just, Just & Coping, Barristers and Solicitors, the lawyers for the plaintiff, at 365 Bay Street - 8701, Toronto, Ontario, M3J 4A9.
2. The copy was given to the courier on January 12, year 1.

FIGURE 8.3   AFFIDAVIT OF PERSONAL SERVICE ON CORPORATION (FORM 16B)

Court file no. 01-CV-1234

ONTARIO
SUPERIOR COURT OF JUSTICE

BETWEEN:

ABIGAIL BOAR

Plaintiff

and

RATTLE MOTORS LTD. and FRED FLOGEM

Defendants

AFFIDAVIT OF SERVICE

I, Joe Splitz, **of the** City of Toronto, **in the** Province of Ontario,
MAKE OATH AND SAY:

1. I am the process server for the law firm of Just &
    Coping, Barristers and Solicitors, and as such have
    knowledge of the matters to which I herein depose.

2. On January 5, year 1 at 2:35 p.m., I served Rattle
    Motors Ltd. with the statement of claim by leaving a
    copy with Sunil Tharper, president and general manager,
    at the corporation's place of business at 1240 Bay
    Street, Toronto, Ontario, M8H 0K8.

3. I was able to identify the person by means of him
    providing me with his name and confirming that he was
    the president and general manager of the corporation.

Sworn before me at the)	
City of Toronto,)	*Joe Splitz*
in the Province of Ontario,)	Joe Splitz
on January 6, year 1.)	

I.M. Just

I.M. Just
Commissioner for Taking Affidavits)

FIGURE 8.4   AFFIDAVIT OF PERSONAL SERVICE ON INDIVIDUAL (FORM 16B)

Court file no. 01-CV-1234

ONTARIO
SUPERIOR COURT OF JUSTICE

BETWEEN:

ABIGAIL BOAR

Plaintiff

and

RATTLE MOTORS LTD. and FRED FLOGEM

Defendants

AFFIDAVIT OF SERVICE

I, Joe Splitz, **of the** City of Toronto, **in the** Province of Ontario, **MAKE OATH AND SAY:**

1. I am the process server for the law firm of Just & Coping, Barristers and Solicitors, and as such have knowledge of the matters to which I herein depose.

2. On January 5, year 1, at 2:35 p.m., I served Fred Flogem with the statement of claim by leaving a copy with him at 21 Cypress Boulevard, Scarborough, Ontario, M8Q 1P3.

3. I was able to identify the person by means of his confirmation that he was Fred Flogem.

Sworn before me at the   )
City of Toronto,   )   *Joe Splitz*
in the Province of Ontario,   )   Joe Splitz
on January 6, year 1.   )

I.M. Just

I.M. Just
Commissioner for Taking Affidavits   )

FIGURE 8.5   AFFIDAVIT OF SERVICE ON DEFENDANT BY MAIL (FORM 16B) WITH ACKNOWLEDGMENT OF RECEIPT CARD (FORM 16A) ATTACHED AS EXHIBIT

Court file no. 01-CV-1234

ONTARIO
SUPERIOR COURT OF JUSTICE

BETWEEN:

ABIGAIL BOAR

Plaintiff

and

RATTLE MOTORS LTD. and FRED FLOGEM

Defendants

AFFIDAVIT OF SERVICE

I, Edward Egregious, **of the** City of Toronto, **in the** Province of Ontario, **MAKE OATH AND SAY:**

1. I am a law clerk for the firm of Just & Coping, Barristers and Solicitors, lawyers for the plaintiff, and as such have knowledge of the matters to which I herein depose.

2. On January 5, year 1, I sent to the defendant Fred Flogem by regular lettermail a copy of the statement of claim.

3. On January 12, year 1, I received the acknowledgment of receipt card, attached here as exhibit A, bearing a signature that purports to be the signature of Fred Flogem.

Sworn before me at the)	
City of Toronto,)	*Edward Egregious*
in the Province of Ontario,)	Edward Egregious
on January 12, year 1.)	

I.M. Just

I.M. Just
Commissioner for Taking Affidavits   )

FIGURE 8.5   CONCLUDED

Court file no. 01-CV-1234

ONTARIO
SUPERIOR COURT OF JUSTICE

BETWEEN:

ABIGAIL BOAR

Plaintiff

and

RATTLE MOTORS LTD. and FRED FLOGEM

Defendants

TO: Fred Flogem

You are served by mail with the documents enclosed with this card in accordance with the Rules of Civil Procedure.

You are requested to sign the acknowledgment below and mail this card immediately after you receive it. If you fail to do so, the documents may be served on you in another manner and you may have to pay the costs of service.

ACKNOWLEDGMENT OF RECEIPT

I ACKNOWLEDGE that I have received a copy of the following documents:

Statement of claim of Abigail Boar, issued January 4, year 1

Fred Flogem
Fred Flogem

(The reverse side of this card must bear the name and address of the sender and the required postage.)

THIS IS EXHIBIT A REFERRED TO
IN THE AFFIDAVIT OF
EDWARD EGREGIOUS,
SWORN BEFORE ME ON
January 10, year 1

I.M. Just

Commissioner for Taking Affidavits

FIGURE 8.6   CERTIFICATE OF SERVICE BY SHERIFF (FORM 16C)

CERTIFICATE OF SERVICE BY SHERIFF

I, Joe Shmoe, sheriff's officer of the Township of Vaughn, certify that on March 1, year 2, at 10 a.m., I served Donald Donaldson with a writ of seizure and sale by leaving a copy with him at 400 Starry Lane, Woodbridge, Ontario L47 9V6. I was able to identify the person by means of his confirmation that he was Donald Donaldson.

Date: March 1, year 2

Joe Shmoe
_____
Joe Shmoe

the document. The certificate is often put right on the copy of the served document that is filed with the court.

If you use the sheriff to serve the enforcement documents, the sheriff's office will provide you with a completed certificate. Although you will not need to prepare the document itself, you should know what it looks like.

Proof of acceptance or admitting of service by the other side

When you are serving a document, very often the lawyer for the other side will admit service. It is a good idea to put the following wording on the backsheet of the document to be filed with the court:

Service of a copy of this
document admitted on
_____
(*date*)
_____
(*signature*)
Lawyers for

The lawyer for the party being served, or one of the staff in his or her office, may be willing to fill in the date and sign for the document. This signature tells the court that the other side agrees that it has been properly served according to the rules. There is no need to prepare an affidavit of service. The copy of the document on which service has been admitted can be filed with the court without any further proof of service being required.

It is not always possible to use this method of proof because the lawyer for the opposite side may not be in the office when the document is served and may not have left instructions with a staff member to admit service. *It is very important that you never admit service of any document unless you have been given specific instructions by the lawyer you work for to do so.* If there is a problem with the service — for example, if it is not in keeping with the rules — and service has been admitted, the service cannot usually be challenged later.

Acceptance of service works the same way as admitting service, but the wording that is put on the backsheet of the document being served is slightly different.

Service of a copy of this
document accepted on
_____
(*date*)
_____
(*signature*)
Lawyers for

The acceptance wording is used when you are serving a lawyer with an originating process under rule 16.03(2) as an alternative to personal service. If you are serving a lawyer of record with a document that is not an originating process under rule 16.05, you use the admittance of service wording.

SERVICE OUTSIDE THE PROVINCE

Sometimes one of the parties to the proceeding lives or is located outside Ontario. When serving a party outside the province, in addition to following rule 16, you must also follow any additional procedures prescribed by rule 17. This means that an originating process served outside the province must still be served personally or by an alternative to personal service under rule 16. However, you must also look at rule 17 to see if there are additional steps that must be taken or additional procedures that must be followed.

Rule 17.01 changes the definition of originating process by adding an additional document to the list contained in rule 1.03. Counterclaims against parties to the main action and crossclaims are also included as originating processes for the purpose of serving someone outside the province.

Not all documents served outside the province can be served without a court order, although many can. To determine whether your case is one in which you can serve outside the province without a court order, you must first look at rule 17.02. If your case is one of the types of cases listed under this rule, you may serve outside the province without leave, or permission, from the court. If your case is not one of the types listed under rule 17.02, you must first bring a motion to get leave from the court to serve the party who is out of the province (rule 17.03). The motion is usually a motion without notice. The court grants leave for a type of case not listed in rule 17.02 only if it can be satisfied that the courts in Ontario are the appropriate courts to hear the case.

Where an originating process is being served outside the province without leave under rule 17.02, you must state in the document which part of the rule you are relying on to serve without leave (rule 17.04(1)). For instance, if you are serving someone in Manitoba with a statement of claim in a case that involves the breach of a contract made in Ontario, your statement of claim must contain a paragraph that states that fact and mentions rule 17.02(f)(i). Rule 17.02(f)(i) says that you do not need leave from the court to serve a document on a party when the case involves a claim relating to a contract made in Ontario.

If you are dealing with a claim that requires leave to serve outside the province, the order that grants leave must also be served along with the originating process (rule 17.04(2)).

Rule 17.05 deals with the method of service you must use when serving documents outside Ontario. Basically, when you want to serve an originating process outside the province, you may do so by having the document personally served or served by an alternative to personal service as described in rule 16. In addition, you may also serve by whatever method of service is permissible in the other jurisdiction as long as that method of service is likely to bring the document to the attention of the person being served.

However, if you want to serve an originating process in a foreign country, you must first find out if that country is a **contracting state** to the *Hague Convention on the Service Abroad of Judicial and Extrajudicial Documents in Civil or Commercial Matters*. This is the international convention, or agreement, that Canada has entered into with many other countries. All the countries that have signed the convention are called "contracting states." They have agreed that they will help litigants from the other countries serve documents. If you are dealing with a country that is part of the convention, you must send your documents to the central authority in Ontario. That central authority then sends the documents to the central authority in the other country. The central authorities are government offices in each country that have signed the treaty. The central authority in the other country takes care of serving the documents and preparing the proof of service, which it will send back to you. A country that is a convention state will provide whatever proof of service is legal in that country, and it will be acceptable as good proof in an Ontario court (rule 17.05(4)).

To find out whether a country is a contracting state to the convention, you may look at the website for the Hague Conference on Private International Law at http://www.hcch.net/index_en.php?act=conventions.status&cid=17. You may also telephone the Foreign Affairs Canada in Ottawa at 613-995-1050 or fax the department at 613-992-2467.

The central authority for Ontario can be contacted as follows:

Ministry of the Attorney General
Courts Administration
Ontario Court of Justice
Court House
393 Main Street
Haileybury, ON P0J 1K0

tel.: 705-672-3395

A party that has been served outside Ontario can bring a motion, in an Ontario court, to set aside service of an originating process or to stay or stop the proceeding as long as the party commences the motion before filing any documents. When dealing with such a motion, the judge looks at whether the documents have been properly served under the rules and whether the Ontario court is the proper court in which to hear the proceeding. When you wish to serve a document in a contracting state, you must complete forms 17A, 17B, and 17C. You are usually required to provide a translation of the document as well.

contracting state
country that is a signatory to a contract or convention

CHAPTER SUMMARY

This chapter introduced the various methods that must be used to serve a document under the rules. Generally, there are specific methods set out for the service of a document that is an originating process and other methods set out for documents that are not.

You must first look to see if there is a specific rule relating to the document you want to serve that requires a specific method of service. If not, an originating process may be served either by personal service through one of the methods listed in rule 16.02 or by an alternative to personal service listed in rule 16.03. Only the alternatives to personal service listed in that rule may be substituted for personal service.

If a document is not an originating process and the party is represented by a lawyer of record, it is possible to serve the document on the lawyer by one of the methods provided in rule 16.05. If the party is representing him- or herself in the proceeding, a document that is not an originating process may be served by mail to the address provided by the party on the originating process or by personal or alternative service.

If it is impossible to serve a person because the person is avoiding service or cannot be found, the party wishing to serve the document may bring a motion to ask for an order of substituted service or an order dispensing with service. It is only in the most extraordinary circumstances that a court will make an order dispensing with service.

Once service has been effected according to the rules or a court order, the person who served the document must make an affidavit that provides evidence of the steps he or she took to serve the document. However, it is not necessary to prepare an affidavit of service if the lawyer for the opposite party admits or accepts service and certifies that he or she has done so on the backsheet of the served document. Likewise, no affidavit is necessary where the document has been left in a document exchange. The stamp of the document exchange on the document is sufficient service.

A document may be served outside Ontario without leave of the court if the case is listed in rule 17.02. If the case is any other type of case, the party wishing to serve the document must obtain a court order first. If you wish to serve a document on a person who is in a contracting state to the *Hague Convention on Service Abroad of Judicial and Extrajudicial Documents in Civil or Commercial Matters*, the person must be served, in accordance with rule 17.05(3), by a central authority in the country where the party is located.

KEY TERMS

service

originating process

sheriff

contracting state

NOTE

1   This is not the same as registered mail. Form 16A must be used.

REFERENCES

Hague Convention on Service Abroad of Judicial and Extrajudicial Documents in Civil or Commercial Matters, November 15, 1965. See *Hague Conference on Private International Law* at http://www.hcch.net/e/status/stat14e.html.

Public Service Act, RSO 1990, c. P.47.

Rules of Civil Procedure, RRO 1990, reg. 194.

REVIEW QUESTIONS

1. How do you effect service on a partnership?

2. When can you serve a motion record on a lawyer by fax?

3. Julie Giudice served the defendant's lawyer of record by mail with a document that was not an originating process. The document was mailed on Friday September 23. What date will service be effective?

4. A process server wants to serve Frasier Croon with a statement of claim. He goes to Frasier's house and finds the cleaning woman there alone. The process server leaves a copy of the statement of claim with the cleaning woman and mails a copy to Frasier at the same address on the same day. Is this good service? Explain your answer.

5. Jaspal wants to serve a 15-page statement of defence on the lawyer of record for the plaintiff. He is running out of time and decides to serve the document by fax at 9:30 a.m. Is this good service?

6. You are a law clerk for Seneca and Associates, Barristers and Solicitors, 1750 Finch Avenue East, Toronto, Ontario, M2J 2X5. Your client is John Ahab, who is suing Moby's Whale of a Time Inc., a chain of restaurants, for negligently leaving a bone in his sushi. You have just served Moby's Whale of a Time Inc. with a statement of claim. You went to the restaurant closest to the law office, at 5910 Yonge Street, North York, Ontario, M7U 4T8 and left a copy with the manager of the restaurant, Ishmael Bosun. Draft an affidavit of service. If there is any necessary information that you think is missing, make it up.

7. You sent the process server out to serve a sole proprietorship personally. When the process server comes back, he produces an affidavit saying he left a copy of the statement of claim with Ginny, the assistant cashier at the place of business. Is this service adequate?

8. In the following situations, will it be necessary to seek leave of the court to serve a party with an originating process outside Ontario.
   a. Joe died in Ontario. His heirs want to sue his nurse, Betty, whom they believe removed some of Joe's property from his home after he died, and they want the property to be returned.

b. Stacey lives in Toronto. She was in a car accident in New York State. She wants to sue the owner of the car that hit hers. He also lives in Ontario.

c. The parties made a contract in Manitoba, but since they knew that one of the parties was moving his business to Toronto the next month, they agreed to a term in the contract that the law of Ontario should govern.

d. George wants to seek custody of his son Benny, who is living with him in Barrie, but the child's mother lives in Montreal.

9. You are a law clerk with the firm of MacDonald, Reed, and Buss. Your supervising lawyer is Jacqueline Reed. The address of the firm is:

MacDonald, Reed, and Buss
Barristers and Solicitors
200 Bay Street, Suite 1100
Toronto, Ontario, M5V 3T3
Tel.:   416-595-5000
Fax: 416-595-5050
E-mail: MDRB@sympatico.ca

Your law firm acts for the plaintiffs, Yorkful Developers Inc. The defendant is Louis LaFrance. The process server is Jacky Dillhopper. Jacky phones and tells you he has effected service on Louis LaFrance by attending at his residence at 100 Bloor Street North, Toronto, Ontario, M6Y 4R7. He left a copy with Louis's wife, Celine, after she identified herself as Louis's wife. Draft an affidavit of service for Jacky to sign when he gets back to the office.

CHAPTER 9

Motions

INTRODUCTION

This chapter is about motions procedure and the preparation of **motion** documents. It includes Appendix I: Motion and Application Procedure in Toronto, which refers to the special motion procedure used in Toronto, and Appendix II: Special Motions, which provides examples of special motions you are likely to encounter in practice. You will notice that both the procedure and the documents are very similar to those used in applications. This is not accidental. Documents and procedures in motions and applications are designed to be dispatched in a summary fashion, with a short timeline between raising a legal issue and obtaining an answer from the court.

motion
proceeding within the main proceeding to settle an issue, usually procedural and usually one that has arisen prior to trial

Purpose of motions

The purpose of a motion is to settle issues that arise in the course of civil litigation, usually before trial.[1] We have already identified some circumstances where motions are required to resolve a problem prior to trial: a motion to join parties to a lawsuit, a motion to strike out pleadings, and a motion to demand particulars. It used to be, and sometimes still is the case, that a party with money to spend would try to delay proceedings by bringing one motion after another and drive up the legal costs at the pretrial stage. The opposing party, if more financially limited, would soon be forced to drop the lawsuit or settle on disadvantageous terms. This practice was sometimes referred to as "motioning the other side to death." The rules discourage this kind of litigation strategy, and the courts have the power to award punitive costs against the parties who resort to them. In some cases, the courts award costs against lawyers who engage in these dark arts (rule 57.07). The court may also bar a party from bringing further motions unless the court's permission is first obtained (rule 37.16).

But there are often good reasons to bring motions. Suppose that I.M. Just, Abigail Boar's lawyer, has read the statement of defence stating that the area around the Super Coupe was properly illuminated and therefore safe. That matter is now an issue between the parties. To help settle it, I.M. Just asks Huey Sue, the defendants' lawyer, to permit a lighting engineer to come to the showroom and examine the lighting. Huey refuses to permit this. So I.M. Just decides to bring a motion to ask the court to order an examination of the premises by the lighting engineer.

Motions with notice: Overview of procedure

While we will look at various aspects of motion procedure in detail, here we set out a general overview of the process of bringing a motion with notice.

The moving party prepares a notice of motion and a supporting affidavit and serves it on the responding party at least four days before the motion is to be heard and files it at least three days before the hearing.

The day picked for the **return of the motion** depends on the practices in the court where the motion is returnable. In Toronto, an appointment for motions before both judges and masters must be obtained before serving the responding party. This is discussed in more detail in appendix I to this chapter.

As of July 2004, motions shall be brought and heard where the proceeding was commenced, unless otherwise ordered (rule 37.03(1)). This is consistent with rule 13.1, governing the place of trial, and with case management requirements; it applies to motions with or without notice.

The responding party may serve an affidavit or other evidentiary material or a cross-motion and supporting documents on the moving party up to three days before the hearing.

A motion record must be prepared, usually by the moving party, consisting of the table of contents, the notice of motion, affidavits, and any other documents the parties intend to refer to on the motion. It is then filed in the court where the motion is to be heard three days before the hearing. This requires the parties to observe time limits for serving each other and requires cooperation. Otherwise, each side files its own motion record: the moving party no later than three days before the hearing, the responding party two days before the hearing.

Either party may ask to cross-examine the maker of an affidavit that is filed on the motion. This is done out of court before a court reporter or **official examiner**, and the transcript, or a part of it, may be used at the hearing. If the parties have not allowed enough time for cross-examination between the date the motion is served and its return date, the request to cross-examine is made on the return date of the motion; if the request is granted, the motion is adjourned pending completion of cross-examination. The rules require that a party who seeks to cross-examine should move to do so "with reasonable diligence." Because cross-examination causes delay, its misuse may lead to an imposition of cost penalties on the party that improperly resorts to it or the court may deny permission for cross-examination altogether (rule 39.02(3)). A party who cross-examines on an affidavit may not file supplementary affidavits responding to what was said in cross-examination without the court's consent. This puts an end to the old practice of serving a responding affidavit after cross-examination, followed by a response to the responding affidavit, and so on, which caused both delay and confusion.

There are some additional burdens on a party who cross-examines. The party bears the expense of ordering a transcript of the cross-examination for the court and for other parties. The party must also pay partial indemnity costs of every adverse party on the motion unless the court orders otherwise (rule 39.02(4)).

Parties may wish to file factums, which are statements of fact, law, and case references; they are not required on all motions, except in Toronto on lengthy, complex motions, but the practice is recommended and encouraged by the judiciary.

Hearings are **summary proceedings**. Oral evidence is usually not heard; instead, counsel make submissions, referring to affidavits and other documentary evidence, including cross-examination transcripts.

return of a motion
day on which a motion is "returned" to court for a hearing; the hearing date is also referred to as "the return date"

official examiner
individual who is licensed to operate a business to conduct out-of-court examinations, such as cross-examinations on affidavits and discoveries

summary proceedings
proceedings designed to be conducted quickly and with reduced formality

The successful party on the motion then drafts the order from the judge's or master's endorsement, obtains approval as to form from the unsuccessful party, and has the order issued and entered by the court.

CHANGES TO MOTION PROCEDURE AS OF JANUARY 1, 2010

There will be earlier deadlines for serving and filing motion materials under rule 37 and application materials under rule 38 in order to allow parties, particularly responding parties, more time to prepare.

MOTIONS WITHOUT NOTICE

There are certain types of motions that may be brought without notice. For example, if you have been unable to serve a defendant with a statement of claim, you may bring a motion for substituted service, as you saw in chapter 8. The motion is brought in the court where the proceeding was commenced (rule 37.03(1)), but no notice to the other side is required. You file the notice of motion and the affidavit or other evidence you will use, appear before the judge or master, or submit the motion in writing, and make submissions. A notice of motion should be filed to set out the issues in advance for the judge or master. Once an order is made, unless the court orders otherwise, any party affected by the order must be served with a copy of the order immediately, along with a copy of the motion, and all the documents used on it. In that way, the process is reasonably transparent because the party, though not present, gets to see what was before the court. If the moving party misled the court, the other party will become aware of that fact and can take action to set the order aside. Because a motion without notice is rather one-sided, an affidavit must give full and fair disclosure and must be more neutral in tone than it would be had the motion been made on notice (rule 39.01(6)).

If the judge or master is of the opinion that the motion should not have been brought without first giving notice, he or she may dismiss the motion or adjourn it until the other party is served, and he or she may direct that any order made be served on the non-attending party (rule 37.07(5)).

JURISDICTION TO HEAR A MOTION

In the Superior Court, there are two types of judicial officials who decide legal issues and who can decide contested motions: a **master** and a judge. Masters have a more limited jurisdiction than judges do, and they sit in courts where the volume of cases is high, such as in Toronto and Ottawa. In other judicial regions, judges hear all motions.

Where you have a choice as to whether the motion is heard by a judge or master, you must decide before whom it should come. As a general rule, a motion that can be heard by a master must be heard by a master. If you schedule it before a judge, he or she will refuse to hear it, and you will have to appear again before a master, wasting both time and money.[2]

master
minor judicial official with limited jurisdiction to hear and decide specific legal issues identified by the rules or a statute

A master's jurisdiction is more circumscribed than a judge's. Rule 37.02(2)(a) to (g) lists those matters that a master *cannot* hear:

- A master cannot hear a matter that has been given exclusively to a judge by a statute or regulation.

- A master cannot change an order that was made by a judge.

- A master cannot shorten or lengthen the time for doing something in an order made by a judge.

- A master cannot give a consent judgment where there is a party under disability — such as a minor — involved.

- A master cannot make an order that affects the liberty of a person — for example, because an order for contempt of court may result in jail time, contempt motions must be brought before judges.

- A master cannot make orders under s. 4 or s. 5 of the *Judicial Review Procedure Act* such as interim orders or orders extending the time for filing applications for judicial review.

- A master cannot make orders on an appeal.

Subject to these restrictions, masters have jurisdiction to hear all other matters.

While masters and judges share jurisdiction over contested motions, the registrar has jurisdiction over some motions if all parties consent to the order being sought on the motion. Rule 37.02(3) provides that if all parties to the proceeding or affected by it consent, and the subject of the motion is one that is listed in the rule, then the motion documents may be submitted to the registrar, who will sign the order, if the documentation is in order. If the registrar has any doubts, he or she will not sign the order, and will return the documents to the moving party, who then has to bring the motion in the ordinary way. This is sensible and practical. Since the motion is being made on consent, there is no need to resort to a legally trained judge or master to make an order. Here, the making of an order is an administrative act that can be performed inexpensively and quickly by a registrar.

OBTAINING A HEARING DATE

In large regions such as Toronto, motions are heard every day. In small centres, there is often a "motion day,"[3] where a judge usually hears all motions filed since the last motion day. Generally, the moving party may choose any date on which motions are heard without needing first to obtain a date from the court office. When choosing a date, however, it is a good idea to check with the responding parties to the motion to be sure that counsel will be available. This will avoid wasting time and money on adjournments and rescheduling.

In Toronto, the practice for obtaining a hearing date for nearly all motions is governed by a motions and applications advisory notice, effective September 3, 2002. In Toronto you must reserve a motion date before serving a motion. This is discussed in more detail in appendix I to this chapter.

Generally, if you are involved with a motion to be heard in a court or region where you are not familiar with local scheduling and hearing practices, it is a good idea to call the court office to find out whether there are special requirements for hearing dates, service, or documents required on the motion.

NOTICE OF MOTION

The primary document you need to prepare is the notice of motion. This tells the other side the issue that you wish to have decided, the remedy you seek, and the reason you believe you are entitled to the remedy. The document also lists the materials you intend to rely on. The prescribed form is form 37A, and the relevant rule is rule 37.06, which sets out the information required:

1. *To whom the motion is made.* Is the motion made to a master or to a judge? Check rule 37.02(2).

2. *Time, date, and place where the motion will be heard.* Try to arrange a convenient time with the responding party. Where applicable, get the date and time reserved with the court.

3. *Whether the motion is to be heard orally or in writing.* The lawyer will make oral or written submissions. Evidence, however, in either case, is by affidavit. You need permission from the court to proceed with oral evidence.

4. *Legal basis or grounds that support the remedy requested.* Briefly list a rule, statute, case, or legal principle if relevant.

5. *Documentary evidence you rely on.* Affidavits and other documents listed on the notice of motion should be identified by the date the document was created and the maker of the document if this is not obvious.

6. *Name, address, and telephone number of the lawyer for the moving party.* Provide the same information for the lawyers who are being served on behalf of the responding party. Many lawyers also include their fax number, although this is not required.

Figure 9.1 sets out Abigail's motion for an order for inspection of the defendants' premises. The relevant rule for inspections is rule 32. Have a look at it, and notice that its language is incorporated into the statement of the grounds of the motion itself.

AFFIDAVITS AS EVIDENCE ON MOTIONS AND APPLICATIONS

One of the ways in which hearings on motions and applications are speeded up is by using affidavit evidence instead of having witnesses give evidence orally. What a witness would have said in examination-in-chief is reduced to a sworn statement. If cross-examination is desired, arrangements need to be made to cross-examine the deponent on the contents of his or her affidavit. The transcript of that cross-examination is used with the affidavit itself at the hearing. The process of adjourning a motion or application to permit cross-examination and obtain transcripts may end up costing more and taking more time than using oral evidence on the motion or affidavit.

Drafting affidavits

The basic requirements for affidavits are set out in rule 4.06. Form 4D sets out a prescribed format.

FIGURE 9.1   MOTION FOR ORDER FOR INSPECTION OF PREMISES
(FORM 37A)

Court file no. 01-CV-1234

ONTARIO
SUPERIOR COURT OF JUSTICE

BETWEEN:

ABIGAIL BOAR

Plaintiff

and

RATTLE MOTORS LTD. and FRED FLOGEM

Defendants

NOTICE OF MOTION

THE PLAINTIFF will make a motion to the court on Monday October 16, year 1 at 10:00 a.m., or as soon after that time as the motion can be heard, at 393 University Avenue, Toronto, Ontario, M5G 1Y3.

PROPOSED METHOD OF HEARING: The motion is to be heard

❑   in writing under subrule 37.12.1 (1);
☒   in writing as an opposed motion under subrule 37.12.1 (4);
❑   orally.

THE MOTION IS FOR an order permitting Eldred Klump, consulting electrical engineer, to inspect the level of lighting in the automobile showroom operated by the corporate defendant at 1240 Bay Street in the City of Toronto, Province of Ontario, on such terms and at such times as the court considers just.

THE GROUNDS FOR THE MOTION ARE that there is an issue between the parties as to the adequacy of lighting in the corporate defendant's showroom, and it is necessary to determine that issue in this proceeding to carry out an inspection of the corporate defendant's premises to examine the lighting, pursuant to rule 32 of the rules of civil procedure.

THE FOLLOWING DOCUMENTARY EVIDENCE will be used at the hearing of the motion:

1. Statement of claim filed January 4, year 1;
2. Statement of defence filed January 12, year 1; and
3. Affidavit of Eldred Klump sworn October 3, year 1.

FIGURE 9.1 CONTINUED

Date: October 16, year 1

                                        Just & Coping
                                        Barristers and Solicitors
                                        365 Bay Street - 8701
                                        Toronto, Ontario, M3J 4A9

                                        I.M. Just
                                        LSUC #12345R
                                        tel. 416-762-1342
                                        fax 416-762-2300

                                        Lawyers for the Moving
                                        Party (Plaintiff)

TO:
Huey Sue
LSUC #23456T
Barrister and Solicitor
65 False Trail
Toronto, Ontario, M6Y 1Z6

tel. 416-485-6891
fax 416-485-6892

Lawyer for the Responding
Parties (Defendants)

USE THE FIRST PERSON FORM

The statements in affidavits are set out in the first person singular ("I"), although joint affidavits may be used where appropriate, in which case the first person plural ("we") must be used.

IDENTIFY THE DEPONENT

Before setting out the first numbered paragraph, give the deponent's full name, followed by the municipality and province where the deponent resides. Set out the deponent's status — for example, as a party, lawyer for a party, or officer of a corporation — so that the testimony can be seen in context. Two examples of paragraphs identifying a deponent are set out below. The second example, although not in conformity with the directions in form 4D, is often used.

I, Eldred Klump, of the City of Brampton, in the Regional Municipality of Peel,[4] consulting electrical engineer, MAKE OATH AND SAY:

I, Eldred Klump, of the City of Brampton, in the Regional Municipality of Peel, MAKE OATH AND SAY:

    1. I am a consulting electrical engineer, retained by the plaintiff, and as such have knowledge of the matters sworn to in this affidavit.

FIGURE 9.2   STANDARD JURAT (FORM 4D)

Sworn before me at the   )

City of Brampton,   )   *Edward Klump*

in the Regional Municipality   )   Edward Klump

of Peel,   )

on October 3, year 1.   )

I.M. Just

I.M. Just

Commissioner for Taking Affidavits   )

SET OUT STATEMENT IN CONSECUTIVE PARAGRAPHS

Much like a statement of claim or defence, the affidavit is divided into consecutively numbered paragraphs, with each paragraph confined as far as possible to a specific statement of fact. Again, this may mean that many paragraphs are just two or three sentences long. The writing should be concise. However, it is not limited to material facts, and evidentiary material may be set out.

SIGN AND SWEAR THE AFFIDAVIT

The deponent must sign the affidavit at the end, or foot, after he or she has been affirmed or sworn by a commissioner for taking oaths and affidavits. Every lawyer is a commissioner and is authorized to swear affidavits. Law clerks employed in law offices may apply through their offices to the provincial government to become commissioners while employed in that law office and doing work for it. A lawyer signs the **jurat** as commissioner when he or she has sworn the deponent. A non-lawyer signs the jurat and also applies his or her commissioner's stamp, identifying the law office for which he or she works and the date of the expiry of the commission. A lawyer's commission does not require use of a stamp.

jurat
part of an affidavit that appears at the bottom on the left side of the page and begins with the words "Sworn (or affirmed) before me"

An affidavit is commissioned when it is being used in an Ontario proceeding. If it is being sworn for use in another province or in a foreign jurisdiction, it should be notarized instead, and the notary's seal should be affixed next to the notary's signature.

Where a lawyer commissions an affidavit without a seal and the signature is an illegible scrawl, the lawyer should print his or her name underneath the signature. The standard jurat[5] is set out in figure 9.2.

WHEN HEARSAY IS PERMISSIBLE

The content of an affidavit, like the evidence on a witness's oral examination-in-chief, is usually restricted to matters of which the deponent has personal knowledge. Hearsay is not permitted unless it falls into one of the numerous exceptions to the hearsay rule. However, this requirement, set out in rule 4.06(2), is subject to the qualifications set out in rule 39.01(4) and (5).

If the affidavit is for use on a motion, it may contain statements of the deponent's information and belief, provided that the deponent identifies the source of

FIGURE 9.3   EXHIBIT STAMP

This is exhibit A **to the affidavit of** Eldred Klump **dated** October 3, year 1 *I.M. Just* ―――――――――――――――――― Commissioner for Taking Affidavits

the information and states that he or she believes the information to be true. In this instance, hearsay is admissible.

This rule also applies to affidavits used on applications, provided that the source of the information is revealed, the deponent states that he or she believes it to be true, and the *facts in question are not contentious*. Therefore hearsay is admissible, provided that it is not disputed. Where a contentious statement is included, the proper response is to move to strike out the objectionable part of the affidavit.

Using an example from Abigail Boar's case, the usual method for expressing information and belief is as follows: "I am informed by Abigail Boar, the plaintiff in this action, and I believe that she was unable to see the oil spill because of inadequate lighting at the site of her fall."

EXHIBITS TO AFFIDAVITS

Occasionally the deponent's statement refers to a document or other material. The document or other material should be clearly described and given an exhibit number (usually a letter), which is stamped on a copy of the document. If the exhibit to be attached or filed is a copy, the deponent should so state. Once it is made an exhibit, the document or other material should be made available to other parties and the court. This can be done in one of two ways: (1) it can be attached to the affidavit or (2) it can be referred to in the affidavit and filed in court. Rule 4.06(3) prescribes language for each of the two ways of dealing with exhibits, and you should take care to use the appropriate word formula. Examples from Abigail's case appear below.

- If the exhibit is attached, write "Now *shown to me*, marked exhibit A, *and attached to this affidavit* is a copy of the bar bill of Abigail Boar from Barbeerian's restaurant, dated September 14, year 0."

- If the exhibit is shown to the deponent and filed in court, write "*Now produced and shown to me*, and marked exhibit A is a copy of the bar bill of Abigail Boar from Barbeerian's restaurant, dated September 14, year 0."

Law firms usually use an exhibit stamp with blank spaces to be filled in with the exhibit number or letter, the name of the deponent, and the date of the affidavit. The person who commissions the affidavit signs in the space provided. The stamp is reproduced in figure 9.3.

Figure 9.4 shows what Eldred Klump's affidavit in the Abigail Boar case looks like. Figure 9.5 sets out the affidavit filed by Sunil Tharper on behalf of Rattle Motors Ltd.

MOTION RECORDS

Assume for the moment that you have now obtained a date for the motion, determined who hears it, prepared a notice of motion and affidavit, and served this on the responding party. The responding party has served its documents on you. You are now ready to prepare a motion record.

Why use a motion record?

Formerly when a motion was brought, the moving party served and filed a motion and affidavit, and the responding party served and filed an affidavit. On each filing, the court clerk stamped the incoming document and put it in the appropriate court file, noting the day of the motion. On the day before the motion, the clerks brought the court file to the judge or master who was to hear the matter. The judicial official then found himself or herself with a court file full of documents in no particular order. If the matter was complex, there might be hundreds of pages in the file. The judge or master would go through the file, looking for the notice of motion and the appropriate affidavits, and reading what he or she hoped was the correct material. To introduce some order into this chaos, the rules now require a motion record to be filed containing all the material necessary for hearing and determining the motion. Only the motion record would be delivered to the judge or master unless a party separately requisitioned the whole file. It was now no longer necessary for judges and masters to fumble around in the court file in search of the appropriate documents.

Contents of a motion record

Rule 37.10(2) sets out what a motion record should have in it in consecutively numbered pages:

- an index, headed by a general heading and title of proceeding, describing each document, identified by its nature or date, including exhibits filed or attached to affidavits and identified by exhibit numbers (figure 9.6 sets out a motion record index for the case of Abigail Boar);

- a copy of the notice of motion;

- a copy of all affidavits and other material served by any party;

- a list of all relevant transcripts (cross-examinations on affidavits, discoveries, or other evidence) in chronological order (if the transcript or the part relied on is short, it may be included in the motion record; if it is too long for that, be sure it is in the court file, and requisition the court file for the motion); and

- a copy of any other material in the court file that might be relevant to the issues on the motion (often lawyers file copies of the pleadings to provide a context) or that may be required by the court.

FIGURE 9.4   AFFIDAVIT OF ELDRED KLUMP (FORM 4D)

Court file no. 01-CV-1234

ONTARIO
SUPERIOR COURT OF JUSTICE

BETWEEN:

ABIGAIL BOAR

Plaintiff

and

RATTLE MOTORS LTD. and FRED FLOGEM

Defendants

AFFIDAVIT OF ELDRED KLUMP

I, Eldred Klump, **of the** City of Brampton, **in the** Regional Municipality of Peel, **MAKE OATH AND SAY:**

1. I am a consulting electrical engineer, retained by the plaintiff, and as such have knowledge of the matters sworn to in this affidavit.
2. I am advised by I.M. Just, lawyer for the plaintiff, and I believe that there is a disagreement between the parties as to whether or not there was adequate illumination in the area where the plaintiff allegedly fell in the showroom of Rattle Motors Ltd.
3. There are Building Code and other standards for safe and adequate lighting for various areas in buildings, including showrooms.
4. It is possible to measure the amount of light at the location in question and check the measurements against known standards.
5. The information obtained from these tests would be relevant in assisting the court in making findings as to the adequacy of the lighting in question.
6. In order to properly measure the light, it is necessary for me to enter the showroom of the corporate defendant, adjust the lights in the location where the plaintiff fell as they were on the day of the accident, and take measurements of the light available.

Sworn before me at the)	
City of Brampton,)	*Eldred Klump*
in the Regional Municipality)	Eldred Klump
of Peel,)	
on October 3, year 1.)	

I.M. Just

I.M. Just
Commissioner for Taking Affidavits)

FIGURE 9.5 AFFIDAVIT OF SUNIL THARPER (FORM 4D)

Court file no. 01-CV-1234

ONTARIO
SUPERIOR COURT OF JUSTICE

BETWEEN:

ABIGAIL BOAR

Plaintiff

and

RATTLE MOTORS LTD. and FRED FLOGEM

Defendants

AFFIDAVIT OF SUNIL THARPER

I, Sunil Tharper, president and general manager of Rattle Motors Ltd., **of the** City of Toronto, **in the** Province on Ontario, **AFFIRM:**

1. I have read the affidavit of Eldred Klump, sworn October 3, year 1 and filed on behalf of the plaintiff in this proceeding.
2. On or about February 1, year 1, the corporate defendant's directors decided to renovate its automobile showroom to better display the automobiles that the company sells.
3. The renovations were extensive, involving a complete gutting of the interior and replacement of flooring, ceilings, showroom windows, and offices.
4. In the course of carrying out this renovation, all of the prerenovation lighting, including spotlights or pot lights, was removed, and new lighting was installed.
5. The new lighting is of a different type from the old lighting and is placed differently. In particular, the spotlighting now used is of the halogen type, rather than the conventional incandescent floodlight type.
6. Since the lighting fixtures and the illumination they cast are completely different from the lighting that was used at the time the plaintiff fell, the inspection proposed by the plaintiff would serve no purpose.
7. The defendants have consulted a lighting expert, Elihu Dunck, who has prepared a report in which he advises that it would now be impossible to carry out the tests and inspections proposed by the plaintiff, and that the inspection would be of no assistance to the court. Now shown to me and attached hereto and marked exhibit A to this affidavit is a report dated October 5, year 1 from Elihu Dunck to the defendant's lawyer, which sets out Mr. Dunck's opinion.

Affirmed before me at the	)
City of Toronto,	)
in the Province of Ontario,	)
on October 6, year 1.	)

Sunil Tharper
Sunil Tharper

Huey Sue

Huey Sue
Commissioner for Taking Affidavits)

Although it is not required, it is a good idea to use tabs to separate documents so the judge or master can easily find what the lawyer is referring to in argument. Rule 4.07 requires that a motion record be bound with a light blue backsheet.

If, as it should, the motion record contains the notice of motion and supporting affidavits, these documents need not be filed separately with the court.

Figure 9.6 sets out the motion record index in the case of Abigail Boar.

Responding party's motion record

If enough time is allowed for both parties serving each other with their motion material and there is cooperation, one motion record can usually be prepared for use by the parties and the court on the motion. This is the approach preferred by judges and masters, who dislike having to shuffle through several sets of documents. However, where the responding party is not satisfied that the record is complete, he or she may prepare a responding party's motion record to include those documents which he or she thinks should be included. The motion record should have a table of contents describing the documents included that were omitted from the moving party's motion record (rule 37.10(3)). It must be served on other parties and filed two days before the hearing. A responding party's motion record is required where the moving party refuses or neglects to include a court document that the responding party wishes included or where the responding party decides that a document is required after the moving party's motion record has been filed.

Factums for use on motions

Factums are required for "long," complex motions and for opposed motions in writing. Otherwise, they are not required, but the rules encourage parties to serve and file a factum for use on a motion. This is particularly useful with long or complex motions involving issues of law. A factum is required if a motion is opposed and in writing. It is also required on certain types of motions in some regions — for example, on a motion for summary judgment in Toronto. A factum can set out in neutral terms the facts of the case, concise arguments on these facts, and statements of the principles of law relied on, including case references. A motion factum is simply a version of the type of factums that have long been filed on appeals (rule 37.10(6)).

SERVICE OF MOTIONS AND MOTION RECORDS

The requirements for service of motion material are scattered through rules 37 and 39. Generally, you should pick a return date that is far enough in advance so that you will have time to serve your documents, receive the responding party's documents, and file a complete motion record on time. It is a good idea to consult the responding party when choosing a date. But where time is of the essence, here are the steps you must follow:

1. *Determine the location.* The place of hearing for the motion shall be the place where the proceeding was commenced (rule 37.03).

2. *Serve the motion.* The notice of motion, supporting affidavit, and other documents must be served at least four days before the hearing (rules 37.07(6) and 39.01(2)).

FIGURE 9.6 MOTION RECORD INDEX

Court file no. 01-CV-1234

ONTARIO
SUPERIOR COURT OF JUSTICE

BETWEEN:

ABIGAIL BOAR

Plaintiff

and

RATTLE MOTORS LTD. and FRED FLOGEM

Defendants

MOTION RECORD INDEX

Tab	Document	Page
1	Notice of motion brought by the plaintiff, returnable on October 16, year 1	2
2	Affidavit of Eldred Klump, sworn October 3, year 1	3
3	Affidavit of Sunil Tharper, sworn October 6, year 1	4
3a	Exhibit A to the affidavit of Sunil Tharper, sworn October 6, year 1: report from Elihu Dunck, dated October 5, year 1	5
4	Statement of claim, issued January 4, year 1	7
5	Statement of defence, dated January 12, year 1	10

3. *File the notice of motion.* The notice of motion with proof of service must be filed at least three days before the day of the hearing (rule 37.08(1)).

4. *File the affidavit.* The moving and the responding parties may file affidavits and other supporting documents at least two days before the hearing, which gives a responding party more time to file (rule 39.02).

5. *File the motion record.* A motion record should be filed at least three days before the date of hearing. If it contains all the documents necessary for the motion, there is no need to follow the separate rules for filing motions and affidavits that are noted above.

6. *File the responding party's motion record.* If required, this should be served and filed at least two days before the hearing (rule 37.10(3)). This rule is also consistent with the rule requiring filing of affidavits two days before the hearing. Everything that is going to be filed must be with the court two days before the hearing so that the judge or master can read the documents before the hearing.

Remember that these are filing and service deadlines. You could find yourself:

- serving the opposing party on day 1;

- filing your motion record on day 2 (in which case the record is likely to be missing the responding party's material);

- being served with the responding party's material on day 3;

- having the responding party filing his or her own motion record, including the affidavit served on you, on day 3; and

- attending the hearing on day 5.

If the matter is an emergency, both the notice and the service and filing rules may be suspended (rules 2.03 and 37.07(2) to (4)). When proceeding this way, it is wise to ask in the notice of motion for "leave to dispense with service of this notice of motion" and "leave to abridge the time for serving and filing the notice of motion and supporting affidavits" on the grounds that the matter is urgent. If leave is granted, you can proceed with the substantive part of the motion.

CONFIRMATION OF MOTIONS

Often, a motion is served on a party and there is no further discussion before the motion hearing. Ideally, however, parties should confer and discuss ways of resolving the issue. If the parties do resolve the issue, they should alert the court that the matter has been resolved and the motion will not proceed. To encourage the resolution of issues arising on motions, rule 37.10.1 requires parties to confer, or to attempt to confer. Then, not later than 2 p.m. two days before the hearing, the moving party shall file with the registrar a confirmation on form 37B that the motion is confirmed to be heard on the date set by the court. If the nature of the confirmation changes, a corrected confirmation must be filed. Under case management, there are similar requirements that parties confer and confirm that a hearing will proceed.

ABANDONED MOTIONS

A party who has made a motion, has served but not filed it, or filed a motion but did not confirm it, and who does not appear in court is deemed to have abandoned the motion. However, a party who makes a motion may abandon it by delivering a notice of abandonment. In either case, the responding party is likely to have done some work and spent some legal fees getting ready to respond. Provided that the moving party served the motion, the responding party is entitled to immediate costs of the motion unless the court specifically orders otherwise. This means that the responding party may move to fix or assess costs without waiting for the trial judgment. If the responding party appears on a motion that has been abandoned, he or she can ask the court to fix costs immediately, saving the need for a separate assessment of costs, and yet another court attendance. A notice of abandonment is set out in figure 9.7.

However, for emergency motions in Toronto, you still need to obtain a date beforehand from the Motions Scheduling Unit. For details, see appendix I to this chapter.

FIGURE 9.7   NOTICE OF ABANDONMENT

Court file no. 01-CV-1234

ONTARIO
SUPERIOR COURT OF JUSTICE

BETWEEN:

ABIGAIL BOAR

Plaintiff

and

RATTLE MOTORS LTD. and FRED FLOGEM

Defendants

NOTICE OF ABANDONMENT

TAKE NOTICE that the moving party, Abigail Boar, wholly abandons
the motion returnable on October 16, year 1.

Date: October 10, year 1

Just & Coping
Barristers and Solicitors
365 Bay Street – 8701
Toronto, Ontario, M3J 4A9

I.M. Just
LSUC #12345R
tel. 416-762-1342
fax 416-762-2300

Lawyers for the Moving
Party (Plaintiff)

TO:
Huey Sue
LSUC #23456T
Barrister and Solicitor
65 False Trail
Toronto, Ontario, M6Y 1Z6

tel. 416-485-6891
fax 416-485-6892

Lawyer for the Responding
Parties (Defendants)

MOTIONS MADE WITHOUT ORAL ARGUMENT

The usual way to argue a motion is for counsel to appear at the hearing on the return date and to make submissions orally with references to the motion, affidavits, transcripts, or other documents. However, there are some circumstances where a motion does not require anyone to appear at a hearing.

Motion on consent

If a motion has been made and the responding party consents to the order sought, the moving party needs to file a consent and a draft order along with the notice of motion. A judge simply signs the order after reviewing the consent (rule 37.12.1(2)). You may wish to contact the court office to find out the procedure for filing a consent motion. Some regions ask moving parties to indicate on the motion that it is returnable during "the week of" followed by a date, for example, rather than on a specific day.

Unopposed motion

If the motion has been served and the responding party signals that he or she does not oppose it, the moving party should file a notice from the responding party that the motion is unopposed, together with a draft order (rule 37.12.1(3)). The notice should indicate that there is no opposition to the order sought. An example of the wording of such a notice is set out in figure 9.8.

Motions without notice

Motions without notice may be made in writing. For example, a motion for substituted service may not require oral argument. The notice of motion should make it clear what the moving party requires, and the affidavit should provide all of the evidence and facts a master would need to grant the order.

Opposed motions in writing

Where a motion is opposed and the issues are not overly complicated, the moving party may propose in the notice of motion that there be no oral argument and that the documents on the motion be submitted to the court. This is attractive because it saves the cost of a hearing, but most lawyers are loath to give up the opportunity for oral argument because it gives them the chance to gauge the court's reaction to the arguments. However, the elimination of oral argument is the way of the future for some procedures since it saves time and money. If the moving party wishes to take this route, the motion must be served 14 days before the return date. The moving party must serve a motion record *with* the notice of motion, a draft order, and a factum for a motion in writing, and at the same time file all of this with the court.

Within 10 days of being served, the responding party must serve and file a consent to the order, a notice that the order is not opposed, or a motion record with a notice that the responding party agrees to have the contested motion dealt with in writing without oral argument. In this case, the responding party must also file a factum.

If the responding party requires oral argument, he or she serves the moving party with notice that the responding party intends to make oral argument as well as file material. The moving party must then decide whether to appear and argue the motion or rely on his or her motion record and factum (rule 37.12.1(4)).

FIGURE 9.8 NOTICE THAT MOTION IS UNOPPOSED

Court file no. 01-CV-1234

ONTARIO
SUPERIOR COURT OF JUSTICE

BETWEEN:

ABIGAIL BOAR

Plaintiff

and

RATTLE MOTORS LTD. and FRED FLOGEM

Defendants

NOTICE THAT MOTION IS UNOPPOSED

TAKE NOTICE that the defendant, Rattle Motors Ltd. (responding party), does not object to the order sought by the plaintiff (moving party) to permit an inspection by a lighting engineer of the defendant's premises at 1240 Bay Street, Toronto, Ontario, M4H 0K8.

Huey Sue
LSUC #23456T
Barrister and Solicitor
65 False Trail
Toronto, Ontario, M6Y 1Z6

tel. 416-485-6891
fax 416-485-6892

Lawyer for the Responding
Parties (Defendants)

TO:
Just & Coping
Barristers and Solicitors
365 Bay Street - 8701
Toronto, Ontario, M3J 4A9

I.M. Just
LSUC #12345R
tel. 416-762-1342
fax 416-762-2300

Lawyers for the Moving
Party (Plaintiff)

CHAPTER SUMMARY

In this chapter, we examined the procedures for making motions, beginning with an overview of the procedure for a motion on notice. We then saw how motions without notice are dealt with, how to determine whether a motion should come before a master or a judge, and how to obtain a hearing date, noting the way in which practice directions in Toronto have complicated motion procedure there. We then examined the requirements for notices of motion and affidavits, focusing on criteria and rules for drafting and preparing these documents. Following this discussion, we turned to the preparation of motion records and to the rules governing time limits for serving motion materials. Finally, we examined the consequences of abandoning a motion and looked at the requirements and procedure for bring a motion in writing without oral argument.

APPENDIX I: MOTION AND APPLICATION PROCEDURE IN TORONTO

Until recently, there was a confusing collection of practice directions for procedures on various types of motions in Toronto. All of these were designed to spread out the motion workload so that the Toronto judges and masters could handle it efficiently, but case-managed and non-case-managed motions were handled differently, as were motions before judges and masters. There were also other specialized procedures for other areas such as estate, commercial list, and construction lien matters.

As of September 2002, there is one procedural guide for scheduling and bringing motions in Toronto, the *Superior Court of Justice Motions and Applications Procedure — Toronto Region*. If you are involved with Toronto motions, you should obtain a copy of this document, and any amendments, from the Toronto Court Office and read it carefully. Highlights are set out here:

1. There is a specific procedure for scheduling masters' and judges' motions in almost all cases, case-managed or non-case-managed. Estate list, commercial list, and some other motions are not covered by this practice direction, and continue to have their own separate scheduling systems.

2. To schedule a motion:

   a. You must check with counsel for the responding party to decide on a suitable date, and estimate how long the motion will take, provided that it will not take more than two hours.

   b. Call 416-327-5292 or e-mail the Motions Scheduling Unit at jus.g.mag .csd.civilmotionscheduling@jus.gov.on.ca to determine whether the date selected is available, and to book it if it is.

3. If the motion will take more than two hours, obtain a special appointment from the Motions Scheduling Unit:

   a. Your notice of motion will not have a fixed date. Instead, it will indicate that it will be heard on a date to be fixed by the court.

   b. With the responding party, you will have to work out a timetable of all steps to be taken prior to the argument of the motion, including the dates on which those steps will be completed. You must also include in the timetable the dates for exchange of motion documents with the responding party.

   c. Serve the timetable with your notice of motion so that the responding party can review it.

   d. As the moving party, you will have to file this timetable with your motion record. There is no special form for the timetable.

   e. If the responding party does not agree to the timetable, either party can ask for a case conference to fix the timetable.

   f. Once the timetable is complete and either fixed by the court or agreed to, the Motions Scheduling Unit will provide the parties with a court date.

4. If a motion is before a judge and will take more than one full day, you will need to have a case conference before the judge in charge of long motions to deal with timetables and other procedural matters. The judge will assign it to a trial list "for the week of" rather than for a specific date. This means that counsel will have to be sure to be available for that week, without having much advance notice of when the motion will actually be heard.

5. All motions, long or regular, must be confirmed by 2 p.m. two business days before the motion is to be heard. Confirmation may be made by fax to 416-327-5484 or by e-mail to jus.g.mag.csd.civilmotionsconfirmation @jus.gov.on.ca. Figure 9.9 shows the confirmation form for all judges/ masters civil motions/applications. Note that this form is similar to, but not identical to, form 37B, which is used in the rest of Ontario.

6. Urgent or emergency motions can be scheduled by calling the manager of the Motions Scheduling Unit at 416-326-1843.

7. If the motion is about discovery undertakings or objections involving more than five questions, there are special procedures. You are required to use a chart in prescribed form (schedule B to the practice direction) to list disputed discovery questions and the issues surrounding them. The chart is virtually identical to form 37C, which is used in the rest of the province.

APPENDIX II: SPECIAL MOTIONS

The following are some examples of special motions commonly encountered in a civil practice with special procedural or substantive requirements.

Interlocutory injunctions and mandatory orders: Rule 40 and section 101(2) of the Courts of Justice Act

Interlocutory injunctions and mandatory orders are used where the moving party wishes to stop the respondent from engaging in acts that continue to cause harm to the moving party that may not be adequately remedied by damages. The injunction prohibits or enjoins the respondent from continuing to persist in doing the acts complained of. A mandatory order is a positive injunction — it directs a party to perform specified actions. Often this motion, by stopping objectionable conduct, will bring the case to an end in a settlement — the real goal of the action.

FIGURE 9.9 CONFIRMATION FORM FOR ALL JUDGES/MASTERS CIVIL MOTIONS/APPLICATIONS

SCHEDULE A

ONTARIO
SUPERIOR COURT OF JUSTICE
CASE MANAGEMENT SCHEDULING UNIT

383 University Avenue, 10th Floor
Toronto ON M5G 1E6
Telephone: (416) 327-5292; Fax: (416) 327-5484
E-mail: jus.g.mag.csd.civilmotionsconfirmation@jus.gov.on.ca

CONFIRMATION FORM FOR ALL JUDGES/MASTERS
CIVIL MOTIONS/APPLICATIONS

COURT FILE NUMBER:

SHORT TITLE: _Boar v. Rattle Motors Ltd. et al._

Jurisdiction of Motion:
☐ Judge   ☒ Traditional Master   ☐ Case Management Master   _Smith_
(Name of Managing Master)

I, _I.M. Just_ , COUNSEL FOR THE MOVING
PARTY/~~APPLICANT~~, CONFIRM:

☒ I HAVE DISCUSSED WITH _Huey Sue_ , OPPOSING
COUNSEL/PARTY, THE MATTER REFERRED TO ABOVE AND CONFIRM,

OR

☐ I HAVE BEEN UNABLE TO CONFIRM WITH OPPOSING COUNSEL/PARTY BECAUSE
_____

THAT THE MOTION/APPLICATION LISTED TO BE HEARD ON _Monday_ THE _16th_ DAY OF _October_, ~~2002~~ _YR 1_ IS:

(TICK ONE BOX ONLY):

☐ WITHDRAWN ON CONSENT   ☐ CONSENTED TO
☐ UNOPPOSED, ALL OTHER ISSUES   ☐ OPPOSED, COST ISSUE ONLY
☐ ADJOURNED ON CONSENT TO: _____(DATE BOOKED WITH SCHEDULING UNIT)
☐ OPPOSED ADJOURNMENT TO BE REQUESTED BY: _____
☒ OPPOSED ON ISSUES AS SET OUT IN THE NOTICE OF MOTION/MOTION FORM
☐ OPPOSED ONLY ON THE FOLLOWING ISSUES: _____

TIME ESTIMATE REQUIRED: _1_ HOURS _25_ MINUTES   ☐ MORE THAN ORIGINALLY ESTIMATED

THE FOLLOWING MATERIALS (MOVING AND RESPONDING) HAVE BEEN FILED FOR USE ON THIS MATTER.

1. Statement of claim, Jan. 4, YR 1
2. Statement of defence, Jan. 12, YR 1
3. Affidavit of Eldred Klump, sworn Oct. 1, YR 1
4. Affidavit of Sunil Tharper, sworn Oct. 6, YR 1
5.
6.

October 12, YR 1
Date & Time

I.M. Just
Solicitor for moving party (please type or print clearly)

416-762-1342   imjust@isp.on.ca
Telephone Number and Email Address

TO: SCHEDULING UNIT
FAX: 416-327-5484   CONFIRMATIONS ONLY — NO FILINGS WILL BE ACCEPTED
EMAIL: jus.g.mag.csd.civilmotionsconfirmation@jus.gov.on.ca

NOTE:
❑ CONFIRMATION OF MOTION MUST BE FAXED OR E-MAILED BY 2:00 P.M. TWO DAYS PRIOR TO THE SCHEDULED DATE OF HEARING
❑ IF CONFIRMATION IS NOT RECEIVED BY THE SCHEDULING UNIT, THE SCHEDULED MOTION/APPLICATION WILL BE NOTED AS ABANDONED
❑ NO LATE MATERIALS WILL BE ACCEPTED BY THE COURT
❑ THIS FORM SHOULD BE COPIED TO OPPOSING COUNSEL/PARTY

The motion may be made only to a judge. The motion may be brought before a proceeding is commenced, provided that the proceeding is eventually commenced. The moving party must undertake to pay damages to the respondent for any unjustifiable harm done to the respondent as a result of the injunction. The order may be obtained without notice, but it is only valid for ten days and may be renewed on notice to the respondent. A factum is required on this motion.

Appointment of a receiver: Rule 41 and section 101 of the Courts of Justice Act

A receiver is a person appointed by the court to exercise the powers granted in a receivership order to step in and stand in the shoes of the responding party in order to carry out the powers granted in the order. In commercial secured debt transactions, the creditor may apply to the court to have a receiver take over control of the debtor in order to liquidate it in an orderly way that will protect the creditor's investment where the debtor's finances and operations are in chaos. In some circumstances, a receiver-manager may also be appointed to take control of and run the debtor's business.

The motion may be brought prior to commencement of proceedings, and must be brought before a judge. The order must name the receiver and specify the security that the moving party is to provide for any damages resulting from the receivership. If the receiver is also a manager, it must set out the management powers. The responding party or any party may require a reference to examine the conduct of the receiver, and a receiver may apply for direction from a judge on a motion.

Certificate of pending litigation: Rule 42 and section 103 of the Courts of Justice Act

A certificate of pending litigation is available when the moving party claims an interest in land in a civil action. Once a certificate has been issued, it may be registered on title; this provides notice to others that the moving party has an interest in the land as a result of the litigation, which may cause others to exercise caution in dealing with the land's current owners.

Certificates of pending litigation may be found on title, for example, where there is litigation over the dissolution of a partnership (or other type of business) where the partners' interests in land is in dispute.

To bring this motion, you must claim leave to obtain a certificate of pending litigation in your action or application, and then bring the motion. Factums are required on any motion to discharge a certificate of pending litigation.

Interpleader order: Rule 43

An interpleader order is one in which the court gives directions to a person in possession of personal property where others are making claims with respect to that property. A trustee, for example, may bring an interpleader motion where two beneficiaries are claiming competing interests in the same property under rule 43.02(1). A sheriff or other person may also do so if holding property as a result of a seizure under a writ of execution where there are competing claims, usually between creditors and a debtor, under rule 43.02(2). There are different requirements under each branch of rule 43.02 for an order, and this should be reflected in the contents of the affidavit in support of the motion. The purpose of the motion is for the interpleading person to obtain court directions as to what should be done with the property that that person is holding and, by doing so, avoid being sued by one of the disputants for mishandling the property.

Where there are substantive issues of law involved, the motion should be brought before a judge. If the matter is under rule 43.02(1), and no proceeding has been commenced, the person seeking an interpleader order shall commence an application. Otherwise, the person proceeds by motion.

Interim recovery of personal property order: Rule 44

An interim order for recovery of personal property directs the sheriff to seize and hold personal property until further order of the court where there is a dispute about property ownership. The court may direct that the property remain with one party or the other, subject to undertakings to pay damages or to post security for the prompt return of the property. The idea behind this order is that where there is a dispute over possession of the property, the property will be safe and secure until the court can hear and decide the issues.

The motion may be made without notice if a party is taking steps that will permanently prevent recovery of the property. In the action or proceeding there must be a claim to recover personal property before the motion may be brought. If an order is made without notice, the sheriff must hold the property for ten days after service of the order so that the defendant may take steps to recover the property. Otherwise, the court may order the sheriff to take possession of the property, or leave it with the defendant, subject to posting of security and undertaking to immediately return the property if ordered to do so. If the defendant is blocking the sheriff in an attempt to seize the property, the sheriff may seize other property belonging to the defendant that is of equivalent value.

Interim preservation order: Rule 45

An interim preservation order may be given not only to secure disputed property, as in the case of an order to recover property under rule 44, but it can also be used to preserve personal property that may be evidence, or to recover personal property held by another who is not a party to the proceeding. This may include the sequestration or control of a specific fund. If the property is perishable, the court may order its sale or disposal. Conditions may be imposed on the order for preservation of property. If a debtor claims that security was wrongfully seized, he may recover the security, but will have to post other security until the matter has been adjudicated.

Motion for security for costs: Rule 56

In some situations, a plaintiff may be obliged to post security for costs in the event that the action is dismissed, and the defendant would be likely to have difficulty enforcing an order to pay costs against a plaintiff. Plaintiffs who reside outside the jurisdiction and have no assets in Ontario, who are nominal plaintiffs with no assets, who have previously failed to pay a judgment owed to the defendant in an earlier proceedings, or who appear to be vexatious litigants may all be compelled to post security for costs before they can proceed further with their lawsuit.

Security for costs can only be ordered on a motion after the defence has been served. Once an order is made, the court may entertain other motions to increase security as the proceeding progresses.

KEY TERMS

motion

return of a motion

official examiner

summary proceedings

master

jurat

NOTES

1 In a proper case, rule 37.17 permits a motion to be brought before a proceeding has been commenced, provided that the moving party undertakes to commence proceedings promptly.

2 A master's motion, as a matter of convention, may be brought before a judge in an emergency if no master is available.

3 Often this is a "motion morning" or a "motion afternoon." Once you know the court where the matter must be heard, call the court office to find out when the motion time is.

4 While the form calls for the municipality and the county or region as a residential description, the City of Toronto, since the abolition of the former Municipality of Metropolitan Toronto, is no longer part of a county or region. The practice has grown up of describing a deponent residing in Toronto as residing in the City of Toronto, Province of Ontario.

5 The wording of the jurat changes slightly when it is sworn by two or more deponents, when it is sworn by a blind or illiterate person, or when it is sworn by a person who does not understand the language in which it is written. If the deponent is blind or illiterate, the jurat must indicate that the deponent had it read to him or her, that he or she understood it, and that he or she signed it or made his or her mark (usually an "X"). If the deponent does not understand the language, the jurat must indicate that a named person interpreted the affidavit and swore to translate it correctly.

REFERENCES

Courts of Justice Act, RSO 1990, c. C.43.

Judicial Review Procedure Act, RSO 1990, c. J.1.

Rules of Civil Procedure, RRO 1990, reg. 194.

REVIEW QUESTIONS

1. What is the purpose of motions?

2. What does the phrase "motioning the other side to death" mean, and how may the practice be prevented?

3. Explain to your client what happens when a motion is brought.

4. Indicate whether a master can hear the following motions:

   a. a motion to strike out parts of a statement of claim

   b. a motion to commit a witness to jail for failure to appear at trial when summonsed

   c. a motion to vary an order made by Judge Jeffreys

d. a motion to join parties to the lawsuit

e. a motion for a judgment on consent where 16-year-old Rory is a party

5. Suppose your firm wishes to bring a "long motion" in Toronto. Is there anything special you should do?

6. When can hearsay be used in an affidavit?

7. What is included in a motion record?

8. What is the purpose of a motion record?

9. a. Today is March 2. Your instructing lawyer wants to bring a motion on notice returnable March 5. Can she do it? Why?

   b. When is the last day the lawyer could have filed a motion record?

   c. When is the last day the responding party could have filed a responding party motion record?

10. Can a law firm bring a motion, change its mind, and abandon the motion without consequences?

11. Suppose your law firm wishes to make a motion in writing, rather than have an oral hearing. Can it?

DISCUSSION QUESTIONS

1. Read and respond to the following memorandum:

   To: E. Egregious, law clerk
   From: I.M. Just, lawyer
   Re: *Boar v. Rattle Motors Ltd. et al.*

   When we brought a motion for inspection of Rattle Motor's showroom, under rule 32, we were surprised to hear that the defendant had gutted the interior of the showroom and destroyed important evidence. I don't believe that this renovation had anything to do with marketing cars. I want to bring a motion to have the defendant found in contempt for the intentional destruction of evidence. But before I do that, I want to examine Sunil Tharper, the manager, on this issue. Write me a brief memo setting out what authority there is for doing this.

2. Read and respond to the following memorandum:

   To: E. Egregious, law clerk
   From: I.M. Just, lawyer
   Re: *Boar v. Rattle Motors Ltd. et al.*

   I have just received a report from Diedre Kuflesnout. She is an automobile engineer and a member of the Society of Automotive Engineers. She is a consultant and expert on assessing mechanical and design defects in cars. Her report indicates that leaking oil pans on new models, affecting about 12 cars in 1,000, have plagued the year 0 Super Coupe. If there were no defect, the expected rate of reported leaking oil pans would be about 1 in 2,000 cars. There is also information that the manufacturer was aware that there might be a problem and did nothing. Although we are about to start discoveries, I want to add Skank Motorcar Company Ltd., the manufacturer of the Super Coupe, as a party defendant in this lawsuit. Find out what rule gives me the right to do this, and then draft the notice of motion and an affidavit in my name setting out the reasons why the proposed defendant should be added. Also research whether we would likely have to pay costs and what rights the other defendants might have.

CHAPTER 10

Default judgment

INTRODUCTION

Once you have served the plaintiff's statement of claim, the defendant must serve you with a statement of defence within the time provided for in the rules. If you receive no statement of defence, the defendant is deemed to have admitted the truth of the facts in the statement of claim and admitted liability. The plaintiff may then obtain a judgment against the defendant in default of a defence. The plaintiff may also obtain a default judgment if a defence was delivered but was struck out without leave to file another (rule 19.01(2)). Where there are several defendants and one has not delivered a defence, and the plaintiff has not noted that defendant in default, a defendant who has delivered a defence can require the registrar to order the plaintiff to note the non-filing defendant in default (rule 19.01(3)).

If a claim is a liquidated amount, there is a quick and straightforward administrative process for obtaining a judgment for the amount due. Most debt collection cases are liquidated claims — for example, claims for payment for goods sold or services rendered or for repayment of loans.

Abigail's claim against Fred and Rattle Motors Ltd., however, is not liquidated. Her claim for general damages cannot be calculated by using a simple, objective formula. Even her special damages, which can be calculated that way, are still accruing, so we do not know what they will total. In this kind of case, even though the defendant is deemed to have admitted the truth of the facts in the statement of claim and to have admitted liability, the plaintiff is obliged to prove the monetary value of damages on a motion to a judge. Evidence may be given by affidavit or orally in a hearing if the court requires it. An affidavit, usually the plaintiff's, details her injuries, pain, treatment, and post-injury disabilities by way of general damages; it also provides details of her special damages. Affidavits of other witnesses provide other evidence that supports the claim for damages.

In this chapter, we examine both the summary method of signing default judgment for liquidated damages before the registrar and the method whereby a judge assesses general damages.

DEFAULT JUDGMENT FOR A LIQUIDATED DEMAND

To obtain or sign default judgment on behalf of a plaintiff, you must prepare certain documents and file them with the registrar of the Superior Court (actually with a clerk at the public counter in the court office of the region where the action is commenced). If the documents are properly prepared and in order, the clerk acts on the registrar's behalf to sign judgment for the full amount of the claim, prejudgment interest, and costs. Be sure that your claim is accurately stated and that your calculations are accurate because it is embarrassing and time-consuming to amend a judgment later to correct an error.

Consider another of Abigail's claims. Hieronymus Bloggs owes Abigail Boar $38,182.79 for the financial analysis services provided by Abigail. Payment should have been made on July 28, year 0, and interest runs on overdue amounts at the rate of 12 percent per annum. On September 26, year 0, I.M. Just issued a claim on Abigail's behalf and served it on Hieronymus. No statement of defence was received, and I.M. Just intends to sign default judgment on October 17, year 0. The cost of issuing a claim is $181. You paid a process server $41 to serve the claim and provide you with an affidavit of service. You have receipts to attach to the bill of costs for all disbursements. GST is chargeable on all fees and on disbursements that are services, such as photocopies, fax, postage, and service of pleadings at 5 percent. GST is not chargeable on government fees, such as the $181 paid to issue the statement of claim.

Forms required to sign default judgment

The following are the forms required to sign default judgment:

- an affidavit of service, proving service of the statement of claim, and the original statement of claim;

- a requisition of default judgment, noting the defendant in default;

- a bill of costs (the original and two copies) to provide a basis for fixing the amount of costs;

- a draft judgment (the original and two copies);

- a cheque payable to the Minister of Finance for filing for default judgment;

- a requisition for a writ of seizure and sale (optional);

- a writ of seizure and sale (the original and two copies) (optional); and

- a cheque, payable to the Minister of Finance, to issue the writ of seizure and sale (rules 19.01 and 19.04).

The defendant may be noted in default separately by filing a requisition to note the defendant in default. But it saves some time and paper to note the defendant in default as part of the requisition for default judgment. The effect of noting the defendant in default is to note pleadings closed, which bars the late filing of a statement of defence.

The requisition for default judgment requires you to state that the claim is liquidated and that it comes within the class of claims for which you may sign default judgment. You also show on this form how much is owing, less payments made by the debtor, if any.

Procedure for signing judgment

Set out below is a step-by-step guide to signing default judgment.

PREPARE A REQUISITION FOR DEFAULT JUDGMENT

You will need the original statement of claim attached to the process server's affidavit of service so that the clerk can see when the claim was served, where it was served, and satisfy himself or herself that the time for filing the defence has elapsed. Remember that the time runs from the time of service, not from the time the claim was issued. Figure 10.1 at the end of the chapter shows a completed requisition for a default judgment.

1. On the requisition itself, after the words "TO THE LOCAL REGISTRAR AT," type in the word "Toronto." After this, type "I REQUIRE you to note the defendant (*name*) in default in this action and that pleadings be noted closed against the defendant on the ground that the defendant has failed to file a statement of defence within the time provided for in the *Rules of Civil Procedure.*"

2. Check off the basis for signing default judgment.

3. Indicate whether any payments have been made on account with respect to the claim. If some payments have been made, complete part A; if none have been made, complete part B.

4. If some payments have been made, indicate the principal amount claimed, without interest. Then show the payment on account, and show how much of that payment is allocated to interest and how much to principal. At common law, amounts received are applied first to outstanding interest. If there is any amount remaining, it is applied to outstanding principal. After allocating the payment received, indicate the principal amount outstanding. This is "total A" on the form.

5. With respect to the calculation of prejudgment interest, indicate the date on which the claim was issued and the date on which the cause of action arose. This allows the clerk (and you) to determine how many days of interest your client is entitled to, and what the appropriate rate is if interest is calculated under the prejudgment interest provisions of the *Courts of Justice Act*. If you have not previously learned how to apply the prejudgment and postjudgment interest rules, see chapter 17.

6. Show how the prejudgment interest is calculated. Calculate simple interest unless you have a contractual right to compound interest. Calculate interest on the principal amount outstanding from the date of the last payment previously identified in the form. To do this, count the number of days from the date of the last payment to the date on which judgment is to be signed (the last "end date" in the form). Then multiply that number by the annual rate of interest, multiply that result by the principal amount owing, and divide by 365. This is "total B" on the form.

7. From the calculations in 6 above, enter total B, and from the calculations in 4 above, enter total A in order to fill in the total amount for which to sign judgment.

8. If no payment was received, then complete part B, indicating amount A, the total amount of the claim less interest. Provide the interest data, including the date on which the claim arose and was issued. Then show your interest calculations, using simple interest unless you have a contractual right to compound interest and have claimed this in your statement of claim. Count the number of days from the date the cause of action arose to the date of judgment, and do the calculations as described previously for part A (part payments received). Add the sum claimed (total A) to the interest claimed (total B) to determine the amount for which the judgment is to be signed.

9. Complete part C, "Postjudgment interest and costs." Insert the rate of postjudgment interest that applies (this is either a rate contractually agreed on between the parties or the rate set by statute for the quarter in which the judgment is signed), and indicate the basis for claiming interest. Then check off whether you wish the registrar to fix costs or have the costs assessed later. The usual practice is to have the registrar fix the costs based on your bill of costs, which you prepare in accordance with the rules. This is much quicker and less expensive than coming back at a later date to have the costs assessed. One might ask to have a bill of costs assessed if costs to the plaintiff had been much higher than is usually the case in a default judgment situation. In this situation, having costs assessed might be worth the time and expense because costs are fixed in accordance with flat rates based on a "normal" proceeding.

PREPARE A BILL OF COSTS

See figure 10.2 at the end of the chapter for Abigail's bill of costs (form 57A). In 2005, amendments to the rules established a procedure for fixing costs at the end of a hearing, rather than referring them for an assessment in a separate proceeding. These procedures are discussed in detail in chapter 18, the chapter on costs. The general theory is that fixing costs is quicker and cheaper than assessing them, and rule 19.04(2)(e) clearly permits a plaintiff to use either method. Generally, plaintiffs opt to have the registrar assess costs using a bill of costs rather than a costs outline (form 57B).

As is usually the case, the defaulting defendant is obliged to pay costs on a **partial indemnity** scale. The basis for assessing a lawyer's fees on a bill of costs is rule 57.01(1), which creates broad discretion in determining the fee component of a costs award. Costs were subject to a notice from the costs subcommittee of the Civil Rules Committee, which established a costs grid. This grid was revoked in 2005. However, in the absence of any other guidelines to interpret rule 57.01(1), the grid figures continue to be used by judges, lawyers, and law clerks, and are included here. The costs grid sets out the following maximum rates to be used:

partial indemnity
usual order for costs, based on a cost grid that establishes hourly rates for tariff items listed in the grid; provides less than full recovery for the client

- law clerk: $80 per hour;

- student-at-law (articling student): $60 per hour;

- lawyer with less than 10 years' experience: $225 per hour;

- lawyer with more than 10 but less than 20 years' experience: $300 per hour;

- lawyer with 20 or more years' experience: $350 per hour.

However, for simpler matters, including obtaining a default judgment, the rates should be well below the maximums, although there is no prescription or formula to tell you with precision what they should be.

A lawyer's out-of-pocket expenses, or **disbursements**, are another story. These are covered in tariff A, part II, "disbursements." Here, cost recovery is usually on a dollar-for-dollar basis. For example, if $41 is paid to a process server to serve a statement of claim, then that is the amount that will be recovered in costs, although there are limits on some part II disbursements. Court fees and sheriff costs can be recovered in full.[1] Always check the tariff and court fees before preparing a bill of costs because the allowable amounts change from year to year. The items usually included in the bill of costs on default judgment are as follows:

disbursements
out-of-pocket expenses incurred by a lawyer for fees and services paid to others as part of proceeding with a case

1. *Pleadings.* Hours spent times the appropriate hourly rate from the costs grid.

2. *Court fees paid to issue statement of claim.* Obtain fees from the schedule of fees that follows tariffs A and B in commercial editions of the Rules of Practice, such as *Ontario Annual Practice* — note that these fees change from time to time.

3. *Fees paid to serve statement of claim.* See tariff A, part II — reasonable costs backed by receipt for payment to process server (this includes GST).

4. *Determination of costs and signing order for default judgment.* Hours spent times the appropriate hourly rate on the costs grid.

5. *Court fees paid to file requisition for default judgment.* As in item 2 above, see the schedule of fees.

In the bill of costs, fees and disbursements are recorded in separate columns and totalled. Disbursements include tariff A, part II items, as well as court fees and sheriff fees. If for any reason you wish to recover costs on a **substantial indemnity** scale, this is a claim for a full recovery of costs and is best dealt with by being set down for hearing before an assessment officer. Recovery on this scale is unusual in default situations, because this scale is usually applied when a party misconducts himself or herself in the course of proceedings.

substantial indemnity
costs scale, usually used as a punitive costs award, that results in near indemnity for the winner on a dollar-for-dollar basis

DRAFT A JUDGMENT

Draft a judgment such as the one shown in figure 10.3 (at the end of the chapter), and make two copies of it. A judgment is a one-paragraph document in which you must insert the sum claimed, composed of the principal amount and interest (taken from the requisition for default judgment), and the costs (taken from the bill of costs). Remember to include a sentence that says "This judgment bears interest at the rate of ___ percent per year from its date." If this statement is not present in the draft judgment, even though interest is claimed in the statement of claim and identified in the requisition for default judgment, the clerk might not insert the phrase for you, and you might not obtain postjudgment interest.

PREPARE A REQUISITION FOR A WRIT OF SEIZURE AND SALE

While a requisition for a writ of seizure and sale and a writ of seizure and sale are not required to obtain a default judgment, these documents are often prepared when obtaining default judgment because you may wish to file the writ of execution as quickly as possible in order to catch the debtor's assets before they are dissipated.

The requisition for a writ of seizure and sale, which is set out in figure 10.4 at the end of the chapter, is directed to the sheriff of each county, region, or district where you think the debtor has assets. If the debtor has assets in more than one area, you must refer in the requisition to each sheriff's office in which you intend to file a writ of seizure and sale. Be sure to set out the name of the debtor accurately. Include the amount to be seized, the amount of costs claimed, and the applicable postjudgment interest rate, all of which can be copied from the judgment.

PREPARE A WRIT OF SEIZURE AND SALE

This writ is set out in figure 10.5 at the end of the chapter. You should prepare an original and one copy of it for each sheriff's office in which you plan to file it. When you obtain the default judgment and pay the fee to issue the writ, file the original and one copy with the sheriff's office, along with a covering letter instructing the sheriff to file the writ in the land registry and land titles system (if there is one). If the writ is not filed in the land titles system, the writ will not attach the execution debtor's land registered in the land titles system. Filing the writ with the sheriff is sufficient to attach an interest in land registered in the land registry system. Check with the sheriff's office to ascertain the fee for filing with the land registry system.

To complete each writ, fill in the blanks, using the judgment and the requisition for a writ of seizure and sale as the source of the relevant information. Keep one copy of each writ for your office file. Remember to complete the backsheet by adding in the fee paid to the province to issue the writ, and the fee paid to the lawyer for doing the work. The sheriff is entitled to add these costs to the amount on the face of the writ that may be collected from the debtor in the future.

PREPARE A CHEQUE PAYABLE TO THE MINISTER OF FINANCE

To cover the cost of issuing each original writ of seizure and sale, check the current court's and sheriff's fees tariff.

DEFAULT JUDGMENT FOR AN UNLIQUIDATED DEMAND

Where a claim is not liquidated and the defendant has defaulted on a defence, or where the registrar is uncertain about a liquidated claim and refuses to sign default judgment, the plaintiff must bring a motion before a judge against the defendant to claim judgment on the statement of claim.

Evidence of damages

Where the claim is unliquidated, more detail is required than in the case of a liqui-dated claim. Initially, this detail is provided by way of affidavit evidence. If the judge is satisfied with the contents of the affidavit, he or she may grant judgment in ac-cordance with the motion. But if there is any doubt, the judge can order that the matter proceed to trial for an assessment of damages. The judge may also decide that the claim is without merit — for example, if the claim concerns a breach of a right of the plaintiff that the law does not recognize. In that case, it does not matter whether the plaintiff can prove damages. If there is no right of action, the claim is dismissed even though the defendant has not put in a defence.

Contents of the affidavit

Where the statement of claim discloses a breach of the plaintiff's rights, the affidavit need only focus on the damages. Abigail's affidavit would describe the accident very briefly and focus on her injuries, convalescence, recovery, treatment, and the consequences of the injury on her social life, employment, and general enjoyment of life. An exhibit should be attached to the affidavit, listing the totals for special damages, such as medications, homecare assistance, and income loss. You may wish to have an affidavit from Abigail's doctor with medical reports about her prog-nosis attached as exhibits. You may want an affidavit from her employer or from the human resources person who has handled her work disability issues. You may also wish to have affidavits from one or two of her acquaintances who can describe the pre- and post-injury Abigail to show how the injuries have affected her daily life.

If a judge decides that oral evidence should be heard, the witnesses who made the affidavits will testify, and the topics covered will be the same as those covered in the affidavits.

Figure 10.6 (at the end of the chapter) shows what Abigail's affidavit might look like. Because it includes both evidence from which factual conclusions can be drawn and the facts themselves, it appears to be like a detailed version of the paragraphs in Abigail's statement of claim that deal with damages. Since liability is deemed to be admitted, little space is devoted to that issue.

SETTING ASIDE DEFAULT JUDGMENT

Often a plaintiff will serve a defendant, and the defendant will not respond. While the plaintiff is entitled to assume that the defendant's lack of response is simply an admission of the plaintiff's case, that is not always the case. Where, for example, the defendant has been served by an alternative to personal service, he or she may have been unaware of the case against him or her because service was ineffective. For example, the plaintiff may have attempted personal service at the defendant's residence and followed up, following rule 16.03(5), by delivering and then mailing the statement of claim to the defendant at his or her residence. Perhaps the defend-ant was out of town, and the letters were just left for him or her. The defendant may return to find that there is now a judgment against him or her. In other cases, the de-fendant is served and turns the claim over to a lawyer with instructions to defend; the lawyer then inadvertently misses the time limit. In these cases, rule 19.08 pro-vides that a judgment signed by the registrar or a judgment made after motion to a

Table 10.1   Routes for setting aside an order on motion

Nature of original order	Before whom motion to set aside should be made
Order of a registrar	Judge or master in accordance with rule 37.03.
Order of a judge	1. Judge who made the order in any place where the judge is sitting. 2. Any other judge in accordance with rule 37.03.
Order of a master	1. Master who made the order in any place where the master is sitting. 2. Any other judge or master in accordance with rule 37.03.
Order of a judge of Court of Appeal or Divisional Court	1. Judge who made the order. 2. If the order was made by a panel of judges, the panel that made it.

judge may be set aside or varied by the court. The noting of the defendant in default may also be set aside, which technically reopens pleadings and allows a statement of defence to be filed. The cases make clear that the defendant must satisfy the court on three factors if the judgment is to be set aside:

1. the default must be adequately explained as the result of a mistake or error on the part of one or more of the parties,

2. the motion to set the judgment aside must be brought promptly, and,

3. the defendant must disclose a plausible defence that cannot be decided without cross-examination or further judicial inquiry.[2]

Figure 10.7 (at the end of the chapter) sets out the kind of affidavit that can be used to set aside a default judgment.

SETTING ASIDE ORDERS ON MOTIONS

What rule 19.08 does for default judgments, rule 37.14 does for orders made on motions. Any order made by a judge or master on a motion, or made by a registrar, may be set aside by bringing a motion to set aside or vary the order in question.

When motion to set aside may be brought

Anyone who is affected by an order made on a motion without notice may move to set the order aside. The person need not be a party to the proceeding. The breadth of this rule demonstrates the safeguards that are built into the rules where a motion is made without notice. Where a motion is made with notice and a responding party or other interested person fails to appear through inadvertence, mistake, or insufficient notice, that person may move to set the motion aside. Here, because of the short minimum period for serving and filing, a responding or interested party may not have enough time to prepare adequately. In a case like this, it is appropriate to tell the moving party that the time period is too short and ask for an adjournment. If the moving party refuses, rule 37.14 provides an adequate, if cumbersome, remedy. If a person is affected by an order of a registrar, he or she may move to set the judgment aside.

Motion procedure

The rule requires that a motion be brought immediately on finding out about the order. The motion is returnable on the first available day that is at least three days after the service of the motion (the minimum notice period under the rules). Rule 37.14(3) to (6) tells you before whom a motion may be brought, depending on who made the original order. This is necessary because of jurisdictional issues. A master does not have the power to set aside a judge's order. Table 10.1 summarizes the routes to follow to set aside an order made on a motion.

CHAPTER SUMMARY

In this chapter we examined the procedure for obtaining a default judgment when the defendant fails to file a statement of defence. We noted the difference between a liquidated claim, where the registrar of the court signs judgment as an administrative act, and an unliquidated claim, where the plaintiff is obliged to present evidence to show what the quantum of damages should be. We noted how to prepare the necessary documentation for a default judgment (requisition, bill of costs, draft judgment, requisition for a writ of seizure and sale, and a writ of seizure and sale). We then examined what is required to set aside a default judgment both for judgments and for orders made on other kinds of motions.

KEY TERMS

partial indemnity

disbursements

substantial indemnity

NOTES

1 *Administration of Justice Act*, O. reg. 293/92, as amended.

2 See *Grieco v. Marquis* (1998), 38 OR (3d) 314 (Gen. Div).

REFERENCES

Carthy, James J., W.A. Derry Millar, and Jeffrey G. Cowan, *Ontario Annual Practice* (Aurora, ON: Canada Law Book, published annually).

Courts of Justice Act, RSO 1990, c. C.43.

Grieco v. Marquis (1998), 38 OR (3d) 314 (Gen. Div.).

Rules of Civil Procedure, RRO 1990, reg. 194.

REVIEW QUESTIONS

1. Under what circumstances can a plaintiff apply to sign default judgment?

2. Explain the difference between a liquidated and an unliquidated claim.

3. What documents must you present to the court in order to sign a default judgment?

4. What is the function of the requisition for default judgment?

5. Suppose the defendant defaults on his or her defence but pays some money on account of the amount claimed. How does this affect the process of signing default judgment?

6. What determines the prejudgment and postjudgment interest rate you ask for?

7. How do you determine the amounts that go into a bill of costs?

8. In what circumstances do you need to requisition more than one writ of seizure and sale?

9. If you wish to set aside a default judgment, what must you show to the court?

10. Explain how setting aside an order under rule 37.14 differs from setting aside a judgment under rule 19.

DISCUSSION QUESTIONS

1. Read and respond to the following memorandum:

   To: Law clerk
   From: Lawyer
   Re: *Ulock v. Foot*
   Date: April 26, year 1

   We issued a claim against Murgatroyd Ulock on March 23, year 1. Ulock had signed a promissory note to our client, Squeezem Ltd., for $20,000 on August 1, year 0. The note was due on December 1, year 0. It provided for interest at 11 percent per year from the time it was past due until payment. Interest has been claimed on this basis. The claim was thus for $20,000 plus interest on the overdue amount. On March 1, year 1, Ulock paid $2,000 on account, but he has paid nothing since. Ulock was served with the statement of claim on March 24, year 1. Because Ulock has not defended, and the time for filing a defence has passed, please prepare the necessary documents to sign default judgment on April 28, year 1. The original statement of claim and affidavit of service is in the file, together with a receipt for $53.21 for service of the claim and a receipt for $181 for the court fee paid to issue the statement of claim. It is rumoured that Foot owns property in Toronto and Oshawa.

2. Read and respond to the following memorandum:

   To: Law clerk
   From: Lawyer
   Re: *Foot ats Ulock*
   Date: April 30, year 1

   I have just learned that default judgment has been signed on April 28, year 1 against our client, Ophelia Foot, on a promissory note made to Murgatroyd Ulock. Foot brought the statement of claim in two weeks ago, and I meant to draft a defence. The defence is to be based on the fact that Ophelia does not speak or read English, she thought she was signing a lease rather than a promissory note, and Ulock misled her and intended to defraud her. Unfortunately, I spilled coffee all over the statement of defence, put it on the radiator in the copier room to dry out, and then forgot about it. I think the cleaners threw it out, so I do not have a copy, though I remember it was a simple claim on a promissory note. Draft a notice of motion and affidavit in support in my name so that we can move to set aside default judgment.

FIGURE 10.1   REQUISITION FOR DEFAULT JUDGMENT (FORM 19D)

Court file no. 01-CV-7777

ONTARIO
SUPERIOR COURT OF JUSTICE

BETWEEN:

ABIGAIL BOAR

Plaintiff

and

HIERONYMUS BLOGGS

Defendant

REQUISITION FOR DEFAULT JUDGMENT

TO THE LOCAL REGISTRAR AT TORONTO

I REQUIRE you to note the defendant, Hieronymus Bloggs, in default in this action and that pleadings be noted closed against the defendant on the ground that the defendant has failed to file a statement of defence within the time provided for in the *Rules of Civil Procedure*.

I REQUIRE default judgment to be signed against the defendant Hieronymus Bloggs.

Default judgment may properly be signed in this action because the claim is for

- ☒ a debt or liquidated demand in money
- ❏ recovery of possession of land
- ❏ recovery of possession of personal property
- ❏ foreclosure, sale or redemption of a mortgage

☒ There has been no payment on account of the claim since the statement of claim was issued. *(Complete Parts B & C.)*
OR
❏ The following payments have been made on account of the claim since the statement of claim was issued. *(Complete Parts A & C.)*

FIGURE 10.1   CONTINUED

Part A — PAYMENT(S) RECEIVED BY PLAINTIFF

(Complete this part only where part payment of the claim has been received. Where no payment has been received on account of the claim, omit this part and complete Part B.)

1. Principal

Principal sum claimed in
statement of claim (without interest) $. . . . .

Date of Payment	Amount of Payment	Payment Amount Principal	Applied to Interest	Principal Sum Owing
TOTAL	$.	$.	$.	A $ . . . .

2. Prejudgment interest

(Under section 128 of the Courts of Justice Act, *judgment may be obtained for prejudgment interest from the date the cause of action arose, if claimed in the statement of claim.)*

Date on which statement of claim was issued . . . .

Date from which prejudgment interest is claimed . . . .

The plaintiff is entitled to prejudgment interest on the claim, calculated as follows:

(Calculate simple interest only unless an agreement relied on in the statement of claim specifies otherwise. Calculate interest on the principal sum owing from the date of the last payment. To calculate the interest amount, count the number of days since the last payment, multiply that number by the annual rate of interest, multiply the result by the principal sum owing and divide by 365.)

Principal Sum Owing	Start Date	End Date (Date of Payment)	Number of Days	Rate	Interest Amount

(The last End Date should be the date judgment is signed.)

TOTAL B $ . . . .

Principal Sum Owing (Total A above) $ . . . .
Total Interest Amount (Total B above) $ . . . .

SIGN JUDGMENT FOR. . . . . $ . . . .

FIGURE 10.1   CONTINUED

PART B — NO PAYMENT RECEIVED BY PLAINTIFF
(Complete this part only where no payment has been received on account of the claim.)

1. Principal

Principal sum claimed in
statement of claim (without interest) A $ 38,182.79

2. Prejudgment interest

(Under section 128 of the Courts of Justice Act, *judgment may be obtained for prejudgment interest from the date the cause of action arose, if claimed in the statement of claim.)*

Date on which statement of claim was issued . . September 26, year 0

Date from which prejudgment interest is claimed . . . . July 29, year 0

The plaintiff is entitled to prejudgment interest on the claim, calculated as follows:

(Calculate simple interest only unless an agreement relied on in the statement of claim specifies otherwise. To calculate the interest amount, count the number of days and multiply that number by the annual rate of interest, multiply the result by the principal sum owing and divide by 365.)

Principal Sum Owing	Start Date	End date (Date of Judgment)	Number of Days	Rate	Interest Amount
38,182.79	July 29, year 0	Oct. 17, year 0	81	12%*	1,016.81

TOTAL B $ 1,016.81

Principal Sum Owing (Total A above) $ . . . 38,182.79
Total Interest Amount (Total B above) $ 1,016.81

SIGN JUDGMENT FOR. . . . . $ . . . 39,199.60

(*Assume that the interest rate is based on the agreed term of a contract.)

FIGURE 10.1   CONCLUDED

PART C — POSTJUDGMENT INTEREST AND COSTS

1. Postjudgment interest

    The plaintiff is entitled to postjudgment interest at the rate of 12
    percent per year,

    ❑ under the *Courts of Justice Act*, as claimed in the statement of
    claim.

    or

    ☒ in accordance with the claim made in the statement of claim.

2. Costs

    The plaintiff wishes costs to be

    ☒ fixed by the local registrar.

    or

    ❑ assessed by an assessment officer.

Date . .October 17, year 0. . .   . .*I.M. Just*. . . . .

Just & Coping
Barristers and Solicitors
365 Bay Street - 8701
Toronto, Ontario, M3J 4A9

I.M. Just
LSUC #12345R
tel. 416-762-1342
fax 416-762-2300

Lawyers for the Plaintiff

FIGURE 10.2   BILL OF COSTS (FORM 57A)

Court file no. 01-CV-7777

ONTARIO
SUPERIOR COURT OF JUSTICE

BETWEEN:

ABIGAIL BOAR

Plaintiff

and

HIERONYMOUS BLOGG

Defendant

BILL OF COSTS

AMOUNTS CLAIMED FOR FEES AND DISBURSEMENTS

FEES OTHER THAN COUNSEL FEES

1. Preparing and drafting statement of claim,
   I.M. Just, October 16, year 1   1 hour
2. Signing default judgment and assessing costs   0.6 hour
   Fee for I.M. Just, Barrister and Solicitor,
                        1.6 hours x $300 = $480.00

TOTAL FEE $480.00
GST* ON FEE $24.00

DISBURSEMENTS**

1. Paid to issue statement of claim $181.00
2. Paid to serve claim (includes GST) $41.00
3. Paid to file requisition for default judgment $127.00

TOTAL DISBURSEMENTS $349.00

GST RO12534

TOTAL FEES AND DISBURSEMENTS $853.00

STATEMENT OF EXPERIENCE
A claim for fees is being made with respect to the following lawyers:

Name of lawyer	Years of experience
I.M. Just	12 years

(* GST of 5 percent as of February 2008. GST is applied to legal fees
   and disbursements paid out to third parties for services other than
   court fees and fixed government fees. Not all lawyers charge GST on
   bills of costs, although the better practice is to do so.
** Court fees under O. Reg. 293/92 of the Administration of Justice Act
   as of February 2008. Note that these fees increase annually.)

FIGURE 10.2   CONCLUDED

TO:

Huey Sue
LSUC #23456T
Barrister and Solicitor
65 False Trail
Toronto, Ontario, M6Y 1Z6

tel. 416-485-6891
fax 416-485-6892

Lawyer for the Defendants

THIS BILL assessed and allowed at $ this   day of

Registrar,
Ontario Superior Court of Justice

FIGURE 10.3   DEFAULT JUDGMENT (DEBT OR LIQUIDATED DEMAND) (FORM 19A)

Court file no. 01-CV-7777

ONTARIO
SUPERIOR COURT OF JUSTICE

BETWEEN:

ABIGAIL BOAR

Plaintiff

and

HIERONYMUS BLOGGS

Defendant

JUDGMENT

On reading the statement of claim in this action and the proof of service of the statement of claim on the defendant, filed, and the defendant having been noted in default,

1. IT IS ORDERED AND ADJUDGED that the defendant pay to the plaintiff the sum of $39,199.60 and the sum of $853.00 for costs of this action.

This judgment bears interest at the rate of 12 percent per year from its date, and the costs bear interest at the rate of 12 percent per year from its date.

Date: October 17, year 0

Signed by: _____

Address of
court office: 393 University Avenue
Toronto, Ontario, M5G 1E6

FIGURE 10.4   REQUISITION FOR WRIT OF SEIZURE AND SALE

Court file no. 01-CV-7777

ONTARIO
SUPERIOR COURT OF JUSTICE

BETWEEN:

ABIGAIL BOAR

and

HIERONYMUS BLOGGS

REQUISITION FOR WRIT OF SEIZURE AND SALE

TO THE LOCAL REGISTRAR at Toronto

I REQUIRE a writ of seizure and sale pursuant to an order of this court made on October 17, year 0 in favour of Abigail Boar

directed to the Sheriff of the City of Toronto
to seize and sell the real and personal property of

Surname of individual or name of corporation/firm, etc.
1. Bloggs

First given name (individual only)	Second given name (individual only) (if applicable)	Third given name (individual only) (if applicable)
Hieronymus		

and to realize from the seizure and sale the following sums:

(a) $ 39,199.60 and interest at 12 percent per year commencing on October 17, year 0

Amount of payment   *Due date*

(a) $_____ and interest at _____ percent per year on the payments in default commencing on the date of default;
(b) 853.00 for costs together with interest at 12 percent per year commencing on October 17, year 0; and
(c) your fees and expenses in enforcing this writ.

Date: October 17, year 0

Just & Coping
Barristers and Solicitors
365 Bay Street - 8701
Toronto, Ontario, M3J 4A9

I.M. Just
LSUC #12345R
tel. 416-762-1342
fax 416-762-2300

Lawyers for the Plaintiff

FIGURE 10.5   WRIT OF SEIZURE AND SALE (FORM 60A)

Court file no. 01-CV-7777

ONTARIO
SUPERIOR COURT OF JUSTICE

BETWEEN:

ABIGAIL BOAR

and

HIERONYMUS BLOGGS

WRIT OF SEIZURE AND SALE

TO the sheriff of the City of Toronto

Under an order of this court made on October 17, year 0, in favour of Abigail Boar

YOU ARE DIRECTED to seize and sell the real and personal property within the City of Toronto

Surname of individual or name of corporation/firm, etc.
Bloggs

First given name (individual only)
Hieronymus

and to realize from the seizure and sale the following sums:

(a) $ 39,199.60 and interest at 12 percent per year commencing on October 17, year 0

Amount of payment   *Due date*

(a) $_____ and interest at _____ percent per year on the payments in default commencing on the date of default;

(b) $853.00 for costs together with interest at 12 percent per year commencing on October 17, year 0; and

(c) your fees and expenses in enforcing this writ.

YOU ARE DIRECTED to pay out the proceeds according to law and to report on the execution of this writ if required by the party or lawyer who filed it.

Date: October 17, year 0

Issued by: _____

Address of
court office: Court House
393 University Avenue
Toronto, Ontario, M5G 1E6

FIGURE 10.5   WRIT OF SEIZURE AND SALE — BACKSHEET (FORM 60A)

ABIGAIL BOAR

and

HIERONYMUS BLOGGS

(Short title of proceeding)

Court file no. 01-CV-7777

ONTARIO SUPERIOR COURT OF JUSTICE

Proceeding comment at Toronto

**WRIT OF
SEIZURE AND SALE**

Creditor's name: Abigail Boar
Creditor's address:
c/o Just & Coping
Barristers and Solicitors
Lawyer's name:
I.M. Just
LSUC #12345R
Lawyer's address:
Just & Coping
365 Bay Street – 8701
Toronto, Ontario, M3J 4A9
Tel. no.: 416-762-1342
Fax no.: 416-762-2300

Lawyer for the Plaintiff

FEES		
Fee	Item	Officer
$100.00	Paid for this writ	
$15.00	Lawyer's fee for issuing writ	
	First renewal	
	Second renewal	
	Third renewal	

RENEWAL		
Date	Officer	

FIGURE 10.6   AFFIDAVIT OF ABIGAIL BOAR

Court file no. 01-CV-1234

ONTARIO
SUPERIOR COURT OF JUSTICE

BETWEEN:

ABIGAIL BOAR

Plaintiff

and

RATTLE MOTORS LTD. and FRED FLOGEM

Defendants

AFFIDAVIT OF ABIGAIL BOAR

I, Abigail Boar, **of the** City of Toronto, **in the** Province of Ontario, **MAKE OATH AND SAY:**

1. I am the plaintiff in this proceeding and as such have knowledge of the matters set out in this affidavit.
2. I slipped on oil on the floor of the showroom of the corporate defendant. My fall and subsequent injuries were solely the result of the negligent acts of the defendants.
3. As a result of the fall, I struck my head, suffered a concussion and lost consciousness. I also fractured my right wrist and several other bones in my right arm. I was taken to the Toronto Hospital emergency room, where my fractures were set and my arm was put in a cast. I was hospitalized and also underwent neurological examination for my head injury.
4. My arm was in a cast for six weeks. I was in great pain for the first two weeks and was unable to sleep or rest without medication to mask the pain. I required homecare assistance. Because I am right-handed and my right arm was immobilized, I was unable to dress myself or look after myself.
5. I had to undergo 10 weeks of physiotherapy to help restore mobility to my right hand and arm.
6. Since the accident, I have also suffered from headaches and chronic lower back pain. I am unable to walk long distances or sit at a desk for long periods. I have not recovered mobility in my right arm, and I am unable to work at a computer keyboard for more than 10 minutes without great pain.
7. As a result of these injuries, I have been far less active and less outgoing than I had been. I have become withdrawn and morose. I can easily become upset by little things that would not have bothered me in the past. I am often tired and have difficulty sleeping because of the chronic pain from my back and head injuries.

FIGURE 10.6   CONCLUDED

8. Before I was injured, I was outgoing and gregarious, an avid tennis player, and a competent amateur violinist. Since I was injured, I have become uninterested in maintaining my social life, and I am unable to engage in the sports and cultural activities from which I formerly derived much pleasure.

9. I have also suffered some memory loss, which has interfered with both my employment and my social life.

10. I have been unable to return to work as a result of my injuries. My work as a securities analyst requires me to sit at a desk and computer keyboard for lengthy periods of time. I also now have difficulty focusing and concentrating on my work because of memory loss and chronic pain. I tried to return to work but was able to work only for a month before my employer and I agreed that I was no longer able to perform my duties. I have been on long-term disability from April 1, year 1 and am unlikely to be able to return to my former employment.

11. At the time of the accident, I was earning $80,000 per year plus benefits worth another $20,000. My work performance was excellent. I expected to work another 25 years and retire early at age 51. I am advised by Eatom Shredlu, the vice-president of human resources at Megadoon Investment Ltd., and believe, that my salary would likely have increased on average about 6 percent per year during my career had I continued my work for this employer.

12. I am advised by Dr. Morris Furgazy, a neurologist, and I believe, that I am unlikely to be employable in any office position on a permanent basis because of my mental disabilities arising from my accident and my physical inability to perform office work.

Sworn before me at the	)	
City of Toronto,	)	*Abigail Boar*
in the Province of Ontario,	)	Abigail Boar
on February 18, year 1.	)	
I.M. Just		
I.M. Just		
Commissioner for Taking Affidavits	)	

FIGURE 10.7   AFFIDAVIT TO SET ASIDE DEFAULT JUDGMENT

Court file no. 01-CV-1234

ONTARIO
SUPERIOR COURT OF JUSTICE

BETWEEN:

ABIGAIL BOAR

Plaintiff

and

RATTLE MOTORS LTD. and FRED FLOGEM

Defendants

AFFIDAVIT OF HUEY SUE

I, Huey Sue, **of the** City of Toronto, **in the** Province of Ontario,
AFFIRM:

1. I am the lawyer for the defendants and as such have knowledge of the matters deposed to in this affidavit.
2. On January 4, year 1, the defendants were served with the statement of claim in this action.
3. On January 6, year 1, I met both defendants and arranged to file a statement of defence. Attached hereto and marked exhibit A to my affidavit is a copy of the proposed statement of defence in this proceeding.
4. The defendants have a good defence to the plaintiff's claim. It is the position of the defendants that the plaintiff was intoxicated at the time of the accident and that her injuries were wholly the result of her intoxicated condition, rather than the result of any alleged act of negligence by either defendant, which negligence, if any, is denied by the defendants.
5. Because of the pressures of practice, I overlooked the passage of the time for filing the statement of defence.
6. I discovered my oversight on January 28, year 1. I attempted immediately to file the statement of defence, but I learned that the defendants had been noted in default and that a default judgment had been entered.
7. On January 29, year 1, I served the plaintiff with a notice of motion to set aside the noting of pleadings closed and the default judgment in this action.

Affirmed before me at the	)	
City of Toronto,	)	*Huey Sue*
in the Province of Ontario,	)	Huey Sue
on January 28, year 1.	)	
Henry Hood		
Henry Hood		
Commissioner for Taking Affidavits	)	

CHAPTER 11

Summary judgment: Rule 20

INTRODUCTION

Once the pleadings have been delivered, one of the parties may take the position that there is no issue that needs to be tried. For example, Abigail Boar, the plaintiff, may believe that the defendants, Fred Flogem and Rattle Motors, have raised no defence known in law to her claim. On the other hand, the defendants may take the position that Abigail does not have sufficient evidence to make a case against them.

In such circumstances, either the plaintiff or the defendant may bring a motion for summary judgment once a statement of defence or notice of motion has been delivered by the defendant. If the plaintiff brings the motion, she will ask the court to make a final judgment in her favour. If the defendants bring the motion for summary judgment, they will ask for a dismissal of all or part of the plaintiff's case. Rule 20 provides the procedure for summary judgments.

Summary judgment is a final decision about the case that is made by the court without a trial. The parties may not rely on their pleadings in trying to persuade the court that there is no issue for trial. They must provide the court with an affidavit setting out the facts on which they are relying. The affidavits may be based on the information supplied by others that the deponent believes to be true. However, basing a motion for summary judgment on affidavit evidence may be risky. The court may **draw an adverse inference** if the affidavits contain material based solely on information and belief and not on the direct, personal knowledge of the deponent. For example, the court may take the view that the reason that no direct personal knowledge evidence has been presented is that there is none.

The affidavits of the party responding to the motion must do more than deny the allegations of the moving party or say that more evidence may be available at trial. The material must set out specifics facts showing that there is a genuine issue for trial (rule 20.04(1)).

In addition to the affidavits they wish to rely on in the motion for summary judgment, each party must also serve and file a factum at least two days before the hearing of the motion (rule 20.03). A factum is a document that gives a concise summary of the facts in the case and sets out the case law and the statutes that the party is relying on to support its position. Factums are dealt with in more detail in chapter 20.

draw an adverse inference
make a factual determination that is contrary to the interests of a party

CHANGES TO THE SUMMARY JUDGMENT PROCEDURE, IN EFFECT AS OF JANUARY 1, 2010

- Judges now have much more explicit directions for the exercise of discretion if, after a motion for judgment, a judgment is refused or granted in part. In particular, a judge may direct a summary trial where circumstances warrant, for example, providing for evidence by affidavit, limited time for cross-examination, mutual consultation and information sharing by expert witnesses, and time-limited discovery.

- Judges will now be able to order oral evidence to be presented by one or more parties, with other evidence being given by affidavit where the procedure will be proportional to the time and expense of proceeding to a full trial.

- A party who thought the opponent's pleadings did not show a triable case could bring a motion for summary judgment based on the pleadings. However, if the moving party lost the motion, he or she had to pay the costs of the responding party. This greatly increased the risk for those who wished to move for summary judgment, and the result was that parties often hesitated to move for summary judgment when they ought to have done so. As of January 2010, a judge hearing a summary judgment motion is not bound to award costs to the respondent if the winner is not successful. The judge must now determine whether the motion was improperly brought (for example, it was of no merit) before awarding costs in these circumstances.[1]

TEST FOR GRANTING SUMMARY JUDGMENT

The test for summary judgment in a simplified procedure is different from the test in a regular action; see chapter 23. In a regular action, the first situation in which summary judgment is available occurs when the court is satisfied that there is no genuine issue for trial. For instance, in Abigail's negligence action, if the defendants can establish that the plaintiff's case is statute barred because it was commenced outside the time set in the *Limitations Act, 2002*, they would be able to satisfy the court that there is no genuine issue for trial. In such a case, the court must grant summary judgment.

The second situation in which summary judgment is available occurs when the parties agree to have all or part of the case dealt with on a motion for summary judgment and the court agrees that it is an appropriate case for this treatment. Summary judgment based on this criterion is discretionary. The court may decide that the matter is better left to trial.

A motion for summary judgment may be brought before a master or a judge. However, if a motion based on a question of law is brought before a master, it must be adjourned for hearing before a judge (rule 20.04(4)).

If the court decides that the only genuine issue for trial is the amount of money to which the moving party is entitled, the court can order a trial limited to that issue or grant judgment in favour of the moving party and direct a **reference** to determine the exact amount (rule 20.04(3)).

reference
judicial proceeding used when it is necessary to delve into an issue in detail before a decision can be reached

Summary judgments are often sought in cases involving debt issues because a plaintiff may obtain judgment for all or part of a debt claim at an early stage in the proceedings without the cost and delay of discovery and trial.

If the court determines on the motion that a summary judgment is not appropriate in a particular case, or is only partially applicable, the court can make a number of orders regarding the trial:

1. It may make an order specifying that certain facts or issues are not in dispute in order to narrow the scope of the trial.

2. It may order that the trial be placed on a special list of cases requiring speedy trial or that the case be set down for trial within a specified time.

3. It may give directions or impose terms, including an order for security for costs, an order for payment into court of all or part of the claim, or an order prescribing the way in which discovery is to be conducted.

Summary judgment can be a very effective litigation tool in that it can, in appropriate cases, avoid costly and time-consuming procedures. However, if a party improperly uses the rule, the court may apply cost sanctions. If the moving party is unsuccessful and the court determines that the motion for summary judgment was unreasonable, it may fix the responding party's costs on a substantial indemnity basis and order the moving party to pay them forthwith (rule 20.06).

Where there are many claims in an action, summary judgment may address only some of those claims, leaving others to be determined through the trial process. A plaintiff who obtains summary judgment may proceed against the defendant for any other relief he or she is claiming. In an appropriate case, the court may order a stay of the summary judgment until the entire matter, including any crossclaim, counterclaim, or third party claim, is dealt with.

CHAPTER SUMMARY

In this chapter, we have seen that summary judgment is a final decision that is made about a case by a court without a trial. Either the plaintiff or the defendant may bring a motion for summary judgment, which must be accompanied by affidavit evidence and factums. The test for granting a summary judgment is that there is no genuine issue for trial. A summary judgment may be granted either in whole or in part.

The parties may agree to have the case determined in this manner; however, the court is not obligated to grant a summary judgment and may direct that the case proceed by way of a full trial. Debt cases are often dealt with by way of summary judgment. Summary judgment may prove to be an effective litigation tool to avoid costly and time-consuming trials, but there can be severe cost consequences for seeking summary judgment in an inappropriate situation.

KEY TERMS

draw an adverse inference

reference

NOTE

1   O. reg. 438/08, ss. 12–16, amending rule 20.

REFERENCES

Limitations Act, 2002, SO 2002, c. 24.

Rules of Civil Procedure, RRO 1990, reg. 194.

REVIEW QUESTIONS

1. Set out the steps you would take and the documents you would prepare to bring a motion for summary judgment.

2. What must a party show to obtain a summary judgment?

3. What sort of evidence should be used in support of the motion?

4. If a party is unsuccessful on a motion for summary judgment, are there consequences?

CHAPTER 12

Counterclaims, crossclaims, and third party claims

INTRODUCTION

A simple proceeding involves only two parties: the plaintiff and the defendant. As you know, the plaintiff can sue more than one defendant in the proceeding, as Abigail Boar is doing. She believes both Fred Flogem and Rattle Motors Ltd. are responsible for her injuries, and she is suing them both. In Abigail's case, there are multiple defendants.

It is also possible to have multiple plaintiffs in a proceeding when several people claim that they suffered damages caused by the defendant or group of defendants. But a proceeding can become more complicated than this. The rules provide for a number of different combinations of plaintiffs and defendants and outline the pleadings and the procedures for each. These pleadings are the counterclaim, the crossclaim, and the third party claim.

When you first try to sort out the nature of these other pleadings, they may seem extremely complicated because of the additional parties and steps involved. However, when reviewing the procedures, keep in mind the basic principle: All parties should know the legal claim made against them and have the opportunity to answer the claim. Remember the basic pleadings in an action: the statement of claim, the statement of defence, and the reply. All of the other pleadings follow the same general principles.[1]

COUNTERCLAIMS: RULE 27

The defendant may wish to sue the plaintiff in the proceeding. Maybe the defendant was seeking legal advice about suing the plaintiff, but the plaintiff was the one who issued the statement of claim first. The legal system and the rules have an interest in resolving disputes between parties in the most cost-effective and efficient manner. To force the defendant who wants to sue the plaintiff to commence a proceeding separate from the one already commenced by the plaintiff would be more expensive and time-consuming than allowing the defendant to bring his or her action against the plaintiff at the same time.

counterclaim
claim made by the defendant in the main action against the plaintiff or against the plaintiff and other persons

main action
primary case brought by the plaintiff against the defendant

When a defendant sues a plaintiff, this is called a "**counterclaim**." The proceeding in which the plaintiff is suing the defendant is then called the "**main action**."

In a counterclaim, the defendant in the main action must be suing the plaintiff in the main action. The defendant can also sue anyone else in his or her counterclaim, as long as the original plaintiff is one of the persons being sued.

There is no restriction as to the basis for the defendant's counterclaim against the plaintiff. It may have the same subject matter as the claim in the main action, or it may have a completely different subject matter. Assume that Abigail Boar did not go to Rattle Motors Ltd. to buy a car on the day that she fell. Assume instead that she had already bought the car and went into the dealership that day to make a payment on the car she had purchased. After she slipped and fell, she refused to make additional payments on the car. Rattle Motors Ltd. wants to enforce its contract of sale against her. Therefore, when she starts her action against Rattle Motors Ltd., it counterclaims against her for the debt owing. Abigail is suing Rattle Motors Ltd. for the tort of negligence, and Rattle Motors Ltd. is suing Abigail on a contract.

Assume as well that Abigail's boyfriend purchased the car with her and also entered into a sales contract with Rattle Motors Ltd. He has made no further payments on the car either, and Rattle Motors Ltd. wants to sue him too. Rattle Motors Ltd. can add him to the counterclaim, even though he is not one of the parties in the main action. As long as Rattle Motors Ltd. is suing Abigail, the plaintiff in the main action, it may also include her boyfriend in the counterclaim.

Pleadings in a counterclaim

The possible pleadings in a counterclaim are:

1. statement of claim (form 14A), delivered by the plaintiff in the main action;

2. statement of defence and counterclaim (form 27A or 27B), delivered by a defendant in the main action who is making a counterclaim against the plaintiff in the main action;

3. defence to counterclaim (form 27C), delivered by the plaintiff in the main action who wishes to defend against the counterclaim; and

4. reply and defence to counterclaim (form 27D), delivered by the plaintiff in the main action who wants to reply to the defendants' statement of defence in the main action and defend against the counterclaim.

Statement of defence and counterclaim

The defendants commence the counterclaim by including it in the same pleading as their defence to the main action. Instead of being called a "statement of defence," it is called a "statement of defence and counterclaim." There are two forms for this pleading: form 27A and form 27B. Form 27A is used when the defendant is suing only people who are parties to the main action. Form 27B is used if the defendant is adding someone to the counterclaim who is not a party to the main proceeding. If Rattle Motors Ltd. were suing only Abigail, it would use form 27A. If it were also suing Abigail's boyfriend, because the boyfriend is not a party to the main action, it would use form 27B. Figure 12.1 at the end of the chapter sets out a statement of defence and counterclaim.

There is a major distinction between the two forms. Because form 27A is not an originating process, it does not need to be issued. However, because form 27B brings in a new party to the proceeding, it is an originating process. It must therefore be issued within the time prescribed in rule 18.01 for delivery of the statement of defence or any time before being noted in default — that is, within 20 days if the statement of claim was served in Ontario, 40 days if it was served elsewhere in Canada or in the United States, or 60 days if it was served anywhere else in the world.

Form 27B must also contain a second title of proceeding showing the plaintiff by counterclaim and the defendants by counterclaim. In our example, Rattle Motors Ltd. is the plaintiff by counterclaim, and Abigail and her boyfriend are the defendants by counterclaim (rule 27.03).

The statement of defence and counterclaim (form 27A or 27B) raises two separate issues for the plaintiff in the main action. She has been served with a defence to her claim in the main action and with a new claim against her by the defendant. In the main action, in which Abigail is suing Rattle Motors Ltd. in negligence, she may want to reply to any new issue that Rattle Motors Ltd. has raised in its defence. In addition, Abigail will want to raise her defence against Rattle Motors Ltd.'s claim for payment for the car. Her boyfriend will also want to raise his defence against Rattle Motors Ltd.

Defence to counterclaim or reply and defence to counterclaim

If Abigail has no reply to Rattle Motors Ltd.'s defence in the main action but wants to defend herself against Rattle Motors Ltd.'s counterclaim, she must file a defence to counterclaim, form 27C, within 20 days after being served with the statement of defence and counterclaim. Figure 12.2 at the end of the chapter sets out a defence to the counterclaim. If Abigail's boyfriend or any other defendant who is not a party to the main action wishes to file a defence to the counterclaim, that person has 20 days, 40 days, or 60 days to file a statement of defence and counterclaim, depending on the place of service (rule 27.05(3)).

If Abigail wants to file a reply to Rattle Motors Ltd.'s defence in the main action and raise a defence on the counterclaim, she must include the defence to the counterclaim in the reply. This means she first addresses all the issues she wishes to address in reply and follows those paragraphs with all the points she wishes to raise in the defence to the counterclaim.

If Rattle Motors Ltd. wants to reply to Abigail or to another defendant's defence and counterclaim, it may do so in form 27D within 10 days after being served with the defence to the counterclaim (rule 27.06).

Amending defence to add counterclaim

If the defendants in the main action deliver a statement of defence and then decide they want to bring a counterclaim, they may amend their statement of defence to add the counterclaim and deliver the amended pleading, as long as the counterclaim is against the plaintiff and someone else who is already a party to the main action. But if the counterclaim brings in a defendant who is not a party to the main action, the defendants may amend their pleading to add the counterclaim only with leave of the court (rule 27.07).

Trial and disposition of the counterclaim

A counterclaim that goes to trial is usually heard at the end of the trial of the main action. However, if it appears that the counterclaim may delay, complicate, or prejudice a party, the court may order separate trials or may order that the counterclaim proceed as an action separate from the main action (rule 27.08(1) and (2)).

Sometimes, the defendant may not dispute the plaintiff's claim in the main action but may want to assert a counterclaim. Conversely, the plaintiff may not dispute the counterclaim but may want to proceed with his or her claim in the main action. In such a situation, the court may either stay or grant a judgment in the undisputed part of the case and then hear the claims that are disputed. If the plaintiff is successful in the main action and the defendant is successful on the counterclaim — that is, if each party wins the part of the case it brought against the other — the court may dismiss the smaller claim and order that the difference between the two damage awards be paid (rule 27.09).

For example, assume that Abigail Boar wins her negligence action against Rattle Motors Ltd., and Rattle is ordered to pay her $75,000. Rattle Motors Ltd., however, also wins its counterclaim for the money still owing on the car, which is $10,000. In this instance, the court may dismiss Rattle Motors Ltd.'s case and order Rattle to pay Abigail $65,000, the difference between the two claims.

CROSSCLAIMS: RULE 28

crossclaim
claim brought by one defendant whom the plaintiff is suing against another defendant whom the plaintiff is suing

A **crossclaim** is a claim made by one defendant against another defendant in the main action. Rule 28 governs the procedure on a crossclaim. The rule provides that crossclaims may be brought only in certain limited circumstances. These circumstances exist if:

1. the **co-defendant** is or may be liable to the defendant for all or part of the plaintiff's claim;

co-defendant
one defendant in multi-defendant proceeding

2. the co-defendant is or may be liable to the defendant for an independent claim for damages or other relief, arising out of the same transaction or occurrence involved in, or related to, the main action;

3. the co-defendant should be bound by the determination of an issue arising between the plaintiff and the defendant; or

4. the defendant is claiming a contribution from a co-defendant under the *Negligence Act* (rule 28.01(1) and (2)).

In short, the crossclaim must have a direct relationship to the main action in terms of subject matter and some level of joint liability to the plaintiff in the main action. For instance, Abigail is suing both Fred Flogem and Rattle Motors Ltd. for negligence. Fred and Rattle Motors Ltd. are therefore co-defendants. If Fred believes that he did nothing to cause Abigail's fall and that Rattle Motors Ltd. created an unsafe showroom and is totally responsible for Abigail's injuries, Fred can bring a crossclaim against Rattle Motors Ltd. However, if Fred wants to start an action against Rattle Motors Ltd. for unpaid wages, that issue has no connection to the main action and is not a proper subject for a crossclaim.

The defendant in the main action who brings the crossclaim is referred to in the rules as the **crossclaiming defendant**. The defendant against whom the crossclaim is brought is called the **defendant on the crossclaim**. In our example, Fred is the crossclaiming defendant, and Rattle Motors Ltd. is the defendant on the crossclaim.

Until now, in our scenario involving Abigail, Fred and Rattle Motors Ltd., Rattle and Fred have used the same lawyer. There was no conflict of interest for the lawyer because both Fred and Rattle were taking the same position against Abigail. Now, however, Fred is suing Rattle on the crossclaim and he cannot use the same law firm.

Pleadings in a crossclaim

The following is a list of pleadings on a crossclaim:

1. statement of claim (form 14A), delivered by the plaintiff in the main action against more than one defendant;

2. statement of defence (form 18A), delivered by any defendant who is not crossclaiming;

3. reply (form 25A), delivered by the plaintiff in the main action to answer any new issues raised in the statement of defence;

4. statement of defence and crossclaim (form 28A), delivered by a defendant who wishes to answer the plaintiff's claim against him or her and bring a crossclaim against one of the other defendants being sued by the plaintiff in the main action;

5. defence to crossclaim (form 28B), delivered by the co-defendant against whom the crossclaim has been commenced; and

6. reply to defence to crossclaim (form 28C), delivered by the defendant who is bringing the crossclaim and who wants to reply to issues raised by the co-defendant he or she is suing on the crossclaim.

Statement of defence and crossclaim

A crossclaim is included in the same document as the statement of defence and is called a statement of defence and crossclaim (form 28A). Figure 12.3 at the end of the chapter sets out a statement of defence and crossclaim. If the defendant has already filed a statement of defence in the main action and then decides he or she wants to bring a crossclaim, the defendant may simply amend the statement of defence under rule 26 and include the crossclaim. No leave of the court is required (rule 28.03).

The statement of defence and crossclaim must be served within the time limits for filing a statement of defence under rule 18.01 or anytime before the defendant is noted in default. It may be served after a noting in default only with leave of the court (rule 28.04(1)). There is no requirement for personal service of the statement of defence and crossclaim, unless the defendant in the crossclaim has failed to deliver a statement of defence or a notice of intent to defend in the main action.

crossclaiming defendant
defendant in the main action who commences a crossclaim against one or more of the other defendants in that action

defendant on the crossclaim
defendant in the main action against whom a crossclaim is brought

Defence to the crossclaim

The defence to the crossclaim, form 28B, must be delivered within 20 days after service of the statement of defence and crossclaim. Figure 12.4 at the end of the chapter sets out a defence to a crossclaim. However, a defence to a crossclaim is not needed in the circumstances specified in rule 28.05. When the crossclaim is only seeking contribution or indemnity under the *Negligence Act* and the defendant to the crossclaim has delivered a defence in the main action that addresses the issues raised in the crossclaim, the defendant need not deliver a specific defence to the crossclaim. He or she can rely on the statement of defence delivered in the main action and is deemed to deny every allegation in the crossclaim.

In a crossclaim, the defendants are being sued by the plaintiff, and the crossclaim must have something to do with the plaintiff's claim in the main action. Very often the defendant on the crossclaim will be liable for damages on the crossclaim only if the plaintiff is successful in the main action. If the plaintiff loses his or her case, none of the defendants bears any liability.

Therefore, rule 28.06 provides a procedure by which the defendant on the crossclaim may raise a defence to the plaintiff's claim against the other defendant — that is, the crossclaiming defendant. If the defendant wants to raise a defence to the plaintiff's claim against the crossclaiming defendant, he or she may do so in a separate part of the defence to the crossclaim. This part of the defence against the crossclaim must be headed with the wording "DEFENCE TO A PLAINTIFF'S CLAIM AGAINST CROSSCLAIMING DEFENDANT."

A defendant who does not defend against the crossclaiming defendant in this way is bound by any order made in the main action between the plaintiff and the crossclaiming defendant.

A defendant may be noted in default on a crossclaim just as a defendant can be noted in default in the main action. If the defendant on the crossclaim is noted in default on the crossclaim, judgment can be obtained against him or her only at the trial of the main action or on a motion to a judge. In other words, a default judgment cannot be obtained from the registrar in this circumstance.

Reply to the defence to the crossclaim

The reply to the defence to a crossclaim must be delivered within ten days of the service of the defence to the crossclaim.

Trial of the crossclaim

The crossclaim is usually heard at the trial of the main action or immediately thereafter. However, if the plaintiff believes that the crossclaim will prejudice or delay the trial of the main action, he or she may bring a motion seeking an order that the crossclaim proceed as a separate action. The court may order a separate trial on the crossclaim, or it may impose any terms necessary to ensure that the main action is not prejudiced or delayed.

THIRD PARTY CLAIMS: RULE 29
Introduction

One or more of the defendants to the main action may take the position that the plaintiff has not named all persons who are liable for his or her injuries. For instance, assume that unbeknownst to Abigail Boar, the car on display in the showroom had a manufacturer's defect in the oil pan that caused it to leak onto Rattle Motors Ltd.'s showroom floor. In its own investigation into Abigail's fall, Rattle Motors Ltd. discovers this defect and believes that Skank Motorcar Company Ltd. is responsible for Abigail's injuries. But Abigail has not sued the car manufacturer. The rules provide a procedure for Rattle Motors Ltd. to bring Skank Motor Company Ltd. into the action. This is called a **third party claim**, and it may be commenced by a defendant against any person who is not a party to the main action but who:

- is or may be liable to the defendant for all or part of the plaintiff's claim,

- is or may be liable to the defendant for an independent claim for damages or other relief arising out of the same transaction or occurrence or series of transactions or occurrences involved in the main action, or

- should be bound by the determination of an issue arising between the plaintiff and the defendant (rule 29.01).

third party claim
claim brought by a defendant in the main action against a person who is not already a party to the main action

Pleadings on a third party claim

A third party claim is a new claim made against a person who is not a party to the main action. It is unlike a counterclaim and a crossclaim because these proceedings involve someone who is already a party to the existing proceeding. For instance, in a counterclaim, the defendant must make a claim against the plaintiff. A crossclaim involves defendants who are already parties by virtue of the fact that they are being sued by the same plaintiff or plaintiffs. There are therefore two sets of pleadings in a third party proceeding: the pleadings in the main action and the pleadings in the third party proceeding.

The pleadings in the main action are the regular pleadings: the statement of claim, the statement of defence, and the reply. The second set of pleadings between the defendant who is making the claim against the third party and the third party are:

- the third party claim (form 29A), delivered by the defendant asserting the claim and resembling a statement of claim in its form and content;

- the third party defence (form 29B), delivered by the third party to raise a defence to the claim being brought against him or her; and

- the reply to the third party defence (form 29C), delivered by the defendant asserting the third party claim.

The third party claim

Because a third party claim brings someone new into the proceeding and asserts a new claim, it is an originating process. It must be issued by the court within ten days after the defendant delivers a statement of defence or anytime before the defendant is noted in default (rule 29.02(1)). However, if the plaintiff replies to the statement of defence in the main action, the third party claim may be issued within ten days of the plaintiff's delivering his or her reply (rule 29.02(1.1)).

There are exceptions to these time limits for commencing a third party claim. A claim may be issued at any time if the plaintiff consents or if the court grants leave, and the court grants leave unless the plaintiff will suffer prejudice (rule 29.02(1.2)).

Like other originating processes, the third party claim must be served on the third party personally or by an alternative to personal service under rule 16.03. At the same time, the third party must also be served with all the pleadings previously delivered in the main action, any counterclaim, any crossclaim, and any other third party claim. Service of the documents must take place within 30 days after the third party claim is issued (rule 29.02(2)).

The third party claim must also be served on every other party to the main action within 30 days after the issuing, but it need not be served personally on these parties (rule 29.02(3)). Figure 12.5 at the end of the chapter sets out a third party claim.

Third party defence

The third party defence must be delivered within 20, 40, or 60 days, depending on where the third party claim is served (rule 29.03).

Once the third party has delivered a third party defence, there are several consequences that affect the third party.

- The third party must be served with any subsequent pleadings filed by any party to the main action.

- The plaintiff cannot obtain a consent judgment or note the defendant in default without notice to the third party.

- The third party has a right of discovery against any defendant to a crossclaim brought by the defendant who asserted the third party claim (rule 29.06).

Where a third party is noted in default for failing to file a third party defence, judgment may be obtained against the third party only at trial of the main action or on a motion to a judge. The registrar cannot issue a default judgment against a third party. Figure 12.6 at the end of the chapter sets out a third party defence.

Reply to third party defence

The defendant who commenced the third party proceeding has a right to reply to a third party defence within 10 days after being served with the defence.

Defence of the main action by the third party

A third party may defend against the plaintiff in the main action's claim against the defendant by delivering a statement of defence, and the third party may raise any defence open to the defendant. The reason for this rule is obvious: Since the defendant's third party claim is based on the allegation that the third party is liable for the plaintiff's damages in whole or in part, if the plaintiff is unsuccessful in the main action, the defendant will have no need or interest in pursuing the third party claim.

The statement of defence must be delivered within the standard time frames of 20, 40, or 60 days from the service of the third party claim, depending on where the third party was served (rules 29.04(3) and 29.03). The plaintiff may reply to that statement of defence within 10 days after being served.

Once the third party has delivered a statement of defence in the main action, he or she has the same rights and obligations in the main action as the defendant. The third party may seek discovery, participate in the trial of the main action, and appeal any decision made at the trial. In addition, he or she is bound by any order made in the main action between the plaintiff and the defendant who made the third party claim. In the event that the third party does not deliver a statement of defence in the main action, he or she is still bound by any order made in that action between the plaintiff and the defendant who made the third party claim.

Trial of the third party claim

After the close of pleadings in the third party claim, the claim must be listed for trial without undue delay in accordance with rule 48. It is to be placed on the trial list immediately after the main action, and it must be tried at the same time or immediately after the main action.

If the plaintiff is concerned that the third party claim will delay or prejudice the main action, he or she may bring a motion. The court may order that the third party claim be tried as a separate action or set terms for a trial of the action that will prevent delay or prejudice. However, the order or terms may not cause any injustice to the defendant or the third party.

Subsequent party claims

A third party may bring a fourth party claim against a person who is not a party to the main action as long as it meets the criteria set out in rule 29.01 for the commencement of a third party action. A fourth party may then assert a fifth party claim under the same criteria, and so on (rules 29.11 and 29.12).

CHAPTER SUMMARY

In this chapter, we have explored counterclaims, crossclaims, and third party claims.

Rule 27 governs counterclaims, a procedure in which the defendant is suing the plaintiff and any number of other persons along with the plaintiff. The basis for the counterclaim does not have to have the same subject matter as the main claim. Pleadings relating only to the counterclaim are the statement of defence and counterclaim, the defence to the counterclaim, or the reply and defence to the counterclaim. A counterclaim that goes to trial is usually heard at the completion of the trial of the main action. However, if it appears that the counterclaim may delay the main action, the court may order it to be tried separately.

Rule 28 governs crossclaims, a procedure that involves one defendant suing another defendant. The crossclaim must be directly related to the main action in terms of its content and the joint liability of the defendants to the plaintiff. Pleadings relating only to the crossclaim are the statement of defence and crossclaim, the defence to the crossclaim, or the reply to the defence to the crossclaim. The trial of the crossclaim is usually held at the same time as or immediately after the trial of the main action. However, the plaintiff may bring a motion to have the crossclaim tried separately if there is a possibility that the crossclaim could delay the main action.

Rule 29 governs third party claims, a procedure in which the defendant commences an action against a person whom the plaintiff is not suing. It must be directly related to the main action respecting subject matter and liability of the parties. The pleadings related solely to a third party claim are the third party claim, the third party defence, and the reply to the third party defence. Since a third party claim brings a new party into the proceeding, it is an originating process and must be issued by the court. The third party action is usually tried at the same time as or immediately after the main action, although the plaintiff may move to have it tried as a separate matter if it will delay the main action. A third party may make a fourth party claim and bring an additional party into the proceeding. A fourth party may bring in a fifth party, and so on.

KEY TERMS

counterclaim	crossclaiming defendant
main action	defendant on the crossclaim
crossclaim	third party claim
co-defendant	

NOTE

1 You may find it helpful to locate in your rules book the chart that deals with the procedure in counterclaims, crossclaims, and third party claims and follow it as you read through this chapter.

REFERENCES

Negligence Act, RSO 1990, c. N.1.

Rules of Civil Procedure, RRO 1990, reg. 194.

REVIEW QUESTIONS

1. John Smith is suing Big Bob's Building Emporium Ltd. Big Bob believes that Diddlehopper Cleaning Ltd. bears some of the liability for the claim. What can Big Bob do? What rule applies?

2. Draft the general heading for this pleading.

3. What is the document used to bring a counterclaim? What is this document's form number?

4. In a counterclaim, is the defendant limited to suing the plaintiff in the main action?

5. What are the pleadings used on a counterclaim?

6. In what circumstances is a crossclaim available and what rule applies?

7. The defendant has already filed a statement of defence. However, he now wants to commence a crossclaim against one of his co-defendants. Do the rules permit him to do this?

8. Which of the proceedings you have studied in this chapter are originating processes?

9. John Green wishes to commence a crossclaim against his co-defendant George Black. What steps must be taken to commence the crossclaim?

10. At what stage of the proceedings may a third party claim be issued?

11. If a third party claim has been commenced, is there any step the plaintiff can take to have the third party claim heard separately from the main action?

DISCUSSION QUESTIONS

1. Kule Kiddie Fashions Inc. is being sued by Mindy McGillicuddy for a breach of contract. Mindy is claiming that Kule Kiddie did not deliver her line of spring clothing to her boutique as required under her contract with it. Kule Kiddie claims that it did not deliver the spring line of clothing because Mindy still owes $40,000 on the winter line and must pay before there will be any more clothing deliveries. What can Kule Kiddie do to recover its money from Mindy? What rule applies?

2. Kule Kiddie Fashions Inc. is being sued by Mindy McGillicuddy for a breach of contract for its failure to deliver a clothing line to Mindy's boutique. Kule Kiddie has had many business dealings with Mindy. Last year, Mindy did some clothing design work for it but did not complete the job because she left to open her own boutique. Kule Kiddie was forced to retain another designer to finish the job. The second designer charged twice as much for the job. Because it was late, Kule Kiddie lost $100,000 in income. Can Kule Kiddie bring a counterclaim in this situation?

3. Kule Kiddie Fashions Inc. wants to sue Mindy's son, Boris, an electrician. When he did some work at its factory last year, he crossed the wires, causing its major knitting machine to blow up. While Kule Kiddie was awaiting a new machine, it lost $20,000 in business. Can Kule Kiddie bring a counterclaim against Boris in the main action that his mother has commenced against it?

FIGURE 12.1   STATEMENT OF DEFENCE AND COUNTERCLAIM (FORM 27B)

Court file no. 01-CV-7890

ONTARIO
SUPERIOR COURT OF JUSTICE

BETWEEN:

ABIGAIL BOAR

Plaintiff

and

RATTLE MOTORS LTD. and FRED FLOGEM

Defendants

AND BETWEEN:

RATTLE MOTORS LTD.

Plaintiff by Counterclaim

and

ABIGAIL BOAR and JAMES JINGLEHIMER

Defendants to the Counterclaim

STATEMENT OF DEFENCE AND COUNTERCLAIM

TO THE DEFENDANTS TO THE COUNTERCLAIM

A LEGAL PROCEEDING has been commenced against you by way of a counterclaim in an action in this court. The claim made against you is set out in the following pages.

IF YOU WISH TO DEFEND THIS COUNTERCLAIM, you or an Ontario lawyer acting for you must prepare a defence to counterclaim in Form 27C prescribed by the Rules of Civil Procedure, serve it on the plaintiff by counterclaim's lawyer or, where the plaintiff by counterclaim does not have a lawyer, serve it on the plaintiff by counterclaim, and file it, with proof of service, in this court, WITHIN TWENTY DAYS after this statement of defence and counterclaim is served on you.

If you are not already a party to the main action and you are served in another province or territory of Canada or in the United States of America, the period for serving and filing your defence is forty days. If you are served outside Canada and the United States of America, the period is sixty days.

If you are not already a party to the main action, instead of serving and filing a defence to counterclaim, you may serve and file a notice of intent to defend in Form 18B prescribed by the Rules of Civil Procedure. This will entitle you to ten more days within which to serve and file your defence to counterclaim.

IF YOU FAIL TO DEFEND THIS COUNTERCLAIM, JUDGMENT MAY BE GIVEN AGAINST YOU IN YOUR ABSENCE AND WITHOUT FURTHER NOTICE TO YOU. IF YOU WISH TO DEFEND THIS PROCEEDING BUT ARE UNABLE TO PAY LEGAL FEES, LEGAL AID MAY BE AVAILABLE TO YOU BY CONTACTING A LOCAL LEGAL AID OFFICE.

FIGURE 12.1   CONTINUED

IF YOU PAY THE AMOUNT OF THE COUNTERCLAIM AGAINST YOU, and $500.00 for costs, within the time for serving and filing your defence to counterclaim, you may move to have the counterclaim against you dismissed by the court. If you believe the amount claimed for costs is excessive, you may pay the amount of the counterclaim and $400.00 for costs and have the costs assessed by the court.

Date: January 12, year 1

Issued by: _____

Address of
court office: Court House
                 393 University Avenue
                 Toronto, Ontario, M5G 1E6

TO:

James Jinglehimer
4747 Memory Lane,
Toronto, Ontario, M7T 8U9

Defendant by counterclaim

TO:

Just & Coping
Barristers and Solicitors
365 Bay Street - 8701
Toronto, Ontario, M3J 4A9

I.M. Just
LSUC #12345R

tel. 416-762-1342
fax 416-762-2300

Lawyer for the Defendant by Counterclaim, Abigail Boar

1. The defendants admit the allegations contained in paragraphs 2, 3, and 4 of the statement of claim.
2. The defendants deny the allegations contained in paragraphs 7, 8, 9, 10, 11, 12, 13, 14, 15, 16, and 17 of the statement of claim.
3. The plaintiff entered the corporate defendant's premises at about 7:30 p.m. on September 14, year 0. She indicated to Linda Lucre, a salesperson on the showroom floor at that time, that she was interested in purchasing a Super Coupe.
4. Lucre showed the plaintiff several automobile models. Then the plaintiff walked over, on her own, to look at another model. She walked around the car and fell.
5. The defendants admit that there was a small pool of oil on one side of the car but claim that it was easily visible to any reasonably prudent person who could have avoided it without difficulty.

FIGURE 12.1 CONTINUED

6. The defendants admit that two of the four spotlights were off but deny that the area was not well illuminated. The defendants state that the area was well and clearly illuminated. Any hazard, if there was one, which is specifically denied, could easily be seen and avoided.

7. The defendants admit that the plaintiff fell and appeared to lose consciousness momentarily. She also appeared to injure her lower right arm in the fall.

8. The defendants state that the plaintiff, before coming to the corporate defendant's place of business, had consumed two glasses of wine and that she was intoxicated when she entered the defendant's premises.

9. The plaintiff fell solely as a result of her intoxication. Any injuries she sustained were solely the result of her own intoxicated state and not any acts of the defendants.

10. With respect to paragraphs 10, 11, 12, 13, 14, and 15 of the statement of claim, the defendants deny that the plaintiff suffered such injuries as described. Further or in the alternative, the defendants state that the plaintiff has exaggerated both the extent of her injuries and the consequences of them.

11. With respect to the plaintiff's allegation that she cannot return to work, the defendants state that the plaintiff is exaggerating her injuries and that she is a malingerer. In the alternative, the defendants state that the plaintiff has failed to mitigate her damages.

12. With respect to the allegations of negligence in paragraph 16, the defendant Flogem states that he knew there was oil on the floor but that it was contained and did not constitute a danger to any reasonably prudent person. The defendant Flogem admits that he turned off two of the four spotlights, but he specifically denies that he created a situation of danger for the plaintiff because the area in question remained well illuminated and safe for a reasonably prudent person.

13. The defendants therefore request that this action be dismissed with costs.

COUNTERCLAIM

14. The plaintiff by way of counterclaim claims:
    a. the sum of $11,275.98;
    b. interest in the said amount of $11,275.98 at the rate of 5 percent per year from September 1, year 1 to the date of payment on the judgment;
    c. its costs of this counterclaim; and
    d. such further relief as seems just to this court.

15. On November 15, year -1, the defendants to the counterclaim, Abigail Boar and James Jinglehimer, entered into a contract of purchase and sale with the plaintiff by counterclaim, Rattle Motors Ltd., for the purchase on credit of a Super Coupe, year 0 model. The full purchase price of the vehicle was $22,472.89. The price was to be paid in monthly instalments of $329.47, commencing December 1, year -1.

FIGURE 12.1 CONCLUDED

16. Between December 1, year -1 and September 1, year 0, the defendants by counterclaim paid the requisite amount owing each month. No payment has been made pursuant to the agreement since September 1, year 0.
17. The defendants by counterclaim have made no payment since September 1, year 0 and are currently 4 months in arrears.

Date: January 12, year 1

Huey Sue
LSUC #23456T
Barrister and Solicitor
65 False Trail
Toronto, Ontario, M6Y 1Z6

tel. 416-485-6891
fax 416-485-6892

Lawyer for the Plaintiff by Counterclaim

FIGURE 12.2 DEFENCE TO COUNTERCLAIM (FORM 27C)

Court file no. 01-CV-1234

ONTARIO
SUPERIOR COURT OF JUSTICE

BETWEEN:

ABIGAIL BOAR

Plaintiff

and

RATTLE MOTORS LTD. and FRED FLOGEM

Defendants

AND BETWEEN:

RATTLE MOTORS LTD.

Plaintiff by Counterclaim

and

ABIGAIL BOAR and JAMES JINGLEHIMER

Defendants to the Counterclaim

DEFENCE TO COUNTERCLAIM

1. The defendants to the counterclaim admit the allegations contained in paragraphs 15 and 16 of the counterclaim.
2. The defendants to the counterclaim deny the allegations contained in paragraph 17 of the counterclaim.
3. The defendants to the counterclaim have no knowledge in respect of the allegations contained in paragraph 14 of the counterclaim.
4. The automobile that was the subject of the contract of sale between the plaintiff by counterclaim and the defendants by counterclaim has required 4 major motor repairs since purchase. For the 7 months that the defendants by counterclaim have had possession of the vehicle, the vehicle has been inoperable for all or part of 5 of those months.
5. On September 14, year 0, the defendants by counterclaim attempted to return the vehicle to the plaintiff by counterclaim, but the sales manager refused to accept the return.
6. The defendants by counterclaim allege that there has been a fundamental breach of the contract of sale by the plaintiff by counterclaim and that they are no longer liable for payments on the contract.
7. The defendants by counterclaim therefore submit that the counterclaim in this action be dismissed.

FIGURE 12.2 CONCLUDED

Date: February 1, year 1

> Just & Coping
> Barristers and Solicitors
> 365 Bay Street - 8701
> Toronto, Ontario, M3J 4A9
>
> I.M. Just
> LSUC #12345R
> tel. 416-762-1342
> fax 416-762-2300
>
> Lawyers for the Defendants by Counterclaim

TO:
Huey Sue
LSUC #23456T
Barrister and Solicitor
65 False Trail
Toronto, Ontario, M6Y 1Z6

tel. 416-485-6891
fax 416-485-6892

Lawyer for the Plaintiff by Counterclaim

FIGURE 12.3 STATEMENT OF DEFENCE AND CROSSCLAIM (FORM 28A)

Court file no. 01-CV-1234

ONTARIO
SUPERIOR COURT OF JUSTICE

BETWEEN:

ABIGAIL BOAR

Plaintiff

and

RATTLE MOTORS LTD. and FRED FLOGEM

Defendants

STATEMENT OF DEFENCE AND CROSSCLAIM OF THE DEFENDANT
FRED FLOGEM

1. The defendant Fred Flogem admits the allegations in paragraphs 1, 2, and 3 of the statement of claim.
2. The defendant denies the allegations contained in paragraphs 7, 8, 9, 10, 11, 12, 13, 14, 15, 16, and 17 of the statement of claim.
3. The plaintiff entered the defendant Rattle Motors Ltd.'s premises at about 7:30 p.m. on September 14, year 0. She indicated to Linda Lucre, a salesperson on the showroom floor at that time, that she was interested in purchasing a Super Coupe.
4. Lucre showed the plaintiff several automobile models. Then the plaintiff walked over, on her own, to look at another model. She walked around the car and fell.
5. The defendant Fred Flogem admits that there was a small pool of oil on one side of the car but claims that it was easily visible to any reasonably prudent person who could have avoided it without difficulty.
6. The defendant Fred Flogem admits that two of the four spotlights were off but denies that the area was not well illuminated. The defendant Fred Flogem states that the area was well and clearly illuminated. Any hazard, if there was one, which is specifically denied, could easily be seen and avoided.
7. The defendant Fred Flogem admits that the plaintiff fell and appeared to lose consciousness momentarily. She also appeared to injure her lower right arm in the fall.
8. The defendant Fred Flogem states that the plaintiff, before coming to the defendant Rattle Motors Ltd.'s place of business, had consumed two glasses of wine and that she was intoxicated when she entered the premises.
9. The plaintiff fell solely as a result of her intoxication. Any injuries she sustained were solely the result of her own intoxicated state and not any acts of the defendant Fred Flogem.
10. With respect to paragraphs 10, 11, 12, 13, 14, and 15 of the statement of claim, the defendant Fred Flogem denies that the plaintiff suffered such injuries as described.

FIGURE 12.3 CONTINUED

Further or in the alternative, the defendant Fred Flogem states that the plaintiff has exaggerated both the extent of her injuries and the consequences of them.

11. With respect to the plaintiff's allegation that she cannot return to work, the defendant Fred Flogem states that the plaintiff is exaggerating her injuries and that she is a malingerer. In the alternative, the defendant Fred Flogem states that the plaintiff has failed to mitigate her damages.

12. With respect to the allegations of negligence in paragraph 16, the defendant Fred Flogem states that he knew there was oil on the floor but that it was contained and did not constitute a danger to any reasonably prudent person. The defendant Fred Flogem admits that he turned off two of the four spotlights, but he specifically denies that he created a situation of danger for the plaintiff because the area in question remained well illuminated and safe for a reasonably prudent person.

13. The defendant Fred Flogem therefore requests that this action be dismissed with costs.

CROSSCLAIM

14. The defendant Fred Flogem claims against the defendant Rattle Motors Ltd.:
    a. contribution and indemnity for any and all claims of the plaintiff,
    b. costs of this action on a substantial indemnity basis, and
    c. such further relief as seems just to this court.

15. The defendant Fred Flogem is the employee of Rattle Motors Ltd.

16. The defendant Fred Flogem states that if the plaintiff has suffered damage, which is not admitted, such damage was caused by the negligence of the defendant Rattle Motors Ltd. and did not result from any act or omission of the defendant Fred Flogem.

17. *(Any additional facts on which the crossclaiming defendant relies are set out in the following paragraphs in the same manner as in a statement of claim.)*

FIGURE 12.3 CONCLUDED

Date: January 12, year 1

Brenda Brilliant
LSUC #86421X
Barrister & Solicitor
1400 Willsa Way
Toronto, Ontario M6V 9T7

tel. 416-766-4321
fax 416-766-9876

Lawyer for the Crossclaiming Defendant

TO:

Huey Sue
LSUC #23456T
Barrister and Solicitor
65 False Trail
Toronto, Ontario M6Y 1Z6

tel. 416-485-6891
fax 416-485-6892

Lawyer for the Defendant in the Crossclaim

FIGURE 12.4 DEFENCE TO CROSSCLAIM (FORM 28B)

Court file no. 01-CV-1234

ONTARIO
SUPERIOR COURT OF JUSTICE

BETWEEN:

ABIGAIL BOAR

Plaintiff

and

RATTLE MOTORS LTD. and FRED FLOGEM

Defendants

DEFENCE TO CROSSCLAIM

1. The defendant Rattle Motors Ltd. admits the allegations contained in paragraph 15 of the crossclaim.
2. The defendant Rattle Motors Ltd. denies the allegations contained in paragraphs 16 and 17 of the crossclaim.
3. The defendant Rattle Motors Ltd. has no knowledge in respect of the allegations contained in paragraph 14 of the crossclaim.
4. *(Any facts relied on as a defence to the crossclaim must be laid out in consecutively numbered paragraphs, as they would be in a statement of defence.)*

DEFENCE TO PLAINTIFF'S CLAIM AGAINST CROSSCLAIMING DEFENDANT

7. *(If the defendant to the crossclaim wishes to defend against the plaintiff's claim against the crossclaiming defendant, pursuant to rule 28.06, further consecutively numbered paragraphs are included here. If no such defence is being raised, this part of the document is not included.)*

Date: January 25, year 1

Huey Sue
LSUC #23456T
Barrister and Solicitor
65 False Trail
Toronto, Ontario M6Y 1Z6

tel. 416-485-6891
fax 416-485-6892

Lawyer for the Defendant in the Crossclaim

TO: Brenda Brilliant
LSUC #86421X
Barrister & Solicitor
1400 Willsa Way
Toronto, Ontario, M6V 9T7

tel. 416-766-4321
fax 416-766-9876

Lawyer for the Crossclaiming Defendant

FIGURE 12.5   THIRD PARTY CLAIM (FORM 29A)

Court file no. 01-CV-1357

ONTARIO
SUPERIOR COURT OF JUSTICE

BETWEEN:

ABIGAIL BOAR

Plaintiff

and

RATTLE MOTORS LTD. and FRED FLOGEM

Defendants

and

SKANK MOTORCAR COMPANY LTD.

Third Party

THIRD PARTY CLAIM OF THE DEFENDANT
RATTLE MOTORS LTD.

TO THE THIRD PARTY

A LEGAL PROCEEDING HAS BEEN COMMENCED AGAINST YOU by way of a third party claim in an action in this court.

The action was commenced by the plaintiff against the defendant for the relief claimed in the statement of claim served with this third party claim. The defendant has defended the action on the grounds set out in the statement of defence served with this third party claim. The defendant's claim against you is set out in the following pages.

IF YOU WISH TO DEFEND THIS THIRD PARTY CLAIM, you or an Ontario lawyer acting for you must prepare a third party defence in Form 29B prescribed by the Rules of Civil Procedure, serve it on the lawyers for the other parties or, where a party does not have a lawyer, serve it on the party, and file it, with proof of service, WITHIN TWENTY DAYS after this third party claim is served on you, if you are served in Ontario.

If you are served in another province or territory of Canada or in the United States of America, the period for serving and filing your third party defence is forty days. If you are served outside Canada and the United States of America, the period is sixty days.

Instead of serving and filing a third party defence, you may serve and file a notice of intent to defend in Form 18B prescribed by the Rules of Civil Procedure. This will entitle you to ten more days within which to serve and file your third party defence.

YOU MAY ALSO DEFEND the action by the plaintiff against the defendant by serving and filing a statement of defence within the time for serving and filing your third party defence.

FIGURE 12.5 CONTINUED

IF YOU FAIL TO DEFEND THIS THIRD PARTY CLAIM, JUDGMENT MAY BE GIVEN AGAINST YOU IN YOUR ABSENCE AND WITHOUT FURTHER NOTICE TO YOU. IF YOU WISH TO DEFEND THIS PROCEEDING BUT ARE UNABLE TO PAY LEGAL FEES, LEGAL AID MAY BE AVAILABLE TO YOU BY CONTACTING A LOCAL LEGAL AID OFFICE.

IF YOU PAY THE AMOUNT OF THE THIRD PARTY CLAIM AGAINST YOU, and $500.00 for costs, within the time for serving and filing your third party defence, you may move to have the third party claim dismissed by the court. If you believe the amount claimed for costs is excessive, you may pay the amount of the third party claim and $400.00 for costs and have the costs assessed by the court.

Date: May 25, year 1

Issued by: _____

Address of
court office: Court House
393 University Avenue
Toronto, Ontario, M5G 1E6

TO:
Skank Motorcar Company Ltd.
349 Losers' Lane
Windsor, Ontario, J4T 6Y7

CLAIM

1. The defendant Rattle Motors Ltd. claims against the third party:
   a. a declaration that the third party is liable to the defendant for all or part of the plaintiff's claim that the defendant may be ordered by this court to satisfy;
   b. further, or in the alternative, contribution, indemnity, and relief in respect to any damages, interest, and costs awarded to the plaintiff as against the defendant;
   c. costs of defending the main action and the third party action on a substantial indemnity basis; and
   d. such further relief as seems just to this court.
2. The plaintiff in the main action alleges that as a result of the negligence of the defendants, she slipped and fell on a patch of oil while viewing automobiles for sale in the showroom of the defendant Rattle Motors Ltd.
3. The plaintiff in the main action alleges that as a result of her fall in the showroom of the defendant Rattle Motors Ltd., she suffered damages totalling $203,649.00, together with interest and costs.
4. The defendant Rattle Motors Ltd. denies that it is negligent and further denies any liability to the plaintiff.

FIGURE 12.5   CONCLUDED

5. *(Each allegation of a material fact relied on must be set out in consecutively numbered paragraphs. The form and content should resemble the form and content of a statement of claim.)*

6. If the defendant Rattle Motors Ltd. is found at trial to be liable for the plaintiff's claim, or any part of it, then the defendant Rattle Motors Ltd. is entitled to contribution, indemnification, or relief from the third party to the full extent of the damages found and the costs of the main and third party actions on a substantial indemnity basis.

Date of issue: February 6, year 1

> Huey Sue
> LSUC #23456T
> Barrister and Solicitor
> 65 False Trail
> Toronto, Ontario, M6Y 1Z6
>
> tel. 416-485-6891
> fax 416-485-6892
>
> Lawyer for the Defendants

FIGURE 12.6   THIRD PARTY DEFENCE (FORM 29B)

Court file no. 01-CV-1357

ONTARIO
SUPERIOR COURT OF JUSTICE

BETWEEN:

ABIGAIL BOAR

Plaintiff

and

RATTLE MOTORS LTD. and FRED FLOGEM

Defendants

and

SKANK MOTORCAR COMPANY LTD.

Third Party

THIRD PARTY DEFENCE

1. The third party admits the allegations contained in paragraphs 2 and 3 of the third party claim.
2. The third party denies the allegations contained in paragraphs 5 and 6 of the third party claim.
3. The third party has no knowledge in respect of the allegations contained in paragraph 1 of the third party claim.
4. *(Each allegation of a material fact must be set out in a consecutively numbered paragraph. The form and content should resemble the form and content of a statement of defence.)*

Date: February 16, year 1

Huey Sue
LSUC #23456T
Barrister and Solicitor
65 False Trail
Toronto, Ontario, M6Y 1Z6

tel. 416-485-6891
fax 416-485-6892

Lawyer for the Defendants

TO: U.R. Smart
LSUC #13579S
Barrister & Solicitor
4700 Bay Street
Toronto, Ontario, M4T 8V2

Lawyer for the Third Party

CHAPTER 13

Amending pleadings

INTRODUCTION

Ideally, before issuing a pleading, you will have carefully investigated the facts, researched the law, and drafted the claim, defence, or crossclaim. All parties should expect to be able to rely on that pleading as an accurate statement of your case right through the pretrial and trial stages. However, after a pleading has been issued, often as the result of discovery, new facts emerge which expand or change a claim or defence, so that the pleading is no longer accurate. For example, if on the eve of trial, further medical tests showed that Abigail had suffered more serious mental impairment than was evident from the description of her injuries when the claim issued and when she appeared for discovery, I.M. Just would need to amend the pleadings. He would do this by adding this information to a description of the consequences of her injuries. He would also have to amend paragraph one to increase the claim for general damages. If her claim was not amended and the evidence at trial showed more serious damages than had been pleaded, Abigail would be limited to judgment for the amount she had claimed in her pleadings. The reason for this is that the defendant expects to answer the case as pleaded. If a plaintiff changes her claim, the defendant is entitled to proper notice; if it is not given, she is confined to the case as pleaded. The balance of this chapter concerns how a party goes about giving that notice.

RIGHT TO AMEND

Rule 26.01 states that the court *shall* amend a pleading at any stage of the action, including trial, unless the prejudice to the other side cannot be compensated by costs or by an adjournment. There are relatively few cases where costs and an adjournment cannot compensate the opposite party when an amendment is sought, even at a late stage. While judges usually grant the request, given the language of the rule, they often remain sceptical of a defence or claim that arises late in the proceeding. If your law firm is going to amend, it should do so at the earliest opportunity. The longer it waits, the more expensive it will be. For example, if an amendment is sought and granted on the eve of trial, it will often be on terms that the case be adjourned and that the opposite party have the opportunity to have discovery, both oral and documentary, on the issues covered by your amendment. In addition, your amendment may trigger an amendment to the opposite party's pleading as he or she pleads to your amendment. The costs of all the procedures spawned by the amendment will be borne by the party seeking the amendment.

WHEN YOU AMEND MAKES A DIFFERENCE

Before pleadings are noted closed, any party may amend his or her pleading without seeking leave of the court and without having terms imposed as a condition for making the amendment, provided that the amendment does not result in new parties being added or existing parties being deleted (rule 26.02(a)). Once pleadings have closed, then you must bring a motion (rule 26.02(b)), in which case the court follows the requirements of rule 26.01, and permits the amendment on terms unless it is so prejudicial that costs and adjournment will not adequately compensate the other party. However, if all parties consent, the amendment may be made without the court's permission on filing the consent. Any new party being added as a result of the amendment must consent as well (rule 26.02(c)).

HOW TO MAKE THE AMENDMENT

Rule 26.03, which governs the making of amendments, predates the age of the word processor. It provides one of the few instances in the rules where interlineations in pen seem to be required.

If the amendment is not extensive, consisting of a phrase or a sentence or two, it can simply be written in the appropriate place on the face of the document and underlined. If the amendment is so extensive that interlineations would make the document difficult to read, the party must file a fresh copy of the original pleading as amended, bearing the date of the original pleading, with the title preceded by the word "amended" (AMENDED STATEMENT OF DEFENCE, for example). The amended parts of the fresh pleading must also be underlined.

In each case, the registrar must note on the pleading the date on which the amendment was made and the authority for it: the order of the judge or master who permitted it, rule 26.02(a) if leave was not required because pleadings were not noted closed, or the filed consent of all parties.

If the pleading is amended more than once, each subsequent amendment is underlined an additional time. The text of the second amendment made is underlined twice to distinguish it from the previous amendment, and so on. So, for example, in figure 13.1, Abigail's claim for relief in her statement of claim set out her damages at $200,000 in paragraph 1a. It was then amended to $250,000 (and underlined once), then later amended to $400,000 (and underlined twice).

AMENDED PLEADINGS MUST BE SERVED

Every party to the proceeding, including any party added by the amendment, is to be served with the amended pleading. This includes not only the opposite party but also those added by crossclaim, third party claim, and counterclaim. Proof of service of the amended pleading must be filed "forthwith."[1] If the amended pleading is an originating process, such as a statement of claim, it need not be served personally on a party that was served with and responded to the original pleading. However, if the party had previously defaulted or is added as a result of the amendment, he or she must be served personally. The defaulting party's opportunity to plead and rejoin the proceeding is revived by being served with the amended pleading

FIGURE 13.1 AMENDED PLEADING

1. The plaintiff claims, against the defendant:

$250,000 $400,000

↑ ↑

a. general damages in the amount of $200,000;

(rule 26.04). The reason for this is that a defaulter with no defence to the original claim might have defence to the amended claim and may now wish to defend.

A party served with an amended pleading has ten days to respond. If the amendment is made at an early date, while the time to respond to the original pleading is still running, then the party has the balance of the time remaining, if it is greater than 10 days (rule 26.05(1)).

If a pleading is amended and the party responded to the original but not the amended version, the party is deemed to be relying on the other party's original pre-amended pleading (rule 26.05(2)). Interestingly, the rules do not specify what form this "response" should take. Refer back to rule 1.04(2), which states that where the rules do not provide for a situation, you should proceed by analogy to the rules — in other words, find a similar process in the rules and adapt it. You might use a reply and modify it to respond to the amended pleading. Alternatively, you could develop a document called a "response to the amended statement of claim," or other amended document, with the usual general heading and title of proceedings. Then set out your response in consecutive numbered paragraphs, following the usual rules for pleadings. However, if your response also requires you to amend your pleadings, you must bring a motion to do so if pleadings are closed.

If an amendment is made at trial and is recorded on the trial record by the court reporter, no formal written order need be drafted, issued, or entered. It is likewise unnecessary to formally amend the pleading (rule 26.06).

CHAPTER SUMMARY

This chapter reviewed the process of amending pleadings. It noted the general rule that amendments are to be made unless they are so prejudicial that the other side cannot be compensated in costs or by an adjournment. We then noted how amendments are made technically on the face of the pleadings by underlining and, in some cases, by issuing a fresh copy of the original pleadings as amended. Once an amendment is made, the pleading must be served on all parties, who then have the opportunity to respond to the amended pleadings and to amend their own pleadings.

NOTE

1 "Forthwith" is not defined as a specific time period, but it means "as soon as possible."

REFERENCES

Rules of Civil Procedure, RRO 1990, reg. 194.

REVIEW QUESTIONS

1. Amir claims that you can amend pleadings at any time. Is he correct?

2. What constitutes prejudice in the context of amending pleadings?

3. When do you need leave to amend and when do you not need it?

4. How do you make amendments?

5. What happens after a pleading is formally amended?

DISCUSSION QUESTION

1. Read and respond to the following memorandum:

To: E. Egregious, law clerk
From: I.M. Just, lawyer
Re: *Boar v. Rattle Motors Ltd. et al.*, amending claim

Although trial is only three weeks away, I have just had a supplementary report and updated prognosis from Ms Boar's neurologist, Dr. Morris Furgazy. In his report, dated May 30, year 2, Dr. Furgazy says that as a result of recent neurological tests, he has found that there is much more brain damage than he originally thought. Specifically, there are neurological lesions present, which cause impaired cognitive function. Originally, these looked to be transient or relatively minor, but it now appears that they are permanent and will result in much reduced ability to reason and to remember information. This changes the nature of the injury sustained and increases the damages that we should be claiming. I called Huey Sue to see if he would consent to the amendments. He refused, saying we should have had this information much earlier. We will need to move to amend.

What do you think the likely outcome of a motion to amend will be? Please draft the motion and affidavit in my name.

PART III

From discovery to trial

CHAPTER 14

Discovery

INTRODUCTION

In terms of time, and therefore cost, **discovery** takes up a large part of the proceedings prior to trial. The purposes of discovery are:

discovery
process that occurs after close of pleadings in which parties obtain more information about each other's cases before trial

- to discover the evidence on which the opponent relies to establish the facts of his or her case,

- to obtain admissions that will help prove your case,

- to obtain admissions that will assist you in weakening the opponent's case,

- to narrow issues for trial by requiring disclosure,

- to assess the credibility of the opposing party and your client as witnesses, and

- to determine if there is a basis for settlement before trial.

CHANGES TO DISCOVERY PROCEDURES, IN EFFECT AS OF JANUARY 1, 2010

While effective litigation counsel usually cooperated in planning both documentary and oral examinations for discovery, the rules did not explicitly require that they do so; however, as of January 1, 2010, cooperation will be mandated by a new rule, rule 29.1.

- Parties will be now required, early in the litigation process, to agree on a discovery plan that covers both documentary and oral discovery. The plan should set out the scope of discovery, how documents will be produced (particularly when they were originally in electronic form), and when pretrial examination for discovery will take place. The goal is to start discovery early and end it quickly, considering the principle of proportionality, by setting up a discovery plan and timetable that the parties will be expected to stick to.

- Because oral discovery can be very slow and time consuming, the amended rules impose caps on the time that can be spent on discovery. Each party will be limited to a total of seven hours of pre-trial examination for discovery unless the parties consent or the court orders otherwise.[1]

OVERVIEW OF THE DISCOVERY PROCESS

Rules 30 to 33 include the basic forms of discovery that can be used. Rules 34 and 35 cover discovery procedures. An overview of these rules is set out in table 14.1.

In addition to the discovery procedures covered by rules 30 to 35, there are three other discovery-like provisions in the rules.

1. The pretrial conference covered by rule 50 creates a forum that enhances settlement and allows for narrowing of the issues if the case proceeds to trial.

2. Rule 51 facilitates a process in which the parties ask each other to admit the authenticity of a document or the truth of a fact, which narrows issues by reducing matters that must be formally proved at trial.

3. Rule 53 requires the disclosure of experts' reports before trial to reduce surprise and narrow issues.

These discovery-like procedures are discussed later in the text. In this chapter, after briefly discussing the deemed undertaking rule (rule 30.1), property inspections (rule 32), and medical examinations (rule 33), we focus on discovery of documents, oral discovery, and following up on undertakings because these procedures are featured in almost every civil action.

Deemed undertaking rule: Rule 30.1

Rule 30.1 codifies a rule, which developed at common law, that parties give an implied undertaking not to use the fruits of discovery other than in the proceeding in which the information was obtained.[2]

The purpose of the rule is to protect the privacy of parties because discovery requires them to disclose information that they might not otherwise need or want to disclose publicly. Remember that court proceedings and the content of this court file are public. Anyone may look at the discovery transcripts and filed documents.

This common law rule has now been incorporated into rule 30.1. All parties and counsel are governed by this rule with respect to any information obtained from any form of discovery under the rules (oral, written, and documentary discovery, medical examinations, and property inspections). The information obtained may be used only in the proceeding in which it was obtained (rule 30.1(1) and (3)).

Table 14.1   Overview of discovery rules

Regulation of the forms of discovery: Rules 30 to 33
    Rule 30: Discovery of documents
    Rule 30.1: Deemed undertaking
    Rule 31: Examination for discovery
    Rule 32: Inspection of property
    Rule 33: Medical examination

Regulation of the procedure for conducting discovery: Rules 34 and 35
    Rule 34: Out-of-court oral examinations
    Rule 35: Out-of-court written discovery by questions

However, if a party uses other investigative techniques to discover information in the course of a proceeding, rule 30.1 does not cover that kind of information — it covers only information obtained through the discovery process (rule 30.1(2)). There are some exceptions: If a party consents to the use of evidence, it may be filed in another proceeding (rule 30.1(4)). If evidence is filed in court or given or referred to in a hearing, or if information is obtained from evidence given at a hearing, either orally or as a document, it may be disclosed. This exception is based on the notion that court proceedings are open, and the information given in court is public and may be disseminated generally (rule 30.1(5)(a) to (c)). Evidence obtained in one proceeding through discovery may be used against a witness to impeach the witness' credibility in another proceeding (rule 30.1(6)). If, for example, Fred gave evidence on discovery in one proceeding and in a separate proceeding gave evidence that contradicted his previous discovery evidence, counsel in the second proceeding is entitled to introduce the discovery evidence in the first proceeding to challenge Fred's credibility. The undertaking rule may be waived by the court where the interest of justice demands it (rule 30.1(8)).

Inspection of property: Rule 32

Rule 32 sets out a procedure for the inspection of property as part of the discovery process. It may be used in conjunction with rule 45, which gives the court the authority to order the preservation of property for inspection and for other purposes in connection with a proceeding. Rule 32.01(1) permits the inspection of real or personal property. The rule is broad and permissive. It allows the court to authorize the entry onto property of any person and may allow the property to be taken out of the possession of its owner, whether the owner is a party to the proceeding or not. The court may permit all kinds of tests and inspections to be carried out, though notice must be given to the party who owns or has possession of the property unless there are good reasons not to give notice (rule 32.01(3) and (4)).

Medical examinations of parties: Rule 33

This form of discovery usually occurs in cases involving claims for damages for personal injury where the plaintiff's own doctors have furnished expert medical evidence. With difficult-to-diagnose injuries, such as back problems or neurological problems, the defendants may wish to have their own expert conduct an examination. Where a party raises his or her own health or medical state as an issue, an opponent can test the allegations. Where an opponent raises the other party's medical condition as an issue, the court is more reluctant to order the party to submit to an examination. However, where the parties cannot agree on an examination, s. 105 of the *Courts of Justice Act* permits a medical examination. Rule 33 governs the procedure to be followed after an order for an examination has been made under s. 105.

MEDICAL EXAMINATION PROCEDURE

Where one party wishes to subject an opponent to an examination, he or she must being a motion, serving all parties, not just the party who is the focus of the inquiry (rule 33.01). An order under s. 105 of the *Courts of Justice Act* may name the practitioner to conduct the examination and set the terms and limits on the examination. If the circumstances warrant, subsequent examinations may be ordered (rule 33.02(1) and (2)). Within seven days of the examination, the party to be examined must provide the party requesting the examination with a copy of relevant medical reports and hospital or other records. However, records that were prepared in contemplation of litigation, and for no other purpose, and that will not be used at trial may be withheld. This may include, for example, preliminary examinations conducted at the behest of the injured party's lawyers to advise the lawyers of the nature of the injury or its cause, where the report is used to guide the lawyer to other experts whose reports eventually will be used (rule 33.04). The medical examination ordered under s. 105 is not a three-ring circus. Unless the court orders otherwise, only the person to be examined, the medical practitioner, and assistants may attend the examination (rule 33.05).

Once an examination has been conducted, its results cannot be swept under the carpet. The practitioner is required to prepare a written report of observations, test results, diagnosis, and prognosis, and deliver it to the party who requested the order for an examination. That party is then obliged to serve the report on every other party to the proceeding (rule 33.06). For a party who does not cooperate with an order under s. 105, there are the usual remedies of striking out pleadings, dismissing the action, or making "such further order as is just."

DISCOVERY OF DOCUMENTS
Discovery of documents: When and what

In every action, within 10 days after the close of pleadings, every party must serve on every other party an affidavit of documents (rule 30.03(1)). The scope of what must be included is broad. The affidavit must list and disclose every document relating to any matter in issue in an action. As a general rule, when in doubt as to its relevance, include it (rule 30.02(1)).

To be disclosed, the document must be or have been in the possession, control, or power of the party. This means that the party has the document, or has the power or right to obtain it, where the other party does not (rule 30.01(b)). If the other party has the document or can get it, you need not list it and can take the position that the other party can satisfy itself by obtaining the document itself (rule 30.01(b)).

Once listed in the affidavit of documents, every document must be produced for inspection if requested unless privilege is claimed for it. If the other party wishes to challenge a claim of privilege, it may do so by bringing a motion (rule 30.02(2)). Whether privilege may be claimed depends on what kind of document you have. There are three categories you need to consider.

1. *Lawyer–client communications to get and receive advice on issues relevant to the action.* This category is covered by lawyer–client privilege and probably includes most of the lawyer's correspondence on the file with the client and with others on the client's behalf.

2. **_Without prejudice_** documents. Typical of this category is settlement correspondence where offers are made on a without prejudice basis. These documents are privileged and may be described as correspondence regarding settlement between the parties.

3. _Documents for which the dominant purpose is litigation._ A document may have been created for several purposes, but if the dominant purpose was litigation, then it may be privileged.[3] For example, in one case, the lawyers for the defendant obtained a police officer's summary report of his investigation of an accident for the dominant purpose of litigation. Although the document had other purposes, such as data for traffic accident statistics, its primary purpose conferred a privilege on it.[4]

without prejudice
term used, usually in correspondence, to indicate that an offer or admission cannot be used against its maker, admitted in evidence, or disclosed to the court

There is a special rule about insurance policies. Where there is an insurance policy that may cover a claim in all or part of a lawsuit, or may cover a settlement of a claim, the insured party, whether plaintiff or defendant, must disclose and produce the insurance policy if requested. However, no evidence about the insurance policy can be admitted into evidence unless it is relevant to an issue in the action. Its purpose is to let other parties know that the judgment can be satisfied from the insurance and to permit other parties to notify the insurer if the insured party has not done so so that the insurer is not able to deny coverage because there was a failure to give timely notice of a claim (rule 30.02(3)). Insurance companies are entitled to use technical defences to deny coverage, and they are not shy about doing so.

Subsidiary corporations, affiliated corporations, and corporations controlled by a party may be forced to produce documents in a lawsuit to which they are not parties. In this situation, the court may order a party to disclose documents in the power, possession, or control of a subsidiary, affiliate, or wholly controlled corporation. The key here is that the party controls these corporations, or at least has a right of access to information from them because of the relationship (rule 30.02(4)). The nature of the corporate relationship that ties a corporation to a party is further spelled out:

1. A subsidiary corporation is one that is directly or indirectly controlled by another. This means that the controlling corporation has a majority of voting shares or at least a large enough minority to give it _de facto_ control in alliance with others.

2. A corporation is affiliated if:

   a. one corporation is a subsidiary of another;

   b. both corporations are subsidiaries of another so that they are linked; or

   c. the same person, where one corporation is a party and the other is not, controls both corporations directly or indirectly (rule 30.01(2)).

A document includes the usual paper, but it also includes all kinds of information that is stored electronically, as well as maps, videos, and films.

Electronic discovery

The document discovery procedures in rule 30 were developed at a time when documents were mostly paper records created by hand. A physical record search of hard copy was involved in finding them, and the result was usually a finite number of identifiable documents.

The use of office and personal computers, as well as various handheld data-generating and data-gathering devices since the mid 1990s has resulted in a growing awareness of the impact of these technological changes on the discovery process, and practitioners have started to talk about electronic discovery or "**e-discovery**." They recognize that e-discovery is different from "paper" discovery in a variety of ways:

e-discovery
a term used to describe discovery of documents where the discovery procedures primarily involve the collection and production of information that is stored electronically

1. The sheer volume of electronic information (e-mails, documents, databases, etc.) that is potentially relevant for discovery purposes is beyond the comprehension of many lawyers and clients.

2. Electronic documents and information can easily be deleted, either intentionally or inadvertently, and data thought to be destroyed in the ordinary course of business can sometimes be recovered, but often at considerable cost.

3. Collections of electronic data will often contain a mixture of business and private communications.

4. The preservation, review, and production of large volumes of electronic data can be time-consuming, costly, and difficult when there are no standard formats or protocols.

5. Protection of privacy and privileged information is much more difficult in the electronic realm.[5]

Rather than amend rule 30 to create new e-discovery rules, the response in Ontario so far has been to rely on the broad definition of "document" in rule 30.01(1)(a), which clearly includes information in electronic form, and to use case law[6] and practice directions to the profession to guide the development of e-discovery procedures. In this regard, the Ontario Bar Association has set out principles designed to alert you to problems and issues with e-discovery and that can also serve as a guide for use in a case where discovery of documents is primarily e-discovery:

1. Electronic documents containing relevant data are discoverable under rule 30 (as is clear from rule 30.01(1)(a)).

2. The obligations of the parties with respect to e-discovery are subject to balancing and may vary with

   • the cost, burden, and delay that may be imposed on parties;

   • the nature and scope of the litigation, the importance of the issues, and the amounts at stake;

   • the relevance of the available electronic documents, and their importance to the court's adjudication in a given case.[7]

3. In most cases, the primary source of electronic documents should be the parties' active data, and any other information that was stored in a manner that anticipated future business use and that still permits efficient search and

retrieval. (This principle may relieve parties of having to search every nook and cranny of a party's computer systems when it is not practical to do so.)

4. Absent an agreement or a court order based on demonstrated need or relevance, a responding party should not be required to search for, review, or produce documents that are deleted or hidden, nor should they have to do this with residual data such as fragmented or overwritten files. (This means that backup data and data that has become corrupted or which is no longer readable because the hardware to read it is obsolete and no longer available does not have to be made available unless there is a clear case for relevance or need, due to the effort and expense required to produce it.)

5. As soon as litigation is contemplated or threatened, parties should immediately take reasonable and good faith steps to preserve relevant electronic documents. However, it is unreasonable to expect parties to take every conceivable step to preserve all documents that may be potentially relevant. (This may require collecting client archives, creating backup and deletion policies, and instructing client's staff to conform to policies of backup and preservation of relevant data, including **meta data**, and the cessation of overwriting disks and tapes.)

meta data
computer technology term that describes information about an electronic document indicating who prepared it, when it was prepared, who it was sent to, etc.

6. Parties should place each other on notice with respect to preserving electronic documents as early in the process as possible because electronic documents may be lost in the ordinary course of business.

7. Parties should discuss the need to preserve or produce meta data as early as possible. If a party considers meta data relevant, it should notify the other party immediately.

8. Counsel should meet and confer as soon as practicable, on an ongoing basis, regarding the location, preservation, review, and production of electronic documents. They should seek to agree on the scope of each party's rights and obligations with respect to e-discovery, and create a process for dealing with them.

9. The scope of e-discovery should be defined by parties and their counsel before commencing oral examination for discovery. This can best be achieved if parties' requests for preservation of electronic documents and pre-discovery meetings between counsel are as specific as possible in identifying what is being requested, what is being produced and what is not being produced, and the reasons for any refusals.

10. A party may satisfy its obligation to produce relevant electronic documents in good faith by using electronic tools and processes such as data sampling, searching, or selection criteria to identify the documents that are most likely to contain relevant data or information. (This means that a party may not have to review every bit of data in an e-file in some circumstances; for example, where the relevance of the data lies in its indicating a trend or direction.)

11. Parties should agree early in the litigation process on the format in which electronic documents will be produced. Such documents may be produced in electronic form where this would

- provide more complete and relevant information,

- facilitate access to the information in the document by means of electronic techniques to review, search, or otherwise use the documents in the litigation process,

- minimize costs to the producing party, and/or

- preserve the integrity and security of the data.

12. During the discovery process, where appropriate, parties should agree to measures to protect privileged information and other objections to the production of electronic documents. (Where databases are large, inadvertent disclosure of privileged information may be a significant problem.)

13. In general, consistent with the rules regarding production of paper documents, pending any final disposition of the proceeding, the interim costs of preservation, retrieval, review, and production of electronic documents will be borne by the party producing them. The other party will, similarly, be required to incur the cost of making a copy of the resulting productions for its own use. However, in special circumstances, it may be appropriate for the parties to arrive at a different allocation of costs on an informal basis, by agreement, or by court order.[8]

Affidavit of documents

The affidavit of documents has a prescribed format (form 30A for individuals and form 30B for corporations). The difference is that an officer or director of a corporation or a partner on behalf of a partnership completes form 30B, whereas an individual party completes his or her own affidavit using form 30A. The deponent must not only search his or her own records but must also take steps to inquire about the kinds of documents that might be relevant and inquire of others who may have control of various types of classes of relevant documents. After a thorough inquiry and search, the deponent swears that he or she has disclosed all documents that are relevant and in his or her power, possession, or control.

The documents are then divided into three schedules:

1. Schedule A documents are those that the deponent has or can get and that he or she will produce if asked.

2. Schedule B documents are those that the deponent has or once had but that he or she objects to producing on the ground of privilege. The basis for privilege must be stated: correspondence subject to lawyer–client privilege, documents for which the dominant purpose is litigation, or correspondence related to settlement made on a without prejudice basis.

3. Schedule C documents are those that were once in the possession, power, or control of the deponent but no longer are. It is necessary to state how control was lost and to give the present location of the documents if known.

There is also a fourth schedule, schedule D, but it is used only in cases brought under rule 76, the simplified procedure rule. Here, in addition to disclosing documents, a party also discloses the names and addresses of persons who might reasonably be expected to have knowledge of transactions or occurrences in issue. Some of these persons may be called as witnesses, and some may not, but those who eventually become witnesses should be on this list. Once the names are known, lawyers for any party may approach the potential witnesses to ask them questions. It is then up to the person contacted to decide whether he or she wishes to talk to the lawyer. There is no obligation to do so. The only obligation is to attend court and give evidence if summonsed to do so. In a proceeding that is *not* conducted under rule 76, names of persons with information can be obtained on oral discovery.

The deponent's signature must appear on the affidavit of documents. A lawyer must also sign the certificate on the form, stating that he or she informed the deponent of the requirement that full disclosure of all documents be made.

Clerk's role in the discovery of documents

Now that we have examined the basic document disclosure and production rules, and the contents of the affidavit of documents, we can turn to your role in the document discovery process.

The law clerk needs to understand both the issues involved in the action and the individual lawyer's approach to the issues in the file. This means that you need to understand the theory of the case, and how that might affect the organization of documents. The theory for Abigail's allegation of negligence, for example, is that she fell because Fred left the oil on the floor so no that one would notice it and hid it by turning down the lights.

The clerk needs to find out how the lawyer prefers information to be presented in the affidavit. The main variation is in how documents are described, for example: "letter from Dr. Morris Furgazy, neurologist, to Dr. Edwina Dhrool, family physician for Abigail Boar, regarding results of PET scan taken June 13, year 1" or "letter from Dr. Morris Furgazy to Dr. Edwina Dhrool, Abigail Boar's family physician." Either version is acceptable. The briefer version will force the opponent's lawyer to review the document and determine its relevance.

The next step is to review the client's documents. If they are numerous, and are composed of ordinary business records, it may be necessary to conduct your review on the client's premises. Otherwise, the documents can be taken to the lawyer's office. Whichever approach is taken, it is important not to disturb the way in which the client arranged the material. If a client keeps account records in a particular sequence in a shoebox, then they should remain in that sequence in that shoebox. Each document should be located, copied, identified, and put back in its original location. With many documents now available electronically, whole folders and files may be downloaded onto CDs, flash memory sticks, or other electronic storage devices. If this is done, all material should be downloaded in the order and format in which it is found, insofar as this is possible.

Table 14.2   Document table

Schedule	Date	Type	Pages	Description	Location

In the schedule column, insert A, B, or C for the relevant schedule on the affidavit of documents.

In the date column, insert the date of the document; leave it blank if the document is undated.

In the type column, indicate whether the document is an original, photocopy, video, or fax copy.

In the pages column, indicate the length of the document in pages.

In the description column, bearing in mind your lawyer's approach, enter a description of the document.

In the location column, indicate the document's location by subfile number and individual document number — for example, F3/D67.

The management of the documents by the law firm may be done on a variety of specialized software programs, or it may be done on a standard word-processing program, using the table and sort functions. What follows is an overview of how to prepare an affidavit of documents from client files.

Go through the client's documents in the exact order that you find them, without disturbing that order, and review them for relevance and privilege, using the guidelines discussed earlier. Number each document in each file in the sequence that they appear. This includes every phone message, invoice, memorandum, letter, videotape, and so on.

Each file can be labelled as a subfile and given a sequential number. The documents in all subfiles can then be numbered in sequence as well, starting with the first document in the first subfile and ending with the last document in the last subfile. This means that the first document in subfile 4 is not F4/D1 but may be F4/D632. In this way, each document has a unique number, allowing you to easily find a document to be produced, or one that is privileged or irrelevant, and to know how many documents there are in total.

When numbering documents, do not write on originals; instead, use small coloured stickers, writing the document number and the subfile number on the sticker.

As you assign document and file numbers, you prepare a table in which a complete list of all documents in all files can be entered. This is a master list for office use, although by using the sort function of your software later, you will be able to select documents for the schedule A list, with all necessary location details. Table 14.2 provides a format for a document table.

List each document, starting with the first document in the first subfile and going to the last document in the last subfile. Then sort the list chronologically. Undated items appear at the head or foot of the list, depending on your preference and the capabilities of your software.

Using this chronological list, you can now prepare the list for schedule A in the affidavit. From the chronological list, sort for all schedule A documents and list them in a separate table in chronological order, undated items first. The schedule A documents should now be listed in sequence (1, 2, 3) on the affidavit, and the document identifier numbers (F1/D3) previously used to locate them can be deleted from the affidavit. Most lawyers do not give individualized lists of documents for which privilege is claimed in schedule B. Rather, they identify and describe a class of documents, as the following examples illustrate:

- "all notes prepared by or on behalf of Abigail Boar in anticipation of litigation or for use in instructing counsel and prosecuting this action,"

- "all correspondence passing between the plaintiff and her lawyers," and

- "narrative prepared by Abigail Boar of events following her fall, prepared for her lawyers."

Abigail Boar's affidavit of documents

In a case such as Abigail's, most of the documentation concerns her injuries and their consequences. But to keep matters simple, let us assume we have looked through Abigail's files and found the following documents:

1. a receipt for dinner at Barbeerian's, September 14, year 0 [D1];

2. a written narrative prepared by Abigail for I.M. Just describing events after the accident, January 21, year 1 [D2];

3. a daily "pain diary" prepared by Abigail and kept on a daily basis, from November 10, year 0, recording pain and other effects of the injuries sustained [D3];

4. Toronto Hospital records from September 14 to 16, year 0 [D4];

5. a letter from Dr. Furgazy to Dr. Dhrool, January 10, year 1, advising on treatment for Abigail [D5];

6. a prescription, October 14, year 0 [D6];

7. a prescription, October 21, year 0 [D7];

8. a prescription, November 3 year 0 [D8]; and

9. a birthday card from Aunt Emma, August 31, year 0 [D9].

Because there are not many documents, and the client hasn't created subfiles, you would not necessarily arrange them in subfiles; but if you did, you could create the following subfiles and place the documents in them:

- F1 receipts: D1, D6, D7, D8;

- F2 medical records: D4; and

- F3 correspondence and memorandums: D2, D3, D5, D9.

D2 is privileged because it was prepared for use by her lawyer in this litigation. You can eliminate D9 from the affidavit because Abigail's birthday is not relevant to the issues in the action. It is included in the office list but will not appear in the affidavit. The rest are clearly relevant to the issues and belong in schedule A.

Figure 14.1 shows Abigail Boar's affidavit of documents.

FIGURE 14.1 AFFIDAVIT OF DOCUMENTS (FORM 30A)

Court file no. 01-CV-1234

ONTARIO
SUPERIOR COURT OF JUSTICE

BETWEEN:

ABIGAIL BOAR

Plaintiff

and

RATTLE MOTORS LTD. and FRED FLOGEM

Defendants

AFFIDAVIT OF DOCUMENTS

I, Abigail Boar, **of the** City of Toronto, **in the** Province of Ontario, **the plaintiff in this action, MAKE OATH AND SAY:**

1. I have conducted a diligent search of my records and have made appropriate enquiries of others to inform myself in order to make this affidavit. This affidavit discloses, to the full extent of my knowledge, information and belief, all documents relating to any matter in issue in this action that are or have been in my possession, control or power.
2. I have listed in Schedule A those documents that are in my possession, control or power and that I do not object to producing for inspection.
3. I have listed in Schedule B those documents that are or were in my possession, control or power and that I object to producing because I claim they are privileged, and I have stated in Schedule B the grounds for each such claim.
4. I have listed in Schedule C those documents that were formerly in my possession, control or power but are no longer in my possession, control or power, and I have stated in Schedule C when and how I lost possession or control of or power over them and their present location.
5. I have never had in my possession, control or power any document relating to any matter in issue in this action other than those listed in Schedules A, B and C.

Sworn before me at the)	
City of Toronto,)	*Abigail Boar*
in the Province of Ontario,)	Abigail Boar
on February 10, year 1.)	
I.M. Just	

I.M. Just
Commissioner for Taking Affidavits)

FIGURE 14.1 CONCLUDED

CERTIFICATE OF LAWYER

I CERTIFY that I have explained to the deponent a) the necessity of making full disclosure of all documents relating to any matter in issue in the action; b) what kinds of documents are likely to be relevant to the allegations made in the pleadings; and c) if the action is brought under the simplified procedure, the necessity of providing the list required under rule 76.03.

Date . . . . January 14, year 1 . . . . *I.M. Just* . . . .

 I.M. Just

SCHEDULE A

Documents in my possession, control or power that I do not object to producing for inspection.

1. Receipt for dinner from Barbeerian's: September 14, year 0
2. Toronto Hospital records: September 16, year 0
3. Prescription: October 14, year 0
4. Prescription October 21, year 0
5. Prescription November 3, year 0
6. Pain diary, November 10, year 0 to date of this affidavit
7. Letter from Dr. Furgazy to Dr. Dhrool, January 10, year 1

SCHEDULE B

Documents that are or were in my possession, control or power that I object to producing on the grounds of privilege.

1. Written narrative describing post-accident events, prepared for counsel for the purpose of conducting litigation: January 21, year 1.
2. All correspondence passing between the plaintiff and her lawyer.
3. All notes, reports, and memoranda prepared by or on behalf of the plaintiff in anticipation of litigation or for use in instructing counsel and conducting this litigation.

Privilege is claimed on the basis that these documents were prepared in contemplation of or for the purpose of litigation or are the subject of lawyer–client privilege.

SCHEDULE C

Documents that were formerly in my possession, control or power but are no longer in my possession, control or power.

There are no such documents.

FIGURE 14.2 REQUEST TO INSPECT DOCUMENTS (FORM 30C)

Court file no. 01-CV-1234

ONTARIO
SUPERIOR COURT OF JUSTICE

BETWEEN:

ABIGAIL BOAR

Plaintiff

and

RATTLE MOTORS LTD. and FRED FLOGEM

Defendants

You are requested to produce for inspection all the documents listed in Schedule A of your affidavit of documents.

Date: January 23, year 1

Huey Sue
LSUC #23456T
Barrister and Solicitor
65 False Trail
Toronto, Ontario, M6Y 1Z6

tel. 416-485-6891
fax 416-485-6892

Lawyer for the Defendants

TO:
Just & Coping
Barristers and Solicitors
365 Bay Street - 8701
Toronto, Ontario, M3J 4A9

I.M. Just
LSUC #12345R
tel. 416-762-1342
fax 416-762-2300

Lawyers for the Plaintiff

Inspection of documents

Once the other parties have received an affidavit of documents, they have a right to inspect any of the documents in schedule A. They may do this by serving a request to inspect documents (form 30C). An example of a request to inspect documents is set out in figure 14.2.

Most lawyers do not bother with the request to inspect; instead, they usually cooperate by producing and providing copies to the other side of their client's documents in schedule A, often bound and tabbed in a binder. With e-discovery, the parties may supply each other with CDs containing relevant documents. The affidavit of documents is not usually filed in court unless it is relevant to an issue on a motion or at trial. Its primary function is to serve as an index to the productions themselves.

However, where a party does not produce documents voluntarily, rule 30.04 sets out a procedure for obtaining them for inspection. If there are further difficulties, a court on a motion may order production. In considering an order for production, a court may order "divided production" (rule 34.04(8)). Such an order may be made where a document that is prejudicial to a party becomes relevant only after an issue in the action has been decided. The court may allow disclosure to be withheld until the issue is decided. If the decision on the issue results in the second issue becoming relevant, then discovery may be had on the other documents.

Without further notice or summons, documents in schedule A are to be produced at discovery of the party who swore the affidavit of documents and at trial (rule 34.04(4)).

Incomplete affidavits of documents

A party may find relevant documents after completing the affidavit of documents and producing documents. In this case, the party must make a supplementary affidavit of documents, indicating which further documents have been discovered and take the necessary steps to produce the documents (rule 37.07). Where the affidavit is incomplete or privilege is improperly claimed, the court may order cross-examination on the affidavit of documents, service of a revised and amended affidavit of documents, and disclosure and production of omitted documents. If a claim of privilege is in issue, the court may inspect the document to determine if the claim of privilege is improper (rule 30.06). Where a party fails to disclose a document or produce it for inspection on the issue whether or not it is privileged, the court may, if the document is favourable to the party withholding it, prohibit its use in evidence in the action. If the document is not favourable, the court may make any order as is just (rule 30.08). There are similar rules with respect to documents for which privilege is improperly claimed. Once a document is privileged, the other side does not get to see it or refer to it in evidence. It would be unfair to allow the party claiming privilege to take the other side by surprise by suddenly waiving privilege and introducing the document in evidence at trial. If a party does wish to waive privilege, it must do so by notice in writing at least 90 days before the commencement of trial. There is one exception to this rule: A party may, without giving advance notice, use the privileged document to challenge the credibility of a witness (rule 30.09).

Production from non-parties

The rules governing discovery of documents apply only to parties. What happens if a non-party has a relevant document that is not privileged and is legally beyond the reach of any party? Rule 30.10 provides an answer by permitting any party to bring a motion for the inspection (as to relevance and privilege, if claimed) and production of a document. The moving party must show that the document is relevant and that it would be unfair to require the party to proceed to trial without it. Because the motion involves someone who is not a party to the proceeding, the non-party must be served with the motion personally or by an alternative to personal service.

ORAL EXAMINATION FOR DISCOVERY
Introduction

Examination for discovery is probably the most important procedure prior to trial in a civil action. It permits a lawyer to obtain admissions to prove his or her case and to undermine the other party's case. It narrows the issues that must be proved at trial and identifies evidence on which the other party relies. It may also reveal the opponent's theory and strategy for proof of the case.

wood-shedded
prepared for later cross-examination by opposing lawyer

Thorough preparation is extremely important. The client must understand the theory of his or her case and be **wood-shedded** so that he or she is prepared to answer questions on cross-examination and deal with various cross-examination styles. The client must review the pleadings, witness statements, documents, and relevant memorandums. The client should also review with counsel the issues to be canvassed and the questions to be asked in examining the opposing party.

Opposing counsel tries to obtain answers that help his or her case and hurt yours. A witness who answers a question without thinking has lost many a case. David Stockwood, an experienced civil litigator, has the following suggestions to aid a witness on examination for discovery or any examination:

1. If the lawyer objects to a question, the client should not answer it unless he or she is told to do so. Objections are used sparingly because they may be seen as an attempt to hide evidence.

2. The client should listen to the question and be sure he or she understands it before answering.

3. If the client does not understand the question, he or she should say so.

4. If the client does not know the answer to a question or does not remember the answer, he or she should say so. This information can be supplied after discovery.

5. Unless the client has clear and accurate figures in writing, he or she should give an estimate.

6. The client should not rush to answer and should take time to think, if it is needed.

7. The client should be concise and should not ramble.

8. The client should not argue with opposing counsel.[9]

The client also needs to know how oral discovery works and what the physical layout is in the place where the examination occurs. Discovery is an out-of-court examination that is arranged and supervised by the lawyers. The lawyer conducting the examination, usually after consultation with opposing counsel, determines the date and time for the examination and reserves space with one of the private reporting services or, in smaller centres, with the official examiner. If a reporting service or an official examiner is used, the service or the official examiner supplies a meeting room with a long table, exhibit stamps, a Bible, and a court reporter who takes down the evidence on tape and later transcribes it. There is no judicial official present. The party being examined and his or her lawyer sit on one side of the table. The lawyer conducting the examination sits on the other side, together with his or her client, who is allowed to be present. The witness is then sworn and questioned by the opposing counsel. If the witness's lawyer believes a question is irrelevant, abusive, or otherwise improper, he or she may object to the question and tell the witness not to answer it. In this case, the lawyer states the basis of the objection for the record. The lawyer may then permit the party to answer, subject to the objection. In this case, the answer cannot be used in court later unless on a motion the court determines that the question was proper. Alternatively, the lawyer may tell the client not to answer, in which case a motion is necessary to compel the answer. Because there is no judge present to rule on an objection, if the examining lawyer wants the question answered, he or she must bring a motion to compel reattendance to answer the question, provided, of course, that the court finds the objection improper. When the witness does not know an answer or does not have information, he or she may be asked to give an undertaking to provide the answer or information. The witness should wait for his or her lawyer to agree or not. A lawyer who is not sure "takes it under advisement." This means that the lawyer will consult with the client and provide an answer later, either refusing to give an undertaking or providing what is required. If a lawyer cuts off the client and answers the question, the client is deemed to have adopted the lawyer's answer as his or her own if the client does not object or correct the lawyer's answer (rule 31.08).

Questioning styles vary. Some lawyers hop around from issue to issue, often returning to a specific issue several times. This may result in a witness's being caught off guard and contradicting himself or herself. But the transcript from this kind of examination is often hard to follow. Other lawyers take a more chronological or sequential approach. Often the lawyer doing the discovery is a junior associate. One purpose here is to save the client from the senior counsel's higher fees. The other purpose is strategic, so that the party being examined is not exposed to and therefore ready for the style of questioning of senior counsel at trial.

Lawyers often agree to certain ground rules to save time. Often counsel adopts an **estoppel** technique in conducting the examination. For example, in Abigail Boar's case, counsel might ask Fred Flogem, "Can you show me anything in the correspondence with Skank Motorcar Company Ltd. that indicates that the problem with the leaking oil pan had been fixed?" This may produce a lengthy wait, while Fred goes through the exhibits to inform himself. Instead, counsel can state, "Unless I hear from you to the contrary, may I take it that there is nothing in the correspondence with Skank Motorcar Company Ltd. to suggest that the problem with the leaking oil pan had been fixed?" In the latter case, no undertaking need be given. Fred can look at the correspondence and report back if he finds something

estoppel
term indicating that a witness is bound by his or her original position and evidence and cannot later take a contrary position

relevant. If he is silent, Fred is estopped, or barred, from taking the position at trial that there is something relevant in the correspondence.

More time is saved when both lawyers consult at the beginning of the examination and come to an agreement about the facts that are not in dispute. The witness can then be asked to adopt the position that certain facts have been agreed to. The facts in question can be set out in writing and made an exhibit to the discovery, so the witness does not have to be taken through each one. If the discussion about which facts might be agreed to takes place in the examination, the lawyer who initiates the discussion may ask to go "off the record." This means that the reporter will not record the discussion. This cuts the length of the transcript and its cost. Not every discussion should be off the record, however. Discussions about the basis for an objection should be on the record, as the transcript of that discussion may be evidence or an exhibit in a motion to compel a party to answer the question objected to.

In dealing with documents on discovery, much time can be wasted making each document a separate exhibit. Each party usually has a pile of documents that are in schedule A of the affidavit of documents. If there are 40 documents in schedule A, the easiest thing to do is to produce copies in a tabbed binder and agree to enter them as exhibits 1 to 40 on discovery and later at trial. Any other documents that emerge can be entered separately as exhibits 41, 42, and so on after a witness has identified them and testified as to their authenticity.

Cross-examination is permitted at discovery, except on issues of credibility, which are explored at trial. This allows a lawyer to lead a witness with simple questions that can be answered "yes" or "no." This saves time and transcript space. It is permissible to ask about evidence that lies behind a statement of fact and to ask for the names and addresses of persons who have knowledge of matters in the action, whether these people become witnesses or not. Because insurance policies must be produced if they cover the liabilities raised by the lawsuit, they can be the subject of questions on discovery. A party may also be asked to disclose findings, opinions, and conclusions of experts who will give evidence, though the report does not have to be produced unless the party intends to rely on it at trial. Parties who subsequently learn the answer to a question they were asked on discovery are obliged to disclose it (rule 31.06).

Once the examination is completed, a lawyer does not terminate it but adjourns it, subject to the fulfillment of undertakings and the bringing of motions on disputed questions.

The lawyer for the party who has been examined may, at the conclusion of the examination, re-examine the party to clarify an answer, or the answer may be clarified by letter later.

In the event information is obtained that requires correction of an answer given on discovery, there is a duty to provide the correct information forthwith in writing. The writing can be treated as evidence, but an adverse party may insist that it be given in affidavit form to have the same weight as the sworn evidence given on discovery (rule 31.09(1) and (2)). If a party fails to disclose new information as required by rule 31.09, if it is favourable, he or she cannot use it at trial. If it is not favourable, the court has broad discretion to do what is just (rule 31.09(3)).

Arranging discoveries

A party to an action may examine every other party who is adverse in interest. The examination may be oral or written but not both. If a corporation or partnership is a party, get directions from your supervising lawyer before arranging for a particular representative to be examined. Counsel may examine any party once. If the corporation's counsel gets to choose who represents the company, the examination may be very uninformative. If counsel has a person in mind to question, that person should be summonsed to the examination (rule 31.03). If a person under disability is a party, the litigation guardian may be discovered, but if the disabled party is competent to give evidence, the disabled party may be examined.[10]

There is some debate over whether it is advantageous to be examined first or to examine first.[11] Some think that it is an advantage to examine first because the examining lawyer gets a chance to assess the credibility and demeanour of the opponent and take him or her by surprise. Others think that by going last, you will know more about your opponent's theory of his or her case and be able to shape your own examination accordingly. Where credibility is an issue, however, whoever goes first, the time between examinations of the plaintiff and defendant should be short, so that a dishonest party does not have the opportunity to tailor evidence. If the examinations are to last a half day each, scheduling back to back is one solution to this problem. Another solution is to have both examinations well underway before transcripts are available.

The governing rules for arranging discoveries are rules 31.04 and 34. A defendant who wishes to examine the plaintiff must have served a statement of defence and an affidavit of documents. A plaintiff who wishes to examine a defendant may do so after the defendant has served a statement of defence and affidavit of documents, or the defendant has been noted in default. The parties may also agree to other arrangements regarding timing. In any event, the person who first issues a notice of examination may examine first and complete his or her examination before being examined by the other party (rule 34.01).

Rule 34.04 sets out the procedure for compelling attendance. A notice of examination, form 34A, must be served on the lawyer of record, if there is one, or on the party personally or by an alternative to personal service. The alternative service procedure may not be used if the person is appearing as a representative of a company or other non-individual. An example of the notice of examination is set out in figure 14.3.

If a lawyer expects that the party being summonsed for examination will not appear, it may be wise to serve the party personally as well as by his or her lawyer. Then if the lawyer brings a motion for contempt, the party can be jailed if he or she has been served personally with the notice (and later with the motion). Usually, however, service on the lawyer of record will suffice.

If the person being examined resides in Ontario, he or she must be given at least two days' notice of the examination (rule 34.05). If the person resides outside Ontario, the terms and conditions of the examination, whether it is held in Ontario or elsewhere, are set by the court (rule 34.07). Examinations outside Ontario, which are governed by rules 34.07 and 36.01, are beyond the scope of this text.

A notice of examination operates like a summons to a witness. Consequently, the party being summonsed must be served with **attendance money** in accordance with tariff A, part II. As of March 2008, $50 is allowed for each day of attendance,

attendance money
formerly called conduct money, composed of the *per diem* witness fee and an amount for transportation and lodging in accordance with tariff A

FIGURE 14.3   NOTICE OF EXAMINATION (FORM 34A)

Court file no. 01-CV-1234

ONTARIO
SUPERIOR COURT OF JUSTICE

BETWEEN:

ABIGAIL BOAR

Plaintiff

and

RATTLE MOTORS LTD. and FRED FLOGEM

Defendants

NOTICE OF EXAMINATION

TO: Abigail Boar

YOU ARE REQUIRED TO ATTEND FOR AN EXAMINATION
FOR DISCOVERY on Tuesday, September 14, year 1, at 10:00
a.m. at the office of

Victory Verbatim Reporting Services
Toronto Dominion Centre
66 Wellington Street West
Suite 3320, PO Box 182
Toronto, Ontario, M5K 1H6

YOU ARE REQUIRED TO BRING WITH YOU and produce at the
examination the documents mentioned in subrule 30.04(4) of the Rules
of Civil Procedure, and the following documents and things: All
documents, as defined in the Rules of Civil Procedure, relating to any
matter in this action within your possession, power, or control.

Date: August 23, year 1

Huey Sue
LSUC #23456T
Barrister and Solicitor
65 False Trail
Toronto, Ontario, M6Y 1Z6

tel. 416-485-6891
fax 416-485-6892

Lawyer for the Defendants

TO:
Just & Coping
Barristers and Solicitors
365 Bay Street - 8701
Toronto, Ontario, M3J 4A9

I.M. Just
LSUC #12345R
tel. 416-762-1342
fax 416-762-2300

Lawyers for the Plaintiff

plus $3 for travel if the party is examined in the county or region where he or she resides. This is usually the case because a party is entitled to be examined for discovery where he or she resides. If the party is travelling farther, the travel allowance is based on the distance travelled. The accommodation and meal allowance is currently $75 per day.[12]

All of this rigmarole can be avoided, and sensible lawyers usually do avoid it, by agreeing to the time, place, and order of the examinations and to the furnishing of documents. Taking the sensible approach can save much time and money, and there is little to be gained by being unnecessarily adversarial in making these procedural arrangements.

Examination of non-parties

An analogy to rule 30.10, requiring production of documents from non-parties in certain circumstances, is found in rules 31.10 and 34.05(4), governing the examination of non-parties. The test for bringing such a motion is set out in rule 31.10(2), and it is a stringent one. Non-parties are strangers to the lawsuit, at least technically, and they ought not to be inconvenienced by being made to participate in it. If non-parties are required for examination, the moving party must show that:

- he or she could not obtain the information from a party on discovery, or from the person who has possession, power, or control of the information or document in question;

- it would be unfair to require the moving party to proceed to trial without the opportunity of examining the person; and

- the examination will not unduly delay the trial, create unreasonable expense for the person, or be unfair to the non-party.

If the moving party is successful, he or she must provide transcripts free of charge to the other parties. The costs of the examination cannot be recovered from other parties as part of a general costs award at trial unless the court expressly permits it. Evidence of a non-party, unlike the evidence of parties, cannot be read into evidence under rule 31.11(1).

Controlling disruptive and uncooperative behaviour

Although lawyers should know better, there are a number who cannot resist engaging in improper or disruptive behaviour, or who do not take steps to prevent their clients from behaving improperly and disruptively. Some members of the legal profession who think this is a growing problem look back to a "golden age," when lawyers behaved with civility toward other counsel and their clients. Whether the problem is or is not on the increase, the Law Society of Upper Canada, in August 2001, mailed a pamphlet on civility to all lawyers in the province, a sort of lawyer etiquette manual. With respect to discovery, and out-of-court examinations generally, the kinds of questionable conduct one might expect to encounter are set out in rule 34.14(3):

- an excessive number of improper questions, interruptions, or objections designed to wear down or distract the person being examined or to disrupt the examination completely;

- an examination conducted in bad faith (for a purpose other than that intended by the rules) or in an unreasonable manner so as to embarrass, intimidate, or oppress the person being examined (examples include using a loud, angry, and sarcastic voice, asking irrelevant and embarrassing questions, making personal remarks, and in one extreme case, pouring coffee on opposing counsel's notes and later on his lap);

- answers from a party that are evasive, unresponsive, or unduly lengthy (examples include answering questions with questions, giving irrelevant answers that do not respond to the question asked, and going on at great length about irrelevant matters); and

- neglect or refusal of a party to produce relevant documents on the examination.

A lawyer faced with this kind of behaviour has several choices. If it is only moderately disruptive, so that he or she is still getting information, it may be best to ignore it. Let the examination transcript speak for itself at trial if the issue of bad faith, non-responsiveness, or credibility arises, or when addressing costs at trial. An examination for discovery is not a chat among friends. Some friction, though it should be avoided, may have to be tolerated. There comes a time, however, when a lawyer is simply being stonewalled or a client is being subjected to stressful and intimidating tactics. At that point, it is appropriate to break off the examination, state that you are adjourning the examination in order to seek directions from the court for the continuation of the examination, or for an order terminating the examination or limiting its scope. If the court finds that there was improper conduct, the court may levy costs against the person who engaged in improper conduct, especially if it was wilful or in bad faith. Costs may be levied personally against a lawyer in this regard (rule 34.14(2)). The same cost penalties may be levied against a moving party who improperly adjourned an examination to bring a motion for directions.

While the motion under rule 34.14 for directions focuses on improper conduct of an examination, rule 34.15 is directed at default or misconduct by a witness on an examination including:

- failure to attend at the time and place fixed for examination,

- refusal to take an oath or make an affirmation,

- refusal to answer a proper question,

- refusal to produce a document or thing that he or she is required to produce, or

- refusal to comply with an order made under rule 34.14 to correct previously noted improper behaviour.

The remedy granted depends on the nature of the default or misconduct. If counsel considers a question to be improper, he or she can state the objection on the record and direct the client not to answer the question. If opposing counsel wishes to challenge the objection, a rule 34.15 motion is the way to do it. If the moving party is successful, the court will order the party to re-attend at his or her own expense and answer the question, and any proper questions that flow from that answer. This is not uncommon. Reasonable lawyers may honestly disagree about whether a question is proper or not. But the other kinds of misconduct identified in rule 34.15 are more likely to be unreasonable and wilful. For this misconduct, a plaintiff's action may be dismissed, or a defendant's defence may be struck out. Lesser penalties include striking out the person's evidence recorded on the transcript or in an affidavit.

The ultimate penalty, where someone refuses to attend or be sworn or continues to obstruct an examination after a rule 34.14 order has been made, is committal to jail for contempt. If a lawyer is seeking committal for contempt, the rule 34.15 motion must be served personally, and the motion must be brought before a judge because a master has no authority to make an order depriving someone of his or her liberty.

Ordering and using transcripts

Check with the lawyer responsible for the file before ordering transcripts of an examination for discovery. Depending on the issues and the complexity of the case, and whether settlement is imminent, the lawyer may not wish to go to the expense of ordering transcripts. On the other hand, it may be important to obtain transcripts quickly, in which case counsel may wish to have the transcripts expedited. This means that instead of taking several weeks, copies will be available in a few days, but the cost is high. The lawyer who conducts an examination usually orders a copy, and a copy is also to be sent to and filed in court (rule 34.17). A party who intends to use a transcript on a motion or at trial is responsible for seeing that the transcript is filed with the appropriate court office (rule 34.18).

The transcript may be used in a variety of ways. At trial, counsel may read into the record, as part of his or her own case, all or part of the discovery transcript of an adverse party or a non-party. Counsel may later call other evidence at trial to rebut the answers given on discovery. This procedure of "reading in" is usually done by referring to the questions and answers by the question numbers. At that point, and not before, the transcript or the relevant parts should be filed with the court (rule 31.11(1)). The opposing party may ask that other parts of the transcript also be included because they qualify the answers or give them a proper context.

The transcript may be used to impeach the credibility of the deponent as a witness at trial when he or she gives an answer that contradicts the answer given on discovery. Counsel puts the discovery question and answer to the witness and asks if he or she gave that answer then. The assumption is that the discovery answer, earlier in time, is more likely to be accurate.

The transcript of any party may be read into evidence if that party has died, is unable to attend the trial, refuses to attend the trial, refuses to be sworn, or stands mute and refuses to answer questions.

If discovery is held in an action, the action is discontinued or dismissed, and a new action dealing with the same subject matter is commenced, the discovery in the first proceeding may be used in the second proceeding as if it had been the discovery transcript in the second proceeding (rule 31.11(2) to (8)).

EXAMINATION FOR DISCOVERY BY WRITTEN QUESTIONS

Written questions and answers as a form of discovery has long been in use in England, where they are called interrogatories, and in the United States, where they supplement oral discovery. Although available here under rule 35, they are rarely used. Most lawyers are not familiar with the format and find it inflexible. Most lawyers prefer the fluidity of an oral examination, where a question may be inspired by the answer to the previous question. An oral examination is especially desirable when the person being examined is uncooperative or evasive, credibility is in issue, or a lawyer needs to get a sense of what the party being examined is like. However, a written examination for discovery is much cheaper because it does not involve court reporters, rental of meeting rooms, out-of-office attendances, or the cost of transcripts. Where credibility is not an issue and the fact situation is simple, a rule 35 written discovery may be more appropriate. With the advent of case management in Toronto, case management masters may start encouraging parties to use this mode of discovery to save time and money where it is appropriate.

Serving a list of questions in form 35A on the person to be examined and on every other party commences a written examination. Once the list is served, the party waives a right to oral discovery. Answers are given by affidavit in form 35B within 15 days after being served with the list of questions. If the party objects to a question asked, he or she must state the objection in the affidavit and give reasons for refusing to answer. The examining party, after receiving the affidavit, has 10 days to serve a further list of supplementary questions, which must be answered in 15 days from the date of service of the supplementary questions. Where there is an unresolved dispute about an unanswered question, the court may order the question answered by affidavit or by oral examination. Similarly, if the answers are evasive, the court may order attendance for a complete oral examination, thereby abandoning the rule 35 process. The questions and the answers given under rule 35 may be filed and treated as transcripts at trial under rule 31.11. Figure 14.4 provides an example of questions on a written examination for discovery, and figure 14.5 provides an example of answers on such an examination.

UNDERTAKINGS AND FOLLOWUP ON DISCOVERY

When a discovery transcript has been prepared, it is often the duty of a law clerk to go through the transcript and do the following:

- prepare a summary of the transcript, noting key points; and

- prepare a list of undertakings to provide information, refusals to provide information or answer a question, and requests taken under advisement.

Many reporters list undertakings, objections, and refusals at the front of the transcript, but you would be wise to scan it yourself to be sure nothing was missed. You will also wish to note questions taken under advisement — that is, questions that the opposing lawyer wishes to think about and advise you on later.

Once you have recorded the necessary material, write to the lawyer for the other party, asking him or her to honour the undertakings, and answer the questions objected to or taken under advisement. You probably will not get a positive

FIGURE 14.4   QUESTIONS ON WRITTEN EXAMINATION FOR DISCOVERY (FORM 35A)

Court file no. 01-CV-1234

ONTARIO
SUPERIOR COURT OF JUSTICE

BETWEEN:

ABIGAIL BOAR

Plaintiff

and

RATTLE MOTORS LTD. and FRED FLOGEM

Defendants

QUESTIONS ON WRITTEN EXAMINATION FOR DISCOVERY

The plaintiff has chosen to examine the defendant Fred Flogem for discovery by written questions and requires that the following questions be answered by affidavit in Form 35B prescribed by the Rules of Civil Procedure, served within fifteen days after service of these questions.

1. On what date and at what time did you notice an oil leak on the showroom floor?
2. What steps did you take upon discovering the oil leak?

• • •

Date: May 15, year 1

Just & Coping
Barristers and Solicitors
365 Bay Street - 8701
Toronto, Ontario, M3J 4A9

I.M. Just
LSUC #12345R
tel. 416-762-1342
fax 416-762-2300

Lawyers for the Plaintiff

TO:
Huey Sue
LSUC #23456T
Barrister and Solicitor
65 False Trail
Toronto, Ontario, M6Y 1Z6

tel. 416-485-6891
fax 416-485-6892

Lawyer for the Defendants

FIGURE 14.5   ANSWERS ON WRITTEN EXAMINATION FOR DISCOVERY (FORM 35B)

Court file no. 01-CV-1234

ONTARIO
SUPERIOR COURT OF JUSTICE

BETWEEN:

ABIGAIL BOAR

Plaintiff

and

RATTLE MOTORS LTD. and FRED FLOGEM

Defendants

ANSWERS ON WRITTEN EXAMINATION FOR DISCOVERY

I, Fred Flogem, of the City of Toronto, in the Province of Ontario, one of the defendants in this action, AFFIRM that the following answers to the questions dated May 15, year 1 submitted by the plaintiff are true, to the best of my knowledge, information and belief:

1. I first became aware of some fluid on the floor of the showroom at about 6:30 p.m. on September 14, year 0.

2. The fluid did not seem to be an urgent problem, so I left it until later to clean up and turned off the lights to discourage customers from wandering into the area.

. . .

Affirmed before me at the)	
City of Toronto,)	*Fred Flogem*
in the **Province of** Ontario,)	Fred Flogem
on May 20, year 1.)	
Huey Sue	
Huey Sue	
Commissioner for Taking Affidavits)	

response on the questions objected to or taken under advisement, but there is no harm in asking. If the information is not provided and the lawyer feels it is necessary for the case, you will have to bring a motion to compel the party to re-attend and answer the questions at his or her own expense.

When you have received the answers, they should be bound together and added as an appendix to the discovery transcript.

Your law firm will be asked to provide answers to undertakings on behalf of your client. If the letter is a general request, you will have to go through your client's transcript and find the undertakings, prepare a list, and ask the client to provide answers, including answers to disputed questions if nothing much turns on them. The letter to the client should request that the answers be in writing, and you should note the question number and page of the transcript on which the question appears. The lawyer should review the client's answers and forward them in a letter to opposing counsel.

In your review of the transcript, if you note any errors in the answers or any answers that are not complete, you have an obligation to provide corrections as soon as possible. Your instructing lawyer should be notified of errors immediately.

Summaries and undertaking lists prepared from transcripts

To demonstrate how an undertaking list and summary is prepared, figure 14.6 sets out an excerpt of the transcript of Abigail Boar's evidence.

Preparation of a transcript summary

Create a two-column table. In the left-hand column, note the question number or numbers and the page number. In the right-hand column, write a brief summary of the point or issue covered. Your table should look like the one set out in table 14.3.

List of undertakings

You also need to prepare a list of undertakings to provide information later where the information was not available to answer a question on discovery. The list also includes refusals or objections to answering questions or providing documents or further information, as well as a list of questions taken under advisement. To record this information, set out a six-column table such as the one in table 14.4. The last two columns, designed for the date you receive an answer and the substance of the answer/disposition by court, are left blank for now. They will be filled in later when and if you get answers to the undertakings, or when a court deals with a refusal to answer. The table can also be used for motions to compel a party to answer an undertaking; it meets the format requirement for form 37C.

CHAPTER SUMMARY

This chapter introduced you to various discovery procedures. We began with an overview of the general purposes of discovery and discussed the deemed undertaking rule, which prevents you from using information obtained on discovery in other proceedings. We then identified and described the various forms discovery

FIGURE 14.6   EXAMINATION FOR DISCOVERY OF ABIGAIL BOAR

EXAMINATION FOR DISCOVERY OF ABIGAIL BOAR ON BEHALF OF FRED FLOGEM AND RATTLE MOTORS LTD., HELD SEPTEMBER 14, YEAR 1

1	Abigail Boar, sworn	
2	By Mr. Sue:	
3	Q1:	Madam, please state your name for the record.
4	A:	Abigail Boar.
5	Q2:	Ms Boar, I understand that on September 14, year 0 you
6		entered the showroom of Rattle Motors Ltd. to look at new
7		cars.
8	A:	Yes.
9	Q3:	What time did you arrive there?
10	A:	About 7:30 p.m.
11	Q4:	What time did you leave work?
12	A:	About 5:30.
13	Q5:	How did you spend the time between leaving work and ar-
14		riving at the car showroom?
15	A:	I walked to a restaurant, Barbeerians, had dinner with a
16		friend, and then I walked on alone to Rattle Motors.
17	Q6:	Ms Boar, I am producing and showing to you a restaurant
18		receipt from Barbeerian's, dated September 14, year 0.
19		Can you identify this receipt?
20	A:	Yes, it is mine for my dinner that evening. I had dinner with
21		a friend.
22	Q7:	I notice that the bill includes two glasses of wine. Did you
23		drink both glasses?
24	A:	Yes, it was a fine Bordeaux. When I drank the first glass, it
25		was very fine, and not the plonk it often is, so I had another,
26		to savour it. And very nice it was, raspberry overtones with
27		a hint of oak. Yes, very fine indeed.
28	Q8:	You mentioned a friend. Please tell me the name and ad-
29		dress of that friend.
30	Mr. JUST:	Just a moment. Who that person is is entirely irrelevant to
31		the issues; Ms Boar will not provide that information.
32	Mr. SUE:	I am entitled to the names and addresses of anyone with
33		knowledge of the matters in issue in this litigation.
34	Mr. JUST:	We will take it under advisement.
35	Q9:	Now, Ms Boar, you claim that the lighting on the premises
36		was inadequate for you to see the oil on the floor. Aside
37		from your own inability to see the oil, do you have any ex-
38		pert evidence or reports that indicate the lighting was not
39		adequate?
40	Mr. JUST:	Just a moment, counsel. You have no right at this time to
41		any experts' reports we might have on hand, and we are
42		refusing to produce any such report at this time.

FIGURE 14.6   CONCLUDED

1	Q10:	Well, Ms Boar, can you summarize what the findings are
2		in any report on the adequacy of lighting that you may
3		have?
4	A:	Well, we have one, but I only glanced at it, and I don't re-
5		member what it actually said.
6	Q11:	Will you undertake to review the report and provide me
7		with a summary of its findings and conclusions?
8	Mr. JUST:	We will examine our records and provide you with the in-
9		formation you request.
10	Q12:	What kind of shoes were you wearing when you got to the
11		showroom?
12	A:	Swamp green dress shoes with a narrow 4-inch heel.
13	Q13:	Would you describe your footwear as giving you good foot
14		and ankle support when you are walking?
15	A:	Well, they are really for office wear. I wouldn't go rock
16		climbing in them.
17	Q14:	Ms Boar, do you have any accident insurance that covers
18		the personal injuries you sustained?
19	A:	Yes, I think Mr. Just gave you the particulars of it.
20	Q15:	Will you please provide me with a copy of the policy?
21	Mr. JUST:	No, we will not give you that undertaking. You have all of
22		the information that you require.

Table 14.3   Summary of transcript of examination of Abigail Boar

Q1-2, p. 1	introduction of Boar, setting context
Q3-8, p. 1	Boar accounts for time after work, dinner with friend with two drinks before going on to Rattle
Q9-11, pp. 1-2	Boar asked for lighting expert's report and her recollection of what it said: didn't recall what it said
Q12-13, p. 2	Boar describes her footwear at time of accident, and whether it was safe or suitable
Q14-15, p. 2	Boar acknowledges she had accident insurance, refusal to provide copy of policy

Table 14.4   Summary of undertakings, objections, and advisements

Refusals and Undertakings, Form 37C

Refusals Chart

Refusals to answer questions on the examination of Abigail Boar				Dated September 14, year 1	
Issue and relationship to pleadings or affidavit	Question no.	Page no.	Specific question	Answer or precise basis for refusal	Disposition by court
1. Provision of expert lighting report	9	1	Will you provide a copy of the expert's lighting report?	Refused on the basis that the report is privileged and prepared for use by counsel	
2. Whether to provide name and address of dinner companion (defence, paras. 8 and 9; reply para. 3)	8	1	Will you provide the name and address of your dinner companion?	Name of individual is not relevant.	
3. Provision of accident insurance policy	15	2	Please provide a copy of your accident insurance policy	Refused on the basis that the policy is not relevant	

Undertakings Chart

Outstanding undertakings given on the examination of Abigail Boar				Dated September 14, year 1	
Issue and relationship to pleadings or affidavit	Question no.	Page no.	Specific undertaking	Date answered or precise reason for not doing so	Answer/ Disposition by court
Provision of summary of lighting expert report	10-11	2	Will you provide a copy of a summary of expert's lighting report?		

takes: discovery of documents, including e-documents, oral examination for discovery, inspection of property, medical examinations, and written discovery. Our primary focus in this chapter was on documentary discovery and oral discovery because these are used in practically all cases, whereas the others are narrower and more specialized in their usage. We then examined the rules for discovery of documents, noting the obligations on a party to identify and produce all non-privileged documents that are relevant. We discussed how to assist clients in collecting documentary material and how to organize it both for office use and for the preparation of an affidavit of documents. We then turned to how to set up an oral examination for discovery and described its scope and how it is conducted. Then, using sample transcripts we saw how a summary and a list of undertakings are prepared by a clerk for use by a lawyer.

KEY TERMS

discovery

without prejudice

e-discovery

meta data

wood-shedded

estoppel

attendance money

NOTES

1   O. reg. 438/08, ss. 25–31, adding rule 29.1 and amending rules 30–35.

2   *Goodman v. Rossi* (1995), 125 DLR (4th) 613 (Ont. CA).

3   *General Accident Assurance Co. v. Chrusz* (1997), 34 OR (3d) 354 (Gen. Div.); var'd. 37 OR (3d) 790 (Div. Ct.); rev'd. 45 OR (3d) 321 (CA).

4   *Ferber v. The Gore Mutual Insurance Co.* (1991), 3 CPC (3d) 41 (Gen. Div.).

5   For an introduction to issues and problems involved in e-discovery, see the Ontario Bar Association's The Discovery Task Force E-Discovery Guidelines and Resources Page, and relevant links to other material on the OBA website at http://www.oba.org/en/main/ediscovery_en/default.aspx.

6   See in particular *Air Canada v. Westjet Airlines Ltd.* (2006), 267 DLR (4th) 483, 81 OR (3d) 48 (SCJ).

7   Ibid. The balance of obligations was the issue in *Westjet* where counsel argued, unsuccessfully in this case, that review for relevant material in the vast volumes of data in various databases would be unduly time-consuming and expensive.

8   The Discovery Task Force, *Guidelines for the Discovery of Electronic Documents in Ontario* (Toronto: Ontario Bar Association, 2003) can be found at http://www.oba.org/en/pdf_newsletter/E-DiscoveryGuidelines.pdf.

9   David Stockwood, *Civil Litigation*, 4th ed. (Toronto: Carswell, 1997), form 25, at 239.

10   Rule 31.03(5); also see (6), (7), and (8) with respect to assignees, trustees in bankruptcy, and nominal parties.

11 Supra note 8, at 74.

12 Tariff A, part II, 21. Always consult the current tariff before issuing a cheque because the tariffs change from time to time.

REFERENCES

Air Canada v. Westjet Airlines Ltd. (2006), 267 DLR (4th) 483, 81 OR (3d) 48 (SCJ).

Courts of Justice Act, RSO 1990, c. C.43.

Ferber v. The Gore Mutual Insurance Co. (1991), 3 CPC (3d) 41 (Gen. Div.).

General Accident Assurance Co. v. Chrusz (1997), 34 OR (3d) 354 (Gen. Div.); var'd. 37 OR (3d) 790 (Div. Ct.); rev'd. 45 OR (3d) 321 (CA).

Goodman v. Rossi (1995), 125 DLR (4th) 613 (Ont. CA).

Ontario Bar Association, Discovery Task Force, *Guidelines for the Discovery of Electronic Documents in Ontario* (Toronto: Ontario Bar Association, 2003) can be found at http://www.oba.org/en/pdf_newsletter/E-DiscoveryGuidelines.pdf.

Ontario Bar Association, The Discovery Task Force E-Discovery Guidelines and Resources Page, http://www.oba.org/en/main/ediscovery_en/default.aspx.

Rules of Civil Procedure, RRO 1990, reg. 194.

Stockwood, David, *Civil Litigation*, 4th ed. (Toronto: Carswell, 1997).

REVIEW QUESTIONS

1. What is the purpose of discovery?

2. What forms of discovery are available in a civil action?

3. What is the deemed undertaking rule?

4. Can you run tests on property during an inspection under rule 32?

5. Under what circumstances will a medical examination be ordered as a form of discovery?

6. What documents must be disclosed?

7. What determines whether a document is privileged?

8. The plaintiff's lawyer would like to see the defendant's insurance policies. Can she?

9. Company A is a defendant in a lawsuit. A minority of company A's and company B's shares are held by company C, but the minority is large enough to give company C total control because the rest of the shares in companies A and B are widely dispersed. Company B has some documents that are relevant to the plaintiff's claim against company A. Can the plaintiff demand this document from company A?

10. Consider the principles that guide e-discovery when answering the following questions.

    a. What should you do if you consider the information about who created a document and when it was created to be as important as the content of the document itself?

    b. What should you do if your opponent insists that you review every bit of data in your client's databases?

    c. What should you do if some of your client's relevant data appears to have been deleted or to be in formats that are no longer readable with the use of available software?

11. How does a law clerk organize client materials for an affidavit of documents?

12. How do lawyers obtain the schedule A documents to inspect them?

13. What should you do if you notice that a document was omitted from the affidavit of documents or that an answer given in oral discovery was in error?

14. Can a lawyer obtain production from a non-party?

15. How should you prepare a witness for an examination for discovery?

16. Describe for the client the physical environment where discovery takes place.

17. How do lawyers control the discovery process?

18. How can lawyers shorten the process of entering exhibits?

19. How do you arrange discoveries?

20. Can a lawyer examine a non-party for discovery?

21. What kinds of misconduct at discovery do the rules contemplate and how is it controlled?

22. How do you obtain transcripts of the examination?

23. When would you be likely to use a written question-and-answer discovery format?

24. What do you need to do with a transcript when it comes back from the reporter?

DISCUSSION QUESTIONS

1. Read and respond to the following memorandum:

   To: Law Clerk
   From: Lawyer
   Re: Examination of Phineas Whipsnade

   We act for Henry in a family law dispute. Wendy claims that the property she owns in which Henry claims a half interest is heavily mortgaged to her father, Phineas Whipsnade. If this is so, Henry's share is likely peanuts. If it is a load of codswallop, as I suspect it is, then Henry may well get a bundle. On discovery, Wendy claimed she had no mortgage documents in her possession, power, or control. She said it was an unregistered equitable mortgage, based on a promissory note giving the property as security. She said she didn't have a copy of the note and claimed her father had the original. I wrote to Phineas requesting that he provide me with a copy and let me examine the original. That was two weeks ago, and I have had no answer.

   Please write a short memorandum telling me what our options are.

2. Read and respond to the following memorandum:

To: E. Egregious, law clerk
From: I.M. Just
Re: *Boar v. Rattle Motors Ltd. et al.*

Attached is a copy of a transcript of the examination of Fred Flogem for discovery. Please prepare a summary and a list of undertakings, objections/refusals, and questions taken under advisement. Also prepare a draft notice of motion to compel Fred to re-attend at his own expense to answer unanswered questions and provide documents. Assume that Fred will not respond to the refusals, objections, or advisements.

EXAMINATION FOR DISCOVERY OF FRED FLOGEM HELD OCTOBER 21, YEAR 1

1	Fred Flogem, affirmed	
2	By Mr. Just:	
3	Q1:	Sir, will you please state your name for the record.
4	A:	Fred Flogem.
5	Q2:	I understand that you are employed as a salesperson for
6		Rattle Motors Ltd. and that you were present on the prem-
7		ises on September 14, year 0.
8	A:	Yes.
9	Q3:	I understand at about 6:30 p.m. you spotted an oil leak on
10		the floor by the Super Coupe.
11	A:	Well, there was some fluid on the floor, but I didn't know
12		for sure it was oil, or that it came from a leak.
13	Q4:	Well, Freddie boy, did you think the spirits of the air sud-
14		denly dropped this stuff out of the sky?
15	Mr. SUE:	I object to that question, and Mr. Flogem will not answer it.
16		It is not necessary to use that sarcastic and flippant tone,
17		calculated as it is to intimidate and harass the witness.
18	Q5:	Well, Mr. Flogem, where did you think this stuff came
19		from?
20	Mr. SUE:	I object to the question. It is not relevant where it came
21		from. He has already acknowledged in his answers that it
22		was there, and that is sufficient.
23	Q6:	Mr. Flogem, do you have an insurance policy covering the
24		damages claimed in this action?
25	A:	Me? Not personally, but I believe Rattle Motors has a
26		policy, or at least so I have been told.
27	Q7:	Can you furnish me with the particulars of the policy?
28	A:	Well, not off hand. Sunil, the manager, has a copy, I think,
29		but I have never seen it, and I have no idea where it is.
30	Q8:	Will you undertake to find out what the particulars are?
31	A:	Well, Sunil has it with him, and he is out of town, so I don't
32		know.
33	Mr. SUE:	We will take it under advisement.

1   Q9:   After you saw the fluid on the floor, what did you do?

2   A: Well, I thought I would clean it up later, and to discourage

3   anyone from going into the area, I turned off two of the

4   four spotlights in that part of the room.

5   Q10:   Why did you put off cleaning this up?

6   A: Well, it wasn't much of a spill, it was mostly under the car,

7   and it didn't seem urgent.

8   Q11:   Did you have any information before September 14, year

9   0 that Skank Motorcars had issued an alert about leaking

10   oil pans on the Super Coupe model?

11 A: Well, I think there were some letters, but I haven't read

12   them.

13 Q12:   Can you provide me with copies of those letters?

14 A: Well —

15 Mr. SUE: No, he cannot because he does not have them or have

16   access to them.

CHAPTER 15

Pretrial procedures

INTRODUCTION

Once the parties have completed the discovery process, it is time to think about going to trial. As we have discussed, the discovery process gives both sides a good opportunity to examine the case of the opposite party and determine whether or not they have a chance of winning their case at trial. During discovery, the parties often decide to settle the case.

Rules 46, 47, 48, 50, and 51 are the major rules dealing with pretrial procedures. The various procedural steps are as follows:

1. determining the place of trial: rule 46;

2. deciding whether the case will be tried with a jury and issuing a jury notice if so: rule 47;

3. listing the case for trial: rule 48;

4. pretrial conference: rule 50; and

5. dealing with admissions: rule 51.

PLACE OF TRIAL: RULES 13.1 AND 46

Usually, the plaintiff may choose where to commence the proceeding. The general rule set out in rule 46.01 is that a trial shall be held in the place where the proceeding was commenced. For example, if a plaintiff chose to issue a statement of claim in the court office in Newmarket, that is where the trial will be held.

However, where a statute or another rule specifies the place of trial, then rule 13.1.01 makes it clear that the plaintiff cannot choose any location to start proceedings. The proceeding must start and the trial must be held where the statute or rule requires.

The court always has the power to change the place of trial on its own initiative or on the motion of any party. The change of place of trial is called a "change of venue." Under rule 13.1.02(1) the court may change the venue or place of trial if the plaintiff has not complied with a statute or rule requiring that a matter be commenced in a specific location. However, this is not the only reason the court might order a change of venue. Rule 13.1.02(2) provides a set of factors to be considered on a request to change the place of trial. First, the court must be satisfied that

- it is likely that a fair hearing cannot be held in the place where proceedings were commenced, or

- a transfer is desirable in the "interest of justice."

The second branch of the rule focuses on a number of factors for the court to consider, such as where most of the events in issue occurred; where damages were sustained; where the subject matter of the proceeding is located; and the convenience of the parties, witnesses, and the court (the core of the old balance-of-convenience test). In addition, whether court facilities and judges are available to try the matter is explicitly a factor to consider, as is the local community's interest in the subject matter of the proceeding. The court may also consider any other relevant matter, indicating that the factors to be considered "in the interest of justice" are not limited to the specific ones referred to in the rule.

Even if no one moves to change the place of trial, rule 13.1.02(4) gives the regional senior judge the power to move on his or her own initiative to order a change of venue, subject to the rights of interested parties to be heard.

Once a change of venue order has been made, the registrar shall transfer the file to the appropriate court office named in the order, and all subsequent filings shall be made in the named court office.

JURY NOTICE: RULE 47
Right to a jury trial

Section 108 of the *Courts of Justice Act* gives any party in a proceeding in the Superior Court of Justice the right to a jury trial. Whether or not a party wants a jury trial will depend on a number of factors, including the complexity of a case, the amount of sympathy or hostility the party believes that it may receive from a jury, and the length of the trial list for jury trials. The role of a jury is to determine the facts of the case. If there is no jury, the judge determines the facts.

If a jury trial is chosen, the jury can hear the entire case and make a determination about whether or not the defendant is liable for damages, or it can be called in to hear only the damages part of the case. In the latter instance, the trial proceeds from the beginning without a jury. The judge makes all the determinations of facts in the case and decides whether or not the defendant is liable to the plaintiff. Then, once the liability issue has been decided, the jury is called in to determine the amount of damages that the plaintiff will receive.

There is no absolute right to a jury trial. Section 108(2) of the *Courts of Justice Act* lists the types of cases in which a jury trial is never permitted. The list includes most family law matters, cases involving equitable remedies, partition or sale of real property, requests for injunctions, and a number of other matters. Even if the case is one where a jury trial is not prohibited under s. 108(2), a judge has the discretion to decide that a jury trial is not appropriate in a particular case.

Procedure for obtaining a jury trial

Either party can decide that it wants to have a jury trial. It then must prepare and serve a jury notice on all the other parties. The jury notice is in form 47A. It may be served any time before the close of pleadings. Once served, the notice is then filed with the court (rule 47.01). A jury notice in Abigail Boar's case is set out in figure 15.1 (at the end of the chapter).

Striking out a jury notice

If any of the other parties does not wish to have a jury trial, they can bring a motion asking that the jury notice be struck out. If the notice is struck out, the trial proceeds without a jury. There are two grounds under rule 47.02 for striking out a jury notice:

1. the jury notice is not in accordance with a statute or the rules, or

2. it is inappropriate to have a jury trial in a particular case.

NOT IN ACCORDANCE WITH A STATUTE OR THE RULES

If there is a statute that governs a particular type of case and the statute prohibits a trial by jury, a party's attempt to have a trial by jury is not "in accordance" with a statute and the jury notice must be struck out. For example, in a case involving the partition or sale of real property, if one of the parties served a jury notice, this notice would not be in accordance with a statute because s. 108(2) of the *Courts of Justice Act* prohibits jury trials in all cases of this nature. The other party would bring a motion to strike the jury notice out and the court would grant that motion (rule 47.02(1)(a)).

Likewise, a jury notice not would be in accordance with the rules if it were served after the close of pleadings. Rule 47.01 requires that the jury notice be served *before* the close of pleadings. If served after pleadings have closed, it is out of time, and it may be challenged on that basis. A motion to strike out a jury notice on the grounds that it is not in accordance with a statute or the rules may be brought before a master.

JURY TRIAL WOULD BE INAPPROPRIATE

If a jury notice cannot be struck out on the basis that it is not in accordance with the rules or a statute, it is still possible to bring a motion under rule 47.02(2) asking that it be struck out on the grounds that it is not appropriate to have a jury hear a particular case. This motion, unlike a motion to strike on the basis of not according with a statute or the rules, must be brought before a judge. A master has no jurisdiction to hear this type of motion.

When deciding whether or not a jury trial is appropriate, the judge will look at a number of issues, including the complexity of the case. If a case involves difficult questions of law, a judge may decide that it is best to proceed without a jury. It is the jury's role in a trial to determine which version of the facts is the most plausible. In a jury trial, it is the role of the judge to decide the legal issues. We call the jury "the finder of fact" for this reason. Sometimes the parties are not in a major dispute about the facts of a case: The source of their disagreement is how the law should be applied to those facts. In a case like this, there is no role for a jury, and a judge would likely decide that the case should proceed without one.

Even if the party wanting to have the jury notice struck is not successful on a motion, that party may try again to have the jury notice struck by the trial judge (rule 47.02(3)).

LISTING THE CASE FOR TRIAL: RULE 48
Setting the action down for trial: Rules 48.01 and 48.02

The court does not automatically schedule a trial once a lawsuit has been started. The parties must first let the court know that they are ready to proceed to trial. The process of letting the other side and the court know that your side is ready for trial is called **setting an action down for trial**.

setting an action down for trial
procedure that a party must follow in order to have its case placed on the trial list

Any party who has not been noted in default can set the case down for trial after the close of pleading, but usually the plaintiff takes this step. The plaintiff is the party who has the most interest in having the case decided. For example, Abigail Boar wants to have the court decide that she is entitled to be compensated by the defendants for her injuries. It is likely that she would be the party to set the matter down for trial.

In order to set a matter down for trial, Abigail must serve and file a **trial record** (rule 48.02(1)). The trial record must be served and filed on all the parties to the action, including the parties to a counterclaim, a crossclaim, or a third party claim. Once this has been done, the trial record is filed with the court along with proof of service. The court is now aware that this case is ready for trial.

trial record
bound set of documents prepared by the party setting the action down for trial and containing the pleadings of all parties, any relevant orders, all notices, and certificates

If there is a third party claim in your action, the third party must be served along with all the other parties, but there are additional procedural requirements. A party that wants to have the third party claim set down for trial must prepare a separate trial record. This third party trial record must be served on all the parties to the third party claim. Therefore, if an action has a third party claim, there are two trial records: one for the main action and one for the third party claim.

When an action is undefended — that is, when the defendant does not file a statement of defence — the plaintiff has the defendant noted in default, and the case does not proceed to trial. However, in rare instances, a judge can order that an **undefended action** proceed to trial. In that case, rule 48.03(2) requires that a trial record be prepared in the usual way, but there is no requirement that it be served on any other party. If you are setting an undefended action down for trial, you file the trial record with the court without serving anyone.

undefended action
an action in which no statement of defence is delivered

Once again, there are slightly different rules for third party claims. If a third party claim is undefended, a party that wants to set it down for trial must prepare a separate trial record for the third party claim. Rule 48.02(4) requires that the trial record for the undefended third party claim be served on the plaintiff in the main action, but no other party in the main action needs to be served. After service on the plaintiff in the main action, the trial record in the undefended third party claim can be filed with the court.

For example, suppose that Abigail Boar, the plaintiff in the main action, is suing Rattle Motors Ltd. and its employee Fred Flogem. Both Rattle Motors Ltd. and Fred Flogem have served and filed statements of defence in the main action. The main action is therefore a defended action. Both Rattle Motors Ltd. and Fred Flogem are planning to defend against Abigail's claim that they are liable to pay her damages because they caused her injuries. Rattle Motors Ltd. has commenced a third party claim against Skank Motorcar Company Ltd., the manufacturer of the Super Coupe, claiming that the oil pan on the car was defective and that it caused the leak that resulted in Abigail's fall. Because Skank Motorcar Company Ltd. has also filed a statement of defence in the third party claim, the third party claim is also defended.

Abigail wants to set the main action involving herself, Rattle Motors Ltd., and Fred Flogem down for trial. I.M. Just prepares the trial record for the main action and it is served on Fred Flogem, Rattle Motors Ltd., and the third party, Skank Motorcar Company Ltd. Abigail really does not care whether Rattle Motors Ltd.'s third party claim against the car manufacturer comes to trial or not. She intends to get all compensation for her injuries from Fred Flogem and Rattle Motors Ltd.

Rattle Motors Ltd., however, cares that the third party claim comes to trial because it thinks Skank Motorcar Company Ltd. caused Abigail's injuries. Rattle Motors Ltd.'s lawyer, Huey Sue, would prepare the trial record in the third party claim, serve it on all the other parties, and file it with the court. There would then be two trial records: one for the main action involving Abigail, Rattle Motors Ltd., and Fred Flogem and the other for Rattle's third party claim against Skank Motorcar Company Ltd.

Let's change the facts. Assume that Rattle Motors Ltd. and Fred Flogem have not filed a statement of defence. There is now no third party claim because Rattle Motors Ltd. never brought one. In this example, there is only one action, the main action, and it is undefended. Nevertheless, a judge has ordered that this undefended action proceed to trial. I.M. Just would prepare the trial record and file it with the court immediately without serving it on Rattle Motors Ltd. and Fred Flogem.

Let's say that the main action between Abigail, Rattle Motors Ltd., and Fred Flogem is a defended action. In this situation, Rattle Motors Ltd. has brought a third party claim, but Skank Motorcar Company Ltd. has not filed a statement of defence. The third party claim is now undefended. If this undefended third party claim is to be set down for trial, Huey Sue must prepare a third party trial record. He does not need to serve the third party or Fred Flogem, but he must serve Abigail, the plaintiff in the main action.

Consequences of setting an action down for trial: Rule 48.04

There can be a very long wait for cases to come to trial. Therefore, a party may be anxious to set the action down as soon as possible, but there are consequences of setting the action down that a party will want to consider before moving too quickly. By setting an action down for trial or consenting to an action's being placed on the **trial list**, a party is advising the court that it is ready for trial. Therefore, rule 48.04(1) prohibits parties from bringing any motions or conducting any further discoveries without leave of the court once they have set the action down. The other parties can bring motions and continue with discoveries if they wish. Only the party that sets the action down is prohibited from continuing these procedures. A party will want to make sure that it has brought all the necessary motions and conducted all the discoveries it will need before setting the action down.

trial list
list kept by the registrar in each courthouse of cases that are ready for trial

The rule prohibiting discoveries for the party setting down the action does not mean that the other parties are not obligated to follow through on their undertakings or their other obligations listed in rule 48.04(2)(b).

The party that sets an action down for trial may seek permission from the court to bring further motions, but the court will be reluctant to grant permission to do so unless the proposed motion concerns a serious issue that could not have been brought before the action was set down. It is rare that the court will give leave to a party to initiate or continue with discoveries after the party has set the action down.

Placing the action on the trial list: Rules 48.05 to 48.13

Once the trial record is filed, the action must be placed on the trial list 60 days later by the registrar of the court (rules 48.05 to 48.09). The parties can agree that the action be listed for trial before the 60-day period has passed, but a party who consents to putting the case on the trial list loses the right to bring any further motions or to initiate or continue discoveries without leave of the court.

In larger cities, the court sits all year long, so it does not matter when the trial record is filed. Once it is filed, the registrar adds the name of the action to the bottom of the list of cases that are ready for trial. However, outside major centres, the judges may not hear civil litigation matters all year. These cases are heard at certain designated periods called **sittings**. For instance, the Superior Court in Milton might have a sitting scheduled from October 15 to December 14. There is a trial list prepared for each sitting of the court. If you want your action added to the list for a particular sitting, you must file the trial record at least 10 days before the start of that sitting (rules 48.05(2) and 48.06(2)). After that time, any new cases are added to the trial list for the next scheduled sitting. The only way a case that is filed less than 10 days before the start of the sitting can go on the list for that sitting is if a motion is brought and the judge orders that the action be placed on that list.

sittings
a time period during which a specific court may hear cases

A place on the trial list does not guarantee that the case will be heard right away. The trial lists are long, and a case is not heard until it reaches the top of the list. Usually the court notifies the lawyers as the case gets close to the top, but it is the responsibility of the parties' lawyers to keep track of where they are on the list. When the case reaches the top, the parties must be ready to go to trial. There are separate trial lists for jury and non-jury trials. Usually the jury trial list is shorter.

Rule 48.12 requires the lawyers for the parties to let the registrar's office know immediately if a case has been settled. Usually you call the registrar's office first, but the rule also requires that the settlement be confirmed in writing. If a case is settled, it is taken off the trial list. This is one of the reasons that the trial list must be monitored closely when your case gets near the top. Your case may be number ten on the list, but if all the cases in front of you are settled and removed from the list, you will move to the top very quickly.

Status notice

Sometimes, an action is commenced and a court file is opened, but nothing much happens on it. A statement of claim and a statement of defence may be filed. Maybe the parties are taking their time negotiating a settlement, or maybe they have settled and have forgotten to terminate the action.

The registrar is responsible for making sure that there are not a lot of these cases cluttering up the court files. Rule 48.14 requires the registrar to send a notification to the parties if an action has not been placed on a trial list within two years after a statement of defence has been filed in the case. To notify the parties, the registrar sends them a status notice in form 48C. The notice says that the action will be dismissed for delay unless it is set down for trial or terminated within 90 days after service of the status notice. A lawyer who receives a status notice is required to give a copy of it to the client immediately.

If the action is not set down for trial or terminated or if a judge does not order an extension of time, the registrar makes an order dismissing the action with costs

90 days after the status notice is served. This order must also be given to the client immediately after it is served on the lawyer.

Sometimes there is a legitimate reason why the action has not been set down for trial. If this is the case, the lawyer for a party served with a status notice may request a status hearing before a judge (rule 48.14(5)). At this hearing, the plaintiff must satisfy the court that the action should not be dismissed for delay. However, the status hearing must be arranged within the 90-day period before the registrar dismisses the case. If the judge determines that there should be an extension of time, the action stays alive for the period specified by the judge. Otherwise, the judge dismisses it. Figure 15.2 (at the end of the chapter) sets out a status notice.

Contents of a trial record

Rule 48.03 specifies the contents of a trial record. The record must include a table of contents, all pleadings, any orders made on motion relating to how the trial is conducted, all notices, and a certificate from the lawyer of record who is setting the action down for trial. The certificate must state, among other things, that the record contains all the required documents and that pleadings have closed. Only one of the parties serves and files the trial record, and it therefore must contain the pleadings of all the parties. It is like a short history of the proceedings.

The following shows I.M. Just's certificate:

CERTIFICATE

I, I.M. Just, lawyer for the Plaintiff in this action, certify as follows:

1. this trial record contains all the relevant documents required by rule 48.03(1)(a) to (g); and
2. the time for delivery of pleadings has expired.

(signed by I.M. Just)

A trial record is put together in the same way as a motion record. It is bound with a light blue backsheet (rule 4.07(1)), and the pages should be numbered consecutively. The various documents should be separated by tabs to make it easy to read. An example of a trial record is set out in figure 15.3 (at the end of the chapter).

Note that the party that filed the trial record will also have to file copies of orders, notices, and other documents filed or delivered after the pretrial conference.[1]

THE PRETRIAL CONFERENCE: RULE 50

The court has a major interest in seeing that matters settle before they come to trial. Litigation is expensive for the parties, but it is costly from the court's perspective as well. There must be courtrooms, court staff, and judges available to accommodate the trial procedure. The courts therefore want to see that as many matters as possible are resolved before they require trial time. The pretrial conference is one of the procedural mechanism to try to achieve settlement.

The pretrial conference is an informal meeting between the lawyers for each party and a judge. Parties who are not represented by lawyers are expected to attend, but those represented by counsel need not be present. However, many lawyers find it advantageous to have their clients with them for the pretrial conference so that the clients can give instructions should a reasonable settlement be proposed by the other side.

The pretrial conference can be requested by a judge or by one or all of the lawyers for the parties. In most jurisdictions, pretrial conferences are held in almost every case. The purpose of the pretrial conference is to settle the case and avoid a trial or, if a trial cannot be avoided, to narrow the issues for trial. A list of issues that may be considered at the conference appears in rule 50.01.

Changes to pretrial conference procedure as of January 1, 2010

Changes to Rule 50 reflect the increased importance given to promoting settlement, narrowing issues, and organizing cases for trial.

- Pretrial conferences will now be mandatory for all actions in order to encourage settlement and help identify or narrow the actual issues for trial.

- Once a case is set down for trial, the registrar shall, within 90 days, give the parties notice to appear before a case conference judge or master.

- Counsel must attend pretrial conferences, and parties are expected to participate.

- Parties will now be required to file a detailed conference brief.

- Pretrial conferences may result in the court establishing timetables that state when the next steps must be completed, or that place the proceedings into case management.

- The judge will prepare a pretrial conference report indicating the steps to be taken prior to trial, the estimated duration of the trial, and stating that the parties are obliged to be ready to try the case on the date fixed for hearing. Lawyers will be obliged to communicate this information to their clients.[2]

Settlement of the case

During the pretrial conference, the lawyers each outline to the pretrial judge the case they intend to present at trial. They tell the judge the evidence they will call and how they intend to present the party's interests. Once the judge has heard the two sides of the case, he or she usually states how he or she would decide the case on the basis of this evidence. The lawyers then discuss the pretrial judge's decision with their client. The pretrial judge is not making the final decision but is merely advising the parties what he or she thinks of their likelihood of success. However, a judge's opinion can be helpful in encouraging a party to accept a reasonable settlement offer if the party thinks there is a possibility that they may lose the case at trial.

It is important to prepare properly for a pretrial conference. The documents that a party intends to use at trial should be made available to the pretrial judge (rule 50.05). Very often, the pretrial memorandum and the documents to be presented at trial can be included together in a pretrial brief. Because there is no formal requirement under the rules for this kind of brief, the contents are up to the party. However, most pretrial memorandums contain separate sections outlining the facts and the law that will be relied on at the trial. Expert reports and other documents can be attached, and a brief summary of each document's contents will be very helpful to the pretrial judge. A well-prepared memorandum can be very helpful in persuading a pretrial judge of the merits of a client's case. An example of a pretrial conference memorandum is set out in figure 15.4 (at the end of the chapter).

Sometimes despite the parties' efforts to settle, the case is not settled and must proceed to trial. The judge who presided at the pretrial conference may not hear the case at trial. He or she may have already heard too much informally about the case to render a decision on the evidence presented at the trial alone (rule 50.04).

Narrow the issues at trial

In many cases, it is not possible for the parties to settle all the issues between them, but it is possible to agree that certain facts are not in dispute. Although the case must go to trial, it can be significantly shorter and less costly when the parties spend time dealing only with the issues that are contested. For instance, in Abigail's case, none of the parties disputes the fact that Abigail fell while at Rattle Motors Ltd.'s showroom. What they do disagree on is the cause of the fall. Abigail alleges that she fell because the defendants negligently left oil on the floor, and Rattle Motors Ltd. claims she fell because she was intoxicated. If the defendants are prepared to admit that the plaintiff fell on their premises, the plaintiff need not call witnesses to prove that she fell.

It is important to determine exactly what the other side admits is true and what is not in dispute in a case. To do this, the parties can use rule 51, which governs admissions.

ADMISSIONS

Under rule 51, a party can formally request that any other party admit the authenticity of certain documents or the truth of certain facts. If a party makes an admission about a document or a fact, the party intending to rely on the document or the fact need not prove that the document is genuine and authentic or that the fact is true.

Every document relied on by a party at trial must usually be proven to be authentic. The person who wrote the letter or took the photograph or prepared the report must give evidence that the document is genuine or is a true copy of the original document. This can be very time consuming, particularly in a trial where a lot of documents are being relied on. Likewise, every fact that a party relies on must also be proved in court. Admissions remove the need for proving every element that is not in dispute.

Rule 51.02 provides that a party may serve a request to admit (form 51A) on the opposite party at any time during a proceeding. The request to admit may ask the other side to admit either a fact or a document. Any document for which a party is seeking an admission of authenticity must be attached to the request to admit unless the other side already has a copy. An example of a request to admit is provided in figure 15.5 (at the end of the chapter).

The party that receives the request to admit must respond within 20 days after the request is served. A party responds to the request to admit by preparing and serving a response to request to admit, which is in form 51B. An example of a response to a request to admit is set out in figure 15.6 (at the end of the chapter). Parties must answer each request to admit a fact or document by saying they admit or deny the fact or document. If they fail to respond to any part of the request to admit or fail to respond to the entire request, they are deemed to have admitted all the facts and documents contained in the request (rule 51.03(2) and (3)).

An admission, either in a pleading or in a response to a request to admit, and all deemed admissions can be withdrawn only with the consent of all the other parties or with leave of the court. The court only grants leave to withdraw if the party asking to withdraw can show that there is something about the fact or document that is an issue between the parties, that the admission was made through inadvertence, and that there will be no injustice to the opposite party that cannot be made up in costs. Therefore, it is important to ensure that no admissions are made without major consideration.

If an admission is significant enough, a party to whom the admission is made can seek an order in the case based on that admission by bringing a motion to a judge. An admission made under oath or affirmation — in an affidavit, in examinations for discovery, or orally in court — can be used by another party to obtain an order in an entirely different proceeding (rule 51.06).

CHAPTER SUMMARY

This chapter dealt with the decisions and the steps that must be taken to get ready for a trial. We noted that rules 46, 47, 48, 50, and 51 are the major rules dealing with pretrial procedures.

The first decision to be made is where the trial is to take place, and we noted the requirements of rule 46 in this regard. The second decision is whether or not the trial should be held before a jury or a judge alone. We noted the procedural requirements for serving and filing a jury notice and for bringing a motion to strike the jury notice under rule 47. Any party can decide to have a jury trial.

We then covered the procedure for setting a case down for trial and examined the consequences of failing to set a matter down for trial within two years of its commencement under rule 48.

We then considered the pretrial conference, an informal hearing before a judge which attempts to effect a settlement between the parties or at least to narrow the issues for trial under rule 50.

Finally we examined the matter of admissions and the procedures involved in the request to admit under rule 51.

KEY TERMS

setting an action down for trial

trial record

undefended action

trial list

sittings

NOTES

1 See rule 48.03(2) of the *Rules of Civil Procedure*, which states:

> (2) It is the responsibility of the party who filed the trial record to place with the record, before the trial, a copy of,
>
> (a) any notice of amounts and particulars of special damages delivered after the filing of the trial record;
>
> (b) any order respecting the trial made after the filing of the trial record;
>
> (c) any memorandum signed by lawyers, or any order made by the court, following a pre-trial conference; and
>
> (d) in an undefended action, any affidavit to be used in evidence.

2 O. reg. 438/08, s. 47, amending rule 50.

REFERENCES

Courts of Justice Act, RSO 1990, c. C.43.

Evidence Act, RSO 1990, c. E.23.

Rules of Civil Procedure, RRO 1990, reg. 194.

REVIEW QUESTIONS

1. If Abigail wants to have her trial held in Toronto, when must she decide this and how must she let the defendants know?

2. Are there any limitations on Abigail's choice of place of trial?

3. If Fred does not want the trial to be held in Toronto, what must he do?

4. If the parties agree that the place for trial should be changed to London, is the court obligated to change the location?

5. Who is most likely to want to set this case down for trial, and how must that party do it?

6. What are the consequences of a party's setting a matter down for trial?

7. What is a status notice, and who sends it?

8. What are the purposes of a pretrial conference?

DISCUSSION QUESTIONS

1. Abigail does not want to have a jury trial. However, Fred believes he will do better with a jury than without one. He thinks the jury will not be sympathetic to Abigail if he can show that she was drunk. Can Fred ask for a jury trial even though he is a defendant?

2. If Rattle Motors Ltd. has brought Skank Motorcar Company Ltd. into the action, what must be done to set the matter down for trial?

3. If Rattle Motors Ltd. has made an admission in its statement of claim that Abigail fell on its premises, what would Rattle have to do to withdraw it? What criteria would determine whether a withdrawal could be made?

FIGURE 15.1   JURY NOTICE (FORM 47A)

Court file no. 01-CV-1234

ONTARIO
SUPERIOR COURT OF JUSTICE

BETWEEN:

ABIGAIL BOAR

Plaintiff

and

RATTLE MOTORS LTD. and FRED FLOGEM

Defendants

JURY NOTICE

THE PLAINTIFF REQUIRES that this action be tried by a jury.

Date: May 3, year 3

Just & Coping
Barristers and Solicitors
365 Bay Street – 8701
Toronto, Ontario M3J 4A9

I.M. Just
LSUC #12345R
tel. 416-762-1342
fax 416-762-2300

Lawyers for the Plaintiff

TO:
Huey Sue
LSUC #23456T
Barrister and Solicitor
65 False Trail
Toronto, Ontario M6Y 1Z6

tel. 416-485-6891
fax 416-485-6892

Lawyer for the Defendants

FIGURE 15.2   STATUS NOTICE (FORM 48C)

Court file no. 01-CV-1234

ONTARIO
SUPERIOR COURT OF JUSTICE

BETWEEN:

ABIGAIL BOAR

Plaintiff

and

RATTLE MOTORS LTD. and FRED FLOGEM

Defendants

STATUS NOTICE

TO THE PARTIES AND THEIR LAWYERS

MORE THAN TWO YEARS HAVE PASSED since a statement of defence in this action was filed. According to the records in the court office, this action has not been placed on the trial list or terminated.

THIS ACTION WILL BE DISMISSED FOR DELAY unless within ninety days after the service of this notice: (a) it is set down for trial; (b) it is terminated; or (c) a judge presiding at a status hearing orders otherwise.

A party may request the registrar to arrange a status hearing.

IF A STATUS HEARING is held, the plaintiff must show cause why the action should not be dismissed for delay, and the presiding judge may set time periods for the completion of the remaining steps necessary to have the action placed on a trial list and may order that it be placed on a trial list within a specified time, or may adjourn the status hearing to a specified date, or may dismiss the action for delay.

Date: February 26, year 3

Signed by: *(signed by local registrar)*
Local Registrar

Address of
court office: Court House
393 University Avenue
Toronto, Ontario, M5G 1E6

FIGURE 15.2   CONCLUDED

TO:

Just & Coping
Barristers and Solicitors
365 Bay Street - 8701
Toronto, Ontario, M3J 4A9

I.M. Just
LSUC #12345R
tel. 416-762-1342
fax 416-762-2300

Lawyers for the Plaintiff

AND TO:

Huey Sue
LSUC #23456T
Barrister and Solicitor
65 False Trail
Toronto, Ontario, M6Y 1Z6

tel. 416-485-6891
fax 416-485-6892

Lawyer for the Defendants

FIGURE 15.3 TRIAL RECORD

Court file no. 01-CV-1234

ONTARIO
SUPERIOR COURT OF JUSTICE

BETWEEN:

ABIGAIL BOAR

Plaintiff

and

RATTLE MOTORS LTD. and FRED FLOGEM

Defendants

TRIAL RECORD

Just & Coping
Barristers and Solicitors
365 Bay Street - 8701
Toronto, Ontario, M3J 4A9

I.M. Just
LSUC #12345R
tel. 416-762-1342
fax 416-762-2300

Lawyers for the Plaintiff

TO:

Huey Sue
LSUC #23456T
Barrister and Solicitor
65 False Trail
Toronto, Ontario, M6Y 1Z6

tel. 416-485-6891
fax 416-485-6892

Lawyer for the Defendants

FIGURE 15.3   CONCLUDED

TRIAL RECORD TABLE OF CONTENTS

Tab	Document	Page
1	Statement of claim, dated January 4, year 1	1
2	Statement of defence, dated January 12, year 1	5
3	Reply, dated February 2, year 1	9
4	Jury notice, dated May 3, year 3	12
5	Certificate of I.M. Just	13

FIGURE 15.4 PRETRIAL CONFERENCE MEMORANDUM

Boar v. Rattle Motors Ltd. and Flogem   Date: May 20, year 3

Counsel for the plaintiff:

Just & Coping
Barristers and Solicitors
365 Bay Street – 8701
Toronto, Ontario, M3J 4A9

I.M. Just
LSUC #12345R
tel. 416-762-1342
fax 416-762-2300

Counsel for the defendants:

Huey Sue
LSUC #23456T
Barrister and Solicitor
65 False Trail
Toronto, Ontario, M6Y 1Z6

tel. 416-485-6891
fax 416-485-6892

Counsel for the plaintiff at trial: I.M. Just

THEORY OF THE PLAINTIFF'S CASE INCLUDING FACTUAL CONTENTIONS

The plaintiff was a customer of the defendant corporation, Rattle Motors Ltd., an automobile dealership. The defendant Fred Flogem is an automobile salesperson for Rattle Motors Ltd. The plaintiff slipped and fell while in the corporate defendant's showroom, sustaining considerable physical and psychological damage. The plaintiff alleges that Rattle Motors Ltd. was negligent in permitting an oil spill to remain on the showroom floor and that Fred Flogem was negligent in lowering the showroom lighting so that the spill could not be detected.

LEGAL ISSUES RAISED IN THE PLEADINGS AND TO BE DETERMINED AT TRIAL

1. Was the defendant Rattle Motors Ltd. negligent?
2. Was the defendant Fred Flogem negligent?
3. Was there any contributory negligence on the part of the plaintiff?
4. What general damages were suffered by the plaintiff?

PLEADINGS AND RELEVANT MATTERS

1. Are the pleadings in order or do they require amendments?
   The pleadings are in order and do not require further amendments.

FIGURE 15.4   CONTINUED

2. Are there any contemplated or outstanding motions?
    No.
3. Are productions complete?
    Yes.
4. Are all the transcripts available?
    Yes.

MOTIONS

Will there be any motions at trial?
No.

ADMISSIONS

The defendants admit that the plaintiff slipped and fell while on the premises of the corporate defendant and momentarily lost consciousness, but they allege that the fall was the result of the plaintiff's intoxicated state and not of any negligence of the defendants.

BUSINESS RECORDS

Will any business records be entered under the *Evidence Act*, and has the appropriate notice been given?
No business records will be produced.

EXPERT EVIDENCE

1. Will any be called?
    Yes.
2. On what issues?
    The long-term physical effects of the injuries that the plaintiff suffered.
3. Identity of Experts
    The plaintiff will call her neurologist, Dr. Morris Furgazy.

TRIAL DATE

1. Are the parties ready for trial?
    Yes.
2. Are there times when the trial cannot proceed because of witness or other matters?
    No.
3. How long will the trial last?
    It is estimated that it will last three days.

SETTLEMENT

What are the prospects of settlement?
Settlement is not likely in this case.

FIGURE 15.4   CONCLUDED

DAMAGES

The plaintiff claims:

1. general damages in the amount of $200,000; and
2. special damages in the amount of $20,769.

IS THIS A CASE WHERE IT MAY BE ADVISABLE TO DIRECT A
REFERENCE?
No.

WHAT PRETRIAL ORDERS ARE REQUESTED?
None.

FIGURE 15.5   REQUEST TO ADMIT (FORM 51A)

Court file no. 01-CV-1234

ONTARIO
SUPERIOR COURT OF JUSTICE

BETWEEN:

ABIGAIL BOAR

Plaintiff

and

RATTLE MOTORS LTD. and FRED FLOGEM

Defendants

REQUEST TO ADMIT

YOU ARE REQUESTED TO ADMIT, for the purposes of this proceeding
only, the truth of the following facts:

1. The plaintiff drank two glasses of wine at Barbeerian's
   before arriving at the corporate defendant's place of
   business on September 14, year 0.

2. The plaintiff was intoxicated at the time that she
   entered the corporate defendant's place of business.

YOU ARE REQUESTED TO ADMIT, for the purposes of this proceeding
only, the authenticity (see rule 51.01 of the Rules of Civil Procedure) of
the following documents:

1. Receipt for dinner from Barbeerian's, dated September
   14, year 0.

Attached to this request is a copy of each of the documents referred to
above.

The above document has not been attached because the
plaintiff has copies.

YOU MUST RESPOND TO THIS REQUEST by serving a response to
request to admit in Form 51B prescribed by the Rules of Civil Procedure
WITHIN TWENTY DAYS after this request is served on you. If you fail to do
so, you will be deemed to admit, for the purposes of this proceeding only,
the truth of the facts and the authenticity of the documents set out above.

Date: March 15, year 3

Huey Sue
LSUC #23456T
Barrister and Solicitor
65 False Trail
Toronto, Ontario M6Y 1Z6

tel. 416-485-6891
fax 416-485-6892

Lawyer for the Defendants

FIGURE 15.5   CONCLUDED

TO:

Just & Coping
Barristers and Solicitors
365 Bay Street - 8701
Toronto, Ontario, M3J 4A9

I.M. Just
LSUC #12345R
tel. 416-762-1342
fax 416-762-2300

Lawyers for the Plaintiff

FIGURE 15.6 RESPONSE TO REQUEST TO ADMIT (FORM 51B)

Court file no. 01-CV-1234

ONTARIO
SUPERIOR COURT OF JUSTICE

BETWEEN:

ABIGAIL BOAR

Plaintiff

and

RATTLE MOTORS LTD. and FRED FLOGEM

Defendants

RESPONSE TO REQUEST TO ADMIT

In response to your request to admit, dated March 15, year 3, the plaintiff:

1. Admits the truth of fact number 1.
2. Admits the authenticity of document number 1.
3. Denies the truth of fact number 2.
4. Denies the authenticity of documents numbers: N/A.
5. Refuses to admit the truth of fact number 2 for the following reasons:
   There is no truth in the allegation that the plaintiff was, in fact, intoxicated when she entered the place of business of the corporate defendant.
6. Refuses to admit the authenticity of documents numbers for the following reasons: N/A.

Date: March 22, year 3

Just & Coping
Barristers and Solicitors
365 Bay Street - 8701
Toronto, Ontario, M3J 4A9

I.M. Just
LSUC #12345R
tel. 416-762-1342
fax 416-762-2300

Lawyers for the Plaintiff

TO:
Huey Sue
LSUC #23456T
Barrister and Solicitor
65 False Trail
Toronto, Ontario, M6Y 1Z6

tel. 416-485-6891
fax 416-485-6892

Lawyer for the Defendants

CHAPTER 16

Trial preparation and trial

INTRODUCTION

If the parties do not settle at the pretrial conference, it is important to start preparing for an eventual trial as soon as possible. If the evidence has not been prepared and the work done well in advance, parties can find themselves pressed for time when they suddenly realize that their action is near the top of the trial list. In order to prepare the evidence for trial, it is important that we understand some very basic principles of the law of evidence.

CHANGES TO PROCEDURES FOR USING EXPERT EVIDENCE AS OF JANUARY 1, 2010

- In an adversarial proceeding, each party calls its own witnesses, whose evidence is expected to be favourable to that party's case. Expert witnesses are, in theory, expected to be objective, dispassionate, and not partisan, but in practice that is not always the case. To reinforce that expert witnesses are intended to assist the court with a neutral evaluation of the issues, they will now be required to certify in writing their duty to the court to be fair, objective, and non-partisan.

- Expert reports will now be served earlier than had previously been the case, and are to contain certain specific details. Previously, reports had to be served 90 days before trial. That time limit has been moved up to 90 days before the pretrial conference, so that the reports can be considered part of the pretrial conference process. Also, a party filing a responding expert's report shall file that report 60 days before the pretrial conference. Experts are no longer free to determine the format of a report because that is now determined by the rule amendments.[1]

SOME BASIC PRINCIPLES OF EVIDENCE
Relevant and material

To be admissible into evidence, a fact must be both relevant and material. To be relevant, a fact must logically lead to something that is important to prove in the case. For example, in Abigail's case, it would be relevant that she had been drinking just before she fell in the Rattle Motors Ltd. showroom because the defendant is claiming that she fell down due to being drunk, rather than because of any danger in their showroom. However, the fact that she may have had wine with dinner two days before the fall would likely be irrelevant.

In order to be material, a fact must relate to the matter in dispute between the parties. In Abigail's case, the issue between the parties is what caused Abigail's injuries or, in other words, who is at fault in causing her injuries. The fact that Abigail graduated from her law clerk course five years ago is not material because it has absolutely nothing to do with who is at fault in causing her injuries.

Reliability

Even though a fact may be relevant and material, it may not be entered into evidence if it is not reliable. Most of the rules of evidence deal with ensuring that evidence is as reliable as possible. The major way that evidence is tested for reliability is through the process of cross-examination of witnesses. Cross-examination of a witness is done by a lawyer for a party that is adverse in interest to the party that called the witness.

Hearsay

Hearsay is an out-of-court statement being admitted in court for the truth of its contents. For example, Tom, a friend of Abigail's boyfriend, would not be permitted to give evidence in court that the boyfriend told him that he saw Abigail drink six glasses of wine just before she fell in the automobile showroom. That would be hearsay. It cannot be tested on cross-examination for its truth. Tom was not present when Abigail was drinking and has no personal knowledge of how much she did or did not drink. All Tom could be cross-examined on is whether Abigail's boyfriend actually told him this. Hearsay is not admissible into evidence unless it fits within one of the exceptions to the hearsay rule.

The exceptions to the rule about the inadmissibility of hearsay are numerous and have developed over many centuries of the common law. These exceptions have grown up primarily because the law recognizes that there are circumstances in which a statement made out of court is likely reliable even though it cannot be tested by cross-examination. One example of an exception to the hearsay rule is that most statements made by a party to a proceeding are admissible. If Abigail herself had told Tom that she had drunk six glasses of wine before her fall, that would be an exception to the hearsay rule. Since her own statement about how much she had to drink weakens her claim that the fall was completely the fault of the defendants, it is regarded as having some intrinsic reliability even though Tom cannot be cross-examined on whether or not the statement is true. The principle underlying this exception to the hearsay rule is that, in accordance with human nature, Abigail is more likely to tell the truth about a fact that would hurt her case and more likely to lie about something that would help her.

However, not only oral evidence or testimony can involve hearsay. In an affidavit, which is evidence in written form, if the deponent states that another person told him or her something, then that too is hearsay. That is why rule 4.06(2) generally restricts an affidavit to matters of which the deponent has personal knowledge. Hearsay is not permitted, but there are some exceptions provided by rules 39.01(4) and (5). These exceptions as they relate to affidavits in support of motions are discussed in chapter 9.

ORGANIZING THE EVIDENCE

There are three types of evidence used at trial: documentary evidence, physical evidence, and the testimony of witnesses. We will examine each type in turn.

Documentary evidence

Documentary evidence consists of all written documents, such as letters and contracts, that a party wants to rely on to prove the facts of the case. Documents also include all the things that are mentioned in rule 30.01(1)(a), such as sound recordings, videotapes, film, and charts.

Most of the work done in relation to documentary evidence is done during discoveries and the preparation of the affidavit of documents. Not all the documents listed in the affidavit of documents will be used at trial. In fact, only a small portion of the existing documentary evidence will be so used. This is because the material often addresses a matter that is not at issue between the parties.

Sometime after the completion of discoveries, check with the lawyer handling the case to see what documents he or she expects will be needed should the case go to trial. Keep a note of these documents, and once the matter has passed the pretrial stage without settling, begin to make copies of the identified documents. You will need enough copies of the documents to provide them to the other side, to the court, and to any witness who will be asked to validate or otherwise give evidence related to that document. Many lawyers tend to make notes on copies of the documents they are using in the case. Make sure that the copies are clean copies — that is, that they do not have a lawyer's notes all over them.

Lawyers are urged by the court to submit joint document books. This cuts down on duplication and provides more manageable material for the judge to review. If you are using a joint document book, you will have to contact the law clerk or lawyer on the other side to determine which documents will go into the joint book.

The rules of evidence do not commonly permit a document to be introduced into evidence without a witness to authenticate it. For instance, if a lawyer wants to introduce a letter into evidence, the lawyer has the writer of the letter come to court to give oral evidence that the letter was indeed written by him or her and that his or her signature appears on the document. However, calling a witness for every single piece of material introduced at trial could add a significant amount of time to a trial. In an effort to keep a trial as short as possible, some documents are treated in a particular manner that does not require their identification by a witness.

BUSINESS RECORDS

If a party wants to introduce records that are kept by a business in the ordinary course of its operation and the records were made at or near the time of the incident that they record, the records may be admitted without calling the person who made them. For instance, if Abigail were taken to the emergency department after her fall at Rattle Motors Ltd., her lawyer could use the emergency room admission records at the trial as business records. Many people may have seen Abigail at emergency: the admission clerk, a series of nurses, a medical intern, a resident doctor, the emergency physician, and perhaps a specialist. All of these people would have written things in Abigail's chart. Without special provisions in the *Canada Evidence Act* and the Ontario *Evidence Act*, in order to admit these records, the lawyer would need to call all these people to verify the records.

The evidence statutes, however, provide that if at least seven days' notice is given to all other parties, the court may admit them without having a person there to verify them. The other parties are given an opportunity to object to the admission of the record, and an objection is argued before the court. If you are dealing with business records, you must ensure that notice of intention to introduce them as evidence at trial is served on all the other parties at least seven days before trial.

The other parties have a right to inspect the documents and may give notice to the party introducing the records that they wish to examine them. The introducing party must then produce the records within five days after receiving the notice.

MEDICAL REPORTS

Section 52 of the Ontario *Evidence Act* provides a procedure whereby medical evidence may be presented through a written report without the presence of the medical practitioner. To comply with the statute, you must give ten days' notice that you intend to introduce the report at trial to all the other parties. The other parties have a right to review the report before trial, and a copy of the report should therefore be included with the notice.

Even if the intention is to call the medical practitioner to give evidence, if the lawyer wishes to introduce the report itself, the other side should be given ten days' notice.

It is important to remember that "medical practitioner" refers not only to a medical doctor. Section 52 also relates to reports prepared by a chiropodist, a physiotherapist, a registered psychologist, a denture therapist, a dentist, a nurse practitioner, and many other types of health care providers covered by the *Regulated Health Professions Act* and the *Drugless Practitioners Act*.

USING A COPY OF AN ORIGINAL DOCUMENT

An original document is usually used at trial. If, for any reason, it is necessary to use a copy of the original at trial, the Ontario *Evidence Act* requires that notice be given to all the other parties at least ten days before the trial. The notice should also provide an appropriate date and time when the other parties may come to inspect the document.

Sometimes a statute may allow for the admission of a certified copy of the original. A certified copy is a copy that the person certifying the document compares to the original and swears to be a true copy.

In title documents pertaining to a real estate transaction, the land registrar certifies the copy to be a true copy of the original. The party wishing to introduce the document must give at least ten days' notice to all the other parties that he or she intends to introduce the certified copy. Any other party may challenge the document within four days of being served with the notice.

Under s. 29 of the Ontario *Evidence Act*, public or official documents may also be certified by the person who has custody or control of the document. They then may be admitted into evidence without further verification.

Physical evidence

Physical evidence consists of an actual object relating to an issue in the action between the parties. It may be brought into court and introduced into evidence. For instance, if a party were suing a manufacturer for damages caused by a faulty or unsafe product, the product may be brought into the court. In our case, Rattle Motors Ltd. may want to claim that the oil spill in its showroom resulted from a faulty oil pan made by Skank Motorcar Company Ltd. and may wish to bring the oil pan into the courtroom.

Sometimes, if the object is too large to be brought into the courtroom, the rules provide a method whereby the judge, jury, and other trial participants can go to a site outside the courtroom to look at the object or the property. This is called a "view," and it is governed by rule 52.05

Testimony of witnesses

The usual way to introduce evidence to be given by a person is to summon that person to court to give oral evidence called "**testimony**." The witnesses are asked questions by the lawyers for the parties. The judge and the jury, if there is a jury, listen to the answers. The testimony is recorded by a court reporter or a recording device that takes down every word said in the courtroom.

testimony
oral evidence given by a witness

It is unusual for evidence at a trial to be given in affidavit form. Affidavits may be used at a trial under the ordinary procedure only with special leave of the court, although they are used in the simplified procedure.

When a witness comes to give evidence at trial, the lawyer for the party who has asked the witness to give evidence asks questions first. This is called **examination-in-chief**.

examination-in-chief
series of questions asked of a witness by the lawyer for the party who called the witness

Any party who is adverse in interest to the party that called the witness then gets to ask questions. This is called **cross-examination**. The purpose of cross-examination is for the opposing side to try to shake the credibility of that witness. Cross-examination can be gruelling, and sometimes witnesses are reluctant to attend voluntarily to give evidence. Witnesses should also be prepared for the fact that the judge may ask some questions. Judges usually only ask questions if they need clarification of some point that a witness has made, but if a witness is unprepared for the situation, it may intimidate and fluster them.

cross-examination
series of questions asked of a witness by a lawyer for a party adverse in interest to the party that called the witness

During the course of a witness's testimony, counsel for an opposing party may make an objection to the question being asked. The objection is often based on a rule of evidence such as relevance or hearsay. As witnesses are being prepared to give their evidence, they should be told to not answer or stop answering a question in the face of an objection until the judge makes a ruling on the objection and instructs them as to whether or not they may give their answer.

In rare cases, a witness's testimony may be essential to a party's case, but the witness may not want to give evidence. Such a situation might arise when the witness is a friend or family member of an adverse party, or even when the witness is afraid. In such instances, counsel for the party calling the witness, who would

FIGURE 16.1 SUMMONS TO WITNESS (AT HEARING) (FORM 53A)

Court file no. 01-CV-1234

ONTARIO
SUPERIOR COURT OF JUSTICE

BETWEEN:

ABIGAIL BOAR

Plaintiff

and

RATTLE MOTORS LTD. and FRED FLOGEM

Defendants

SUMMONS TO WITNESS

TO:
Donny Dilhouse
1700 Bloor Street East
Toronto, Ontario, M6Y 3K9

YOU ARE REQUIRED TO ATTEND TO GIVE EVIDENCE IN COURT at the hearing of this proceeding on July 10, year 3 at 10:00 a.m. at the Court House at 393 University Avenue, Toronto, and to remain until your attendance is no longer required.

YOU ARE REQUIRED TO BRING WITH YOU and produce at the hearing the following documents and things: N/A

ATTENDANCE MONEY for one day of attendance is served with this summons, calculated in accordance with Tariff A of the Rules of Civil Procedure, as follows:

Attendance allowance of $50.00 daily	$50.00
Travel allowance	$ 3.00
Overnight accommodation and meal allowance	$ Nil
TOTAL	$53.00

If further attendance is required, you will be entitled to additional attendance money.

IF YOU FAIL TO ATTEND OR REMAIN IN ATTENDANCE AS REQUIRED BY THIS SUMMONS, A WARRANT MAY BE ISSUED FOR YOUR ARREST.

Date: June 1, year 3

Signed by: _(signed by local registrar)_

Local Registrar

Address of
court office: Court House
393 University Avenue
Toronto, Ontario, M5G 1E6

FIGURE 16.1 CONCLUDED

This summons was issued at the request of, and inquiries may be
directed to:

```
Huey Sue
LSUC #23456T
Barrister and Solicitor
65 False Trail
Toronto, Ontario, M6Y 1Z6

tel. 416-485-6891
fax 416-485-6892

Lawyer for the Defendants
```

---

normally only be entitled to ask non-leading questions in examination-in-chief, may
seek leave of the judge to cross-examine their own witness.

SUMMONS TO A WITNESS

Witnesses can, however, be compelled to attend the trial. They can be served with
a summons in form 53A if they are in Ontario or in form 53C if they are outside Ontario. An example of a summons in form 53A is provided in figure 16.1. A summons
is a court order to a person to attend a court hearing at a certain date and time. It
can also direct a person to bring certain documents with him or her. A person who
does not appear can suffer severe legal consequences. A warrant may be issued for
his or her arrest, and he or she can then physically be brought to court.

It is important to serve each witness with a summons even if the witness is your
client's best friend and says he or she is more than willing to attend to give evidence.
If witnesses have not been served with a summons and they do not appear, it is
much more difficult to convince the judge to adjourn the matter until they do. If witnesses are important to your client's case and they come down with the flu or are
in a car accident on their way to the courthouse, and you have not served them
with a summons, it is possible that their evidence will never be heard and your client's case will be irreparably damaged.

The summons to a witness must be issued by the court. You may request a
blank summons from the court office, and it will be signed by the registrar and
sealed. You can then fill in the rest of the form later, at your office.

The summons must be served personally on the witness, and a cheque for the
full amount of the attendance allowance and any travel allowance must accompany
the summons. Attendance money is a small allowance that is set by tariff A, part II
"Disbursements."

Witnesses are entitled to a payment of $50 for each day they are expected to at-
tend a trial and give evidence. In addition, if they live in the same city or town as
the courthouse, they are entitled to $3 per day travel allowance. If they live within
300 km of the courthouse, they are entitled to a travel allowance of $0.24 per km. If
they live further away than 300 km, they are entitled to return airfare, mileage to the
airport, overnight accommodation, and meal allowances of $75 per night.

If a witness requires an interpreter in a language other than French, the person calling the witness must provide the interpreter. In larger centres, the court usually keeps lists of interpreters who have been approved to interpret in various languages, including sign language. French interpreters are usually provided by the court.

EXPERT WITNESSES

An expert witness is permitted to give opinion evidence. An ordinary witness must stick strictly to what they saw, heard, or otherwise perceived. For instance, Fred Flogem can say that he saw oil under the car directly beneath the oil pan. He can describe the oil pan and the car, but he cannot say that, in his opinion, a defective oil pan in the car caused the leak onto the floor of the showroom. However, an engineer, qualified to design and examine cars can give his or her opinion about what caused the leak.

Before being classified as experts, witnesses must satisfy the court that they have the necessary qualifications and experience. They must also be experts in some area that the court recognizes as a valid area of study. For instance, a person may have studied UFOs for years, but the court may not find that to be a legitimate area of study.

A party who intends to call an expert must serve all the other parties with a report, signed by the expert, setting out his or her name, address, qualifications, and the substance of his or her proposed testimony. This report must be served at least 90 days before the commencement of the trial.

If any of the other parties wishes to call another expert to challenge the testimony of the first expert, the party must serve a similar report containing the same information pertaining to the expert. This report must be served on all the other parties at least 60 days before the start of the trial (rule 53.03).

These timelines must be met, or the court may refuse to hear the expert witness.

PREPARATION OF WITNESSES

The law clerk may be asked to help prepare the witnesses for trial. Most witnesses are not accustomed to being in a courtroom and will need some help and reassurance in getting ready to give evidence.

leading a witness
asking a witness a question that suggests the answer

Most lawyers run their witnesses through the proposed examination-in-chief and may rehearse a possible cross-examination to give them experience in answering difficult questions asked by a lawyer who is challenging their testimony. Witnesses should be told some basic things about giving evidence, such as the fact that in examination-in-chief, the lawyer asking the questions is not able to help the witness find the answer. This technique is called "**leading a witness**," and it violates the rules of evidence if used during examination-in-chief. However, the opposing counsel may lead the witness in cross-examination, and witnesses must be aware that an opposing lawyer may attempt to lead them into giving answers that they do not wish to give.

Witnesses should be told that they may ask the lawyer to repeat the question. They do not need to rush their answers, but if they are too slow, they may appear to be avoiding the question. If they do not understand the question or do not recall something, they should say so.

Finally, witnesses should understand that they must, for the most part, rely on their recollections of the event or incident. If they use notes that were made at the time of the incident, they must be prepared to show their notes to the other party's counsel. They may not use notes unless the notes were made at the same time or almost immediately after the incident at issue. They cannot write down what they want to say just before they are called to give evidence and then use these notes to jog their memories while they are in the witness box.

In the event that the trial lasts more than one day, the witnesses may be released by the court and called back to give their evidence as the proceedings progress. Often, if an expert witness is to give testimony in a case, the court will permit them not to be at court but to be available by telephone to be called when they are needed.

Trial brief

Once all the material is organized, it is time to prepare a trial brief. A trial brief is not the same as a trial record. A trial record is for the use of the court. A trial brief is for a lawyer's use at trial. It helps the lawyer keep his or her material organized as he or she is presenting the case.

Lawyers have their own preferences for the organization of a trial brief, but it must be composed in such a way that lawyers are able to find things easily while they are on their feet and making their case in the courtroom.

Unlike the documents filed with the court, which are usually spiral-bound, the trial brief is usually in a three-ring binder so that the material can be moved around freely. A trial does not always follow a straight path, particularly if something unexpected arises, and a lawyer must be able to adapt the organization of the material to the flow of the trial.

Most lawyers will want the material organized by type and placed in the binder in chronological order. For instance, the opening and closing arguments will be in one binder, the pretrial motions in another, the witness statements and summaries of evidence in another, and the discoveries in yet another. If the material is not voluminous, some of these binders may be combined in a single binder.

The binders should be different colours so they can easily be distinguished from one another when they are sitting on the counsel table in a courtroom. There should be clearly marked tabs separating the material.

Once the trial brief has been prepared, it is time to go back and ensure that sufficient copies of proposed exhibits and transcripts have been made.

Brief of authorities

A brief of authorities puts together all the legal cases, statutes, and regulations that support your client's action. It should be organized with an index, listing the cases and the legislation. The cases and legislation must be properly cited. Tabs should be used to separate the material, and the index should identify the tab at which the material can be found. These briefs are usually spiral-bound. The judge is given a copy of the brief of authorities as are counsel for the other side. Remember that if a lawyer is referring a judge to an authority, the judge must be able to find it easily.

TRIAL PROCEDURE

Trial by judge and jury, or judge alone

As we learned in chapter 15, in accordance with s. 108 of the *Courts of Justice Act*, a trial may be conducted with or without a jury. If the party has an option under the statute for a jury trial, the decision to try the matter before a jury or by judge alone will be made on the basis of a number of factors that include the complexity of the case, the amount of sympathy or hostility the party believes that it may receive from a jury, and the length of the trial list for jury trials.

If the trial is conducted before a jury, it is the role of the jury to be the "trier of fact." That is, the jury must decide which of the facts presented in evidence they will accept as the truth. The judge in a jury trial ensures that the law is properly applied and the jury is properly instructed on the law. In a jury trial, the judge is the "trier of law."

In a trial by judge alone, the judge is both the trier of fact and the trier of law. In other words, the judge both applies the law and determines the facts that are accepted as true.

Overview of a trial

Generally, a trial proceeds as outlined below.

1. Preliminary motions are dealt with, including any motions dealing with the amendment of pleadings, adjournment of trial, and striking out of the jury notice.

2. Jury selection takes place, when there is to be a jury.

3. Order excluding witnesses. Rule 52.06 provides that the judge may, at the request of a party, exclude a witness from the courtroom until the witness is called to give evidence. It is a common practice for parties to ask for such an order so that a witness cannot hear other witnesses testifying and have what they hear influencing their own testimony. There can be no communication with an excluded witness until the witness has been called to give evidence. An exclusion order does not apply to a party to the proceeding or to a witness who is necessary to instruct counsel; however, such an instructing witness may be required to give evidence first.

4. Opening statement of the plaintiff in which counsel for the plaintiff presents an overview of the case to be presented. The defendant's counsel may make an opening statement at this time (leave of the judge will be required to do so at this time in a jury trial), or he or she may wait until the start of the presentation of the defence. Any document briefs or agreed statements of facts are presented to the court at this time.

5. Presentation of the plaintiff's evidence by calling witnesses and reading into the record any admissions from examinations for discoveries or requests to admit. The plaintiff's witnesses are examined-in-chief by the plaintiff's counsel and cross-examined by counsel for any party that is adverse in interest to the plaintiff.

6. Presentation of the defendant's case. Counsel for the defendant will examine the witnesses in-chief and then the adverse parties will cross-examine.

7. Reply evidence may be called.

8. Closing arguments take place. In a trial by judge alone, the plaintiff's closing argument is presented first, followed by the defendant's closing argument. In a jury trial, the defendant closes first, unless the defendant has called no evidence.

CHAPTER SUMMARY

In this chapter, we discussed the two steps involved in getting ready for a trial: (1) organizing the evidence and (2) assembling the materials that will be needed in the courtroom for the presentation of the case. We also discussed three general types of evidence: (1) documents, (2) physical evidence, and (3) testimony.

We observed that much of the documentary evidence in a trial is identified through discoveries. The rules of evidence require most documents to be verified in the course of the trial by calling the person who made the documents as a witness. However, there are special rules of evidence permitting business records and medical reports to be entered into evidence without calling the person who made them. In connection with testimony, we discussed summons and the need to summons even witnesses who agree to appear voluntarily.

Finally, we covered the drafting of a trial brief and the compilation of a brief or a book of authorities.

KEY TERMS

testimony

examination-in-chief

cross-examination

leading a witness

NOTE

1 O. reg. 438/08, s. 48, amending rules 53.01 and 53.02.

REFERENCES

Canada Evidence Act, RSC 1985, c. C-5.

Courts of Justice Act, RSO 1990, c. C.43.

Drugless Practitioners Act, RSO 1990, c. C.18.

Evidence Act, RSO 1990, c. E.23.

Regulated Health Professions Act, 1991, SO 1991, c. 18.

Rules of Civil Procedure, RRO 1990, reg. 194.

REVIEW QUESTIONS

1. What is a trial brief, and who uses it? How does it differ from a trial record?

2. What are the three types of evidence that may be introduced in a trial?

3. How is evidence usually admitted at a trial?

DISCUSSION QUESTIONS

1. Your instructing lawyer is calling Dr. Hardy Ames as an expert witness. Dr. Ames is an engineering professor at Trent University. He has a PhD in chemical engineering. What must the lawyer do to ensure that Hardy's evidence will be heard?

2. John Doe is suing Mary Smith. Draft a summons in the case for the plaintiff's witness Dan Doe. Dan lives at 1400 Winding Lane, Peterborough, Ontario, L4T 7Y6. The trial is to take place in Newmarket. There is a distance of about 120 km between Peterborough and Newmarket. The trial starts on March 15, year 1, and the witness will be needed for one day of testimony.

CHAPTER 17

Judgments

PROCEDURE FOR DRAFTING, ISSUING, AND ENTERING JUDGMENTS AND ORDERS

Introduction

When a court makes a decision, that decision is a command to one or more of the parties to do something: to pay money or to cease doing something in the case of an injunction, for example. These commands from the court are referred to as orders. They take three forms under the rules:

1. an order in form 59A, called an "order" and used for a decision on motions and applications;

2. an order in form 59B, called a "judgment" and used for a final decision in actions; and

3. an order in form 59C, called an "order on appeal" and used for a decision by an appellate court (the Court of Appeal and the Superior Court when it acts in an appellate capacity).

Make sure to determine the type of order you are drafting so that you use the correct form.

DRAFTING ORDERS AND JUDGMENTS

Order-drafting process

There are several steps to the creation of a final order or judgment:

1. obtaining the judge's or master's endorsement of the record,

2. drafting a formal order from the endorsement,

3. approving and signing the order, and

4. entering the order.

Obtaining the judge's or master's endorsement

In any proceeding, whether it is a motion or a trial, when a judge makes a decision, he or she writes or endorses the decision on the back of a trial or motion record, notice of motion, or other court document. If a judge or master wishes to give reasons for the decision, he or she may write them as part of the endorsement, if that is practical, or may state "reasons to follow" (rule 59.02). (In an appellate court, if reasons are given, an endorsement is not required.) In the rare cases where written reasons are given, they are usually written separately, typed by the judge's secretary, released to the parties, and filed in the court file.

Figure 17.1 shows what an endorsement in Abigail Boar's case might look like.

Drafting a formal order

The court does not create the final order for you. It is the responsibility of the parties to prepare the order. One of the parties, usually the one who has been successful and has a real interest in completing the process, prepares the order. You begin by going to the court file, finding, and photocopying or writing out the endorsement. Using the appropriate version of form 59, you then prepare a draft order. All orders contain the following:

- the name of the judge or officer who made it;
- the date on which it was made;
- the recital, which gives a context for the order and may include the date of the hearing and whether parties or counsel or both were present; and
- the operative parts of the order or the commands.

Each command is set out in a separately numbered paragraph. The paragraphs usually begin with "THIS COURT ORDERS AND ADJUDGES" or some variation of this phrase, depending on the court and the type of order (rule 59.03(1) to (4)). Damages are usually expressed as a total consisting of general and special damages together with prejudgment interest, if awarded, calculated to the date of the order. Costs are listed in a separate paragraph.

If the order requires payments to a minor directly or through a trustee, the order must show the minor's date of birth and address, and it must contain a direction that it be served on the children's lawyer. This ensures that an independent public agency has notice of the minor's interest, and that there is an indication of when the minority status ends (rule 59.03(5)). At that point, the minor, on becoming an adult, has the right to take charge of funds held on his or her behalf under the terms of the order.

An order for the payment of costs must direct that the costs be paid to the party, and not to the lawyer for the party. This prevents the lawyer's obtaining the funds for his or her own use. It is permissible for the payer to pay the costs to the lawyer in trust for the client, however. In this way the lawyer has to account for what is held in trust (rule 59.03(6)).

Where postjudgment interest is payable, you draft the order with a provision for the payment of postjudgment, setting out the rate at which it is payable and the date from which it begins to run. Sometimes the rate and date are left blank and filled out by the counter clerk when the order is signed.

Support orders must set out the last-known addresses of the support creditor and support debtor.

Figure 17.2 sets out what a draft judgment in form 59B might look like if Abigail Boar succeeded in getting judgment for $200,000 for general damages, $25,000 for special damages, and costs.

An order in form 59A has a somewhat different format. Set out in figure 17.3 is an order on a motion to compel Fred Flogem to re-attend and answer questions on his examination for discovery.

FIGURE 17.1 ENDORSEMENT

(Short title of proceeding)

ABIGAIL BOAR

Plaintiff(s)

and

RATTLE MOTORS LTD. ET AL.

Defendant(s)

Court file no. 01-CV-1234

ONTARIO SUPERIOR COURT OF JUSTICE

Proceeding commenced at Toronto

TRIAL RECORD

Name, address and telephone number of plaintiff's lawyer or plaintiff:

I.M. Just
LSUC #12345R

Just & Coping
Barristers and Solicitors
365 Bay Street - 8701
Toronto, Ontario, M3J 4A9

tel. 416-762-1342
fax 416-762-2300

Lawyers for the Plaintiff

July 12, year 3:

Judgment for the plaintiff in the amount of $53,000 with interest thereon at the rate of 3.8 percent from August 13, year -1. Costs fixed at $8,000.

Snork, J

FIGURE 17.2   JUDGMENT (FORM 59B)

Court file no. 01-CV-1234

ONTARIO
SUPERIOR COURT OF JUSTICE

The Honourable   Friday, the 12th day
Madam Justice Snork   of July, year 3

BETWEEN:

ABIGAIL BOAR

Plaintiff

and

RATTLE MOTORS LTD. and FRED FLOGEM

Defendants

JUDGMENT

THIS ACTION was heard on July 10, 11, and 12, year 3,
without a jury at Toronto, in the presence of counsel for
all parties,
  ON READING THE PLEADINGS AND HEARING THE EVIDENCE and the
submissions of counsel for the parties,

1. THIS COURT ORDERS AND ADJUDGES that the plaintiff
   recover from the defendants the sum of $200,000.00 for
   general damages.
2. THIS COURT ORDERS AND ADJUDGES that the plaintiff
   recover from the defendants the sum of $25,000.00 for
   special damages.
3. THIS COURT ORDERS AND ADJUDGES that the plaintiff
   recover prejudgment interest at the rate of 4 percent
   from July 3, year 0 to the date of judgment.
4. THIS COURT ORDERS AND ADJUDGES that the defendants pay
   to the plaintiff her partial indemnity costs of this
   action forthwith after assessment.

THIS JUDGMENT BEARS INTEREST at the rate of _____ percent
per year commencing on _____.

_____
Registrar, Superior Court of Justice

FIGURE 17.3 ORDER (FORM 59A)

Court file no. 01-CV-1234

ONTARIO
SUPERIOR COURT OF JUSTICE

MASTER BELLWETHER   Friday, the 3rd
                                           day of June, year 2

BETWEEN:

ABIGAIL BOAR

Plaintiff

and

RATTLE MOTORS LTD. and FRED FLOGEM

Defendants

ORDER

THIS MOTION, made by the plaintiff for an order that the
defendant Fred Flogem re-attend at his own expense to answer
questions 4, 5, and 7 on his examination for discovery was
heard this day at Toronto,
    ON READING the affidavit of Dianne Swan, sworn and filed,
and on reading the transcript of the examination for
discovery of the defendant Fred Flogem and on hearing the
submissions of counsel for both parties,

1. THIS COURT ORDERS that the plaintiff's motion be
   dismissed.
2. THIS COURT ORDERS that costs be in the cause.

_____

Registrar, Superior Court of Justice

Approving and signing the order

Once you have drafted the judgment or order from an endorsement, you must obtain approval as to the form of the order from the other parties who are affected by it and who were present and participated in the proceeding. The lawyer for the other party checks the draft against the endorsement to see that your draft is fair and accurate. If it is, the lawyer writes on the face of the order "approved as to form" and signs his or her name and capacity as lawyer for a party in the proceeding. Then he or she returns the signed copy to you. Approval can also be given over the phone, by e-mail, or by faxing a copy that has been marked approved. The rule is not restrictive here.

You then take the approved copy and an original to the office of the local registrar. If all parties who were present at the hearing have approved the order, the registrar examines the order and, if satisfied with the form, signs the order on behalf of the court.[1] If the registrar is not satisfied, he or she rejects the order and returns it unsigned. In this case, the party can either make the required corrections or, if he or she believes the registrar is in error, can obtain an appointment before the judge or master who made the order to settle the terms of the order (rule 59.04(5) to (9)).

Where the parties cannot agree on the form of the order and a party has withheld approval, the other party may obtain an order to settle the terms of the order before the registrar. The registrar examines the draft order and the endorsement and, if satisfied, signs the order. If the registrar is uncertain, he or she refers the order to the judge or master who made the order to determine whether or not it should be signed (rule 59.04(10)). If a party disagrees with the registrar's decision, he or she may obtain an appointment with the judge or master to settle the terms of the order (rule 59.04(12)).

If the referral is to a court consisting of more than one judge, the application to settle the terms of an order should be brought before the presiding judge in that court. Once the order has finally been settled, the registrar signs it (rule 59.04(12) to (16)). If a case is urgent, a lawyer can ask the judge who issued the order to sign it. In this case, the judge may do so without approval if he or she is persuaded that the matter is urgent. The judge will then sign a draft order, which you need to prepare beforehand, and write on the face of the order: "let this judgment issue and enter."

Entering the order

Once the order has been signed, it must be officially recorded and filed by the court. The court's seal is applied in the upper left-hand part of the order, just below the name of the judge or master who made the order. At the bottom, a note is affixed identifying the entry book in which the order is inserted. If the order is entered in the court records electronically or is microfilmed or photocopied, the note on the order will provide appropriate information to retrieve the order. This is done in the office of the court where the proceeding commenced. If an order is amended or varied by a subsequent order, the subsequent order is entered in the same court office as the original order, as well as in the office where the subsequent order was made. If the order is made in the Court of Appeal, it is entered both in the Court of Appeal office and in the office of the court where the action commenced (rule 59.05).

An order found to contain an inadvertent error resulting from an accidental slip or omission may be corrected on motion to the court that made the order (rule 59.06).

Where an outstanding judgment has been paid to the judgment creditor's satisfaction (even if not paid in full), it can no longer be enforced. A document attesting to the satisfaction of the judgment creditor, called a "satisfaction piece," may be filed and entered in the office of the court where the order was entered (rule 59.07).

PREJUDGMENT INTEREST
Introduction

When a party obtains judgment in a lawsuit for money to which he or she is entitled, the party is also entitled to interest because he or she has been deprived of the use of the money or its value from the time it was owing. Interest is paid on the amount owing to compensate the party for what he or she might have earned as profit on that money or to compensate the party for the loss of the use of it. Another reason for awarding interest is to make it less attractive for the defendant to stall proceedings in the hope that the plaintiff will run out of money or the will to pursue the case. A defendant who knows that interest is running on the amount of the claim may be more inclined not to waste time and to settle the claim.

Sections 127 to 129 of the *Courts of Justice Act* set out the rules for calculating prejudgment interest. Section 127 sets out definitions of relevant terms and the formula for determining prejudgment and postjudgment interest. The person designated by the deputy attorney general calculates the basic interest rate for each quarter of the year. The rate for each quarter is available on the Attorney General's website at http://www.attorneygeneral.jus.gov.on.ca/english/courts/interestrates.asp. The rates are also posted at court offices, but are no longer published in the *Ontario Gazette*. There is also a computerized source of rate information that even does the calculations: http://www.judgmentcalc.com. Whatever source you use, all you need to do is determine what the relevant quarter is and look up the interest rate for that quarter in the given year. The rates are set out in table form, using two tables. The first table covers rates for prejudgment interest for causes of action that arose before October 23, 1989 and for postjudgment interest in all cases, both before and after 1989. The second table sets out the rates for prejudgment interest for all causes of action that arose after October 23, 1989. Prejudgment interest is calculated differently before and after that date as a result of an amendment to the *Courts of Justice Act*, which is why we need the second table for post-1989 prejudgment interest.

Step-by-step calculation instructions

1. *Determine whether you should claim interest under the prejudgment interest rules or whether you have an alternative right to interest.* Contracts often provide an interest rate and method of calculation for any amount that may be payable under the contract, including when there is a default in payment. A contract for a loan will certainly contain an interest rate. A penalty clause may also provide for interest. Sections 128(3)(g) and 129(5) of the *Courts of Justice Act* state that neither prejudgment nor postjudgment interest is payable under ss. 127 to 129 if there is a right to interest that arises other than under these sections. If you have a right to interest that arises outside the Act, it is still a good idea to claim prejudgment interest under the Act in the alternative in the statement of claim. If your claim to a right to interest arising outside the Act is unsuccessful, you can then fall back on the Act's provisions. The clause in the claim for relief might read: "prejudgment and postjudgment interest at the rate of 14 percent in accordance with the provisions of s. 3 of the contract between the parties or, in the alternative, prejudgment and postjudgment interest in accordance with the provisions of the *Courts of Justice Act*."

2. *If you have a right to claim interest under the Act, you must classify the damages on which interest may be charged because this may determine what the rate of interest is and how interest is calculated.* There are three types of damages for the purpose of s. 128:

a. *General rule: Section 128(1).* Money awarded under an order is generally subject to the appropriate quarterly rate for the quarter when the proceeding was commenced.

b. *First exception: Section 128(2) damages for non-pecuniary loss for personal injury.* The rate of interest on damages for **non-pecuniary** loss (for personal injuries) does not use the quarterly rates, but instead uses the rate determined under rule 53.10, which is still 5 percent. The type of damages you are looking for is a non-monetary loss in a personal injury action. This means the amount of general damages awarded by the court for pain and suffering or the emotional shock that results from a personal injury. Because no money was actually lost, the s. 128(2) rule was meant to limit interest to 5 percent, which was lower than the usual quarterly rates at the time the rule was made. If Abigail is awarded $100,000 in general damages for pain and suffering, use 5 percent as the interest rate for this head of damages.

> **non-pecuniary**
> non-monetary

c. *Second exception: Section 128(3) special damages accruing over time.* Special damages are liquidated damages. These include out-of-pocket expenses and other sums that can be determined with precision using a simple formula. They may occur all at once at the time the cause of action arises, or you may have continuing out-of-pocket expenses from the time the cause of action arose. If so, you must calculate interest every six months on these damages as they accrue. If Abigail had continuing out-of-pocket expenses for medications, you would add up her expenditures for each six-month period. Beginning with the date the action arose, you would calculate interest using the quarterly rate on the day the action was commenced on the total for the first six-month period and do the same for any other six-month period, and for any part period up to the date of the order. You may not calculate interest on interest from any previous six-month period. Total the interest separately from the special damages for each six-month or part period to determine interest under this head of damage. This interest is added to any other interest arising under other heads of damage and added to the amount of the total judgment.

> **exemplary damages**
> damages over and above the plaintiff's actual loss, paid to compensate the plaintiff for hurt feelings or mental stress caused by the defendant's particularly outrageous behaviour

3. *Identify amounts on which no interest may be charged.* Section 128(4) identifies amounts that are not subject to interest calculation. They are listed below.

a. *Exemplary or punitive damages.* **Exemplary damages** (also called aggravated damages) are awarded to compensate the plaintiff for emotional harm when a defendant's conduct has been particularly outrageous. **Punitive damages** are also awarded when a defendant's behaviour is particularly outrageous, but the purpose here is to punish the defendant to deter him or her from behaving in the impugned way again. Because these damages are penalties, interest on these amounts as a further penalty could be said to be overly harsh.

> **punitive damages**
> damages in the nature of a fine paid to the plaintiff when the defendant's behaviour has been particularly outrageous

b. *Interest under s. 128.* Interest is not compounded and generally there is no interest charged on accrued interest. It is calculated separately and then added in with the other damages. However, when postjudgment interest is calculated, it is calculated on the entire judgment, including the component that is prejudgment interest.

c. *Award of costs.* The costs awarded at the time of judgment, whether fixed or to be assessed, are not subject to prejudgment interest, though they are subject to postjudgment interest.

d. *Pecuniary loss that is identified as occurring after the date of the judgment.* Sometimes a judge can identify a plaintiff's loss that is connected to the cause of action but that has not yet accrued. For example, in Abigail's personal injury action, a judge may be able to determine an amount for her future loss of income because she will continue to be unable to work. On this amount, no interest may be charged.

e. *Advance payment of the amount to settle a claim before judgment after the payment was made.* Suppose you owe $100 as of January 1, and you pay $75 as an advance payment to settle the claim on February 1. If the plaintiff continues to go after you for the balance, prejudgment interest on the $75 will run only from January 1, when the cause of action arose, to February 1, when that amount was paid. But interest will run on the balance, $25, for the whole period from the time the cause of action arose until judgment: from January 1 until the date of the judgment.

f. *Where the order is made on consent.* There is no prejudgment interest on an order made on consent unless the debtor agrees.

g. *Where interest is payable by a right other than under s. 128.* As noted earlier, if you have a right of interest arising, for example, under a contract, you must claim interest under the contract and not under the Act.

4. *Establish the prejudgment interest rate that applies to your damages claim.* Except for damages for non-pecuniary loss on personal injuries, where the interest rate is 5 percent, the applicable rate of interest is the rate for the quarter in which the action was commenced. Do not confuse this with the quarter in which the cause of action arose. The right to sue always arises earlier than the day on which you commence proceedings, and it may well be in a different quarter. You do not have to do the calculations in s. 127 to determine the rate. This is done for you in the table that is updated quarterly by the Ministry of the Attorney General. Remember, as noted earlier, that there are two tables. Use the first table (beginning with 1985) for prejudgment interest on cases where the cause of action arose before October 23, 1989 and for postjudgment interest in all cases. Use the second table (beginning with October 23, 1989) for prejudgment interest in cases where the cause of action arose *after* October 23, 1989.

5. *Having established the rate, calculate the prejudgment interest.* You will need to determine the following dates: (a) the date on which the cause of action arose (interest is calculated from this date); (b) the date on which proceedings commenced (the interest rate is the rate for the quarter in

which proceedings commenced); and (c) the date on which the order or judgment was made (interest runs to this date). The prejudgment interest calculation formula for simple interest is:

$$I = P \times R \times T$$

where

    I = interest,

    P = amount for the head of damage on which the claim is made,

    R = rate of interest from the rate for the quarter when the action was commenced, and

    T = number of days from the day the cause of action arose to the day of judgment, which is expressed as a fraction of a year — for example, 40 days is expressed as $^{40}/_{365}$.

Suppose Abigail Boar sues her employer for wrongful dismissal when her employer terminates her employment without notice on August 12, year 0. She sues the employer on October 1, year 0 and recovers judgment with general damages of $80,000 on November 15, year 1.

1. *Determine if you have a right to interest under the Act.* In this case, there is no rate set out in a contract and no other right to interest. Therefore prejudgment interest can be claimed under the Act.

2. *Classify the damages to determine the rate and calculation mode.* The damages are general damages and come within neither exception to the general rule: They are not damages for personal injuries and they are not special damages accruing over time before judgment.

3. *Identify the amount on which no interest may be charged.* Interest may be charged on the general damages claimed; there are no claims that are exempt from prejudgment interest on these facts.

4. *Establish prejudgment interest rate for this claim.* The rate is the rate for the quarter in which the cause of action arose. August 12, year 0 is in the third quarter of year 0, and the rate must be taken from the second table for proceedings where the cause of action arose after 1989. Assume that the rate is 5.3 percent.

5. Calculate the prejudgment interest:

$$I = P \times R \times T$$

August 12, year 0 to August 11, year 1 (one year):

$80,000 \times 0.053 = $4,240$

August 12, year 1 to November 14, year 1 (95 days, not including the day on which judgment is given):

$80,000 \times 0.053 \times {}^{95}/_{365} = $1,103.56$

$I = $5,343.36$

POSTJUDGMENT INTEREST

Introduction

Postjudgment interest is also available. If a party has a right to interest from the time the cause of action arose, a party has that right after judgment until he or she is paid. Postjudgment interest therefore compensates a party for the loss of the use of money that he or she should have had. It also encourages a judgment debtor to pay what he or she owes. The longer the delay, the greater the amount that must be paid.

The general principles are the same as for prejudgment interest but the calculation rules are slightly different. If an order awards periodic payments, such as in a divorce support order, postjudgment interest runs from the date each payment becomes due.

Step-by-step calculation instructions

1. *Determine the amount of the judgment.* This includes the amount of the damages, the interest on that amount, and the costs awarded.

2. *Determine the postjudgment interest rate.* This requires you to use the rate in the first table for the quarter in which judgment was given.

3. *Calculate the postjudgment interest.*

    a. Determine the day of judgment, when the interest begins to run.

    b. Count the days from the day after the order is made to the day on which payment is received. Since prejudgment interest was calculated to include the day the judgment was given, postjudgment interest starts on the next day.

    c. Calculate the postjudgment interest using the formula: $I = P \times R \times T$.

4. *Calculate the amount due on the date of payment.* Add the postjudgment interest just calculated to the amount of the outstanding judgment.

Let's assume Abigail Boar had her costs assessed at $2,000 and that she was paid on November 30, year 1.

1. *Determine the amount of the judgment.*

    Judgment was for $80,000 + costs of $2,000 + interest of $5,343.36 = $87,343.36.

2. *Determine the postjudgment interest rate.*

    The day of judgment is November 15 in the fourth quarter of year 1, and assume that the rate in table 1 is 7 percent.

3. *Calculate the postjudgment interest.*

    Interest runs from the day after the judgment to the date of payment:

    November 16, year 1 to November 30, year 1 = 15 days
    $87,343.36 \times 0.07 \times {}^{15}\!/_{365} = $251.26

4. Calculate the amount due on November 30, year 1.

    $87,343.36 + $251.26 = $87,594.62

CHAPTER SUMMARY

In this chapter, we examined the procedural requirements involved in drafting, approving, signing, and entering orders, including challenging and varying orders that are not in accordance with a judge's endorsement. We distinguished between orders generally and orders on applications, motions, and from the Court of Appeal. We also distinguished orders generally from judgments after trial, noting the differences in form. We then turned to prejudgment and postjudgment interest, noting that prejudgment interest runs from the time the cause of action arises to the day of judgment, and is calculated on the amount of the judgment at an interest rate determined by a formula and set out in a table. We also made note of exclusions and types of damages using special calculations methods and special rates. We then turned to the calculation of postjudgment interest from the date of the order to payment, noting how the rate is established and the amount of the judgment on which it is calculated.

KEY TERMS

non-pecuniary

exemplary damages

punitive damages

NOTE

1 The procedure varies. In some places, a court clerk signs the order on behalf of the registrar. Judges can sign their own orders but rarely do so.

REFERENCES

Courts of Justice Act, RSO 1990, c. C.43.

Rules of Civil Procedure, RRO 1990, reg. 194.

REVIEW QUESTIONS

1. What is the difference between a judgment and an order?

2. What is an endorsement?

3. What does it mean to "approve the order as to form"?

4. Describe the process of signing an order.

5. What happens if the order is not approved as to form?

6. What happens if the registrar refuses to sign an order because he or she is not satisfied that it is in proper form or that it correctly reflects the contents of the endorsement?

7. Where are orders entered?

8. What should you do if you pay the amount due on an order or an amount that satisfies the judgment creditor?

9. What happens if there is an inadvertent error in the judgment?

10. On what can you obtain prejudgment and postjudgment interest?

11. How do you determine the appropriate interest rate to calculate prejudgment interest?

12. How do you determine the interest rate for calculating postjudgment interest?

13. How do you calculate the interest for special damages where they continue to accrue after the cause of action arose?

DISCUSSION QUESTIONS

1. Suppose Abigail is not successful at trial. You are asked to draft the judgment. You get the court file and find this endorsement on the back of the trial record: "September 27, year 1. Action dismissed with costs. Palardeau J." The trial took place in Toronto on September 10, 12, 13, 14, 26, and 27. Counsel and parties were all present and evidence was given orally. Draft the judgment.

2. Assume the same trial dates as in question 1, but suppose that Abigail is successful. The endorsement reads: "Judgment for the plaintiff. General damages $225,000. Special damages $87,242.03. Partial indemnity costs for the plaintiff together with prejudgment interest in the amount of $12,098.21."

3. Determine how much is owing to Abigail. Assume that Abigail obtained judgment for $100,000 for general damages for pain and suffering and $50,000 for out-of-pocket expenses or special damages, which accrued as follows: September 14, year 0 to March 13, year 1: $22,000; March 14, year 1 to September 13, year 1: $23,000; September 14 to 28, year 1: $5,000. The accident occurred on September 14, year 0. The action commenced on October 23, year 0, and judgment was granted on September 28, year 1.

4. Assume that Abigail obtained judgment on June 5, year 0 for $150,000, her costs were assessed at $10,000, and prejudgment interest was $3,000. Assume also that she was paid on October 15, year 0. Determine the amount of postjudgment interest and the total amount payable on October 15, year 0.

CHAPTER 18

Costs

INTRODUCTION

Although there are exceptions, a judge usually orders that the losing side pay part of the legal costs of the winning side. When speakers of legalese say "the costs are in the cause" or "the costs follow the event," this is what they mean: the winning side recovers some of its legal expenses from the losing side.

The jurisdiction of the court to award costs is provided in s. 131 of the *Courts of Justice Act*. The amount of costs or whether costs are awarded at all are matters totally in the discretion of the court. Although costs usually "follow the event" (that is, are awarded to the winner), the court sometimes awards costs or denies costs to express its disapproval of the way that one of the parties has conducted itself during the proceeding (rule 57.01(2)). For instance, if a party has prolonged the proceedings unnecessarily, the court may refuse to award costs to the party, even if the party wins the case. Moreover, depending on the inappropriateness of the conduct during the litigation, the court may even order the winning party to pay costs to the losing side.

HOW COSTS ARE DETERMINED

In determining whether costs are to be awarded, the court uses the factors set out in rule 57.01(1). These factors include such things as the amount of money the winning party recovered in the proceeding; the complexity of the proceeding; the importance of the issues; and the conduct of any party, including conduct resulting from negligence, mistake, or excessive caution. These factors now also include consideration of the experience of the lawyer for the party awarded costs, the rates charged, and the time spent. (The implication here is that the costs awarded bear some resemblance to what the client is actually paying for legal services.) Also to be considered is the amount of costs the party paying those costs might reasonably be expected to pay in the circumstances of the case.[1]

Rule 57.01(4)(e) now permits costs to be awarded to a party who represented himself or herself. Formerly, because the party did not pay fees to a lawyer, no costs were awarded in respect of fees. Now, the court may recognize the time and trouble spent by an unrepresented party on his or her own case and award an amount for expenses incurred by the unrepresented party, such as the loss of a day's pay. In addition, rule 57.04 provides costs sanctions if the case was brought improperly in the Superior Court rather than in the Small Claims Court. As you can see, in providing for the awarding of costs, the rules encourage parties to move their cases speedily and efficiently through the litigation process.

Although rule 57.01(4)(d) now explicitly permits the court to fully indemnify a costs recipient, costs in Ontario courts are rarely awarded on that basis. Rather, they usually cover only a portion of the actual legal costs of the party. The portion of the real legal costs covered depends on what scale is used to calculate the costs awarded. The court determines which scale is to be used when it awards costs. The two usual scales used are the partial indemnity scale and the substantial indemnity scale. In most cases, the partial indemnity scale is used. The court usually orders that the substantial indemnity scale be used only if the party who must pay costs has done something blameworthy during the litigation. Substantial indemnity costs, if awarded, are 1.5 times what they would have been if they had been awarded on a partial indemnity basis. On very rare occasions of particularly obnoxious conduct by a party, the court may order full indemnification.

Before January 1, 2002, when the rules relating to costs went through substantial change, the trial judge could determine both which party would be awarded costs and the actual monetary amount of the costs. Alternatively, the judge might make an order determining which party was to be awarded costs and leave the actual calculation of the amount of those costs to a court official called an assessment officer. When the judge determines not only who receives costs but also how much that person receives, this is called **fixing costs**. When the judge decides which party receives costs but leaves the assessment officer to decide the amount, this is called making an **assessment of costs**.

fixing costs
making an order that a specific party pay a specific amount of costs

assessment of costs
a costs order made by a judge where the actual amount of the costs is determined at a separate hearing by an assessment officer

When is it appropriate to follow the procedure for fixing costs rather than assessing them? Rules 57.01(3) and (3.1) indicate that when the court awards costs, it shall fix them unless the case is "exceptional." This clearly indicates a default rule that costs should be fixed rather than assessed whenever costs are ordered. It is not entirely clear what makes a case exceptional, so that an assessment should be ordered. If "it is more likely that the assessment process would be more suited to effect procedural and substantive justice," it should be used.[2] The fact that the case is complex or involves great expense will not make it exceptional. Rather, "there must be some element that is out of the ordinary or unusual that would warrant deviating from the presumption that costs are to be fixed."[3]

Whether costs are to be fixed or assessed, rules 57.01(5) and (6) indicate that after a trial, or on an application or a motion that finally disposes of an issue, it is appropriate to serve and file a **bill of costs** in form 57A and, presumably, have the costs assessed, provided the judge has so ordered. If costs have been awarded on a step in a proceeding, for example, after a motion, it is usual to fix costs at the end of the hearing rather than leave the costs of the motion to be dealt with by the trial judge at the end of the proceeding. In this case, where costs are ordered to be fixed, unless the parties have agreed on costs for that step, each side is expected to come to the hearing with a copy of a costs outline in form 57B, and give a copy to every other party. The costs outline is not to exceed three pages and it should summarize the disbursements and the basis for the claim for partial indemnity fees to be requested, focusing on the discretionary factors used to determine costs in rule 57.01.

bill of costs
list of allowable fees and disbursements that is used by an assessment officer to assess a litigant's costs after the litigant is successful in obtaining judgment; differs from an account because it does not include all fees charged to a client

In Toronto, at least, the practice appears to be to continue to assess costs after trial notwithstanding the suggestion in the rules that assessment is limited to "exceptional" cases. Bills of costs, which look a lot like a client's account in terms of detail, are used on the assessment, often with additional written submissions that may mirror some of the submissions in the costs outline, touching on relevant rule

57.01(1) factors. The costs outline is usually restricted to motions or other steps in a proceeding where costs are ordered to be fixed. If the assessment process was expected to wither away in favour of fixing costs in most cases, that does not appear to be happening.[4]

Prior to 2002, rule 57.01 set out the general factors that judges and assessment officers were to use in exercising their discretion in fixing or assessing costs. Rule 57.01 was substantially amended in 2002 and again in 2005. The purpose of the changes was:

- to encourage judges to fix costs in the quickest and least formal way possible, rather than to leave the determination of amounts to the more formal, expensive, and cumbersome assessment process;

- to make costs awards more predictable, uniform, and consistent; and

- to ensure that all relevant factors affecting costs are considered in making an award.

In 2002, a costs grid was introduced into tariff A, part I, which created a formula for determining hourly rates for fees for lawyers based on years of practice experience. Rates were also set for law clerks and students-at-law (articling students). The grid did create a more uniform and consistent pattern of awards, but it was perceived by the lawyers for clients who had to pay costs as being overly generous. The judges and masters began to treat the grid as a ceiling for fees and exercised their discretion to award less than the ceiling in most cases, thereby reducing consistency and predictability.

In 2005, the costs grid was repealed, and tariff A, part I, fees, now directs a judge, master, or assessment officer to set fees for lawyers, clerks, and students-at-law for any step or steps in the judicial process in accordance with the discretionary factors set out in rule 57.01(1). While primary reliance in determining costs is placed on the factors in rule 57.01(1), the Civil Rules Committee has attempted to resurrect the costs grid in a simplified form. In an undated "Information for the Profession,"[5] it proposed an abbreviated version of the repealed costs grid, with suggested maximum rates for clerks, articling students, and lawyers at three experience levels to be used in determining partial indemnity and substantial indemnity costs. The Information for the Profession referred to above that contains this "baby costs grid" is not part of the rules, nor is it a practice direction. Consequently, it has no legal force and, considering the criticism levelled at the old costs grid, it might be thought that the courts would ignore the old grid as well as the baby costs grid. It is clear, however, that that is not what is happening. In *Magnusson Furniture Inc. v. Mylex Ltd.*, decided in March 2008, the court of appeal held that a trial judge was entitled to use the old costs grid as a reference or guide in considering costs, particularly in assessing counsel fees at trial.

The mixed messages on factors to be considered to determine costs have created some confusion. However, to help guide the exercise of discretion to fix costs and to assist parties in focusing on those factors, form 57B, costs outline, has been introduced. Figure 18.1 shows the costs outline for the Boar–Rattle proceeding. Unless the parties have agreed on costs for a proceeding or a step in it, each party must give a copy of the costs outline to other parties involved, and bring a copy to any hearing to fix costs.

In the costs outline, each party seeking costs sets out the fees for services at each step of the proceeding other than appearing in court, an estimated counsel fee for each day or part of a day spent in court, and all disbursements, which should be set out as an appendix to the form. The form sets out rule 57.01 costs factors, where parties can indicate information relevant to each factor. For example, for "the amount claimed and the amount recovered in the proceeding," a party may indicate that he or she claimed $100,000 in damages but obtained judgment for $60,000. Because the party did not obtain full recovery, this factor might be given a lower weight than it otherwise would have been and might reduce the costs awarded.

Specifically, the form requires that the hours docketed for each step be given, along with the hourly rate charged to the client for the lawyer, clerk, or student-at-law doing it. The form then requires the partial indemnity rate sought for each person providing service. This rate should clearly be below the rate actually charged, although how much lower is hard to determine. Prior to the introduction of the cost grid, the costs awards varied from one-third to two-thirds of the fees actually charged based on fees for each step in the proceeding, set out in tariff A. The amounts in tariff A prior to 2002 had not changed in years and were unrealistically low, given the actual costs of litigation. But, as deficient as the old tariff was, it at least provided monetary amounts for each step. Now, with no objective means of determining the appropriate fee, outcomes will, at least initially, be hard to predict. One thing is clear: if substantial indemnity costs are ordered, they will be 1.5 times what the partial indemnity costs would have been. As substantial indemnity costs should be somewhat less than the costs charged to the client, a "cap" of sorts is created for partial indemnity costs; because the scales are still subjective, it is hard to be more precise than this in stating what proportion partial indemnity costs should be to costs charged to the client. After determining the fee to be claimed, the lawyer completing form 57B must then also complete the certificate indicating that the hours claimed, rates for fees, and disbursements incurred are correctly stated.

Rule 57.01(7) indicates that the court shall keep cost and delay to a minimum when fixing costs by keeping the process as simple as possible. In particular, the court may require written submissions, including copies of the costs outline, without holding oral hearings.

Costs may be fixed after a trial, and also in other proceedings, including contested motions. Rule 57.03 requires judges and masters to fix costs on contested motions, rather than refer them to the trial judge, unless there is a good reason for doing otherwise. The costs outline is clearly designed for use here.

After a trial, the party that has been awarded costs must prepare a bill of costs in form 57A. The amounts in the bill of costs for fees are based on tariff A, as was the case for the costs outline. The disbursements are found in tariff A, part II. If the costs are fixed after a trial, a party prepares and files a bill of costs with the court and, if there is a dispute, a copy of the costs outline as well. If costs have been ordered to be assessed under rule 58 by an assessment officer, the parties must follow the procedures in rule 58.

FIGURE 18.1   COSTS OUTLINE (FORM 57B)

Court file no. 01-CV-1234

ONTARIO
SUPERIOR COURT OF JUSTICE

BETWEEN:

ABIGAIL BOAR

Plaintiff

and

RATTLE MOTORS LTD. and FRED FLOGEM

Defendants

COSTS OUTLINE

The Plaintiff provides the following outline of the submissions to be made at the hearing in support of the costs the party will seek if successful:

Fees (as detailed below)	$ 1,712.50
Estimated counsel fee for appearance	3,750.00
GST on fees	273.13
Disbursements (as detailed in the attached appendix)	791.00*
Total	$6,526.63

The following points are made in support of the costs sought with reference to the factors set out in subrule 57.01(1):

- the amount claimed and the amount recovered in the proceeding

  $203,649.00 was claimed, and the amount recovered was $190,000.00

- the complexity of the proceeding

  personal injury action, made more complicated factually by corporate defendant's destruction of lighting system prior to discovery; inadequate lighting was central to the plaintiff's allegation of negligence

- the importance of the issues

  injury to plaintiff was severe, causing her serious financial loss

- the conduct of any party that tended to shorten or to lengthen unnecessarily the duration of the proceeding

  the corporate defendant unnecessarily resisted inspections of premises under rule 32

- whether any step in the proceeding was improper, vexatious or unnecessary or taken through negligence, mistake or excessive caution

  not applicable

---

*   Fees are calculated at the partial indemnity rate claimed. In this case, 50 percent of the rate is charged to the client. The partial indemnity rate is subjective and could be between 40 and 60 percent of the rate charged to the client.

FIGURE 18.1   CONTINUED

- a party's denial or refusal to admit anything that should have been admitted

  the defendants refused to cooperate on admissions under
  rule 51

- the experience of the party's lawyer

  I.M. Just, 9 years' experience

- the hours spent, the rates sought for costs and the rate actually charged by the party's lawyer

FEE ITEMS (e.g., pleadings, affidavits, cross-examinations, preparation, hearing, etc.)	PERSONS (identify the lawyers, students, and law clerks who provided services in connection with each item together with their year of call, if applicable)	HOURS (specify the hours claimed for each person identified in column 2)	PARTIAL INDEMNITY RATE (specify the rate being sought for each person identified in column 2)	ACTUAL RATE*
Drafting statement of claim	I.M. Just, year of call year –9	1.5 hrs	150.00	300.00
Drafting reply to statement of defence	I.M. Just	0.75 hrs	150.00	300.00
Drafting affidavit of service	Edward Egregious, Law Clerk	0.5 hrs	50.00	80.00
Drafting affidavit of documents	Edward Egregious, Law Clerk	4.5 hrs	50.00	80.00
	I.M. Just	0.5 hrs	150.00	300.00
Attendance at discovery	I.M. Just	5.0 hrs	150.00	300.00
Attendance at pretrial	I.M. Just	2.0 hrs	150.00	300.00

* Specify the rate being charged to the client for each person identified in column 2. If there is a contingency fee arrangement, state the rate that would have been charged absent such arrangement.

- any other matter relevant to the question of costs

  not applicable

LAWYER'S CERTIFICATE

I CERTIFY that the hours claimed have been spent, that the rates shown are correct and that each disbursement has been incurred as claimed.

Date: September 5, Year 3   I.M. Just

FIGURE 18.1 CONCLUDED

APPENDIX A: DISBURSEMENTS

```
DISBURSEMENTS SUBJECT TO GST
Paid to process server to serve statement of claim    $ 60.00
Paid to official examiner                              200.00
                                                      $260.00
GST                                                     13.00*
Total disbursements subject to GST                    $273.00

DISBURSEMENTS NOT SUBJECT TO GST

Paid to issue statement of claim                      $181.00
Paid to set matter down for trial                      337.00
Total disbursements not subject to GST                $518.00
TOTAL DISBURSEMENTS                                   $791.00
```

* GST calculated at 5 percent.

GST AND COSTS

Charging clients GST on legal fees and disbursements

Fees charged by lawyers and paralegals for legal services are subject to GST and some, but not all, disbursements are also subject to GST. When preparing bills of costs, costs outlines, and client accounts, GST, where appropriate, should be included. Below is a list of disbursements that are subject to GST and a list of those that are not. Generally, fees paid to the court to issue or file documents are exempt from GST. Services paid for, such as expert reports and transcript preparation, are subject to GST.

When making claims for costs, you should always ask for costs inclusive of GST to maximize the costs award.

Common disbursements exempt from GST

Court fees paid to file claims, defences, motions, and pleadings, or to set a matter down for trial, file a trial record, obtain an order, obtain a summons or subpoena, or file an enforcement document. Generally, any fee paid to a court to file a document or take a step in a proceeding is not subject to GST.

Common disbursements subject to GST

- Witness fee, whether set by legislation or agreed to by the parties; this includes witnesses' travel and accommodation expenses.

- Fees for recording services, transcript production, and special examiner fees, whether prescribed by statute or not.

- Fees to serve documents.

- Fees for expert report/attendance, including the costs of preparing a report.

- Fee to obtain court transcript.

For further information about GST on legal fees and disbursements, including information on various practice areas, see Canada Revenue Agency Policy Statement P-209R, available on the CRA website at http://www.cra-arc.gc.ca. Search for P-209R.

PREPARATION OF A BILL OF COSTS

A bill of costs is form 57A and appears as figure 18.2. In order to complete the form, you need the time dockets for the client's files, showing specific work that has been done on the file and the amount of time it took to accomplish each task.

You must then sort the time dockets into tasks that involve procedures authorized by the rules, such as drafting of pleadings or attendance at a mandatory mediation session, and tasks that are services provided to the client but that are not covered by the rules, such as meetings with clients for the purpose of taking instruction.

A step-by-step guide for calculating costs is provided below.

1. *Determine the scale that the costs are to be calculated under.* This can be determined from the order or judgment.

2. *Divide the time dockets for the file into items that cannot be included in the bill of costs, items to be included as non-counsel fees, and items to be included as counsel fees.* Counsel fees are those fees directly related to the lawyer's appearance in court and are flat amounts per day or, if for less than a full day, for a half day. It is up to the lawyer to determine his or her counsel fees, usually based on years of experience.

3. *Determine the years of experience for each lawyer involved in the file, and the actual rate charged the client, as well as the partial indemnity rate your firm wishes to claim.*

4. *Determine whether any procedure to be included in the bill of costs was performed by a law clerk or a student-at-law and determine the rate charged the client, as well as the partial indemnity rate your firm wishes to claim.*

5. *Calculate allowable disbursements.* Look at part II of tariff A to determine whether a particular type of disbursement is an allowable item in the bill of costs, and ascertain how much can be billed for each type.

6. *Attach time dockets.* You must attach the actual time dockets for the fees claimed to the bill of costs.

7. *Attach evidence of disbursements.* For disbursements claimed, you must attach copies of invoices, cancelled cheques for payment of issuing fees, and any other evidence that proves the disbursements were incurred.

ASSESSMENT OF COSTS

If the court does not fix costs at the completion of the motion or trial, the court awards costs to a particular party and refers the matter to an assessment officer for an assessment of costs. The assessment officer is a court official who has the responsibility of determining the exact monetary amount to be awarded to that party. In assessing the costs, the assessment officer looks to rule 58, which determines the assessment procedure.

A party entitled to costs files a bill of costs, including supporting documents (such as receipts and docket sheets), and a copy of the order awarding costs (rule 58.03(1)). Once these documents are filed, the entitled party can then obtain

FIGURE 18.2   BILL OF COSTS (FORM 57A)

Court file no. 01-CV-1234

ONTARIO
SUPERIOR COURT OF JUSTICE

BETWEEN:

ABIGAIL BOAR

Plaintiff

and

RATTLE MOTORS LTD. and FRED FLOGEM

Defendants

BILL OF COSTS

AMOUNTS CLAIMED FOR FEES AND DISBURSEMENTS

FEES OTHER THAN COUNSEL FEES

1. Drafting and issuing statement of claim	1.5 hours	
I.M. Just, January 3, year 1		
2. Receiving and drafting reply to statement of defence	0.75 hours	
I.M. Just, February 5, year 1		
3. Drafting affidavit of service	0.5 hours	
Edward Egregious, law clerk, January 5, year 1		
4. Drafting affidavit of documents		
Edward Egregious, February 7, year 1	4.5 hours	
I.M. Just, February 9, year 1	0.5 hours	
5. Attendance at examination for discovery	5.0 hours	
I.M. Just, February 10, year 1		
6. Attendance at pretrial conference	2.0 hours	
I.M. Just, May 20, year 3		

FEES OTHER THAN COUNSEL FEES   1,712.50

COUNSEL FEE

7. Attendance at trial of the matter
    I.M. Just, July 10, 11, 12, year 3
    3 days x $1,250

COUNSEL FEE   3,750.00

TOTAL FEES (BEFORE GST) $5,462.50

GST FEES   273.13

TOTAL FEES $5,735.63

FIGURE 18.2 CONCLUDED

```
DISBURSEMENTS SUBJECT TO GST
Paid to process server to serve
  statement of claim                          $ 60.00
Paid to official examiner                      200.00
                                              $260.00
GST                                             13.00*
Total disbursements subject to GST            $273.00

DISBURSEMENTS NOT SUBJECT TO GST

Paid to issue statement of claim              $181.00
Paid to set matter down for trial              337.00
Total disbursements not subject to GST        $518.00

TOTAL DISBURSEMENTS                           $791.00
TOTAL FEES AND DISBURSEMENTS                $6,526.63


STATEMENT OF EXPERIENCE

A claim for fees is being made with respect to the following
lawyers:
Name of lawyer                  Years of experience
I.M. Just                       9 years
```

TO:

```
Huey Sue
LSUC #23456T
Barrister and Solicitor
65 False Trail
Toronto, Ontario, M6Y 1Z6

tel. 416-485-6891
fax 416-485-6892

Lawyer for the Defendants
```

* GST calculated at 5 percent.

---

a notice of appointment for assessment of costs, form 58A, from the office of the assessment officer. The notice of appointment for assessment and the bill of costs must be served on all parties who have an interest in the assessment at least seven days before the date of the assessment (rule 58.03(2)). A sample notice of appointment for assessment of costs appears as figure 18.3.

If the party entitled to costs does not serve the bill of costs for assessment within a reasonable time, the party who has been ordered to pay the costs may obtain a notice to deliver a bill of costs for assessment, form 58B, from the assessment officer and serve it on every party who has an interest in the costs issue at least 21 days before the date set for the assessment. A sample notice to deliver a bill of costs for assessment appears as figure 18.4.

FIGURE 18.3   NOTICE OF APPOINTMENT FOR ASSESSMENT OF COSTS (FORM 58A)

Court file no. 01-CV-1234

ONTARIO
SUPERIOR COURT OF JUSTICE

BETWEEN:

ABIGAIL BOAR

Plaintiff

and

RATTLE MOTORS LTD. and FRED FLOGEM

Defendants

NOTICE OF APPOINTMENT FOR ASSESSMENT OF COSTS

TO THE PARTIES

I HAVE MADE AN APPOINTMENT to assess the costs of the plaintiff, a copy of whose bill of costs is attached to this notice, on Tuesday July 30, Year 3 at 2:00 p.m., at the Court House, 393 University Avenue, Toronto, Ontario, M5G 1E6.

Date: July 20, Year 3

_____
Assessment officer

TO:
Huey Sue
LSUC #23456T
Barrister and Solicitor
65 False Trail
Toronto, Ontario, M6Y 1Z6

tel. 416-485-6891
fax 416-485-6892

Lawyer for the Defendants

FIGURE 18.4   NOTICE TO DELIVER A BILL OF COSTS FOR ASSESSMENT (FORM 58B)

Court file no. 01-CV-1234

ONTARIO
SUPERIOR COURT OF JUSTICE

BETWEEN:

ABIGAIL BOAR

Plaintiff

and

RATTLE MOTORS LTD. and FRED FLOGEM

Defendants

NOTICE TO DELIVER A BILL OF COSTS FOR ASSESSMENT

TO THE PARTIES

I HAVE MADE AN APPOINTMENT, at the request of the defendant Rattle Motors Ltd., to assess the costs of the plaintiff on Tuesday July 30, year 3, at 2:00 p.m., at the Court House, 393 University Avenue, Toronto, Ontario, M5G 1E6.

TO:
Just & Coping
Barristers and Solicitors
365 Bay Street - 8701
Toronto, Ontario, M3J 4A9

I.M. Just
LSUC #12345R
tel. 416-762-1342
fax 416-762-2300

Lawyers for the Plaintiff

YOU ARE REQUIRED to file your bill of costs with me and serve your bill of costs on every party interested in the assessment at least seven days before the above date.

Date: July 21, Year 3

_____
Assessment officer

Once the party entitled to costs is served with the notice to deliver a bill of costs for assessment, the entitled party must file and serve a bill of costs on every interested party at least seven days before the date set for the assessment. If the entitled party does not serve a bill of costs as required, then the assessment officer may proceed to fix the costs, without the bill of costs.

On the date of the assessment, the interested parties appear before the assessment officer. The items in the bill of costs are examined, and the parties make submissions orally and in writing on any items that they wish to challenge or defend. The assessment officer then reviews the items and determines whether they reflect a reasonable amount of time spent on a particular step. For instance, the assessment officer might not allow a party to claim 3.5 hours for drafting a simple notice of motion. That amount of time is excessive for a routine matter. In deciding whether the expenditure of time or any other item in the bill of costs is reasonable, the assessment officer may take into consideration the factors listed in rule 58.06(1).

The assessment officer must apply tariff A, parts I and II with respect to fees and disbursements. Part I, fees, directs the officer to the factors in rule 57.01. Part II lists the disbursements that are allowable. These include court fees and necessary expenses incurred by or on behalf of a party, such as the costs of serving documents. Sometimes, with an unusual disbursement, it may be necessary to prepare an affidavit to prove the disbursement. The assessment officer also has the authority under the rules to require a party to produce books and records for the purpose of the assessment.

In addition, the assessment officer is bound to follow any direction given by the court that made the order for costs. Pursuant to rule 57.02, the court that awards costs may provide specific directions to the assessment officer as to how the costs are to be assessed. If there is such a direction on any item, the assessment officer must follow it. For example, the court may order that an item that is not included in part II of tariff A be assessed as a legitimate disbursement.

As you can see, an assessment hearing requires the lawyers to provide ample documentary evidence to support claimed fees and disbursements, and each side can cross-examine the other on any of the material presented. The process is, in effect, an accounting, which is by its nature a time-consuming process. In a complex matter, an assessment hearing could take days. It is no wonder that rules 57.01(3) and (3.1) direct that costs be fixed rather than assessed unless the case is exceptional.

Following the assessment, the assessment officer must provide a certificate of assessment of costs, form 58C, that sets out the amount of the costs allowed. Once the certificate is completed, it has the same effect as an order of the court and may be enforced in the same way as a court order. A sample of a certificate of assessment of costs appears as figure 18.5.

If, at the completion of the assessment, any of the parties is unhappy with the assessment officer's decision, he or she may ask the assessment officer to withhold the certificate for seven days. During the period that the certificate is withheld, the objecting party must serve a written copy of his or her objections on every other interested party and file them with the assessment officer. Any party served with the objections may prepare a reply to the objections, serve them on the other parties, and file the reply with the assessment officer. The assessment officer, on receiving an objection, must reconsider the initial assessment and then complete the certificate

FIGURE 18.5   CERTIFICATE OF ASSESSMENT OF COSTS (FORM 58C)

Court file no. 01-CV-1234

ONTARIO
SUPERIOR COURT OF JUSTICE

BETWEEN:

ABIGAIL BOAR

Plaintiff

and

RATTLE MOTORS LTD. and FRED FLOGEM

Defendants

CERTIFICATE OF ASSESSMENT OF COSTS

I CERTIFY that I have assessed the costs of the plaintiff in this proceeding under the authority of the order of the Honourable Madam Justice Snork, dated July 12, year 3, and I ALLOW THE SUM OF $12,000.

THE COSTS ALLOWED IN THIS ASSESSMENT BEAR INTEREST at the rate of 6.75 per cent per year commencing on July 12, year 3.

Date: July 12, year 3

_____
Assessment officer

of assessment, which may be amended as a result of the reconsideration. A party that is still not satisfied may appeal the assessment officer's decision to the court that made the original costs order.

ASSESSMENT OF COSTS ON SETTLEMENTS AND ABANDONED CASES

It is usually costs that have been awarded by the court at the completion of a trial or a motion that are referred to assessment. However, sometimes a case settles or is abandoned before it gets to trial. In such cases, the parties may agree that costs are appropriate. Especially where a case is abandoned, one party may believe it is entitled to costs.

It is often a condition of the settlement of a proceeding that one party pay costs. Parties that agree to costs being a condition of settling a case usually draft minutes of settlement that contain the specific amount of costs to be paid. However, where the payment of costs is a condition of settlement and the amount is not included in the settlement, the costs may be assessed pursuant to rule 57.04 by one of the parties filing a copy of the minutes of settlement in the office of the assessment officer.

Likewise, the costs on an abandoned motion, application, or appeal may also be assessed if one of the parties files

- the served notice of motion or application and an affidavit stating that the document was not filed within the time prescribed by the rules or that the initiator of the proceeding did not appear on the court date;

- a served notice of abandonment; or

- a copy of any order dismissing the case as abandoned.

COST IMPLICATIONS OF OFFERS TO SETTLE

The legal system has a major interest in having matters settle without trial. The rules provide many methods of encouraging parties to settle their disputes. One of these rules is rule 49, which deals with offers to settle. An offer to settle is a proposal made by a party to the litigation that attempts to resolve one or more of the issues between the parties. For example, the defendant may offer the plaintiff a portion of the damages being sought.

Rule 49 provides procedures for making and withdrawing offers. Rule 49.10 deals with the cost consequences when reasonable offers to settle are made by one party but not accepted by the party to whom they are made. The rule sets out three criteria regarding the offer to settle and its acceptance:

1. the offer to settle must have been made at least seven days before the commencement of the hearing;

2. the offer to settle must not be withdrawn and must not expire before the commencement of the hearing; and

3. the offer must not be accepted by the opposite party.

The consequences that flow from meeting these criteria are set out below.

Offer to settle made by plaintiff

If all three of these criteria are met and the offer to settle is made by a plaintiff who obtains an order at the end of the proceeding that is *as good as, or better than, the offer made*, the plaintiff is entitled to partial indemnity costs to the date the offer to settle was served and substantial indemnity costs from that date onward unless the court orders otherwise.

Stated another way, the plaintiff makes an offer to the defendant to settle the case for less money than the plaintiff is suing for. The defendant does not accept the plaintiff's offer, and the case goes to trial. At the end of the trial, the plaintiff wins the case, and the court awards the plaintiff the same amount of money or more than the amount that the plaintiff offered to settle the case for. The defendant may be ordered to pay higher costs than he or she would usually have to pay because the costs are based on the substantial indemnity scale from the date that the offer was made until the end of the trial. The higher costs for the defendant are ordered because the defendant, by refusing a "good" offer, was the cause of an unnecessary trial.

Offer to settle made by defendant

If all three of the criteria are met and the offer to settle is made by a defendant and the plaintiff obtains an order at trial that is *only as good as, or is worse than, the offer made*, the plaintiff is entitled to partial indemnity costs to the date the offer was served, and the defendant is entitled to partial indemnity costs from that date onward, unless the court orders otherwise.

In this situation, the defendant has made an offer to settle the case for less money than the plaintiff is seeking from the court. The plaintiff does not accept the offer and ultimately wins the case. However, the court does not accept the plaintiff's claim for damages and instead orders the defendant to pay damages to the plaintiff in an amount that is equal to, or lower than, the amount contained in the defendant's offer to settle. Because the plaintiff could have saved the time and expense of the trial by accepting an offer that was as good as, or better than, he or she ultimately received in the judgment, the plaintiff is entitled to costs on a partial indemnity scale only to the time the offer was made. After that date, the plaintiff must pay partial indemnity costs to the defendant.

The obvious intention of this rule is to ensure that parties think carefully about rejecting any reasonable offer to settle. If they reject an offer that turns out to be either as good as, or better than, the order eventually made by the court, the rejecting party suffers cost consequences.

Because of this rule, it is wise to structure all offers to settle a case in such a way that they automatically expire either within a specified period or at the commencement of the trial. If the offer to settle does not contain an automatic expiry period, it is important to withdraw it before the commencement of a trial, unless it is intended as a rule 49 offer.

Offer made in a case with multiple defendants

In many cases, the plaintiff names more than one defendant and claims they are jointly and severally liable for damages. Rule 49.10 does not apply to the situation of multiple defendants unless the plaintiff makes an offer to settle that includes all the defendants. If the offer is made by the defendants to the plaintiff, rule 49.10 does not apply unless the offer includes all the defendants or the defendants making the offer also agree to pay the costs of any defendant not joining in the offer (rule 49.11).

Offer to contribute

If the plaintiff is suing more than one defendant and claiming that the defendants are jointly and severally responsible for the damages, one defendant can make an offer to another defendant under rule 49.12. The offer would be to contribute to the plaintiff's claimed damages in a specific amount.

A plaintiff who is suing more than one defendant, claiming that they are jointly and severally liable, is saying that they each are totally liable for all the damages. A plaintiff who wins such a case can go after any of the defendants for all the money. He or she need not take a specific portion from each of them unless the court orders otherwise. The plaintiff obviously wants to go after the defendant with the most money to collect the amount owing with the least trouble. For instance, if Abigail is successful against both the defendants Fred Flogem and Rattle Motors Ltd., unless the court orders otherwise, she is likely to seek all the money from Rattle Motors Ltd.

Rattle Motors Ltd. is more likely to have the money available because Rattle Motors Ltd. is a business, whereas Fred, who is an individual employed as a car salesman, may or may not have the funds available.

Rule 49.12 provides that Rattle Motors Ltd. can offer to split Abigail's claim with Fred on a 50/50 basis. If this offer is accepted, Rattle Motors Ltd. will pay half of Abigail's damages, and Fred will pay the other half. Rattle Motors Ltd. initiates this by serving Fred with a offer to contribute, form 49D.

If Fred rejects Rattle Motors Ltd.'s offer and Abigail eventually wins her case against both of them, the court can take Fred's rejection of Rattle Motors Ltd.'s offer to contribute into account when awarding costs. The court may require Fred to pay Rattle Motors Ltd.'s costs, and it may require Fred to pay not only his own share of the costs to Abigail, but Rattle Motors Ltd.'s share as well.

Discretion of the court to consider any offer to settle

Rule 49.13 gives the court discretion to consider any offer to settle when making an order as to costs. This means that the court is not restricted to addressing cost issues in the manner set out in the rules.

SECURITY FOR COSTS

If a plaintiff is unsuccessful, the defendant is usually entitled to costs. Collecting costs from a plaintiff who does not have sufficient assets in Ontario is difficult. Rule 56 therefore provides a method for a defendant to bring a motion to the court asking that a plaintiff be required to pay money into court to be held for the duration of the proceeding. If the plaintiff is the successful party, the money is returned at the conclusion of the case. However, if the plaintiff is unsuccessful and the defendant is awarded costs, the costs are paid out of the money held by the court. The money held in the court is called "security for costs."

Rule 56.01(1) lists the circumstances in which security for costs is available. Security is most commonly sought and granted when plaintiffs reside outside the jurisdiction and may not have sufficient assets in Ontario to satisfy an order for costs made against them.

A defendant who is not certain where a plaintiff normally resides can demand in writing that the plaintiff's lawyer declare in writing whether the plaintiff is a resident of Ontario (rule 56.02). Failure of the plaintiff's lawyer to answer the demand may result in the court dismissing or staying the case. Staying a case means suspending it.

When the case is brought by way of an action, the motion for security for costs can be brought only after the defendant has delivered a defence. Notice of the motion must be served on the plaintiff and on every defendant who has delivered a defence or a notice of intent to defend.

When the case is brought by way of application, the motion for security can be brought only after the respondent has delivered a notice of appearance. Notice of the motion must be served on the applicant and every other respondent who has delivered a notice of appearance.

Once security for costs has been ordered, the plaintiff cannot take any further steps in the proceeding until the security has been paid into court. If the plaintiff does not comply with the order for security, the court may dismiss or stay the case.

When the plaintiff has posted the security, he or she must immediately give notice to every other party that he or she has complied with the order.

CHAPTER SUMMARY

In this chapter, we have seen that s. 131 of the *Courts of Justice Act* gives the court jurisdiction to award costs and that rules 57 and 58 deal with the procedure for awarding costs and the assessment of costs. Generally, the losing party must pay costs to the successful party, but we have noted exceptions to this. The rules require that the court fix costs in all but exceptional cases, where the court may refer the case for an assessment of costs.

We observed that costs may be awarded on either a partial indemnity scale, a substantial indemnity scale, or a full indemnity scale. The ordinary scale is partial indemnity. Tariff A, part I refers to the factors in rule 57.01 that guide discretion in determining costs. Part II of the tariff deals with the disbursements that may be included in an award of costs.

At the end of the proceeding, we saw that the party who is awarded costs must prepare, serve, and file a bill of costs or a costs outline, depending on the costs order and the nature of the proceedings. A guide was provided for preparing a costs outline and a bill of costs.

Since the court wants to encourage litigants to settle cases wherever possible, there are cost penalties for rejecting a reasonable offer to settle made by the opposite party pursuant to the rules. We reviewed rule 49 in this regard. Finally, we examined rule 56, which provides a procedure for requiring a plaintiff to post security for costs.

KEY TERMS

fixing costs

assessment of costs

bill of costs

NOTES

1   See rule 57.01(1) for a complete list of the factors to be considered in the awarding of costs.

2   *Authorson (Litigation Guardian of) v. Canada* (2002), 215 DLR (4th) 544 (Ont. CA).

3   *Boucher v. Public Accountants Council for the Province of Ontario* (2002), 28 CPC (5th) 25 (SCJ).

4   The authors wish to thank Toronto litigators D. Barry Prentice, Austin Riley, and Gregory W.M. Cooper for sharing their experience with the costs fixing and assessment process in Toronto.

5   See rule 57 in James J. Carthy, W.A. Derry Millar, and Jeffrey G. Cowan, *Ontario Annual Practice* (Aurora, ON: Canada Law Book, 2008-9), 1124-25.

REFERENCES

Carthy, James J., W.A. Derry Millar, and Jeffrey G. Cowan, *Ontario Annual Practice* (Aurora, ON: Canada Law Book, published annually).

Magnusson Furniture Inc. v. Mylex Ltd. (2008), 89 OR (3d) 401 (CA).

Rules of Civil Procedure, RRO 1990, reg. 194.

REVIEW QUESTIONS

1. The plaintiff in the case of *Smith v. Jones* sued for $150,000 in damages and was successful. No offer to settle was made. What costs is a court likely to award?

2. The plaintiff in the case of *Mahoud v. Balucci* sued for $25,000. She won the case, but the court awarded her only $7,000 in damages. How might the court approach a cost award in this case? What rule would apply? Why do you think this rule exists?

3. Explain the difference between the fixing of costs and the assessment of costs.

4. Your law firm acted for an unsuccessful plaintiff in a proceeding. The court awarded costs to the defendant. Two months have passed since the making of the order, and the defendant has not yet served and filed a bill of costs. How should your firm proceed? What rule or rules should it look to for guidance?

5. Your client is a defendant being sued by a plaintiff who lives in New York State. What are the cost implications? What must be done to protect your client? What rule applies?

6. The plaintiff is suing the defendant for damages in the amount of $300,000. Following the examinations for discovery, the defendant makes an offer to settle for $200,000. The plaintiff rejects the offer. A trial takes place. The plaintiff is successful and is awarded $200,000 in damages by the court. What are the cost implications? What rule applies?

DISCUSSION QUESTIONS

1. You are the law clerk for B.A. Doowright and Associates, the lawyers for the plaintiff in the case of *Sam Sunshine v. Fast and Loose Delivery Services Ltd.* Sam has won his case against the defendant, and you must now draft a bill of costs. The court has ordered that the plaintiff shall have costs on a partial indemnity scale up to January 10, year 1 and substantial indemnity scale after that date. This order was made because the defendant had rejected an offer to settle made by the plaintiff. However, at the end of the case, the court awarded the plaintiff larger damages than those he proposed in the rejected offer. The various members of the firm who worked on this file are:

B.A. Doowright, lawyer: 21 years' experience

M.A. Blitz, lawyer: 2 years' experience

Sally Smart, law clerk

The file shows the following time docket items:

a. institution of action, including drafting pleadings: July 10, year 0
   i. Doowright: 0.5 hours
   ii. Blitz: 3.0 hours
   iii. Smart: 2.0 hours

b. discovery of documents, including drafting affidavit of documents: September 16, year 0
   i. Smart: 1.5 hours
   ii. Blitz: 1.0 hours

c. examination for discovery: October 11 and 12, year 0

  i. Doowright: 1.5 hours
  ii. Smart: 1.0 hours

d. counsel fee at trial: February 1, 2, and 3, year 1

  i. Doowright: 3 days

e. drafting judgment, February 6, year 1

  i. Smart: 0.5 hours

The disbursements on the file are as follows:

a. paid court $181 for issuing of statement of claim

b. paid $40 for service of statement of claim

c. paid $40 for service of affidavit of documents

d. paid $250 to expert witness at trial

e. paid $337 to file the record

Draft a bill of costs.

2. Your law firm represents the plaintiff. The defendant brought a motion to dismiss your client's action. Your law firm spent a great deal of time preparing the necessary documents, serving and filing them, and taking other necessary steps to deal with the defendant's motion, including appearing in court to argue it. Neither the defendant nor his counsel appeared on the motion. You telephoned the office of the defendant's counsel and were told that the client no longer intends to ask for a dismissal of the case. Your client asks if there is anything you can do to force the defendant to pay some of her legal expenses. Is there something you can do? What is it? What rule applies?

CHAPTER 19

Statement of accounts

INTRODUCTION

If Abigail Boar wins at trial and there is no appeal, the work on her case is done, and I.M. Just will send out her final account. If the law practice is managed well, Just & Coping will have sent her interim accounts at the end of various stages in the proceeding. In most civil litigation cases, interim accounts are sent out at the close of pleadings, the conclusion of discoveries, and near the beginning of trial when pretrial preparation gets underway. Just & Coping may also have asked Abigail to **refresh the retainer** by making further deposits on account of fees when each interim account is rendered. If Just and Coping had taken Abigail on as a client on a contingency fee basis, she would not have paid them anything prior to trial. But her lawyers will be able to take between 15 and 30 percent of a judgment as their fee (and will get nothing if Abigail loses the case). Before reading this chapter, review the section of chapter 2 that deals with client accounts, particularly docketing and disbursements.

refresh the retainer
make a further deposit against future fees as a case progresses

GATHERING INFORMATION TO PREPARE THE CLIENT'S ACCOUNT

The following is a step-by-step guide to gathering the relevant information.

1. *Collect all docket slips or sheets.* If a file has been well managed, this information will have been entered periodically on docketing software. If this has not been done and paper dockets have been used, collect these for entry. If other lawyers or law clerks have worked on the file, you should include their dockets. Lawyers who are not partners (as well as those who are) have their salaries tied directly or indirectly to their billings. It is important for them to have their hours properly billed.

   If, in reviewing the file, you see that there has been work done for which there are no dockets, you should alert the lawyer with **carriage** of the file. Do not try to solve this problem yourself, and do not manufacture docket slips after the fact, even if you think they are likely to be accurate, because the law society considers this to be unprofessional conduct.

   carriage
   responsibility for a file or a case

2. *Check billable disbursements.* Disbursements are expenses paid by the law firm out of the firm's general account. These include charges for photocopying, long distance calls, courier services, fees paid to witnesses, fees paid for expert reports, and filing fees. Some expenses, such as

courier services, that generate receipts will probably be properly entered on the client ledger card, but others, such as photocopying, may not be, and you may need to search out this information.

3. *Check credits to the client's account recorded on the ledger card.* Credits include any retainer/deposits not yet billed or accounted for, and any receipts by the lawyer in trust for the client — for example, payment of a judgment. You should be able to use this information to summarize trust account transfers in a trust statement at the end of the account.

You should now be ready to prepare the draft account.

COMPONENTS OF A CLIENT ACCOUNT

An account is usually prepared on the firm's letterhead or on special account letterhead and addressed to the client. The format may vary. Some lawyers favour sending out a brief account, which simply says "for professional services rendered," followed by the total fees and disbursements. This is accompanied by a reporting letter from the lawyer, describing the work done, giving further advice if required, and informing the client that details of the account will be furnished on request. Other lawyers favour a more detailed account with a reporting letter. What follows is a description of what goes into a detailed account.

Description of fees

This is almost always presented in chronological order and tells a story that shows what work the lawyer did on a case. It may be in one long narrative paragraph, setting out the date of an activity, its description, and the time taken to do it, in 10ths of an hour — for example, .1 hour or .2 hour. If the account covers several months, it may list all activities for each month under a subheading for each month. Whatever variation is used, you should describe the activity, the date(s) on which it occurred, the person who did it, and the amount of time taken to do it.

Totalling of fees

When you have finished describing the work done, add up the work done by each lawyer or law clerk on the file, and multiply the hours by the appropriate rate. For example:

> I.M. Just, lawyer: 18.3 hours × $250 per hour = $4,575
> Edward Egregious, law clerk: 10 hours × $75 per hour = $750

Then, total the fees. To the total of $5,325 in the above example, you must then add 5 percent GST ($5,325 × 0.05 = $266.25), for a grand total of $5,591.25.

GST

GST is the federal goods and services tax. It applies to some, but not all, of the items that are billed by lawyers in an account. There is some room for interpretation as to how the tax applies to specific items, but you should note that GST is chargeable on the fees charged by lawyers for their professional services, including the services of clerks, articling students, and associates, as well as disbursements where a service is provided. Court fees are not subject to GST. See the note on GST and legal services in chapter 18 on page 391.

Adjusting the fee

In preparing a draft account, multiply the hourly rate by the hours of work done; the lawyer may adjust the fee, usually by discounting it. Lawyers often adjust the fee based on the results for the client, the benefit to the client from those results, the complexity or difficulty of the work undertaken, and other subjective factors. For example, where the unadjusted fee is high in comparison to the benefit to the client, the lawyer may lower the fee. This reflects what an assessment officer might do if a client moves to assess the account because he or she thinks it too high.

Disbursements

After identifying all of the disbursements charged to the client's ledger, and any others not yet posted to the ledger, divide them into disbursements subject to GST and disbursements not subject to GST. Then you can add each subset of disbursements, and calculate and add in the GST.

Total fees and disbursements

You are now ready to total all fees and disbursements, including the GST. The total GST on fees and disbursements should be set out on a separate line below the total, along with the firm's GST number so that commercial clients can include this amount in any tax credits available to them.

Deduct credit balance in trust from total

If the client has a retainer/deposit held in trust, it should be credited against the amount due on the account, thereby reducing the amount owing from the client.

Balance now due

On this line, you can now record the net amount due after deducting credits from the client funds held in trust.

Signature line

Only a lawyer can sign an account. This job should not be delegated to a law clerk or other office staff.

E&OE

This acronym is a standard business account notation and means "errors and omissions excepted." This means that the lawyer is not bound by the account if the lawyer finds that he or she left something out. The lawyer can still bill for that amount subsequently.

Interest on overdue accounts

At one time, lawyers could not charge on overdue accounts because it was considered improper for professionals to do so. Times change. Interest can now be charged at up to 1.5 percent per month or 18 percent per year, putting lawyers in the same league as bank credit cards. There should be a statement just below the signature that interest will be charged at a specified rate on accounts that remain unpaid for more than 30 days after they are rendered.

Trust statement

A trust or ledger statement should appear at the end of the account to record transfers of money held in trust by the lawyer, including the purpose of the transfer. The trust statement underlies the lawyer's right to transfer money from the lawyer's trust account to his or her general account when an account is rendered to the client.

ABIGAIL BOAR'S FINAL ACCOUNT
Account information and data

Let's suppose that Abigail's case went to trial on some of the issues raised in the pleadings, that the trial lasted three days (July 10, 11, and 12, year 3), and that Abigail obtained judgment for $100,000. On July 14, year 3, I.M. Just rendered his final account, covering the period from July 1, year 3, after completion of some of the pretrial work, through to the end of trial. Abigail's previous account was rendered on June 30, and was paid for by an amount on deposit in her trust account. She has refreshed the retainer with a cheque for $10,000, deposited to I.M. Just's trust account on July 2. I.M. Just's hourly rate is $250. When attending court, litigation lawyers often charge a flat counsel fee for each day or half day in court. I.M. Just's counsel fee is $2,500 per day and $1,200 per half day. The rate charged by the firm for Edward Egregious, the law clerk, is $75.

Edward's dockets are as follows:

- July 6: arranging for issuing and serving summonses to witnesses: 0.5 hours

- July 8: meeting with witnesses: 1.0 hours

- July 10: organizing files and documents for trial: 1.0 hours

- July 10–12: attending court to assist I.M. Just, 6 hours per day for 3 days: 18 hours

- July 14: preparing account and telephone calls arranging for payment of judgment by defendants: 0.6 hours

I.M. Just's dockets are as follows:

- July 2: reading law and preparing trial brief: 8.0 hours

- July 3: reading law and preparing trial brief: 6.0 hours

- July 5: interviewing witnesses: 4.0 hours

- July 6: meeting client and preparing client for trial: 3.0 hours

- July 10, 11, 12: attending trial: 3 full days

- July 13: reporting to client: 1.0 hour

The client's ledger card shows the following entries:

- July 2, year 3: received from client further retainer of $10,000

- July 5, year 3: paid witness fees, 3 summons at $53 each per court-prescribed fee ($159)

- July 6, year 3: paid to serve summonses $45.00

- July 8, year 3: photocopying $73.20

Draft account

Figure 19.1 shows what the draft account in Abigail's case might look like.

CHAPTER SUMMARY

In this chapter, we continued to explore the docketing of hours and the recording of disbursements on the client's account, and we used this information to render an account to a client. From assembled docket sheets and disbursements recorded from the client's ledger card, we created a draft account. The account described the work done and the time taken to do it. It established the fee and total disbursements and recorded the GST charged on all fees and disbursements that are subject to GST. We also accounted for any monies received from the client in trust, using these funds to reduce the balance owing.

KEY TERMS

refresh the retainer

carriage

FIGURE 19.1 DRAFT ACCOUNT

JUST & COPING
Barristers and Solicitors
365 Bay Street – 8701
Toronto, Ontario, M3J 4A9

July 14, year 3

TO:
Abigail Boar
72 Sumach Street
Toronto, Ontario M4R 1Z5

RE: BOAR v. RATTLE MOTORS LTD. AND FLOGEM

FOR ALL PROFESSIONAL SERVICES from and after July 1, year 3, including:
I.M. Just, July 2-3, reading law and preparing trial brief: 14 hours; I.M. Just, July 5, interviewing witnesses: 4 hours; I.M. Just, July 6, meeting client and preparing client for trial: 3 hours; E. Egregious, July 6, arranging for issuing and serving witness summonses: 0.5 hours; E. Egregious, July 8, meeting witnesses: 1 hour; E. Egregious, July 10, organizing files and documents for trial: 1 hour; E. Egregious, July 10, 11, 12, attending court to assist counsel: 6 hours per day for 3 days: 18 hours; I.M. Just, July 13, reporting to client: 1 hour; E. Egregious, telephone calls arranging for payment of judgment: 0.6 hours

OUR FEE:	$7,082.50
COUNSEL FEE: I.M. Just, 3 days at trial at $2,500 per day	$7,500.00
TOTAL FEE:	$14,582.50
*GST:	$729.13
TOTAL FEES INCLUDING GST:	
	$15,311.63
DISBURSEMENTS SUBJECT TO GST:	
Photocopies	$73.20
Service of summonses	$45.00
TOTAL SUBJECT TO GST:	$118.20
GST:	$5.91
TOTAL DISBURSEMENTS AND GST	$124.11
DISBURSEMENTS NOT SUBJECT TO GST:	
Court prescribed witness fee,	
3 summonses at $53.00 per summons	$159.00
TOTAL NOT SUBJECT TO GST:	$159.00
TOTAL FEES AND DISBURSEMENTS:	$15,594.74
(TOTAL GST IS $735.04 — GST # RO12534)	

* GST calculated at 5 percent.

FIGURE 19.1   CONCLUDED

LESS TRANSFERRED FROM TRUST: −$10,000
BALANCE NOW DUE AND OWING: $5,594.74
THIS IS OUR ACCOUNT HEREIN

JUST & COPING
Per: _____

Interest will be charged at the rate of 18 percent per annum on all accounts outstanding for over 30 days.
E&OE

TRUST STATEMENT

Date	Transaction	Disbursement	Receipt
July 2, year 3	Received from client in trust		10,000.00
July 14, year 3	Paid to Just & Coping, Transfer of funds for fees and disbursements, invoice # year 3-1298	10,000.00	
	TOTAL TRUST	10,000.00	10,000.00
	TRUST BALANCE	NIL	NIL

REVIEW QUESTIONS

1. In a well-managed law practice, does the lawyer usually wait until the trial is over before billing the client?

2. Does a client usually make a single deposit payment when he or she retains a lawyer?

3. What must you do before drafting an account?

4. What should you do if dockets are missing for work you know has been done?

5. What is subject to GST?

6. Does a lawyer always establish a fee by adding up all of his or her billable hours?

7. What does "E&OE" mean?

8. May a lawyer charge interest on overdue accounts?

DISCUSSION QUESTION

1. Read and respond to the following memorandum:

   To: Law clerk
   From: Lawyer
   Re: *Farthbottle v. Blob*

   We opened this file on September 16, year 0, and it has just settled. Please draft an account to Fabian Farthbottle for the end of November of this year. My hourly rate is $250. Charge $50 for your time on the file.

   An examination of docket sheets reveals the following:

   Law clerk's dockets:

   - September 16: attending meeting with client: 1.0 hours

   - October 25: meeting client to review documents: 3.0 hours

   - October 26: organizing documents and drafting affidavits of documents: 3.5 hours

   Lawyer's dockets:

   - September 16: initial meeting with client: 1.0 hours

   - September 25: drafting statement of claim: 0.5 hours

   - September 26: telephone conversation with client concerning amendments to statement of claim: 1.0 hours

   - October 5: reviewing statement of claim and defence: 2.0 hours

   - October 10: drafting reply and defence to counterclaim: 0.5 hours

   - November 21: preparing for examination for discovery: 3.0 hours

   - November 21: preparing client for discovery by telephone: 2.0 hours

   - November 22: attending examination for discovery: 5.0 hours

- November 24: negotiating on telephone with defendant's lawyer: 2.0 hours

- November 24: discussing offer with client on telephone: 0.2 hours

- November 25: discussion with defendant's lawyer accepting offer: 0.1 hours

Client's ledger card shows the following:

- September 16: received in trust $2,000.00

- September 16–November 25: photocopies $25.00

- September 26: fee to issue statement of claim $181.00

- September 26: service of statement of claim
  by process server $41.00

- October 1: postage $6.00

- October 26: fax charges $3.00

- October 30: examiner's fee for notice of
  examination $9.50

- November 24: discovery transcript $16.00

- November 24: court reporter's fees $100.00

- November 24: examination facilities $80.00

CHAPTER 20

Appeals

INTRODUCTION

An appeal is not a retrying of the case. Many clients misunderstand this. They think an appeal is a redetermination of the case by a higher court that will hear all the evidence presented to the **court of first instance**. This is not the function of the higher court hearing the appeal.

The client must be helped to understand that an appeal can be commenced only if the court of first instance made a legal error. It is not the role of the appeal court to hear new evidence, make new determinations of facts, or reassess the credibility of witnesses. In fact, the appeal court does not hear any witnesses. An appeal is conducted by way of written documentation and submissions of the lawyers for the parties. The submissions centre on the legal error that the appealing party claims the court of first instance made. The party commencing the appeal is called the **appellant** and the party responding to the appeal is called the **respondent**.

Rules 61, 62, and 63 deal with procedure on appeals. You also must look to the *Courts of Justice Act* to determine which level of court has jurisdiction to hear an appeal. In addition, there is a lengthy practice direction that governs civil appeals in the Court of Appeal that must be followed when bringing an appeal to that court.

NATURE OF THE ORDER APPEALED FROM

Once it has been decided that there are arguable legal grounds for an appeal, the next step in determining which procedure to follow is to establish whether the order appealed from is final or interlocutory in nature.

All orders can be classified as either final or interlocutory. A **final order** is one that determines all the outstanding issues in the proceeding. An **interlocutory order** is one that resolves only a particular issue in the proceeding on a temporary basis. It is not a complete determination of all the issues between the parties.

Many, but not all, motions lead to interlocutory orders. Similarly, most orders made at a trial of an issue are final. However, it is important to look at the content of the order, not the proceeding in which it was granted, to determine whether it is final or interlocutory in nature. For instance, a successful motion for summary judgment results in a final order. The order is final because all the issues in the proceeding are dealt with on the basis of summary judgment.

When trying to decide whether a particular order is final or interlocutory, it is a good idea to ask whether the order resolves all the outstanding issues between the parties or whether there are still issues to be litigated. The issue is not always cut

court of first instance
court that made a decision that is under appeal

appellant
party that commences an appeal

respondent
party that answers or defends against an appeal

final order
order that resolves all the outstanding issues between the parties

interlocutory order
order that decides some of the matters at issue

and dried, and there are many cases in which the courts have been asked to determine whether a particular order is final or interlocutory in nature.

There are different routes through the court system for appeals of final orders and interlocutory orders. Therefore, determining whether a particular order is final or interlocutory is the first step in establishing the procedure to be followed on an appeal.

RIGHT TO APPEAL

There is not always an automatic right to appeal an order of the court. In many instances, permission or **leave of the court** must be sought in order to commence an appeal. If the rules require that leave must be granted before an appeal can be commenced, the party wishing to appeal must bring a motion to the court that is to hear the appeal, asking for permission.

leave of the court
permission of the court to take a procedural step

WHICH COURT HEARS THE APPEAL?

After establishing whether the order is interlocutory or final, the next step is deciding which court has the jurisdiction to hear the appeal. There are three courts that can hear appeals:

1. the Ontario Superior Court of Justice,

2. the Divisional Court, and

3. the Court of Appeal.

To determine which court has jurisdiction in each particular appeal, you must look at the *Courts of Justice Act*. Section 17 of the Act, provides that a judge of the Superior Court of Justice has jurisdiction to hear appeals from the following orders:

(a) an interlocutory order of a master or case management master;

(b) a certificate of assessment of costs issued in a proceeding in the Superior Court of Justice, on an issue in respect of which an objection was served under the rules of court.[1]

Section 19 of the *Courts of Justice Act* provides that the Divisional Court may hear appeals from the following orders:

(1) An appeal lies to the Divisional Court from,

(a) a final order of a judge of the Superior Court of Justice, as described in subsections (1.1) and (1.2);

(b) an interlocutory order of a judge of the Superior Court of Justice, with leave as provided in the rules of court;

(c) a final order of a master or case management master.

(1.1) If the notice of appeal is filed before the day section 3 of Schedule A to the *Access to Justice Act, 2006* comes into force, clause (1) (a) applies in respect of a final order,

(a) for a single payment of not more than $25,000, exclusive of costs;

(b) for periodic payments that amount to not more than $25,000, exclusive of costs, in the 12 months commencing on the date the first payment is due under the order;

(c) dismissing a claim for an amount that is not more than the amount set out in clause (a) or (b); or

(d) dismissing a claim for an amount that is more than the amount set out in clause (a) or (b) and in respect of which the judge or jury indicates that if the claim had been allowed the amount awarded would have been not more than the amount set out in clause (a) or (b).

(1.2) If the notice of appeal is filed on or after the day section 3 of Schedule A to the Access to Justice Act, 2006 comes into force, clause (1) (a) applies in respect of a final order,

(a) for a single payment of not more than $50,000, exclusive of costs;

(b) for periodic payments that amount to not more than $50,000, exclusive of costs, in the 12 months commencing on the date the first payment is due under the order;

(c) dismissing a claim for an amount that is not more than the amount set out in clause (a) or (b); or

(d) dismissing a claim for an amount that is more than the amount set out in clause (a) or (b) and in respect of which the judge or jury indicates that if the claim had been allowed the amount awarded would have been not more than the amount set out in clause (a) or (b).

The Divisional Court, pursuant to s. 31 of the *Courts of Justice Act*, also has jurisdiction to hear appeals from Small Claims Court matters in which the amount of the claim was in excess of $500, excluding costs.

Section 6(1)(a) through (c) of the *Courts of Justice Act* provides that the Court of Appeal has jurisdiction to hear an appeal of the following orders:

(a) an order of the Divisional Court, on a question that is not a question of fact alone, with leave of the Court of Appeal as provided in the rules of court;

(b) a final order of a judge of the Superior Court of Justice, except an order referred to in clause 19(1)(a) [an order that should be appealed to the Divisional Court] or an order from which an appeal lies to the Divisional Court under another Act;

(c) a certificate of assessment of costs issued in a proceeding in the Court of Appeal, on an issue in respect of which an objection was served under the rules of court.[2]

In summary, a final order of a judge of the Superior Court of Justice may be appealed to the Divisional Court if the monetary value of the order is $50,000 or less. A final order for more than $50,000 from a judge of the Superior Court goes to the Court of Appeal. An interlocutory order of a master goes to the Superior Court of Justice on appeal, but a final order of a master goes to the Divisional Court. Table 20.1 sets out the various routes of appeal.

APPEAL TO THE DIVISIONAL COURT OR THE COURT OF APPEAL

Rule 61 applies to appeals to the Divisional Court or the Court of Appeal, except for an appeal of a certificate of assessment of costs issued in a Court of Appeal proceeding. Rule 62 governs that type of appeal. In addition, on appeals to the Court of Appeal, the practice direction relating to those appeals must also be followed.

Section 20(1) of the *Courts of Justice Act* requires that an appeal to the Divisional Court be brought in the region where the proceeding is commenced. Since there is only one Court of Appeal in Ontario, at Osgoode Hall in Toronto, an appeal to that court is commenced through the court office there.

Table 20.1   Appeal routes

Nature of the order made	Court to which the appeal goes
Final order of a judge of the Superior Court of Justice in an amount over $50,000 (exclusive of costs)	Court of Appeal
Final order of a judge of the Superior Court of Justice in an amount of $50,000 or less (exclusive of costs)	Divisional Court
Interlocutory order of a judge of the Superior Court of Justice (with leave)	Divisional Court
Final order of a master	Divisional Court
Interlocutory order of a master	Judge of the Superior Court of Justice
Certificate of assessment of costs issued in a proceeding in the Court of Appeal	Court of Appeal
Certificate of assessment of costs (where objection served) in a proceeding in the Superior Court of Justice for an amount of $50,000 or less	Superior Court of Justice
Certificate of assessment of costs (where objection served) in a proceeding in the Superior Court of Justice for an amount over $50,000	Court of Appeal
Small Claims Court order for an amount over $500	Divisional Court

Title of proceeding on appeals

In an appeal, the parties are identified as the appellant and the respondent. Rule 61.04(2) requires that the title of the proceeding be in accordance with form 61B. This means that the plaintiff and defendant are still identified as such, and remain in the same order in the general heading as they did in the original proceeding, but for the appeal documents, under the words "Plaintiff" and "Defendant" in the general heading, the nature of the parties' roles in the appeal should be identified. For instance, if Abigail Boar is appealing, the word "Appellant" should appear under the word "Plaintiff" in the general heading. Rattle Motors Ltd. and Fred Flogem would still be identified as the defendants, but the word "Respondents" should appear under the word "Defendants." See figure 20.3.

Motions for leave to appeal

There is not always a right to appeal a decision. Sometimes it is necessary to seek leave from the appellate court to appeal a judgment of a lower court. The procedure on motions for leave to appeal to the Divisional Court is similar to the procedure on motions for leave to appeal to the Court of Appeal. Because there are some procedural differences, however, we will deal with these appeals separately.

MOTION FOR LEAVE TO APPEAL TO THE DIVISIONAL COURT: RULE 61.03

A motion for leave to appeal to the Divisional Court must be served within 15 days of the making of the order or the decision being appealed unless the matter is governed by a statute that provides a different time limit. If the court reserves a decision, the 15 days starts to run on the day the decision is released.

The notice of motion, along with proof of service, must then be filed within 5 days of service in the office of the registrar of the Divisional Court in the region where the proceeding resulting in the appeal was commenced. A notice of motion for leave to appeal, which appears as figure 20.1, is generally in the same format as a regular motion. (See chapter 9 on motions.) However, in the portion of the form that requires a date, instead of including a date, you write "on a date to be fixed by the registrar" (rule 61.03(1)(a)).

In addition, the questions that the Divisional Court is being asked to answer, should leave be granted, must be included in the notice of motion.

On the motion for leave, you need a motion record. A motion record on an application for leave to appeal is similar to a regular motion record. The pages must be consecutively numbered, and the contents must be arranged in the following order:

1. a table of contents, describing each document, including each exhibit by its nature and date and, in the case of an exhibit, by its exhibit number or letter;

2. a copy of the notice of motion;

3. a copy of the order or decision from which leave to appeal is sought as signed and entered;

4. a copy of the reasons of the court or tribunal from which leave to appeal is sought with a further typed or printed copy if the reasons are handwritten;

5. a copy of any order or decision that was the subject of the hearing before the court or tribunal from which leave to appeal is sought;

6. a copy of any reasons for the order or decision with a further typed or printed copy if the reasons are handwritten;

7. a copy of all affidavits and other material used before the court or tribunal from which leave to appeal is sought;

8. a list containing each relevant **transcript** of evidence in chronological order, but not necessarily the transcripts themselves; and

> **transcript**
> written record of proceedings transcribed word for word

9. a copy of any other material in the court file that is necessary for the hearing of the motion.

In addition to the motion record, the factum and the transcripts of the proceeding must be provided. A factum is a statement of the facts and the law on which the moving party is relying. Facts are determined by going through the transcripts of the trial and listing each fact, as found by the court at the trial.

The facts and law are to be set out in the document. They are to be presented in the form of a concise argument. For the overview of the contents of a factum on appeal, see the section in this chapter dealing with motions for leave to appeal to the Court of Appeal.

FIGURE 20.1 NOTICE OF MOTION FOR LEAVE TO APPEAL

Court file no. 03-DC-5678

DIVISIONAL COURT
SUPERIOR COURT OF JUSTICE

BETWEEN:

ABIGAIL BOAR

Plaintiff

and

RATTLE MOTORS LTD. and FRED FLOGEM

Defendants

NOTICE OF MOTION FOR LEAVE TO APPEAL

THE DEFENDANT Rattle Motors Ltd. will make a motion to the court on a date to be fixed by the Registrar.

PROPOSED METHOD OF HEARING: The motion is to be heard orally.

THE MOTION IS FOR: Leave to appeal the order of the Honourable Madam Justice Snork, made July 12, year 3.

THE GROUNDS FOR THE MOTION ARE:

1. Should leave to appeal be granted, the questions the court will be asked to address on the appeal are:
   a. Did the Honourable Trial Judge err in finding that the defendant Rattle owed a duty of care to the plaintiff?
   b. …
2. *(List all further grounds for the motion.)*
3. …

THE FOLLOWING DOCUMENTARY EVIDENCE will be used at the hearing of the motion:

1. The order of the Honourable Madam Justice Snork made July 12, year 3.
2. *(List all other documents on which you will be relying in the motion.)*

Date: July 30, year 3

Just & Coping
Barristers and Solicitors
365 Bay Street - 8701
Toronto, Ontario, M3J 4A9

I.M. Just
LSUC #12345R
tel. 416-762-1342
fax 416-762-2300

Lawyers for the Plaintiff

FIGURE 20.1 CONCLUDED

```
TO:
Huey Sue
LSUC #23456T
Barrister and Solicitor
65 False Trail
Toronto, Ontario, M6Y 1Z6

tel. 416-485-6891
fax 416-485-6892

Lawyer for the Defendants
```

Three copies of the motion record, factum, and transcripts must be filed with the court, along with proof of service, within 30 days after filing of the notice of motion for leave. Three copies are required because the Divisional Court usually sits as a panel of three judges, but one judge alone may hear a motion for leave. In addition to the copies for the court, you will need copies for each of the other parties, as well as a copy for your own lawyer.

The responding party may file a motion record if he or she believes that the moving party's record is not complete. It must be filed with proof of service, within 15 days after the responding party is served with the moving party's record. The responding party's motion record must have a table of contents, followed by any additional material that the respondent believes should be before the court on the motion for leave. Responding parties may also file a factum, and in most cases they do.

Once all the documents are filed, the registrar fixes a date for the hearing of the motion. The Divisional Court is made up of judges from the Superior Court of Justice, but since the motion for leave cannot come before the same judge that made the order or judgment being appealed, the motion cannot be scheduled for any date that the judge will be sitting as a member of the Divisional Court.

Should the moving party be granted leave to appeal, the party must file a notice of appeal within seven days after leave to appeal has been granted.

One of the orders or judgments that cannot be appealed without leave is an order for costs. If only costs are being appealed, then a motion for leave must be brought in the usual way. But often costs are appealed along with another issue that does not require leave. An appeal that does not require leave of the court is called an **appeal as of right**. If the costs appeal or cross appeal is brought along with an appeal as of right, or cross-appeal as of right, the leave to appeal costs is included in the notice of appeal as part of the relief sought. The motion for leave to appeal is then heard at the start of the appeal on the other issues and not on a separate date.

appeal as of right
appeal that a party has a legal right to bring and for which leave to appeal is not required

MOTION FOR LEAVE TO APPEAL TO THE COURT OF APPEAL: RULE 61.03.1

Rule 61.03.1 provides the procedure for bringing a motion for leave to appeal to the Court of Appeal. The rule must be read in conjunction with the practice direction that governs appeals to the Court of Appeal. In many ways, the procedure mirrors that of a similar motion to the Divisional Court, but there are some major differences prescribed by both the rules and the practice direction.

Most motions in the Court of Appeal are heard by one judge of the court, but a motion for leave to appeal, a motion to quash an appeal, or any other motion specified in the rules is heard by a panel of at least three judges of the court.

A motion for leave to appeal to the Court of Appeal is usually considered based on the appeal documents submitted without any of the parties or their counsel attending before the court. However, once all the necessary documents have been filed on the motion, the court may decide to order that the motion be heard orally. If that is the case, the registrar will fix a date for the hearing and advise the parties.

The Court of Appeal is now equipped to conduct motions and appeals by way of videoconferencing. If parties wish to have a motion conducted by way of videoconferencing, they should contact the registrar for the Court of Appeal at 416-326-1029 when a date has been set for the motion, or is about to be set, and make appropriate arrangements.

The notice of motion must state that the court will hear the motion in writing 36 days after service of the moving party's motion record, factum, and transcripts, or on the filing of the moving party's reply factum, whichever is earlier. Since the Court of Appeal has its own filing system, do not put the court file number of the lower court on the notice of appeal. The registrar's office will assign a new file number to the case.

The notice of motion must be served within 15 days after the date of the order or decision that the party wants to appeal. It must then be filed, along with proof of service, with the Court of Appeal within five days of service. A motion record, factum, and transcripts must also be served on the respondent and filed with the court along with proof of service.

Although the factum and transcripts for the motion may be filed in person at the court, the practice direction regarding appeals to the Court of Appeal encourages parties to file the factum and transcripts electronically by e-mail. See the practice direction and the section in this chapter that deal with the formatting of electronically filed documents on appeals to the Court of Appeal.

Unlike the rule regarding motions for leave to appeal to the Divisional Court, rule 61.03.1(4) spells out exactly what is to be put into a factum used on a motion for leave to appeal. It should contain the following sections:

1. Part I, which identifies the moving party, the order or decision they want to appeal, and the content of the order.

2. Part II, containing a concise statement of the facts with any references to the transcripts given by page and line.

3. Part III, outlining any specific questions that would be put to the Court of Appeal if the motion for leave is granted.

4. Part IV, containing a concise statement of each issue raised, immediately followed by a statement of the law and the citation for the authorities supporting that legal point.

5. Schedule A, containing a list of all the authorities used in part IV.

6. Schedule B, containing the text of all relevant provisions of statutes, regulations, and bylaws upon which the moving party will be relying.

All the paragraphs in the factum should be numbered consecutively from start to finish. This means that if the last paragraph in part I is number 5, the first paragraph in part II would be number 6.

As with all documents that are prepared for court, the presentation of a factum is important. You should use tabs if it will help make the document more accessible. You should always put tabs in for the schedules in all cases, even if you do not use them in any other part of the factum. If there are only a few authorities being used, you can put them right in the back of the factum. However, if there are a lot of authorities, prepare a separate book called a "book of authorities" and put all the cases in it.

There should be a list of the cases at the front of the book of authorities, and each case should be separated by a tab. Number all the pages in the book of authorities. The court must be provided with three copies, and the opposite parties should each be served with one. It is also necessary to prepare a book for the lawyer from your firm who is arguing the motion. Books of authorities may also be used on motions for leave to appeal to the Divisional Court, and they are always used on the appeal itself.

Three copies of the moving party's motion record, factum, transcripts, and book of authorities must be filed, with proof of service, within 30 days after the notice of motion has been filed. In addition to the filing of the hard copy of the factum and transcript, the practice direction requests that counsel also file an electronic copy of the factum or transcript. For more details on the specifics of this requirement, see the section further on in this chapter that relates to the practice direction requirements for filing electronic versions of factums and transcripts.

The responding party may serve a motion record as well, if it is his opinion that the moving party's motion record is incomplete. In any event, the responding party must file a factum organized as follows:

1. Part I, containing a statement of the facts that identifies those facts given by the moving party that he accepts and those with which he disagrees. In addition, the responding party must incorporate a summary of any facts that he believes the moving party has not included in her factum, along with reference to the evidence in the transcripts that supports these facts.

2. Part II, containing the responding party's position with respect to each issue raised by the moving party, immediately followed by a concise statement of the law and the citations for the authorities related to the issue in question.

3. Part III, containing a statement of any additional issues raised by the responding party, followed by a concise statement of the law on the issue and the citations for the relevant authorities.

4. Schedule A, containing a list of the citations for the authorities referred to in the factum.

5. Schedule B, with photocopies of the portion of the relevant statutes, regulations, and bylaws upon which the responding party is relying.

The factum must be laid out in the same fashion as the moving party's factum, with all the paragraphs numbered consecutively throughout the parts.

The three copies of the factum, any book of authorities, and the motion record of the respondent, if any, must be filed with the court, along with proof of service, within 25 days of the service of the moving party's factum and other documents. This means that you will need to prepare at least five copies of the documents, one for your lawyer, three for the court, and at least one for the opposite party. Of course, if there is more than one opposite party, you must prepare a separate set of documents for service on each of them. In addition, the responding party must also file an electronic copy of his or her factum with the court.

In the event that the responding party has raised some new issue that is not addressed by the moving party in his factum, the moving party is entitled to serve and file a reply factum, including an electronic copy, within ten days after service of the responding party's factum.

As with a motion in Divisional Court for leave to appeal costs, which is joined to another issue that can be appealed as of right, the request for leave to appeal must be included in the notice of appeal as part of the relief sought. The panel of the Court of Appeal that hears the appeal as of right decides whether or not to grant leave on the costs appeal.

Practice direction requirements for motions to the Court of Appeal

First, the practice direction requires that all parties include their telephone number, fax number, e-mail address, and, in the case of counsel, Law Society number on the documents filed with the court.

The registrar will not set a date on a motion for leave to appeal until the moving party has filed the motion record, factum, and transcript, if any. All motions before a panel of judges, such as a motion for leave to appeal, will be limited to 15 minutes for the moving party, 10 minutes for the responding party, and 5 minutes for reply. If the motion is expected to take more time than this, a special request must be made to the List Judge. This can be arranged through the Appeals Scheduling Unit by fax at 416-327-6256.

Once the hearing date is set, the moving party must attempt to confer with the responding party and then, not later than 2 p.m., two days before the hearing, give the registrar of the Court of Appeal a confirmation of motion in form 37B. The confirmation can be sent by fax to 416-327-5032. If the confirmation is not given, the motion will not be heard unless the court orders otherwise. If there are any changes to the confirmation once it has been given to the registrar, the moving party must send a corrected copy of the confirmation.

Commencement of appeals: Rule 61.04

The document that commences an appeal is a notice of appeal in form 61A, which is set out in figure 20.2. If leave to appeal is sought and granted, the moving party has 7 days to file the notice of appeal after leave is granted. On an appeal as of right, the notice of appeal must be served on every party whose interest may be affected and on every person entitled by statute to be heard within 30 days of the granting of the order or decision that is being appealed. The only exception to the 30-day rule comes into play if a statute or the rules prescribe another time limit for filing of the notice.

FIGURE 20.2 NOTICE OF APPEAL TO AN APPELLATE COURT (FORM 61A)

Court file no. 03-CA-1234

COURT OF APPEAL FOR ONTARIO

BETWEEN:

ABIGAIL BOAR

Plaintiff
(Appellant)

and

RATTLE MOTORS LTD. and FRED FLOGEM

Defendants
(Respondents)

NOTICE OF APPEAL

THE PLAINTIFF APPEALS to the Court of Appeal from the judgment of the Honourable Justice Snork, dated July 12, year 3, made at Toronto.

THE APPELLANT ASKS that the judgment be set aside and judgment be granted as follows:

1. the respondent Rattle Motors Ltd. be found jointly and severally liable for the appellant's injuries along with the respondent Fred Flogem;
2. damages be awarded to the appellant in the full amount of her claim; and
3. the appellant be awarded costs of this appeal.

THE GROUNDS OF APPEAL are as follows:

1. the learned trial judge erred in finding that the defendant Rattle Motors Ltd. did not owe a duty of care to the plaintiff;
2. the learned trial judge erred in finding that the defendant did not breach the standard of care owed to the plaintiff; and
3. such further and other grounds as counsel may advise and this court permit.

THE BASIS OF THE APPELLATE COURT'S JURISDICTION IS:

1. the appellant relies on s. 6(1)(b) of the *Courts of Justice Act*;
2. the order appealed from is a final order of a judge of the Superior Court of Justice for an amount of damage exceeding $50,000; and
3. no leave to appeal is necessary.

FIGURE 20.2 CONCLUDED

Date: July 30, year 3

Just & Coping
Barristers and Solicitors
365 Bay Street – 8701
Toronto, Ontario M3J 4A9

I.M. Just
LSUC #12345R
tel. 416-762-1342
fax 416-762-2300
e-mail im.just@justcoping.com

Lawyers for the Appellant

TO:

Huey Sue
LSUC #23456T
Barrister and Solicitor
65 False Trail
Toronto, Ontario M6Y 1Z6

tel. 416-485-6891
fax 416-485-6892

Lawyer for the Respondents

FIGURE 20.3 GENERAL HEADING FOR APPEAL (FORM 61B)

Court file no. 03-CA-1234

COURT OF APPEAL FOR ONTARIO

BETWEEN:

ABIGAIL BOAR

Plaintiff
(Appellant)

and

RATTLE MOTORS LTD. and FRED FLOGEM

Defendants
(Respondents)

As with all court documents, there is no need to serve the notice of appeal on a party to an action who has been noted in default or a respondent in an application who has failed to file a notice of appearance unless that respondent was given permission by the court to participate in the hearing in which the order being appealed was made.

The notice of appeal must set out the relief sought by the appellant and the grounds for the appeal and the basis for the appellate court's jurisdiction. In some cases, the notice of appeal is filed to protect the party's right to appeal. After the transcripts have been ordered, the appellant may wish to make some changes to the grounds or the relief sought. The notice of appeal may be amended without leave of the court at any time before the appeal is perfected. **Perfecting an appeal** means completing the procedural steps to ensure that the appeal is ready to be heard by the court. Perfecting an appeal is discussed in more detail later in this chapter.

In order to amend the notice of appeal, the appellant must serve a supplementary notice of appeal in form 61F and file it with the registrar, along with proof of service. The appellant must obtain leave of the court to rely on grounds or seek relief not specified in the original or supplementary notice of appeal.

The precedent for the general heading on an appeal is in form 61B. The court file number on the appeal is not the same as the file number in the lower court. The Divisional Court and the Court of Appeal both have their own filing systems and issue the file a new number within that system. Therefore, initially leave the court file number blank when you prepare the notice of appeal. The file number will be given to you by the court office.

Along with the notice of appeal, the appellant must also serve a certificate in which he or she sets out the portion of the evidence that he or she believes to be required for the appeal. The precedent for this document is form 61C. Within 15 days of service of the appellant's certificate, the respondent must serve a responding certificate on the appellant in which he or she either confirms the appellant's certificate or sets out any additions or deletions that he or she wants to make. If the respondent fails to serve and file a certificate within the required time, the respondent is deemed to have accepted the appellant's certificate.

Instead of complying with the rules about the certificate of evidence, the parties may choose to consult each other and come to an agreement respecting the evidence to be used on the appeal and included in the appeal book and compendium. If they choose this option, within 30 days of the service of the notice of appeal they must make the decision about which documents and portions of the transcripts will be needed for the court on the appeal. If the appellant has already placed an order for portions of the transcript that both parties agree will not be needed, the appellant may provide the court reporter with an amended order for the transcripts.

The purpose of the certificate of evidence or the agreement respecting the evidence is to cut down on the amount of documentation with which the Court of Appeal must deal. Not all the evidence given at a trial is required on the appeal because much of it covers issues that are not being appealed. These two procedures ensure that only the necessary evidence is filed with the court and that only one copy of each document is filed. Without the rule, both parties might file all the transcripts and copies of identical documents.

perfecting an appeal
taking all the necessary procedural steps to ensure that an appeal is ready to be heard

During the trial, a court reporter or a recording device would have taken down every word said in the courtroom. The written version of the trial is called the transcript. The appellant must order all the transcripts of the trial within 30 days of filing the notice of appeal and must file proof that he or she has ordered them. However, the appellant need only order the copies of the transcript of the evidence that the parties have agreed should be admitted on the appeal. It is important to keep the quantity of transcript to a minimum because transcripts are expensive and take a great deal of time to read. If the respondent has not agreed to the appellant's certificate of evidence and has required unnecessary additional parts of the transcript to be prepared, the court may impose costs against the respondent.

In any event, the transcript must not include:

- any challenge of the jury;

- the opening address of the judge;

- the opening and closing addresses of counsel;

- any part of the proceeding that took place in the absence of the jury, except an objection to the charge to the jury by the judge; or

- any objections to the admissibility of evidence, but the ruling of the judge on the objection is to be included.[3]

The court reporter should be aware of these automatic exclusions and not include them unless there is a court order requiring a normally excluded part of the transcript to be included. Therefore, if there is an order for inclusion, you should provide the court reporter with a copy when you order the transcript or as soon as possible after the order is made.

The transcripts are ordered through the court reporter who recorded the oral proceedings in the court of first instance. If more than one reporter was involved in recording the proceeding, transcripts may be ordered through the coordinator for reporters. The reporter will provide a confirmation to you and to the court that the transcripts have been ordered. You must order five copies for the court, a copy for yourself, and one for each of the other parties. Transcripts being prepared for the Court of Appeal are expected to be completed within 90 days of being ordered. If they are not, the court will look into the delay to see if the preparation can be facilitated. Once the transcripts are ready, the reporter will notify all the parties and the registrar in writing.

Where it appears that the appeal is frivolous and vexatious, and the appellant does not have sufficient assets to pay costs, or if an order for security for costs could be made under rule 56.01, or, for any other good reason, the respondent may bring a motion asking that the appellant be required to provide security for costs and the court may order the appellant to do so. If the appellant fails to comply with the order for security, the court may dismiss the appeal.

Court reporters have been instructed that once a transcript has been ordered for an appeal in the Court of Appeal, they may not suspend completion of the transcript on the request of a party. A court order is required to suspend completion except in legal aid cases.

On some appeals to the Court of Appeal, the parties do not have a different version of the facts. Instead, they are appealing the manner in which the trial judge applied the law to these facts. If there is no dispute as to the facts, the parties may file an agreed statement of facts rather than a transcript. This saves money and time in bringing the appeal before the court.

Cross-appeals: Rule 61.07

In some cases, the respondent may also want to appeal the same judgment that the appellant is setting to overturn, or the respondent may be satisfied with that judgment but wish to seek different or additional relief in the event that the appellant is successful on the appeal. The appeal of the respondent is a cross-appeal. The respondent wishing to cross-appeal must, within 15 days after service of the notice of appeal, serve a notice of cross-appeal on all parties whose interests may be affected or who are entitled to be heard.

No leave to appeal is required on a cross-appeal if there is an appeal as of right or if leave to appeal has already been granted. If the respondent requires leave to bring the cross appeal, he or she may bring a motion for leave pursuant to the same rules that the appellant would rely on in seeking leave: rule 61.03 if the appeal is to the Divisional Court, and rule 61.03.1 if it is to the Court of Appeal.

A notice of cross-appeal is in form 61E. It must state the relief sought and the grounds for the cross-appeal and must be filed, along with proof of service, in the office of the registrar within ten days of service. If the respondent does not deliver a cross-appeal, no cross-appeal may be heard, except with leave of the court.

Perfecting the appeal: Rule 61.09

Perfecting the appeal means completing all the necessary legal steps to ensure that the appeal is ready to be heard by the court. There are different time limits for perfecting the appeal depending on whether or not transcripts need to be ordered. If the appeal does not require transcripts, it must be perfected within 30 days after the notice of appeal was filed. If transcripts are required, the appeal must be perfected within 60 days of the court reporter's giving notice that the transcripts are available.

In addition to the oral evidence set out in the transcripts, the appellant or cross-appellant may require for the appeal any or all of the exhibits presented in the court of first instance. To obtain these exhibits for the appeal, the party must bring a motion before a judge of the appellate court seeking an order that they be sent to the registrar of the court hearing the appeal.

In order to perfect the appeal, the appellant must

(3)(a) serve on every other party to the appeal and any other person entitled ... to be heard on the appeal,

(i) the appeal book referred to in rule 61.10,

(ii) the exhibit book, if any, referred to in rule 61.10.1,

(iii) a typed or printed copy of the transcript of evidence,

(iv) an electronic version of the transcript of evidence, unless the court reporter did not prepare an electronic version, and

(v) a typed or printed copy of the appellant's factum referred to in rule 61.11;

(b) file with the Registrar, with proof of service,

(i) three copies of the appeal book, and where the appeal is to be heard by five judges, two additional copies,

(ii) one copy of the exhibit book,

(iii) a typed or printed copy of the transcript of evidence,

(iv) an electronic version of the transcript of evidence, unless the court reporter did not prepare an electronic version,

(v) three typed or printed copies of the appellant's factum, and where the appeal is to be heard by five judges, two additional copies, and

(vi) an electronic version of the appellant's factum; and

(c) file with the Registrar a certificate of perfection,

(i) stating that the appeal book and compendium, exhibit book, transcripts, if any, and appellant's factum have been filed, and

(ii) setting out, with respect to every party to the appeal and any person entitled ... to be heard on the appeal,

(A) the name, address and telephone number of the party's or other person's lawyer, or

(B) the name, address for service and telephone number of the party or other person, if acting in person.

Preparation of all the documentation on an appeal may cost a great deal and take a long time to prepare. Where compliance with the rules for perfecting the appeal would cause undue expense or delay, on motion a judge of the appellate court may make an order giving special instructions and direction.

When all of the above steps have been taken, the appeal is perfected. Once it has been perfected, the registrar sends both counsel a notice of listing for hearing in form 61G. This notice does not contain the date set for the appeal. Counsel are notified of the date at a later point.

Appeal book and compendium: Rule 61.10

Rule 61.10 sets out in detail the required content and organization of the appeal book and compendium. The registrar may refuse to accept any appeal book and compendium that does not comply with the rules or is not legible. The appeal book must contain, in consecutively numbered pages arranged in the following order, a copy of

1. a table of contents describing each document by its nature and date;

2. the notice of appeal and any notice of cross-appeal or supplementary notice of appeal or cross-appeal;

3. the order or decision appealed from, as signed and entered;

4. the reasons of the court or tribunal appealed from with a further typed or printed copy if the reasons are handwritten;

5. any earlier order or decision that was the subject of the hearing before the court or tribunal appealed from, as signed and entered, and a copy of any reasons for it, with a further typed or printed copy if the reasons are handwritten;

6. the pleadings or notice of application or any other document that initiated the proceeding or defines the issues in it;

7. any excerpts from a transcript of the evidence referred to in the appellant's factum;

8. any exhibits that are referred to in the appellant's factum;

9. any other documents relevant to the appeal that are referred to in the appellant's factum;

10. the certificates of agreements respecting evidence referred to in rule 61.05;

11. any order made in respect to the conduct of the appeal; and

12. a certificate (form 61H) signed by the appellant's lawyer, or on the lawyer's behalf by someone he or she has specifically authorized, stating that the contents of the appeal book and compendium are complete and legible.

In addition to the requirements in rule 61.10, the practice direction also stipulates that the appeal book and compendium for the Court of Appeal be indexed in such a way that the court can easily locate documents referred to in the appellant's factum. For example, number 8 above requires that if the appellant has referred to an excerpt from a transcript, copies of the excerpts must be included in the appeal book and compendium. This means that each excerpt included should indicate the tab number (if tabs are used in the factum), page number, and line number where the reference to the excerpt is made in the factum. Sample wording might be: "This is the excerpt from the transcript of evidence referred to at tab 3, page 7, line 35 of the appellant's factum." If no tabs were used in the factum, then reference would only be made to the page and paragraph numbers.

If the evidence in the court of first instance is presented, in whole or in part, by affidavit, relevant extracts and exhibits from the affidavit must also be included in the compendium. Do not include the entire affidavit or all the exhibits unless they are relevant to the appeal. It is important to remember that the appeal book and compendium is an important working document for the members of the court in preparing for and conducting the appeal. It is essential that it be as easy to read and accessible as possible, and not cluttered up or made unwieldy by the inclusion of material that is not needed for the appeal. The respondent must also serve and file a compendium indexed in the same manner as the appellant's to make it easy to locate documents referred to in the respondent's factum.

Although the practice direction applies only to the Court of Appeal and not to Divisional Court, it would be a good idea to prepare your materials for both courts with the practice direction in mind.

Appellant's factum: Rule 61.11

An appellant's factum, which is set out in figure 20.4, is laid out in essentially the same form as the factum on a motion for leave to appeal, described earlier in this chapter. However, in addition to the four parts and the two schedules required on motions for leave to appeal, the factum for the appeal must contain a fifth part, stating the precise order that the appellate court will be asked to make, including any order for costs. The factum must also be signed by the appellant's lawyer or someone the lawyer has specifically authorized to sign in his or her place. In addition, the factum must contain a certificate that states

FIGURE 20.4 APPELLANT'S FACTUM

Court file no. C42798

COURT OF APPEAL FOR ONTARIO

BETWEEN:

ABIGAIL BOAR

Plaintiff (Appellant)

and

RATTLE MOTORS LTD. and FRED FLOGEM

Defendants (Respondents)

APPELLANT'S/RESPONDENTS' FACTUM

Just & Coping
Barristers and Solicitors
365 Bay Street - 8701
Toronto, Ontario M3J 4A9

I.M. Just
LSUC #12345R
tel. 416-762-1342
fax 416-762-2300
e-mail im.just@justcoping.com

Lawyers for the Appellant

TO:

Huey Sue
LSUC #23456T
Barrister and Solicitor
65 False Trail
Toronto, Ontario M6Y 1Z6

tel. 416-485-6891
fax 416-485-6892

Lawyer for the Respondents

Part I: Statement identifying the appellant, the court appealed from, and the judgment appealed from

1. The appellant, Abigail Boar, is the plaintiff in a negligence action brought in the Superior Court of Justice. She appeals from the judgment of the Honourable Justice Snork, dated October 15, 2008, wherein the learned trial judge dismissed the plaintiff's action and awarded costs to the defendants, Fred Flogem and Rattle Motors Ltd., in the amount of $72,000.00.

FIGURE 20.4 CONTINUED

Part II: Overview statement describing the nature of the case and the issues on appeal

2. The plaintiff brought an action in negligence in the Superior Court of Justice against the defendants after she was injured in a slip and fall at the place of business of the corporate defendant, Rattle Motors Ltd., a motor vehicle dealership. At the time of the injury, the plaintiff was a customer of Rattle Motors Ltd. and was being escorted through the property by the defendant Fred Flogem, an employee of Rattle Motors Ltd.

3. The plaintiff alleges
   a. that the defendants owed a duty of care to the plaintiff as a customer at their place of business,
   b. that they breached the required standard of care by failing to safely maintain the property, and by failing to warn the plaintiff of a known dangerous condition, and
   c. that the injuries suffered by the plaintiff were reasonably foreseeable given the state of repair and the failure of the defendants to warn the plaintiff.

4. The plaintiff says that the learned trial judge erred in
   a. finding that the defendants did not owe a duty of care to the plaintiff, and
   b. finding that the defendants did not breach the standard of care owed to the plaintif in the maintenance of their property.

Part III: Statement of the facts relevant to the appeal

5. On September 14, 2006, the appellant, while a customer at Rattle Motors Ltd., slipped and fell on a patch of oil leaking from a vehicle in the showroom.

6. The respondent, Rattle Motors Ltd., is a corporation in the business of selling automobiles to the public.

7. The respondent, Fred Flogem, is an employee of the respondent corporation, Rattle Motors Ltd.

8. … etc.

Part IV: Statement of each issue raised

9. The two issues on this appeal are:
   a. Did the learned trial judge err in finding that the defendants did not owe a duty of care to the plaintiff?
   b. Did the learned trial judge err in finding that the defendants did not breach the standard of care owed to the plaintif in the maintenance of their property?

FIGURE 20.4   CONCLUDED

Issue 1: Did the trial judge err in finding that the defendants did not owe a duty of care to the plaintiff?

10. It is respectfully submitted that the appellant was a customer at the respondent Rattle Motors Ltd.'s place of business and as such was owed a duty of care by the respondent.

    M'Alister (or Donoghue) v. Stevenson, [1932] AC 562 (HL)

    Hercules Managements Ltd. v. Ernst & Young, [1997] 2 SCR 165.

Issue 2: Did the learned trial judge err in finding that the defendants did not breach the standard of care owed to the plaintiff in the maintenance of their property?

11. It is further respectfully submitted that the respondent Rattle Motors Ltd. breached the standard of care when its employee, Fred Flogem, dimmed the lights in the automobile showroom to hide the spillage of oil underneath one of the vehicles.

    LeBlanc v. Marson Canada Inc. (1995), 139 NSR (2d) 309 at 312.

12. It is further respectfully submitted ….

13. It is further respectfully submitted …. Etc.

Part V: Order requested

14. It is therefore respectfully submitted that the appeal should be allowed, with costs, and that
    a. the respondent Rattle Motors Ltd. be found jointly and severally liable with the respondent Fred Flogem,
    b. the appellant be awarded the full amount of her claim,
    c. the appellant be awarded costs of this appeal and the trial below,
    d. such further relief as counsel may advise and this honourable court deem just.

I.M. Just
_____

I.M. Just

Just and Coping, Barristers and Solicitors
365 Bay Street - 8701
Toronto, Ontario M3J 4A9

I.M. Just, LSUC #12345R
tel. 416-762-1342
fax 416-762-2300

Lawyers for the Appellant

You must also include two schedules:
  - *Schedule A, containing a list of the authorities referred to, and*
  - *Schedule B, containing a list of all relevant provisions of statutes, regulations, and bylaws, followed by the text of those provisions.*

- that an order requiring the forwarding of the original record and exhibits has been obtained or is not needed, and

- how long the party will require for his or her oral argument on the appeal to the closest quarter hour.

Remember, the factum, the appeal book and compendium, and the exhibit book must all be cross-referenced so the court may easily locate the various documents referred to. In the factum, when references are made to the transcript, it must be done by tab, page number, and line number in the appeal book and compendium. References to exhibits must be by page number in the exhibit book and by tab and page number in the appeal book and compendium.

The practice direction for the Court of Appeal requires a motion be brought to the chambers judge for leave to file a factum that is more than 30 pages long. The proposed factum must be included in the motion record.

Respondent's factum and compendium: Rule 61.12

The respondent must prepare, serve, and file the requisite copies of a factum and compendium as well. It must be delivered within 60 days after the service of the appeal book and compendium, transcripts, exhibit book, if any, and appellant's factum. In addition to the hard copies that must be delivered, the respondent must also file an electronic version of the factum with the court within that time period. The factum must be signed by the respondent's lawyer or someone specifically authorized by the lawyer to sign the document in his or her place. It is laid out in the same general manner as other factums,[4] and it must also contain a certificate

- stating that an order requiring the forwarding of the original record and exhibits has been obtained or is not needed, and

- stating how long the party will require for his or her oral argument on the appeal to the closest quarter hour.

A respondent who is cross-appealing must deliver an appellant's factum in the cross-appeal. It can be a separate factum from the respondent's factum or can be incorporated into the respondent's factum, and it must be delivered within the allowable times for delivery of the respondent's factum.

The appellant on the main appeal, who is also the respondent on the cross-appeal, may file a respondent's factum on the cross-appeal within ten days after service of the respondent's factum.

RESTRICTIONS ON THE LENGTH OF FACTUMS

The rules require that the factum contain a "concise" summary of the facts and the applicable law. Although there is no limit on the length of a factum in the rules, a practice direction of the Court of Appeal states that factums usually should be no more than 30 pages unless the case is exceptional. A lawyer who believes that the case is exceptional and that the factum must exceed 30 pages must bring a motion seeking leave to file a longer factum from a judge of the Court of Appeal.

Exhibit book: Rule 61.10.1

This book is a collection of the documentary evidence, filed as exhibits, in the trial that the parties intend to rely on in the appeal. The parties can agree that certain exhibits from the trial may be omitted; however, unless both parties consent to the omission, the exhibit must be included.

The exhibit book is to be bound and laid out in consecutively numbered pages. There is to be a table of contents describing each exhibit by its nature, date, and exhibit number or letter. A copy of each exhibit must follow. The exhibits can be arranged in order of their date, or they can be arranged in groups, with similar documents sharing common characteristics grouped together. Do not arrange the exhibits by their trial exhibit numbers.

Book of authorities

Although there is no specific requirement for a book of authorities in the rules, it is helpful to both the court and the lawyers to prepare bound books containing copies of all the case law that a party will rely on in the appeal. The practice direction that provides guidelines for preparing these books. They should:

- include only the cases which have been referred to in the factum — passages being specifically referred to should be highlighted;

- indicate whether the appellant or the respondent filed them (lawyers for the parties should consult each other beforehand to ensure that they are not filing duplicate copies of cases) — a joint case book is acceptable if the parties can agree;

- have a tab for each case with either a number or a letter on the tab;

- have an index of the cases and indicate the tab number or letter where the case can be found;

- have consecutively numbered pages unless the actual page number of each case is clear on the photocopy; and

- be filed, if possible, with the factum, but if this is not possible, then not later than the Monday of the week preceding the hearing of the appeal so that the judges on the panel have an opportunity to read them before the appeal.

Copies of case law in the book of authorities may be either photocopies from law reports or cases obtained from Internet legal reporting services or other electronic databases, but if an Internet or electronic database is used, the case must have the same paragraph numbers as the judgment released by the court. The citation from the law report should be given as well as the electronic citation, and the date the copy was obtained from the Internet or electronic source should be included. It is important to ensure that the copy submitted to the court is the most current one available from the electronic source.

You must prepare three or five copies of the book of authorities to be filed with the court, depending on how many judges will be sitting on the panel. Then there must be a copy for the lawyer for each of the parties.

Dismissal for delay: Rule 61.13

A notice of appeal must be filed within a specifically limited period of the making of the order being appealed. Sometimes a lawyer for a party files the notice to protect the party's right to appeal, but the party may decide not to proceed. In other cases, a party may file a notice of appeal as a tactical matter in order to create a delay. The party does not order the transcript as required and may delay in perfecting the appeal.

In such instances, either the respondent or the registrar may take procedural steps to dismiss the appeal for delay. The respondent may make a motion to the registrar to dismiss the appeal with ten days' notice to the appellant.

However, the registrar does not need to wait for the respondent to take action. Where the appellant has not

- filed a transcript within 60 days after the court reporter has provided written notice that it is ready,

- perfected the appeal within one year of filing the notice of appeal, or

- perfected the appeal within 30 days of filing the notice of appeal where no transcript is needed for the appeal,

the registrar may serve notice on the appellant to correct the default within ten days, or the appeal will be dismissed.

Within the ten days following the service of the respondent's motion or the registrar's notice, the appellant must perfect the appeal, order the transcript or obtain an order from the court providing him or her with an extension of time in which to take these steps. If the appellant does nothing, the registrar will dismiss the appeal for delay and award costs to the respondent.

It is not only the appellant who must act in a timely fashion on the appeal. If the respondent has brought a cross-appeal and has not delivered a factum on the cross-appeal within 60 days after he or she has been served with the appeal book and compendium, the appellant may make a motion on 5 days' notice to the respondent to have the cross-appeal dismissed for delay. The respondent has 5 days in which to file the factum or obtain an order for an extension of time. If the respondent does neither, the registrar will dismiss the cross-appeal with costs.

Similar consequences apply to a party who does not act in a timely fashion on a motion seeking leave to appeal. If the moving party has not served and filed a motion record and other documents within 60 days of filing the notice of motion, the registrar may give notice to the moving party to file the record and documents within 10 days. If the defect has not been cured within 10 days, the registrar will dismiss the motion for leave with costs.

The responding party on the motion for leave need not wait the 60 days for the registrar to take action. If the motion record and other documentation has not been filed within 30 days of the notice of motion being filed, the responding party may bring a motion, on 10 days' notice, to dismiss the motion for leave (rules 61.03(2) and 61.03.1(4) to (6)). Once again, the appellant has 10 days to correct the defect or obtain an order for an extension of time. If he or she does neither, the registrar will dismiss the motion for leave to appeal with costs.

Abandoned appeals: Rules 61.14 and 61.15

After filing the notice of appeal, if the appellant decides that he or she does not wish to continue with it, the proper thing to do is to file a notice of abandonment in form 61K. A party who serves a notice of appeal but does not file it with the court within ten days of service is deemed to have abandoned the appeal. A party who abandons an appeal or a cross-appeal may be liable for costs to the opposite party or parties.

If the main appeal has been dismissed for delay or abandoned, and a cross-appeal has been commenced, the respondent on the main appeal must deliver a notice of election to proceed with the cross-appeal in form 61L or bring motion to the court for directions. Otherwise, the cross-appeal will be deemed to be abandoned without costs.

Motions in appellate court: Rule 61.16

In the event a party finds it necessary to bring a motion relating to the appeal to the appellate court, parts of rule 37,[5] the general rule for motions, and rule 61.16 govern. The two rules must be read together.

There are a number of different types of motions that may be made in an appeal. Some of the motions are heard by only one judge of the appellate court. Others are heard by a panel of judges.[6] Motions in appellate courts are commenced in the same manner as other motions — that is, with a notice of motion. The notice of motion for an appellate court must, however, include a certificate stating how long the party estimates the motion will take. The notice must be served at least four days in advance and filed at least three days before the motion is to be heard. A motion record must also be served and filed along with a factum.

If a motion is to be heard by more than one judge, the notice of motion should not set a date but should rather state that the motion is to be heard on a date to be fixed by the registrar. The registrar then arranges for a date when a panel of judges is sitting and notifies the parties.

In addition to rule 61.16, there is a practice direction that pertains to motions in the Court of Appeal. This practice direction provides specific, additional requirements to the rule, depending on whether the motion is being brought before a single judge or a panel of judges. Both the rule and the practice direction must be followed for motions in this court.

APPEALS FROM INTERLOCUTORY ORDERS AND OTHER NON-APPELLATE COURT APPEALS

Rule 62 deals with the procedure on appeals of interlocutory orders. Appeals of this type of order lie either with a judge of the Superior Court of Justice or with the Divisional Court.

If the order being appealed is an interlocutory order of a master, a certificate of assessment of costs, or an appeal under any statute that does not specifically require another procedure for appeal, the appeal will proceed to a single judge of the Superior Court of Justice. Unlike an appeal of a final order, it will not proceed to an **appellate court**. Interlocutory orders that fall within any of these three categories may be appealed without leave.

appellate court
the court of appeal or the divisional court

If the order being appealed is an interlocutory order of a judge of the Superior Court of Justice, the appeal must be heard by the Divisional Court. However, there is no automatic right to appeal an interlocutory order of a judge. A party that wants to appeal this type of order must bring a motion seeking leave to the Divisional Court. Since the judges of the Divisional Court are the same as those who sit in the Superior Court of Justice, the judge hearing the motion for leave must be different from the judge who made the order being appealed.

The procedure on these appeals is different from the procedure on appeals of final orders, which we looked at earlier under rule 61. Rule 62.01 deals with the procedure on the appeal of interlocutory orders that do not require leave. Rule 62.02 sets out the procedure on seeking leave for appeal, when leave is required.

Commencement of the appeal when no leave is required

If the appeal does not require leave, it is commenced by serving a notice of appeal on all parties whose interests may be affected by the appeal. The prescribed form is form 62A. The notice of appeal must be served within seven days of the making of the order being appealed. The notice must then be filed with the court, along with proof of service, no later than four days before the appeal is to be heard.

The notice of appeal must set out the relief sought and the grounds of the appeal. The grounds must be specific and only those grounds stated in the notice may be relied on at the hearing unless the presiding judge orders otherwise. Therefore, the grounds must be carefully drafted and be as comprehensive as possible.

Rule 37.03 governs the place of hearing of motions. The appeal must be commenced in the same place where the original proceeding was commenced.

Material for use on the motion

The appellant must prepare, serve, and file both an appeal record and a factum. These must be filed in the court office, along with proof of service, at least four days before the hearing of the appeal.

Rule 62.01(7) sets out the required contents of an appeal record. It must contain, in consecutively numbered pages,

- a table of contents describing each document, including each exhibit, by its nature, date, and exhibit number, if there is one;

- a copy of the notice of appeal;

- a copy of the signed and entered order or certificate of costs appealed from, along with a copy of any reasons for judgment relating to the order or certificate; and

- any other material used at the hearing at which the order being appealed was made, which is necessary for the hearing of the appeal.

The contents of the appeal record must be set out exactly in the order listed above. The appeal record must also have a blue back cover, not the buff-coloured back cover required for appeals to appellate courts.

The title of proceedings does not change for this type of appeal, except that the words "plaintiff" and "defendant" are changed to "appellant" and "respondent." If there is more than one defendant and the appeal does not involve all of them, the names of those involved must be underlined in the title of proceedings.

The respondent must also prepare a factum and any other material that was before the judge who made the order being appealed, which is necessary for the hearing of the appeal and which has not been provided by the appellant in his or her appeal record. The factum and the additional material must be served and filed with the court at least two days before the hearing of the appeal.

The judge hearing the appeal may dispense with the requirements of the parties to file any or all of this material.

If the appellant commences the appeal by serving and filing the notice of appeal and then decides not to proceed with it, he or she should serve and file a notice of abandonment. If the appellant does not file the necessary documentation on the appeal at least three days before the hearing date, he or she will be deemed to have abandoned the appeal.

Motions for leave to appeal

If the order being appealed is an interlocutory order of a judge of the Superior Court of Justice, leave is required to bring the appeal and the prospective appellant must serve a motion within seven days after the order to be appealed was made. Rule 62.02 sets out the procedure on the motion for leave to appeal.

It is usually quite difficult to obtain leave to appeal. Leave will not be granted if one of the tests in rule 62.02(4) is met.

In preparing a motion record for leave to appeal, it is not necessary to reproduce an entirely new motion record. Remember, what is being appealed here is likely an order made on a motion. The original motion record may be requisitioned for the motion for leave. A supplementary motion record should then be prepared, containing the notice of appeal, a copy of the order being appealed, and any reasons given by the judge for making the order.

Both parties must serve and file factums on the motion. The moving party must serve their documents at least four days in advance of the hearing. The respondent must serve at least two days in advance. Both parties must file their documents with the court at least two days in advance.

If the motion is successful and leave to appeal is granted, the moving party, who now becomes the appellant, must serve and file a notice of appeal as required by rule 61.04, along with the appellant's certificate of evidence required by rule 61.05(1). This must be done within seven days after the order granting leave to appeal is made.

STAYS PENDING APPEAL: RULE 63

During the appeal process, both final and interlocutory orders for the payment of money, other than orders for family support, are usually stayed or suspended. Only a judge of the appellate court can order that the judgment remain in effect while it is being appealed. Without such an order, the order appealed from is automatically stayed, and it cannot be enforced.

A party may bring a motion to have an automatic stay lifted while the appeal is winding its way through the system. The court may lift the stay totally or partially on terms that are just.

If the order being appealed is an order for relief other than the payment of money, the order is not automatically stayed when the appeal commences. A party may apply to the appellate court or to the court that made the order being appealed, however, to request a stay during the appeal. If a stay is ordered, it may be varied or set aside later through motion. An order for a stay that was made by the same court that made the order expires if a notice of appeal or a motion for leave to appeal is not commenced within the time required under the rules.

The stay comes into effect when the notice of appeal is filed, or the order granting the stay is made. Once the stay takes effect, no enforcement action can be taken. In order to ensure that the sheriff's office does not commence enforcement on a stayed order, a party may requisition a certificate of stay from the registrar of the court that granted the stay or the court to which the appeal was taken. This certificate can then be filed with the sheriff's office to notify the sheriff that he or she may not take any further enforcement action until the stay is lifted. If the stay is granted by an order, particulars of the order must be included in the certificate. A certificate of stay is in form 63A.

CHAPTER SUMMARY

This chapter has dealt with appeals and rules 61, 62, and 63, which govern the procedure for appeals. We have seen that rule 61 governs appeals of final orders, rule 62 governs appeals of interlocutory orders, and rule 63 governs stays pending an appeal. We have noted that there are three courts that may hear appeals in Ontario: the Superior Court of Justice, the Divisional Court, and the Court of Appeal. The *Courts of Justice Act* sets out the types of appeal that each court may hear, and we have provided an overview of the courts' jurisdiction.

We have addressed the matter of commencing an appeal, with or without the necessity of seeking leave. We have noted the various time limits and procedures in this regard. An appeal must be perfected before it is ready to be heard. An appeal is perfected when the appellant has taken all the procedural steps, including the service and filing of such material as an appeal book, an exhibit book, the transcript, and a factum. Finally, we have examined automatic stays of orders under appeal and the lifting of such stays by means of motion.

KEY TERMS

court of first instance

appellant

respondent

final order

interlocutory order

leave of the court

transcript

appeal as of right

perfecting an appeal

appellate court

NOTES

1 An objection to an assessment may be made pursuant to rule 58.10.

2 Ibid.

3 Practice direction of the chief justice of Ontario, May 1, 1993.

4 See rule 61.12 for specific detail of the content of the respondent's factum on an appeal.

5 Rules 37.02 to 37.05, 37.07(6), 37.08, 37.10, and 37.17 do not apply to motions to an appellate court.

6 See rule 61.16(2), (2.1), and (2.2).

REFERENCES

Courts of Justice Act, RSO 1990, c. C.43.

Rules of Civil Procedure, RRO 1990, reg. 194.

REVIEW QUESTIONS

1. What is the difference between a final and an interlocutory order?

2. What factors determine which court will hear an appeal?

3. What three courts hear appeals?

4. What types of appeals are heard in the Superior Court of Justice?

5. What types of appeals are heard in Divisional Court?

6. What types of appeals are heard in the Court of Appeal?

7. Identify the court to which the following judgment or orders should be appealed:

   a. a decision by a judge that Widgets Inc. has breached its contract with John Doe and that John should be awarded $60,000;

   b. a decision by a master to permit an amendment of a pleading after pleadings have closed;

   c. a decision by a Small Claims Court judge to award the plaintiff $1,500 in damages caused by his neighbour's negligence;

   d. a decision by a judge at the end of trial that the defendant is not liable for the plaintiff's claim of $100,000;

e. a decision by a judge at the end of trial that the defendant is liable for the plaintiff's claim but awarding the plaintiff only $20,000; and

f. a decision by a judge of the Superior Court to strike out a jury notice after hearing the motion brought by the defendant.

8. Where does the Ontario Court of Appeal sit?

9. How much time do you have to serve a motion for leave to appeal to the Divisional Court? What rule applies?

10. How is a factum for leave to appeal to the Court of Appeal arranged? What rule applies?

11. What document commences an appeal?

12. How long does an appellant have to order the transcript for an appeal?

13. Your law firm is appealing a matter to the Court of Appeal and needs some of the exhibits from the trial. How do you obtain them?

14. In an appeal to the Divisional Court, must the respondent file a factum?

15. A party does not wish to continue with an appeal after filing a notice of appeal. How does the party terminate the appeal process?

DISCUSSION QUESTION

1. The defendant, Global Steel Works Inc., wishes to appeal a decision of the Superior Court of Justice. The decision ordered it to pay its former employee, Romeo Capulet, $250,000 for wrongful dismissal. Draft a general heading for the notice of appeal.

CHAPTER 21

Case management

INTRODUCTION

What is case management?

Case managment is a system designed to give the courts control over the pace at which a case moves to trial. Before the introduction of case management, lawyers, and to some extent their clients, determined the pace at which a case moved forward. Once originating process was issued, lawyers could waive many time limits imposed by the rules. For example, the statement of defence is due 20 days from the time the statement of claim is served in most cases. Defence counsel would often ask for, and get, an extension of time, simply as a matter of courtesy. And so the case would progress, at a stately and leisurely pace. The court was passive, waiting for lawyers and litigants to take the next step.

The result was that cases could take a long time to get to trial, particularly if one litigant or the other decided to employ delaying strategies, or one of the lawyers had many files on the go. Lawyers used to joke about files so old that they had moss growing on their north side.[1] In addition, there was the natural tendency among many lawyers to procrastinate about getting things done. As a student, you may be familiar with this tendency and will appreciate how it could prevent a case from moving forward quickly to trial.

These kinds of delays did not matter all that much in judicial regions where the volume of cases was low. But in larger centres, such as Toronto, it created problems. Because lawyers controlled the pace a case took getting to trial, individual decisions about when a case was to move forward at various stages of the proceeding resulted in uneven flows of cases through the court system. This created backlogs at points where court time was needed: at motions, at discovery, and at trial. In Toronto, a case could take a year or more getting to trial. In addition, because the court was not proactive in assisting the parties to explore settlement in a rational way, settlement was often left to the last minute, with a deal being struck at the courtroom door. This approach to settlement was wasteful for both the court system and the litigants. If a deal had been explored earlier in the process, much time and money might have been saved for the litigants. For the courts, a last minute settlement often meant collapse of the trial list because the next cases on the list were not necessarily ready to start immediately. This sometimes resulted in empty courtrooms and judges with nothing on their schedule for the day — hardly a good use of public funds.

Case management is an attempt to solve problems of cost and delay and to promote settlement at earlier stages by having the court intervene and oversee the case as it moves along, making procedural decisions and ensuring that the case adheres to a timetable so that it either settles or comes to trial within a reasonable time.

Under the case management system, once a proceeding is commenced, the plaintiff must select a track (fast or standard) with a timetable to which the litigants *must* adhere unless the court agrees to change it. The case is assigned to a case management master or, in some cases, a judge who may call a **case conference** to discuss changes to the timetable, make orders enforcing time limits, discuss settlement, and deal with a host of procedural issues. A party can also request a case conference. The case management masters and judges have powers to enforce strict compliance with set timetables, but they can also alter timetables if circumstances warrant.

Once the first defence[2] is filed, the parties are obliged to enter into and complete **mandatory mediation**, within strict time limits, early in the proceeding. This gives the parties an opportunity to explore settlement before spending time and money on what may turn out to be unnecessary litigation. It also diverts cases from the courts at an early stage, lessening the burden on the court system.

Motions are simpler and less formal than in the ordinary system. Often something that would be the subject of a motion may be disposed of informally at a case conference.

Settlement conferences are now automatic and mandatory, following mediation. Within 150 days of filing the first defence in a fast track action, and within 240 days in a standard track, all discoveries must be completed. Parties must be prepared to seriously discuss settlement and will be assigned a trial date if settlement discussions fail.

There is an optional trial management conference to narrow issues and promote speedy trials.

case conference
conference managed by the case management judge or master, who controls timetables and settles all procedural matters

mandatory mediation
process in which disputants are required to allow a neutral third party to facilitate their communication and assist them in negotiating a settlement

Purpose of the rule

In stating the purpose of the rule, we can do no better than to quote rule 77.02 in its entirety:

> 77.02 The purpose of this Rule is to establish a case management system throughout Ontario that reduces unnecessary cost and delay in civil litigation, facilitates early and fair settlements and brings proceedings expeditiously to a just determination while allowing sufficient time for the conduct of the proceeding.

What's in?

Although rule 77.02 speaks of all of Ontario, at the time of writing, case management applies only in the following areas:

- all civil cases commenced in the Superior Court in Ottawa and the municipalities around it that formerly constituted the Regional Municipality of Ottawa-Carleton (now called the City of Ottawa); the province has reserved the right to name other areas at a later date by listing them in the schedule referred to in rule 77.01(1);

- all civil cases commenced in the former Municipality of Metropolitan Toronto and present City of Toronto before July 1, 2001 and randomly assigned to case management by the court registrar;

- all civil cases commenced in the Superior Court in the City of Toronto after July 1, 2001 but before January 1, 2005, subject to some exceptions (as of January 1, 2005, case managment is no longer mandatory in Toronto under rule 77); and

- all civil cases commenced in the Superior Court in the County of Essex (Windsor) after July 2, 2002, with some exceptions.

It is also open to the court under rule 77.01(1.1) and rule 77.11 to bring cases that are not case managed into case management. While the language is broad enough to bring a case anywhere in Ontario into case management, it would be hard to do this outside Windsor, Toronto, or Ottawa.

What's out

The case management rules do not apply to cases commenced outside Ottawa and Windsor. Rule 77.01(2) also excludes certain types of cases. Simplified procedure cases under rule 76 are also excluded from case management under rule 77.[3] A summary of the types of exclusions is set out below, but when considering whether a case is within the case management rules, you should read rule 77.01(2) carefully.

Exclusions to the case management rules include:

- some Superior Court family law cases in Toronto and Ottawa that are subject to family law case management rules or are otherwise excluded;

- commercial list actions in Toronto, which go on a separate civil trial list before judges with a commercial litigation background;

- a variety of estate, guardianship, and trust proceedings, many of which are governed by statutory procedural rules in addition to the *Rules of Civil Procedure*;

- mortgage actions;

- construction lien proceedings, which are governed by procedural rules and time limits found in the *Construction Lien Act*;

- bankruptcy proceedings, where there is a prescribed procedure dictated in part by the *Bankruptcy and Insolvency Act*;

- class proceedings, unless certification as a class proceeding has been denied;

- simplified proceedings under rule 76; and

- applications.

THE RETREAT FROM CASE MANAGEMENT?

When case management was made mandatory in Toronto in July 2001, the view was that a case timetable that was enforced and controlled by the court would bring an end to the high costs and lengthy delays in the Superior Court. But by 2004, it was apparent that case management was not working the way the rules committee thought it would. There were continued and increasing delays in getting motions heard and actions tried. It was also clear that rather than cutting costs, case management increased them by requiring extra appearances at case conferences and an increased number of formal steps. The case timetables, with the insistence that a case be ready for a settlement conference 240 days after the first defence was filed, were often too rigid for cases with complex issues or many parties.

The rules committee responded by issuing a practice direction for civil cases in Toronto, which took effect on December 31, 2004.[4] It can be summed up, in the words of the practice direction itself, as "case management as necessary, but not necessarily case management." Cases in Toronto are no longer automatically be under rule 77, the case management rule; instead, case management may be chosen by the parties, or imposed by the courts in its pure form or in a modified form, as determined by the court. The details of the practice direction, rule 78 (which is designed to implement it), and its effect on case management in Toronto are described at the end of the chapter.

THE FURTHER RETREAT FROM CASE MANAGEMENT AS OF JANUARY 1, 2010

While the basic case management system under rule 77 continues to exist with minor modifications, there are some changes:

- Case management will no longer be automatic, but will be available in Toronto, Ottawa, and Windsor under rule 77.

- Rule 78, the modified case management rule for Toronto, will be revoked.

- Parties will now have greater responsibility for managing actions and moving them quickly to trial or other resolution. A judge may order, at any time, or the parties may request, that a case be moved into case management.

- Case management rules will continue to apply in Toronto, Ottawa, and Windsor.[5]

COMMENCEMENT OF PROCEEDINGS

The steps taken when proceedings commence are somewhat different from those in an ordinary proceeding. Originating process is the same as in an ordinary proceeding, but there are differences.

Forms prescribed by rule 77, including notices, certificates, and orders referred to in the rule, may be single spaced and do not require backsheets (rule 77.05(2)). The idea behind this is to save paper and reduce the size of court files to save storage space.

When commenced as part of a main proceeding, third party proceedings keep the same court file number as the main proceeding but have a suffix added. For example, if the main case number is CM1234, the third party proceeding is identified as CM1234-A (rule 77.05(1)).

When a notice of action or statement of claim is issued, the party files the pleadings as in an ordinary action along with form 14F, "Information for Court Use." There is a place on the form to check off that rule 77 applies and that the plaintiff is choosing either the fast or the standard track. The former requirement to file a notice of commencement of proceedings, but not the pleadings, was revoked.[6]

The plaintiff must choose a track on which the case is to proceed. The criteria for choosing is set out in rule 77.06(6). In general, fast track cases

- have simpler facts or issues of law,

- involve issues that are of importance to the parties rather than the public,

- have few parties,

- will not require much intervention by the case management master, and

- will not have lengthy discoveries.

All other cases go on the standard track.

While the initial choice is the plaintiff's, the defendant has the opportunity to move to change tracks, but he or she must do so before the close of pleadings or within ten days of the filing of the respondent's affidavit. By that time, the defendant has the basic outline of the case before him or her and has enough information to decide which track is appropriate.

The choice of track involves different time limits.

Within 150 days on the fast track and within 240 days on the standard track from the filing of the first defence, the plaintiff must complete all productions of documents, discovery, and all motions arising from discovery and be ready for a settlement conference. Not later than ten days before the settlement conference, the plaintiff must serve and file a settlement brief. The defendant must respond to this by filing his or her settlement brief within five days of the settlement conference.

Defendants serve on the plaintiff and file in court a statement of defence or notice of intention to defend just as in a regular action.

Commencement of proceedings sets the clock running

Issuing a claim or commencing an application sets timetables and deadlines running. Because the times allotted for completing pretrial procedures and getting a matter to trial are shorter and under the control of the courts, a lawyer must be careful about when to commence proceedings. In the days before case management, lawyers issued claims before they completed their investigation and research, and they did repair work on the pleadings later if required, adding parties and amending claims or defences. But with the timetable out of their hands, there may not be time to correct mistakes if, for example, the time for completing discoveries has passed, and the matter is being set down for a pretrial conference. Lawyers are now advised to complete as much of their investigative and research work on a case as possible before commencing proceedings, unless a limitation period is about to expire. Once a proceeding is commenced, it is expected to move from stage to stage within the time allowed by the case timetable.

CASE TIMETABLE
Deadlines that arise when proceeding commences

Once a claim is issued, regardless whether or not it is served, three time limits begin to run:

1. the six-month period to serve a statement of claim pursuant to rule 14.08(1);

2. the 180-day period in which either a defence must be filed or a default judgment must be obtained, failing which the registrar will dismiss the action as abandoned pursuant to rule 77.08; and

3. the 180-day period in which a timetable must be agreed to by all parties, or a case conference must be convened to impose one.

Periods of 180 days or six months may sound like a lot of time, but they are not. Consider what happens if you have difficulty in serving the claim after it is issued. If the claim is unliquidated and not defended, the plaintiff will need time to move for an assessment of damages under rule 19.05. Consider what will happen if you have several defendants to serve, some of whom are overseas and may have up to 60 days to file a defence. You could easily run up against the 180-day limit without having been able to obtain a default or undefended judgment. You then run the risk of having the registrar dismiss your action. You can see why you should do as much preparation ahead of time, before issuing your claim. And once having issued it, move to serve it as quickly as possible.

Deadlines that arise when the first defence is filed

If you serve some of the parties but not all of them, you may run into a second problem. A second set of time limits begins to run when the first defence is filed, regardless whether some defendants have not yet been served:

1. Within 30 days from the date the first defence is filed, the parties must name a mediator; if they fail to do so, the court will appoint one pursuant to rule 24.1.09(5).

2. Within 90 days from the filing of a first defence, the parties must complete mandatory mediation or, in the case of standard track cases, consent to an extension of time for mediation.

3. Within 150 days, the parties must complete all production and discovery and motions arising from discovery in fast track actions.

4. Within 240 days, the parties must complete all production and discovery and motions arising from discovery in standard track actions.

To put it succinctly, you have 240 days from the filing of the first defence to complete all pretrial proceedings in most cases. In a straightforward case with one plaintiff and one defendant where no motions are necessary, this is not a difficult timetable to meet. But if the case is factually and legally complex, there are multiple parties, difficulties with service, and disputes about procedure that result in motions, 240 days may be very tight indeed.

Defendants and timetables

It is not only the plaintiff who must move quickly once proceedings have commenced. The defendant has even less room to manoeuvre. Because the registrar must dismiss an action if no defence has been filed and the case has not been disposed of within 180 days of the claim issuing, the plaintiff cannot extend extra time for filing a defence.

If a defendant does not have counsel at the time a claim is served, the defendant may put off retaining counsel until near the end of the time for filing a defence. This leaves little time for the defendant's newly retained counsel to conduct necessary research and investigate the matter before issuing a statement of defence. There may be a need to make crossclaims against other defendants, third-party claims, or a counterclaim against the plaintiff. Since these are part of the main action, they are all subject to the main action timetables on which time is already beginning to run. This in turn creates a situation where counsel will need to ask a **case management judge or master** to extend the time for filing a defence, and extend other running time limits. Asking for more time creates an extra procedural step, which makes for more cost and delay. But the important point is that someone other than counsel is overseeing the progress of the case and preventing it from getting bogged down, as often used to be the situation when a simple case became complex.

Because a third party proceeding, spawned from the main action, brings in a new party, the proceeding is subject to a separate timetable. It gets a case file number that is the same as that in the main action, but it has a letter added at the end to distinguish it, while keeping the two proceedings linked.

Because timelines start to run when the claim issues, it is important to do as much investigation and negotiation, including mediation, before it is required under rule 24.1. In this way, if negotiations fail, you will have done all the necessary preliminary work and will have possibly selected a mediator so that you are ready to move within the timelines set by rule 77, when the action commences.

Case management timetable

Once the case is underway under case management, the court expects to see the parties create a case management timetable. Initially, under rule 77.10(2), it is the responsibility of the plaintiff to do this when a mediator files a report or when an order exempting the case from mediation has issued. The purpose of the timetable is to set up a "schedule for the completion of one or more steps required to advance the proceeding" (rule 77.03). This means that dates may be set for the delivery of affidavits of documents, examinations for discovery, other types of discovery, or motions. Here, the parties can set their own timelines, provided that they fit them within the boundaries set by the rules. For example, depending on the track chosen, the timetable must provide for the completion of discoveries and related motions within 150 or 240 days after the first defence is filed and within 10 days before the settlement conference (rule 77.10(4)). Within those 150 or 240 days, the parties are free to arrange discoveries as they see fit. But remember to be realistic about allowing

case management judge or master
court official assigned to each case managed case to ensure court control over the case on its way to trial

enough time to carry out the steps required in the case. Lawyers, as well as other folk, often underestimate the time required to complete a series of tasks, and it is important to stay within the deadlines established under rule 77 and other rules.

Timetable must comply with deadlines in the rules

If a timetable is filed that does not comply with the rules, the court has the power to call a case management conference to review and, if necessary, impose a timetable that complies with rule 77. The timetable should at least take the parties to completion of discoveries and right up to the settlement conference within the 150- or 240-day time limits. The parties cannot themselves extend the time limits in the rules.

Customizing the timetable and extending the deadlines in the rules

If the parties think they are going to need more time than the fast or standard track provides to complete pretrial procedures, rule 77.10 gives the court power on a motion by a party, or on the motion of a case management judge or master, to convene a case conference. At the conference, a timetable can be arranged. If the parties are uncooperative, they can be subject to sanctions.

In changing or customizing the case management timetable, counsel should be aware that some rules trigger automatic dismissal and that some timelines are running simultaneously. For example, if a lawyer is moving to extend time for mandatory mediation, he or she must also remember to extend other rule 77 times, such as the date for completing pretrial discovery before scheduling a case conference. Otherwise, lawyers may give themselves enough time for mediation but not leave enough time to complete discoveries. They then need to ask for a second case management conference.

Time requirements

Case management time requirements, and any time requirement in any rule, may be extended or abridged only by order of a case management judge or master. The key time requirements are set out below.[7]

Within 180 days from the commencement of proceedings:

1. The plaintiff must file a timetable agreed to by all parties or request a case conference to establish one (rule 77.10(2)).

2. If no defence is filed, the plaintiff must obtain default judgment or an order extending time for filing a defence by motion or case conference, or the registrar will dismiss the action (rule 77.08(1)).

3. If the statement of claim is not served in six months, an order is required to extend time for service (rule 14.08(1)).

Within 30 days from the filing of the first defence:

1. The parties must name a mediator and provide the name to the mediation coordinator or obtain an order from the case management judge or master to extend the time for doing this; otherwise, the mediation coordinator will appoint a mediator, who will unilaterally set a date for mediation (rule 24.1.09(6) and (7)).

Within 90 days from the filing of the first defence:

1. The parties must complete a mandatory mediation session. In standard track cases, you may extend the time to do this on consent, or you may obtain an order. In fast track cases, you must obtain an order (rule 24.1.09(1) and (3)).

2. Rule 24.1 (mandatory mediation) requires the parties to file a statement of issues with the mediator, and the plaintiff must file a copy of the pleadings at least seven days before the first mediation session. Failure to comply with the requirements for mandatory mediation will result in a certificate of non-compliance, which automatically triggers an appearance before a case management judge or master.

Within 150 days for fast track actions and 240 days for standard track actions from the filing of the first defence:

1. The parties must complete all production and discovery and all motions arising from discovery and be ready for a settlement conference (rule 77.14(1) and (2)).

2. At least 10 days before the date of the settlement conference, the plaintiff must file a settlement conference brief, including a witness list with a summary of evidence to be given by each witness. All other parties must file their brief and witness list within 5 days of the settlement conference (rule 77.14(4) to (6)).

3. If the parties are not ready for a settlement conference, the court will schedule a case conference, revise the timetable, and possibly impose sanctions.

At least 90 days prior to trial:

1. Each party must deliver any expert reports on which he or she intends to rely at trial (rule 53.03(1)).

At least 60 days before trial:

1. Each party must deliver responding expert reports on which he or she intends to rely at trial (rule 53.03(2)).

2. Each party must answer any undertakings if he or she wishes to rely at trial on the information that is the subject of the undertakings (rule 31.07(2)).

At least 30 days before trial:

1. Each party must deliver any supplementary experts' reports on which it intends to rely at trial (rule 53.03(3)(b)).

At least 7 days before trial:

1. The trial record must be filed (rule 77.14(8)).

2. Notice must be given under s. 35(3) of the Ontario *Evidence Act* regarding introduction of records made in the ordinary course of business.

Missing a time limit often triggers a case conference, which can occur automatically or at the instance of another party. This in turn can lead to the imposition of timetables or sanctions, raising costs for your client. Rule 77 procedures and time limits will cause lawyers to introduce a form of case management to their office operations to control their practice. Gone are the days when lawyers take on all files that come in the door. It will be much more important to manage the flow of cases in the office, so that the lawyer is able to meet all deadlines, and does not end up, for example, with two cases being tried back to back, while he or she is trying to complete discoveries in a third and schedule mediation in a fourth. This will be particularly problematic for sole practitioners, who do not have a stable of associates or articling students to hand work to. Case Management Master MacLeod has set out 10 ideas to make case management work:

1. *Complete all research and investigation before you commence proceedings.*

2. *Once the claim issues, serve it immediately because time limits start running.*

3. *Once all parties have appointed counsel, try to get agreement on an early timetable.* If extensions of times beyond the limits in the rules are required, be ready to apply for an order.

4. *Watch your time limits.* Use ticklers with multiple time warnings — for example, at one month, two weeks, five days, two days, and one day before a deadline.

5. *Organize documentary production.* Organize production as soon as possible, and seek extensions over the ten-day time period where necessary.

6. *Consider the timing of mediation.* After the first defence is filed, you must name a mediator in 30 days and complete mediation in 90 days. This may be too short a time for mediation to work in some cases. Consider applying for an order to extend time, and be careful to extend other times that will be affected by the extension of mediation.

7. *Consider the timing of discoveries and the need for post-discovery motions.* It may not be possible to complete discoveries in 150 or 240 days of the filing of the first defence if, for example, there are a dozen defendants. Consider applying to extend the time.

8. *Consider using requests to admit facts and documents to narrow issues before trial.* Consider also whether you can proceed by stated case, with an agreed statement of facts, in whole or in part.

9. *Continue to watch time limits.* If the case timetable is becoming unrealistic, consider obtaining the consent of all parties to schedule a case conference and revise it or revise it on a consent motion.

10. *Focus on results.* Avoid useless procedural wrangling. The court is likely to be far less tolerant of delaying tactics than it was before mandatory case management was put in effect.

Case timetable forms

There is no prescribed form for setting out a case timetable. Lawyers have therefore been creating their own forms, such as the one for standard track actions, which appears as figure 21.1, and the one for fast track actions, which appears as figure 21.2 (at the end of the chapter). These forms have been completed and show realistic times between stages in an action.

MOTIONS

Rule 77.12 provides special rules governing motions in the case management system. To the extent that this rule conflicts with rule 37, which sets out motion procedures generally, the specific procedures in rule 77.12 prevail. There are certain unique features to motions under case management. Generally, the case management judge or master assigned to a case hears all motions. As part of the "hands-on" management by the court, a judge or master may initiate a motion if neither party does. More routine motions may be brought informally in a case conference without serving documents or making complicated scheduling arrangements. Some motions, such as a motion to change tracks, must be brought within specific time periods. There is an abbreviated check-off motion form, form 77C, that is used on case-managed motions, and generally there is less documentation required. There is usually no need to draft, issue, or enter an order after a decision has been rendered.

Motions made before case management judge or master

Once a case is commenced, a case management judge or master must hear all motions. Motions that were within the master's jurisdiction under rule 37.02(2) must be brought before a case management master. Motions that are within the exclusive jurisdiction of a judge must be brought before a case management judge.

A case management master is assigned to the case to oversee its progress to trial or settlement. The assignment usually takes place when a case conference is convened, a party proposes to bring a motion, or a party asks for a review of a proposed case timetable. When the case is commenced, it is automatically assigned to a team of judges, and judges from that team hear the motions. In exceptional cases, the senior regional judge may assign a single judge to manage the action, and that judge will hear all motions. In some cases, the regional senior judge may assign a single judge and master or two masters to case manage a complex case (rules 77.04 and 77.09.1).

Motions before specific judicial officers

There are some motions, however, that must be brought before specific judicial officers. If you believe that your case falls under rule 77.09.01, requiring the appointment of a specific judge to manage the case and hear motions, you must bring your motion before the senior regional judge to request that a specific judge be appointed. Certain motions concerned primarily with procedural matters, which are either unopposed or on consent, may be brought before the registrar under rule 77.12(5). The registrar must then make the order requested. This removes routine motions from the usual case management motion procedure designed for contested motions. The types of motions that may be brought before the registrar include motions to amend pleadings, add parties, or remove a lawyer from the record, provided that they are on consent or unopposed. The complete list of included motions is set out in rule 77.12(5) 1, i to ix. The registrar may also make orders on motions where no responding material is filed. This presumably identifies the motion as unopposed. However, a responding party on a case-managed motion is not required to file a case management motion form, even if opposing a motion (rule 77.12(2.1) and (2.2)). This may be a drafting oversight, and it would be unsafe to assume that all motions on which no material is filed should be treated as unopposed. A call to responding counsel will soon settle the matter.

It is also clear that in some circumstances under rule 77.11(2), a case management judge or master may initiate hearings that will lead to orders of a type usually associated with motions. For example, rule 77.10(7) provides that where the parties have failed to comply with a timetable, the judge or master may strike out pleadings filed by the non-compliant party.

Where motions are brought

If a case commences under case management, the motion is brought before the case management judge or master to whom the case is assigned.

Case management motion procedure

In some cases, procedural matters may be resolved without bringing a formal motion, even where the issue is contested. If no case conference had been held and no case management master has been formally assigned, you would usually need to call a case conference to have a master or judge assigned to manage the case and to hear the motion. Then you would need to schedule the motion and argue it in a separate proceeding. But you can use the case conference and rule 77.13(5) and (6) to ask the case management judge at a case conference to make procedural orders and give directions on procedural issues.

The first case conference may also be used to discuss the scheduling of a longer or more complex motion, possibly eliminating or narrowing some issues. You should raise the possibility of a long motion at the first opportunity at a case conference so that the master will have the opportunity to schedule it at an early and convenient date.

Where a long motion is in respect to refusals to answer questions or honour undertakings on discovery, you must complete and file a chart that sets out the details of each objection or unanswered undertaking. The chart must be in the form indicated in schedule B of the Toronto Motions Practice Direction Advisory (see appendix I to chapter 9). An example of the chart is provided in table 14.4 in chapter 14.

Saving trees: Form 77C

A motion under case management uses form 77C, which appears at first glance to be a document requiring little creative drafting. In fact, it does allow for persuasive writing. In addition, you are not prohibited from providing additional information and attaching other documentation. Rule 77.12(2.1) contemplates that a motion may be made without supporting material or a motion record. However, most counsel want to attach an affidavit to set out supporting facts, and it is probably wise to attach the pleadings to sketch out the basic facts and positions of the parties. The responding party may want to file evidence in the form of an affidavit or may want to file a responding party's motion form, but there is no requirement that this be done.

Once a motion has been decided, rule 77.12(8) indicates that no formal order need be issued and entered, unless there is an appeal or the presiding judicial officer requires an order to be issued and entered. The judicial officer's endorsement on the motion form is the only necessary notation, and this form usually stands in for a written order.

An example of a case management motion form in form 77C is set out in figure 21.3 (at the end of the chapter).

Costs on a motion

Rule 77.12(4) requires counsel to address costs at the end of the motion. This is not new, but this rule contemplates that the judicial officer hearing the motion will fix costs at the end of the motion and order them payable forthwith. In a contested complex motion, it is a good idea to prepare a cost outline and include receipts for disbursements so that counsel can make a complete and convincing argument on the costs issue.

Scheduling motions

Motions concerned with discovery and productions must all be completed at least 10 days before a settlement conference (rule 77.10(5)). As for the time for filing motions, the old requirement of three days' notice under rule 37 is gone, replaced by the requirement of rule 77.12(2) that form 77C be submitted to the court before the motion is heard. However, the scheduling of motions in case management cases in Toronto is subject to the provisions for scheduling motions in the Toronto courts, as set out in the Motions Practice Direction Advisory (see appendix I to chapter 9).

CASE CONFERENCE
What the case conference does

The case conference is the device used to steer a case-managed proceeding. It creates a forum where a case management judge or master can do whatever is necessary to keep a case moving forward effectively. In particular, it allows a judge or master to

- resolve issues arising under mandatory mediation;
- make procedural orders, even where no motion has been brought;
- arrange for a motion on a fixed hearing date;
- create or revise a case timetable, extending or abridging time for completing pretrial tasks;
- make arrangements for related actions and third party proceedings to be settled or tried together;

- engage in settlement discussions, if appropriate, at an early date before a formal settlement conference;

- narrow issues and establish agreed facts; and

- oversee the readying of a case for trial so that a fixed trial date remains realistic.

How and when to convene a case conference

There is no single prescribed method or time for convening a case conference. A case conference can be convened at the request of any party — for example, when a party wishes to bring a motion or on the initiative of a judge or master.

Rule 77 sets out some circumstances where the court can compel parties to attend a case conference on the initiative of either party or the court.

1. *Rule 77.10(1).* If a party fails to meet a time limit established by rule 77, a case management judge or master will convene a case conference.

2. *Rule 77.10(2) and (3).* This is the rule that a case timetable must be established once mediation is completed or dispensed with. If the plaintiff has not proposed one and no other party has acted, the court will initiate a case conference.

3. *Rule 77.10(6).* If the timetable turns out to be unrealistic or the parties are otherwise not meeting timetable requirements, a case management judge or master may convene a case conference to amend the timetable or sanction uncooperative parties.

4. *Rule 77.11(2).* This is the catch-all rule that covers the general oversight function of case management judges and masters. These judges and masters can call case conferences at any time in connection with any case management matter, including failure to comply with the rules.

5. *Rule 24.1.13.* If a party has refused to comply with the mandatory mediation rules, the mediation coordinator must refer the problem to a case management judge or master, who may convene a case conference to establish a mediation timetable, or make punitive orders for non-compliance, including striking out pleadings, dismissing actions, and awarding costs.

If no case management judge or master has been appointed to your case because there has been no need for a case conference or motion, you will need to call the case management appointments and scheduling clerk. The clerk will advise you which master is assigned to handle the case. You will then need to book the case management conference through the assigned master's registrar.

When a party requests a case conference, some masters require completion of a request for a case conference form. If you must use the form, the reason for the case conference should be stated concisely and without argument. The purpose of the form is to give notice of the issues to other parties and the case management master. Examples of request for case conference forms are set out at the end of the chapter in figures 21.4 (Toronto) and 21.8 (Ottawa).

Once a case conference is initiated, the master's office sends a copy of a notice to attend a case conference to the plaintiff's lawyer, who is then responsible for serving copies on counsel for other parties and on unrepresented parties. An example of a notice to attend a case conference in person is provided in figure 21.5. An example of a notice to attend a case conference by telephone conference call is set out in figure 21.6. (Both figures appear near the end of the chapter.)

Case management judge or master

When a situation arises requiring a case conference, the party seeking it needs to consider whether a judge or master is required. If, for example, a lawyer is bringing a motion that only a judge can hear, you should make that clear to the case management scheduling office. There is a team of case management judges, and one will be assigned to hold the case conference, hear the motion, and hear all subsequent motions. Usually, however, an assigned master will handle case management matters until trial. In some circumstances, where a case is complex, has many parties, involves several related proceedings, or has other peculiarities, a particular judge, two judges, or a judge and a master can be assigned to manage the case under rule 77.09. This can be done on consent of all parties or on a motion brought by any party.

Making effective use of case conferences

The case conference is designed to make the litigation process more efficient, and less expensive. To make good use of the conference, lawyers and legal staff need to prepare for it. An early meeting of counsel may avoid the need for convening case conferences. When a case conference is called, counsel with carriage of the file in your office should attend. Alternatively, another lawyer must be thoroughly briefed so that the conference time is not wasted. The lawyer should bring his or her calendar or scheduler so that conflicts can be avoided. A calendar is also necessary if you are seeking to extend time or amend the timetable or if another party is doing so. Lawyers may wish to consider holding the case conference by conference telephone call. This may be done by pre-arrangement with the case management master's registrar or by submissions in writing.

Powers of case management judges and masters

Masters' powers are not as extensive as judges' powers. Under rule 77.11(1), either can extend or abridge a timeline, transfer a proceeding from one track to another, adjourn a case conference, set aside an order made by a registrar, and generally make orders to carry out the purposes of rule 77. In addition, a master may make a procedural order, on consent of the parties refer a matter to alternative dispute resolution, and convene a settlement conference. A judge may do all of the things a master may do and in addition may convene a hearing and give directions for trial. Rule 37 does not fade into the sunset: A master's jurisdiction on motions is subject to the same limitations under case management as in motions that are not case managed.

SETTLEMENT CONFERENCE

The settlement conference is much like a pretrial conference in that it is designed to promote settlement before trial. But there are significant differences. Under rule 50, a pretrial conference is an option, but under rule 77.14 a settlement conference is mandatory, and so is the timing. Rule 77.14(1) says that the registrar is required to give 45 days' notice of the date of the settlement conference, which is to occur no later than 240 days after the first defence is filed for standard track actions (150 days for fast track actions).

The settlement conference is usually held far enough ahead of the date fixed for trial that trial preparation, and the attendant preparation costs, have not yet been incurred. This means significant savings for the client if the case settles at the settlement conference.

Completion of pretrial steps before settlement conference

The reason why lawyers must keep track of the timing of the settlement conference is that they cannot continue to conduct pretrial proceedings, such as motions, after the settlement conference. Rule 77.14(2) requires that all examinations, production of documents, and motions arising out of examinations and productions are to be completed before the settlement conference. If that does not seem to be happening, a case conference is necessary to alter the timetable. There must be a good reason — something other than procrastination or sloth — because the case management judge or master can refuse the extend the time or apply cost penalties. The idea behind this rule is that the parties should have had full disclosure so that they know and can assess their own cases and their opponent's before discussing settlement at a settlement conference.

You should also be sure to have all medical and other expert witness reports completed and available since rule 77.14(6)(d) requires such reports to be exchanged before the settlement conference.[8]

Settlement conference brief

In order to give structure and focus to settlement conferences, all parties are required by rule 77.14(4) and (5) to file a settlement brief. The plaintiff's brief and certification under rule 77.14(2) that all discoveries and related motions have been completed must be delivered not later than 10 days before the settlement conference, with the defendant's due not later than 5 days before the settlement conference. If the parties need more time to file a settlement brief, particularly a defendant responding to issues in the plaintiff's brief, he or she should ask to convene a case conference to extend the time.

Contents of the brief

Rule 77.14(6) lists what should be in the brief:

- a concise summary of the facts, including agreed upon facts, which helps to distinguish between facts that are admitted and facts that must be proved at trial;

- a concise summary of the legal issues and the law to be relied on in the form of legal principles and their authorities, such as cases;

- a list of witnesses and a summary of each witness's evidence;

- relevant portions of transcripts, experts' reports, and other documentary evidence to be adduced at trial; and

- pleadings, including any particulars produced as a result of a demand for particulars.

The defendant's brief is shorter, consisting of anything the plaintiff omitted from his or her brief. Although the rule is silent, the brief should be cerlox-bound, have covers, and have a table of contents. It is also a good idea to include tabs for each section of material.

The contents of the brief allow a case management judge or master to know enough about the case to give a reasoned opinion on the parties' chances of success at trial, the likely costs, and the amount of time the trial will take.

Who attends the settlement conference?

Rule 77.14(3) is clear: In order to get anything done on settlement, counsel need instructions to make a deal. The lawyer with carriage of the file should be present and so should the client or a representative of the client with authority to settle the lawsuit. The conferences are scheduled to last about an hour. If more time is needed, it should be arranged through a case conference or should be spoken to in trial-scheduling court. A settlement conference is not like mediation, where the focus is on getting parties to talk their way to a deal regardless of their legal rights. A settlement conference is based on an assessment of the rights of the parties, with the case management judge or master giving views on the outcome. With properly prepared briefs, oral submissions should not be lengthy, and the conference should not take long.

Orders arising from the outcome of a settlement conference

Ideally, the only order that should arise is an order for dismissal of the action in accordance with the terms of a settlement or an order fixing a trial date in accordance with rule 77.14(7). However, a case management judge or master may also make procedural orders to carry out the intent of rule 77, including ordering a case conference or trial management conference.

TRIAL MANAGEMENT CONFERENCE

Rule 77.15 governs the trial management conference. Unlike the settlement conference, the trial management conference is optional. It may be convened at the request of a party or on the initiative of the trial judge or a case management judge or master once a trial date has been set.

The trial management conference is likely to be used when the settlement conference has not resulted in a clear picture of what will happen at trial. As noted earlier, the settlement conference is held when disclosure is complete and before trial preparation has been commenced. It is not until trial preparation is well underway that counsel decides which witnesses will be called, which facts will be admitted on a request to admit, and which facts can generally be agreed to without formal proof. The trial management conference is likely to be used in cases where one side is uncooperative or inefficient in making full disclosure, where several related cases have been joined together for trial, or where a case is complex.

Whoever is presiding over the trial management conference may exercise the powers that all judicial officers may exercise at a case management conference under rule 77.11. In addition, there are powers to ensure the parties organize the presentation of evidence in the most effective way. Before the conference is held, the plaintiff and defendant must file form 77D, the trial management conference form, at least 4 days before the trial management conference is held. If no trial management conference is convened, the form must be filed at least 14 days before trial. A review of the forms filed by the case management judge or master, or the trial judge, may identify issues that need to be resolved, and the filing may result in a judicial official convening a trial management conference if no party has requested one. The form is useful in requiring parties to think carefully about the evidence to be used, the issues outstanding, and the time it will take to try the matter. Each party completes its own form, and the picture is not complete until both plaintiff and defendant have filed their respective forms. It is important that the information on the form be complete and accurate. A sample of form 77D is set out in figure 21.7 (at the end of the chapter).

OTTAWA

Case management under rule 77 also operates in civil cases in Ottawa. However, there are some differences in practice. These distinctions may evolve over time, but at the time of writing the principal ones are set out below.

The rule does not mandate a case conference request form, but Ottawa has created one for all cases. It is simpler than the ones some case management masters in Toronto have developed for their own use (see figure 21.4). The Ottawa form is set out in figure 21.8 (at the end of the chapter).

Rule 77.10, requiring plaintiffs to file a timetable or request a case conference within 180 days of the commencement of proceedings, does not apply in Ottawa.

Motions are heard on Tuesday and Thursday mornings or by teleconference at other times. Motions must be confirmed with a motion confirmation form two days before the day of the motion. Factums and books of authorities are not required, but an outline of the summary of the argument is suggested. Dispositions are not faxed to parties. Copies can be obtained from the court file or from a computer in the civil filing office.

Settlement conference briefs are required by rule 77.14. Although there are no penalties specified in that rule, in Ottawa failure to file will result in a plaintiff's action being dismissed and a defendant's defence being struck out.

TORONTO: MODIFICATIONS TO CASE MANAGEMENT

Rule 77, in its "pure form," will continue to apply to actions in Windsor and Ottawa that must be case managed under rule 77.01, but it no longer applies automatically in Toronto. By 2003 it was apparent, given the high volume of Toronto cases, that the case management system was not working in Toronto. Instead of reducing cost and delay and moving cases through the system quickly, cases were becoming backlogged and more expensive for litigants as a result of increased attendances for case conferences and the taking of extra steps not otherwise required. Motions were no longer heard promptly and cases were taking as long to get to trial as they had been prior to the introduction of case management.

To address the problem, Toronto was taken out of mandatory case management under rule 77 and a hybrid system was created, one that is best described as "case management if necessary, but not necessarily case management." The authority for this hybrid system is a practice direction called "The Backlog Reduction/ Best Practices Initiative," dated November 22, 2004, and rule 78, The Toronto Civil Case Management Pilot Project. In order to understand the procedural requirements for Toronto actions, rule 78 and the practice direction have to be read together, with rule 78 filling in some of the procedural details outlined in the practice direction. Unfortunately, rule 78 does not provide a complete procedural code in the way that rule 77 does.

The hybrid system was designed as a three-year pilot project that began on January 1, 2005 and was to end in May 2008. As of the time of writing, the system has had its life extended to December 31, 2010 by a practice direction.[9] The life of rule 78 has also been extended to July 1, 2009, which is presumably an oversight that will be remedied, because the rule and the pilot project described in the practice direction operate together and will presumably continue to operate together until December 31, 2010. Because this system seems to be working, it is possible that it will continue beyond 2010, perhaps with modifications.

Highlights of the Toronto rule 78 system are set out below:

- *Full or modified case management may apply:* Under this system, full rule 77 case management may be imposed under rule 78.12 only if the parties request it, or there has been obstruction or unreasonable delay. If the order is made, rule 77 applies, with necessary modifications; for example, if a case is ordered into case management after pleadings have closed, some parts of rule 77 that include scheduling mediation or discovery might not apply. In fact, the court has broad discretion to customize the case management procedure of any action.

- *Commencement of proceedings:* Rule 78 applies to actions commenced in the City of Toronto, other than those excluded under rule 78.01. While form 14E, Information for Court Use is required, it is not necessary to choose a track when commencing an action.

- *Forms:* Court forms may be, but do not have to be, single spaced, and do not require backsheets (rule 78.05(2)).

- *Abandoned actions:* The registrar, on 45 days notice, may issue a dismissal notice where an undefended action has not been disposed of within two years of its commencement. The notice is to be served on all parties, after which counsel must take steps to move the action along (rule 78.06).

- *Dismissal for delay:* If one party moves to dismiss for delay, the court may order a case timetable or, if that is not practical, a case conference. The parties then must adhere to the timetable requirements, provided that the court is of the view that the action should proceed (rules 78.07 and 78.09).

- *Status notices:* If a defended action has not been disposed of within two years of the filing of a defence, the registrar serves a status notice under rule 48.14 requiring that the case be dismissed unless, within 90 days, the action is set down for trial, terminated, or a master at a status hearing overrides the registrar and orders that it not be dismissed. In addition, under rule 78 the parties may request a status hearing, and if they file a timetable and a draft order establishing the timetable, the hearing can be held in writing without the attendance of parties. They will then have to follow the timetable agreed to.

- *Mediation:* Mediation is mandatory under rule 78 and the practice direction; parties are encouraged to schedule mediation as soon as possible, but are not required to do it as early as is the case under rule 77. Under rule 78, mediation must be conducted within 90 days of setting down an action — after the completion of pleadings and discovery, when the parties have enough information about the case to rationally weigh their chances. In wrongful dismissal and simplified procedure cases, mediation must be scheduled within 150 days after the close of pleadings. Note that the requirements of rule 24.1 apply under rule 78 (other than with respect to the timing of the mediation) and, in particular, the mediator's report must be filed within 10 days after the mediation session. Mediation must be completed prior to the pretrial conference, or there may be cost consequences.

- *Pretrial conferences:* Actions are set down for trial in the usual way under rule 48. After the record is filed, the registrar will give at least 90 days' notice of the date of the pretrial conference under rule 50. One adjournment of the pretrial is permitted. Rule 78 goes on to require that at least five days prior to the pretrial, each party must file a pretrial memorandum that covers the issues, identifies witnesses, and indicates the steps to be completed prior to trial. The judge or master on the pretrial may establish a timetable to complete the remaining pretrial steps and may set a date for trial, in which case he or she must prepare a pretrial conference report to be placed with the record for the information of the trial judge (rule 78.10). If the parties have not engaged in mediation, the court may impose sanctions or put the action under case management. Failure to comply may result in dismissal of the action or the striking out of a defence.

- *Trial dates:* Trial dates are expected to be fixed by the judge or master at the pretrial, and the date is not notional or suggested, but firm. The parties are therefore well advised to consult and discuss the estimated length of trial and the availability of witnesses and counsel so that the date and the expected number of days of trial can be determined. It follows that trial scheduling courts will now cease to be used.

- *Contact information:* The court may be contacted with respect to
  scheduling under rule 78 at Toronto.SCJ.Civil.Status.Hearings@jus.gov.on.ca.

CHAPTER SUMMARY

This chapter introduced you to the mandatory case management procedure for
most civil actions in Windsor, Toronto, and Ottawa. Case management was introduced to help reduce cost and delay in civil litigation and to reduce case volumes in
the overcrowded Windsor, Toronto, and Ottawa courts. We noted that once a proceeding commences, plaintiffs must select a fast or standard track for the proceeding. The track imposes fixed deadlines before which various steps in the proceeding
must be completed. Cases are assigned to case management masters or judges, who
hear all motions and generally oversee the case. The case management authorities
have the powers to enforce compliance with set timetables and to amend those timetables in appropriate cases.

The case management system has a simplified procedure for motions, allowing some motions to be made informally at case conferences. All motions involve
minimal paperwork. Settlement conferences are now automatic and mandatory. If a
case fails to settle, a specific trial date will be fixed by a trial-scheduling court, usually before the settlement conference is held. To ensure trials are conducted effectively, there is an optional trial management conference to narrow the issues,
arrange for the effective presentation of evidence, determine who the witnesses will
be, and decide how long the trial will take. Some difference between practices
under rule 77 in Toronto, Windsor, and Ottawa were identified. In Toronto, case
management appeared to cause more cost and delay than it prevented. Rule 77 is
now no longer mandatory in Toronto, having been replaced by a practice direction
that has been codified under rule 78. An overview of the rule 77 process is set out
in figure 21.9 (at the end of the chapter) in the form of a case management checklist. It has been left blank so that you can make use of it in practice, if you wish.

KEY TERMS

case conference   case management judge or master

mandatory mediation

NOTES

1 Delay in the courts is nothing new. Charles Dickens's novel *Bleak House*
   involves an estate litigation case, *Jarndyce v. Jarndyce*, that went on for more
   than a generation, with lawyers dying or retiring and being replaced by others,
   until most of the beneficiaries were dead, and the estate had been consumed by
   legal fees. This is a fictional and extreme example, but it shows that problems
   with cost and delay have been constant. A large part of the cause is attributed to
   delaying tactics and procrastination by the legal profession. The 19th-century
   reform that attacked this problem was the abolition of the Court of Chancery,
   combining law and equity in one superior court. The late 20th-century solution

has been case management, which transfers control of how a case progresses from the lawyers to the courts.

2 The phrase "first defence" contemplates actions where there are several defendants filing separate defences as well as cases with only one defendant or one statement of defence for several defendants.

3 Simplified procedure cases were originally included under rule 77 but then excluded as of January 2, 2002. Rule 76 cases have their own form of case management.

4 Superior Court of Justice, Ontario Region Practice Direction of Regional Senior Judge Winkler, December 2004, "Backlog Reduction/Best Practices Initiative." See also rule 78, which incorporates the practice direction changes, in James J. Carthy, W.A. Derry Millar, and Jeffrey G. Cowan, *Ontario Annual Practice* (Aurora, ON: Canada Law Book, 2008-9) and http://www.ontariocourts.on.ca/scj/en/notices/pd/toronto/casemanagement.htm. The civil justice reforms that take effect on January 1, 2010 will bring the Toronto case management system under rule 78 to an end, with a single, hopefully flexible, case management system for Toronto, Ottawa, and Windsor.

5 O. reg. 438/08, ss. 61–65, amending rules 77 and 78.

6 O. reg. 457/01, which was proclaimed on December 22, 2001 and came into force on January 2, 2002. It was not surprising to find that when the courts opened after New Year's Day, there was a certain amount of confusion.

7 Adapted from C. MacLeod, "Commencing an Action and the Key New Concept: The Early Timetable," in *Civil Litigation — 100% Case Management Alert*, Advocates' Society conference, held in Toronto, May 31, 2001.

8 Rule 53.03 requires a report prepared by an expert witness that a party intends to call at trial to be served on the other parties 90 days before trial.

9 http://www.attorneygeneral.jus.gov.on.ca. Follow the links to civil courts, superior court, and practice directions.

REFERENCES

Bankruptcy and Insolvency Act, RSC 1985, c. B-3, as amended.

Construction Lien Act, RSO 1990, c. C.30.

Evidence Act, RSO 1990, c. E23.

MacLeod, C., "Commencing an Action and the Key New Concept: The Early Timetable," in *Civil Litigation — 100% Case Management Alert*, Advocates' Society conference, held in Toronto, May 31, 2001.

O. reg. 457/01.

Rules of Civil Procedure, RRO 1990, reg. 194.

Short, Donald, "Case Timetable (Fast Track)," in *Civil Litigation — 100% Case Management Alert*, Advocates' Society conference, held in Toronto, May 31, 2001.

Short, Donald, "Case Timetable (Standard Track)," in *Civil Litigation — 100% Case Management Alert*, Advocates' Society conference, held in Toronto, May 31, 2001.

REVIEW QUESTIONS

1. Why was case management introduced in Toronto, Windsor, and Ottawa?

2. What are the key features of case management?

3. What cases does case management cover?

4. What specific procedures must you follow when commencing a proceeding?

5. What time limits are set by the fast and standard tracks?

6. What do defendants have to do in a case-managed proceeding that is different from what they usually have to do?

7. When do the time limits in case management begin to run?

8. What is included in a case timetable?

9. Once a case timetable is set, is it rigidly fixed?

10. What needs to be done within 180 days of the commencement of proceedings?

11. What must be done after the filing of the first defence?

12. What is the procedure for bringing motions in case management?

13. For what purposes is a case conference convened and by whom?

14. How and when is a case conference convened?

15. What powers can case management judges and masters exercise in a case conference?

16. What are the principal features of a settlement conference?

17. What is the purpose of a trial management conference?

18. How does the application of rule 77 in case-managed proceedings in Ottawa differ from the application of the rule in Toronto?

19. What are the main features of case management in Toronto under the 2004 pilot project and rule 78?

DISCUSSION QUESTIONS

1. Read and respond to the following memorandum:

   To: E. Egregious, law clerk
   From: I.M. Just, lawyer
   Re: *Boar v. Rattle Motors Ltd. et al.*

   We have served our statement of claim, which was issued on January 4, year 2, and we have asked that the case be on the standard track in Toronto. Huey Sue is acting for both defendants and served us with his statement of defence on January 12, year 2. Because the date to choose a mediator is fast approaching, I would like to have a case conference convened to discuss early implementation of a case timetable. Please find out who we call to schedule a case conference and assign a case management master to this case, and then prepare a draft request for a case conference. Even though all masters don't require this, I think it is a good idea to use one. Also prepare a draft case timetable that fits sensibly within the standard track that I can use as a basis for discussion at the case conference.

2. Return to discussion question 2 in chapter 9 and reread I.M. Just's memorandum about Diedre Kuflesnout's engineering report. Respond to the memorandum, drafting the appropriate documents to bring the relevant motion under case management in Toronto. Also let I.M. Just know what is necessary to bring the matter before the case management master.

FIGURE 21.1 CASE TIMETABLE FOR STANDARD TRACK ACTION

Court File No. 03   /2001

ONTARIO SUPERIOR COURT OF JUSTICE

D. SHORT

Plaintiff(s)

- and -

A. LINE

Defendant(s)

CASE TIMETABLE [STANDARD TRACK]

X **AGREED**

☐ **DATES TO BE RESOLVED**

A. Date Action Commenced: July 10, 2001   + 180 days =   January 6, 2002
                                                                   (Last Date to File Timetable)

   Date First Defence Filed: September 4, 2001   + 240 days =   April 25, 2002
                                                                      (Last Date for Settlement Conference)

B. Enter dates by which the various steps are to be completed. Ensure that sufficient time is allowed to accomplish the step. If counsel cannot agree on an element enter "To Be Resolved" and then each party should prepare and attach a separate schedule setting out their position on the items that cannot be agreed upon for submission to the court. The Court may by Order extend any time period.

1.	Mediator Selected By [within 30 days of First Defence]:	Date: October 1, 2001
2.	Affidavits of Documents Exchanged By:	Date: November 15, 2001
3.	**Mediation Completed By [within 90 days of First Defence] [60 more days available Rule 24.1.09(3)]:**	**Date: November 30, 2001**
4.	Discoveries Completed By:	Date: February 5, 2002
5.	Undertakings/Refusals Completed By:	Date: April 4, 2002
6.	Discovery Motions Completed By:	Date: April 29, 2002
7.	Other: PLAINTIFF'S EXPERT REPORT	Date January 15, 2002
8.	**Settlement Conference Completed By: (Max. 240 days from first defence unless Court varies)**	**Date: April 25, 2002**

TIMETABLE DATE: September 9, 2002

FIGURE 21.1 CONCLUDED

ACTION NO:

1) Is this action settled? YES ☐ NO ☐

If the action is settled **ALL** counsel and self-represented parties must confirm this in writing and return the consent with this form. Otherwise, personal attendance is required. Counsel are not required to gown.

2) If not settled – what is the status of <u>this action</u> and <u>any other related proceeding</u>?

Comment: _____

ACTION NO. OF ALL RELATED PROCEEDINGS: _____

_____

a) Pleadings completed? YES ☐ NO ☐

b) Affidavits of documents completed? YES ☐ NO ☐

c) Discovery completed? YES ☐ NO ☐

d) Experts reports available? YES ☐ NO ☐

3) Any Motions intended to be brought? YES ☐ NO ☐

<u>If yes</u> –   What Motions? _____

Under which rules? _____

4) Is this action ready for a pre-trial conference? YES ☐ NO ☐

5) Is this action ready for a trial? YES ☐ NO ☐

6) Have the parties attended mediation? YES ☐ NO ☐

7) Approximately how long will the trial take? _____ Days

8) JURY ☐ NON-JURY ☐

9) Has the action been affected by Bankruptcy or other transmission of interest? YES ☐ NO ☐

FIGURE 21.2 CASE TIMETABLE FOR FAST TRACK ACTION

Court File No. __04__ /2001

ONTARIO SUPERIOR COURT OF JUSTICE

D. SHORT

Plaintiff(s)

- and -

S. SWEET

Defendant(s)

CASE TIMETABLE [FAST TRACK]

X **AGREED**

☐ **DATES TO BE RESOLVED**

A. Date Action Commenced: __July 10, 2001__ + 180 days = __January 6, 2002__

(Last Date to File Timetable)

Date First Defence Filed: __September 4, 2001__ + 150 days = __February 1, 2002__

(Last Date for Settlement Conference)

B. Enter dates by which the various steps are to be completed. Ensure that sufficient time is allowed to accomplish the step. If counsel cannot agree on an element enter "To Be Resolved" and then each party should prepare and attach a separate schedule setting out their position on the items that cannot be agreed upon for submission to the court. The Court may by Order extend any time period.

1.	Mediator Selected By [within 30 days of First Defence]:	Date: October 1, 2001
2.	Affidavits of Documents Exchanged By:	Date: October 15, 2001
3.	**Mediation Completed By [within 90 days of First Defence] [60 more days available Rule 24.1.09(3)]:**	**Date: November 30, 2001**
4.	Discoveries Completed By:	Date: December 3, 2001
5.	Undertakings/Refusals Completed By:	Date: January 15, 2001
6.	Discovery Motions Completed By:	Date: January 25, 2002
7.	Other:	Date: N/A
8.	**Settlement Conference Completed By: (Max. 150 days from first defence unless Court varies)**	**Date: February 1, 2002**

TIMETABLE DATE: __September 10, 2001__

FIGURE 21.2   CONCLUDED

Counsel to sign to evidence agreement to above schedule. Signed schedules to be exchanged with other counsel and copies of schedule to be filed at Court Office.

Counsel for Plaintiff(s):		Counsel Defendant 1:	
(party)	D. Short	(party)	S. Sweet
(name)	Joe Blow	(name)	Huey Dewey
(sgd)		(sgd)	
(date)		(date)	
(firm)	Tried and True	(firm)	Dewey Cheetham & Howe
(phone)		(phone)	
(fax)		(fax)	
(email)		(email)	

Counsel for Defendant 2:		Counsel Defendant 3:	
(party)		(party)	
(name)		(name)	
(sgd)		(sgd)	
(date)		(date)	
(firm)		(firm)	
(phone)		(phone)	
(fax)		(fax)	
(email)		(email)	

IN THE MATTER OF UNRESOLVED DATES:

CASE CONFERENCE DISPOSITION *(If necessary)*

1.   The dates entered on the above Case Timetable in the areas previously noted "To Be Resolved" and initialed by me above are hereby established for this case.

2.

_____   _____
Date   Case Management Master

FIGURE 21.3   CASE MANAGEMENT MOTION FORM (FORM 77C)

Court file no. 01-CV-1234

ONTARIO
SUPERIOR COURT OF JUSTICE

BETWEEN:

ABIGAIL BOAR

Plaintiff

and

RATTLE MOTORS LTD. and FRED FLOGEM

Defendants

CASE MANAGEMENT MOTION FORM

JURISDICTION ☐ Case management judge
☒ Case management master

THIS FORM FILED BY *(Check appropriate boxes to identify the party filing this form as a moving/responding party on this motion AND to identify this party as plaintiff, defendant, etc. in the action)*

☒ moving party
☐ Plaintiff _____
☐ responding party
☐ defendant/respondent name _____
☐ other — specify kind of party and name _____

MOTION MADE

☐ on consent of all parties   ☐ on notice to all parties and
                                         unopposed

☐ without notice   ☒ on notice to all parties and
                                         expected to be opposed

Notice of this motion was served on: October 6, year 2.
by means of: service on the lawyer for the defendants by courier.

METHOD OF HEARING REQUESTED

☒ by attendance
☐ in writing only, no appearance
☐ by fax
☐ by telephone conference under rule 1.08
☐ by video conference under rule 1.08

Date, time and place for attendance or for telephone or video conference

September 16, year 1, at 10:00 a.m., Court House,
393 University Avenue, Toronto, Ontario, M5G 1E6

FIGURE 21.3 CONTINUED

ORDER SOUGHT BY THIS PARTY *(Responding party is presumed to request dismissal of motion and costs)*

❑ Extension of time — until *(give specific date)*: _____
❑ serve claim/application   ❑ file or deliver defence
❑ complete discoveries
❑ other _____
❑ Assignment of proceeding (and related proceedings if applicable) to judge(s) for case management.
☒ Other relief — be specific

1. The plaintiff seeks an order permitting Eldred Klump, lighting engineer, to inspect the level of lighting in the automobile showroom operated by the corporate defendant at 1240 Bay Street, Toronto, Ontario, M8H 0K8 on such terms and times as the court considers just.
2. The costs of this motion.

MATERIAL RELIED ON BY THIS PARTY

☒ this form   ☒ pleadings   ☒ affidavits - specify
❑ transcript — specify   ❑ other — specify

Affidavit of Eldred Klump, sworn October 3, year 1

GROUNDS IN SUPPORT OF/IN OPPOSITION TO MOTION (INCLUDING RULE AND STATUTORY PROVISIONS RELIED ON)

There is an issue between the parties as to the adequacy of lighting in the corporate defendant's showroom, and it is necessary to carry out an inspection of the corporate defendant's premises to examine the lighting, pursuant to rule 32 of the *Rules of Civil Procedure*, in order to determine that issue.

CERTIFICATION BY LAWYER

I certify that the above information is correct, to the best of my knowledge.

Signature of lawyer *(If no lawyer, party must sign)*

I.M. Just   *LSUC #12345R*

Date: September 4, year 1

FIGURE 21.3 CONCLUDED

THIS PARTY'S LAWYER *(if no lawyer, give party's address for service, telephone and fax number)*

OTHER LAWYER *(if no lawyer, give other party's name, address for service, telephone and fax number)*

Name and firm
I.M. Just, Just & Coping
LSUC #12345R

Address
365 Bay Street - 8701
Toronto, Ontario, M3J 4A9

Telephone 416-762-1342

Fax 416-762-2300

Name and firm
Huey Sue
LSUC #23456T

Address
65 False Trail
Toronto, Ontario, M6Y 1Z6

Telephone 416-485-6891

Fax 416-485-6892

DISPOSITION BY CASE MANAGEMENT JUDGE/MASTER

❑ order to go as asked
❑ order refused

❑ adjourned to
❑ order to go as follows:

_____

_____

_____

_____

Hearing method _____ Hearing duration _____ min.

Heard in: ❑ courtroom ❑ office
❑ Successful party MUST prepare formal order for signature
❑ No copy of disposition to be sent to parties
❑ Other directions — specify

_____

_____

Date _____   Judge's/Master's Name _____   Judge's/Master's Signature _____

FIGURE 21.4   TORONTO CASE CONFERENCE REQUEST FORM

Master Albert's Chambers
Superior Court of Justice
Toronto Region

Chambres des Pronotaire Albert
Cour suprieure de justice
Région de Toronto

Court House
393 University Ave.
Toronto, Ontario
M5G 1E6

Registrar: (416) 326 3272
Facsimile: (416) 326 5416

Request for Case conference with Master Albert

Court file number: _____

Short Title of Proceeding: _____ v. _____
Date of request: _____

Party requesting case conference:
- Name of party:
- Plaintiff, defendant, third party, etc?
- Counsel (name, address, telephone and fax):

_____

_____

_____

_____

_____

_____

_____

Purpose of case conference (if seeking to vary an order, attach a copy):

_____

_____

_____

_____

Proposed participants in case conference:

Party (plaintiff, defendant)	Name of Counsel	Counsel's Phone/Fax
_____	_____	_____
_____	_____	_____
_____	_____	_____

>>

(To be completed by registrar):   **Date and time of case conference appointment:** _____

Appearance _____   or   **Telephone Conference Call** _____

If tel. conference call, telephone arrangements to be made by _____.

FIGURE 21.5   NOTICE TO ATTEND CASE CONFERENCE IN PERSON

Court File Number: _____

SUPERIOR COURT OF JUSTICE

_____ v _____

NOTICE CONVENING A CASE CONFERENCE
(Appearance)

TAKE NOTICE that pursuant to Rule 77.13(1) of the Rules of Civil Procedure, you must attend a case conference before Master Albert in this proceeding and all related proceedings on _____, _____, at 393 University Avenue, 6th Floor, to discuss the issues raised in the litigation and to establish an appropriate timetable to meet the requirements of Rule 77 in this proceeding and any third and fourth party and other related proceedings.

COUNSEL AND UNREPRESENTED PARTIES in this proceeding and any third or fourth party or other related proceedings are required to participate in the case conference. In the event counsel cannot participate, it will be their responsibility to brief and arrange for fully informed alternate counsel to participate. At the case conference a timetable will be established or if one is in place it will be reviewed to ensure that the requirements of Rule 77.14 are met and any necessary consequential orders will be made.

THOSE PARTICIPATING must have with them calendars reflecting the future availability of counsel, parties and witnesses and should be fully familiar with the proceeding and its conduct to date. They must be prepared to schedule future events and discuss the issues in dispute.

COUNSEL FOR THE PLAINTIFF SHALL FORTHWITH SERVE A COPY OF THIS NOTICE on all counsel and unrepresented parties in this proceeding and all related proceedings to whom the notice has not been directed as set out below. If you have any questions please contact my registrar, Annette Bidlofsky, by telephone at (416) 326-3272 or by fax at (416) 326-5416.

DATED at Toronto _____.

_____
Master Carol Albert, Case Management Master

TO: _____, *lawyer for the plaintiff*
FAX: _____

FIGURE 21.6　NOTICE TO ATTEND CASE CONFERENCE BY TELEPHONE

Court File Number: _____

SUPERIOR COURT OF JUSTICE

_____ v _____

NOTICE CONVENING A CASE CONFERENCE
(Telephone Conference Call)

TAKE NOTICE that pursuant to Rule 77.13(1) of the Rules of Civil Procedure, you must participate in a case conference with Master Albert by conference telephone call on _____, at _____. _____ counsel for _____ shall make the conference call arrangements. Telephone conference arrangements are made by the responsible person connecting all parties on the telephone conference line and then calling in to Master Albert at (416) 326-3239. Any administrative inquiries shall be directed in advance to Master Albert's registrar at (416) 326-3272. If your office does not have conference facilities, use the Conference Operator service provided by your telephone service provider.

THE PURPOSE of the case conference is to discuss the issues raised in the litigation and to establish an appropriate timetable to meet the requirements of Rule 77 in this proceeding and any third and fourth party or other related proceedings.

COUNSEL AND UNREPRESENTED PARTIES in this proceeding and any third or fourth party or other related proceedings are required to participate in the case conference. In the event counsel cannot participate, it will be their responsibility to brief and arrange for fully informed alternate counsel to participate. At the case conference a timetable will be established or if one is in place it will be reviewed to ensure that the requirements of Rule 77.14 are met and any necessary consequential orders will be made.

THOSE PARTICIPATING must have with them calendars reflecting the future availability of counsel, parties and witnesses and should be fully familiar with the proceeding and its conduct to date. They must be prepared to schedule future events and discuss the issues in dispute.

COUNSEL FOR THE PLAINTIFF SHALL FORTHWITH SERVE A COPY OF THIS NOTICE on all counsel and unrepresented parties in this proceeding and all related proceedings to whom the notice has not been directed as set out below. If you have any questions please contact my registrar, Annette Bidlofsky, by telephone at (416) 326-3272 or by fax at (416) 326-5416.

DATED at Toronto _____.

_____
Master Carol Albert, Case Management Master

TO:　　_____, *lawyer for the plaintiff*

FAX:　_____

FIGURE 21.7 TRIAL MANAGEMENT CONFERENCE FORM (FORM 77D)

Court file no. 01-CV-1234

ONTARIO
SUPERIOR COURT OF JUSTICE

BETWEEN:

ABIGAIL BOAR

Plaintiff

and

RATTLE MOTORS LTD. and FRED FLOGEM

Defendants

TRIAL MANAGEMENT CONFERENCE FORM

Filed on behalf of the plaintiff, Abigail Boar

Trial Management Judge or Case Management Master: Master Slow
Date of Trial Management Conference: October 30, year 2
Trial Lawyer: Plaintiff

I.M. Just LSUC #12345R
Just & Coping, Barristers and Solicitors
365 Bay Street - 8701,
Toronto, Ontario M3J 4A9
tel. 416-762-1342; fax 416-762-2300

Defendant

Huey Sue LSUC #23456T
Barrister and Solicitor
65 False Trail, Toronto, Ontario M6Y 1Z6
tel. 416-485-6891; fax 416-485-6892

Jury: yes _____   no _____x_____

1. **Issues Outstanding**
   a) liability: admitted by the defendant
   b) damages: general damages are still in issue
   c) other: N/A

2. **Plaintiff's Witnesses**

Names	Estimated time for Examination-in-chief *(to be completed by plaintiff)*	Estimated time for Cross-examination *(to be completed at trial management conference)*
Abigail Boar	3 days	
Dr. Morris Furgazy	1 day	
Dr. Edwina Dhrool	1/2 day	

FIGURE 21.7 CONTINUED

3. **Defendant's Witnesses**

Names	Estimated time for Examination-in-chief (*to be completed by plaintiff*)	Estimated time for Cross-examination (*to be completed at trial management conference*)

4. **Document Brief**
   a) Prepared: yes ____x____ no _____
   b) If no, will be prepared by lawyer for the_____
      and delivered by _____ (date)
   c) Comment: Joint document brief including all documents
      of all parties.

5. **Expert's Reports**
   a) Are any "reply" reports anticipated?

      yes ____x____ no _____

   b) If "yes," do they create any timing problems regarding readiness
      for trial? yes _____ no ____x____

6. **Admissions Made**
   a) By plaintiff
      none
   b) By defendant #1
      on issue of liability
   c) By defendant #2
      same as defendant #1

7. **Notice To Admit Facts/Documents**
   a) Served by plaintiff: yes ____x____ no _____
   b) If no, will be served by: _____ (date)
   c) Served by defendant(s): yes ____x____ no _____
   d) If no, will be served by: _____ (date)
   e) Comment: N/A
   f) Would a chronology, cast of characters or chart of corporate
      parties with shareholders, directors, officers, etc. be useful and if
      so, who will prepare them?
      Yes, a chronology of treatment of Abigail Boar's
      injuries will be prepared by the plaintiff.

FIGURE 21.7 CONCLUDED

8. **Amendments to Pleadings**
   a) Have all parties considered the pleadings and are any amendments likely to be sought?
   No
   b) If amendments are likely, will this create problems with readiness for trial?
   N/A

9. **Damages**
   a) Has a damages brief been delivered?

   yes _____ no ____x____

   b) If "no," will one be delivered before trial?

   yes ____x____ no _____

10. **Brief of Authorities**
   a) Has a brief of authorities been delivered?

   yes ____x____ no _____

   b) If "no," will one be delivered before trial?

   yes _____ no _____

11. **Settlement Conference**
   a) Already held on September 12, year 2 by Master Slow.
   b) Further settlement conference will be conducted:

   yes _____ no ____x____

   c) If yes, lawyer to arrange for such conference to be held prior to (date)

12. **Readiness for Trial**
   a) Estimated trial time required: 8 days
   b) Are there any special circumstances which should be noted to assist in scheduling this matter for trial? (i.e. witnesses from out of town; large courtroom required due to number of lawyers or documents?)
   Dr. Furgazy is on vacation during the first three weeks of November, year 2 and will not be available at that time.

FIGURE 21.8   OTTAWA CASE CONFERENCE REQUEST FORM

ONTARIO SUPERIOR COURT OF JUSTICE

SHORT TITLE OF PROCEEDING: BOAR v. RATTLE MOTORS ET AL.

CASE CONFERENCE FORM

REQUESTED BY:

DATE SCHEDULED:

1.   Brief Statement of facts and law:

2.   Purpose of the Case Conference
     a) Identification of Issues
     b) Explore methods to resolve contested issues
     c) Secure parties' agreement on a specific schedule
     d) Review and amend the timetable for the proceeding
     e) Other procedural matter (specify)

3.   Disposition of the Case Management Judge/Master:

_____

_____

_____

_____

_____

_____   _____

Date   Judge/Master

Prepared by: (Law Firm)

FIGURE 21.9 CASE MANAGEMENT CHECKLIST (STANDARD TRACK ACTIONS)

* = Rule 77 Mandated action or time

EVENT	DATE	DATE EXTENDED OR AMENDED BY ORDER OF	DATE EXTENDED OR AMENDED BY ORDER OF
STATEMENT OF CLAIM ISSUED (Standard or Fast Track?)		N/A	N/A
* Defence must be filed or default obtained by 180 days or action is dismissed. (*See Note 1*)			
* Plaintiff must file consent timetable or obtain Case Conference Date by 180 days. Defendant may consider proposing one. (*See Note 2*)			
STATEMENT OF DEFENCE # of Defendants			
* When was the first Statement of Defence filed? (Obtain Case History — *See Note 1*)			
Other Defences to be filed			
MANDATORY MEDIATION (*See Note 3*)			
* Mediator must be selected and Mediation Coordinator advised failing which the Mediation Coordinator appoints a mediator from the roster (30 days after first defence).			
* Notice of Mediation must be served on all parties by lawyers 20 days before mediation.			
* Statement of Issues (Form 24.1C) to be filed 7 days before mediation.			
* Mediation to be held within 90 days of 1st defence (or in a standard track case only, may be extended a further 60 days on consent filed with Mediation Coordinator).			

FIGURE 21.9   CONTINUED

EVENT	DATE	DATE EXTENDED OR AMENDED BY ORDER OF	DATE EXTENDED OR AMENDED BY ORDER OF
Draft Timetable to be delivered. (With SOD? *See Note 2*)			
Affidavit of Documents served.			
Examinations for Discovery completed.			
Discovery Motions to be completed.			
Undertakings and Refusals answered.			
Plaintiff's Reports to be delivered.			
Defendant's Reports to be delivered.			
Third Party Reports to be delivered.			
Reply Reports to be delivered.			
SETTLEMENT CONFERENCE			
* Notice to be sent to parties (105 days after 1st defence filed)			
* Plaintiff's SC Brief must be filed 10 days before SC (ie. 230 days after 1st defence filed)			
* SC Briefs of other parties filed 5 days before SC (ie. 235 days after 1st defence)			
* SC is to be held (240 days after 1st defence filed)			
TRIAL MANAGEMENT CONFERENCE * Parties to file TMC form (Form 77D - earlier of 14 days before trial date or 4 days before TMC date)			
TRIAL DATE (set at TMC)			

NOTES:

1. **When acting for a Plaintiff**, if, within 180 days of the issuance of the claim, a) at least one defendant has not defended OR b) default judgment has not been obtained, the registrar will dismiss the action.

    When acting for a Defendant, when a Defence file comes in, obtain instructions to get the Case History from the Court which will tell you the two key dates: a) when the claim was issued, and b) when the first defence was filed.

    NO MORE WAIVERS OF DEFENCE WILL BE GIVEN BY THE PLAINTIFF

FIGURE 21.9   CONCLUDED

2. **Timetable:** The obligation is on the Plaintiff to file a consent timetable within 180 days of issuing the claim, or convene a Case Conference with the Master to set one. If acting for a Plaintiff, consider suggesting one with the SOC, or on receipt of the (first?) defence. If acting for the Defendant, consider sending a suggested timetable with the SOD.

   Make sure the client can abide by the timetable as well.

   Case Management and Timetables mean more events in a shorter period of time. Carefully coordinate timetables on files to prevent double booking or other conflicts.

3. **Mandatory Mediation:** The rates of the Mediator are fixed by Regulation for the mandated 3 hour session (plus 1 hour mediator prep time). If the mediation extends beyond the prescribed time, the rate of the mediator must be negotiated between the mediator and the parties.

Source: "Case Management Checklist (Standard Track Actions)," in *Civil Litigation — 100% Case Management Alert*, Advocates' Society conference, held in Toronto, May 31, 2001.

CHAPTER 22

Mandatory mediation

WHAT IS MEDIATION?

Mediation is a form of **alternative dispute resolution** (ADR). It is one way for people to settle disputes or lawsuits without going to court. When a dispute is mediated, a neutral third party — the mediator — assists the parties in identifying their chief concerns and interests and helps them to negotiate a settlement that they can each live with. Mediators do not impose settlements by deciding disputes the way judges or arbitrators do. The mediator's job is to facilitate communication between the parties in a constructive way so that the parties can find their way to a satisfactory agreement. In mediation, the aim is not to identify winners or losers but to solve a problem that has led to a dispute or disagreement. The solution the parties fashion with a mediator's help may be based on factors other than the parties' legal rights.

Mandatory mediation in Ontario

In the last decade of the 20th century, the civil courts began to come to grips with problems of cost and delay in the civil court system by looking for new ways of doing things. The court system was overhauled, and the civil court rules were amended to introduce procedures, such as case management, to cut cost and delay. Another approach was to divert some cases out of the civil courts to be dealt with under various alternatives to dispute settlement in court. This approach has a history going back to the mid-20th century, when courts were divested of jurisdiction over various types of disputes. Labour relations disputes, for example, began to be dealt with by arbitrators or in some cases by labour relations boards, but not by courts. Boards and tribunals often deal with disputes without the parties being able to go to court. The court's role in these situations is restricted, ensuring that the boards or arbitrators or mediators provide a basically fair system.

The Ministry of the Attorney General introduced mandatory mediation in 1999 in the form of selected pilot projects. The original intention was to have mediation apply across the province as part of the civil litigation process. However, it is currently mandatory under rule 24.1 only in certain types of actions:

- case managed actions under rule 77 in Ottawa and Windsor;

- actions governed by rule 78 in Toronto where, under rule 78.12, an action is moved into case management under rule 77; and

- simplified procedure actions under rule 76, when ordered by a judge.

mediation
process whereby a neutral third party facilitates communication between disputants and assists them in negotiating a solution

alternative dispute resolution
term used to describe various ways of settling disputes without going to court, including arbitration, mediation, and conciliation

Mediation is not mandatory under rule 24.1 in actions under the *Substitute Decisions Act, 1992*, under part V of the *Succession Law Reform Act*, or in cases where there has been mediation under s. 258.6 of the *Insurance Act* within a year of the delivery of the first statement of defence.[1]

Mediation requirements for Toronto

A hybrid form of mediation is required in civil actions under rule 78 in Toronto. While rule 78 is largely silent on the subject of mandatory mediation, the rule must be read with the Practice Direction of Regional Senior Judge Winkler, December 2004, "Backlog Reduction/Best Practices Initiative."[2] The Toronto Civil Case Management Project that is based on the practice direction is to be continued until 2010. Under this regime, cases in Toronto will not automatically be governed by rule 24.1; mediation is mandatory, although it will take place later in the court process than it does under rule 24.1. Parties should mediate at the earliest stage at which counsel think it will be effective, but mediation must be conducted within 90 days of setting the case down for trial, prior to the pretrial conference. At this point, all pretrial procedures will have been completed, and each side will have a good idea of the merits of both their case and their opponent's case. Note that if the case is a wrongful dismissal or a simplified procedure case, parties must engage in mediation within 150 days after pleadings have closed. This reflects the expedited pretrial procedure in these types of proceedings.

In all Toronto actions under rule 78, aside from timelines, all other requirements of rule 24.1 apply, including the requirement to file a mediator's report within ten days of completion of the mediation process.

Whether or not it is not required under the rules, lawyers and their clients often resort informally and unofficially to the use of mediation and other ADR techniques as an alternative to a time-consuming, expensive, and unpredictable court process.

Does mandatory mediation work?

That was the question the pilot project had to answer. The answer was that mandatory mediation was generally successful.[3] It resulted in significant reductions in the time taken to dispose of cases — a plus for clients and the courts, which can deal with the remaining cases more easily when the case load is reduced. Not surprisingly, the costs for litigants were also reduced when mediation was wholly or partially successful.[4] A high proportion of cases, over 40 percent in both Toronto and Ottawa, were settled at or within seven days of the completion of mediation. An additional 13 percent of cases in Ottawa and 21 percent of cases in Toronto were partially settled, with some issues being taken from the table, speeding up the proceedings and reducing costs. However, there were concerns voiced by some members of the bar, particularly in Toronto. One was that mediation came too early in the proceeding under rule 24.1, before the parties were ready to consider it. Generally, the Toronto bar was more critical than the Ottawa or Windsor bar of the mandatory mediation process.

MANDATORY MEDIATION IN CIVIL PROCEEDINGS: RULE 24.1

As you can see, mandatory mediation has broad application under rule 24.1 in case managed cases in Ottawa and Windsor, as well as in Toronto, where, with relaxed timelines, a form of it is required in most civil cases. Even where it is not required, for example under the *Substitute Decisions Act* or in estate matters, it is often because there is already a form of mediation available in those cases.[5]

Note that while mediation is mandatory, it may not be possible to apply it to certain cases. If the parties are so antagonistic toward one another that there is no reasonable prospect for a successful mediation, then mediation should not be attempted. Indeed, rule 24.1.05 permits a party to bring a motion for an order for exemption of a particular case from mandatory mediation.

Who conducts the mediation?

Because there is a high volume of mediation cases, it is necessary to have a great many mediators, and some administrative coordination of them. Rule 24.1.08 provides for the establishment of a mediation committee with the responsibility of developing criteria for appointing mediators, screening them, and approving them to be included on a list or roster of mediators. A mediation coordinator for each county or region where mandatory mediation has been imposed administers the list. There are a variety of certificate and diploma courses where one may train to be a mediator. There are no clear professional standards that all mediators must adhere to, and there is no single body that certifies mediators as professionals in the way that doctors and lawyers are certified. The mediation committee has broad discretion in appointing individuals to the list of mediators, and the Ministry of the Attorney General has provided some guidelines for exercising that discretion.

In any case, the litigants have some choices about who does the mediation (rule 24.1.08(2)). The mediation may be conducted by:

- a person the parties agree to, whether on the list or not, and whether the person holds himself or herself out as a mediator or not, or

- a person assigned by the mediation coordinator.

An appointment is made where the parties fail to give notice within 30 days after the filing of the first defence that they have appointed a mediator. It also occurs where no mediation session has taken place within 90 days from the time that the first defence was filed. The coordinator also appoints a mediator if he or she has not received a notice postponing mediation on consent (rule 24.1.09(1), (3), (5), and (6)). The person chosen or assigned to mediate must comply with the requirements of rule 24.1. and, in particular, must file a mediation report under rule 24.1.15(1). This procedure also applies to Toronto cases under rule 78 if no mediation session has been scheduled within 90 days of the action being set down for trial.

Choosing a mediator

Counsel is entitled to information from any mediator, on the list or off it, and there are questions a lawyer or client should ask before a mediator is selected.

- Where did the mediator train?

- What kind of mediation experience does he or she have?

- Is the mediator familiar with rule 24.1, the court processes, and the role of mediation in a civil proceeding?

- What references can the mediator provide?

- Will the mediator agree to the fee schedule established under the rule?

- What are the mediator's fees for services above and beyond the fee schedule for the first three hours of mediation?

CHANGES TO MANDATORY MEDIATION PROCEDURES AS OF JANUARY 1, 2010

- The timelines for mandatory mediation sessions will be extended. This will allow parties more time to prepare for a productive and meaningful mediation. The first session is to take place 180 days after the first defence is filed, *not* 90 days. And the process may be deferred to a later date if the parties consent[6] and the mediation coordinator is notified.

  However, at the time an action is set down for trial, the parties must indicate the status of the mediation process, and the mediation coordinator may appoint a mediator to commence and, within 90 days, at least attempt mediation if it has not occurred.

- If an insurer (not a party to the action) might be liable for damages on behalf of a party, the insurer's representative shall attend the mediation in place of the party.

- Mandatory mediation will continue to apply only in Toronto, Ottawa, and Windsor.[7]

MEDIATION PROCEDURE STEP BY STEP
Arranging the mediation

The parties need to contact each other as soon as possible after proceedings are commenced to select a mediator because a mediation session must take place within 90 days of the filing of the first defence. However, if there are many parties or complex issues and pleadings, a lawyer can bring a motion to extend (and also to abridge or shorten) the time for mediation (rule 24.1.09(1) and (2)). The rule suggests that in addition to the number of parties and the complexity of the issues, the court will also consider extending time for mediation if a party brings a motion for determination of an issue before trial because this might change the focus of mediation if the court removes an issue from mediation by ruling on it. The court will also hold off on mediation if there is a motion for summary judgment. If the motion is successful, the lawsuit is over, and there is nothing to mediate. If a party argues that he or she cannot proceed to mediation without more facts and information, the court may extend the time to permit discovery to take place before mediation begins.

In addition, the parties may also consent to postpone a mediation session for up to 60 days without bringing a motion by filing a consent with the mediation coordinator.

While mediation can be delayed, the choice of a mediator should be made within 30 days of the filing of the first defence. It is the duty of the plaintiff to file with the mediation coordinator a notice in form 24.1A[8] setting out the mediator's name and the date of the mediation session. A sample notice appears in figure 22.1.

If the parties do not themselves choose a mediator and fix a date for the first mediation session, under rule 24.1.09(6) it is the responsibility of the mediation co-ordinator to assign a mediator from the list. The assigned mediator immediately fixes a date for the mediation and serves a notice in form 24.1B on all parties at least 20 days before the day for which the mediation is scheduled. This puts the mediator in a peculiar position: He or she is expected to conduct a mediation with parties who may not wish to mediate and who are not cooperating with respect to the mediation process. The mediator is also acting as the court's police force, compelling the parties to attend or risk penalties. A sample mediator's notice form is reproduced in figure 22.2.

Preparing for mediation

The lawyer needs to run the client through the requirements for mandatory mediation, including the penalties for not cooperating in the process. A lawyer must also advise the client as to the choice of mediator, whether the mediator is from the list or not. The choice may involve some negotiation with other parties. The lawyer also has to prepare the statement of issues in form 24.1C[9] and provide a copy to other parties at least seven days before the mediation session. The statement of issues is like an agenda for a meeting; it tells the parties and the mediator, who knows nothing about the case, what is going to be "on the table." A statement of issues appears in figure 22.3.

The lawyer then must prepare the client for the mediation session and provide legal and strategic advice during the mediation process. Mediation is not something to send the client to alone. The lawyer, as an officer of the court, is obliged to protect the integrity of the mediation process by participating in the process in good faith and ensuring, as far as possible, that the client participates in the process in good faith too.

Preparing the client for mediation

Unlike a pretrial conference or a settlement conference, where the client says little and the lawyer does most of the talking, a client is expected to be an active participant in mediation. This means that an intelligent and articulate client may have an advantage, which is something a lawyer with a less articulate client may have to counter by participating more actively. But a client will require careful preparation. In particular, the lawyer must

- give the client an overview of the mediation strategies and goals;

- explain to the client what the client's role is;

FIGURE 22.1   NOTICE OF NAME OF MEDIATOR AND DATE OF SESSION (FORM 24.1A)

Court file no. 01-CV-1234

ONTARIO
SUPERIOR COURT OF JUSTICE

BETWEEN:

ABIGAIL BOAR

Plaintiff

and

RATTLE MOTORS LTD. and FRED FLOGEM

Defendants

NOTICE OF NAME OF MEDIATOR AND DATE OF SESSION

TO: MEDIATION CO-ORDINATOR,

1.   I certify that I have consulted with the parties and that the parties have chosen the following mediator for the mediation session required by Rule 24.1: Marielle Moosetrap.
2.   The mediator is named in the list of mediators for the City of Toronto.
3.   The mediation session will take place on December 13, year 1.

Date: November 17, year 1

Just & Coping
Barristers and Solicitors
365 Bay Street - 8701
Toronto, Ontario M3J 4A9

I.M. Just
LSUC #12345R
tel. 416-762-1342
fax 416-762-2300

Lawyers for the Plaintiff

FIGURE 22.2   NOTICE BY ASSIGNED MEDIATOR (FORM 24.1B)

Court file no. 01-CV-1234

ONTARIO
SUPERIOR COURT OF JUSTICE

BETWEEN:

ABIGAIL BOAR

Plaintiff

and

RATTLE MOTORS LTD. and FRED FLOGEM

Defendants

NOTICE BY ASSIGNED MEDIATOR

TO: Abigail Boar
AND TO: Rattle Motors Ltd. and Fred Flogem

The notice of name of mediator and date of session (Form 24.1A) required by rule 24.1.09 of the *Rules of Civil Procedure* has not been filed in this action. Accordingly, the mediation coordinator has assigned me to conduct the mediation session under Rule 24.1. I am a mediator named in the list of mediators for the City of Toronto.

The mediation session will take place on December 13, year 1 from 10:00 a.m. to 1:00 p.m., at JPR Arbitration and Mediation Services, 365 Bay Street – 400, Toronto, Ontario, M3J 4A9.

Unless the court orders otherwise, you are required to attend this mediation session. If you have a lawyer representing you in this action, he or she is also required to attend.

You are required to file a statement of issues (Form 24.1C) by December 6, year 1 (7 days before the mediation session). A blank copy of the form is attached.

When you attend the mediation session, you should bring with you any documents that you consider of central importance in the action. You should plan to remain throughout the scheduled time. If you need another person's approval before agreeing to a settlement, you should make arrangements before the mediation session to ensure that you have ready telephone access to that person throughout the session, even outside regular business hours.

YOU MAY BE PENALIZED UNDER RULE 24.1.13 IF YOU FAIL TO FILE A STATEMENT OF ISSUES OR FAIL TO ATTEND THE MEDIATION SESSION.

November 20, year 1

Marielle Moosetrap
1200 Yonge Street
Toronto, Ontario, M5R 1Z6
tel. 416-490-8765
fax 416-490-8766

cc. Mediation coordinator

FIGURE 22.3   STATEMENT OF ISSUES (FORM 24.1C)

Court file no. 01-CV-1234

ONTARIO
SUPERIOR COURT OF JUSTICE

BETWEEN:

ABIGAIL BOAR

Plaintiff

and

RATTLE MOTORS LTD. and FRED FLOGEM

Defendants

STATEMENT OF ISSUES

1. Factual and legal issues in dispute

The plaintiff states that the following factual and legal issues are in dispute and remain to be resolved:

1. whether oil leaking from an automobile in the corporate defendant's showroom caused the plaintiff to fall and be seriously injured;
2. whether the defendant Fred Flogem failed in his duty to the plaintiff by not cleaning up the oil spill when he became aware of it; and
3. whether the damages sustained by the plaintiff were solely the result of the defendants' negligence.

2. Party's position and interests (what the party hopes to achieve)

1. The plaintiff's position is that all of her injuries and subsequent losses and damages resulted from the negligent acts of the defendants.
2. The plaintiff hopes to receive adequate compensation for both special and general damages arising from her injuries.

3. Attached documents

Attached to this form are the following documents that the plaintiff considers of central importance in the action:

1. Statement of claim and defence
2. List of general damages sustained by the plaintiff
3. List of special damages sustained by the plaintiff

Date: December 1, year 1   _Abigail Boar_

FIGURE 22.3   CONCLUDED

```
                              Just & Coping
                              Barristers and Solicitors
                              365 Bay Street - 8701
                              Toronto, Ontario, M3J 4A9

                              I.M. Just
                              LSUC #12345R
                              tel. 416-762-1342
                              fax 416-762-2300

                              Lawyers for the Plaintiff
```

NOTE: When the plaintiff provides a copy of this form to the mediator, a copy of the pleadings shall also be included.

NOTE: Rule 24.1.14 provides as follows:

All communications at a mediation session and the mediator's notes and records shall be deemed to be without prejudice settlement discussions.

- remind the client that the goal is to find a mutually acceptable solution, not to beat the other side;

- discuss particular strategies with the client;

- be sure the client or the client's representative has authority to settle the lawsuit, and establish settlement ceilings;

- discuss with the client the cost, risks, and benefits of not settling during mediation;

- ensure that the client understands the theory of his or her own case, and its strengths and weaknesses;

- ensure that the client understands the theory of the other party's case, and its strengths and weaknesses;

- advise the client how to present his or her position in the most positive and persuasive way;

- advise the client about any confidential information that should not be disclosed; and

- work with the client to develop an opening statement.

Mediation session

The parties and their lawyers must attend the mediation session. Since the session is confidential and things said in it are said without prejudice, the sessions are not public. The three-hour mediation session usually opens with the mediator's explaining to the parties the mediation process and reviewing the terms of the mediation and the issues set out in the issues statement. The mediator usually then initiates the discussion and structures it. Each party gives his or her side of the story, sets out what is important, and asks questions. Once the mediator has a sense of where the parties are, he or she helps them to develop solutions to the problem. The mediator may meet the parties while they are face-to-face or may shuttle back and forth between them while the parties stay in separate rooms. The lawyer, sitting with the client, can determine when the client needs additional advice or a break. During the break, the client can get advice from the lawyer about how to negotiate and about possible solutions.

Rule 24.1.11 makes it clear that both the client and the lawyer, if there is one, must attend the mediation session. If the claim for damages is covered by insurance, a representative with authority to bind the insurer to any agreement must also attend. Where authority to settle is required and the person with authority cannot be present, the party must arrange to have telephone access to whoever is appearing for him or her at the mediation session.

Minimal attendance requirements

Rule 24.1 mandates a three-hour mediation session, meaning that the parties must attempt mediation for at least three hours. The session may be less than that if the parties settle or if the mediator decides that there is no point in continuing. Mediation also may last more than three hours if the parties and the mediator consent. Further sessions may be scheduled if the parties agree, but no one is obliged to attempt more than three hours of mediation.

If a mediation is scheduled and a party does not appear within 30 minutes of the scheduled commencement time, the mediator cancels the session and files a certificate of non-compliance in form 24.1D [10] with the mediation coordinator. A certificate of non-compliance appears in figure 22.4.

When the mediation coordinator receives a notice of non-compliance, the coordinator refers the matter to the case management master or judge assigned to the case. If none has been assigned at this early stage in the proceedings, one will be assigned, and he or she is likely to convene a case conference. Issues of rescheduling can be dealt with and costs may be awarded to those who showed up and had costs "thrown away" because they spent time preparing for a meeting that did not happen and will need to spend time preparing again. Costs usually include payment of the mediator's fee for the cancelled session.

Completion of the mediation process

Rule 24.1.15 requires the mediator to file a report on the outcome of the mediation with the parties and the mediation coordinator within 10 days after the mediation is concluded. Because the matters discussed in mediation are confidential, the report states no more than the fact that the parties attended the mediation session and complied with the rules.

If the parties reach an agreement on some or all of the issues, you can record the terms of the agreement using a standard minutes of settlement format. If the agreement settles the matter, the minutes of settlement should be filed in court, together with an order consenting to judgment or dismissal in accordance with the terms of the minutes of settlement.

FIGURE 22.4   CERTIFICATE OF NON-COMPLIANCE (FORM 24.1D)

Court file no. 01-CV-1234

ONTARIO
SUPERIOR COURT OF JUSTICE

BETWEEN:

ABIGAIL BOAR

Plaintiff

and

RATTLE MOTORS LTD. and FRED FLOGEM

Defendants

CERTIFICATE OF NON-COMPLIANCE

TO: MEDIATION CO-ORDINATOR

I, Marielle Moosetrap, mediator, certify that this certificate of non-compliance is filed because:

( ) (*Identify party(ies)*) failed to provide a copy of a statement of issues to the mediator and the other parties (*or* to the mediator *or* to *party(ies)*).
( ) (*Identify party(ies)*) failed to provide a copy of the pleadings to the mediator.
(x) The defendant Fred Flogem failed to attend within the first 30 minutes of a scheduled mediation session.

December 13, year 1

Marielle Moosetrap
1200 Yonge Street
Toronto, Ontario, M5R 1Z6
tel. 416-490-8765
fax 416-490-8766

Who pays for mediation?

Mediator's maximum fees for the mandatory three-hour mediation session are set by regulation,[11] in response to charges of critics that mediation is an added, open-ended expense for clients. The fee covers one hour of preparation time for the mediator as well as the three-hour session. The client must pay lawyer's fees connected to the mediation process in addition to the cost of the mediator. The fee rises along with the number of parties involved and is shared by the parties. The current schedule is set out in table 22.1.

If the client has a legal aid certificate, or is of modest means and meets the Ministry of the Attorney General's financial eligibility requirements, mediation is provided at no cost to the client. The ministry's eligibility form is set out in figure 22.5.

Table 22.1   Mediator fees

Number of parties	Maximum fees for mandatory session
2	$600 plus GST
3	$675 plus GST
4	$750 plus GST
5 or more	$825 plus GST

Over and above the fees set out in table 22.1, a mediator may charge reasonable expenses, such as those incurred for renting space to conduct the mediation. However, the parties must agree to payment of these fees in advance.[12]

MANDATORY MEDIATION IN ESTATE, TRUST, AND SUBSTITUTE DECISION PROCEEDINGS: RULE 75.1

Introduction

This section provides an overview of mandatory mediation as it applies to what is generally called estates litigation, which concerns litigation about estates, trusts, and substitute decisions under rule 75.[13] A related rule, rule 75.1, requires that a form of mandatory mediation be applied to estates cases under rule 75. Mandatory mediation under rule 75.1 closely parallels rule 24 but is adapted to suit the procedures in estates litigation. Mandatory mediation under rule 75.1 applies to cases in Toronto and Ottawa to disputed matters relating to estates, trusts, and substitute decisions (rule 75.1.01). Not every type of estate litigation requires mediation, and you should refer to rule 75.1.02(1) for the kinds of estate cases to which mandatory mediation applies.

How rule 75.1 works

There are reasons for the differences between mandatory mediation under rule 24.1 and mandatory mediation under rule 75.1. Cases under rule 75 are not under case management and follow a different timetable. Cases under rule 75 are usually brought by notice of application, which sets out a different and shorter pretrial procedure. Procedure is further complicated by rules in statutes that govern rule 75 matters. It is usual in estate cases to have a great number of parties, consisting of estate beneficiaries and classes of estate beneficiaries, not all of whom are interested in all of the issues. A mechanism is needed to avoid dragging all parties into mediation that does not concern them.

When a rule 75 proceeding has been commenced, an applicant on a notice of application is required to bring a motion for directions relating to the conduct of the mediation within 30 days of the last day on which the respondents may serve a notice of appearance. The rule does not specify a time limit for when the motion must be heard (rule 75.1.05).

On the return of the motion for directions, the order may be a formality and a foregone conclusion, or it may be lengthy and customized. Estate litigation that

FIGURE 22.5 FINANCIAL ELIGIBILITY FORM

FINANCIAL ELIGIBILITY FORM
ONTARIO MANDATORY MEDIATION PROGRAM

To be completed by litigants seeking pro bono mediation services under the MMP Access Plan.

Date: _____ Location (county): _____
      yy mm dd

Name: _____
      First   Last

1. How many people are in your family unit, including you, your spouse and any dependent children?

   1 2 3 4 5+

2. What is the total gross income of your family unit annually (or monthly)?

   ❑ No income ❑ Under $18,000 ($1,500) ❑ $18,000-26,999 ($1,500-2,249)
   ❑ $27,000-30,999 ($2,250-2,582) ❑ $31,000-36,999 ($2,582-3,082)
   ❑ $37,000-43,000 ($3,083-3,583) ❑ Over $43,000 ($3,583)

3. Does the total amount of your liquid assets exceed $1,500 including all bank accounts, bonds, stocks, RRSPs, GICs, mutual funds and similar assets? (Do not include vehicles, real property and household effects)

   ❑ yes ❑ no

4. Does your net worth exceed $6,000?

   ❑ yes ❑ no

Declaration: I, _____, of the _____ of ____ _____, declare that the above information is true and correct and I make this statement conscientiously believing it to be true and knowing that it is of the same force and effect as if made under oath.

Declare before me at the _____ of _____ in the province of Ontario this

_____ day of _____ 20 ___.

_____   _____
Local Mediation Coordinator Signature Litigant Signature Counsel Signature
(if applicable)

involves a challenge to a will or raises issues interpreting a will can be very complex. There may be scores of beneficiaries, some of whom will be affected by the order but some of who may not be. Some may be affected in different ways, or some may have one position on the outcome, and others may have another. In the complex estate case, the court may have to:

- identify the issues to be mediated and the order in which they are mediated,

- determine who has carriage of the mediation (usually the estate administrator or trustee),

- set the timetable for conducting the mediation when there are many parties with different interests, and

- decide which parties may attend the mediation and how the cost is to be shared among the parties or classes of parties.

Once an order for directions is made, the parties must select a mediator within 30 days (rule 75.1.07). The parties may choose their own mediator or select one from the roster. Care should be taken to select a mediator who has some general knowledge of substantive and procedural estate law. Once the parties have agreed to a mediator, the party with carriage of the mediation is required to give the mediator a copy of the order for directions. If the parties fail to select a mediator within 30 days, the party with carriage of the mediation is responsible for filing a request to assign a mediator with the local mediation coordinator.

When the mediator is selected (or assigned), he or she must immediately fix a date for the mediation and, at least 20 days before that, must serve on every party designated by the order for directions notice of the place, date, and time of the mediation (rule 75.1.07). At least 7 days before the mediation, designated parties must provide the mediator and the other designated parties with a statement of issues. The statement of issues, in form 75.1C, must identify the factual and legal issues in dispute and briefly set out the position and interest of the party making the statement. The party should also attach any documents that that party considers to be of relevance to its position (rule 75.1.08). Form 75.1C[14] is set out in figure 22.6. It is completed in much the same way as is the statement of issues in form 24.1C under rule 24.1.

The mediator is obliged to give a copy of his or her report on the mediation to every party and to the mediation coordinator within 10 days of the conclusion of the mediation (rule 75.1.12). An agreement is to be reported, and a breach of an agreement by any party can be enforced. If the standard three-hour mediation is not enough, and with many parties or issues it is likely not to be, the parties may consent to an order for further sessions. The fees are then to be negotiated between the parties and the mediator.

CHAPTER SUMMARY

This chapter briefly explained the purpose of mediation and its role in diverting civil cases from the court system by promoting settlement at an early date. The encouraging results of the mediation pilot project have resulted in mediation becoming mandatory for all proceedings that are case managed under rule 77 and, with

FIGURE 22.6   STATEMENT OF ISSUES (FORM 75.1C)

Court file no. E-1111-01

ONTARIO SUPERIOR COURT OF JUSTICE

IN THE ESTATE OF Abigail Boar,   deceased,
late of the City of Toronto, in the Province of Ontario,
occupation investment analyst,
who died on   October 21, year 4

STATEMENT OF ISSUES

1. Factual and legal issues in dispute

The undersigned designated party states that the following factual and
legal issues are in dispute and remain to be resolved.

Whether or not there is a last will and testament of Abigail
Boar, subsequent to that which is dated April 4, year -4, for
which an application for probate has been made in this
court.

2. Party's position and interests (what the party hopes to achieve)

This party is the brother of Abigail Boar, who is excluded
from the beneficiaries mentioned in the Last Will and
Testament of Abigail Boar, dated April 4, year -4. This
party believes there is a subsequent will dated April 9,
year -4, and that this will includes this party as a
beneficiary of the estate of Abigail Boar.

3. Attached documents

Attached to this form are the following documents that the designated
party considers of central importance in the proceeding:

1. Affidavit of Bill Boar, sworn November 5, year 1 and
   filed in this proceeding
2. Photocopy of a Last Will and Testament of Abigail Boar,
   executed by her on April 9, year -4

Date: October 23, year 4   Bill Boar
                                          2311 Baybottom Crescent
                                          Toronto, Ontario, M5R 8X3

NOTE: Rule 75.1.11 provides as follows:

All communications at a mediation session and the mediator's notes and
records shall be deemed to be without prejudice settlement discussions.

modifications, in actions in Toronto under rule 78. We discussed the lawyer's role in the mediation process and his or her duty in explaining to the client how mediation works.

Once a proceeding is commenced, except in Toronto where mediation comes at a later stage in the proceedings, we noted that the parties have 30 days after the first defence is filed to choose a mediator. Within 90 days of the filing of the first defence, the parties are expected to complete mediation, which is envisaged as a three-hour session. If necessary, time limits can be extended by calling a case conference under rule 77. At least 7 days before the mediation session, the parties must provide the mediator with an issues statement. On completion of the mediation, the mediator must, within 10 days, report to the mediation coordinator on the outcome of the mediation. The costs of mediation are borne by the parties, and the fees are fixed for the first three hours. The parties may, on consent, go on to further sessions, but the mediator's fees are no longer fixed. If a party does not cooperate with the process, the court may impose penalties. However, in appropriate cases, the court may order that the case proceed without mediation.

We also briefly discussed mandatory mediation under rule 75.1 for contentious and disputed estate, trust, and substitute decision cases, noting differences from mandatory mediation under rule 24.1.

KEY TERMS

mediation

alternative dispute resolution

NOTES

1 Rule 24.1.04. This rule sets out the details of which actions are or are not included for the purposes of rule 24.1.04.

2 Superior Court of Justice, Ontario Region Practice Direction of Regional Senior Judge Winkler, December 2004, "Backlog Reduction/Best Practices Initiative," in James J. Carthy, W.A. Derry Millar, and Jeffrey G. Cowan, *Ontario Annual Practice* (Aurora, ON: Canada Law Book, 2008-9) and http://www .ontariocourts.on.ca/scj/en/notices/pd/toronto/casemanagement.htm.

3 The description here of the results of the evaluation of mandatory mediation is adopted from R.G. Hann and Carl Baar et al., *Evaluation of the Ontario Mandatory Mediation Program: Executive Summary and Recommendations* (Toronto: Queen's Printer, March 2001). See also "Report of the Evaluation Committee of the Ontario Civil Rules Committee for the Mandatory Mediation Rule Pilot Project," in *Civil Litigation — 100% Case Management Alert*, Advocates' Society conference, held in Toronto, May 31, 2001.

4 But costs increase where mediation fails because the parties must pay the mediator, and there are the additional costs of lawyers preparing for mediation.

5 See rule 75.1 regarding mediation in estate matters, for example.

6 The mediation pilot projects' expiry dates are extended to January 2010, and will likely be extended beyond that date.

7 O. reg. 438/08, ss. 15–24, amending rule 24.1

8 Form 24.1A appears to have been revoked by O. reg. 453/98, s. 2(2) as of July 1, 2001, but still seems to be in use.

9 This form, like form 24.1A, appears to have been revoked by O. reg. 453/98, as of July 1, 2001, but seems to be still in use.

10 Form 24.1D, like forms 24.1A and 24.1C, appears to have been revoked by O. reg. 453/98, s. 2(1) as of July 1, 2001, but seems to be still in use.

11 O. reg. 451/98, as amended by O. reg. 241/01.

12 Ibid.

13 The discussion is brief. Estate, trust, and substitute decisions litigation, known collectively as "estate litigation," is specialized and based on several statutes and a vast amount of case law.

14 This form has technically been revoked, like other mediation forms, by O. reg. 453/98, s. 2, but appears to be still in use.

REFERENCES

Hann, R.G. and Carl Baar et al., *Evaluation of the Ontario Mandatory Mediation Program: Executive Summary and Recommendations* (Toronto: Queen's Printer, March 2001).

Insurance Act, RSO 1990, c. I.8.

O. reg. 241/01.

O. reg. 451/98.

O. reg. 453/98.

"Report of the Evaluation Committee of the Ontario Civil Rules Committee for the Mandatory Mediation Rule Pilot Project," in *Civil Litigation — 100% Case Management Alert*, Advocates' Society conference, held in Toronto, May 31, 2001.

Rules of Civil Procedure, RRO 1990, reg. 194.

Substitute Decisions Act, 1992, SO 1992, c. 30.

Succession Law Reform Act, RSO 1990, c. S.26.

REVIEW QUESTIONS

1. What is mediation?

2. What are the advantages and disadvantages of mediation?

3. What cases are subject to mandatory mediation?

4. Must every case-managed proceeding go through mediation?

5. How are mediators selected?

6. What must be done to prepare for mediation?

7. Who must attend the mediation?

8. How long is a mediation session?

9. What are the costs of mediation?

10. What happens if a party is not cooperative in the mediation process?

11. What happens when mediation is complete?

12. How does mandatory mediation under rule 24.1 differ from mediation under rule 75.1?

DISCUSSION QUESTION

1. Draft a statement of issues to be filed on behalf of Fred Flogem and Rattle Motors Ltd. You will want to review figures 7.2 (statement of claim), 7.3 (statement of defence), and 22.3 (Abigail Boar's statement of issues).

CHAPTER 23

Simplified procedure: Rule 76

INTRODUCTION

As we have seen in our look at the *Rules of Civil Procedure*, litigation in the Ontario Superior Court of Justice can be a complicated, expensive, and time-consuming process. A party who is suing for less than $10,000 can take the case to Small Claims Court with its straightforward and relatively fast procedure. However, if a party wants to sue for more than $10,000, there is no option but to use the Superior Court.

Not all actions in the Superior Court warrant the use of the usual lengthy procedure. Therefore, the rules provide a little halfway point between the Small Claims Court and the regular Superior Court process. This halfway point is called the simplified procedure, and it is contained in rule 76. This procedure reduces the time and expense associated with litigation.

CHANGES TO SIMPLIFIED PROCEDURE, IN EFFECT AS OF JANUARY 1, 2010

Amendments to the *Rules of Civil Procedure* made in December 2008 indicate the following changes to simplified procedure as described in this chapter.

- The monetary jurisdiction for a case brought under the simplified procedure will be raised from $50,000 to $100,000. This is generally consistent with other changes in monetary jurisdiction that will increase the monetary jurisdiction in the Small Claims Court to $25,000. This partly reflects inflation since the limit was last changed, and partly reflects a desire to remove cases of small value from the more complex, regular procedure in the Superior Court.

- Parties will now have an opportunity to obtain more information about the opposing case before trial through the use of examination for discovery. Previously, discovery was not permitted under rule 76, as it was regarded as a major source of cost and delay prior to trial. Each party will be allowed up to two hours in which to conduct an examination for discovery of all other parties. It is thought that this will help to encourage earlier and more meaningful settlement discussions.

- At a summary trial, both the plaintiff and defendant may examine their own witnesses on their affidavits for up to ten minutes. Previously, a party could cross-examine an opponent's witness on an affidavit, but could not examine his or her own witness on his or her affidavit.[1]

APPLICATION OF THE SIMPLIFIED PROCEDURE

The simplified procedure *must* be used in all cases in the Superior Court in which a party is claiming $50,000 or less, exclusive of interest and costs. It may also be used for claims over $50,000, provided that the defendant does not object. The limit does not apply only to claims for money. It also applies to claims for real and personal property valued at $50,000 or less. The assessment of the value of the property is its fair market value at the time the action is commenced.

The simplified procedure is not available for actions brought under the *Class Proceedings Act, 1992* or the *Construction Lien Act*, except for trust claims. Actions following the simplified procedure are not subject to rule 77 and are therefore not case managed.

If there is more than one plaintiff in the action, each plaintiff's claim must independently meet the requirements for application of the rule.

For example, if Abigail Boar sued Rattle Motors Ltd. and Fred Flogem for $25,000, and her boyfriend also decided to sue the defendants for the loss of Abigail's companionship as a result of her injuries, his claim would have to be for $50,000 or less and satisfy the other criteria as well.

If the plaintiff is suing more than one defendant in the same action, she must use the simplified procedure if each claim is for $50,000, or less. For instance, if Abigail sues Rattle Motors Ltd. for $50,000 and Fred Flogem for $40,000, she must use the simplified procedure. However, if she sues Rattle Motors Ltd. for $100,000 and Fred Flogem for $40,000, it is not mandatory for her to use the simplified procedure; however, she could use it if the defendant does not object.

All the other rules apply to actions brought under the simplified procedure unless rule 76 specifically provides that another procedure applies.

COMMENCEMENT OF AN ACTION

Since it is the plaintiff who commences the action, it is also the plaintiff who must use the simplified procedure if the amount claimed is $50,000 or less. It is also the plaintiff who may elect to use the procedure for claims of more than $50,000. The statement of claim must indicate that the action is being brought under the simplified procedure. The proper wording is "This action is brought against you under the simplified procedure provided in rule 76 of the *Rules of Civil Procedure*." This wording is added at the top of the page on which the claim is commenced.

An action commenced under the simplified procedure will proceed under rule 76 unless the defendant objects. The ground for the objection would be that the claim does not fit within the monetary requirements of the rule. The objection is made in the statement of defence.

Once the defendant objects to the matter proceeding under rule 76, the plaintiff, in his or her reply to the statement of defence, may state that he or she is aban-

FIGURE 23.1   NOTICE WHETHER ACTION UNDER RULE 76 (FORM 76A)

NOTICE WHETHER ACTION UNDER RULE 76

The plaintiff states that this action and any related proceedings are:

- ❑   continuing under Rule 76
- ❑   continuing under Rule 77 — fast track
- ❑   continuing under Rule 77 — standard track
- ❑   continuing as an ordinary procedure.

doning forever the portion of the claim that is above $50,000 and the proceeding will continue under the simplified procedure. If he or she does not take the option to abandon the excess amount, the action will then continue under the ordinary procedure and case management will apply if it is the type of case that would fall under the case management rule.

In a situation where there is more than one plaintiff, the simplified procedure is to be used if each plaintiff's claim independently meets the requirements under the rule. Similarly, in an action with multiple defendants, rule 76 may be used if each claim, against each defendant, considered separately, falls within the rule.

Any counterclaim, crossclaim, or third-party claim attached to the main action will also proceed by way of the simplified procedure even if it does not meet the requirements, unless

- the defendant, by crossclaim, counterclaim, or third-party claim, objects in the statement of defence to the use of the simplified procedure and the claim is not amended so that it falls within the requirement of the rules, or

- the defendant brings a crossclaim, counterclaim, or third-party claim that does not meet the requirement of rule 76 and states in the pleading that the crossclaim, counterclaim, or third-party claim is to proceed under the ordinary procedure.

In either of these cases, the ordinary procedure will then apply.

In the same way, an action that has been commenced under the ordinary procedure may continue under the simplified procedure if

- all the parties consent and a consent is filed with the court, or

- no consent is filed, but

    - the plaintiff has followed rule 26 to amend the claim so that it falls within the requirements for the use of the simplified procedure, and

    - all the other claims, counterclaims, crossclaims, or third-party claims meet the requirements to proceed under rule 76.

If an action changes stream, from simplified to ordinary procedure or vice versa, the plaintiff must serve and file form 76A, which states what change has been made. A sample form 76A is shown in figure 23.1.

DIFFERENCES BETWEEN THE SIMPLIFIED AND THE ORDINARY PROCEDURE

The major differences between the ordinary and simplified procedures are set out below.

1. *Discovery.* No discovery is permitted on the simplified procedure, but the parties are required to have discussions within 60 days after the first statement of defence or notice of intent to defend has been filed to determine whether all the documents relating to the disputed issues have been disclosed (rule 76.08).

2. *Cross-examination.* No cross-examination on an affidavit is permitted under the simplified procedure.

3. *Examination of a witnesses.* No examination of a witness on a pending motion is permitted under the simplified procedure.

4. *Affidavit of documents.* The affidavit of documents under the simplified procedure must contain an additional schedule, schedule D, setting out the names and addresses of all potential witnesses to be called at trial. A witness who is not included in schedule D cannot be called to give evidence at the trial without an order of the court. When the affidavit of documents is served, copies of all the documents listed in schedule A must be served as well. The affidavit of documents must be served within 10 days of the close of pleadings.

5. *Motions.* Motions under the simplified procedure are significantly different from those under the ordinary procedure. These differences are discussed below.

MOTIONS

A motion is commenced with a simplified procedure motion form, form 76B, rather than with a notice of motion. Reflecting the less complicated process under the simplified procedure, this form, for the most part, involves filling in the blanks and requires little drafting. A sample of a motion in form 76B is set out in figure 23.2.

The motion is to be heard in the same court where the action was commenced unless the parties consent or the court orders that it be heard in another location. In many instances, the motion may be heard without a motion record and other supporting documents.

Many motions can be dealt with by the registrar and do not require a hearing before a judge. For example, the registrar may deal with the following types of motions if they are on consent, a consent is filed, no party is under a disability, and no responding material is filed:

- an amendment of a pleading or a notice of motion;

- an addition, deletion, or substitution of a party whose consent is filed;

- the removal of a lawyer of record;

- setting aside a noting in default;

FIGURE 23.2   SIMPLIFIED PROCEDURE MOTION FORM (FORM 76B)

SIMPLIFIED PROCEDURE MOTION FORM

JURISDICTION   ❏ Judge
                   ❏ Master
                   ❏ Registrar

THIS FORM FILED BY (*Check appropriate boxes to identify the party filing this form as a moving/responding party on this motion AND to identify this party as plaintiff, defendant, etc. in the action*)

❏ moving party
❏ plaintiff

_____

❏ responding party
❏ defendant

_____

❏ other — specify kind of party and name

_____

_____

MOTION MADE

❏ on consent of all parties   ❏ on notice to all parties and
                                              unopposed

❏ without notice   ❏ on notice to all parties and
                                              expected to be opposed

Notice of this motion was served on (date):

_____

by means of:

_____

_____

METHOD OF HEARING REQUESTED

❏ by attendance
❏ in writing only, no attendance
❏ by fax
❏ by telephone conference under rule 1.08
❏ by video conference under rule 1.08

Date, time and place for conference call, telephone call or appearances

_____ _____ _____

   (date)   *(time)*   *(place)*

FIGURE 23.2   CONTINUED

ORDER SOUGHT BY THIS PARTY *(Responding party is presumed to request dismissal of motion and costs)*

❑ extension of time — until (give specific date): _____
❑ serve claim
❑ file or deliver statement of defence
❑ other relief — be specific

_____

_____

MATERIAL RELIED ON BY THIS PARTY

❑ this form
❑ pleadings
❑ affidavits — specify
❑ other — specify

_____

_____

GROUNDS IN SUPPORT OF/IN OPPOSITION TO MOTION (INCLUDING RULE AND STATUTORY PROVISIONS RELIED ON)

_____

_____

CERTIFICATION BY LAWYER

I certify that the above information is correct, to the best of my knowledge.

Signature of lawyer *(if no lawyer, party must sign)*

_____

Date   _____

THIS PARTY'S LAWYER *(if no lawyer, give party's name, address for service, telephone and fax number)*	OTHER PARTY'S LAWYER *(if no lawyer, give party's name, address for service, telephone and fax number)*
Name and firm:	Name and firm:
Address:	Address:
Telephone:	Telephone:
Fax:	Fax:

FIGURE 23.2 CONCLUDED

DISPOSITION
❑ order to go as asked
❑ adjourned to
❑ order refused
❑ order to go as follows:

_____

_____

Hearing Method: _____ Hearing duration: _____ minutes
Heard in: ❑ courtroom ❑ office

❑ Successful party MUST prepare formal order for signature
❑ No copy of disposition to be sent to parties
❑ Other directions — specify

_____

_____

Date _____ Name _____ Signature _____
Judge/Master/Registrar

- setting aside a default judgment;

- discharge of a certificate of pending litigation;

- security for costs in a specified amount; and

- dismissal of a proceeding without costs.

There is no need to take out a formal order unless the court specifically orders that it be taken out or the order is being appealed. The endorsement on the motion form is all that is necessary to establish that an order was made.

DISMISSAL BY THE REGISTRAR

Actions proceeding under the simplified procedure rule are not case managed under rule 77. Instead, rule 76 sets up a process through which the registrar will dismiss a case that is not proceeding in a timely fashion. Rule 76.06 requires the registrar to treat an action as abandoned and dismiss it if the following conditions apply:

- no statement of defence has been filed, 180 days have passed since the originating process was filed, and nothing further has been done either to set the matter down for trial or to terminate it; or

- a statement of defence has been filed, more than 150 days have passed since the first statement of defence or notice of intent to defend has been filed, and nothing further has been done either to set the matter down for trial or to terminate it.

Before dismissing an action as abandoned, the registrar must give 45 days' notice of the pending dismissal. At the end of the 45-day period, if the parties do nothing further, the registrar will make an order dismissing the action as abandoned.

SUMMARY JUDGMENT

Either party may move for summary judgment after the close of pleadings. The motion can be brought only before a judge in the county in which the action was commenced unless the parties agree or the court orders otherwise.

As with any motion, a motion for summary judgment under the simplified procedure must be supported by evidence in the form of affidavits. A responding party is not permitted merely to deny all the allegations in the moving party's material. Responding parties must prepare their own affidavits setting out specific facts that support the refusal of summary judgment. Affidavits may be based on what the deponent was told or what he or she believes, but the court may draw an adverse inference if no direct evidence is provided from a person who has personal knowledge of the alleged facts.

A motion record must also be prepared for the motion. The record must contain the following material, arranged in the following order on consecutively numbered pages:

1. a table of contents, describing each document and exhibit by its nature, date, and in the case of an exhibit, by its exhibit number;

2. a copy of the notice of motion;

3. a copy of all the affidavits to be used; and

4. a copy of all the pleadings.

Every party must also file a factum, along with proof of service, at least two days before the hearing of the motion.

A judge must grant the summary judgment under the simplified procedure unless he or she determines that it is not possible to decide the matters at issue without cross-examination or that it would not be fair to decide the issues on the motion. If the motion for summary judgment is not granted, the judge shall determine the appropriate method of trial for the matter.

SETTLEMENT DISCUSSIONS, SETTING THE MATTER DOWN FOR TRIAL, AND THE PRETRIAL CONFERENCE

Within 60 days after the first defence or notice of intent to defend has been filed, the parties are required to have a meeting or a telephone discussion to determine whether all the documents relating to the case have been disclosed and whether a settlement of any or all of the issues is possible. Within 90 days after the first statement of defence or the notice of intention to defend has been filed, the plaintiff must serve a notice of readiness for pretrial conference, form 76C, on all the parties and file it with the court, along with proof of service. A sample form 76C is shown in figure 23.3. If the plaintiff does not take this step, any other party may do it. The filing of the notice of readiness for pretrial conference sets the case down for trial. Following the filing of the notice of readiness, the registrar schedules a pretrial conference and gives the parties at least 45 days' notice.

**FIGURE 23.3   NOTICE OF READINESS FOR PRETRIAL CONFERENCE
(FORM 76C)**

Court file no. 01-CV-6789

ONTARIO
SUPERIOR COURT OF JUSTICE

BETWEEN:

MABEL MADDENLY

Plaintiff

and

JIMMY JINGLE

Defendant

NOTICE OF READINESS FOR PRE-TRIAL CONFERENCE

The plaintiff, Mabel Maddenly, is ready for a pre-trial conference and is
setting this action down for trial. A pre-trial conference in the action will
proceed as scheduled and the trial will proceed when the action is reached
on the trial list, unless the court orders otherwise.

CERTIFICATE

I CERTIFY that there was a settlement discussion under rule 76.08.

Date: January 10, year 2

_____
Signature

Belinda Smart
Barrister & Solicitor
LSUC #13579C
47 Tempest Road
Toronto, Ontario M6Y 5R7

tel. 416-555-1234
fax 416-555-1235

Lawyer for the Plaintiff

TO:
George Fandoddle
Barrister & Solicitor
LSUC #24681B
2001 Space Lane
Toronto, Ontario M8U 9I4

tel. 416-666-8910
fax 416-666-8911

Lawyer for the Defendant

*(Name, address and telephone and fax numbers of lawyer or moving
party giving notice)*

The parties and their lawyers are required to attend the pretrial conference unless the court orders otherwise. In addition, a party who needs approval from someone else to accept a settlement of the action must ensure that he or she has the ability throughout the conference to contact that person by telephone.

At least five days before the conference, each party must file:

- a copy of the party's affidavit of documents and copies of the documents relied on for the party's claim or defence,

- a copy of any expert's report, and

- any other material necessary for the conference.

It is not necessary to serve this material on the other parties because they will already have copies. In addition, the parties must *serve* and file:

- a two-page statement setting out the issues and the party's position with respect to them, and

- a trial management checklist (form 76D).

A sample trial management checklist is provided in figure 23.4.

The pretrial judge or master sets the trial date. The trial may be an ordinary trial or a summary trial under rule 76.12. If the parties cannot agree about the type of trial, the pretrial judge or master will determine which type of trial is most appropriate for the case.

Immediately after the pretrial conference, the registrar will place the action on the appropriate trial list. At least 10 days before the trial, the party that set the matter down for trial by filing the notice of readiness for the pretrial conference must serve a trial record and file it with the court with proof of service. All the parties to the main action, counterclaim, crossclaim, or third party claim must be served with the trial record.

If the trial is proceeding as an ordinary trial, the trial record is prepared in exactly the same way as the trial record for an action under the ordinary procedure (rule 48.03). If the trial is proceeding as a summary trial, the trial record must contain, in consecutively numbered pages arranged in the following order:

1. a table of contents that describes each document, including each exhibit, by its nature and date and, in the case of an exhibit, by its exhibit number or letter;

2. a copy of the pleadings, including those relating to any counterclaim, crossclaim, or third party claim;

3. a copy of any demand or order for particulars of a pleading and the particulars delivered in response;

4. a copy of any order respecting the trial;

5. a copy of all the affidavits served by all the parties for use in the summary trial; and

6. a certificate signed by the lawyer of the party filing the trial record, stating that it contains the documents listed above.

FIGURE 23.4 TRIAL MANAGEMENT CHECKLIST (FORM 76D)

TRIAL MANAGEMENT CHECKLIST

Trial Lawyer — Plaintiff (s):

Trial Lawyer — Defendant (s):

Filed by Plaintiff
Filed by Defendant
Filed by Subsequent Party

1. Issues Outstanding
   (a) liability:
   (b) damages:
   (c) other:

2. Names of Plaintiff's Witnesses

3. Names of Defendant's Witnesses

4. Admissions
   Are the parties prepared to admit any facts for
   the purposes of the trial or summary trial?   ❏ yes   ❏ no

5. Document Brief
   Will there be a document brief?   ❏ yes   ❏ no

6. Request to Admit
   Will there be a request to admit?   ❏ yes   ❏ no
   If so, have the parties agreed to a timetable?   ❏ yes   ❏ no

7. Expert's Reports
   Are any expert's reports anticipated?   ❏ yes   ❏ no

8. Amendments to Pleadings
   Are any amendments likely to be sought?   ❏ yes   ❏ no

9. Mode of Trial
   Have the parties agreed to a summary trial?   ❏ yes   ❏ no
   Have the parties agreed to an ordinary trial?   ❏ yes   ❏ no
   If the parties have not agreed about the mode of
   trial, what mode of trial is being requested by
   the party filing this checklist?

10. Factum of Law
    Will the parties be submitting factums of law?   ❏ yes   ❏ no

SUMMARY TRIAL

In an ordinary trial, each party calls its witnesses into the courtroom, and the witness is first questioned by the lawyer for the party who called the witness. This is called examination-in-chief. The lawyers for the other parties are then entitled to ask the witness questions on cross-examination.

In a summary trial, parties present their evidence in affidavits, eliminating examination-in-chief of witnesses at trial. Opposite parties are entitled to cross-examine witnesses in court, if necessary. Rule 76.12 sets out the order for presenting the evidence and examining witnesses at a summary trial.

A party who wants a witness presented at trial for cross-examination on affidavit must give ten days' notice to the party who presented the affidavit. The notice is to allow the party presenting the affidavit to arrange for the deponent's attendance at trial for cross-examination.

If the parties agree to a summary trial or the pretrial judge or master orders that it proceed in that manner, a timetable for delivery of all the affidavits will be established at the pretrial conferences and the parties must abide by that schedule.

Unlike cross-examination in an ordinary trial, in a summary trial time limitations are placed on cross-examination of witnesses and closing arguments. All of a party's cross-examinations must be completed within 50 minutes, and each party has only 45 minutes to present a closing oral argument.

COSTS CONSEQUENCES

Since the purpose of simplified procedure is to reduce both expense and delay of litigation involving smaller amounts, there are severe cost consequences for failure to use the simplified procedure in appropriate actions. For instance, if the plaintiff proceeds to trial under the ordinary procedure seeking more than $50,000 in relief but at the end of the trial is awarded only $50,000 or less, the court will deny the plaintiff costs unless it is satisfied that it was reasonable for the plaintiff to proceed under the ordinary procedure. This ensures that plaintiffs will put appropriate thought into correctly valuing their claim before they begin the litigation.

Defendants also face potential cost consequences if they object to the actions proceeding under the simplified procedure because they say the property at issue is worth more than $50,000 and, as a result of their objection, the matter is continued under the ordinary procedure. If the court finds that the property is in fact worth $50,000 or less, the defendant will be ordered to pay the extra costs of the plaintiff that were incurred because he or she could not proceed under the simplified procedure. Any such costs will be awarded based on the substantial indemnity scale.

Any party who amends a pleading so that the action is changed from the ordinary procedure to the simplified procedure is liable for the other party's costs that were incurred because the action was originally commenced under the ordinary procedure. These costs will be awarded on a substantial indemnity basis.

CHAPTER SUMMARY

In this chapter, we have seen that the simplified procedure is a process for dealing with claims of $50,000 or less. It is not available for class action, construction lien, or family law matters. Cases involving a claim of less than $50,000 must use the

simplified procedure, but cases involving a claim of more than that amount may also use this route if the parties consent. The plaintiff elects to proceed under simplified procedure but the defendants, a third party, or a party in a crossclaim or counterclaim may object by way of motion.

We have noted that the major differences between simplified procedure and ordinary procedure are that no discovery or cross-examination of witnesses on affidavits is permitted in simplified procedure, and the affidavit of documents contains an additional schedule, schedule D, which sets out the names and addresses of all the witnesses a party intends to call at trial. Motion records are not required, and the registrar has the power to deal with most simple or uncontested motions. Summary judgment is easily obtained.

We also examined the various time limits in simplified procedure. Within 60 days of the first defence being filed, the parties must hold a settlement conference to decide whether all the necessary documents have been produced and whether settlement is possible. Within 90 days, the plaintiff must set the action down for trial. The registrar will then give notice of a pretrial conference date to the parties. The parties and the lawyer must attend the pretrial conference, and if no settlement can be reached, the judge or master will set a trial date.

The trial may be a regular trial, but the matter may also proceed to a summary trial, if appropriate. In a summary trial, the parties present their evidence in affidavits and the witnesses may be cross-examined under strict time limitations.

There are severe cost consequences for failing to use the simplified procedure in an appropriate case.

NOTE

1 O. reg. 438/08, ss. 51–60, amending rule 76.

REFERENCES

Class Proceedings Act, 1992, SO 1992, c. 6.

Construction Lien Act, RSO 1990, c. C.30.

Rules of Civil Procedure, RRO 1990, reg. 194.

REVIEW QUESTIONS

1. Consider whether simplified procedure is available in the following situations:

   a. a claim for damages in the amount of $50,000;

   b. a construction lien in the amount of $25,000;

   c. a divorce action in which the total value of the net family property is $45,000;

   d. a claim for damages in the amount of $75,000; and

   e. a damages claim for $40,000 each by Melinda March and her daughter against George Speedy whose snowmobile ran into the March's toboggan.

2. What is the purpose of the simplified procedure?

3. What is the difference between the statement of claim in an ordinary action and the statement of claim in an action under the simplified procedure?

4. What are the major differences between the regular procedure and the simplified procedure?

5. How is an action under the simplified procedure set down for trial?

6. Your law firm's client, the CEO of a corporation, says he is too busy to attend the pretrial conference but will send his executive assistant as a representative of the corporation. Is this acceptable?

7. What is the difference between a summary trial and an ordinary trial?

8. Why is it important to use the simplified procedure in the appropriate cases?

DISCUSSION QUESTION

1. Read and respond to the following memorandum:

    To: Law clerk
    From: I.M. Smug, lawyer
    Re: *Tome Inc. v. Joseph Apostiledes*

    Our client, Joe Apostiledes, was sued by Tome Inc. for non-payment of a debt of $35,000. We have filed a statement of defence in the case, but Mr. Apostiledes has now decided he does not want legal representation and he is going to represent himself in the action. Counsel for Tome is not objecting to this motion and will not be filing any material in response.

    Please prepare a motion having me removed as lawyer of record on the case.

    You look in the file and see that Tome Inc. is located at 1300 Winding Lane, Toronto, Ontario, M8U 5Y7. It is represented by the firm of Tilley and Tidy, 400 Bay Street, Suite 2200, Toronto, Ontario, M7K 2Y6. Howie Tilley is the lawyer with carriage of the case. The firm's telephone number is 416-878-0000 and their fax is 416-878-0001.

    Joe lives at 14 Foolhardy Way, Windsor, Ontario, N0P 4T8, and his telephone number is 613-555-1222.

    Your firm is located at 1750 Cornucopia Crescent, London, Ontario, L7T U8P. The telephone number is 613-566-6666 and the fax is 613-566-6667.

    Prepare the necessary form to commence the motion.

CHAPTER 24

The commercial list

INTRODUCTION

The commercial list was established in the Superior Court of Justice in Toronto for the hearing of actions, applications, and motions related to corporate and commercial matters. It is a completely voluntary method of proceeding, except for bankruptcy cases, which must be heard by placing them on the commercial list. Other cases that may be placed on the list are cases dealing with or related to

- the *Bank Act*;

- the *Ontario Business Corporations Act*;

- the *Canada Business Corporations Act*;

- the *Companies' Creditors Arrangement Act*;

- the *Limited Partnerships Act*;

- the *Pension Benefits Act*;

- the *Personal Property Security Act*;

- receivership applications and all interlocutory motions to appoint, or give directions to, receivers;

- the *Securities Act*;

- the *Winding-Up and Restructuring Act*;

- the *Credit Union and Caisses Populaires Act* relating to credit unions and caisses populaires under administration or that are being wound up or liquidated; and

- any other commercial matters that a judge presiding over the commercial list may direct be placed on the list.

Lawyers dealing with commercial law often want to have their cases on the list because the procedure for dealing with the list is speedier than the ordinary list.

The list was initially established in 1991 by a practice direction of the chief justice. As of April 2002, the original practice direction was replaced by a new practice direction that governs the procedure for the list. There is no rule dealing with any of the procedure. It is all found in the practice direction of the Honourable Justice Patrick LeSage, chief justice of the Superior Court of Justice, dated February 18, 2002.

The list is administered through the Commercial List Office, 10th floor, 393 University Avenue, in Toronto. Cases are usually heard on the 8th floor of the Court House at that address. Only matters originating in the Toronto judicial region can be heard on the list unless the supervising judge orders otherwise.

If a case is started in the usual manner and the parties wish to transfer it to the list for hearing, the court staff in the Commercial List Office, will transfer it if all parties consent to the transfer, the proper documents are submitted, and the case involves one of the statutes or matters listed above, including bankruptcy matters.

COURT DOCUMENTS

The name of the court in the title of proceeding for cases on the list is "Superior Court of Justice — Commercial List." All notices of application or notices of motion involving the list state that the application or motion will be made to "a judge presiding over the commercial list at 393 University Avenue, Toronto."

Originating process may be issued in the Commercial List Office. In addition to the court documents needed for all actions or applications, cases to be heard on the commercial list must be accompanied by a fully completed request form and a case timetable form. These forms are not forms created by the rules and they change often. Copies of the current forms may be obtained from the Commercial List Office.

In addition, there are several model orders or templates related to bankruptcy matters that are posted on the website of the Superior Court of Justice at http://www.ontariocourts.on.ca/scj/en/commerciallist/index.htm. These include a standard template receivership order, a model receiver discharge order form, and an approval and vesting order form. Other model orders or templates may be added from time to time, so it is a good idea to check this site regularly for updated information and guidelines related to the commercial list.

DATES FOR APPLICATIONS, MOTIONS, AND TRIALS

A realistic estimate of the time required for the hearing must be stated in the request form. Staff in the Commercial List Office schedule hearings that will take less than one day of court time. These are called "short hearings." The supervising judge schedules hearings that will take longer than one day. Each day, the supervising judge is in chambers at 9:30 a.m. to deal with urgent matters, matters without notice, consent matters, and scheduling matters. If your hearing is expected to take more than one day, the office staff will book a time for the lawyers to appear. No matter can take more than ten minutes of the time in chambers, and all matters heard on the chambers list must be completed by 10 a.m. Materials to be used at the chambers appointment must be filed with the court office the day before the hearing.

If the initial hearing date is not one set by the office staff or by the supervising judge in chambers, the first court date for applications and motions is the assignment court, held on the first Monday of each month or on the first Tuesday if the Monday is a holiday. Matters in the assignment court are all scheduled for 9:30 a.m. When preparing the notice of application or the notice of motion for this type of matter, state in the notice that the application or motion is to be heard on the initial return date "and thereafter as the judge may direct."

Dates for hearing a petition in bankruptcy are also set at the assignment court on the first Monday of the month.

In order to obtain a trial date, a motion must be brought to a supervising judge in chambers, or a special appointment must be made with the court office. A trial date will not be set unless the parties have completed a case timetable. The current version of this form may be obtained from the Commercial List Office.

Counsel for the parties are expected to discuss the case timetable and, if possible, to agree on it. If they cannot agree on the schedule for the case, they must attend before the supervising judge in chambers.

If parties are not certain as to the appropriate scheduling, largely because they are negotiating scheduling issues or some other matter, the notice may simply state that the matter will be heard "on a date to be established by the Commercial List Office." The court office keeps a list of cases like this. A case remains on the list for three months, at which time it is struck off unless a judge orders otherwise.

As indicated above, a reasonable estimate of time must be made in the request form, which is to be completed for each case. The estimate should be made in conjunction with the other parties and, where possible, all counsel should sign the form. If a request form that is not signed by all counsel is submitted, the initial date will be scheduled for only a 10-minute scheduling hearing. Sometimes, although the best effort has been made to accurately estimate the time needed, it becomes obvious before the court date that more time will be required. In that case, the Commercial List Office must be advised and provided with a reason for the change.

ADJOURNMENTS AND SETTLEMENTS

Once a date has been set, the matter is expected to go ahead. Adjournments are granted in only the most exceptional circumstances. If an adjournment cannot be avoided, counsel must advise the Commercial List Office at the earliest opportunity to permit staff to reschedule the list so that time is not wasted. Counsel waiting on standby can be alerted that their matter may be scheduled, on short notice, in the vacated time slot resulting from the adjournment.

If a case has been adjourned so that settlement discussions can continue and the case is not settled within a reasonable time, a report must be made to advise the court of the status of the discussions. The report must be made within 30 days after the adjournment and may be made in court, in chambers or by letter, depending on which method is most appropriate in the circumstances.

Cases may be scheduled to be heard on a standby basis for a particular date. When a case is listed in this way, the parties should be prepared to proceed on short notice because they may get a call from the court office telling them to appear because their matter is the next on the list for that day.

CASE MANAGEMENT AND CASE SETTLEMENT

Case management under rule 77 does not apply to matters on the commercial list. However, the operation of the list is a form of informal case management. It is expected that the same judge will hear the matter through to completion. This means that if there is to be a motion on an important matter, the continuing judge must be contacted in writing by counsel in advance so that the matter may be scheduled before that judge wherever possible. The letter advising the judge of the need for a hearing on a particular issue in the case must contain a list of times when the lawyers are available to deal with the issue.

Sometimes a case-managed matter on the regular list is transferred to the commercial list, or a party may want a commercial list matter to be case managed and bring a motion requesting that direction from the judge. In such instances, the matter will be case managed, and there is a provision in the practice direction for a scheduling conference. The conference is held in order to develop a plan for the timely processing of the case through the list.

A case conference is also held no later than a month after discoveries. The purpose of the conference is to monitor the progress of the case and make efforts to settle it before trial. The plaintiff or the applicant has the responsibility of arranging the conference. The plaintiff then confers with the other parties and the court to determine a mutually agreeable date.

There is no mandatory mediation on the commercial list. However, at any time the case management judge, on the consent of the parties, may refer any issue for alternative dispute resolution. If alternative dispute resolution is ordered on a particular case, the parties must keep the case management judge apprised of the progress of the matter while it is in such resolution.

Pretrial conferences may be scheduled for entire cases or for particular issues within a case. At least five days before the conference, each party must deliver a pretrial brief to all the other parties. The brief must contain the following:

- a concise statement of facts, including the agreed facts and admissions;

- a concise summary of the issues where necessary;

- any outstanding procedural issues;

- the current settlement position of each party; and

- an estimate of the trial time.

MATERIALS FOR USE OF THE COURT AT THE HEARING

All materials that are required by the court must be filed within the times prescribed by the rules for your particular type of hearing. However, the court encourages filing of documents as early as possible. Everything must be filed by at least 2 p.m. two days before the hearing.

Commercial cases can be voluminous and to avoid huge files being carted around from filing to courtroom, parties are expected to notify court staff of the specific materials they want at hearings. In addition, in an effort to keep huge files in an easily accessible manner, the court suggests that counsel coordinate a common numbering scheme for the various records, transcripts, factums, authorities, and other materials intended for use by the judge. Usually, the law clerks to counsel for the parties go to the court office before the hearing to ensure that the correct materials are available to the judge.

In addition to the documents and records used for matters on the regular list, a commercial list case may require a **compendium**. A compendium is a type of record that gives an overview of a complex case and organizes the documents to be referred to at the hearing in a way that makes it as easy as possible for the judge to locate them. A compendium usually contains a statement of the relief sought by the party and a copy of any pages from motion records, applications, or other documents that a party intends to rely on. The portions to be referred to should be highlighted. There should be a cover sheet that identifies the document from which the page has been extracted. The cover sheet should also summarize the general content of the document from which the page or pages have been extracted. If a document is only a few pages, the entire document may be included in the compendium, but if a document is lengthy and the party wishes to refer only to a portion of the document, only the portion to be referred to should be included.

compendium
summary of material to be referred to at a hearing, designed for easy access by judge

The compendium should also contain the headnotes and the pages of any case authorities on which a party is relying. There is no need to include the entire case in the compendium, although it should be in the book of authorities. Only the issues being referred to should be included, and the *ratio decidendi* of the case should be highlighted.

ratio decidendi
the legal reason for the judge's decision in a case

All of these materials should be placed in a looseleaf binder. All the photocopies must be clear. The binder contents should be kept to a minimum, and wherever possible the parties should prepare a joint compendium.

If the evidence is complex or technical, the court encourages the use of diagrams, charts, lists of persons involved, point-form chronologies, and other summaries to assist in clarifying the issues and the parties. For trials, the court asks that sworn witness statements be used to replace examination-in-chief, in whole or in part, where appropriate. Statements must be exchanged with all parties well in advance of the hearing. The maker of a statement must be available at the trial for cross-examination on the statement unless the court has ordered otherwise.

In addition, draft orders should be prepared and presented by counsel for signing at the end of the hearing. Counsel for the moving party, or counsel for the plaintiff, must assist court staff in preparing the order by presenting a draft for the judge to edit. In order to facilitate the judge's editing, an electronic version of the draft order, on a disk, should be presented to the court office along with a hard copy of the draft, any handwritten endorsement of the judge, or a copy of the dictation tape. Sometimes judges' handwritten endorsements can be difficult to read. If the person drafting the order has difficulty reading the endorsement, any illegible parts should be highlighted on the copy of the endorsement so that the judge can clarify the wording of the decision.

PROTOCOL CONCERNING COURT-TO-COURT COMMUNICATIONS IN CROSS-BORDER CASES

The commercial list has seen a proliferation of cross-border proceedings, particularly in relation to insolvency and corporate restructuring. As a result, a set of guidelines called "Guidelines Applicable to Court-to-Court Communications in Cross-Border Cases," drawn up by the American Law Institute, have been approved for use in cross-border matters on the commercial list. The guidelines provide cooperative procedures for insolvency proceedings and other types of commercial disputes involving cross-border proceedings where communications between the courts in the different jurisdictions might facilitate in harmonizing proceedings to help ensure consistent results and increase efficiency. They are not automatically applied, but will be used in specific cases and notice will be given to the parties.

Although the guidelines were prepared for court-to-court communications between courts in Canada and the United States, the commercial list has also endorsed their application in court-to-court communications between Canada and other countries, and between Ontario and the other provinces and territories. They are to apply only in a manner that is consistent with the *Rules of Civil Procedure* and the practice in Ontario.

The guidelines are not meant to be static, but are meant to be adapted and modified to fit the circumstances of individual cases, and to change and evolve as experience is gained from working with them.

The guidelines may be viewed online at http://www.ali.org/doc/Guidelines.pdf or a copy may be obtained from:

Commercial List Office
393 University Avenue, 10th Floor
Toronto, ON M5G 1E6

telephone 416-327-5043
fax 416-327-6228

CHAPTER SUMMARY

This chapter provided an overview of the practice direction that outlines the procedure followed for cases on the commercial list. The commercial list is a specialized list of corporate and commercial cases dealt with through an informal case management process, which allows for a speedy and efficient flow of cases through the court. Except for bankruptcy cases, which must go on the commercial list, the use of the list is voluntary.

The practice direction works with the general rules and adds to the regular procedure for cases on the commercial list. Pleadings are prepared in the same manner as regular pleadings, but the title of proceedings must appear as follows: "The Superior Court of Justice — Commercial List."

KEY TERMS

compendium

ratio decidendi

REFERENCES

American Law Institute, *Guidelines Applicable to Court-to-Court Communications in Cross-Border Cases* (Philadelphia: American Law Institute, 2003), http://www.ali.org/doc/Guidelines.pdf.

Bank Act, SC 1991, c. 46, as amended.

Business Corporations Act, RSO 1990, c. B.16.

Canada Business Corporations Act, RSC 1985, c. C-44.

Companies' Creditors Arrangements Act, RSC 1985, c. C-36.

Credit Union and Caisses Populaires Act 1994, SO 1994, c. 11.

Limited Partnerships Act, RSO 1990, c. L.16.

Pension Benefits Act, RSO 1990, c. P.8.

Personal Property Security Act, RSO 1990, c. P.10.

Rules of Civil Procedure, RRO 1990, reg. 194.

Securities Act, RSO 1990, c. S.5.

Winding-up and Restructuring Act, RSC 1985, c. W-11.

REVIEW QUESTIONS

1. What matters may be heard on the commercial list?

2. Where are commercial list matters issued?

3. If a matter is placed on the regular list and a party wants to have it transferred to the commercial list, what is the procedure?

4. How do you obtain a hearing date for a commercial list matter?

5. When you are preparing a motion for hearing on the commercial list and no date has yet been set, what date do you put on the notice of motion?

6. What is the proper procedure for adjourning a matter on the commercial list?

7. What material is required for a pretrial hearing?

8. What is the purpose of a compendium?

Glossary of terms

absentee   person whose rights or interests are being determined in a proceeding and whose whereabouts are unknown

action   one of the two procedures by which a civil matter is commenced in the Superior Court; the other such procedure is an application

affidavit   written statement setting out the evidence of the person who swears or affirms its contents are true

alternative dispute resolution   term used to describe various ways of settling disputes without going to court, including arbitration, mediation, and conciliation

appeal as of right   appeal that a party has a legal right to bring and for which leave to appeal is not required

appellant   party that commences an appeal

appellate court   the court of appeal or the divisional court

application   one of the two procedures by which a civil matter is commenced in the Superior Court; the other such procedure is an action

assessment of costs   a costs order made by a judge where the actual amount of the costs is determined at a separate hearing by an assessment officer

assignee   person to whom rights, usually contract benefits, are granted by an assignor

assignor   person who grants contract rights to an assignee

attendance money   formerly called conduct money, composed of the *per diem* witness fee and an amount for transportation and lodging in accordance with tariff A

backsheet   part of every court document, it contains the name, LSUC number, address, and telephone and fax numbers of the lawyer who prepared the document, the short title of proceedings, the court and court file number, the fax number of the person to be served (if known), and a large space reserved for court officials to make entries on

bill of costs   list of allowable fees and disbursements that is used by an assessment officer to assess a litigant's costs after the litigant is successful in obtaining judgment; differs from an account because it does not include all fees charged to a client

boilerplate   standard wording that is part of every copy of a particular type of document

carriage   responsibility for a file or a case

case conference   conference managed by the case management judge or master, who controls timetables and settles all procedural matters

case management judge or master   court official assigned to each case managed case to ensure court control over the case on its way to trial

cause of action   legal right to sue to obtain a legal remedy

children's lawyer   official of the Ontario Ministry of the Attorney General whose office oversees the rights of some minors involved in civil litigation and custody disputes

chose in action   intangible personal property whose value lies in what it represents

class proceeding fund   public fund of the Law Foundation of Ontario, administered by the Law Society of Upper Canada, to provide funding for the costs of class actions which otherwise might be beyond the financial reach of the parties

co-defendant   one defendant in multi-defendant proceeding

common law   law that is made by judges following precedents set by higher courts; often called "case law"

compendium   summary of material to be referred to at a hearing, designed for easy access by judge

contingency fee   fee payable to a lawyer only if he or she wins the case for a client

contracting state   country that is a signatory to a contract or convention

counterclaim   claim made by the defendant in the main action against the plaintiff or against the plaintiff and other persons

court of first instance   court that made a decision that is under appeal

cross-examination   series of questions asked of a witness by a lawyer for a party adverse in interest to the party that called the witness

crossclaim   claim brought by one defendant whom the plaintiff is suing against another defendant whom the plaintiff is suing

crossclaiming defendant   defendant in the main action who commences a crossclaim against one or more of the other defendants in that action

damages   compensation awarded by a court for harm done

defendant on the crossclaim   defendant in the main action against whom a crossclaim is brought

deponent   person who makes an affidavit

disbursements   amounts lawyers pay on behalf of clients to third parties that lawyers can recover from clients; out-of-pocket expenses incurred by a lawyer for fees and services paid to others as part of proceeding with a case

discovery   process that occurs after close of pleadings in which parties obtain more information about each other's cases before trial

draw an adverse inference   make a factual determination that is contrary to the interests of a party

e-discovery   a term used to describe discovery of documents where the discovery procedures primarily involve the collection and production of information that is stored electronically

endorsement   judge's handwritten order or judgment from which a successful party is expected to prepare a formal draft of the order or judgment

estate administrator   person appointed by a court to administer an estate where there is no will or where the appointment of an executor is ineffective

estoppel   term indicating that a witness is bound by his or her original position and evidence and cannot later take a contrary position

examination-in-chief   series of questions asked of a witness by the lawyer for the party who called the witness

executor   person appointed by a will maker to administer an estate under the provisions of the will; a female executor is sometimes called an executrix

exemplary damages   damages over and above the plaintiff's actual loss, paid to compensate the plaintiff for hurt feelings or mental stress caused by the defendant's particularly outrageous behaviour

factum   document that sets out the facts, statutes, and cases that a party relies on to obtain a favourable decision

fees   payment to lawyers for services rendered

fiduciary relationship   one-sided relationship where one party relies on the other party's honesty and advice given in the reliant party's best interests

final order   order that resolves all the outstanding issues between the parties

fixing costs   making an order that a specific party pay a specific amount of costs

garnishee   order directed to a third party who owes money to a defendant as a means of enforcing a judgment

general damages   monetary damages for pain and suffering that cannot be determined on the basis of a formula

general heading   heading on all court documents identifying the court, the parties, and the status of the parties

impecunious   insolvent

interlocutory order   order that decides some of the matters at issue

issuing   official commencement of court proceedings whereby documents that are originating processes are signed by the registrar, dated, sealed with a court seal, and given a file number

judgment *in personam* judgment that is binding only on the parties to the proceeding

judgment *in rem* judgment that is binding on everyone, whether a party to the proceeding in which the judgment is pronounced or not

judgment-proof unlikely to be able to pay any amount of a judgment

jurat part of an affidavit that appears at the bottom on the left side of the page and begins with the words "Sworn (or affirmed) before me"

law of equity type of law developed several hundred years ago in England wherein judges, rather than following precedents, look at the issues in a case and apply certain principles to ensure a fair outcome

lawyer of record lawyer recognized by the court as the legal representative of a party in a proceeding

leading a witness asking a witness a question that suggests the answer

leave of the court permission of the court to take a procedural step

limitation period specified time within which court proceedings must be commenced

litigation guardian competent adult who directs and takes responsibility for the litigation of a legally disabled party, such as a minor, an absentee, or a mentally disabled person

main action primary case brought by the plaintiff against the defendant

mandatory mediation process in which disputants are required to allow a neutral third party to facilitate their communication and assist them in negotiating a settlement

master minor judicial official with limited jurisdiction to hear and decide specific legal issues identified by the rules or a statute

mediation process whereby a neutral third party facilitates communication between disputants and assists them in negotiating a solution

meta data computer technology term that describes information about an electronic document indicating who prepared it, when it was prepared, who it was sent to, etc.

motion proceeding within the main proceeding to settle an issue, usually procedural and usually one that has arisen prior to trial

narrow questions questions in which the interviewer tries to elicit specific information

non-pecuniary non-monetary

notice of action document informing defendants that they have been sued

official examiner individual who is licensed to operate a business to conduct out-of-court examinations, such as cross-examinations on affidavits and discoveries

open-ended questions   questions that allow the persons interviewed to choose what they want to talk about to the interviewer

order   generic term used in the *Rules of Civil Procedure* to describe commands issued by courts on motions and at trials

originating process   first document in a lawsuit that tells parties that they are being sued

partial indemnity   usual order for costs, based on a cost grid that establishes hourly rates for tariff items listed in the grid; provides less than full recovery for the client

pecuniary   of monetary value

perfecting an appeal   taking all the necessary procedural steps to ensure that an appeal is ready to be heard

personal representative   under the *Estates Administration Act*, this term refers to the person charged with administering an estate, whether the person is an executor appointed by the deceased, or an administrator appointed by the court

practice direction   instructions set out by a chief justice to inform lawyers about special procedures that must be followed in particular courts as a result of administrative needs

principle of proportionality   requires that the time spent on and the expense of a lawsuit be in proportion to the value of the case that is at stake for the parties

pro bono   abbreviation of a Latin term *pro bono publico*, meaning "for the public good," used where a lawyer takes on a case without charging a fee as part of a duty to see that justice is done

punitive damages   damages in the nature of a fine paid to the plaintiff when the defendant's behaviour has been particularly outrageous

ratio decidendi   the legal reason for the judge's decision in a case

reference   judicial proceeding used when it is necessary to delve into an issue in detail before a decision can be reached

refresh the retainer   make a further deposit against future fees as a case progresses

request to admit   document in which one party requires the other to admit the truth of a fact or the authenticity of a document

res judicata   Latin phrase meaning that a matter decided by a court is final and incapable of being relitigated in a subsequent proceeding

respondent   party that answers or defends against an appeal

retainer   contract between a lawyer and client describing the services to be provided by the lawyer and the terms of payment by the client; also refers to a cash deposit to be used by a lawyer to pay future fees and disbursements as they are incurred

return date   the date on which the motion will be heard by the court

return of a motion   day on which a motion is "returned" to court for a hearing; the hearing date is also referred to as "the return date"

reverse search   a reverse search allows you to submit an address, telephone number, or e-mail address to obtain the name of a resident or subscriber

service   process by which documents are brought to the attention of a party in accordance with the rules or a court order

setting an action down for trial   procedure that a party must follow in order to have its case placed on the trial list

sheriff   official appointed by the provincial government to assist in various court-related functions, such as the enforcement of orders and judgments

sittings   a time period during which a specific court may hear cases

special damages   monetary damages that are specific, ascertainable, and measured on an objective basis; sometimes referred to as out-of-pocket expenses

stay proceedings   stop proceedings for a given or indefinite period, pending the fulfillment of a condition, without dismissing the proceedings

stayed   a legal proceeding may be stopped from proceeding further, or stayed by a judge, until one of the parties does something they are obliged to do; for example, a plaintiff who is suing using an unregistered business name will have the proceeding stayed until he proves that he has registered the name as he is legally required to do

substantial indemnity   costs scale, usually used as a punitive costs award, that results in near indemnity for the winner on a dollar-for-dollar basis

summary proceedings   proceedings designed to be conducted quickly and with reduced formality

summons to a witness   order of a court telling the person named on the summons to attend a trial and give evidence

testimony   oral evidence given by a witness

third party claim   claim brought by a defendant in the main action against a person who is not already a party to the main action

title of proceedings   part of the general heading that identifies the parties and their status in a lawsuit

transcript   written record of proceedings transcribed word for word

trial list   list kept by the registrar in each courthouse of cases that are ready for trial

trial record   bound set of documents prepared by the party setting the action down for trial and containing the pleadings of all parties, any relevant orders, all notices, and certificates

trier of fact   judge or jury whose job is to determine the facts of the case from the evidence

true copy   copy of an original document that is like the original in every particular, including copies of alterations, signatures, and court file numbers

truing up   making a handmade copy of a document at the court counter, usually by adding a seal and the registrar's signature inside quotation marks, by hand, to a photocopy of the original document

undefended action   an action in which no statement of defence is delivered

unincorporated association   association of persons formed to carry out a specific purpose and not formally incorporated

viva voce evidence   oral evidence

without prejudice   term used, usually in correspondence, to indicate that an offer or admission cannot be used against its maker, admitted in evidence, or disclosed to the court

wood-shedded   prepared for later cross-examination by opposing lawyer

writ of seizure and sale   order from a court to a sheriff to enforce the court's order by seizing and selling the defendant's property and holding the proceeds to satisfy the judgment debt to the plaintiff; also known as a writ of execution

Index

Italicized page numbers indicate sample forms and precedents.